INTERNATIONAL
MANAGEMENT
BEHAVIOR

The KENT Series in Management

SECOND EDITION

INTERNATIONAL MANAGEMENT BEHAVIOR

From Policy to Practice

Henry W. Lane
Joseph J. DiStefano

University of Western Ontario

in collaboration with

Lorna L. Wright, Queen's University

and

R. William Blake, Memorial University

 PWS-KENT PUBLISHING COMPANY
Boston
First Edition published by Nelson Canada

PWS-KENT
Publishing Company

20 Park Plaza
Boston, Massachusetts 02116

Sponsoring Editor: Rolf A. Janke
Assistant Editor: Marnie Pommett
Production Editor: Susan L. Krikorian
Production Services: The Book Company
Interior Designer: Wendy Calmenson
Cover Designer: Susan L. Krikorian
Compositor: Thompson Type
Text Printer/Binder: Maple-Vail Book Manufacturing Group
Cover Printer: Henry N. Sawyer Company

PWS-KENT Publishing Company is a division of Wadsworth, Inc.

 This book is printed on recycled, acid-free paper.

Printed in the United States of America.

6 7 8 9—99 98 97 96

Library of Congress Cataloging-in-Publication Data

Lane, Henry W.
    International management behavior / Henry W. Lane, Joseph J. DiStefano. — 2nd ed.
        p.   cm.
    Includes bibliographical references and index.
    ISBN 0-534-92933-8
    1. International business enterprises — Management.
    2. Organizational behavior.   3. Culture.   I. DiStefano, Joseph J.   II. Title.
HD62.4.L36   1991   91-36044
658'.049 — dc20   CIP

To my parents and grandparents, whose
combined legacy of deep pride in our Old World
roots and openness to New World diversity,
has provided me with a wonderfully rich cultural life.

JOSEPH J. DISTEFANO

To all the friends who have helped me learn about
other cultures, and my own.

HENRY W. LANE

PREFACE

Nancy J. Adler

*Japanese and American management is 95 percent the same
and differs in all important respects.*

T. FUJISAWA, COFOUNDER OF HONDA MOTOR CORPORATION

Managing the global enterprise and modern business management are becoming synonymous. "International" can no longer be relegated to a subset of organizations or to a division within the organization. Definitions of success now transcend national boundaries. In fact, the very concept of domestic business may have become anachronistic. As the authors aptly describe, "The modern business enterprise has no place to hide. It has no place to go but everywhere."

To succeed, corporations must develop global strategies. The 1980s made the importance of such recognition commonplace, at least among leading firms and management scholars. New approaches to managing research and development (R&D), production, marketing, and finance incorporating today's global realities have evolved rapidly. Yet, only now is an equivalent evolution in managing global human resource systems beginning to emerge. Although the other functional areas increasingly use strategies that were largely unheard of or that would have been inappropriate only one and two decades ago, many firms still conduct the world-wide management of people as if neither the external economic and technological environment, nor the internal structure and organization of the firm, had changed.

In focusing on global strategies and management approaches from the perspectives of people and culture, this book is an important step in helping us, as managers and scholars, to create effective worldwide human resource systems. *International Management Behavior* allows us to examine the influence of national culture on organizational functioning. Rather than becoming trapped within the more commonly asked, and unfortunately misleading, question of *if* organizational dynamics are universal or culturally specific, the authors ask us to focus on the crucially important question of *when* and *how* to be sensitive to national culture. They allow us to investigate the implications of global approaches for traditional human resource management decisions, as well as for those decisions that will only make sense from the perspective of firms in the 1990s and the twenty-first century.

How important are cultural differences to organizational effectiveness? Some observers of corporate behavior say "not at all," while others claim that cultural differences are and will remain extremely important. The first group, those adherents of the cultural convergence perspective, argue that organizational characteristics across nations are free, or are becoming free, from the particularities of specific cultures. Their position suggests that as an outcome of "common industrial logic" — most notably of technological origin — institutional frameworks, patterns and structures of organizations, and management practices across countries are converging (Adler and Doktor, 1986, pp. 300–301). In counterdistinction, other scholars argue that organizations are culturebound, rather than culture free, and are remaining so. These scholars conclude that there is no one best way to manage; that is, the principle of equifinality applies to organizations functioning in different cultures. Their research findings indicate that many equally effective ways to manage exist, with the most effective depending, among other contingencies, on the cultures involved (Adler and Doktor 1986, p. 301).

Perhaps this dilemma has not been solved because we have been asking the wrong question. If we question the influence of cultural diversity within the context of the history of the multinational firm, it becomes clear that national cultural differences are important and that the extent of their impact depends on the stage of development of the firm, the industry, and the world economy. Thus, the relevant question to ask is *when* does culture influence organizational functioning rather than *if* it does or does not. Using a model originally developed by Vernon in 1966, and enhanced by Ghadar in the 1980s for the post World War II development of multinational firms, one can deduce distinct variations in the relative importance of cultural diversity and, consequently, equally distinct variations in the most appropriate approaches to managing people worldwide.

Immediately after World War II, firms operated primarily from an ethnocentric perspective. Firms produced unique goods and services that they offered almost exclusively to the domestic market. The uniqueness of a product and the lack of international competition negated a firm's need to be sensitive to cultural differences. When organizations exported goods, they did so without altering them for foreign consumption. Any cultural differences were absorbed by the foreign buyers, not by the country product design, manufacturing, or marketing teams. In some ways, the implicit message to foreigners was, "We will *allow* you to buy our product" and, of course, the assumption was that foreigners would want to. During this initial phase, home country nationals and philosophies dominated management. Culture and multinational human resource management were perceived as close to irrelevant.

Foreign competition ushered in phase two, and with it the beginning of a need to market and produce abroad. Totally unlike the first phase, sensitivity to cultural differences became critical in implementing effective corporate strategy. The first phase's product orientation shifted to a market orientation, with each foreign domestic market needing to be addressed differently. Whereas the unique technology of phase one products fits well with an ethnocentric "one best way" approach, now firms began to assume equifinality; that is, that there were many good ways to manage, with each dependent on the nation involved. Successful companies no longer expected foreigners to absorb cultural mismatches between buyers and sellers. Rather, home country representatives had to modify their style to fit with that of their clients and colleagues in foreign markets. Moreover, while cultural differences became important in designing and marketing culturally appropriate products goods and services, they became critical in producing goods in factories worldwide. Managers had to learn the culturally appropriate ways to manage their human resource systems in each of the countries in which they operated.

By the 1980s, many industries had entered a third phase. The environment for these industries had changed again, and with it the demands for cultural sensitivity. Within phase three industries, a number of companies produce very similar products (almost commodities), with the only significant competition being on price. From this global, price-sensitive perspective, cultural awareness falls again to marginal importance. Price competition among almost identical goods and services produced by numerous international competitors negates the importance of most cultural differences and any advantage gained by cultural sensitivity. The primary product design and marketing assumption is no longer "one best way" or even "many best ways" but rather "one least cost way." The primary market has become worldwide, with no significant market segmentation. Firms can only gain competitive advantage through process engineering, sourcing critical factors on a worldwide basis, and benefiting from economies of scale. Price competition reduces culture's influence to negligible.

While some observers believe that the third phase is the ultimate phase for all industries, I do not. While many industries today exhibit phase three dynamics, a fourth phase has begun to emerge. In it, top quality, least possible cost goods and services have become the base line, the minimally acceptable standard. Competitive advantage comes from strategic thinking and mass customization. Product ideas are drawn from worldwide sources, as are the factors and locations of production. However, final goods and services and their marketing are tailored to very discrete market niches. One of the critical components of this market segmentation, again, becomes culture. Successful phase four firms need to know how to understand their potential clients' needs, quickly translate them into goods and services, produce those goods and services on a least cost basis, and deliver them back to the client in an acceptable fashion. By this phase, the product, sales, and price orientations of the past almost completely disappear. They are replaced with a responsive design orientation accompanied by a quick, least cost production function. Needless to say, culture is critically important to this most adavanced stage. Similarly, the ability to manage cross-cultural interaction, multinational teams, and global alliances becomes fundamental. Whereas an effective international human resource management strategy in the past varied from being irrelevant to helpful, by this fourth phase it becomes essential, a minimum requirement for organizational survival and success.

This book addresses questions involving people, culture, and the corporation. It allows us to examine the implications of alternative approaches to managing people and to managing cultural diversity. It encourages us to maintain the perspective of the multinational manager. More than merely being interesting and important, *International Management Behavior* is fundamental to our understanding of management in the 1990s and the twenty-first century.

References

Adler, Nancy J., and Fariborz Ghadar, "Strategic Human Resource Management; A Global Perspective," in Rudiger Pieper (ed.), *Human Resource Management in International Comparison* (Berlin: de Gruyter, 1990), pp. 235–260.

Adler, Nancy J., and R. Doktor (in collaboration with S. G. Redding), "From the Atlantic to the Pacific Century: Cross-Cultural Management Reviewed," *Journal of Management*, 12, no. 2 (1986): 295–318.

Vernon, R., "International Investment and International Trade in the Product Cycle," *Quarterly Journal of Economics* (May 1966).

ACKNOWLEDGMENTS

The course on which this book is based was formulated and launched in 1972 by Professor DiStefano at the University of Western Ontario Business School. The advice and encouragement received by him and Professor Lane since that time ensures that this list of acknowledgments is lengthy. Dean J. J. Wettlaufer provided the initial encouragement and funding for course development through the school's Plan for Excellence. Professor David S. R. Leighton graciously invited Professor DiStefano to audit the existing International Marketing course and shared his expertise in this area. Mrs. Doreen Sanders, O.C., editor of the *Business Quarterly*, provided important exposure of the ideas contained in this book by devoting a special issue of that magazine to international business, with Professor DiStefano as guest editor. Our colleagues in the organizational behavior area group and throughout the school supported our efforts, shared their experiences, and provided invaluable opportunities for overseas activity to both of us.

Even earlier experiences need to be acknowledged. Professor Douglas Bunker, now at the State University of New York at Buffalo, admitted Professor DiStefano, then an MBA student, into the Harvard Business School doctoral seminar on Culture and the Organization of Work. This comparative management course sharpened Professor DiStefano's conviction that a new, cross-cultural and transactional perspective was needed, while simultaneously providing a framework and inspiring intellectual enthusiasm and commitment lasting a quarter century.

Professor Lane's interest in the field also began at Harvard. The Organizational Behavior Teaching Conference was held at the Harvard Business School while he was a doctoral student, and one of the conference sessions was on cross-cultural management. He found the insights and experiences of the speakers, and the issues they were discussing, to be fascinating. During his doctoral studies, he also developed an intercultural orientation similar to Professor DiStefano's that formed the basis for their later collaboration.

Various other people and organizations also merit thanks. Professor DiStefano is especially indebted to colleagues at the World Bank; the Canadian Departments of Indian and Northern Affairs and National Defense; the Society for Intercultural Education, Training, and Research; IMD Management Development Institute in Lausanne; the U.S. Peace Corps; and to companies and executives around the world. Ray Rouse, program associate at The Niagara Institute, has continually challenged and stretched Professor DiStefano's application of his ideas. Stephen Rhinesmith, twice President of the American Field Service and former Ambassador for the United States for U.S.–U.S.S.R. exchanges, provided ideas and opportunities for new experiences. Nancy Adler, professor at McGill University, has added significantly to his thinking by her own research and writing, by her generous exchange of ideas and experience, her agile intellectual sparring, and her warm emotional support.

Both of us appreciate the support of the Canadian International Development Agency and the Department of External Affairs for their funding of numerous projects with which we have been involved at Western.

Don Simpson, a former colleague at Western who is currently Vice-President and Director of the Banff Centre for Management in Banff, Alberta and the single most impressive "servant leader" in the international development field known to us, has given freely of his mind and spirit over the many years of our friendship. When Professor Lane decided to take over responsibility for the course, and to pursue further his interest in international business, he teamed up with Professor Simpson to help companies start joint ventures in developing countries; to write cases; and to learn what it really meant to be international and not just to be able to talk about it.

Friends and colleagues at two business schools in Europe, l'Institut Superieur des Affaires in France and the Koblenz School of Corporate Management in Germany have helped Professor Lane continue to learn through experience. They have been very supportive of him and the International Management Behavior course that he has taught at both schools.

Our casewriters and research assistants have also provided significant help over the years and deserve special thanks. Bill Blake coauthored many of the cases in this book, including the remarkable "Polysar" series. Lorna Wright, who has impressive international credentials and experience, and who is devoted to improving cross-cultural management, constantly challenged the status quo and pushed to improve the course. She was a true champion of making the course more relevant. She kept pushing for more experiential material to balance the cognitive/analytic orientation, and, as a result, this second edition contains a realistic and interesting case/in-basket exercise: Hazelton International and The International Project Manager's Day. Both Bill Blake and Lorna Wright have continued to provide support, ideas, and material for the book even after leaving Western to begin their professional careers as faculty members at business schools elsewhere. Peter Green, whose personal experience as an Arctic administrator gave him instant appreciation of our orientation and goals, wrote many of the early cases that informed our ideas. Marie Solange Perret gambled her Ph.D. dissertation on the application of the Kluckhohn-Strodtbeck framework to international budgeting systems (and won).

We also thank Dean C. B. Johnston of the School of Business Administration and Professors James Hatch and Terry Deutscher, current and past Directors of Research and Publications at the School, respectively, for their encouragement and support. Similarly, members of the Advisory Board of The Centre for International Business Studies have given valuable advice, access, and encouragement.

We have been fortunate to have been able to work with a series of terrific editors, editorial staffs, and production and marketing people in the publishing companies that have played a role in the two editions of this book and want to recognize their contributions. Joerg Klauck of Methuen was first to believe in the authors' approach and the book, and he helped make it a reality. After Nelson Canada purchased Methuen, we found the same professionalism, support, and encouragement from Ric Kitowski, who was always available to work with us to promote the book to ensure that it received the best reception possible. Currently, Rolf Janke of PWS-KENT is carrying on the tradition of professionalism, enthusiasm for the book, encouragement, and support that his predecessors established. The fact that this edition is being published by PWS-KENT is a tribute to Ric's and Rolf's dedication to doing what was best for the book and for the authors. Moving the publication of a book from one country to another is not an easy task, even with the same corporation. It was an exercise in international business and cross-cultural cooperation. We are appreciative of their efforts and others at Nelson Canada and PWS-KENT who made it possible.

We would also like to acknowledge the time spent in reviewing the book and the constructive critiques of numerous colleagues. Bob Moran of the American Graduate School of International Management provided a thoughtful and timely review of our material, and Ed Miller of the University of Michigan also made helpful comments on the manuscript for the first edition. The second edition has benefited greatly from very helpful post-experience and pre-second edition reviews by Bob Dennehy of Pace University, Jerry O'Connell of Bentley College, John Stanbury of Ohio State University, and Christa Walck of Michigan Technological University. Many other colleagues, who also have adopted the book, have provided to us, and to other colleagues who were considering the book, suggestions for improvements as well as positive feedback on their experiences with it and their students' reactions to it. These comments at conferences, by letter, and by phone have been greatly appreciated.

None of the cases would have been possible without the cooperation of companies and managers from around the world. We thank them for the time, assistance, and information they have provided, often at the risk of embarrassment, in the service of others' learning. To our students we give a special thanks for their trust, interest, hard work, effective criticism, and affection. These people and our friends on every continent have sustained us in our effort to better understand the complex phenomena about which we have written.

Our families, too, have earned our gratitude, but not just for the usual support in a book-writing venture. International work means frequent and, sometimes, prolonged time away from home. Our wives, Anne and Lynne, both professionals with their own careers have endured, if not celebrated, our absences without complaint. Our children have been especially patient and understanding. Our families have welcomed myriad visitors from other lands into our homes with graciousness and generosity, even when it inconvenienced them. Although the benefits to us and our visitors have been mutual, without the support of our families these personal exchanges, which have provided deep understanding and long friendships, would never have enriched us so much.

Finally, we close with special thanks to our stalwart secretaries, Sue O'Driscoll, Linda Minutillo, and Beth Smith. Even with the advantages of word processing, we have tested their reserves of good cheer with multiple revisions. They have remained calm and efficient throughout, managing effectively, and with dispatch, during our absences. We are equally grateful for their continued insights about both the people and ideas in our work.

Notwithstanding this lengthy list of acknowledgments, we close with the usual caveat that we alone remain responsible for the contents of this book.

H. W. Lane
J. J. DiStefano
London, Canada
May 1991

CONTENTS

I

The Influence of Culture on Management Behavior

INTRODUCTION

Conducting Business Internationally

This book is different. This is not just another book about international business. This book is about people who conduct business internationally. The cases depict typical situations that managers encounter: their problems and opportunities, their joys and frustrations, their successes and failures, and the decisions they must make. The cases describe situations that anybody could confront in pursuing an international business career. One does not have to wait until he or she is the chief executive officer or president of a company to experience these situations. Issues and dilemmas that people at all levels in an organization face in doing business internationally are presented in the cases. They deal primarily with managers who interact with, or manage, people from cultures outside of their own.

This book is concerned with the practice of international business and international management rather than the theory of international business or the theory of culture. The knowledge and concepts of culture and international business are used so the practice of international management may be improved.

International business is not impersonal, so international business should not be studied in a conceptual but impersonal way. For example, it is useful to know trade theories, to know how to hedge the future value of currencies in which a corporation is dealing, to be able to weigh the pros and cons of exporting versus licensing, or to evaluate entering a joint venture versus establishing a wholly owned subsidiary. Such knowledge, although it may be necessary, is not enough. Eventually, one reaches the point where the conceptual work has to be stopped and something must be done. It is not sufficient to sit in headquarters and debate alternatives. Action is essential. One must leave headquarters to experience what it really means to do business internationally.

When the manager leaves headquarters, he or she starts interacting with people from other cultures. The problems associated with implementing a project or managing operations in another culture are experienced. International business is more personal and relationship oriented than domestic business. In North America, for example, business is done first and out of that business a personal relationship might develop. In most of the world, however, people want to establish the personal relationship first, and out of that relationship may come some business. In order to deal with these and other aspects of international management, this book focuses attention on the implementation of strategic or other corporate decisions and on operating issues and problems.

The authors wish to make clear the distinction between theory and practice. There is a difference between studying about working with people from other cultures and experiencing working with such people. In the first instance, one is able to talk about it. In the second instance, one is able to do it. One may be extremely knowledgeable about art, music, or drama — a real student of these activities. However, this does not mean that one is a good artist, musician, or actress. Similarly, knowing about and talking about management is not the same as managing. Being a good practitioner requires knowledge and experience.

It should not be assumed that studying the few cases in this book is a substitute for experience. However, they provide for initial practice. It is the authors' hope that the cases will increase the student's understanding of, and appreciation for, the delays, frustration, and complexity of putting ideas to work.

The readings and text in this book, along with other readings in the student's course, provide knowledge about concepts and theories of international business and culture. The cases put the student in the position of a manager interacting with people from other cultures. They are intended to increase sensitivity to important cultural differences and assumptions underlying management behavior and to issues managers are likely to encounter in other countries. The emphasis is on understanding behavior and working with people in a business context. Understanding the impact of culture on behavior is important for managers — not in the abstract or for itself — but rather to improve management practice. The business and cultural contexts are important for management action and both must be considered.

In taking a manager's role, the student puts himself or herself psychologically in a particular person's place and situation, sorts out the business issues and cultural issues involved in that situation, and plans action. In this way, the student simulates real life. It is the authors' belief that a combination of the knowledge and the experience that can be gained from immersion in the case situations will improve the judgment of managers who work internationally. This is critical because management is not the application of a technique, but the exercise of judgment. Knowledge of other cultures is a vital component of management judgment in international business.

The authors have been involved in writing most of the cases for this book. The authors have lived in or traveled to many of the locations in the cases as teachers, consultants, managers, or specifically for casewriting. They have worked with the managers described in the cases, and have tried to bring the flavor, feeling, and tempo of these people and the countries they live in to students in the classroom and to those who use this book. It is the authors' belief that the cases are as close to experiencing working in these other countries as one can get in the classroom.

The authors note that the genders of the people in the cases are the same as the real people in the real situations. They recognize that in some societies men are given preferential treatment in organizational life and that in other societies, there are attempts to provide equal opportunity to men and women managers. The cases represent the current reality in international business, not what is necessarily desirable. Readers should be wary of a superficial reading of the cases. Careful analysis is necessary to make accurate judgments about the quality of management exhibited by either the men or the women in the situations described. For the most complete treatment of the topic of women in international management, see Nancy J. Adler, *Women in Management Worldwide*, Armonk, N.Y.: M. E. Sharp, 1987.

The situations described in this book may seem like unusual dilemmas to a reader with no international business experience. Although each situation is unique, each case describes a class of problems or situations that managers encounter throughout the world. Before one jumps too quickly to say, "I'll never go to those countries," or "I will never find myself in these situations," the experience of one individual who said that should be recounted. This person was completing a management-training program and, as part of that program, a speaker came from the firm's operation in Germany to address the class. As the speaker discussed all of the problems and hassles associated with the operation, the listener was saying, "I'm glad I'll never be sent there." He was quite surprised when, soon afterwards, he was sent to Germany as a manager. He wished he had listened more carefully to the speaker.

Why do people start having difficulties when they leave their own country and enter another culture? It is because peoples' world views and mental programs change. These mental programs exert a pervasive, yet hidden, influence on behavior. Culture has been called "the collective programming of the mind which distinguishes the members of one human group from another."[1] As a result of having different mental programs, people often see situations differently and have different approaches and solutions to problems. Each tends to believe that his or her way makes the most sense and is best. The result of such beliefs can be conflict.

Since people within a culture have similar mental programs, it is not easy to observe one's own culture. One student, a Chinese person from Hong Kong, was asked by fellow students to explain the Hong Kong Chinese culture. His answer was, "What do you mean?" He had never thought about what his culture was, nor could he express facts about his culture. Those of us living in the Canadian or American culture are equally blind. If asked to describe the Canadian or American culture, one most likely would be at a loss. However, one might be able to say something about the culture of which one is *not* a member. Canadians and Americans know their culture because they behave like Canadians or Americans; their behavior is directed by the rules of their culture. This is what makes culture so difficult to conceptualize. It is pervasive, but it is hidden. All people are influenced by it, even though people do not see it.

When Canadians or Americans go to another country or start to work with people from other cultures, they notice quickly that the people in these other cultures are different. The danger is that these differences are focused upon, although it may not be understood how one's self is different. One tends to think of people in cultures different than his or her own as the ones who are deviating from the norm. The outsider may overlook the simple fact that he or she is deviating from another culture's norms. It is important not only to understand how another's culture influences their behavior, but also how one's own culture influences one's own behavior. It is usually in the interaction of cultures that difficulties are experienced, because North American behaviors and decisions are based on different assumptions and are the result of different mental programs.

Culture influences the practice of management. Many management concepts, techniques, and systems developed and taught in North American business schools are based upon North American cultural beliefs, values, and assumptions. These may work well in North America. These concepts, techniques, and systems may not work as intended, however, in other cultures. If they are transferred from North America to another country and used improperly, they can compound managers' problems. For example, management by objectives (MBO) is based on an assumption that subordinates will share their objectives with their superior. This is an unrealistic assumption in many cultures that have strong status differentials and that maintain rigid hierarchies. Cultural differences, if not understood, can be significant barriers to the implementation and success of a business venture. One of the tenets of good marketing practice is "to know your customer." Understanding the culture of people with whom one does business is simply good business practice.

In the final analysis, international business is conducted with and through people from various cultural backgrounds. Ultimately, a manager, or a subordinate of that manager, will have to travel to another country and/or work with someone from another culture to implement a business plan. The manager and his or her family may even have to live in another country. Often, when thinking about international business, places like London, Paris, Frankfurt, Geneva, Sydney, Singapore, and Hong Kong come to mind. However, international business does not always take place in these cities, and living and working in a foreign country are not always glamorous.

Corporations pursue business opportunities in remote places and under difficult conditions. Managers whose only experience is with the domestic market will find these situations difficult to understand. Some countries in which large corporations operate and earn substantial revenue have difficult economic, political, and living conditions. Subsidiaries are not always located in England, Switzerland, or France. They also are located in Colombia, Nigeria, and the Philippines.

International business is not an activity that just is transacted from North America or Europe, for example. Nor is it only concerned with operating in the developed world. It also means living in and managing operations in developing countries. International business is just that — it is international and takes place everywhere.

Objectives of This Book

This book is designed to help develop the knowledge and skills needed to manage effectively in different cultural environments and to work effectively with people from other cultures. The authors' intention is to develop, to the extent possible using this medium, an appreciation of what it is like to work with people from other cultures and to work in other countries.

The basic premise of this text is that it is possible and desirable to develop both intellectual understanding and behavioral skills pertinent to the management problems arising from the interaction of people from different cultures in work settings. The authors also believe that this understanding and these skills are generalizable and transferable from one situation to another. People can become better international managers by using the material contained in this text.

Specifically, the objectives of this book are

1. To develop an awareness of the concept of culture and its pervasive and hidden influence on behavior, particularly with respect to management and management practices. This includes understanding how cultural beliefs in North America influence North Americans' practices, as well as how the cultural beliefs of other people influence their practices.
2. To develop familiarity with the types of situations and issues that managers confront when working internationally.
3. To develop an appreciation of the impact of living and working in another culture on one's personal behavior.

Orientations

This book presents a distinct set of orientations to the study of international business. Essentially, these orientations describe the authors' perspective on the conduct of international business. The authors believe it to be a realistic perspective that has been developed, refined, and tested in teaching a course of this type for 20 years to undergraduates, to graduate students, and to practicing managers. The authors, and others, have tested the materials in this text all around the world with participants from every continent and with both culturally homogeneous and heterogeneous groups.

1. *Management orientation.* The book presents a problem-solving and decision-making approach to international business. The implications of differences and similarities in cultures to management can be examined, not in isolation, but in light of actual management situations where an appreciation of cultural influences on behavior can make a difference in outcome and performance.

2. *Behavioral orientation.* The human element in managing effectively across cultures is just as important and, sometimes, more important than the technical or business elements. However, the "people" skills are likely to be less developed than are the technical or business skills. This does not mean that on some absolute scale people skills are more important than technical or business skills, and that the ability to work with people alone will lead to success. A package of skills is needed to be successful — business, technical, and people skills.[2] People chosen to work in other countries, or to work in the international side of business, generally will have developed a basic set of business or technical skills. The skills of relating to and working with people from other cultures are needed to complement those basic skills. If a person does not have these people skills, he or she may never get the opportunity to use his or her business or technical skills. Unfortunately, North Americans tend to emphasize the importance of the technical and business skills over cultural adaptation skills.[3]

3. *Intercultural orientation.* The primary focus of the material in this text is on the interaction between people of different cultures in work settings. This

intercultural orientation is distinct from a comparative approach, in which management practices of individual countries or cultures are examined and compared. The intercultural perspective has been chosen for this text because it reflects reality. It is in the interaction of cultures that managers experience difficulties. Although study of practices within a single culture may be helpful, it is the interaction of people with different beliefs and management practices that has impact on managers.

4. *Culture-general orientation* This book is intended for use in training general managers (meaning management generalists rather than the specific position) and international staff who must function effectively in a realm of cultural diversity. This book is also useful to people who aspire to such positions in international management and as staff of multinational corporations. The material also will interest people who would like to know more about the subject of international management, but may never become corporate managers.

Culture-specific training is more appropriate upon a person's assignment to a specific country in which he or she will live and work.[4] Culture-specific training also may be appropriate for staff specialists concentrating on a particular country or a limited regional area. The authors believe that since the people using this book will have diverse career goals and geographical interests, the culture-general model is more appropriate to their needs and development. This is not to say that culture-specific learning will not take place. The cases and readings will convey information and knowledge specific to given cultures. However, one or two cases will not make one an expert in managing in a specific culture.

The demand for managers with international expertise is increasing as international activities become a larger part of businesses and sales and profits. One study found a concern for managers to develop a "sensitivity and understanding necessary to operate effectively in a wide variety of (cultural) contexts."[5] This study supports the need for culture-general training. Thus, there is a need for developing a framework within which country-specific learning can take place more rapidly as necessary, and for learning culture-related generalizable skills. The culture-general orientation addresses these needs.

The philosophy on which this book is based is that learning is a lifelong, continuous process for which the individual has primary responsibility. Ideally, prior to an international posting, the manager should engage in in-depth country and culture-specific study. He or she should also study the language within the framework of issues, concepts, and attitudes covered in this book.

The material presented in this book may be a student's first encounter with culture. Other students may have been exposed to different cultures through previous courses or personal experience. For student with prior exposure to different cultures, the journey continues. For those without prior experience, welcome to an interesting journey.

Components of Effective Management Action

The interest of this text is to contribute to the development of people who will become effective international managers. A number of components contribute to becoming an effective manager. One is technical and/or business knowledge. For example, in the consulting engineering industry, technical knowledge could include the engineering principles involved in building bridges or roads. Business knowledge, in this example, could include an understanding of project management and systems analysis. There is also a practical or specific dimension of this knowledge that is required. This includes knowledge of a company's products, accounting procedures, computer systems, production methods, planning techniques, and so on. These types of knowledge and their associated skills are not addressed in this book. It is assumed that students are acquiring this knowledge and developing these skills in other courses, and that practicing managers who may be using this book have developed them.

A second component is cultural knowledge. This knowledge includes understanding the dimensions of culture, the role and impact of culture on behavior, and how culture is disseminated. There is a practical and specific dimension of cultural knowledge, also. It is hoped that people will learn some specifics that relate to practices and beliefs in the countries in which the cases in this book take place. The material in this text also permits the development of some cross-cultural communication skills. Development of the following skills can be pursued in culture-general training.[6] The cases and readings in this text, combined with the case method pedagogy, permit students to work on developing these critical communication skills. These cross-cultural communication skills include

1. The capacity to accept the relativity of one's own knowledge and perceptions.
2. The capacity to be nonjudgmental. It becomes necessary to suspend premature judgment, since this may cut off dialogue and become a barrier to communication and learning.
3. A tolerance for ambiguity. As one begins to understand the relativity of one's culture, and suspends judgment in order to learn about another culture, a tremendous amount of uncertainty and ambiguity develops. As some of one's own beliefs and values are called into question, and as one learns about the beliefs and values of other people, ambiguity is often heightened. The case situations in this text can create ambiguity and uncertainty for students. This uncertainty reflects the reality faced by people in those cases.
4. The capacity to communicate respect for other peoples' ways, their country, and their values.
5. The capacity to display empathy. Empathy is the ability to understand and to share another's feelings. Empathy is *not* sympathy or feeling sorry for others.
6. The capacity to be flexible. Often, to accomplish goals in a foreign environment, flexibility is critical.

7. The capacity for turn taking (for example, in business negotiations and in class discussions).
8. The humility to acknowledge what one does not know. One needs to admit when he or she lacks understanding and knowledge. One should seek to learn, rather than act as if he or she knows.[7]

Managers, undoubtedly, would argue that there is a third essential component to effective management action — experience. No traditional university course is an adequate substitute for experience. Experience-based training, combined with conceptual development, would perhaps be the ideal to train managers to be effective in cross-cultural business situations. A combination of the case method, experiential exercises, and projects may be the closest approximation to reality that a student will encounter. Such an approach speeds up the acquisition of experience through exposure to typical situations in a shortened period of time. The cases presented in this book provide a rich background of experiences. When one is put into these real situations and assumes the role of the manager, one develops a perspective and understanding that is improved upon only by real international experience. The case situations include establishing joint ventures, selecting a joint venture partner, problems with a local work force, project management problems, bribery, and setting up a business in another country.

A summary diagram of the components of effective international management action is shown in Figure 1.

INTRODUCTION TO THE READINGS

Some Basic Messages

People involved in international business must have a global perspective. North America functions as part of a worldwide market in which countries and their economies are interdependent. It is no longer possible for companies to hide in their home markets. Competition will come in and take these markets away. North Americans have to compete at home and have to compete by entering competitors' markets. The old saying, "the best defense is a good offense," is nowhere more true than in international business. This attitude has recently been proven true by Eastman Kodak. Under pressure from Japanese competitors in the United States and Europe, Kodak entered the Japanese market at great expense in 1984 and has succeeded in achieving sales of $1.3 billion in Japan and in diverting Fuji's thrust into the United States.[8]

People doing business internationally need to have an expanded role concept. People selling a product or developing a project need to think of themselves more as entrepreneurs than as salespeople. Financing may have to be secured for a product, as well as finding a buyer for that product. The financing might come from the World Bank. Or, aid agencies like the Canadian International Development Agency (CIDA) or the United States Agency for International Development (USAID) may

FIGURE 1 Components of Effective International Management Action

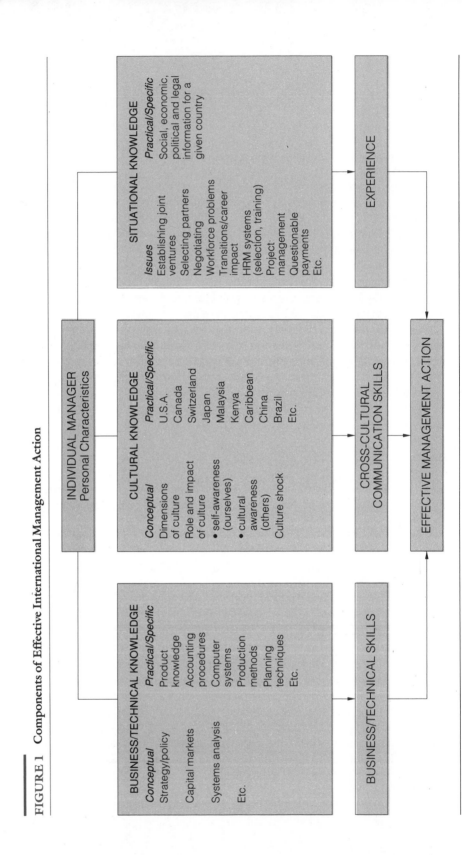

provide financing, rather than the traditional sources of finance, such as commercial banks. The idea of selling a product to a customer who already has money to spend for that product, or does not need help getting that money is no longer appropriate — particularly in the developing world. The new international manager understands this reality and operates accordingly.

Companies and their representatives need to have a broad product image and concept. A narrow product focus on the excellence of a company's technology is not sufficient. Offering a better mouse trap is not a guarantee to success. Nor does a good product necessarily sell. Customers in other countries are not only buying the technology. They are also buying after-sales service and support, and a good relationship with a supplier. These countries want a product and a supplier they can trust. What were formerly nonbusiness issues are now business considerations. If a customer (who often is a foreign government) has a need for training or staffing, then a supplier may have to help with these problems. These issues are not always considered as part of a product in North America.

A student once said that this advice only means that "paying attention to the customer's needs and wants is just good business." Most certainly! However, the subtle difference is that North Americans understand intuitively or through experience what the customer wants and needs in the North American culture. In international business, more time must be spent to find out what the customer in his or her environment wants or needs. Error is risked by applying North American needs and wants to other cultures.

Organizations have to be committed to a global perspective and to an expanded product concept. They must be committed to doing business internationally. They must support their products once they have sold them and they must produce a quality product. Finally, organizations must support their employees around the world. James Brown, the vice president of Northern Telecom, which manufactures and markets telecommunication systems around the world, states:

> Commitment is the single most critical factor for successful entry into foreign markets. Commitment is basically the willingness to put in the time and effort and make the manpower available to solve problems when they arise and to meet the necessary demands of breaking into markets. It's a commitment to spending money and time to be successful. Spending time and being willing to finance the travel and people may be the single most important characteristic in being successful internationally.[9]

Developing and maintaining commitment is a long-term undertaking. Organizations need to be committed to understanding the politics, the economics, and the culture of the countries in which they are operating.

Organizations should select their people carefully and prepare them systematically for international assignments. People working internationally must be patient, sensitive, and politically aware. They must be patient because doing business internationally takes longer than it does domestically. They must be willing to wait for an appointment with the Minister of Communications to talk about a project, for example. They must be willing to return two or three times after this appointment to talk about their project. Then, they must be patient to wait the year, two, or more, that it may take to get a contract for this same project.

It is easy to talk about patience, the long term, and commitment in a university setting. These characteristics can be understood intellectually. But, in business life, they must be understood behaviorally — in a way that affects actions. What do these words mean?

One student, who worked for Northern Telecom before returning to university for an M.B.A., commented that he and some fellow workers used to think poorly of one of the international salespeople. This salesperson did not have a sale in three years, yet had the highest expenses in the division. This salesperson obviously was not performing very well — he thought. After learning how long it could take to sell a telecommunication system, the student had a more positive perspective on the salesperson.

Other students were shocked when the international sales manager for Clark Equipment Company told them of a nine-year effort to close a deal with the USSR. Countless trips, intimidating threats of temporary incarceration as visa expirations drew near, bugged conference rooms, restricted services in hotels, and expenses well into six figures added up to enormous frustrations. But, commitment overcame the personal and corporate hardships. In the end, a multimillion dollar deal for fork lift equipment was signed.

It took General Motors' Diesel Division, which manufactures diesel locomotives, seven years to make a sale to Indonesia. The examples presented here span three to nine years! This is long term, and one must have patience to see a sale or project through. One must be committed to international business to make this kind of investment! Telecommunication systems and locomotives are expensive, complex products. Although it may not take quite as long to sell less complex products, it may take much longer than first anticipated.

People must be flexible in international business. Travel plans, accommodations, meeting schedules, and vacation plans must be adjusted as necessary, to accommodate the customer in another country. Attitudes towards business practices, and attitudes towards other cultures, must be flexible. People involved in international business must be willing to adapt the way they do things.

Walter Light, the former CEO of Northern Telecom, characterizes the person with this cluster of attributes as the Renaissance Manager. The renaissance manager has an open mind, is willing to learn constantly, has an attitude of constant self-renewal, has an awareness of other values and cultures, and has a keen political awareness. These attributes provide an exciting challenge — personally and professionally — for those who work internationally.

The need to develop certain perspectives to be successful in international business has already been discussed. These included having a global world view, commitment, a long-term time orientation, cultural sensitivity and understanding, and an expanded role and product concept. These characteristics will help anybody interested in an international career. However, process — behaving, interacting, learning, and moving forward to objectives — should also be discussed.

Too often, particularly in North America, the focus is on outcome and end result rather than on the activities necessary to achieve the end result. For example, a person may want to become a doctor because of the money and prestige associated with being a famed surgeon. The reality of obtaining this position, however, may not be understood. The day-to-day routine of required courses, the late nights of study, the incredibly difficult exams, the bad professors and difficult students met along the way, and the part-time job that keeps one in groceries usually are overlooked. Some people who begin medical studies find the process overwhelming and drop out. It is important to have an idea of what one wants and where one wants to go, but the difficulty, hard work, and commitment it might take to get there should not be underestimated.

International business is an undertaking characterized by uncertainty. Information must be collected to put pieces of the puzzle together. An orientation that moves one closer to one's objectives is needed. This is accomplished through process, a series of interactions with other people. It could be said that process equals behavior.

Structure, as in the structure of an organization, facilitates the continuity of relationships. Process and structure are not mutually exclusive. They coexist. However, the interactions and the process give life to structure. Process is ongoing interaction; structure is a slice in time of these activities. Process is the drama in organization while structure is a snapshot of the actors in a particular scene. Structure defines relationships and creates expectations. However, the interaction between people in various roles is what provides meaning and accomplishes the work in an organization. The interaction between people, and reactions to events, over a period of time create feelings, meanings, and perceptions such as sincerity, trust, mistrust, and so forth. Each interaction or each event can become a barrier to understanding or a facilitator of understanding. The accumulation of these behaviors is what fractures or enhances mutual commitment and loyalty.

Process conjures up words that are active and interactive. Words like exporting, managing, trading, negotiating, and licensing. Words like selecting, training, entering, leaving, and relating also come to mind. These words imply an ongoing process. These ongoing processes are necessary to be a successful exporter, manager, trader, or negotiator. These ongoing interactions involve relationships with other people in other organizations. Relationships should be thought about carefully.

Another example of the importance of process is a joint venture. A joint venture is an organizational choice, a structural choice. There are numerous benefits in joint ventures such as reduced financial risk, access to local markets, and so forth. However, this example is like the previous example of the student who wished to be a doctor. One tends to concentrate on the end result and desired outcome, and may not think carefully about the process of getting there. People contemplating a joint venture need to think about the people, the events along the way, and the relationships that must be built in the process of getting to the joint venture. These people need to think more accurately, not about the joint venture, but about joint venturing. As soon as it is expressed this way, action and behavior are focused upon.

Actions to create events, to react to events, and to work with people are what eventually produce success or failure in international business.

The Selected Readings:
Reinforcing the Basic Messages

The basic premise or theme of this book is that there is a link between successful international business and cultural awareness and sensitivity. Good business practice, coupled with good cultural skills, should be an unbeatable combination. One would think that in doing business internationally, good business practice automatically would include good intercultural skills. Unfortunately, this is not always the case and, therefore, the combination of the two needs to be stressed.

The basic messages from the previous section can be divided into the following categories:

1. the reality of the global marketplace and what it takes for companies to be successful in that marketplace
2. the awareness of some patterns of behavior in one's own culture, and other cultures
3. the orientations, attitudes, and skills people need to be successful in foreign environments and with people from other cultures
4. the importance of proceeding in conditions of uncertainty and ambiguity that characterize international business

The selected readings in this book have been chosen carefully. These readings provide excellent information, insights, and recommendations based on the experience or research of the authors, who are business people and/or academics. These readings were chosen because, in all cases, they are thoughtful and written for managers. The authors communicate the realities they have discovered through their experiences, their observations of successful managers, or through their research. The emphasis is on improving managerial practice in other cultures.

The scope of readings selected for this book is by no means complete. There are many more excellent selections by outstanding and thoughtful business people and academics. If all these selections were to be included, this book would become a reader rather than a casebook. Similarly, if these selections were to be summarized, this book would then be a textbook.

This book strives to be a balance between text, readings, and cases in which the reader can begin to develop some of the skills needed to do business abroad. Therefore, the readings have been chosen in such a way as to reinforce the perspective that is communicated in this book. Each of the readings develops a part of that perspective in more detail.

Will the readings help to solve the cases in the book? In instances, the readings may be invaluable in helping to solve the problems in the cases, or to provide reasons why the problems exist. However, the purpose of the readings is to reinforce the orientations, perspectives, and attitudes that are requirements for being a successful manager internationally. It is hoped that the readings will motivate the reader to think about issues from a different perspective than he or she has had before. In this way, the readings complement the text and the cases.

Reading 1, "Developing Leaders for the Global Enterprise," looks at the evolution of the global enterprise and the necessary leadership skills and development requirements for this type of organization. It also reinforces the need for flexibility and adaptation of financial, technical, and human resources.

Readings 2 and 3, "The Silent Language in Overseas Business" and "Motivation, Leadership, and Organization: Do American Theories Apply Abroad?" deal with some dimensions of culture of which the global manager needs to be aware. Reading 2, by Edward Hall, is a classic. It focuses primarily on the interpersonal level of intercultural communication and interaction. Reading 3 emerges from one of the more recent, and most complete and ambitious, research projects on variations in cultures. This article draws the link between different cultural orientations and the motivation, leadership, and organization theories of cultures, particularly the American culture.

Reading 4, "Zen and the Art of Management," provides a philosophical underpinning for the notion of a "proceeding" rather than a "deciding" mentality. This reading contrasts the North American and Japanese approach. In situations of ambiguity, proceeding may be the appropriate mode of operation. The North American focus on quick results very often obscures the fact that one needs to proceed and to make progress — rather than to make quick decisions — in order to get results.

Reading 5, "Partner Selection Criteria for Developed Country Joint Ventures," identifies and discusses criteria for evaluating potential partners and makes the point that selecting partners with compatible skills is not the same as selecting compatible partners. An emphasis on long-term compatibility, including trust and commitment as essential elements of the relationship, is suggested.

Readings 6, 7, and 8 deal with different facets of international human resource management. "International Strategy from the Perspective of People and Culture" sets the scene by providing a sweeping overview of the stages of internationalization in operations and human resource management through which corporations have progressed. It places international human resource management in the context of global strategy. "Expatriate Selection, Training, and Career Pathing" reviews the current state of the art of what is known about the processes of choosing managers for international assignments, preparing them, and returning them home to continue their careers. "Pacific Basin Managers: A Gaijin, Not a Woman" reports a study of 52 successful women in international management and describes how they were chosen as well as their professional experiences.

Reading 9, "Bribery in International Business: Whose Problem Is It?" discusses how to do business in the face of pressure for bribes. There are many myths surrounding the issue of bribery and this reading sheds light on the issue from different perspectives. The authors of the reading suggest that there are acceptable alternatives.

It is hoped that these selections will increase one's substantive knowledge and add to one's repertoire of behaviors as action plans are considered. The readings, text, and cases together can help one improve the implementation of policy in practice.

A Note About Disguised Cases

Ideally, the authors of this text would prefer to use the real names of companies, countries, and places portrayed in the cases. However, there are many reasons why this cannot always be done. Often, the issues involved in the case are sensitive or are perceived to be sensitive by the people in the company who have cooperated in writing the case. Also, some of the comments made about other people or other countries in the cases are not always flattering. Many of the companies depicted in the cases have ongoing business relationships with these same people and countries, and do not wish to cause offense. In allowing others to write and use these cases,[10] some companies insist on disguising the names of people, places, and countries. The companies and people involved in these cases have cooperated with the authors of this text so that the student may benefit from their experience. Therefore, their requests have been honored.

Though it might be preferable that the cases not be disguised, the fact that they are is not a critical issue with a culture-general orientation. The emphasis should be on identifying the issues and analyzing the problems in the cases. The issues are important, and many of them in the cases are classic. These issues may be found in South America, Africa, or Europe. A good example of this is the Thurlow case. Five experienced and knowledgeable people who read the case have identified it as a project with which they were involved or knew a significant amount about. Yet all five projects these people were working on were different projects in different countries! Similarly, a manager who had worked in the office of the International Bank of Malaysia insisted that he knew the situation to be exactly the one he had heard about in another company on another continent.

Sometimes, only the management of a company is sensitive to having the real names of people and companies in print. In such cases, a light disguise can be used in which all the remaining data in the case is real. Sometimes, companies are sensitive to financial data in a case and want such data disguised as well. In these situations, a factor is applied to the data but the important relationships in the data are maintained.

Sometimes, the sensitivity to all the issues contained in a case is very high and, therefore, mythical countries have been created in these instances so that no one is offended. There is nothing mythical about the situation described in such a case, only the name of the country. The number of mythical countries contained in the cases of this book has been kept to a minimum. Where they do occur, they are Malindrania, a Latin American country that exhibits many of the problems of countries in that region; and Soronga, an island nation in the Pacific. An indication has been made on each case whether or not the case has been disguised. The main point is that, despite the disguise, the essential elements of the problems are intact.

The cases accurately describe the reality experienced by managers in actual situations.

THE IMPACT OF CULTURE ON MANAGEMENT

"Reforms, when the ground has not been prepared for them, especially if they are institutions copied from abroad, do nothing but mischief."

—Dostoevsky, from *The Brothers Karamazov*,
in which the Devil speaks to Ivan in his
nightmare about changes in Hell.

A fundamental part of any international manager's reality is the intercultural nature of his or her interactions. Most managers recognize that interactions within one's own culture are difficult enough to manage effectively, as is evidenced by the clamor in the business press for more training in interpersonal skills in the world's business schools.[11] Interactions with people from different cultures present a special challenge for the international manager, since there is potential for distortion or misunderstanding in these interactions. The challenge is to correctly interpret the meaning of a person from a different culture. Even if interaction is aided by slowing speech, speaking more distinctly, listening more carefully, or asking more questions, there still remains the problem of interpreting the message. The conceptual frameworks presented in this part of the book are offered to help in this interpretive act.

An even more difficult challenge may arise when management systems are applied in an intercultural context. Consider, for example, the introduction of a piece-rate incentive system in a small sewing operation in Botswana by a well-meaning expatriate manager.[12] Instead of producing more garments in order to receive more pay, the workers, who had previously enjoyed a close relationship with the manager, went on strike. Striking was an extremely unusual action in the rural community where the workers lived. Their actions puzzled the expatriate manager, especially since the workers were highly dependent on their jobs to support their families. Furthermore, the walkout was led by the most productive workers, those people who should have benefited from the new scheme. In this case, the manager's confusion about the reasons for the walkout could easily have led to charging the workers with laziness and a rapid deterioration of working relationships could have resulted. Fortunately, the manager asked the workers and other experienced people in the village for advice. This culturally based conflict was resolved by the manager adopting a group-based incentive that was more consistent with the values of the workers. This incentive, however, violated the expatriate manager's own sense of equity when less productive workers received the same financial rewards as the best producers.

The problem posed by this real-life example may be more difficult to resolve than interpersonal difficulties. The values underlying managerial systems, in this case a reward system, are less obvious. It would be easier to conclude that workers are the problem than it would be to examine the assumptions underlying an incentive scheme. And, if the scheme is one's own design, it is even less likely that one would consider it a source of a problem.[13]

Whether a problem occurs between people or involves managerial systems, the resolution of the problem depends on the manager's willingness to attempt to explain rather than to blame. The quality of the explanation depends, at least in part, on the manager's ability to get outside his or her own cultural mind-set in analyzing the problem.

The Interpersonal Level

A source of potential problems when working across cultures is interpersonal communication. Although language is an important part of communication, communication is not simply a matter of understanding and speaking a language. Communication is broader than language. It involves transmitting an idea and understanding someone else's idea. People from different cultures think about various issues differently than North Americans. The ability of a North American to speak in three different languages still may not enable him or her to understand the issues from the viewpoint of those from another culture.

Most people have been exposed to a general communications model and a description of the barriers to communication in courses at business schools or in management development programs. The general model of communication portrays people as senders and receivers of information. People are simultaneously receivers and transmitters of information. Cross-cultural communication is similar to other communication situations. It can be viewed as a variation of an interpersonal behavior model. Cross-cultural communication differs from familiar communication situations in that there are systemic, substantive differences in assumptions made by people of different cultures. Being aware of and understanding these different assumptions can help improve communication and relationships with people in different cultures.

The major problems of intercultural communication occur in perception and attribution of meaning. Communication is defined as a "dynamic process whereby human behavior both verbal and nonverbal is perceived and responded to."[14] People respond according to their perceptions, not necessarily according to what the transmitter believes he or she is communicating. This is an interactive process. Difficulties arise from:

> . . . error in social perception brought about by cultural variations that affect the perceptual process. The attribution of meaning to messages is in many respects influenced by the culture of the message decoder. When the message being interpreted was encoded in another culture, the cultural influences and experiences that produced that message may be entirely different from the cultural influences and experiences that are being drawn upon to decode the message. Consequently, grave errors in meaning may arise that are not intended nor really the fault of the communicators. They are the result of entirely different backgrounds being unable to accurately understand one another.[15]

Two basic ideas that come from cross-cultural communication studies should be stressed:[16]

1. One must understand the cultural influences (differences and similarities) on communication that affect the person from another culture and one's self.

2. One must want to communicate interculturally. Samovar and Porter state, "the parties to the intercultural communication must have an honest and sincere desire to communicate and seek mutual understanding. This assumption there-fore requires favorable attitudes on the part of intercultural communicators and an elimination of superior-inferior relationships based upon membership in particular cultures."

The second condition infers that an appropriate communication climate must be established for understanding to take place. Perceptual distortions can be asso-ciated with defensive behavior or defensive communication climates as well as with cultural variables. Differences in supportive and defensive communication climates are described in Table 1.[17]

The characteristics in the table describing a supportive climate strongly reflect, and in some instances are identical with, the cross-cultural communication skills discussed earlier in this book. In addition to creating a supportive communications climate, however, one must be aware of two different categories of assumptions that influence communication. These have been categorized as *process* assumptions and *substantive* assumptions.

Process assumptions are assumptions made about a communication or inter-action situation. These assumptions include the following:[18]

1. The other person sees the situation the same way you do.
2. The other person is making the same assumptions you are.
3. The other person is (or should be) experiencing the same feelings as you are.
4. The communication situation has no relationship to past events.
5. The other person's understanding is (or should be) based on your logic, not their feelings.

From experience, the authors of this text would add two more assumptions:

6. The other person is the one who has the "problem" or does not understand the logic of the situation.
7. Other cultures are changing and becoming, or want to become, more like your own culture and, therefore, the other person is becoming more like you.

Substantive assumptions are those that deal with things, concepts, and facts more than process. Some examples would include assumptions made about hier-archy and status, the role of the individual versus the group, the role of government,

TABLE 1   **Communication Climates**

Defensive Climate		Supportive Climate
Evaluation	Speech or other behavior that appears to "judge" the other person increases defensiveness.	Description
Control	Speech used to control the listener evokes resistance.	Problem orientation
Strategy	When the sender is perceived as engaged in a strategy involving ambiguous motivations, receivers become defensive because they don't want to be manipulated.	Spontaneity
Neutrality	When neutrality in speech appears to listeners to indicate a lack of concern for their welfare, they become defensive.	Empathy
Superiority	When people communicate to another that they feel superior in position, power, wealth, intellectual ability, physical characteristics, or in other ways, they arouse defensiveness.	Equality
Certainty	Those who are dogmatic, who seem to know the answers, to require no data, tend to put others on guard.	Provisionalism

contracts, and so forth. These assumptions are discussed in more detail in later sections.

When one interacts with people from very different backgrounds — people who have been exposed to different historical and social development, who speak different languages and have different values, and who see and interpret events and behavior differently — it is easy to see that the potential for misunderstanding, conflict, and unintended consequences exists. The assumptions, perceptions, and feelings model of interpersonal behavior[19] is a useful foundation for conceptualizing and thinking about intercultural management situations.

Assumptions, Perceptions, Feelings Model

A model relating assumptions, perceptions, and feelings has been found to be helpful to organize information and interpret meaning within one's own culture. This model can be extended to help explain and understand intercultural situations.

FIGURE 2   Cognitive and Emotional States

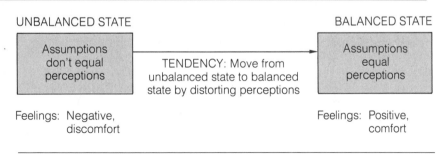

Assumptions, notions of what underlies whatever is observed, thought about, or experienced, are extremely important in daily functioning. If one did not make innumerable assumptions about the world, one would be paralyzed by the need to constantly inquire about the meaning of things and the motives of others. The key to adequate use of assumptions, however, is the assumptions' accuracy. Most assumptions made are accurate enough for communication and effective relations to occur. A crucial element in the accuracy of assumptions is the *commonality* of the assumptions made. The more that others share one's assumptions, the more likely it is that effective exchange will occur. So it is not surprising that one's assumptions are most effective when one operates within one's own culture.

However, even within one's own culture, assumptions can sometimes be barriers, rather than facilitators, of effective relations. One reason for this is that assumptions influence perceptions. The expression "we see what we want to see and hear what we want to hear" is not only a statement of the influence of one's needs on one's perceptions, but also a reflection of how one's assumptions affect one's perceptions. There is little difficulty if what is perceived fits or is consistent with what is assumed. But if perceptions do not fit with assumptions, then difficulties occur.

These difficulties are usually reflected in feelings and behavior. In each of the *cognitive* states (consistency or inconsistency between perceptions and assumptions) there are different *emotional* states. When assumptions equal perceptions, the associated feeling is one of comfort or harmony, or minimally, of neutral feelings. When assumptions do not equal perceptions, the feeling is discomfort. It is the feeling of discomfort that provokes reaction, and the usual reaction is to distort what is perceived to make it consistent with assumptions (see Figure 2). Why is this done? The simple answer is that people seek pleasure and avoid pain. If there is a clash between what is seen and what is assumed, people manage to reduce the negative feelings associated with the clash by distorting what they see.

Although the usual mode of reducing the gap between assumptions and perceptions is to distort perceptions, there is another option. People do not normally consider altering their assumptions, but this is a clear possibility. Unfortunately, this

is usually an unexamined alternative. Furthermore, the closer the relationship between the assumptions in question and one's self-concept, the less likely one is to
consider changing one's assumptions.

This tendency to make perceptions congruent with assumptions is often a
source of misunderstanding between people in the same cultural milieu. It is an
even bigger problem when it is moved into an intercultural context where there is a
lack of shared assumptions. The definitions of how one ought to behave and,
therefore, the explanations of why one is behaving in a particular way, are often
different when one moves from one culture to another. In this situation, people get
into difficulty by making inaccurate assumptions about a person or situation in a
different culture.

If assumptions could be identified and understood, the capacity to verify their
accuracy would increase. Differences in the assumptions might be anticipated and
errors in perception might be avoided. This process is similar to the requirement
that Coleridge posed for readers of poetry, namely, "the willing suspension of
disbelief." In the case of poetry, the poet's power of insight often enables him or her
to juxtapose two images or ideas that most people do not normally associate with
each other. The reader of poetry should not let his or her assumptions overwhelm
the poet's creativity in linking the elements (to disbelieve the unusual association).
The challenge is to be open intellectually to the poet's assumptions about what is
normal. The reward is a new vision! However, the more unusual the poet's perception of what belongs together, the more the reader's assumptions are challenged and
it is less likely that the poet will be appreciated or understood. Unfortunately, the
more abstract the poet, the less likely the reader is to even try to understand his or
her perception. Even more regrettable is the likelihood that the reader will justify
his or her assumptions by dismissing the poet as "impenetrable," "impossible,"
"weird," or whatever favorite pejorative is preferred. In intercultural situations, a
similar process is often employed in which the other culture is negatively stereotyped as, for example, "primitive" or "lazy."

These tendencies are overcome through description rather than evaluation.
Literary critics help people to understand poets by developing categories of poetry,
supporting conventions adopted by certain classes of poets, and by offering their
understanding of a poet's symbolism. Similarly, one could better suspend one's
culturally based assumptions if there were ways of identifying, describing, and
organizing them. Fortunately, anthropologists and other researchers perform a
function similar to this and have provided conceptual resources based upon their
studies. Edward T. Hall, in the reading "Silent Language in Overseas Business"
identifies some important culturally based assumptions and shows how they impact
on people's interpersonal behavior. One of the most extensively researched frameworks, by Geert Hofstede, is presented in the article "Motivation, Leadership and
Organization: Do American Theories Apply Abroad?" This article identifies basic
value patterns of cultures around the world and specifically links these values to
management theories and practices. In the next sections, another framework[20] is
presented that has been found to be easily adaptable and useful in an international
business context. Examples are provided on how the framework is linked to managerial issues and systems.

The Kluckhohn and Strodtbeck framework was developed in 1961. Since this time, many anthropologists have contributed ideas useful to managers in international situations. However, the authors of this text believe that few have conceptualized the complexity of their insights into a framework so easily adaptable and applicable to the world of business. These three frameworks are offered in the hope that readers will find one framework that is meaningful and useful for them. The authors, and others, have found them applicable, adaptable, and useful.

Variations in Value Orientations

To paraphrase the anthropologists Kluckhohn and Strodtbeck, culture consists of a shared, commonly held body of general beliefs and values that define the "shoulds" and the "oughts" of life. These beliefs and values are given to people so early and so unobtrusively that people are usually unaware of their influence. Awareness of the extent to which values shape assumptions, perceptions, and behavior usually emerges only as a different set of values guiding the views and practices of other people are confronted. If people are exposed to new experiences, part of their response will include an examination of their own guiding values as well as the more common reaction of rejecting the other's values as "strange."

It is important to note that the preceding definition of culture did not refer to country. Culture does not mean country, although country labels are often used as shorthand and notation for groups of people who hold "shared, common beliefs and values." Indeed, in the following discussion this shorthand will be employed, but one should not be seduced by the labels into mistaking culture for country or vice versa.

Figure 3 is a pictorial representation of the influence pattern of culture on assumptions, perceptions, and management behavior. It should be read from the bottom up. The value orientations and the factors that have contributed to their development represent the hidden bedrock upon which the guiding imperatives of activities rest. As one moves from abstract and general formulations to concrete and specific manifestations, the influence of the value orientations continually pervades one's ways of thinking and behaving. People may not be conscious enough about their basic belief about human nature to be able to articulate it. But, if somebody asked about how people were likely to behave if they found a large amount of money in an unidentified package on the street, they would probably be able to reply. It is even more likely that somebody would reply with greater clarity and certainty if they were asked a more specific question about what kind of management control system should be in place to prevent the theft of money by dishonest employees. In general, people are more consciously aware of how they ought to behave in situations that are specific and concrete. What people are usually not aware of is the root of the imperative "ought." The framework in Figure 3 provides a way to connect hidden, abstract values to conscious beliefs and behaviors associated with management. This linkage provides a way of analyzing a situation and behaving more effectively when the management practices embedded in two different cultural contexts cause problems. The cultural problems, at least intellectually, can be separated from strictly business problems.

FIGURE 3 Influence Pattern of Culture on Assumptions, Perceptions, and Management Behavior

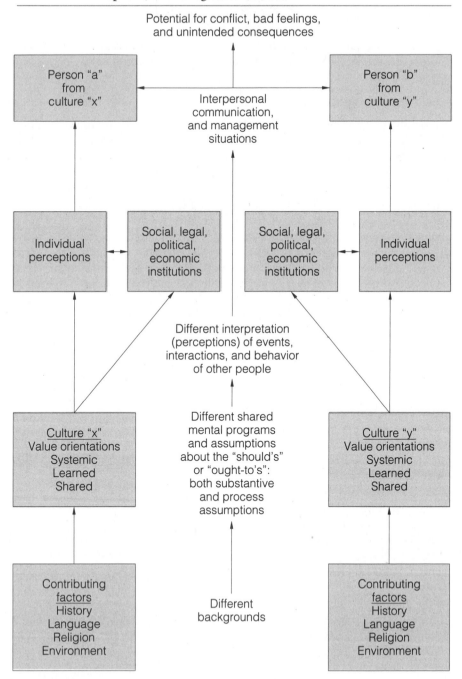

The basic premise underlying the value orientation framework is that there are common themes in the issues or problems that different societies have faced throughout time, and that these universal issues provide a way of viewing culture more objectively.[21] Six issues or problems have been identified as being faced by all societies throughout recorded history. Anthropologists have also discovered that different societies developed different ways of coping with these issues. These differences in preferred ways of dealing with the same issues or problems have been labeled "variations in value orientations." The six issues are

1. relationship of humans to nature
2. time orientation
3. belief about basic human nature
4. activity orientation
5. relationships among people
6. orientation to space

In this application of the value orientation framework, the terminology has been simplified and the links between the abstract concepts underlying each issue and the practical influence of the values and the variations on management have been made explicit.[22] For each of the six issues, the nature of the values underlying the issue will be explained and the variations that occur will be described. Examples of how the value orientation might influence general managerial activities (such as goal setting) will be given. It will be demonstrated how specific variations of the value orientation could yield different ways of dealing with those managerial activities.

An important assumption is that all variations of a particular value orientation exist in a given culture. That is, no culture is assumed to be so pure that only one way of dealing with a given issue is seen as most appropriate by all members of the culture. Rather, some of the variations are held to be more appropriate than others as the desirable way to cope with a particular issue. Each culture has an *ordered preference* of variations for solving a particular problem. One can imagine a dominant variation as reflecting the values of a majority of the people in the culture. This dominant variation may reflect the most influential preference within a culture as compared to other variations, which may also be important, but less so. Even though a culture may be described only in terms of its most dominant variation in the discussion, the reader should not confuse this device for simplifying a description of a culture (stereotyping it) with the reality of a culture's complexity or richness.

1. Relation to Nature

The issue of people's relationship to nature reflects how people in a society ought to orient themselves to the natural world around them, and to the supernatural. Three main variations seem to exist in the human experience. One is, "subjugation to nature," as the preferred mode. At one extreme, people are enjoined to see themselves at the mercy of physical forces and/or subject to the will of a supreme being.

Life in this context is viewed as predetermined, preordained, or as an exercise in chance. It is felt that one ought not to try to alter the inevitable by acts of will, for such actions will be futile at best and blasphemous at worst. The parenthetical addition of "God willing" to a stated intention to meet with a friend in the future is an example of how this variation finds its way into language, if not into literal meaning. To a devout Muslim, the expression "Inshallah," which has the same meaning as "God willing," has a much more serious impact. The Muslim expression reflects a dominant world view which is taken much more literally than the casual use of the similar expression by most Christians.

The second orientation is "harmony with nature," the imperative to behave in concert with the physical environment. To a Native American in the Southwest, this may mean designing a road to skirt a clump of trees on a lovely hill. In contrast, an Anglo-Saxon civil engineer might alter the terrain by leveling the trees and the hill. In doing so, the engineer would exhibit the dominant North American value of "mastery over nature." A good example of the mastery orientation in this century was the goal of landing a person on the moon at a time when the technology did not exist for accomplishing the task. The audacity of announcing that this mission was to be achieved by the end of the 1960s reflected not only a politically astute move to recapture America's confidence after Sputnik; it also reflected a profound belief that if enough time, money, and brains are applied to a goal, nearly anything is achievable. This is the meaning of the mastery notion.

The influence of this cultural dimension on North American perceptions of events is shown in the language used to describe them. When Sir Edmund Hilary reached the summit of Mount Everest, headlines throughout the English-speaking world screamed, "MAN CONQUERS EVEREST." Chinese colleagues have said that the same event reported in Mandarin would have been translated as "Man Befriends the Mountain." Religious writings also reflect culture's influence. The mastery notion seems to pervade Genesis 26, which states: "Let them have dominion over all the Earth." In contrast, the Tao Te Ching states, "Those who would take over the Earth and shape it to their will, never, I notice, succeed." Much of the basis of culture is manifested in religious writings and literary works. International managers would be well advised to read the literature of the countries in which they operate for clues to understanding the cultural roots of the managerial practices which they may experience in the workplace.

The relation to nature value can be seen to impact managerial activity in two areas: goal setting and budgeting. If one is operating in a culture with a subjugation variation as the dominant influence, then it is likely that the goals set in a managerial context in this culture will be more qualified and vague (if set at all) than in a cultural setting where harmony or mastery themes are dominant. In a harmony-dominated culture, goals are more likely to be moderated by the culture's need to fit with the environment. The appropriate contingencies that recognize such external parameters are likely to be stated. For example, environmentalists who reflect a harmony orientation would say, "If we must consume goods, we should minimize the packaging, recycle the waste, and use biodegradable ingredients." The manager in a mastery-oriented culture, on the other hand, is likely to confidently state specific, unambiguous, and ambitious goals. The distinction between individual personality and the impact of culture is worth noting here. The goals set do not depend exclusively on individual differences in personality, such as the need to achieve. Nor do goals reflect ethnicity or race. Rather it is the underlying influence of cultural orientation on the level and types of goals that is being emphasized here. Cultural orientation defines the way an individual *should* set goals.

The second managerial activity affected by the relation to nature value is budgeting. One study reported the differences between French and United States subsidiaries of a large multinational corporation (MNC) with a supposedly Uniform Budget System.[23] This budgeting system had bound volumes of procedures, rules, forms, schedules, and deadlines to be followed worldwide. The French subsidiaries, who showed a very weak preference for the mastery orientation over the harmony orientation, considered the budget system an elegant exercise. They treated only the actual accounting results as real. The United States subsidiaries, who showed a strong preference for the mastery orientation over the harmony view, treated the budget as real, relevant, and useful. They were confident of their ability to at least partially control events by using this managerial tool.

A budget system forced onto a subsidiary operating in a cultural context where the subjugation orientation is dominant might be a futile exercise. The outcomes of the system, intended to assist managers to shape events, would be seen as predetermined by local employees in such a setting. Local managers would likely resist the process and complete the forms involved in the system with reluctant predictions. This is distinct from what could occur if managers made specific choices as part of their activities. Some North American managers have reported such experiences with Indonesian managers.

An example of the impact of these variations in orientation to nature on management occurred when a civil engineer in a large North American construction company was given responsibility to select a site for, design, and construct a large fish-processing plant in a West African country. The engineer classified potential sites according to the availability of reliable power, closeness to transportation, nearness to the river for access by fishing boats from the Atlantic Ocean, location near the main markets, and availability of housing and people for employment. After evaluating these criteria and ranking the few sites in the final list, the engineer chose the optimum location. Just prior to requesting bids from local contractors for some of the site preparation, the engineer discovered, in talking to local authorities, that the site was located on ground considered sacred by the local people. These people believed this site was the place where their gods resided. None of the local people upon whom the engineer was depending to staff the plant would ever consider working there! The engineer quickly revised the priorities previously drawn up and relocated the plant. In this case, it was lucky that the cultural gaffe was discovered prior to construction. Too often these errors are realized only after a project has been completed. This true story points out the hidden workings of culture and also demonstrates that having a prior framework could assist in avoiding the problems of culturally bounded criteria for decision making.

A perhaps extreme, but dramatic, example of the harmony variation was reported in November 1986 by the Associated Press. A factory in India had been closed for over two months because a cobra occupied the owner's office. The Press

FIGURE 4   Variations in Relation to Nature and Examples of Managerial Impact

ISSUE	VARIATIONS		
Relation to nature	Subjugation to nature	Harmony with nature	Mastery over nature

MANAGERIAL IMPACT			
GENERAL	SPECIFIC BY VARIATION		
Goal setting	Qualified, hesitant, vague	Contingent, moderated	Specific, confident, unambiguous, high level
Budget systems	Futile, outcomes predetermined	Exercise, "actuals" are real	Real, relevant, useful

Trust of India (PTI) explained that since snakes are worshipped by many Hindus, the manager and the workers went to a temple for advice. They were told not to disturb the "cobra god." PTI went on to say that despite prayers, offerings, and creditor complaints, the factory remained closed for over two months. If this factory was part of a joint venture with a North American company, one can see the potential for conflict and hard feelings with North American executives who have a different orientation.

The relation to nature orientation is summarized in Figure 4. Under each of the variations are examples of how the cultural values manifest themselves in managerial spheres of activity. The examples in this and later figures are based on research or case studies and have been further reinforced by the experiences of the authors and their associates.

2. Time Orientation

There are two ways to think about time. The first has to do with one's general orientation toward time, rather than how one thinks about or uses specific units of time.[24] This can be illustrated in how people respond to new events. If people respond to a new challenge by looking to tradition and wondering, "How have others dealt with this kind of problem before?" the dominant value might well be past-oriented. If people primarily consider the immediate effects of an action, then the dominant orientation is more likely present-oriented. Similarly, if the chief concern were to be "What are the long-term consequences of this choice?" then the dominant orientation could be described as future-oriented.

One author of this text remembers vividly his Sicilian grandfather's pattern of response to questions. The grandfather would invariably frame his answers in the form of vignettes and start with, "Well, I remember that my father would always tell me. . . ." In contrast, the author's father, who had been born in the United States, almost always answered, "What is it that you want to accomplish?" Then he would give his advice, usually in the form of alternatives, rather than answers. This example illustrates that variations in the time orientation may be intergenerational as well as intercultural. However, it would be a mistake to think that this holds true in all cultures.

The planning horizon is the most obvious point of impact on managers of this cultural variable. Past-oriented cultures are more likely to recreate past behavior for planning. Present-oriented managers will have shorter-term concerns in planning. Future-oriented managers are more likely to consider long-term effects. The influence of precedence, current realities, or effects desired in the future may also influence decision making. Reward systems, too, may fall under the hidden effects of time orientation. Rewards in past-oriented cultures are more likely to be based on historically determined systems. An emphasis on currently contracted arrangements which can be revised to reflect new realities is more likely to be found in cultures where the present time orientation is dominant. Bonus systems and other incentive schemes tend to reflect a future orientation. However, since rewards are also mediated by other variables, there are exceptions and there is not a simple one-to-one relationship between a value orientation and a management system.

One's perception of one's own time orientation may be a source of distortion. Most North American managers would like to think of themselves as future-oriented people, for whom planning is an important part of the managerial function. However, North American managers probably are much more present-oriented than they think. This contradiction is seen in the heavy emphasis given to long-term planning in managerial textbooks and the relative absence of long-term planning in actual behavior. Corporate planners and corporate planning departments appear to have been a fad and are on the way out.[25] Although it may make better sense for line managers to do strategic planning, Henry Mintzberg demonstrated how short the cycle time of activities is for even senior executives, and how little planning is done as a percentage of time available.[26]

Although North Americans may think of themselves as long-term planners, the meaning and implications of North America's propensity to send planeloads of politicians, government bureaucrats, and business executives on trade missions to foreign countries should be pondered. One such mission targeted a blitz of several Brazilian cities by government officials and businesspeople. Upon their return, two weeks after departure, one of the managers remarked that the travel had been a waste of time since no orders had been secured during the whole trip. In contrast, a Japanese manager was sent to Rio de Janeiro by a company who gave the manager a simple mission: "Get to know the people and learn Portuguese during your first year there. Then worry about starting the business." That is future-oriented behavior! Of course, the measurement system of the Japanese company did not require their expatriates to recoup the foreign investment in the first year, either. Part of the reason for that is the structure of the Japanese economy and the close links in that country between companies, government, banks, and investors. The confluence of factors facilitating the longer-term planning of Japanese companies as compared to their North American counterparts is not entirely an accident. Neither is it an accident that North American managers are constrained in their planning horizons by concern for earnings per share reported quarterly, and even by daily shifts in stock prices. A good example of the influence of North Americans' present-time orientation on management behavior was the decision of Levi Strauss to privatize the company. Their motivation was significantly related to shareholders' pressure to maximize profitability in the short term. The executives believed that this pressure constrained future-oriented, strategic decision making that would be more beneficial to the company in the longer run.

Some effects of these preoccupations are useful; some are detrimental. The important points are to understand that some of the forces that shape such behavior are cultural, that these forces operate in several spheres that tend to reinforce each other, and that these forces are not easily altered. Figure 5 summarizes the time orientation and points of potential managerial impact.

There is another aspect to orientation to time that strongly influences behavior and appears to be related to the Kluckhohn and Strodtbeck dimensions. This aspect is the specific units of time that are used. This is the time dimension addressed by Hall in the reading "Silent Language in Overseas Business."

To North Americans, time is a valuable commodity. For example, North Americans save, spend, and waste time. This leads North Americans to live their lives by sacrosanct schedules. For others, such as some Arab and Latin cultures, time schedules are less critical.

There are contrasting units of time. For most North Americans, punctuality is defined as being within five to ten minutes of a time previously set. For others, the period before an apology or explanation for being late is expected might be forty-five minutes to one hour. North Americans, with their present/future orientation divide the hour into quarters, but some subcultures treat five-minute intervals as the appropriate guide to behavior.

It is quite possible, therefore, that differences in definitions of timeliness can have significant effects on business dealings. If one is driven to meet schedules and deadlines, one is likely to be viewed as lacking patience, tact, or perseverance. This is even more complicated if those who use more lengthy time units see the usefulness of the less-hurried pace as a way to build relationships. One's need to "get down to business" and preserve one's schedule will then clash with the other's view of the right pace and the right way to conduct business such as contract negotiations.

We are not suggesting that it is wrong to establish schedules or deadlines when they are reasonable. However, "reasonable" is a cultural variable. Since much of the world has a more elastic and relaxed attitude toward time, North Americans have to learn what is reasonable in other countries and adapt to their definitions, especially when these countries act as hosts. Otherwise, at best one will rush from one country,

FIGURE 5   Variations in Time Orientation and Examples of Managerial Impact

ISSUE	VARIATIONS		
Time orientation	Past	Present	Future

MANAGERIAL IMPACT			
GENERAL	SPECIFIC BY VARIATION		
Planning	Extension of past behavior	Short–term	Long–term
Emphasis in decision criteria	Precedence	Current impact	Desired effects
Reward systems	Historically determined	Currently contracted	Contingent on performance

city, or meeting to another without ever taking sufficient time to achieve closure. At worst, one offends others with insensitivity and risks erecting permanent barriers to doing business.

3. Basic Nature of Human Beings

The belief about basic human nature does not reflect how one thinks about individuals but, rather, one's belief about the inherent character of the human species. Does one believe that humans are changeable or unchangeable? And, apart from the malleability of basic human nature, does one believe people are primarily evil, good, neutral (neither good nor evil) or mixed (a combination of good and evil)? In addressing these questions, the influence of religious traditions as reflecting and shaping culture can be seen. In Christian faiths, the story of Adam and Eve in the Garden of Eden is pertinent. Adam's eating of forbidden fruit symbolized the "fall of man," as Adam gave in to the devil's evil. Note, however, that men and women are perfectible if they follow and worship God. In the language of the value-orientation framework these beliefs parallel the evil/changeable orientation. Fundamentalists, of course, may hold a more dominant view of human beings as evil. Christians with stronger secular perspectives tend to hold a more neutral or mixed orientation. Although the authors claim no expertise in comparative religion, their understanding of Muslim and Shinto faiths, and personal communications from

Arab and Japanese proponents, suggest that orientations emerging from these traditions may be closer to the "good" end of the spectrum.

The most obvious impact on business of the human nature value may be on control systems. A dominantly evil orientation is likely to contribute a tight control system based on an underlying suspicion of people. Cultural orientations dominated by a neutral or mixed value are likely to produce moderately tight controls, with modifications based on managers' experience with the people involved. People operating with an assumption that the basic nature of humans is evil are less likely to modify a control system if there are no violations, because they will attribute the goodness of people to the existence of the control system, not to people's innate goodness. Thus, there is a tendency to explain events in a way consistent with cultural values, even when other possible explanations are available. Similarly, managers who operate with an assumption of goodness as the basic human trait are likely to favor control systems based primarily on the need for management information, rather than for surveillance, checking, and control. One can imagine the opportunities for misunderstanding and mistrust in a Japanese–North American joint venture, for example, when, for cultural reasons, there might exist such basic differences in why information is collected and how it is used.

There is a cultural basis in sanctions against violation of codes of conduct. An executive who was negotiating a large contract in Saudi Arabia was shopping in an open-air market. On stepping up to a currency exchange booth the executive was very surprised to see about one quarter of a million dollars clipped to a board in the stall. The currency dealer wandered away from the board to get some coffee after completing a transaction. The executive was stunned that such a large amount of money should be left unattended, but remembered the Islamic code's punishment for stealing—cutting off the hand at the wrist. The severity of the punishment explained the apparently cavalier behavior of the money dealer. The executive also assumed, erroneously, that Saudis viewed basic human nature the same way as North Americans. This assumption led the executive to believe the punishment and the punishers were inhumane. However, consider an alternative explanation. If the Saudis hold human nature to be basically good, then it may follow that anyone behaving evilly is less than human. If one is not behaving according to the expectations of what is human, then one may deserve to be identified in a dramatic way—by having a hand cut off.

Note that this value orientation may explain the executive's feelings towards crime and the punishment system. To most North Americans, people are, at best, mixed. Therefore, one should not be surprised if money were to be stolen from a neglected stall in an open-air market. A North American would feel that a violator should be punished, but not severely (North Americans slap the wrist, not cut it off!). In fact, in North America, the currency dealer would probably be examined for mental stability for leaving money unattended. Simply put, control and punishment systems are created based on expectations about behavior, and the expectations are based on cultural values.[27]

The ironic end to this story was that the employees who were to go to Saudi Arabia after the executive had the contract signed were sent to a cross-cultural training session for one week. The first program was held at a hotel. Soon after the executive made the speech in which the personal incident cited previously was reported, the hotel, as part of a chainwide campaign to reduce customer theft, had put a sign on the bathroom counters in each room. The sign read, "Love is leaving the towels here when you leave!" Thus, all employees about to embark on their first trip into a markedly different culture had their own culture's view of human nature reinforced just before they left home.

The value orientation regarding basic human nature affects areas of management beyond control and punishment systems. Management style is likely influenced by this dimension of culture. A culture with a dominant evil orientation is likely to be populated by managers with autocratic tendencies who practice very close supervision (Theory X). Neutral or mixed dominant orientations are likely to encourage moderate supervision and consultative managers. At the good end of the spectrum, managers are likely to prefer a *laissez faire* style or to practice participative management (Theory Y).

Organizational climate may be consistent with the orientation on the human nature dimension. At one extreme is an adversarial climate and a stress on contractual relations. At the other extreme, collaborative and informal relations may occur. Organizational climates probably are consistent with control systems and management styles. The consistency of managerial systems is at least partially explained by their common roots in a particular value orientation. Organizations develop management systems to achieve a congruence or fit with their environments and between the people and the tasks they perform. The systems also are likely developed to fit with cultural values which act as hidden enforcers on their consistency. Figure 6 summarizes this human nature orientation and its variations and probable impact on managerial practices.

4. Activity Orientation

The activity orientation does not refer to a state of activity or passivity, but rather the desirable focus of activity. The "being" orientation is characterized by spontaneity. One acts out one's feelings as they are experienced. This is the Dionysian mode (the god of wine and good times). The "doing" orientation is the Promethean mode. Prometheus stole fire from Olympus and gave it to humans to use. As a punishment he was chained to a rock and tormented by vultures. Throughout eternity, he strained to break free of his chains but new chains constantly reappeared when he was successful. The relentless striving to achieve and compulsive attempt to accomplish are the core of the doing orientation. In between the being and doing extremes is the containing/controlling orientation. This is the Apollonian mode, in which the senses are moderated by thought, and mind and body are balanced.

The activity dimension affects how people approach work and leisure, how preoccupied they are with work, and the extent to which work-related concerns pervade their lives. In a strongly doing-oriented culture, people are more likely to view work and work-related activities as a central focus to their existence. It is likely that decisions are made on pragmatic criteria, reward systems are results-based, and

FIGURE 6   Variations in Basic Human Nature and Examples of Managerial Impact

ISSUE	VARIATIONS		
	Changeable		Unchangeable
Basic human nature	Evil	Neutral or mixed	Good

MANAGERIAL IMPACT			
GENERAL	SPECIFIC BY VARIATION		
Control system	Tight, suspicion-based	Moderate, experience-based	Loose, information-based
Management style	Close supervision, autocratic	Moderate supervision, consultative	Laissez-faire, participative
Organization climate	Adversarial, contractual		Collaborative, informal

there is a compulsive concern for performance. In a being-dominated culture, it is more likely that decision criteria are emotional, rewards are feelings-based, and the degree of concern for output and performance is variable, a function of individual spontaneity. In cultures with a dominant containing/controlling orientation, decisions more likely would be based on rational criteria, rewards would be distributed logically, and output would be measured against balanced objectives (such as long- and short-term profitability, quality as well as quantity of production, and so on).

In a study of French and United States subsidiaries, Perret found effects of the activity orientation on the information and measurement systems of companies.[28] In the comptroller departments of the companies, the more doing-oriented United States managers acted on the Uniform Budget System in a highly selective way. They stressed simple, operational indices and were concerned with making the system serve operational objectives. The more contained/controlled-oriented French managers treated the system as a complex exercise and were concerned with the qualitative and broad implications of the system itself, as distinct from what the data implied for action. The French were preoccupied with absolute accuracy for all parts of the system and its calculations. The Americans were satisfied with approximations, as long as these provided data which could be used to make a difference in

FIGURE 7   Variations in Activity and Examples of Managerial Impact

ISSUE	VARIATIONS		
Activity	Being	Containing and controlling	Doing

MANAGERIAL IMPACT			
GENERAL	SPECIFIC BY VARIATION		
Decision criteria	Emotional	Rational	Pragmatic
Reward systems	Feelings–based	Logic–based	Results–based
Concern for output	Spontaneous	Balanced objectives	Compulsive
Information and measurement systems	Vague, feeling–based, intuitive	Complex, qualitative, broad	Simple, operational, few indices

manufacturing departments. Although no comparative data were gathered for the being orientation, that kind of dominant variation would likely yield more of an intuitive system that was less preoccupied with quantitative indicators. The activity orientation is summarized in Figure 7.

5. Relationships Among People

Relationships among people concern the responsibility one has for others. What responsibility does one have for the welfare of others? One response is that one should take care of oneself—"individualism." This attitude is dominant in North America. The nuclear family tends to be the outer limit of formal responsibility. Even that changes after children reach the age of majority. Independence is valued, and "Stand on your own two feet!" is the injunction. Parents with offspring in their twenties still living with them are viewed as having failed in their obligations to instill the "rugged individualism that made this country great!" Perhaps it is only in an individualistic society, such as the United States, that a book entitled *Looking Out for #1* could have appeared on the best-seller list. Yet quite different attitudes toward responsibility exist.

One alternative to individualism is the "group" orientation dominant in many Mediterranean and Asian cultures. In this type of society, one's allegiance and loyalty are to the extended family or group (tribe) of which one is a part. In such a culture, cousins are treated with as much concern and love as siblings are in an individualistic culture.

A corollary often exists in such cultures that if one does treat a stranger with the concern normally reserved for a member of one's group, then the person so treated for all intents and purposes becomes a member of the group with all the rights and responsibilities associated with such membership. This can give rise to misunderstandings, as exemplified by the apocryphal story of an American assisting a pedestrian brushed by a passing car in a busy street in an Asian city. Appalled by the lack of attention to the injured stranger, the American yelled at a nearby police officer, provided first aid, and insisted on hailing and paying for a taxi to take the person to a hospital. Afterward, the American muttered about the inhumanity of the local population and concluded that the incident confirmed his personal theory, "How cheap human life is in the overpopulated Asian cities." Meanwhile, the police officer's family listened, appalled, as the officer told about the American who was so dumb as to treat a stranger like a family member, and then was so indifferent as to send the person off in a taxi, rather than accompany the injured to the hospital personally and to attend to the victim properly afterwards!

A further variation on the relationship dimension is "hierarchical," although the concept is more complex than is implied by this single word. In this variation, society defines the proper relation to others as group-oriented, but with two additional characteristics. One is that the group is nested in a hierarchy of other groups in society. Secondly, the group's position in the hierarchy is stable over time. This is characteristic of aristocratic society and caste systems. One is to look after one's own kind, but one knows where one's kind stands on the status ladder. Mobility between groups is highly unlikely, if not impossible. The hierarchical notion may be one of the reasons that Americans tend either to dismiss English society as consisting of stuffy snobs or wish to be a part of it. It also explains why some British wish they were Americans or find Americans insufferably familiar and informal.

The relationship variable seems to have a pervasive influence on managerial practice and policy. Organizational structures, communication and influence patterns, reward systems, teamwork, and other managerial processes are all influenced by the relationship orientation. In cultures where individualistic values are dominant, individuals are given much attention in the organizational structure. The focus is on the leader in the pyramidal structures. However, no matter how the organization is structured, the arrangement of relationships is treated informally. Behavior within the structures is flexible. Two-boss relationships are possible, as with a matrix organization.

In a group-dominated culture, more attention is given to horizontal differentiation. Differences between groups are the preoccupation, and the structures of work organizations reflect this concern. Similarly, in hierarchical cultures, there is emphasis on both vertical and horizontal differentiation. Of all three possible variations, the most rigidly obeyed structures are likely to be found in the hierarchical situation. Perret found, for example, that French managers could not conceive of working in a matrix structure and faithfully reported any budget anomalies exclusively to their immediate superior, even if there were serious implications for lateral departments. In contrast, American managers operated much more independently of the structure. They reported findings to anyone who had an interest in the data, regardless of his or her position in the structure.

An interesting reversal based on the same cultural differences was found with respect to the importance of interpersonal relations at work. The French spontaneously raised the topic of interpersonal relations several times in unstructured interviews; the Americans mentioned interpersonal relations much less frequently, and only in an instrumental context regarding work. The French valued the relations as ends in themselves. This difference between French and American managers in relating at work also shows up in communication and influence patterns. Hierarchical cultures use authority-based communications. Group-oriented cultures stress within-group patterns. Individualistic cultures maintain multiple, open arrangements to be used on an as-needed basis.

Similarly, the relations variations have impact on reward systems. Individually based, group-based, and status-based systems are characteristic of each of the three types of relationship patterns. Teamwork and cooperation are also affected by the dominant pattern. In hierarchical cultures, teamwork is regulated and formal. In the French controller's departments studied by Perret, the hierarchical orientation was reflected in the regular work group meetings held by the managers, who controlled the agenda, data, and meeting processes rigidly. On the other hand, the American managers scheduled no routine group meetings. Instead, they dealt with others on a voluntary, informal basis whenever (but only when) the circumstances required such activity.

The vaunted skill of the Japanese in group management deserves special mention. Careful examination of Japanese culture[29] shows a more complex pattern than the popular literature leads one to believe. The group orientation is combined with a strong sense of hierarchy, which coexists with an egalitarian educational and social system that depends on merit (doing orientation) rather than class consciousness. The managerial implications of this include the commonly described group decision making. It also includes the less frequently mentioned respect given to a superior, who is invariably an older, experienced manager with all that implies for practice and skill in managing groups. Another implication is that Japanese managers are encouraged to move laterally and diagonally through the organization in their careers. This is partly due to their skills in managing groups of functional experts and partly because companies can depend on investment in such experience paying off in the future (lifetime employment). In contrast, the individualistic orientation in North America stresses individual expertise that gives rise to increased specialization and career paths, primarily within a particular function. The relations orientation of the Japanese provides an explanation for the finding that within Japanese-owned companies in the United States, the greater the Japanese presence in the

FIGURE 8   Variations in Relationships and Examples of Managerial Impact

ISSUE	VARIATIONS		
Relationships	Hierarchical	Group	Individualistic

MANAGERIAL IMPACT			
GENERAL	SPECIFIC BY VARIATION		
Organizational structure	Attention on vertical differentiation	Attention on horizontal differentiation	Informal, flexible behavior vis a vis structures
Communication and influence patterns	Authority–based	Within group emphasis	Multiple, as–needed, open
Reward system	Status–based	Group–based	Individually–based
Teamwork	Regulated, formal	Normative, routine	Voluntary, informal

company, the less the functional differentiation. The greater the United States presence in the companies, the greater the functional differentiation.[30] The relationships orientation is summarized in Figure 8.

6. Orientation to Space

People's orientation to space was not completely conceptualized by Kluckhohn and Strodtbeck, nor investigated as part of their work. It is important enough to discuss, however. The words private, mixed, and public have been chosen to apply to the variations of this orientation. The variable in space orientation has to do with how one is oriented towards surrounding space.[31] How does one view its use, especially the sense of "ownership" of space relative to others? The private perspective holds that space is for the exclusive use of an occupant. The private orientation holds that space is for an occupant's benefit and defines a large area surrounding the occupant as part of that person's territory. Protective action is taken if this larger area is seen as being invaded by others. In contrast, the public orientation sees space as available for anyone's use. The sense of territory is small, and defensive action to guard against invasion is taken only in the immediate area around the occupant. The mixed orientation is a blend of the private and public perspectives, or an intermediate position.

Communication, influence, and interaction patterns are all influenced by the spatial dimension as are physical realities, such as office and building layout. Managers operating in a culture dominated by a private orientation are more likely to find themselves communicating on a one-to-one basis with a secretive, serial pattern. Physically, these managers are most comfortable with a fair amount of distance between them when they are talking directly to each other. On the other hand, managers interacting in a culture dominated by a public orientation are more likely to engage in a wide variety of interactions with an open style. Their conversations may involve several people simultaneously, and physically close relations will not be uncommon. Cultures with a mixed orientation influence managers to be more selective in their communications, with moderately separated space between people and somewhat more organized, semiprivate arrangements.

The layout of the space within which interactions occur show parallel effects of the dominant orientation to space. Private orientations are characterized by barriers. Office doors are closed; private offices are favored; large desks and formal spaces are usual. In public-oriented cultures, offices are more likely to be arranged in an open concept. Where private offices do exist, doors are more likely to be left open and fewer barriers, such as office furniture, will appear in them. The mixed orientation features a blend of these characteristics, for example, an office containing specialized spaces. Part of the layout might be formal, with an official desk providing a barrier between the occupant and visitors. An adjoining space in the same office may be furnished with more comfortable, informal furniture.

The perils of ignoring the cultural factors of space can be extremely costly. One Ontario government ministry, caught in the grips of architectural fads, decided it would modernize its office space and save money at the same time. The ministry planned to consolidate several departments in a new building and use an open office layout. Not wishing to traumatize the managers, they decided that movable partitions would provide the appropriate degree of privacy in the new situation. The move involved a total of 1,300 people. Arrangements were made to purchase sufficient dividers for all, even though the merger was to be accomplished in several steps. The first move involved 300 people, but partitions allotted for 800 people were requisitioned from storage. Puzzled, the planners went to inspect and found that most people had insisted on their own dividers. Duplicate partitions had been placed back-to-back to satisfy the managers' need for privacy and ownership!

In another situation, the CEO of a large insurance company was frustrated by the inability of divisions in the company to better integrate their efforts. Yet, the CEO was surprised when a consultant who had been in the company a total of only fourteen hours had to introduce several of the 120 headquarters executives to each other. Closer scrutiny of the office layouts revealed a highly private orientation that explained both situations. Long corridors in the company formed a maze that separated people from each other. The suites of offices off the corridors all had the

FIGURE 9 Variations in Spatial Orientation and Examples of Managerial Impact

ISSUE	VARIATIONS		
Space	Private	Mixed	Public

MANAGERIAL IMPACT			
GENERAL	SPECIFIC BY VARIATION		
Communication and influence patterns	One-to-one, secret	Selective, semiprivate	Wide, open
Office layout	Emphasis on barriers (closed doors, large desks, etc.)	Specialized spaces (informal furniture next to formal desk)	Open concept
Interaction patterns	Physically distant, one-to-one, serial	Moderately spaced, moderated numbers, organized	Physically close, frequent touching, multiple relations (sometimes spontaneously)

doors accessing the reception areas closed. Inside, each of the offices that formed the group of suites also had all their doors closed. The company had operated in a French-speaking milieu for over a century. However, the company was staunchly British in its culture, and the private orientation to space overwhelmed the CEO's wish for stronger integration among the departments. Even the language used in the company acknowledged the dominance of privacy; the executives openly referred to the high degree of isolation between business units as "functional solitudes." The senior management of the company, including those who used this highly descriptive language in reference to their own situation, seemed genuinely puzzled about their failure to achieve the desired degree of integration. They were, in short, oblivious to the effects of their own company culture, firmly embedded in their own broader cultural values, on the management processes in the company.

In addition to the spatial sense discussed, the space orientation value also may apply to physical goods or property. People with a dominantly private orientation are likely to have a strong sense of ownership of things as well as of space. This manifests itself in the degree to which physical items are shared or viewed as com-

FIGURE 10   Completed Matrix*

ISSUE	VARIATIONS IN ADDRESSING ISSUES		
Relation to nature	Subjugation to	Harmony with	Mastery over
Time	Past	Present	Future
Basic human nature	Unchangeable		Changeable
	Evil	Mixed Neutral	Good
Activity	Being	Containing and controlling	Doing
Relationships	Hierarchical	Group	Individualistic
Space	Private	Mixed	Public

* The vertical columns are not meant to suggest association of variations across issues. For example, a culture with a dominant "being" mode on the "activity" dimension is not more likely to reflect hierarchical relationships and private, spatial orientations. Variations within each issue are assumed to be independent of those on other issues.

munity property. Links between these orientations and forms of economic activity, such as capitalism and socialism, are also possible. Figure 9 summarizes spatial orientation.

Summary

The discussion of each of the variables in the cultural framework has demonstrated the variety of ways in which the effects of values seep into one's assumptions and perceptions and influence behavior in one's managerial life. Figure 10 shows the full matrix. It is worth repeating that dominant values on one dimension are independent of dominant values on another. As one inspects the overall matrix, it is tempting to impose a correlation of dominant values that seem to cluster together naturally. This tendency to associate values across the dimensions as fitting with each other is most likely a result of North American cultural conditioning. Thus, North Americans probably feel that mastery, present/future, mixed/neutral, doing, individualistic, and mixed space values belong together. They also are likely to associate other combinations of values with cultures they have read about or experienced directly. However, the associations are empirical, not inevitably brought about by natural law.

Earlier, the idea of a framework itself being culture-bound was discussed. Conceptualizing culture as an activity reflects a mastery orientation. An emphasis on using these conceptualizations reflects a doing value. Suggestions as to how these

conceptualizations may be employed reflects neutral and individualistic orientations. Culture reaches into the very mental programs that people use to structure
and process their ideas and experience. There is a danger when only a dominant
variation is applied to a society. It should not be forgotten that all variations of each
of the value orientations occur in most societies. The North American tendency to
abbreviate (to save time and achieve efficiency) masks the complexity of culture and
can be deceptive in trying to sort out aspects of another system of living. This needs
to be kept in mind as applications of the framework are discussed in the next section.

Applications of the Framework

There are several approaches to the application of the framework and the cultural
impact these have on work organizations. One can try to anticipate the problems
that might be encountered in an intercultural situation. Or one can wait until actual
problems are experienced and then use the framework to help deal with them.
Another approach in the application of the framework is to differentiate the level of
managerial issue involved in a situation. A problem may occur between people, or
it may involve organizational-level issues, such as structure or systems. If the personal
and organizational aspects are combined, a systematic way of using the framework
can be developed (see Figure 11).

To avoid cross-cultural problems (column 1 of Figure 11) at the personal or
organizational level, appropriate preparation is needed. For example, if a North
American manager is going to another country, that manager should be oriented
to the culture in which he or she will operate. The manager can organize the
information, observations, and advice provided in such an orientation by using the
cultural categories. The manager can then evaluate his or her own dominant value
orientations, analyze those of the culture destination, and then decide where the
main differences exist. For each value dimension where there are differences, one
can deduce the likely areas of managerial problems by examining the framework, or
by careful thought.

A similar approach can be taken if a manager in a MNC is attempting to
introduce organizational structures or systems from headquarters into a foreign
subsidiary. The difference here is that the issues involved include organizational
design elements, rather than people. In either case, the usefulness of the framework
is dependent upon

1. being explicit about one's own culture
2. organizing what is known about another culture
3. providing for a systematic comparison of dominant values
4. noting value differences and predicting from these the areas in which man-
    agerial problems are likely to arise

This four-step process may be approached by making a copy of Figure 10 and
drawing a line connecting the cells in the matrix that designate one's own dominant
cultural values. Then, one could draw a line with a different color designating the

---

FIGURE 11   **Two Approaches to Applying the Framework**

PURPOSE OF APPLICATION

	Avoiding	Resolving
LEVEL OF ISSUE		
Personal	Managerial preparation	Social analysis and action
Organizational	Structural and systems planning	Organizational analysis and action

---

dominant variations of another culture. It is then easier to see the areas where managerial problems might exist, either with oneself, with others, or with respect to organizational issues.

Even though areas of potential managerial and personal problems may be predicted, the international executive still has a basic choice to make. For each kind of problem, one can elect to plan its avoidance by an approach of dominance (deciding which culturally defined management practice should be followed), or a mixed strategy (blending the foreign and North American practices). One also could develop a synergistic approach by "recognizing and transcending the individual" elements of both cultures.[32]

It is probably unwise to select a single strategy for all kinds of problems. Some situations may require different approaches. For example, the Canadian National Railway found it necessary to insist that Inuit employees, running their trains on a single-line track, always call in by radio if they stopped to rest. (An Inuit harmony value was, "When tired, sleep.")[33] In this situation, safety demanded that a dominant strategy be adopted. But when oil companies in the Arctic found that native people failed to show up for work in order to go hunting when the geese were migrating (again a harmony-influenced behavior) or when they felt like visiting relatives (a being- and group-oriented behavior), the companies hired more workers than needed and paid them only when they worked. Rather than complain about "unreliable" employees, they adopted a synergistic solution.

In addition to choosing among the strategies of dominance, mixed, and synergistic, there is the additional issue of deciding which party needs to adapt. A number of factors influence the decision of who should adapt and how the adaptation should be made. As a general rule, the onus for adaptation rests with the party seen as the foreigner. This probably is influenced by the sheer force of numbers. However, location is probably the strongest determinant. When North Americans are hosts to other cultures, these other cultures should adapt to North America; when North Americans are guests of other cultures, North Americans should make the effort to adapt. Technological dependence might alter this equation. A joint venture in Beijing may choose to emphasize North American cultural values and management practice in spite of the location and overwhelming majority of Chinese population, simply as a recognition of the need to acquire information.

Individual preference may also enter the equation. A North American dealing with Chinese in Beijing may attempt to adapt to Chinese traditions, even though there is no necessity to do so. The motives for adaptation in this situation might range from showing courtesy to a desire to learn and to increase one's own repertoire of behavior.

The behavior of people in the variety of examples discussed serve to remind one that several different values can influence people simultaneously. This makes the use of a framework even more valuable, in that it provides a checklist against which to analyze a situation for cultural causes. One should not fixate on single explanations for events and miss the complexity of causes involved. This can lead to error in framing solutions for problems.

Although it is desirable to attempt to avoid problems, in intercultural management situations it is more usual to find oneself immersed in problems that one failed to anticipate and must resolve (column 2 of Figure 11). In such cases, it is critical that the tendency to blame the other party be avoided. An explanation for the problem should be sought. It is equally important to consider cultural causes as potential explanations for problems. If it appears that there is a cross-cultural component to a problem, then the choice of strategy remains as described earlier. The key factor, however, is the careful analysis of the causes of a problem and the isolation of those elements that are cultural in nature. If there are no culturally linked causes, then conventional approaches can be followed for resolving problems.

Some Caveats

Notwithstanding the usefulness of a conceptual scheme for avoiding or for resolving cross-cultural problems, a number of caveats are offered here for the reader. The first caution is, "Beware of the Ecological Fallacy." This is such a common error that sociologists have named it. To avoid the error, apply concepts only at the level of analysis from which they have been derived. The concept of culture is, by definition, a group-based concept (commonly held, widely shared set of values). Therefore, one should not project cultural values known to be held by a group onto an individual who is a member of the group. For example, it does not automatically follow that if the Chinese people in general have harmony and hierarchical dominant values, that a particular Chinese person also has such dominant values. Similarly, if one knows a Nigerian from the Ibo tribe, one should be careful not to assume that by knowing her values that one knows anything about the Ibo culture.

Just as care should be taken not to project from groups to individuals, neither should cultural homogeneity within any country be assumed. In fact, the authors of this text have not been in any country where local jokes did not exist about the cultural characteristics of one region versus another. For example, in Brazil, the story goes that the Paulistas (Sao Paulo) earn the money (doing subculture) so that the Cariocas (Rio) can spend it (being subculture).

The main source of cultural homogeneity types of error is the existence of subcultures. Within larger cultures, there are pockets of smaller cultures that can be identified as holding different dominant values. Both the United States and Canada are familiar with the "Down Easterners" and the "Maritimers," who hold values distinctly different from those of the broader cultures in which they exist. Even in a small country such as Switzerland subcultures exist, and these may be further divided by the different language groupings that make up the country.

Another potential error has to do with cultural change. Cultures are dynamic. Although a culture's basic values change very slowly, they do change over time. It is important to note the time period associated with any information used to analyze a culture. For any particular aspect of a culture being examined, the rate of change for that element should be considered, especially if important decisions are to be based on the analysis. Of course, errors can be made by superficial judgments, too. If the adoption of Western business suits were seen as a sign of the cultural change of Japanese managers, then many cultural and business mistakes would surely follow. On the other hand, intergenerational studies of Japanese families have demonstrated discernible changes in the patterns of dominant values from grandparents to grandchildren. However, even though change is taking place and societies may become more modern, it does not mean that these societies are becoming more Westernized.

A more difficult barrier to using a framework effectively has nothing to do with misunderstanding or misapplying the concepts involved in it. The problem has to do with the gap between understanding and behavior. It is quite possible to appreciate fully that another person's values are different from one's own and to see clearly the managerial implications of different values. One may even try to avoid a problem by changing one's own behavior to accommodate another person. Yet it may be impossible to do so, or doing so may exact such a high cost that it renders one impotent. One can test his or her own ability to adapt by trying to alter the normal talking distance from a person by standing closer. A common reaction is to return quite quickly to normal distance (if the other person does not readjust the distance first!). If one has the ability to maintain the closer distance, one may begin perspiring, or using awkward pauses, gestures, or speech patterns. Some form of interference with usual effectiveness is likely to emerge as one forces oneself to behave against usual cultural norms. If the example discussed seems difficult to carry out, imagine what is likely to happen when cultural forces operating on an individual are unknown.

These caveats to applying the framework presented in this book do not, of course, contradict the main message. That is, a systematic analysis of culture's influence on management is both possible and helpful. An overall caution is that a conceptual scheme be employed as an aid to understanding, not as a simplistic answer. It would be easy to end up using the cultural categories to reinforce the stereotyping of countries and ethnic groups. Such misuse of the framework would be lamentable,[34] for the ultimate usefulness of the framework depends on the learning subsequent to the initial analysis of a situation with the concepts as a guide. No sterile, mechanical application of the concepts will produce useful insights. Only a dynamic, organic approach assisted by the analytic rigor of the scheme will lead to continued growth of understanding about a culture.

Descriptions, Interpretations, and Evaluations

One final suggestion for maximizing the effective use of a conceptual framework involves three different ways of responding to phenomena in other cultures. One mode is to stay with the objective facts of an experience and to describe events. Another is to interpret events by ascribing meaning to them. The third mode is to evaluate a situation by labeling it as good or bad. In North America, there seems to be an unfortunate tendency to move quickly from description to interpretation and to evaluation. In cross-cultural situations, the greater the tendency to judge events, the greater the probability of making errors. Interpretations tend to be made from one's own cultural perspective and are prone to ethnocentric error. Resisting the interpretive and evaluative modes while maintaining a descriptive posture for as long as possible is the best protection against cultural gaffes. While this may be difficult to do, it is still to be encouraged. As the reader proceeds to the analysis of the cases that follow, an explicit separation of these categories by establishing three headings under which notes may be made could prove to be useful.

A Final Caveat: The Reality of Culture Shock[35]

This chapter has discussed the impact of culture on management in an analytic and almost impersonal way. It is important to know how culture works — how it impacts behavior and what some of its dimensions are. Knowledge and understanding should be the bases from which one takes action. There is a danger, however, in assuming that because one has learned something, one can take such action automatically.

Intellectual understanding may not translate directly into a high degree of skill. Skills take practice. Imagine hearing someone explain, using physics and mathematical equations, how to ride a bicycle. Undoubtedly, the explanation would be correct and would display a thorough understanding of the facts and laws that would have to be observed for a person to ride a bicycle successfully. But no one would stand a chance of riding a bicycle for the first time after such a scientific lecture. Parents, teaching their son or daughter to ride a bicycle, talk about balance, not turning the handle bars (and therefore the front wheel) too sharply, pedaling fast enough to keep the bicycle upright, and so on. Keeping these principles in mind and practicing these principles usually leads to success.

Putting knowledge into action is a skill. It is this skill that brings success. Just as the notion of "lecture and ride" is naive, so is "read and go." The child riding the bicycle has reality to deal with (hills, bumps, sand on sidewalks, other bicycles), and so do managers working in other cultures. Managers who are to do business in another culture cannot be told about all the hills and bumps they will face. This section discusses one significant bump, culture shock, and suggests that an open mind and a willingness to learn from experiences will help the international manager get over many problems and adapt to new cultures. However, in the process of adapting, one can expect to fall off one's bicycle occasionally.

Notwithstanding a strong desire to understand and to adapt in order to be effective as a manager, nearly everyone experiences disorientation when entering another culture. This phenomenon, called culture shock, is rooted in our psychological processes.[36] The normal assumptions that the manager uses in his or her home culture to interpret perceptions and to communicate intentions no longer work. When this happens, whether in normal attempts to socialize or in a business context, confusion and frustration result. Frustration occurs because the manager is used to being competent in such situations, and now, the manager finds that he or she is unable to operate effectively.

One can sense the power of such a condition by blindfolding oneself and having dinner with family or friends. It is soon realized that eyes filter enormous amounts of information carried by sound as well as sight. Noises never noticed before become overwhelming. This exercise also reveals other potential aspects of culture shock. An obvious one is that people give information in ways that are difficult to understand . . . "the peas are over in the corner of your plate . . . cut your meat before eating all that!" One finds out that one's own behavior is seen differently than intended . . . "I meant to pick up my wine glass, not put my fingers in it!"

A frivolous example perhaps, but the disorientation stemming from the inability to interpret surroundings and to behave competently can lead to anxiety, frustration, and sometimes, to more severe depression. Most experts agree that some form of culture shock is unavoidable, even by experienced internationalists.[37] People who repeatedly move to new cultures likely dampen the emotional swings they experience and probably shorten the period of adjustment, but they don't escape it entirely.

The pattern usually experienced by people who move into a new culture comes in three phases: first, the elation of anticipating a new environment and the early period of moving into it; second, the distress of dealing with one's own ineffectiveness and, as the novelty erodes and reality sets in, the realization that one has to function in a strange situation; and, third, the adjustment and effective coping with the new environment.

The critical aspect of these phases is that during the first and second periods, performance is usually below one's normal level. The period of adjustment to normal or above-average performance takes from three to nine months, depending on previous experience, the degree of cultural difference being experienced, and the individual personality. It should be noted that culture shock is not a shock experienced as, for example, a result of conditions of poverty. Culture shock is more a behavioral pattern associated with a loss of control and a loss of sense of mastery in a situation.

During a person's adaptation to a new environment, frequently observed symptoms are similar to most defensive reactions. People reject their new environment and the people that live there, often with angry or negative evaluations of "strangeness." Other culture shock symptoms include fatigue, tension, anxiety, excessive concern about hygiene, hostility, an obsession about being cheated, withdrawal into work, family, or the expatriate community, or, in extreme cases, excessive use of drugs and alcohol.

The vast majority of people eventually begin to accept their new environment and adjust. Most emerge from the adjustment period performing adequately and some people perform more effectively than before. A smaller percentage (Sargent estimates about 10 percent) either "go native," usually not an effective strategy, or experience very severe symptoms of inability to adjust (alcoholism, nervous breakdown, or early return home).

These types of reactions seem to occur independently of the type of cultural change or the direction of a move. North Americans going to the Soviet Union exhibit patterns similar to Soviets coming to North America. However, one does not have to leave one's own country to experience culture shock, as the following demonstrates. A man went to Ghana as part of a volunteer group assisting with development. He experienced the symptoms of culture shock, even after participating in an orientation program organized by the sponsoring agency. He reported even more severe symptoms of culture shock upon his return to an urban-based M.B.A. program. However, the ultimate culture shock came when he graduated from the program and went to work for a manufacturer located in a small, rural community in one of Canada's Maritime provinces. In all three experiences the patterns were the same, and the sharpest disorientation occurred within his native country, perhaps because he least expected it. It is important to note that this individual experienced a "reverse culture shock" when he returned home. "Return shock," or "reentry shock," also is an adjustment phenomenon that people experience and need to be prepared for.[38]

Different people have different ways of coping with culture shock. Normal stress management techniques, regular exercise, rest, and balanced diet are helpful. As noted earlier, some use work as a bridge until they adjust. Usually, the work environment does have some similarities to that of one's home culture. But for the spouse who does not work, and who is often left to cope with the new environment on his or her own, the effects can be more severe. Language training is one very effective way of coping and provides an entry into the host culture. Education about the local history, geography, and traditions of the new culture, and then exploration of the new environment also help adjustment. Whatever methods are employed, it is wise to remember that everyone experiences culture shock. One can moderate its effects through diligent preparation.

Support systems are especially important during the adjustment period. One obvious source of support is the family. Doing more things together as a family, more often, is a way to cope with the pressures. Another is to realize that it is acceptable to withdraw from the new culture, temporarily, for a respite. Reading newspapers from home or enjoying familiar food is a good cultural insulator — if not carried too far. After eight months in Switzerland, one person asked her grandfather to bring her cheddar cheese and a Hershey bar on a visit, even though she had grown to enjoy Swiss fondue and Swiss chocolate! It is important that the use of such temporary interruptions to one's reality be restricted to bridges to the new culture, not as permanent anchors to an old environment.

In company situations, it must be understood that the international manager in a new culture goes through these stresses. Local colleagues should not be surprised at less than perfect performance or strange behavior, and can provide crucial sources of support for the managers and their families.

When one goes overseas or sends someone overseas, there are two jobs to accomplish. There is the functional or technical job, for example, the engineering, finance, marketing, or plant management responsibilities. This is obvious. However, too often it is only this job that people identify, focus on, and prepare for. The other job is cultural adaptation. If one cannot adapt successfully, one may be requested to go (or may be sent) home early — often in a matter of months. One may never get a chance to use one's technical or functional skills. The financial and psychological costs of this are heavy. A high failure rate may be a significant problem for North American companies. One study found that of the United States companies sampled, only 24 percent had an early return rate of 10 percent of less, compared with 97 percent for the European companies and 86 percent for Japanese companies.[39]

The single most pervasive reason why expatriates fail is because their spouses fail to adjust. It is not only important for expatriate managers to prepare for their new jobs, but also to see that their spouses are prepared as well.[40]

If one has the opportunity to work in a foreign environment, one should take that opportunity. The personal and professional development can be significant. If one is properly prepared, the total experience will be rewarding and, possibly, one of the more important adventures of one's life.

NEW REQUIREMENTS: THE GLOBAL MANAGER

To this point, the emphasis of the text and the examples used in the discussion of the conceptual frameworks in the preceding pages have had an international perspective describing managers involved in interactions primarily between two countries and cultures — their home country culture and another culture. Similarly, concepts have been applied to situations involving two interacting cultures. Until very recently, this has been an adequate model for much of the world's international business activity. However, as Nancy Adler has so well described in her preface to this book, globalization means transforming our international perspective to a global perspective.

What does the emergence of the term global manager really imply? In the broadest terms, it means reorganizing the way one thinks as managers and as students of management. As one executive put it, "to think globally really requires an alteration of our mind-set."[41] Thinking globally means *extending* concepts and models from one-to-one relationships (we to them) to holding multiple realities and relationships on one's head simultaneously and *acting* skillfully on this more complex reality. The shift means that even if one has a regional responsibility, say as marketing manager for Central and South America, it is likely that more will be required than an understanding of Latin cultures and a capacity to speak Spanish and Portuguese. One also may have to deal with R&D labs in Japan, Europe, and North America to provide them with customer information and to get updates on emerging new products. Similarly, the regional marketing manager may have to discuss product problems with manufacturers in Southeast Asia late at night, North American time, and then send a facsimile about the potential solution to an alternative supplier in Eastern Europe.

Many of the requirements of a global manager were articulated at a symposium organized by the Board of Governors of the American Society for Training and Development and reported as "Executive Traits Now and in the Future."[42]

Now	*The Future*
all-knowing	leader as learner
domestic vision	global vision
predicts future from past	intuits the future
caring for individuals	caring for institutions and individuals
owns the vision	facilitates vision of others
uses power	uses power and facilitation
dictates goals and methods	specifies processes
alone at the top	part of an executive team
values order	accepts paradox of order amidst chaos
monolingual	multicultural
inspires the trust of boards and shareholders	inspires the trust of owners, customers, and employees

This list encompasses many of the particular skills required by global managers.[43] Reviewing a wide range of literature dealing with global strategy, global marketing, global operations management, and global human resource management, the authors identified a profile of effective global executives:

- ability to develop and use global strategic skills
- ability to manage change and transition
- ability to manage cultural diversity
- ability to design and function in flexible organization structures
- ability to work with others and in teams
- ability to communicate
- ability to learn and transfer knowledge in an organization

To assist the reader in advancing his or her understanding of what the emerging world requires of global managers, each of these abilities are explored in the following sections. The development of these skills is a lifelong process and it is unlikely that a single executive will master all of them.

Ability to Develop and Use Global Strategic Skills

A new global economy is emerging that is shaped and driven by money flows as well as by goods and services.[44] It is characterized by volatile foreign exchange, government policies, resistance to standardized products, and changing economies of scale of flexible manufacturing technologies.[45] The result is a shift in the world-wide business base that is forcing managers and corporations to adjust and to shed their parochial views.

Players in this new global environment have a fast response capability, are comfortable with cross-cultural influences, and are entrepreneurial and flexible. Global managers will require a working knowledge of international relationships and foreign affairs, including global financial markets and exchange rate movements.[46] These expanded business management skills will need to be coupled with global responsibilities to take advantage of manufacturing rationalization, "mass customization" of products, and low-cost, global sourcing.

The global mind-set required by these new economic and competitive realities will be needed at all levels in the firm. Managers with this global perspective will need to strike a balance between national responsiveness and exploitation of global economies of scale. This is the vaunted ability to "think globally, but act locally."

Although some respected marketing experts argue that the trend is toward standardization,[47] more recently the evidence is that managers must be sensitive to both local idiosyncrasies and global imperatives in reaching strategic decisions.[48] A few examples illustrate the need to think globally but to adapt to local conditions to avoid the pitfalls of inappropriate standardization.

- Procter & Gamble's liquid detergent failed in Europe when it was introduced in the early 1980s because European washing machines were not equipped for liquid detergent. Modifications to the detergent were made and sales subsequently improved.
- McDonald's sells beer in Germany and tropical shakes in Hong Kong, whereas Dunkin' Donuts sells cake donuts in the United States but yeast donuts in Brazil. Marketing strategies for global recognition were successfully implemented by adapting to local preferences.
- Kellogg's Cornflakes were (mis)used as a snack when first introduced in Brazil. With educational advertising, Cornflakes gained in acceptance as a breakfast food.
- Procter & Gamble introduced Pampers in Japan and were delighted with the initial success. But it did not know that Japanese do laundry daily and were using Pampers only at night. Mooney, a Japanese company, introduced a disposable diaper with reusable parts, which had great appeal to the savings-conscious Japanese. P&G's market share for disposal diapers

dropped from 90% to 10%. P&G regained share by retaliating with a smaller, thinner diaper.
▪ After years of uniform ads, Phillip Morris introduced local ads for the first time in 1987 for its Marlboro cigarettes; each country was given a choice of five ad campaigns.

These examples suggest that global success is contingent on striking a balance between capitalizing on resources and needs within national boundaries and the ability to capture a vision of a world without boundaries. One aspect of managing this balance will likely include moving decision-making authority as close to the customer as possible to ensure that local requirements are satisfied. But local managers will need to know and understand the global strategy and yet enact it within the context of their local environment.

Ability to Manage Change and Transition

Managing change in the unstable environment described earlier will be an unending challenge. Constantly fine-tuning the balance between global and local pressures under changing competitive conditions will contribute to the need for frequent reorganization of resources, human networks, technology, and marketing and distribution systems. The shortening of product life cycles, driven by technological change in the products and how they are manufactured and delivered, contributes to the acceleration of change.

As difficult as these constant changes are to manage, the *overall* transition to global operations represents a formidable challenge in itself. Existing international operations, often marked by standardization of products and uniformity of procedures, may be a barrier to effective globalization. For example, a long history of mass-producing standard products may make it especially difficult to invest in and operate effectively flexible factories, one way that firms may offer differentiated products to different markets on a global scale.[49]

For a successful transition to global operations, it is also important that country managers are in agreement with the strategy. If poorly implemented, the move to globalization can pit headquarters managers against country or field managers. There is a tendency for autonomous units in a firm to protect their own turf. If global strategy is perceived as a move toward a centralization of responsibility, a local manager's role may become less strategic. Subsidiary managers who joined a company because of its commitment to local autonomy and adapting products to local environments may become disenchanted or even leave the organization.[50]

In terms of organization structure, effective global managers will need the skills to manage the transition from independence/dependence to interdependence, from control to coordination and cooperation, and from symmetry to differentiation. In personal terms, global managers will need to act more as equals and less as dominant decision makers operating from a dominant headquarters.

Another method of making the transition to global operations is through the formation of a strategic alliance, or the formation of a network to reduce, for example, the high cost of R&D. Whichever method is selected to make the transition to globalization, the ability to manage change will be an essential skill of an effective global manager.

Ability to Manage Cultural Diversity

The first imperative for effectively managing cultural diversity is cultural sensitivity. The marketers of Coca-Cola, probably the world's most recognized brand, attribute their success to the ability of their people to hold and to understand the following perspectives simultaneously:

- their corporate culture
- the culture of their brand
- the culture of the people to whom they market the brand[51]

Sometimes cultural sensitivity leads to marketing one's products to a particular market segment *across* cultural boundaries, basically finding common subcultures within otherwise diverse cultures. In a classic study of international marketing practices of several bed-linen companies headquartered in the United Kingdom, findings stressed the ability to develop a high level of cultural awareness in order to

- obtain high product acceptance in light of the fact that culturally rooted differences have a significant impact on a product's success in a global market
- understand that the older the consumption pattern, the less likely a global product will be a success
- recognize universal themes by segmenting according to similarities instead of geographical differences[52]

Lack of cultural awareness can be devastating to organizations competing globally. An organization not managed according to values felt by its members is likely to experience conflict. Hidden values and beliefs must be recognized and understood in order to manage effectively. In the 1970s in the Republic of Panama, there were more than twenty serious disputes between MNCs and local labor that were related to popular culture. Also during that period, all six Central American republics imposed restrictions on expatriate managers, which resulted in their replacement by nationals.[53]

Global managers must have the ability to recognize that cultural differences operate internally and externally. It is important to understand the influence of the home office's own cultural filters when dealing with foreign affiliates and to accept that the home office way of doing things will not be appropriate in all instances. In today's global environment, a firm's home culture must no longer dominate the entire organization's culture.[54]

The recognition of cultural differences in global management does not come easily to North American executives, who often have less exposure to multicultural realities in their workplace than, for instance, their European counterparts. For example, Nestlé has a long history of having many nationalities among its top 100 executives (one count had it over 40), whereas IBM in one survey had the largest number among large United States companies — only 11! Although these types of anecdotal reports may be misleading, the limited language ability of many North American managers makes the same point another way. Language training, cross-cultural, and expatriate experiences early in careers, membership on international task forces, and global content in all management training programs are among a few ways to counter the ethnocentricity of domestic managers, regardless of their country of origin.

Learning to manage global cultural diversity effectively can start with the recognition of cultural diversity at home. The requirement to hire African-Americans, Hispanics, and native people in the United States is forcing many firms to come to grips with new mixes of employees. Demographic projections, which suggest that early in the next century white males will represent only one in five of the workforce, also mean cultural diversity will be a domestic reality. In addition to the obvious Anglophone/Francophone mix in Canada, which is regrettably marked more by division than by synergy, there are large minorities of people newly arrived from India, Pakistan, Vietnam, Hong Kong, Central America, and Eastern Europe. The opportunities to gain insight and experience in managing cultural diversity are local as well as global.

To manage diversity, domestically or globally, a modern human resource strategy requires some minimal orientations:

- an explicit recognition by headquarters that its own way of managing reflects the home culture values and assumptions
- an explicit recognition by headquarters that foreign subsidiaries may have different ways of managing people, which may be more effective
- a willingness to acknowledge cultural differences and to take steps to make them discussable and, thus, usable
- building a belief that more creative and effective ways of managing people could be developed as a result of cross-cultural learning[55]

Ability to Design and to Function in Flexible Organizations

Given the complexities of the global economy and its attendant demands on managers, it is unlikely that any single organizational form will be adequate to the tasks. Global managers will surely need significantly increased creativity in organizational design, but limited organizational capability may represent the most critical constraint, as suggested by Bartlett and Goshal, in responding to the new strategic demands.

As mentioned earlier, an individual manager alone cannot be expected to develop and use all the diverse skills required for successful global management. It is essential, then, that the organization itself be of as much assistance to global managers as possible. Global managers will, therefore, be called on to design and operate the very organizations that will help them to be more effective.

The best managers are already creating borderless organizations where the ability to learn, to be responsive, and to be efficient occurs within the firm's administrative heritage.[56] This suggests that a wide range of people in such firms must demonstrate the capacity for strategic thinking and action, assisted by open communication of plans, decentralization of strategic tasks, early opportunities for development of top management capabilities, and control systems measuring performance across many dimensions.[57]

These new organizations will be characterized by flexibility and multidimensionality. Many centers, with frequent movement between centers and jobs, will be common and will displace hierarchy and promotion "up the ladder."

To ensure that the potential cultural diversity in such situations is taken advantage of, managers will need the ability to create an alignment of authority and responsibility between home office and field offices that moves decision making as close as possible to the customer. Balance is required though and, as noted earlier, the ability to coordinate manufacturing interdependencies to maximize economies of production will be a key task of the global manager.

To operate effectively in these radically different, global organizations will take new skills and old skills honed to a new sharpness. Some of the abilities and characteristics needed by the global manager to function in flexible organizations will be

- high tolerance for ambiguity
- new levels of creativity and inventiveness in organizational design
- the ability to learn, be responsive, and be efficient, all simultaneously
- the ability to identify and implement diverse managerial behaviors for ongoing renewal of the organization
- the ability to coordinate complicated financial, human resource, marketing, and manufacturing interdependencies — interdependencies not only across functions but also within each business activity
- ability to recognize different manufacturing, marketing, and organizational problems and priorities across different locations and to accommodate these with new structures and processes[58]

Ability to Work with Others and in Teams

Even before the advent of global companies, effective teamwork was becoming essential for managerial success. As specialization of people and differentiation in organizations increased (often driven by technological improvements, fragmentation of markets, explosions in product variations, and so on), there was a concomitant increased need for integration — for putting the specialized units back together in the service of the organization's objectives. Teams, committees, and task forces were among the devices used to accomplish the desired integration.

With the increased complexity of global operations, the ability to function in work teams — especially in culturally diverse groups — is even more important. A Conference Board Report on the experiences of thirty major MNCs in building teams to further their global interests showed the following:

- Teams used solely for communication or to provide advice and counsel still exist, but more and more firms are also using teams in different and more participative and powerful ways.
- Global teamwork can do more than provide improved market and technological intelligence. It can yield more flexible business planning, stronger commitment to achieving worldwide goals, and closer collaboration in carrying out strategic change.
- Teams that span internal organization boundaries or that span the company's outside boundary (joint venture partners, suppliers, customers) are often required.[59]

The need for transnational teamwork shows up in different ways in different functions. Consider the different assumptions, about the nature and purpose of accounting and auditing in various parts of the world, for example. In one country, financial statements are meant to reflect fundamental economic reality and the audit function is to ensure that this is so. In another country the audit is to check the accuracy of the statements vis-à-vis the economic records. In still another country it is only to make sure legal requirements have been met.[60] Imagine, then, the need for cross-cultural understanding and sensitivity in auditing an international subsidiary or the teamwork needed to develop international audit standards.[61]

Other functions pick up the teamwork theme differently. In operations management, there is a need to develop system-sensitive outlooks and processes that will develop personal relationships across subsidiaries.[62] In managing human resources, it is necessary to develop capabilities for leading multinational teams in flexible and responsible ways. In global marketing, a manager needs the ability to take advantage of a local execution strategy where "not invented here" becomes "now improved here."[63] Using this strategy, an international core team is formed to gather ideas and to pass them to local levels where the final marketing decisions are made and implemented.

The ability to work effectively with other people and in teams will be critical to the successful implementation of a global strategy. Participation in global teams should, therefore, occur early in the careers of managers in order to transform these developing people into globally effective managers.

Ability to Communicate

Strong emphasis was given to the importance of intercultural communication earlier in this chapter. It is obvious that in a global environment managers will need to be able to communicate with diverse groups of people. To do so effectively will require multilingual skills and high levels of cross-cultural awareness and sensitivity.

In addition to the skills necessary for effective interpersonal communication, managers will need to be able to take advantage of increasingly global communications systems resulting from broadcast deregulation and growth in global media firms such as Sky Channel and Pan European Press. Data gathered in 1987 indicate that the market for Pan European advertising campaigns has been growing at a rate of more than 25 percent per year, in spite of the many technological difficulties encountered by the new satellite technology. As always, the need to be sensitive to local requirements is evidenced by several lawsuits launched against the global media by local advertisers wishing to retain advertising revenue and by regulatory bodies seeking to retain control over advertising content.[64]

In addition to the positive effects of good communication skills among colleagues and with customers, there is another advantage of effective communication of particular importance to geographically dispersed and culturally diverse organizations. Sensitive communications will also build trust, and a common message can help build a strong corporate culture emphasizing shared, global value systems.

Ability to Learn and to Transfer Knowledge in an Organization

Given the diversity of market requirements and needs, the dispersion of manufacturing and sourcing, the rise of R&D leadership in Europe and Japan, and the importance of technological advances for product and process innovations, learning and transfer of knowledge are key to global success. Managers who are globally competent will be deeply curious; organizations that are successful will be able to coordinate, transfer, and use the knowledge gained by curious executives rapidly and effectively.

At the individual level, broad interests, an openness to a variety of experiences, and a willingness to experiment and to take risks are all ingredients of success. A visiting scholar from the People's Republic of China typified these characteristics for the authors. She soon knew more people than several others who had been at our institution for many months. Although her specialty was finance, she audited classes across all functions. She interviewed the oldtimers, secretaries, researchers, students, and seasoned teachers. Nor were her interactions confined to work. She learned humor, visited churches, traveled across the country by air, bus, train, and boat, went to country fairs and even insisted on trying golf! By the end of her year, she understood the institution better than most who had been in it for several years; she understood the country almost as well as any native. Then, she transferred her knowledge to her colleagues in China and abroad through an extraordinary report[65] and through a series of lectures and seminars.

At an organizational level even more can be done. For example, at Citicorp operating managers are encouraged to look for opportunities in one country that can be transferred elsewhere. These opportunities or experiments are the responsibility of national managers, while their transfer is the responsibility of corporate management.[66] The use of cross-national task forces for problems of corporate level concern (or for problems that reoccur in various parts of the world) is also a feature of that company.

The transfer of technology is also important. Global Management Information Systems (MIS) systems are now required and a manager must have the skills necessary to access and interpret worldwide information. One way to transfer technology is through the development of strong functional management to allow the building and transference of core competencies.

Yet there are indications that too often companies neglect the rich information available to them by expatriates in other countries, especially when they return. These organizations lose out on a valuable opportunity to transfer some cross-cultural managerial knowledge and cause the expatriate to experience some potentially serious reentry difficulties.[67] Similarly, as companies increase the number and variety of managers from other countries on temporary assignment at their corporate offices, they need to understand, tap, and apply their special knowledge, and skills. If domestic executives view such transfers only as career-development assignments for the "foreigners," they will lose important opportunities for mutual learning.

The ability of organizations to learn and transfer knowledge will only increase in importance as markets continue to globalize. In a global environment, the ability of people to learn from diverse sources and to transfer knowledge within their organization is essential for success.

Summary Profile

This review might lead the reader to conclude that an effective global manager is superhuman. But keeping in mind the necessity of teamwork and the support of organizational design, systems, and processes, the prospect of growing global skills might be seen as an exciting challenge rather than an impossible task. To develop skills to the level necessary will be a lifelong process because the demands will likely expand along with the global economy. Each of us needs to continue to improve in the following areas as we move toward the new century:

- the ability to envision and implement the strategy of thinking globally, acting locally
- the ability to manage change and transition
- the ability to manage cultural diversity, to be culturally adept and comfortable with cross-cultural influences
- the ability to design and function in flexible organization structures, including the ability to deal with stress and ambiguity
- the ability to work with others and in teams
- the ability to be an excellent communicator, commanding more than one language
- the ability to learn and to transfer knowledge in an organization, including the ability to search for and combine elements in new ways

- the ability to enter into trusting alliances and to operate with a high degree of personal integrity and honesty
- the ability to implement, to turn ideas to action
- the ability to take risks and to experiment
- the ability to develop high mobility, with a stateless perception of the world

INTRODUCTION TO THE CASES AND THE CASE METHOD

A case is a description of a situation faced by a decision maker. The case method of teaching is an extremely effective method of accelerating management development. The case method has an applied, rather than a theoretical, focus. Although the use of theory and concepts is encouraged in specific situations, the emphasis is on improving the practice of management, not on demonstrating one's knowledge or ability to manipulate abstract ideas. Although names, places, and other data sometimes are disguised, the cases in this book describe actual business situations faced by real people. Each case is written to leave the student at a decision point which the manager in the case confronted. Just as the real manager was required to do, the student will need to analyze the situation to determine the problems and opportunities; set objectives; develop and assess alternative courses of action; and recommend a plan of action. Unlike the real managers, however, the student will not have an opportunity to actually implement his or her recommendations.

The case method has an active, rather than passive, orientation. A general theme is that of learning by actively participating rather than passively listening. Class sessions are discussions that emphasize developing skills in problem solving and decision making. A typical case discussion will involve students interacting with one another and with the instructor as everyone works toward a solution of the particular problem being addressed. People who have had management experience in the countries in the cases, or people who have lived or traveled to these countries, are encouraged to bring their perspectives to the discussion as well.

There can be difficulties associated with the case method. A prime feature and strength of the case method is that such a method mirrors reality. However, this can create some initial concerns.

The concerns and frustrations experienced by those using the case method are similar to those faced by the decision maker:

1. There is not enough time to do all the reading and to make the decision. Practicing executives often complain about not having enough time for all the things they must do.

2. There is not enough information to make the decision, and one thinks, "If only I had more data." Managers never have enough data. Cases probably contain more data, more clearly organized, than the manager usually has. Also, the cost of securing more information may be unrealistically high. If it is

thought that more data are needed and a recommendation is made to obtain more information, make sure the cost-benefit ratio of that action is thought through.

3. One might think, "I don't know anything about that country. If I did I would make the right decision." It is not the lack of country-specific knowledge that usually causes problems, but rather a framework for thinking about cultural problems and within which to use country-specific data. A framework, patience, and a willingness to learn are the prime requisites for success.

4. There is uncertainty about whether one has made the right decision or how that decision will work. Very often the answer lies in the process by which the solution is found: developing a better way of defining problems and thinking about them.

Just as managers become more capable of making decisions under uncertainty with experience, the difficulties described above usually subside as students become more familiar with the case method. The case method is not the traditional approach to education that most people experience, hence the initial frustration and concern. However, after a period of adjustment people usually feel that the benefits of the case method far outweigh the difficulties first encountered.

Action planning is another skill that can be developed with the case method. Analysis and understanding of a situation are necessary managerial activities, but understanding alone is not sufficient. Management is an active, not a passive, profession. The cases place students in situations where action is required. The emphasis is on realistic, specific action plans that recognize constraints on managerial action.

By putting students in the position of managers and requiring an action plan, the cases simulate, to the extent possible, the students' accepting responsibility for solving the problem and for their solutions to that problem. The case method helps to develop skills in establishing priorities. The case method also helps students to acquire a sense of urgency appropriate to a given situation. In order to encourage these developments, action plans should consider the following issues:

1. Does the action plan flow logically from the problem definition? Is the plan *consistent* with the individual, group, and company goals? Is it consistent with the culture?
2. When must action be taken? What must be done in the short term? medium term? long term?
3. In what order must action be taken? Who must take the action?
4. Does the plan consider likely responses and counterresponses? Is the plan tentative or conditional based upon anticipated responses?

In developing action plans, avoid some unrealistic assumptions, which may include the following:

1. Hiring two more people or sending a potential employee and her family to Africa to see if they like it may not be possible given the financial constraints of

a company. It is often assumed that companies have *unlimited resources* that can be used to solve problems. This usually is not true.

2. *Unlimited time is usually not available.* In many instances, things must be done quickly.

3. *A single project focus is often not possible.* One may assume that a project in a case or a business deal is the only one that the manager has to worry about. This often is not true. Managers may have multiple projects or objectives that they are working on simultaneously. As one reads a case and thinks solely about the described problem, it can become the total focus. Managers' time usually is stretched thin by multiple activities. One should try to put oneself in the manager's position. Sometimes, a staff person in a North American company may spend most of his or her time on a specific project and may get frustrated when that project does not move faster (as does the boss). Nobody, it seems, is taking the time to push the project as fast as it should be pushed. Very often there is a mismatch of expectations. One of the reasons this expectation gap is experienced is because people have different priorities and assumptions about the importance of a particular project. People in the field are busy and things may take longer than expected. They may be pushing the project as fast as it can go, given local conditions. Usually, the cases include the complex contexts in which most managers operate. Often, this reality is overlooked because of single-mindedness.

What about the student's perception of the case method? The following discussion of the case method is from a student's perspective. It was written by second year M.B.A. students to help students just entering the first year of the M.B.A. program.

THE CASE METHOD[68]

The case method is a rich experience. Cases are written about all types of business problems. They are all based on real situations in real enterprises — varying in size from a one-person entrepreneurial endeavor to Northern Telecom and General Motors. It is impossible to fully capture that experience in written words. Our aim is to highlight some aspects of the method, to illustrate how it differs from the lecture method, and to give you an idea of the demands the process will make on you, the student.

The teaching aims of the case method are broad and ambitious.

What Is Being Taught?

The lecture method of teaching involves a one-way dispensation of accepted truths and ideas from the professor to the student. The aim is to increase the students' knowledge base. It is assumed that increased knowledge will facilitate better judgment.

The case method is more ambitious. Business management is not just a technical matter requiring technical knowledge. It is also a human matter. It involves "getting things done through people." It requires an understanding of how people — employees, consumers, investors, bankers, salespeople — will respond to specific actions. The objective is to develop problem-solving and decision-making skills in addition to learning technical knowledge.

Students develop skills in objectively analyzing business situations through cases. They learn to identify problems. They develop decision-making skills and the capacity to make sound judgments on their perceptions of the facts and the problems. They develop skills in communicating their decisions to others in a manner that produces the desired action. They learn how to develop and present arguments; how to listen to and understand the views of others; how to sense the needs of others. Each class is, to some extent, a business meeting. Students develop the confidence that they can make a contribution.

The skills are developed through class discussions, arguments, role plays, and presentations. The process is vastly different from conventional lecturing. It involves different roles for both the students and the professor.

Role of the Professor

In a case discussion, students put their collective knowledge, experience, and brainpower together to analyze and solve a problem. They learn from each other, stimulate each other, inspire each other's thoughts. The role of the professor is to stimulate and guide the discussion. Suggestions may be made but, unlike a lecture, solutions are not given.

The professor is present to keep the discussion moving toward meaningful goals with a minimum amount of intervention. He or she is a catalyst attempting to conduct the orchestra, to inspire, to light fires, to challenge superficial thinking. "That sounds good, but do you really believe it?

The professor may attempt to start fights, figuratively speaking, and then act as referee. "But Carole, over here, maintains that your plan will be disastrous for this company; it will lead to bankruptcy! Surely you can't accept that!" He or she wants you to get involved, to fight back. Learning begins when differences of opinion arise.

If the professor finds you on a wrong track, he or she may encourage you to continue. The professor's challenging questions will lead you along the road of your proposal until you see the consequences for yourself. When you discover your error, it will have a deeper impact than if you had been told. You learn, and the class learns; that's the objective.

Occasionally, the professor will play devil's advocate, purposely making misleading statements to determine your alertness, your conviction in your point of view, or your ability to defend an argument. He or she wants you alert and thinking sharply.

The performance may become theatrical if the professor wants to uncover an issue in a case which the class has missed. The professor doesn't name the issue but begins a probing search. "We've got ourselves to this conclusion; but does it feel right? Is that all that's involved here? Have we got to the bottom of this case?" The search begins. Brains struggle. The tension rises. "If you were the firm's banker, would you be happy with this conclusion?" The probing questions and the hints continue until someone cracks it. The professor may even ask you to be the banker and break into a spontaneous role play.

The case method places heavy demands on the professor. He or she must be alert, and be on top of the discussion. He or she must keep an open mind towards the students' contribution; know the case facts backwards and forwards; and know when and how to intervene. A good case professor has to be, to some extent, an actor.

Despite the need for a committed, highly competent professor, the value of the discussion and the learning experience depend more on the students than on the professor. The conductor must have good musicians in the orchestra. The case method also places heavy demands on you, the student.

Demands on the Student

With the lecture method of teaching, the student faces the relatively simple task of more or less verbatim reception and repetition of facts and ideas. The case method aims at developing skills. If you want to improve your skill at golf or tennis, you must practice; you must participate. The case method of learning demands the active participation and cooperation of the student.

In the traditional lecture method, you are dependent on a lecturer. You are fed information. The case method tries to move you from dependence to dependable self-reliance. You must think for yourself. You must develop your own skills. You must seek knowledge.

You are not expected to have all the insights into every case. You may not be capable of that. You are, however, required to be prepared. You must learn from the contributions of others. You have a duty to make your best contribution. You are part of an information exchange. This exchange usually occurs at two levels after your individual preparation. First you share ideas within a small study group; later you exchange perspectives within a larger classroom.

Skills are developed by this process of participation. You may gather valuable information from observing the process, but you are responsible for developing your own skills. As in any skills-development program, you receive in proportion to your effort and contribution. Don't sit back and be educated. Take the opportunity to educate and develop yourself.

Focus on Action and Utility

The case method brings authentic business situations into the classroom. The situations are analyzed. Alternative courses of action for the decision maker are identified and evaluated. The process leads inexorably to an action plan: "If you were the decision maker, what would YOU do? YOU must make a decision on what to do. YOU must decide on HOW to do it.

The case method forces you to decide on action under realistic conditions. You cannot remain a passive observer. It trains you to be decisive and action oriented. Very often, you will wish you had more information. You never have perfect information in the real world. The case method teaches you to minimize the uncertainty through analysis and then take decisive action, living with the uncertainty that cannot be eliminated.

The focus is on utility, not just on the development of intellectually active theories of business divorced from practice. If some concept is useful, that's great! If it is not, throw it out! You are encouraged to accept what you find useful. If you use a theoretical concept, be sure that it is appropriate for the application you are making.

Many business people will tell you that you can only learn real decision making in the "school of hard knocks." The unfortunate problem with the "school of hard knocks" is that it is not very efficient. The case method gives you the essential background for responsible decisions without the risks to yourself or to the company which are inseparable from amateurish action. Cases provide the opportunity to solve real problems and obtain immediate feedback from your peers. You can afford to make mistakes and learn from them because there is no risk involved. It is as close to the real world of action as we can get — safely and efficiently.

Common Adjustment Problems

There are some common problems in adjusting to the case method.

Burden of Independent Thinking

Many students become habituated to the role of receiver in a lecture situation. Some students find it difficult to actively think, to make independent judgments which can be openly challenged and criticized by their peers. Instead of forcing themselves to think and make personal decisions, they find excuses for not doing so. Common excuses are:

1. "This is not realistic! How can we reach a decision on a major business issue like this in eighty minutes?"
2. "There's not enough information in this case. The real decision maker would have had a lot more information."
3. "We don't have enough theory to solve this problem!" You will always wish you had more time, information, and knowledge. That's true of the real world too. You must realize that you are being trained to make decisions under uncertainty and under conditions as realistic as is practical. You are being thrown in at the "deep end" without the danger of drowning.

It is true that, in some cases, the decision maker had more information than the case presents. You may need to base your decision on assumptions that flow logically from the information presented. In other cases, you have more information than you need. The important thing is to make a decision on the basis of the information you have.

Time

You may complain that there is not enough time to do it all. It is important that you learn to manage your time effectively. Probably the most important piece of advice you can get is, "Work smart, not hard." This sounds great, but how do you use it?

You need to be sharp and alert in class. The most intense learning takes place in class. It follows that if you overwork at home to the extent that you are not in top form in class, you are operating inefficiently. You are not being smart. Your class learning and participation will suffer. At the beginning with the case method, overworking is often more of a problem than underworking. Many minds can dig deeper into a case than one can. This is one of the reasons for study groups.[69] It also means that if you are having particular problems with a case, you should allow others to help you. If you spend four hours trying to "crack" a case on your own, you are working hard—not smart. Working smart means setting priorities and working on the tasks that you can efficiently accomplish on your own, and working with others on tasks you cannot accomplish alone.

Reluctance to Accept the Power of Many Minds

The case method is going to make you realize very soon that a class of sixty students can come up with a lot more ideas than you can as an individual. This realization disturbs some people. They spend a lot of time studying a case. They discuss it in a study group. They go to class and find they uncovered only a fraction of the issues. They feel discouraged and inadequate. They think they are not sufficiently bright and begin to lose self-confidence.

The fact that many minds can collaborate to achieve a deep understanding of a problem is the basis of the success of the case method.[70] Instead of worrying about being inadequate, the student should accept the need for cooperative help. He or she should learn to draw more fully on the ideas of fellow students. The mutual exchange of ideas and assistance makes the program a worthwhile and enjoyable experience.

Impatience

After a couple of weeks, many students feel the case method is not working for them. "I am not learning anything here! I knew more before I got here! I'm just getting more confused!" The problem here is twofold. When you are developing a skill, like learning to play tennis, you initially feel you are not making progress. You have to make significant progress before you realize you are making any progress. Second, there is a steep learning curve involved with the case learning process. Students are unfamiliar with the method. They do not fully understand their role. The professor does not yet know the students. The students do not know each other. The class must become comfortable together before students can freely criticize, argue, and reach their maximum contribution potential. You may hear comments like, "50 percent of what people say in class is rubbish!" Statements like this are often due to the learning curve.

Low Tolerance of Ambiguity

Many students, particularly those with quantitative backgrounds, insist on finding the "right" answer. They come to class and hear arguments and counterarguments. Solutions are proposed and their shortcomings are pointed out. At the end of eighty minutes, the class may not have resolved the issues in the case. Someone asks the professor: "What is the solution?" He or she replies: "I don't know." The seekers of "right" answers leave the class frustrated and discouraged. They question the professor's competence! If this happens to you, realize you have missed the point. The message being communicated is that there is no simple answer. There is no one, right approach to the problem. Business decision making is not a science. Business is a human matter. There may be more than one right approach. If you can derive a solution and then back it up against assailants and it works, it is a "right" solution. Besides, where will the professor be when you are in the business world facing a tough international problem?

Business decision making is an art, a skill; not a science. Quantitative techniques may provide guidelines. In the final analysis, however, you must rely on skill. The case process is designed to help you develop that skill.

Concerns About Class Participation

A percentage of your grade may be based on the professor's evaluation of your contributions in case classes. This fact generates a lot of concern for some students. A lot of students are afraid to participate because they fear the criticism of their peers. They are afraid they are not "right." This attitude reduces the value of the learning experience. It is difficult to determine what is "right" and "wrong" in a lot of cases. Even if you are on a wrong track, the professor will be happy if you contribute because it allows him to illustrate a point. You will learn. The class will learn.

Some students feel that their contribution should aim to please the professor. This is not the objective. What is important is whether you can support your views against the counterattacks and disagreements of other students in the class or, failing to do so, whether you can accept cooperatively the merits of your classmates' views.

Developing a skill requires commitment and an ability to persist in the face of temporary setbacks. You must approach class participation in this manner. Success has to come from you. You have to keep trying until you master it. It's like learning to play tennis all over again!

Recommendations

Often you will be expected to make "recommendations." After one and a half years of the process, we automatically feel obliged to make recommendations!

Keep an open mind. If you are unfamiliar with the case method, you will have to make some adjustments. You should trust the method. It has worked well in numerous places. Don't worry about allowing yourself to change to suit it. Don't come to class with the attitude: "Here I am, professor. Teach me business." You will face problems until you change that attitude. You must be prepared to take the initiative, to work on developing your own skills and abilities.

If you are in search of deep, rational, intellectually pleasing theories, you may be disappointed. Business is real-world stuff. The focus is on action and utility. You will be primarily taught how to analyze and act in business situations. With the case method, theory is a process by-product. Concepts developed earlier are tested for their *usefulness*, refined, and reworked. The interaction between theory and practice is iterative.

It is important that you plan your work. Set priorities and keep asking yourself: "What is the most efficient way for me to accomplish this? How can I use the knowledge and experience of others? How can I contribute to them?" Work smart, not hard.

If you know the answer to a case before you have analyzed it, you are more than likely in trouble. You are either relating the case too closely to your past experience or you are being subjective. The case may not be identical to your past experience. No two business situations are totally identical. You must analyze each individual situation. Keep asking yourself the question "Am I being objective?" especially when you have experience with, or know something about, the company or the industry being studied.

This note simply gives you some food for thought.

A Final Thought (from the Professor's Perspective)

Your willingness to engage the case experience actively and fully might be increased by recognizing the experience of others as reflected in the students' note which you have just read. It might also be encouraged by part of an essay written by an Etonian schoolmaster in the last century (circa 1875):

> At school you are not engaged so much in acquiring knowledge as in making mental efforts under criticism. A certain amount of knowledge you can indeed with average faculties acquire so as to retain, nor need you regret the hours you spend on much that is forgotten, for the shadow of lost knowledge at least protects you from many illusions. But you go to a great school not so much for knowledge as for arts and habits; for the habit of attention, for the art of expression, for the art of assuming at a moment's notice a new intellectual position, for the art of entering quickly into another person's thoughts, for the habit of submitting to censure and refutation, for the art of indicating assent or dissent in graduated terms, for the habit of regarding minute points of accuracy, for the art of working out what is possible in a given time, for taste, for discrimination, for mental courage and mental soberness.

Notes

1. G. Hofstede, *Culture's Consequences: International Differences in Work-Related Values* (Beverly Hills, Calif.: Sage Publications, 1980), 25.

2. We believe that the concept of a package of skills contributing to success is important. It should be noted, however, that in a 1984 study for the Institute for International Education entitled "International Expertise in American Business or How to Learn to Play with the Kids on the Street," Stephen Kobrin cites a clear ranking of the importance of certain skills needed to be effective in international management in the minds of executives of 217 large, industrial companies and banks. The ranking was as follows.

Factor	Median Rank	% Ranking #1
people skills	1.5	48.8
functional knowledge	2.2	32.0
industry knowledge	2.8	20.8
company knowledge	2.9	25.6
country knowledge	3.1	11.2
technical knowledge	4.6	10.4

3. In June of 1973, Dr. Edwin L. Miller of the University of Michigan published an article in the *Academy of Management Journal* (Vol. 16: No. 2) entitled, "the International Selection Decision: A Study of Some Dimensions of Managerial Behavior in the Selection Decision Process." He found that in the international selection process, companies placed primary emphasis on technical (job knowledge and proven performance in similar job) and managerial (leadership skills, company knowledge, and administrative skills) qualifications. At the bottom of the list of criteria, in terms of importance, were past performance in overseas assignments, ability to work with foreign employees, and the spouse's attitudes about the overseas assignment. The attributes related to a person's ability to live and work abroad, which are probably the most critical for success overseas and which are at the top of Kobrin's list, were ignored in favor of those attributes found at the bottom of Kobrin's list. Experience and reading suggests this inversion is still taking place.

4. G. Hofstede, *Culture's Consequences*, 398.

5. Stephen J. Kobrin, *International Expertise*.

6. G. Hofstede, *Culture's Consequences*, 398, referring to the work of B. D. Ruben, "Guidelines for Cross-Cultural Communication Effectiveness," *Group and Organizational Studies* 2, No. 4, University Associates Inc. La Jolla, Calif.; 1977, 470–479.

7. We added this last skill to the list based on personal experiences. The following vignette reinforces our belief. A CEO of a large United States company, when asked what the most important element for success was in international business, replied, "Knowing what you don't know" (personal communication).

8. "The Revenge of Big Yellow," *The Economist*, November 10, 1990, p. 77.

9. "Competing Successfully in the International Marketplace," Case 9-85-CO16, Case and Publications Division, School of Business Administration, The University of Western Ontario.

10. Cooperating managers and companies provide permission for the use and publication of these materials, unless they are taken from public sources.

11. See, for example, Curtis W. Tarr, "How to Humanize MBA's," *Fortune* (March 31, 1986): 153–154; MBA's Learn a Human Touch," *Newsweek* (June 16, 1986): 48–50.

12. See "The Botswana Uniform Agency [Pty] Ltd." (A) and (B), Cases 9-79-CO20 and 9-79-CO21, Case and Publications Division, School of Business Administration, The University of Western Ontario, London, Canada, N6A 3K7.

13. The tendency to attribute success to one's own skill and to blame others for failure is not a cultural universal, however. An Oriental perspective might well reverse the direction of explanation for success and failure and credit others for positive outcomes while assuming the blame for problems. The writers take a North American perspective in discussing examples in the text unless otherwise noted.

14. Richard E. Porter, and Larry A. Samovar, "Communicating Interculturally, in *Intercultural Communications: A Reader*, Larry A. Samovar and Richard E. Porter (Eds.), 2nd ed. (Wadsworth Publishing Company, Belmont, Calif., 1976), 5. This definition was elaborated in "Approaching Intercultural Communication" in the 5th ed. (pp. 15–30) of this book in 1988, but the basic approach, which is the attribution of meaning to behavior, remained the same.

15. Ibid., 23.

16. Ibid.

17. David R. Hampton, Charles E. Summer, and Ross A. Webber. *Organizational Behavior and the Practice of Management*, 4th ed. (Scott Foresman and Company, Glenview, Ill., 1982), 210–211.

18. John J. Gabarro, "Understanding Communication in One-to-One Relationships" in *Managing Behavior in Organizations: Text, Cases and Readings*. Leonard A. Schlesinger, Robert G. Eccles, John J. Gabarro, (McGraw-Hill, New York, 1983), 139.

19. Ibid., 131–141.

20. F. R. Kluckhohn, and F. L. Strodtbeck, *Variations in Value Orientations* (New York: Row, Peterson and Company, 1961).

21. This premise itself is a manifestation of the culture from which the two anthropologists were operating. The assumption that such common themes can be found, or even ought to be sought, reflects a "doing" orientation and a sense that it is possible, even desirable, to "master" one's environment. The meaning of these labels and the cultural roots of the scheme will be apparent as the reader proceeds through the framework.

22. In simplifying the terminology, we recognized that we may distort the original meaning of the authors and/or blur the distinctions made by the more precise use of the specialized language of social science. However, we have consciously elected to run this risk in the hope that by making the ideas more accessible to managers, greater benefits will accrue than would be otherwise possible.

23. M. S. Perret, "The Impact of Cultural Differences on Budgeting," unpublished Ph.D. dissertation, The University of Western Ontario, 1982.

24. For a fuller treatment of the time variable, see Edward T. Hall, *The Silent Language* (New York: Doubleday & Co. Inc., 1959).

25. *Business Week* (January 20, 1986).

26. H. Mintzberg, *The Nature of Managerial Work* (Englewood Cliffs, N.J.: Prentice Hall, 1980).

27. Another example of this kind of reasoning is available in Huston Smith's *The Religions of Man* (New York: New American Library, 1958). According to traditional Hindu tenets, punishment varied by the caste of the offender. For the same offense, a Follower (unskilled laborers) would receive "X" punishment, a Producer (craftsmen, farmers, artisans) would receive "2X," an Administrator (organizers, doers, men of affairs) would receive "4X," and a Brahmin (intellectual and spiritual leaders) would receive "8 to 16X."

28. M. S. Perret, *Impact of Cultural Differences*. Subsequent to her dissertation research, Perret replicated the original study in a consulting/accounting organization across four countries (France, United States, England, and Holland). With quality of service being the focus, she found many of the same patterns of cultural effects. (Personal communication from Professor Perret, Naval Postgraduate School, Monterey, California, 1984.)

29. One of the most readable and thorough is Edwin O. Reischauer's *The Japanese* (Cambridge, Mass.: Harvard University Press, 1977).

30. See *American Sociological Review* 43 (December 1978): 829–847.

31. E. R. Hall, *op. cit.* In his book, *The Hidden Dimension* (Garden City, N.Y.: Doubleday, 1966) the subject of space is even more fully developed.

32. Nancy J. Adler, *International Dimensions of Organizational Behavior* (Boston: Kent Publishing, 2nd ed., 1991), 115. For a fuller description of cultural synergy, see Chapter 4 of this text which is devoted to the topic. For an even more extensive treatment of the subject, see Robert T. Moran and Philip R. Harris, *Managing Cultural Synergy* (Houston: Gulf Publishing, 1981).

33. See "The Great Slave Lake Railway," Case 9-71-CO11, Case and Publications Division, School of Business Administration, The University of Western Ontario, London, Canada, N6A 3K7.

34. There is evidence that effective international managers use stereotypes as devices to approximate reality as they enter another culture. However, after some time in a country, when they encounter the richness and variety of behavior, they drop the simplification of the stereotype and describe the mosaic of what they have experienced. Less effective managers hold on to their initial stereotypes; they exempt those who do not fit the stereotypes as the exceptions which prove the rule. See Indrei Ratui, "Thinking Internationally: A Comparison of How International Executives Learn," *International Studies of Management and Organization* XII, no. 1–2 (Spring-Summer 1983): 139–150.

35. Some suggested readings on the topic of culture shock include: Ingemar Torbiorn, *Living Abroad: Personal Adjustment and Personnel Policy in the Overseas Setting* (Sussex, England: John Wiley, 1982); Nancy Adler, *International Dimensions of Organizational Behavior* Chapters 8, 9; Kalvero Oberg, "Culture Shock: Adjustment to New Cultural Environments," *Practical Anthropology* 7 (1960): 177–182; C. L. Grove and I. Torbiorn, "A New Conceptualization of Intercultural Adjustment and the Goals of Training," *International Journal of Intercultural Relations* 9, no. 2 (1979).

36. Research on stress and adapting to stressful situations also suggests that there are physiological contributors as well. One reference that links physiology and culture shock is Gary Wederspahn, "Culture Shock: It's All in Your Head . . . and Body," *The Bridge* (Winter 1981): 10.

37. For these generalizations we are drawing on Torbiorn, *Living Abroad*; the research literature described by Adler, *International Dimensions*; an excellent, but unpublished, paper by Clyde B. Sargent, "Psychological Aspects of Environmental Adjustment"; Kalvero Oberg, "Culture Shock"; and our own experience with numerous executives and students around the world.

38. See Adler, *International Dimensions of Organizational Behavior*, Chapter 8.

39. See Rosalie L. Tung, "Selection and Training Procedures of U.S., European and Japanese Multinationals," *California Management Review* 25, no. 1 (Fall 1982): 57–71.

40. For discussions of the adjustment problems experienced by expatriate spouses see, Adler, *International Dimensions of Organizational Behavior*, Chapter 9; "Role Shock: A Tool for Conceptualizing Stresses Accompanying Disruptive Role Transitions," M. Minkler and R. P. Biller, *Human Relations* 32, no. 2 (1979).

41. Personal communication from Mr. Bernard Daniel, Secretary-General, Nestlé, Vevey, Switzerland.

42. Patricia A. Galagan, "Executive Development in a Changing World," *Training and Development Journal* (June 1990): 23–41.

43. Brenda McMillan, Joseph J. DiStefano, and James C. Rush, "Requisite Skills and Char-

acteristics of Global Managers," Working Paper, National Centre for Management Research and Development, School of Business Administration, The University of Western Ontario, London, Canada N6A 3K7. This portion of the book on "The Global Manager" draws directly from this working paper with the permission of the authors.

44. J. Phillip Samper, "Changing Face of the Global Corporation: Reflections on the Fabled Phoenix," presented at the World Management Congress, New York City, September 22, 1989.

45. See a pair of articles by Christopher A. Bartlett and Sumantra Ghoshal, "Managing Across Borders: New Strategic Requirements" and "Managing Across Borders: New Organizational Responses" *Sloan Management Review* (Summer and Fall 1987): 7–17 and 43–53, respectively; or their book *Managing Across Borders: The Transitional Solution* (Boston: Harvard Business School Press, 1989).

46. Stephen H. Rhinesmith, John N. Williamson, David M. Ehlen, and Denise S. Maxwell, "Developing Leaders for the Global Enterprise," *Training and Development Journal* (April 1989): 25 – 34. Reading no. 1 in this book.

47. Theodore Levitt, "The Globalization of Markets" *Harvard Business Review*, May–June 1983, pp. 92–103; Ralph T. Kreutzer, "Marketing Mix Standardization: An Integrated Approach to Global Marketing," *European Journal of Marketing*, 22, issue 10 (1988): 19–30.

48. Teresa J. Domzal and Lynette S. Unger, "Emerging Positioning Strategies in Global Marketing," *Journal of Consumer Marketing* 4, issue 4, (Fall 1987): 23–40.
Somkid Jatusripitak, Liam Fahey, and Philip Kotler, "Strategic Global Marketing: Lessons from the Japanese," *Columbia Journal of World Business* 20, issue 1 (Spring 1986), pp. 57–53, and Michael E. Porter, "The Strategic Role of International Marketing," *The Journal of Consumer Marketing* 3, no. 2 (Spring 1986): 17–21.

49. Sandra M. Huszagh, Richard J. Fox, and Ellen Day, "Global Marketing: An Empirical Investigation," *Columbia Journal of World Business* 20, issue 4 (1986): 31–43.

50. John A. Quelch and Edward J. Hoff, "Customizing Global Marketing," *Harvard Business Review* (May–June 1986): 59–68.

51. Harold F. Clarke, Jr., "Consumer and Corporate Values: Yet Another View on Global Marketing," *International Journal of Advertising* 6 (1987): 29–42.

52. Jeryl M. Whitelock, "Global Marketing and the Case for International Product Standardization," *European Journal of Marketing (UK)* 21, issue 9 (1987): 32–44.

53. Antonio Grimaldi, "Interpreting Popular Culture: The Missing Link Between Local Labor and International Management," *Columbia Journal of World Business* 21, issue 4 (Winter 1986): 67–72.

54. Nancy J. Adler and Fariborz Ghadar, "International Strategy from the Perspective of People Culture: The North American Context," Reading 6 in this book.

55. Andre Laurent, "The Cross-Cultural Puzzle of International Human Resource Management," *Human Resource Management* 25, issue 1 (Spring 1986): 91–102.

56. C. A. Bartlett and S. Ghoshal, "Managing Across Borders."

57. For an extraordinary article describing these and other organizational innovations, see Gunnar Hedlund, "The Hypermodern MNC — A Heterarchy?" *Human Resource Management* 25, no. 1 (Spring 1986): 9–35.

58. K. Ferdows, J. G. Miller, J. Nakane and T. E. Vollmann, "Evolving Global Manufacturing Strategies: Projections into the 1990s," *International Journal of Operations and Production Management* 6, no. 4 (1986): 6–16.

59. Ruth G. Shaeffer, "Building Global Teamwork for Growth and Survival," *The Conference Board Research Bulletin*, no. 228.

60. Leslie G. Campbell, *International Auditing* (New York: St. Martin's Press, 1985): 141.
61. William S. Albrecht, Hugh L. Marsh Jr., and Frederick H. Bentzel Jr., "Auditing an International Subsidiary," *Internal Auditor* 45, issue 5 (October 1988): 22–26; Joseph Soeters and Hein Schreuder, "The Interactions Between National and Organizational Cultures in Accounting Firms," *Accounting, Organizations and Society* 13, no. 1 (1988): 75–85; and Nicholas M. Zacchea "The Multinational Auditor: Overcoming Cultural Differences to Apply Audit Standards," *Internal Auditor* 45, issue 5 (1988): 16–21.
62. Briance Mascarenhas, "The Coordination of Manufacturing Interdependencies in Multinational Companies," *Journal of International Business Studies* (Winter 1984), pp. 91–106.
63. Domzel and Unger, *"Emerging Positioning Strategies."*
64. Laurel Wentz, "Global Marketing and Media: TV Nationalism Clouds Sky Gains," *Advertising Age* 58, issue 53 (December 14, 1987): 56.
65. Jiping Zhang, "The Building and Operation of a North American Business School" (Chinese), Tsinghua University Press (Beijing, 1990) (English Version published March 1987 by the School of Business Administration, The University of Western Ontario, London, Ontario N6A 3K7.)
66. Alan J. Zakon, "Globalization Is More Than Imports and Exports," *Management Review* 77, issue 7 (July 1988): 56–57.
67. Robert T. Moran, "Corporations Tragically Waste Overseas Experience," *International Management (UK)* 43, issue 1 (January 1988): 74.
68. J. Knight, M. Slattery, "The Case Method: A Note for First Year Students," School of Business Administration, The University of Western Ontario, December 1984. Minor editing was done on this note by Professors Henry W. Lane and Joseph DiStefano. For a fuller treatment of casewriting and case teaching from a faculty perspective, see Michiel R. Leenders and James Erskine, *Case Research: The Casewriting Process*, 2nd ed., 1978; and James A. Erskine, Michiel R. Leenders and Louise A. Mauffette-Leenders, *Teaching With Cases*. Both books are published by Research and Publications Division, School of Business Administration, The University of Western Ontario, London Ontario.
69. Footnote from the authors: We advocate that students within a class form three- to five-person groups to discuss each case after individually preparing it but before coming to class. Initial differences in assumptions, interpretations, analysis, and recommendations emerge in the study group. Quieter students also develop more confidence in their participation skills.
70. Another footnote from the authors: In the world of increasing technological and managerial complexity, increased specialization is a reality. As differentiation increases there is a concomitant need for more effective integration. The *human skills* required in collaboration and integration can be practiced and developed within the case context.

READING 1

Developing Leaders
for the Global Enterprise

Steven H. Rhinesmith, John N. Williamson,
David M. Ehlen, and Denise S. Maxwell

A global company is more than just a U.S. company with some offshore operations; it takes more than a lot of frequent flyer miles to become a global leader. Today's cosmopolitan executive must know what to do when competitive advantage is fleeting, when change becomes chaos, and when home base is the globe.

$\mathbf{A}$ major new organizational form has emerged in the 1980s. The "Global Enterprise" is rapidly coming to dominate competitive behavior in many industries around the world. It operates basically without the constraints or traditions of national boundaries and seeks to compete in any high-potential marketplace on earth.

The Global Enterprise is a consequence of several new and sophisticated forces that have come to shape the world economy over the last decade, including

- aggressive and massive financial accumulation and relatively free-flowing resource transfer;
- well-defined and highly efficient communication channels and information transfer and control systems;
- technology development and application that seek both leading-edge and low-cost positions in product creation and production;
- clear recognition of the potential for mass markets, mass customization, and global brands.

Rhinesmith is president of AFS Intercultural Programs, and an educational and management consultant. Williamson, Ehlen, and Maxwell are with Wilson Learning Corporation, 7500 Flying Cloud Drive, Eden Prairie, MN 55344-3795, where Williamson is senior vice president of business strategy and marketing, Ehlen is principal consultant for strategic organizational change, and Maxwell is project specialist and senior writer.

EVOLUTION OF THE
GLOBAL ORGANIZATION

A business goes through four conceptually distinct and progressively more complex stages as it evolves from a successful domestic organization to a global corporation:

- **Domestic enterprise**. This business operates solely within its own country—using domestic suppliers and producing and marketing its services and products to customers at home.
- **Exporter**. This is a successful national business that sells or markets its products and services in foreign countries, but operates primarily from its sense of domestic competitiveness and advantage. This firm has little information about marketplace conditions outside its national boundaries and will most often operate through independent agents or distributors. The exporter tends to be opportunistic and transitional in form, as trends and events that it does not anticipate or understand affect its success.
- **International or multinational corporation**. This organization supplements its international sales and distribution capability with localized manufacturing. Such organizations often turn over their foreign operations to locals. Import/export activities move freely within the infrastructure of the multinational corporation; technology and manufacturing may be as equally distributed as sales and logistics. The parent company operates with a centralized view of strategy, technology, and resource allocation, but decision making and customer service shift to the local or national level for marketing, selling, manufacturing, and competitive tactics. Many multinational firms are more accurately characterized as multidomestic, because each national or regional operation acts quite independently of the enterprise's other operations.
- **Global enterprise**. This organization is an extension of the international or multinational corporation. It is constantly scanning, organizing, and reorganizing its resources and capabilities so that national or regional boundaries are not barriers to potential products, business opportunities, and manufacturing locations.

Such an organization is always looking for potential products or businesses. It delivers them in the best markets from the lowest cost positions and with the most appropriate management resources, largely without regard to where dollars, people, resources, and technology reside. The mindset of the Global Enterprise is to reach and penetrate marketplaces before local or international competitors are equipped to exploit the opportunities.

When an organization moves from an international to a global perspective, an essential shift takes place—a shift from the tight control of a bureaucracy to an entrepreneurial, flexible, rapid-response capability that is totally comfortable with cross-cultural influences and conditions.

The Global Enterprise, as Kenichi Ohmae describes it in his book, *Triad Power*, is one that becomes an "insider" in any market or nation where it operates, much as a domestic enterprise operates in a local market. The difference is a global strategic perspective, with cross-cultural integration and a highly localized sense of customers and competitors.

For many international organizations, one of the central executive-suite issues of the late '80s and into the '90s is how to organize, integrate, and manage their activities to become global players. That will become particularly true for the large U.S. firms that are just now beginning to understand that an export mentality — or having offshore divisions or businesses — does not necessarily mean they are equipped to compete effectively on a global basis.

Increasingly, the issue of global strategy deals with a series of differentiation and integration decisions. On one hand, companies have a clear need for a sense of global strategic intent, or for broad-based resource, technology, and market allocation schemes. At the same time, they need a sense of localized customer focus and competitiveness that deals with regional or local conditions as well as culture, behavior, and values.

Interestingly, most of the current writing and thinking about global organizations focuses on marketing, resource allocation, technology transfer, and organizational configuration as they relate primarily to information-flow, strategy, and control requirements. Little attention is given to the management and human-development needs that arise in the evolution from a domestically postured business to one that operates from a true global perspective.

GLOBAL LEADERSHIP-DEVELOPMENT AGENDA

What are the leadership-development requirements of an organization that is moving through those phases to a global outlook? How can it successfully develop its human resources to meet the changing, emerging, and increasingly complex conditions?

The "Leadership Agenda" (Figure 1) shows the leadership-development requirements that face a company as it evolves toward a global perspective. Several premises lie behind the agenda:

- The customer is the center or focus of development and training. In other words, the primary focus of training and development is serving customers increasingly well and with competitive advantage.
- The company's global strategy "wraps around" the training and development approaches; the organization's essential sense of competitiveness and strategic intent is embedded in all training programs and interventions.
- The six leadership-development clusters have a contemporary management viewpoint. The clusters are organized around requirements for global competitive success rather than traditional skill or behavior sets.

Let us define briefly what each of the leadership-clusters comprises and then seek to organize them against the framework of the evolving enterprise.

FIGURE 1   The Leadership Agenda

GLOBAL STRATEGIC INTENT/
STRATEGIC CONTEXT

Managing the
competitive
strategy

Managing the
environmental
scan

Managing
organizational
versatility

LOCAL
CUSTOMER
FOCUS

Managing
personal
effectiveness

Managing
teams and
alliances

Managing
change and
chaos

Managing the Environmental Scan

This cluster represents the systematic process of assessing and understanding the major internal and external influences on the enterprise's ability to achieve competitive advantage. In a larger sense, the cluster focuses on changing the frame of reference from a local or national orientation to a truly global perspective. It involves understanding influences, trends, and directions in technology, financial resources, marketing and distribution practices, political and cultural influences, and international economics.

Operationally, information systems and data-collection processes need to be reframed and revised to enable the organization to collect and utilize, in a timely and strategic way, the information required to proactively manage the business. That often requires an extensive reorganization of the company's data- and information-collection capacities. The process must ensure that the information to be collected is useful, and that the necessary systems, analytical processes, and human-resource-development schemes are in place to support the business's strategic information requirements.

For many organizations, that task appears complex. For others, it simply means augmenting and enhancing the systems already in place, or taking a new look at the company's strategic intent and articulating the information that is necessary to support the current strategy.

Whatever the degree of revision, it requires an understanding of today's critical success factors — those few things that must go right for the business to prosper — and the appropriate data about them. That often means narrowing, not enlarging, the information agenda and being careful about specifying information and data sets that are crucial to the firm's success.

Managing the Competitive Strategy

The focus of this cluster is understanding and developing competitive strategies, plans, and tactics that operate outside the confines of a domestic marketplace orientation. Again, much of the requirement deals with changing the basic frame of reference or point of view from which competitive activities and strategies are addressed. Several new dimensions need to be addressed and internalized.

One of the first "new understandings" is that the competitive environment operates in a greatly expanded and increasingly complex manner. Market strategy can be complicated by new issues and problems arising from unknown new competitors, the possibility of new entrants or players, and the implications of legislation such as tariffs and quotas.

In another sense, the resources and assets of the enterprise need to be looked at in dramatically expanded ways. For instance, the role of the enterprise's brand positioning has to be considered in terms of global strategic presence, as well as local marketing and competitive conditions.

The internationalization of taste, modified by local culture and values, supports the practice of mass customization and segmentation, but always from the perspective of the global brand, product offering, or business franchise. The issues of quality, resource efficiency, and cost leadership are becoming elements of marketing as well as financial strategy. And innovation and creativity have strong strategic implications as the organization confronts different competitors in virtually every local marketplace.

A customer-back business definition — with the organizational responsiveness and value-adding activities that support changing tastes and needs — still must be the fundamental driving force behind the organization's sense of competitiveness. Being close to customers remains a crucial element of success in the global model.

Such marketing tactics as pricing and promotional plans, which historically have operated on a local basis, must have a strategic or global coherence, as well as a localized sense of advantage and competition.

Managing Organizational Versatility

The advent of the global organization will bring dramatic new changes and learning requirements for individuals; other changes will be reflected in the architecture of the organizational models for tomorrow's successful global enterprises.

The most basic shift will take place as an organization moves from the classical, bureaucratic-control model to one that is characterized by flexible and responsive structures, adaptive and sometimes temporary operating systems, control mechanisms driven by information networks, and decision-making and behavior processes that are entrepreneurial, rapid-response, and risk-oriented.

Unstable business environments and irregular competitive and customer changes will contribute to a state of continuous organization and re-organization of resources, technologies, marketing and distribution systems, and human networks. Such changes will be necessary for adapting to the new success factors that will be critical for the business.

The underlying issue and challenge will be one of rapid and continuous response to opportunities and threats in terms of resource allocation, strategies, and human behavior. Certainly those needs seem straightforward, but the new approaches and systems may seem foreign to the conventional thinking that characterizes management practice in today's successful international enterprises.

Managing Teams and Alliances

The central operating mode for the Global Enterprise will be the creation, organization, and management of multinational teams and alliances — groups that represent diversity in functional capabilities, experience levels, and cultural values.

The effective global manager will need to understand how to organize and lead multinational teams; deal with issues of collaboration and cross-cultural variances; and develop processes for coaching, mentoring, and assessing performance across a variety of attitudes, beliefs, and standards. That requires the ability to effectively lead and direct a diverse group of people, most of whom will have values, beliefs, behaviors, business-practice standards, and traditions that are likely to be culturally different from those of the manager or leader.

Success in the global model will also come from the ability to create links across traditional organizational and national boundaries. Strategic partnerships will be formed to "achieve higher performance and/or lower costs through joint, mutually-dependent action of independent organizations or individuals," according to John Henderson of MIT. The basis for such alliances will be a mutually-shared purpose that transcends cultural differences.

In that sense, the requirements of global leadership extend well beyond traditional management practices, to reflect sensitivity to cultural diversity and perspective, and understanding of different — and sometimes conflicting — social forces without prejudice. Often, a manager will be required to operate in an unfamiliar and uncomfortable organizational setting.

Within the architecture of cross-cultural teams, managers need to recognize and focus on the subtle requirements for organizational loyalty and commitment, despite the presence of different cultural values and beliefs. At the same time, they must manage in the context of continuous change and diversity.

Managing Change and Chaos

Continuous change — not stability — is the dominant influence in global business activities today. That demands not only new skills, but also new realities, and even new comfort zones for global managers, who must realize and understand that global management will operate largely in the face of continuous change. The traditional role of making order out of chaos will shift to one of continuously managing change and chaos in ways that are responsive to customers and competitive conditions.

The idea that change — not stability — will be the regular and understood frame of reference for global management underlies the need for training, development, and understanding for managers who operate in international or global enterprises.

Only recently has the subject of change been given legitimate status in managerial training and learning activities. The real nature of the training and development need remains vague and largely undefined.

The concepts and metaphors that describe the management of change are increasingly visual. Peter Vaill of George Washington University describes it as learning how to "navigate in perpetual whitewater." Others see it as the process of continuous learning and improvement, of dealing with the personal requirements of constantly changing environments, and of viewing success as the process of improving (changing) faster than competitors — learning more quickly about opportunities and responding more completely when information and strategy point the way.

A significant learning opportunity in the domain of managing change is contextual: creating the mindsets, metaphors, beliefs, and attitudes that support and define the impact of irregular and chaotic change at a personal level. That means developing self-management and personal growth practices that can provide the stability, energy, and managerial confidence that are crucial to effectively handling such conditions.

Managing Personal Effectiveness

The personal growth and adaptation requirements for many U.S. managers, as they move toward operating in Global Enterprises, will be far-reaching, primarily because U.S.-based managers generally lack the experience, diversity, and globetrotting skills of so many of their offshore counterparts.

Personal adaptation to the changing conditions, cultures, and operating requirements of the Global Enterprise represents a significant and largely unfunded training need. Development of global managers in most businesses is done ad hoc, rather than as a systematic and orderly movement toward the skills, perceptions, and attitudes of effective global management.

In many respects, the global leader will need to have a cosmopolitan perspective new to many U.S. firms. A working knowledge of international relations and foreign affairs will be required, as well as a careful and complete sensitivity to the diversity of cultures, beliefs, social forces, and values, and a commitment to treating that diversity largely without prejudice.

Global managers will also have to manage accelerated change in their own lives, family relations, living conditions, and perhaps even economic constraints. A true world view and sense of world citizenship will be a valuable frame of reference.

At the same time, managers must remain grounded in their skills, capacities, and personal sense of energy and balance, often under the continuing impact of destabilizing organizational and personal influences. That will be particularly true as they move across cultures. Even aspects of their life as mundane as personal living requirements will be challenging and at times difficult.

We believe the effective manager will emerge as a kind of global citizen, always anchored in a nationalistic framework, but embodying the openness, adaptability, and personal versatility necessary to live under new and often unpredictable conditions.

Many of the attitudes, skills, and perceptions of global adaptation can be provided in well-structured learning and training experiences. But complete growth will come only when training and personal on-the-job experiences are integrated to reflect a thoughtful, institutionalized development process. For most global managers, that process can and will be a lifelong journey.

The six development clusters represent the essence and focus of the leadership development and training necessary to support the Global Enterprise. They may lack definitive clarity in today's operating climate, but they point to the direction in which attention and resources must be applied if the successful international organization of today is to make the transition to Global Enterprise.

The "Global Management Matrix" (Figure 2) summarizes the focus of leadership attention as an organization increases in complexity from a domestic to a global entity.

THE AMERICAN LEADERSHIP CHALLENGE

It is somewhat ironic that conventional wisdom about the inability of U.S. firms to compete effectively in the global marketplace usually focuses on inadequate spending in technology, plants, and equipment. The real vulnerability may lie in the lack of attention to training and developing key managers in the approaches, concepts, and experiences required to be effective global managers and leaders.

It is equally ironic that the presumed strength of U.S. firms is the level and quality of management and leadership training — either in academic or corporate settings. Our managers are believed to be better trained than their offshore counterparts. The reality as it relates to the global organization may be just the opposite.

U.S. businesses increasingly recognize the need for achieving a global-marketplace perspective. However, they do not have the training and experience needed for developed and seasoned management teams capable of operating at the same skill level as companies from such countries as Japan and Germany. Such nations have been forced by the nature of their competitive positions to compete nationally — and even globally — over the last 10, 20, or more years. Until recently, the United States has had the luxury of being able to remain domestic.

We in the United States are an insular society. That quality is present in our schools, our government, our corporations, and our values and beliefs. To change the pattern in a fundamental way may take years, if not a generation. During that process, we may well be managerially unprepared to meet the requirements for global competitiveness.

FIGURE 2 The Global Management Matrix

Leadership Development Clusters / Corporate Type	Managing the environmental scan–How do we determine what must go right?	Managing the competitive strategy–How do we allocate and align resources?	Managing organizational versatility–How do we organize for success today and tomorrow?	Managing teams and alliances–How do we connect with others for advantage?	Managing change and chaos–How do we thrive in times of unpredictable change?	Managing personal effectiveness–How do we change and grow successfully as individuals?
Global Enterprise	Global trends, conditions, and resources.	Integrate holistic strategies.	Create free-flowing resource-allocation schemes.	Create global strategic partnerships–inter- and intra-organizational links.	Pro-actively create destabilized conditions for advantage.	Transcend cultural differences.
International or Multinational Corporation	Multidomestic trends, environmental conditions, and strategic resources.	Proliferate successful domestic market model with cultural adaptation.	Adapt systems and processes to international competitive conditions.	Develop multinational alliances and ventures; manage cross-cultural work teams.	Respond and adapt to destabilizing change by flexibly reallocating resources across national markets.	Work effectively in cross-cultural situations.
Exporter	Offshore market trends and conditions; domestic strategic resources.	Extend domestic success to offshore markets.	Respond to emerging foreign-market opportunities.	Manage cross-cultural distribution links.	Adapt to destabilizing change by flexibly entering or withdrawing from foreign markets.	Understand cross-cultural needs.
Domestic Enterprise	Domestic market trends, resources, and environmental conditions.	Penetrate and segment markets.	Respond to local competitive and market changes.	Manage cross-functional teams.	Flexibly protect ourselves against unpredictable change.	Understand self and associates.

What will it take to change and effectively compete?

First, we need to recognize that the new game will not be played or driven by the U.S. business model. To cling to traditional U.S. views of competitiveness and marketplace success will increasingly threaten an organization's ability to compete in the years ahead.

That shift in thinking will be particularly difficult for those American enterprises that have done little in the last 30 or 40 years to educate and train their managers to organize and manage the firm's resources from a multicultural or international perspective. Feeding that deficiency is the failure of the American educational system to provide students with international business skills and cross-cultural knowledge to bring to organizations.

We also need to modify certain barriers, misconceptions, and beliefs, if American enterprise is going to grapple with the question of managerial competitiveness. Some of the barriers appear in research by Andre Laurent, who has studied multinational corporations and has made several key observations:

- Multinational companies do not and cannot submerge the individuality of different cultures. As strong as corporate culture is, people never give up their own backgrounds and preferences. People can adapt, but in periods of crisis or uncertainty, they will retreat to their own sets of beliefs and cultural values.
- Contact with other nationality groups can even promote determination to be different. It is interesting that many people withdraw when confronted with cultural differences, and reinforce their determination not to adjust and not to give up their own values.
- It is useless to present new kinds of management theory and practice to individuals who are culturally unable or unwilling to accept it. For example, performance reviews are difficult in most multinational corporations because of differences in personal style. Americans tend to be open, direct, and blunt; Asians tend to be much more indirect, oblique, and subtle in giving feedback. Thus, something as apparently basic and common as a performance-appraisal system probably cannot be implemented uniformly on a global basis.

Several other key paradigms about cross-cultural awareness that affect our ability to re-think the new game are worth observing:

- The "we are all alike" syndrome is one that many of us have experienced when we have visited a foreign land and come back with the initial perception that all people are very much alike — we are just one, big human race.
- The second stage of understanding comes when we begin to uncover differences — some subtle, some specific. Then we realize that although people have some significant similarities, we can also have strong differences.
- Third comes the realization that we are really both different and similar, and that in an organization, a leadership and management model must

address both common and uncommon threads, as well as diverse behaviors and beliefs.

The prevailing attitude of senior executives in American companies seems to be a point of view that suggests, "If we can get our enterprise's corporate culture and values right—no matter where it operates around the globe—then the issue of strategy and local behavior will be predictable and appropriate."

They are saying that the template for values, beliefs, and behaviors of the enterprise must necessarily come from the values, beliefs, behaviors, and attitudes of the parent corporation. We believe that holding on to that viewpoint means starting from the wrong place.

The difficult task for senior management today is to flip-flop the traditional thinking that suggests that values, beliefs, and behaviors need to be highly standardized from a central, corporate perspective, and that strategies and resource-allocation schemes can be played out from a local point of view. We believe the opposite reflects today's reality and is the fundamental operating condition for an organization that wants to achieve true global status.

We believe that in the '90s the challenge for most enterprises as they move toward the global model will lie in successfully managing international teams. And U.S. corporations have done little in the last 30 or 40 years to educate, train, and provide experience for managers to manage a multicultural workforce.

Meeting that challenge will be expensive in terms of both resources and time. U.S. firms need to get on with the task of building a new model for leadership development in a global community—a model that derives not from the traditional management skill base of planning, staffing, and control, but rather from a recognition of a whole new array of leadership requirements:

- The capacity to manage, live with, and operate under conditions of continuous change and turmoil.
- The recognition that global advantage is transitory and that the role of managers and global leaders will be to continuously assess and adjust resources, technologies, organizational structure, and human beings to reflect simultaneously a centralized view of strategy and a localized view of customers and cultures.
- An acknowledgement that the U.S. business model is not necessarily the best point of departure for evaluating the implications and meaning of global-marketplace trends and opportunities. A fundamental shift in thinking needs to take place in setting assumptions and beliefs about the role enterprises can play in the global marketplace. U.S. businesses have to move from a perspective that considers the rest of the world from a U.S. viewpoint, to a more global outlook that views the home country in the context of the world marketplace.
- A heightened awareness of strategic marketing and global competitiveness. On one hand, brands, technologies, and franchises need to be played out from the advantage of scale and clout that only a global point of view can

provide. At the same time, businesses need to recognize and acknowledge the "close to the customer" conditions that operate locally or inside major national marketplaces.

- The development of skills and capabilities to lead multinational teams in flexible and responsive ways. Human resources need to reflect the same capacity for adaptation and flexibility as technology and financial resources. The new organizational model that emerges will shift from the traditional bureaucratic control scheme that drives so many large enterprises today to a contemporary entrepreneurialism characterized by flexibility, resource fluidity, and continuously changing beliefs and attitudes about competitiveness. It will embody a willingness to shed old assumptions and beliefs quickly, and a recognition that home base is really the globe.
- The understanding that managers, particularly in the United States, need cross-cultural and expatriate experiences early on and continually throughout their careers.

The challenge for all of us involved in both management and the development of management is to begin to change the context in which we think about our human-development responsibilities. We clearly need to discard traditional models and views and begin to think from a global rather than a domestic paradigm. In the process, we must challenge and change many of our views about hiring, training, controlling, offering incentives, and measuring our managers.

It is a long-term assignment, probably three to five years for most large enterprises simply to get moving; in all likelihood, it will take a full generation to implement the approach.

By that time, we will have a whole new game to worry about.

READING 2

The Silent Language
in Overseas Business

Edward T. Hall

With few exceptions, Americans are relative newcomers on the international business scene. Today, as in Mark Twain's time, we are all too often "innocents abroad," in an era when naiveté and blundering in foreign business dealings may have serious political repercussions.

When the American executive travels abroad to do business, he is frequently shocked to discover to what extent the many variables of foreign behavior and custom complicate his efforts. Although the American has recognized, certainly, that even the man next door has many minor traits which make him somewhat peculiar, for some reason he has failed to appreciate how different foreign businessmen and their practices will seem to him.

He should understand that the various peoples around the world have worked out and integrated into their subconscious literally thousands of behavior patterns that they take for granted in each other.[1] Then, when the stranger enters, and behaves differently from the local norm, he often quite unintentionally insults, annoys, or amuses the native with whom he is attempting to do business. For example:

> In the United States, a corporation executive knows what is meant when a client lets a month go by before replying to a business proposal. On the other hand, he senses an eagerness to do business if he is immediately ushered into the client's office. In both instances, he is reacting to subtle cues in the timing of interaction, cues which he depends on to chart his course of action.

> Abroad, however, all this changes. The American executive learns that the Latin Americans are casual about time and that if he waits an hour in the outer office before seeing the Deputy Minister of Finance, it does not necessarily mean he is not getting anywhere. There people are so important that nobody can bear to tear himself away; because of

the resultant interruptions and conversational detours, everybody is constantly getting behind. What the American does not know is the point at which the waiting becomes significant.

In another instance, after traveling 7,000 miles an American walks into the office of a highly recommended Arab businessman on whom he will have to depend completely. What he sees does not breed confidence. The office is reached by walking through a suspicious-looking coffee-house in an old, dilapidated building situated in a crowded non-European section of town. The elevator, rising from dark, smelly corridors, is rickety and equally foul. When he gets to the office itself, he is shocked to find it small, crowded, and confused. Papers are stacked all over the desk and table tops — even scattered on the floor in irregular piles.

The Arab merchant he has come to see had met him at the airport the night before and sent his driver to the hotel this morning to pick him up. But now, after the American's rush, the Arab is tied up with something else. Even when they finally start talking business, there are constant interruptions. If the American is at all sensitive to his environment, everything around him signals, "What am I getting into?"

Before leaving home he was told that things would be different, but how different? The hotel is modern enough. The shops in the new part of town have many more American and European trade goods than he had anticipated. His first impression was that doing business in the Middle East would not present any new problems. Now he is beginning to have doubts. One minute everything looks familiar and he is on firm ground; the next, familiar landmarks are gone. His greatest problem is that so much assails his senses all at once that he does not know where to start looking for something that will tell him where he stands. He needs a frame of reference — a way of sorting out what is significant and relevant.

That is why it is so important for American businessmen to have a real understanding of the various social, cultural, and economic differences they will face when they attempt to do business in foreign countries. To help give some frame of reference, this article will map out a few areas of human activity that have largely been unstudied.

The topics I will discuss are certainly not presented as the last word on the subject, but they have proved to be highly reliable points at which to begin to gain an understanding of foreign cultures. While additional research will undoubtedly turn up other items just as relevant, at present I think the businessman can do well to begin by appreciating cultural differences in matters concerning the language of time, of space, of material possessions, of friendship patterns, and of agreements.

LANGUAGE OF TIME

Everywhere in the world people use time to communicate with each other. There are different languages of time just as there are different spoken languages. The unspoken languages are informal; yet the rules governing their interpretation are surprisingly *ironbound*.

In the United States, a delay in answering a communication can result from a large volume of business causing the request to be postponed until the backlog is cleared away, from poor organization, or possibly from technical complexity requiring deep analysis. But if the person awaiting the answer or decision rules out these reasons, then the delay means to him that the matter has low priority on the part of the other person — lack of interest. On the other hand, a similar delay in a foreign country may mean something altogether different. Thus:

> In Ethiopia, the time required for a decision is directly proportional to its importance. This is so much the case that low-level bureaucrats there have a way of trying to elevate the prestige of their work by taking a long time to make up their minds. (Americans in that part of the world are innocently prone to downgrade their work in the local people's eyes by trying to speed things up.)

> In the Arab East, time does not generally include schedules as Americans know and use them. The time required to get something accomplished depends on the relationship. More important people get fast service from less important people, and conversely. Close relatives take absolute priority; nonrelatives are kept waiting.

In the United States, giving a person a deadline is a way of indicating the degree of urgency or relative importance of the work. But in the Middle East, the American runs into a cultural trap the minute he opens his mouth. "Mr. Aziz will have to make up his mind in a hurry because my board meets next week and I have to have an answer by then," is taken as indicating the American is overly demanding and is exerting undue pressure. "I am going to Damascus tomorrow morning and will have to have my car tonight," is a sure way to get the mechanic to stop work, because to give another person a deadline in this part of the world is to be rude, pushy, and demanding.

An Arab's evasiveness as to when something is going to happen does not mean he does not want to do business; it only means he is avoiding unpleasantness and is side-stepping possible commitments which he takes more seriously than we do. For example:

> The Arabs themselves at times find it impossible to communicate even to each other that some processes cannot be hurried, and are controlled by built-in schedules. This is obvious enough to the Westerner but not to the Arab. A highly placed public official in Baghdad precipitated a bitter family dispute because his nephew, a biochemist, could not speed up the analysis of the uncle's blood. He accused the nephew of putting other less important people before him and of not caring. Nothing could sway the uncle, who could not grasp the fact that there is such a thing as an *inherent* schedule.

With us the more important an event is, the further ahead we schedule it, which is why we find it insulting to be asked to a party at the last minute. In planning future events with Arabs, it pays to hold the lead time to a week or less because other factors may intervene or take precedence.

Again, time spent waiting in an American's outer office is a sure indicator of what one person thinks of another or how important he feels the other's business to be. This is so much the case that most Americans cannot help getting angry after waiting 30 minutes; one may even feel such a delay is an insult, and will walk out. In Latin America, on the other hand, one learns that it does not mean anything to wait in an outer office. An American businessman with years of experience in

Mexico once told me, "You know, I have spent two hours cooling my heels in an executive's outer office. It took me a long time to learn to keep my blood pressure down. Even now, I find it hard to convince myself they are still interested when they keep me waiting."

The Japanese handle time in ways which are almost inexplicable to the Western European and particularly the American. A delay of years with them does not mean that they have lost interest. It only means that they are building up to something. They have learned that Americans are vulnerable to long waits. One of them expressed it, "You Americans have one terrible weakness. If we make you wait long enough, you will agree to anything."

Indians of South Asia have an elastic view of time as compared to our own. Delays do not, therefore, have the same meaning to them. Nor does indefiniteness in pinpointing appointments mean that they are evasive. Two Americans meeting will say, "We should get together sometime," thereby setting a low priority on the meeting. The Indian who says, "Come over and see me, see me anytime," means just that.

Americans make a place at the table which may or may not mean a place made in the heart. But when the Indian makes a place in his time, it is yours to fill in every sense of the word if you realize that by so doing you have crossed a boundary and are now friends with him. The point of all this is that time communicates just as surely as do words and that the vocabulary of time is different around the world. The principle to be remembered is that time has different meanings in each country.

LANGUAGE OF SPACE

Like time, the language of space is different wherever one goes. The American businessman, familiar with the pattern of American corporate life, has no difficulty in appraising the relative importance of someone else, simply by noting the size of his office in relation to other offices around him:

> Our pattern calls for the president or the chairman of the board to have the biggest office. The executive vice president will have the next largest, and so on down the line until you end up in the "bull pen." More important offices are usually located at the corners of buildings and on the upper floors. Executive suites will be on the top floor. The relative rank of vice presidents will be reflected in where they are placed along "Executive Row."

> The French, on the other hand, are much more likely to lay out space as a network of connecting points of influence, activity, or interest. The French supervisor will ordinarily be found in the middle of his subordinates where he can control them.

Americans who are crowded will often feel that their status in the organization is suffering. As one would expect in the Arab world, the location of an office and its size constitute a poor index of the importance of the man who occupies it. What we experience as crowded, the Arab will often regard as spacious. The same is true in Spanish cultures. A Latin American official illustrated the Spanish view of this point while showing me around a plant. Opening the door to an 18-by-20-foot office in which seventeen clerks and their desks were placed, he said, "See, we have nice spacious offices. Lots of space for everyone."

The American will look at a Japanese room and remark how bare it is. Similarly, the Japanese look at our rooms and comment, "How bare!" Furniture in the American home tends to be placed along the walls (around the edge). Japanese have their charcoal pit where the family gathers in the *middle* of the room. The top floor of Japanese department stores is not reserved for the chief executive — it is the bargain roof!

In the Middle East and Latin America, the businessman is likely to feel left out in time and overcrowded in space. People get too close to him, lay their hands on him, and generally crowd his physical being. In Scandinavia and Germany, he feels more at home, but at the same time the people are a little cold and distant. It is space itself that conveys this feeling.

In the United States, because of our tendency to zone activities, nearness carries rights of familiarity so that the neighbor can borrow material possessions and invade time. This is not true in England. Propinquity entitles you to nothing. American Air Force personnel stationed there complain because they have to make an appointment for their children to play with the neighbor's child next door.

Conversation distance between two people is learned early in life by copying elders. Its controlling patterns operate almost totally unconsciously. In the United States, in contrast to many foreign countries, men avoid excessive touching. Regular business is conducted at distances such as 5 feet to 8 feet; highly personal business, 18 inches to 3 feet — not 2 or 3 inches.

In the United States, it is perfectly possible for an experienced executive to schedule the steps of negotiation in time and space so that most people feel comfortable about what is happening. Business transactions progress in stages from across the desk to beside the desk, to the coffee table, then on to the conference table, the luncheon table, or the golf course, or even into the home — all according to a complex set of hidden rules we obey instinctively.

Even in the United States, however, an executive may slip when he moves into new and unfamiliar realms, when dealing with a new group, doing business with a new company, or moving to a new place in the industrial hierarchy. In a new country the danger is magnified. For example, in India it is considered improper to discuss business in the home on social occasions. One never invites a business acquaintance to the home for the purpose of furthering business aims. That would be a violation of sacred hospitality rules.

LANGUAGE OF THINGS

Americans are often contrasted with the rest of the world in terms of material possessions. We are accused of being materialistic, gadget-crazy. And, as a matter of fact, we have developed material things for some very interesting reasons. Lacking a fixed class system and having an extremely mobile population, Americans have become highly sensitive to how others make use of material possessions. We use everything from clothes to houses as a highly evolved and complex means of ascertaining each other's status. Ours is a rapidly shifting system in which both styles and people move up or down. For example:

> The Cadillac ad men feel that not only is it natural but quite insightful of them to show a picture of a Cadillac and a well-turned out gentleman in his early fifties opening the door. The caption underneath reads, "You already know a great deal about this man."

> Following this same pattern, the head of a big union spends an excess of $100,000 furnishing his office so that the president of United States Steel cannot look down on him. Good materials, large space, and the proper surroundings signify that the people who occupy the premises are solid citizens, that they are dependable and successful.

The French, the English, and the Germans have entirely different ways of using their material possessions. What stands for the height of dependability and respectability with the English would be old-fashioned and backward to us. The Japanese take pride in often inexpensive but tasteful arrangements that are used to produce the proper emotional setting.

Middle East businessmen look for something else — family, connections, friendship. They do not use the furnishings of their office as part of their status system; nor do they expect to impress a client by these means or to fool a banker into lending more money than he should. They like good things, too, but feel that they, as persons, should be known and not judged solely by what the public sees.

One of the most common criticisms of American relations abroad, both commercial and governmental, is that we usually think in terms of material things. "Money talks," says the American, who goes on talking the language of money abroad, in the belief that money talks the *same* language all over the world. A common practice in the United States is to try to buy loyalty with high salaries. In foreign countries, this maneuver almost never works, for money and material possessions stand for something different there than they do in America.

LANGUAGE OF FRIENDSHIP

The American finds his friends next door and among those with whom he works. It has been noted that we take people up quickly and drop them just as quickly. Occasionally a friendship formed during schooldays will persist, but this is rare. For us there are few well-defined rules governing the obligations of friendship. It is difficult to say at which point our friendship gives way to business opportunities or pressure from above. In this we differ from many other people in the world. As a general rule in foreign countries friendships are not formed as quickly as in the United States but go much deeper, last longer, and involve real obligations. For example:

> It is important to stress that in the Middle East and Latin America your "friends" will not let you down. The fact that they personally are feeling the pinch is never an excuse for failing their friends. They are supposed to look out for your interests.

Friends and family around the world represent a sort of social insurance that would be difficult to find in the United States. We do not use our friends to help us out in disaster as much as we do as a means of getting ahead — or, at least, of getting the job done. The United States systems work by means of a series of closely tabulated favors and obligations carefully doled out where they will do the most good. And the least that we expect in exchange for a favor is gratitude.

The opposite is the case in India, where the friend's role is to "sense" a person's need and do something about it. The idea of reciprocity as we know it is unheard of. An American in India will have difficulty if he attempts to follow American friendship patterns. He gains nothing by extending himself in behalf of others, least of all gratitude, because the Indian assumes that what he does for others he does for the good of his own psyche. He will find it impossible to make friends quickly and is unlikely to allow sufficient time for friendships to ripen. He will also note that as he gets to know people better, they may become more critical of him, a fact that he finds hard to take. What he does not know is that one sign of friendship in India is speaking one's mind.

LANGUAGE OF AGREEMENTS

While it is important for American businessmen abroad to understand the symbolic meanings of friendship rules, time, space, and material possessions, it is just as important for executives to know the rules for negotiating agreements in various countries. Even if they cannot be expected to know the details of each nation's commercial legal practices, just the awareness of and the expectation of the existence of differences will eliminate much complication.

Actually, no society can exist on a high commercial level without a highly developed working base on which agreements can rest. This base may be one or a combination of three types:

1. Rules that are spelled out technically as law or regulation.
2. Moral practices mutually agreed on and taught to the young as a set of principles.
3. Informal customs to which everyone conforms without being able to state the exact rules.

Some societies favor one, some another. Ours, particularly in the business world, lays heavy emphasis on the first variety. Few Americans will conduct any business nowadays without some written agreement or contract.

Varying from culture to culture will be the circumstances under which such rules apply. Americans consider that negotiations have more or less ceased when the contract is signed. With the Greeks, on the other hand, the contract is seen as a sort of way station on the route to negotiation that will cease only when the work is completed. The contract is nothing more than a charter for serious negotiations. In the Arab world, once a man's word is given in a particular kind of way, it is just as binding, if not more so, than most of our written contracts. The written contract, therefore, violates the Moslem's sensitivities and reflects on his honor. Unfortunately, the situation is not so hopelessly confused that neither system can be counted on to prevail consistently.

Informal patterns and unstated agreements often lead to untold difficulty in the cross-cultural situation. Take the case of the before-and-after patterns where there is a wide discrepancy between the American's expectations and those of the Arab:

> In the United States, when you engage a specialist such as a lawyer or a doctor, require any standard service, or even take a taxi, you make several assumptions: (a) the charge will be fair; (b) it will be in proportion to the services rendered; and (c) it will bear a close relationship to the "going rate."
>
> You wait until after the services are performed before asking what the tab will be. If the charge is too high in the light of the above assumptions, you feel you have been cheated. You can complain, or can say nothing, pay up, and take your business elsewhere the next time.
>
> As one would expect in the Middle East, basic differences emerge which lead to difficulty if not understood. For instance, when taking a cab in Beirut it is well to know the going rate as a point around which to bargain and for settling the charge, which must be fixed before engaging the cab.
>
> If you have not fixed the rate *in advance*, there is a complete change and an entirely different set of rules will apply. According to these rules, the going rate plays no part whatsoever. The whole relationship is altered. The sky is the limit, and the customer has no kick coming. I have seen taxi drivers shouting at the top of their lungs, waving their arms, following a redfaced American with his head pulled down between his shoulders, demanding for a two-pound ride ten Lebanese pounds, which the American eventually had to pay.

It is difficult for the American to accommodate his frame of reference to the fact that what constitutes one thing to him, namely, a taxi ride, is to the Arab two very different operations involving two different sets of relationships and two sets of rules. The crucial factor is whether the bargaining is done at the beginning or the end of the ride! As a matter of fact, you cannot bargain at the end. What the driver asks for he is entitled to!

One of the greatest difficulties Americans have abroad stems from the fact that we often think we have a commitment when we do not. The second complication on this same topic is the other side of the coin, i.e., when others think we have agreed to things that we have not. Our own failure to recognize binding obligations, plus our custom of setting organizational goals ahead of everything else, has put us in hot water far too often.

People sometimes do not keep agreements with us because we do not keep agreements with them. As a general rule, the American treats the agreement as something he may eventually have to break. Here are two examples:

> Once while I was visiting an American post in Latin America, the Ambassador sent the Spanish version of a trade treaty down to his language officer with instructions to write in some "weasel words." To his dismay, he was told, "There are no weasel words in Spanish."

A personnel officer of a large corporation in Iran made an agreement with local employees that American employees would not receive preferential treatment. When the first American employee arrived, it was learned quickly that in the United States he had been covered by a variety of health plans that were not available to Iranians. And this led to immediate protests from the Iranians which were never satisfied. The personnel officer never really grasped the fact that he had violated an iron-bound contract.

Certainly, this is the most important generalization to be drawn by American businessmen from this discussion of agreements: there are many times when we are vulnerable *even when judged by our own standards*. Many instances of actual sharp practices by American companies are well known abroad and are giving American business a bad name. The cure for such questionable behavior is simple. The companies concerned usually have it within their power to discharge offenders and to foster within their organization an atmosphere in which only honesty and fairness can thrive.

But the cure for ignorance of the social and legal rules which underlie business agreements is not so easy. This is because:

- The subject is complex.
- Little research has been conducted to determine the culturally different concepts of what is an agreement.
- The people of each country think that their own code is the only one, and that everything else is dishonest.
- Each code is different from our own; and the farther away one is traveling from Western Europe, the greater the difference is.

But the little that has already been learned about this subject indicates that as a problem it is not insoluble and will yield to research. Since it is probably one of the more relevant and immediately applicable areas of interest to modern business, it would certainly be advisable for companies with large foreign operations to sponsor some serious research in this vital field.

A CASE IN POINT

Thus far, I have been concerned with developing the five check points around which a real understanding of foreign cultures can begin. But the problems that arise from a faulty understanding of the silent language of foreign custom are human problems and perhaps can best be dramatized by an actual case.

A Latin American republic had decided to modernize one of its communication networks to the tune of several million dollars. Because of its reputation for quality and price, the inside track was quickly taken by American company "Y."

The company, having been sounded out informally, considered the size of the order and decided to bypass its regular Latin American representative and send instead its sales manager. The following describes what took place.

The sales manager arrived and checked in at the leading hotel. He immediately had some difficulty pinning down just who it was he had to see about his business.

After several days without results, he called at the American Embassy where he found that the commercial attaché had the up-to-the-minute information he needed. The commercial attaché listened to his story. Realizing that the sales manager had already made a number of mistakes, but figuring that the Latins were used to American blundering, the attaché reasoned that all was not lost. He informed the sales manager that the Minister of Communications was the key man and that whoever got the nod from him would get the contract. He also briefed the sales manager on methods of conducting business in Latin America and offered some pointers about dealing with the minister.

The attaché's advice ran somewhat as follows:

1. "You don't do business here the way you do in the States; it is necessary to spend much more time. You have to get to know your man and vice versa.

2. "You must meet with him *several times* before you talk business. I will tell you at what point you can bring up the subject. Take your cues from me. [Our American sales manager at this point made a few observations to himself about "cookie pushers" and wondered how many payrolls had been met by the commercial attaché.]

3. "Take that price list and put it in your pocket. Don't get it out until I tell you to. Down here price is only one of the many things taken into account before closing a deal. In the United States, your past experience will prompt you to act according to a certain set of principles, but many of these principles will *not* work here. Every time you feel the urge to act or to say something, look at me. Suppress the urge and take your cues from me. This is very important.

4. "Down here people like to do business with men who *are* somebody. In order to be somebody, it is well to have written a book, to have lectured at a university, or to have developed your intellect in some way. The man you are going to see is a poet. He has published several volumes of poetry. Like many Latin Americans, he prizes poetry highly. You will find that he will spend a good deal of business time quoting his poetry to you, and he will take great pleasure in this.

5. "You will also note that the people here are very proud of their past and of their Spanish blood, but they are also exceedingly proud of their liberation from Spain and their independence. The fact that they are a democracy, that they are free, and also that they are no longer a colony is very, very important to them. They are warm and friendly and enthusiastic if they like you. If they don't, they are cold and withdrawn.

6. "And another thing, time down here means something different. It works in a different way. You know how it is back in the States when a certain type blurts out whatever is on his mind without waiting to see if the situation is right. He is considered an impatient bore and somewhat egocentric. Well, down here, you have to wait much, much longer, and I really mean *much, much* longer, before you can begin to talk about the reason for your visit.

7. There is another point I want to caution you about. At home, the man who sells takes the initiative. Here, *they* tell you when they are ready to do

business. But, most of all, don't discuss price until you are asked and don't rush things."

The Pitch

The next day the commercial attaché introduced the sales manager to the Minister of Communications. First, there was a long wait in the outer office while people kept coming in and out. The sales manager looked at his watch, fidgeted, and finally asked whether the minister was really expecting him. The reply he received was scarcely reassuring, "Oh yes, he is expecting you but several things have come up that require his attention. Besides, one gets used to waiting down here." The sales manager irritably replied, "But doesn't he know I flew all the way down here from the United States to see him, and I have spent over a week already of my valuable time trying to find him?" "Yes, I know," was the answer, "but things just move much more slowly here."

At the end of about 30 minutes, the minister emerged from the office, greeted the commercial attaché with a *doble abraso*, throwing his arms around him and patting him on the back as though they were long-lost brothers. Now, turning and smiling, the minister extended his hand to the sales manager, who, by this time, was feeling rather miffed because he had been kept in the outer office so long.

After what seemed to be an all too short chat, the minister rose, suggesting a well-known café where they might meet for dinner the next evening. The sales manager expected, of course, that, considering the nature of their business and the size of the order, he might be taken to the minister's home, not realizing that the Latin home is reserved for family and very close friends.

Until now, nothing at all had been said about the reason for the sales manager's visit, a fact which bothered him somewhat. The whole setup seemed wrong; neither did he like the idea of wasting another day in town. He told the home office before he left that he would be gone for a week or ten days at most, and made a mental note that he would clean this order up in three days and enjoy a few days in Acapulco or Mexico City. Now the week had already gone and he would be lucky if he made it home in ten days.

Voicing his misgivings to the commercial attaché, he wanted to know if the minister really meant business, and, if he did, why could they not get together and talk about it? The commercial attaché by now was beginning to show the strain of constantly have to reassure the sales manager. Nevertheless, he tried again:

"What you don't realize is that part of the time we were waiting, the minister was rearranging a very tight schedule so that he could spend tomorrow night with you. You see, down here they don't delegate responsibility the way we do in the States. They exercise much tighter control than we do. As a consequence, this man spends up to 15 hours a day at his desk. It may not look like it to you, but I assure you he really means business. He wants to give your company the order; if you play your cards right, you will get it."

The next evening provided more of the same. Much conversation about food and music, about many people the sales manager had never heard of. They went to a night club, where the sales manager brightened up and began to think that perhaps he and the minister might have something in common after all. It bothered him, however, that the principal reason for his visit was not even alluded to tangentially. But every time he started to talk about electronics, the commercial attaché would nudge him and proceed to change the subject.

The next meeting was for morning coffee at a café. By now the sales manager was having difficulty hiding his impatience. To make matters worse, the minister had a mannerism he did not like. When they talked, he was likely to put his hand on him; he would take hold of his arm and get so close that he almost "spat" in his face. As a consequence, the sales manager was kept busy trying to dodge and back up.

Following coffee, there was a walk in a nearby park. The minister expounded on the shrubs, the birds, and the beauties of nature, and at one spot he stopped to point at a statue and said: "There is a statue of the world's greatest hero, the liberator of mankind!" At this point the worst happened, for the sales manager asked who the statue was of and, being given the name of a famous Latin American patriot, said, "I never heard of him," and walked on.

The Failure

It is quite clear from this that the sales manager did not get the order, which went to a Swedish concern. The American, moreover, was never able to see the minister again. Why did the minister feel the way he did? His reasoning went somewhat as follows:

"I like the American's equipment and it makes sense to deal with North Americans who are near us and whose price is right. But I could never be friends with this man. He is not my kind of human being and we have nothing in common. He is not *simpatico*. If I can't be friends and he is not *simpatico*, I can't depend on him to treat me right. I tried everything, every conceivable situation, and only once did we seem to understand each other. If we could be friends, he would feel obligated to me and this obligation would give me some control. Without control, how do I know he will deliver what he says he will at the price he quotes?"

Of course, what the minister did not know was that the price was quite firm, and that quality control was a matter of company policy. He did not realize that the sales manager was a member of an organization, and that the man is always subordinate to the organization in the United States. Next year maybe the sales manager would not even be representing the company, but would be replaced. Further, if he wanted someone to depend on, his best bet would be to hire a good American lawyer to represent him and write a binding contract.

In this instance, both sides suffered. The American felt he was being slighted and put off, and did not see how there could possibly be any connection between poetry and doing business or why it should all take so long. He interpreted the delay as a form of polite brush-off. Even if things had gone differently and there had been a contract, it is doubtful that the minister would have trusted the contract as much as he would a man whom he considered his friend. Throughout Latin America, the law is made livable and contracts workable by having friends and relatives operating from the inside. Lacking a friend, someone who would look out for his interests, the minister did not want to take a chance. He stated this simply and directly.

CONCLUSION

The case just described has of necessity been oversimplified. The danger is that the reader will say, "Oh, I see. All you really have to do is be friends." At which point the expert will step in and reply:

"Yes, of course, but what you don't realize is that in Latin America being a friend involves much more than it does in the United States and is an entirely different proposition. A friendship implies obligations. You go about it differently. It involves much more than being nice, visiting, and playing golf. You would not want to enter into friendship lightly."

The point is simply this. It takes years and years to develop a sound foundation for doing business in a given country. Much that is done seems silly or strange to the home office. Indeed, the most common error made by home offices, once they have found representatives who can get results, is failure to take their advice and allow sufficient time for representatives to develop the proper contacts.

The second most common error, if that is what it can be called, is ignorance of the secret and hidden language of foreign cultures. In this article I have tried to show how five key topics — time, space, material possessions, friendship patterns, and business agreements — offer a starting point from which companies can begin to acquire the understanding necessary to do business in foreign countries.

Our present knowledge is meager, and much more research is needed before the businessman of the future can go abroad fully equipped for his work. Not only will he need to be well versed in the economics, law, and politics of the area, but he will have to understand, if not speak, the silent languages of other cultures.

Note

1.   For details, see Edward T. Hall, *The Silent Language* (New York: Doubleday & Company, Inc., 1959).

READING 3

Motivation, Leadership, and Organization: Do American Theories Apply Abroad?

Geert Hofstede

A well-known experiment used in organizational behavior courses involves show-ing the class an ambiguous picture — one that can be interpreted in two different ways. One such picture represents either an attractive young girl or an ugly old woman, depending on the way you look at it. Some of my colleagues and I use the experiment, which demonstrates how different people in the same situation may perceive quite different things. We start by asking half of the class to close their eyes while we show the other half a slightly altered version of the picture — one in which only the young girl can be seen — for only five seconds. Then we ask those who just saw the young girl's picture to close their eyes while we give the other half of the class a five-second look at a version in which only the old woman can be seen. After this preparation we show the ambiguous picture to everyone at the same time.

The results are amazing — most of those "conditioned" by seeing the young girl first see only the young girl in the ambiguous picture, and those "conditioned" by seeing the old woman tend to see only the old woman. We then ask one of those who perceive the old woman to explain to one of those who perceive the young girl what he or she sees, and vice versa, until everyone finally sees both images in the picture. Each group usually finds it very difficult to get its views across to the other one and sometimes there's considerable irritation at how "stupid" the other group is.

CULTURAL CONDITIONING

I use this experiment to introduce a discussion on cultural conditioning. Basically, it shows that in five seconds I can condition half a class to see something different

Reprinted from *Organizational Dynamics*, Summer 1980. © 1980. All rights reserved, Geert Hofstede. This article is based on research carried out in the period 1973–78 at the European Institute for Advanced Studies in Management, Brussels. The article itself was sponsored by executive search con-sultants Berndtson International S.A., Brussels. The author acknowledges the helpful comments of Mark Cantley, André Laurent, Ernest C. Miller, and Jennifer Robinson on an earlier version of it.

from what the other half sees. If this is so in the simple classroom situation, how much stronger should differences in perception of the same reality be between people who have been conditioned by different education and life experience — not for five seconds, but for twenty, thirty, or forty years?

I define culture as the collective mental programming of the people in an environment. Culture is not a characteristic of individuals; it encompasses a number of people who were conditioned by the same education and life experience. When we speak of the culture of a group, a tribe, a geographical region, a national minority, or a nation, culture refers to the collective mental programming that these people have in common; the programming that is different from that of other groups, tribes, regions, minorities or majorities, or nations.

Culture, in this sense of collective mental programming, is often difficult to change; if it changes at all, it does so slowly. This is so not only because it exists in the minds of the people but, if it is shared by a number of people, because it has become crystallized in the institutions these people have built together: their family structures, educational structures, religious organizations, associations, forms of government, work organizations, law, literature, settlement patterns, buildings and even, as I hope to show, scientific theories. All of these reflect common beliefs that derive from the common culture.

Although we are all conditioned by cultural influences at many different levels — family, social, group, geographical region, professional environment — this article deals specifically with the influence of our national environment: that is, our country. Most countries' inhabitants share a national character that's more clearly apparent to foreigners than to the nationals themselves; it represents the cultural mental programming that the nationals tend to have in common.

NATIONAL CULTURE
IN FOUR DIMENSIONS

The concept of national culture or national character has suffered from vagueness. There has been little consensus on what represents the national culture of, for example, Americans, Mexicans, French, or Japanese. We seem to lack even the terminology to describe it. Over a period of six years, I have been involved in a large research project on national cultures. For a set of 40 independent nations, I have tried to determine empirically the main criteria by which the national cultures differed. I found four such criteria, which I label dimensions; these are Power Distance, Uncertainty Avoidance, Individualism-Collectivism, and Masculinity-Femininity. To understand the dimensions of national culture, we can compare it with the dimensions of personality we use when we describe individuals' behavior. In recruiting, an organization often tries to get an impression of a candidate's dimensions of personality, such as intelligence (high-low); energy level (active-passive); and emotional stability (stable-unstable). These distinctions can be refined through the use of certain tests, but it's essential to have a set of criteria whereby the characteristics of individuals can be meaningfully described. The dimensions of national culture I use represent a corresponding set of criteria for describing national cultures.

Characterizing a national culture does not, of course, mean that every person in the nation has all the characteristics assigned to that culture. Therefore, in describing national cultures we refer to the common elements within each nation—the national norm—but we are not describing individuals. This should be kept in mind when interpreting the four dimensions explained in the following paragraphs.

The Research Data

The four dimensions of national culture were found through a combination of theoretical reasoning and massive statistical analysis, in what is most likely the largest survey material ever obtained with a single questionnaire. This survey material was collected between 1967 and 1973 among employees of subsidiaries of one large U.S.-based multinational corporation (MNC) in 40 countries around the globe. The total data bank contains more than 116,000 questionnaires collected from virtually everyone in the corporation, from unskilled workers to research Ph.D.s and top managers. Moreover, data were collected twice—first during a period from 1967 to 1969 and a repeat survey during 1971 to 1973. Out of a total of about 150 different survey questions (of the precoded answer type), about 60 deal with the respondents' beliefs and values; these were analyzed for the present study. The questionnaire was administered in the language of each country; a total of 20 language versions had to be made. On the basis of these data, each of the 40 countries could be given an index score for each of the four dimensions.

I was wondering at first whether differences found among employees of one single corporation could be used to detect truly national culture differences. I also wondered what effect the translation of the questionnaire could have had. With this in mind, I administered a number of the same questions in 1971–1973 to an international group of about 400 managers from different public and private organizations following management development courses in Lausanne, Switzerland. This time, all received the questionnaire in English. In spite of the different mix of respondents and the different language used, I found largely the same differences between countries in the manager group that I found among the multinational personnel. Then I started looking for other studies, comparing aspects of national character across a number of countries on the basis of surveys using other questions and other respondents (such as students) or on representative public opinion polls. I found 13 such studies; these compared between 5 and 19 countries at a time. The results of these studies showed a statistically significant similarity (correlation) with one or more of the four dimensions. Finally, I also looked for national indicators (such as per capita national income, inequality of income distribution, and government spending on development aid) that could logically be supposed to be related to one or more of the dimensions. I found 31 such indicators—of which the values were available for between 5 and 40 countries—that were correlated in a statistically significant way with at least one of the dimensions. All these additional studies (for which the data were collected by other people, not by me) helped make the picture of the four dimensions more complete. Interestingly, very few of these studies had ever been related to each other before, but the four dimensions provide a framework that shows how they can be fit together like pieces of a huge puzzle. The fact that data obtained within a single MNC have the power to uncover the secrets of entire national cultures can be understood when it's known that the respondents form well-matched samples from their nations: They are employed by the same firm (or its subsidiary); their jobs are similar (I consistently compared the same occupations across the different countries); and their age categories and sex composition were similar — only their nationalities differed. Therefore, if we look at the differences in survey answers between multinational employees in countries A, B, C, and so on, the general factor that can account for the differences in the answers is national culture.

Power Distance

The first dimension of national culture is called *Power Distance*. It indicates the extent to which a society accepts the fact that power in institutions and organizations is distributed unequally. It's reflected in the values of the less powerful members of society as well as in those of the more powerful ones. A fuller picture of the difference between small Power Distance and large Power Distance societies is shown in Figure 1. Of course, this shows only the extremes; most countries fall somewhere in between.

FIGURE 1   The Power Distance Dimension

Small Power Distance	*Large Power Distance*
Inequality in society should be minimized.	There should be an order of inequality in this world in which everybody has a rightful place; high and low are protected by this order.
All people should be interdependent.	A few people should be independent; most should be dependent.
Hierarchy means an inequality of roles, established for convenience.	Hierarchy means existential inequality.
Superiors consider subordinates to be "people like me."	Superiors consider subordinates to be a different kind of people.
Subordinates consider superiors to be "people like me."	Subordinates consider superiors as a different kind of people.
Superiors are accessible.	Superiors are inaccessible.
The use of power should be legitimate and is subject to the judgment as to whether it is good or evil.	Power is a basic fact of society that antedates good or evil. Its legitimacy is irrelevant.

(Continued)

FIGURE 1 Continued

Small Power Distance	Large Power Distance
All should have equal rights.	Power–holders are entitled to privileges.
Those in power should try to look less powerful than they are.	Those in power should try to look as powerful as possible.
The system is to blame.	The underdog is to blame.
The way to change a social system is to redistribute power.	The way to change a social system is to dethrone those in power.
People at various power levels feel less threatened and more prepared to trust people.	Other people are a potential threat to one's power and can rarely be trusted.
Latent harmony exists between the powerful and the powerless.	Latent conflict exists between the powerful and the powerless.
Cooperation among the powerless can be based on solidarity.	Cooperation among the powerless is difficult to attain because of their low–faith–in–people norm.

Uncertainty Avoidance

The second dimension, *Uncertainty Avoidance*, indicates the extent to which society feels threatened by uncertain and ambiguous situations, and tries to avoid these situations by providing greater career stability, establishing more formal rules, not tolerating deviant ideas and behaviors, and believing in absolute truths and the attainment of expertise. Nevertheless, societies in which uncertainty avoidance is strong are also characterized by a higher level of anxiety and aggressiveness that creates, among other things, a stronger inner urge in people to work hard. (See Figure 2.)

Individualism — Collectivism

The third dimension encompasses *Individualism* and its opposite, *Collectivism*. Individualism implies a loosely knit social framework in which people are supposed to take care of themselves and of their immediate families only, while collectivism is characterized by a tight social framework in which people distinguish between in-groups and out-groups; they expect their in-group (relatives, clan, organizations) to look after them, and in exchange for that they feel they owe absolute loyalty to it. A fuller picture of this dimension is presented in Figure 3.

FIGURE 2   The Uncertainty Avoidance Dimension

Weak Uncertainty Avoidance	Strong Uncertainty Avoidance
The uncertainty inherent in life is more easily accepted and each day is taken as it comes.	The uncertainty inherent in life is felt as a continuous threat that must be fought.
Ease and lower stress are experienced.	Higher anxiety and stress are experienced.
Time is free.	Time is money.
Hard work, as such, is not a virtue.	There is an inner urge to work hard.
Aggressive behavior is frowned upon.	Aggressive behavior of self and others is accepted.
Less showing of emotions is preferred.	More showing of emotions is preferred.
Conflict and competition can be contained on the level of fair play and used constructively.	Conflict and competition can unleash aggression and should therefore be avoided.
More acceptance of dissent is entailed.	A strong need for consensus is involved.
Deviation is not considered threatening; greater tolerance is shown.	Deviant persons and ideas are dangerous; intolerance holds sway.
The ambiance is one of less nationalism.	Nationalism is pervasive.
More positive feelings toward younger people are seen.	Younger people are suspect.
There is more willingness to take risks in life.	There is great concern with security in life.
The accent is on relativism, empiricism.	The search is for ultimate, absolute truths and values.
There should be as few rules as possible.	There is a need for written rules and regulations.
If rules cannot be kept, we should change them.	If rules cannot be kept, we are sinners and should repent.
Belief is placed in generalists and common sense.	Belief is placed in experts and their knowledge.
The authorities are there to serve the citizens.	Ordinary citizens are incompetent compared with the authorities.

FIGURE 3   **The Individualism Dimension**

Collectivist	*Individualist*
In society, people are born into extended families or clans who protect them in exchange for loyalty.	In society, everybody is supposed to take care of himself/herself and his/her immediate family.
"We" consciousness holds sway.	"I" consciousness holds sway.
Identity is based in the social system.	Identity is based in the individual.
There is emotional dependence of individual on organizations and institutions.	There is emotional independence of individual from organizations or institutions.
The involvement with organizations is moral.	The involvement with organizations is calculative.
The emphasis is on belonging to organizations; membership is the ideal.	The emphasis is on individual initiative and achievement; leadership is the ideal.
Private life is invaded by organizations and clans to which one belongs; opinions are predetermined.	Everybody has a right to a private life and opinion.
Expertise, order, duty, and security are provided by organization or clan.	Autonomy, variety, pleasure, and individual financial security are sought in the system.
Friendships are predetermined by stable social relationships, but there is need for prestige within these relationships.	The need is for specific friendships.
Belief is placed in group decisions.	Belief is placed in individual decisions.
Value standards differ for in–groups and out–groups (particularism).	Value standards should apply to all (universalism).

Masculinity

The fourth dimension is called *Masculinity* even though, in concept, it encompasses its opposite pole, *Femininity*. Measurements in terms of this dimension express the extent to which the dominant values in society are "masculine" — that is, assertiveness, the acquisition of money and things, and *not* caring for others, the quality of life, or people. These values were labeled "masculine" because, *within* nearly all societies, men scored higher in terms of the values' positive sense than of their negative sense (in terms of assertiveness, for example, rather than its lack) — even

FIGURE 4   The Masculinity Dimension

Feminine	*Masculine*
Men needn't be assertive, but can also assume nurturing roles.	Men should be assertive. Women should be nurturing.
Sex roles in society are more fluid.	Sex roles in society are clearly differentiated.
There should be equality between the sexes.	Men should dominate in society.
Quality of life is important.	Performance is what counts.
You work in order to live.	You live in order to work.
People and environment are important.	Money and things are important.
Interdependence is the ideal.	Independence is the ideal.
Service provides the motivation.	Ambition provides the drive.
One sympathizes with the unfortunate.	One admires the successful achiever.
Small and slow are beautiful.	Big and fast are beautiful.
Unisex and androgyny are ideal.	Ostentatious manliness (''machismo'') is appreciated.

though the society as a whole might veer toward the "feminine" pole. Interestingly, the more an entire society scores to the masculine side, the wider the gap between its "men's" and "women's" values (see Figure 4).

A SET OF CULTURAL MAPS OF THE WORLD

Research data were obtained by comparing the beliefs and values of employees within the subsidiaries of one large multinational corporation in 40 countries around the world. These countries represent the wealthy countries of the West and the larger, more prosperous of the Third World countries. The Socialist block countries are missing, but data are available for Yugoslavia (where the corporation is represented by a local, self-managed company under Yugoslavian law). It was possible, on the basis of mean answers of employees on a number of key questions, to assign an index value to each country on each dimension. As described on pages 100–101, these index values appear to be related in a statistically significant way to a vast amount of other data about these countries, including both research results from other samples and national indicator figures.

Because of the difficulty of representing four dimensions in a single diagram, the position of the countries on the dimensions is shown in Figures 5, 6, and 7 for two dimensions at a time. The vertical and horizontal axes and the circles around clusters of countries have been drawn subjectively, in order to show the degree of proximity of geographically or historically related countries. The three diagrams thus represent a composite set of cultural maps of the world.

Of the three "maps," those in Figure 5 (Power Distance × Uncertainty Avoidance) and Figure 7 (Masculinity × Uncertainty Avoidance) show a scattering of countries in all corners — that is, all combinations of index values occur. Figure 6 (Power Distance × Individualism), however, shows one empty corner: The combination of Small Power Distance and Collectivism does not occur. In fact, there is a tendency for Large Power Distance to be associated with Collectivism and for Small Power Distance with Individualism. However, there is a third factor that should be taken into account here: national wealth. Both Small Power Distance and Individualism go together with greater national wealth (per capita gross national product). The relationship between Individualism and Wealth is quite strong, as Figure 6 shows. In the upper part (Collectivist) we find only the poorer countries, with Japan as a borderline exception. In the lower part (Individualism), we find only the wealthier countries. If we look at the poorer and the wealthier countries separately, there is no longer any relationship between Power Distance and Individualism.

THE 40 COUNTRIES
(SHOWING ABBREVIATIONS USED IN FIGURES 5, 6, AND 7.)

ARG	Argentina		JAP	Japan
AUL	Australia		MEX	Mexico
AUT	Austria		NET	Netherlands
BEL	Belgium		NOR	Norway
BRA	Brazil		NZL	New Zealand
CAN	Canada		PAK	Pakistan
CHL	Chile		PER	Peru
COL	Colombia		PHI	Philippines
DEN	Denmark		POR	Portugal
FIN	Finland		SAF	South Africa
FRA	France		SIN	Singapore
GBR	Great Britain		SPA	Spain
GER	Germany (West)		SWE	Sweden
GRE	Greece		SWI	Switzerland
HOK	Hong Kong		TAI	Taiwan
IND	India		THA	Thailand
IRA	Iran		TUR	Turkey
IRE	Ireland		USA	United States
ISR	Israel		VEN	Venezuela
ITA	Italy		YUG	Yugoslavia

FIGURE 5 The Position of the 40 Countries on the
Power Distance and Uncertainty Avoidance Scales

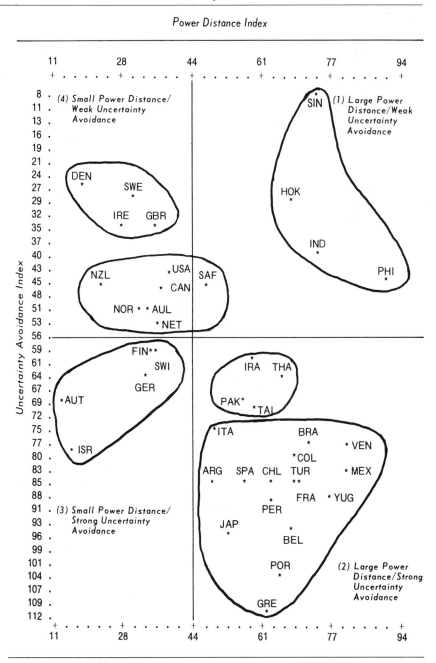

FIGURE 6   The Position of the 40 Countries on the
Power Distance and Individualism Scales

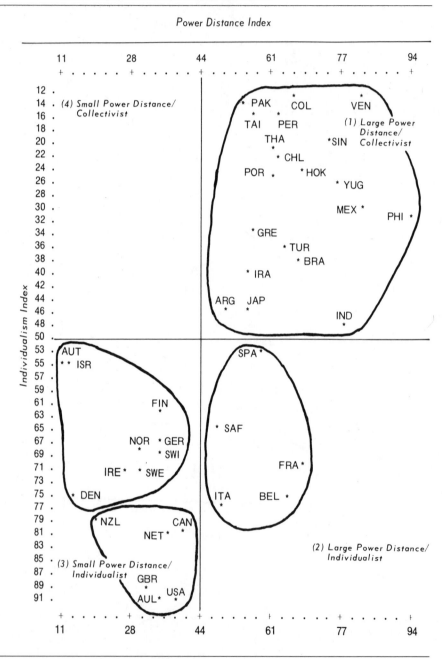

FIGURE 7   **The Position of the 40 Countries on the
Uncertainty Avoidance and Masculinity Scales**

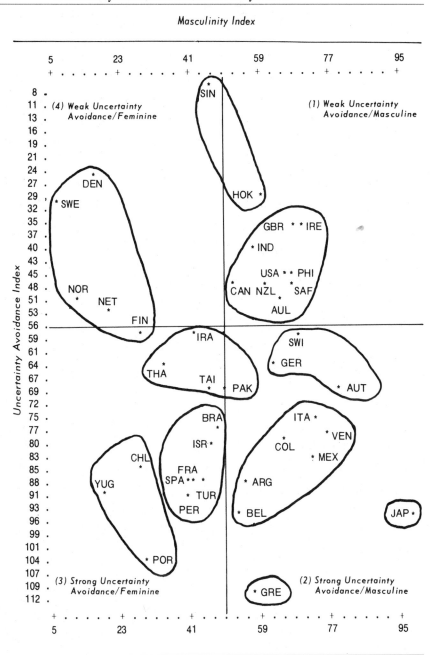

THE CULTURAL RELATIVITY
OF MANAGEMENT THEORIES

Of particular interest in the context of this discussion is the relative position of the United States on the four dimensions. Here is how the United States rates:

- On *Power Distance* at rank 15 out of the 40 countries (measured from below), it is below average but it is not as low as a number of other wealthy counties.
- On *Uncertainty Avoidance* at rank 9 out of 40, it is well below average.
- On *Individualism* at rank 40 out of 40, the United States is the single most individualist country of the entire set (followed closely by Australia and Great Britain).
- On *Masculinity* at rank 28 out of 40, it is well above average.

For about 60 years, the United States has been the world's largest producer and exporter of management theories covering such key areas as motivation, leadership, and organization. Before that, the centers of theorizing about what we now call "management" lay in the Old World. We can trace the history of management thought as far back as we want—at least to parts of the Old Testament of the Bible, and to ancient Greece (Plato's *The Laws* and *The Republic*, 350 B.C.). Sixteenth-century European "management" theorists include Niccolò Machiavelli (Italy) and Thomas More (Great Britain); early twentieth-century theorists include Max Weber (Germany) and Henry Fayol (France).

Today we are all culturally conditioned. We see the world in the way we have learned to see it. Only to a limited extent can we, in our thinking, step out of the boundaries imposed by our cultural conditioning. This applies to the author of a theory as much as it does to the ordinary citizen. Theories reflect the cultural environment in which they were written. If this is true, Italian, British, German, and French theories reflect the culture of Italy, Britain, Germany, and France of their day, and American theories reflect the culture of the United States of its day. Since most present-day theorists are middle-class intellectuals, their theories reflect a national intellectual middle-class culture background.

Now we ask the question: To what extent do theories developed in one country and reflecting the cultural boundaries of that country apply to other countries? Do American management theories apply in Japan? In India? No management theorist, to my knowledge, has ever explicitly addressed himself or herself to this issue. Most probably assume that their theories are universally valid. The availability of a conceptual framework built on four dimensions of national culture, in conjunction with the cultural maps of the world, makes it possible to see more clearly where and to what extent theories developed in one country are likely to apply elsewhere. In the remaining sections of this article I shall look from this viewpoint at most popular American theories of management in the areas of motivation, leadership, and organization.

MOTIVATION

Why do people behave as they do? There is great variety of theories of human motivation. According to Sigmund Freud, we are impelled to act by unconscious forces within us, which he called our id. Our conscious conception of ourselves — our ego — tries to control these forces, and an equally unconscious internal pilot — our superego — criticizes the thoughts and acts of our ego and causes feelings of guilt and anxiety when the ego seems to be giving in to the id. The superego is the product of early socialization, mainly learned from our parents when we were young children.

Freud's work has been extremely influential in psychology, but he is rarely quoted in the context of management theories. The latter almost exclusively refer to motivation theories developed later in the United States, particularly those of David McClelland, Abraham Maslow, Frederick Herzberg, and Victor Vroom. According to McClelland, we perform because we have a need to achieve (the achievement motive). More recently, McClelland has also paid a lot of attention to the power motive. Maslow has postulated a hierarchy of human needs, from more "basic" to "higher": most basic are physiological needs, followed by security, social needs, esteem needs and, finally, a need for "self-actualization." The latter incorporates McClelland's theory of achievement, but is defined in broader terms. Maslow's theory of the hierarchy of needs postulates that a higher need will become active only if the lower needs are sufficiently satisfied. Our acting is basically a rational activity by which we expect to fulfill successive levels of needs. Herzberg's two-factor theory of motivation distinguishes between hygienic factors (largely corresponding to Maslow's lower needs — physiological, security, social) and motivators (Maslow's higher needs — esteem, self-actualization); the hygienic factors have only the potential to motivate negatively (demotivate — they are necessary but not sufficient conditions), while only the motivators have the potential to motivate positively. Vroom has formalized the role of "expectancy" in motivation; he opposes "expectancy" theories and "drive" theories. The former see people as being *pulled* by the expectancy of some kind of result from their acts, mostly consciously. The latter (in accordance with Freud's theories) see people as *pushed* by inside forces — often unconscious ones.

Let us now look at these theories through culture-conscious glasses. Why has Freudian thinking never become popular in U.S. management theory, as has the thinking of McClelland, Maslow, Herzberg, and Vroom? To what extent do these theories reflect different cultural patterns? Freud was part of an Austrian middle-class culture at the turn of the century. If we compare present-day Austria and the United States on our cultural maps, we find the following:

- Austria scores considerably lower on Power Distance.
- Austria scores considerably higher on Uncertainty Avoidance.
- Austria scores considerably lower on Individualism.
- Austria scores considerably higher on Masculinity.

We do not know to what extent Austrian culture has changed since Freud's time, but evidence suggests that cultural patterns change very slowly. It is, therefore, not likely to have been much different from today's culture. The most striking thing about present-day Austrian culture is that it combines a fairly high Uncertainty Avoidance with a very low Power Distance (see Figure 5). Somehow the combination of high Uncertainty Avoidance with high Power Distance is more comfortable (we find this in Japan and in all Latin and Mediterranean countries — see Figure 5). Having a powerful superior whom we can both praise and blame is one way of satisfying a strong need for avoiding uncertainty. The Austrian culture, however (together with the German, Swiss, Israeli, and Finnish cultures) cannot rely on an external boss to absorb its uncertainty. Thus Freud's superego acts naturally as an inner uncertainty-absorbing device, an internalized boss. For strong Uncertainty Avoidance countries like Austria, working hard is caused by an inner urge — it is a way of relieving stress. (See Figure 2.) The Austrian superego is reinforced by the country's relatively low level of Individualism (see Figure 6). The inner feeling of obligation to society plays a much stronger role in Austria than in the United States. The ultrahigh Individualism of the United States leads to a need to explain every act in terms of self-interest, and expectancy theories of motivation do provide this explanation — we always do something *because* we expect to obtain the satisfaction of some need.

The comparison between Austrian and U.S. culture has so far justified the popularity of expectancy theories of motivation in the United States. The combination in the United States of weak Uncertainty Avoidance and relatively high Masculinity can tell us more about why the achievement motive has become so popular in that country. David McClelland, in his book *The Achieving Society*, sets up scores reflecting how strong achievement need is in many countries by analyzing the content of children's stories used in those countries to teach the young to read. It now appears that there is a strong relationship between McClelland's need for achievement country scores and the combination of weak Uncertainty Avoidance and strong Masculinity charted in Figure 7. (McClelland's data were collected for two historic years — 1925 and 1950 — but only his 1925 data relate to the cultural map in Figure 7. It is likely that the 1925 stories were more traditional, reflecting deep underlying cultural currents; the choice of stories in 1950 in most countries may have been affected by modernization currents in education, often imported from abroad.)

Countries in the upper righthand corner of Figure 7 received mostly high scores on achievement need in McClelland's book; countries in the lower lefthand corner of Figure 7 received low scores. This leads us to the conclusion that the concept of the achievement motive presupposes two cultural choices — a willingness to accept risk (equivalent to weak Uncertainty Avoidance; see Figure 2) and a concern with performance (equivalent to strong Masculinity; see Figure 4). This combination is found exclusively in countries in the Anglo-American group and in some of their former colonies (Figure 7). One striking thing about the concept of achievement is that the word itself is hardly translatable into any language other than English; for this reason, the word could not be used in the questionnaire of the multinational corporation used in my research. The English-speaking countries all appear in the upper righthand corn   of Figure 7.

If this is so, there is reason to reconsider Maslow's hierarchy of human needs in the light of the map shown in Figure 7. Quadrant 1 (upper righthand corner) in Figure 7 stands for *achievement motivation*, as we have seen (performance plus risk). Quadrant 2 distinguishes itself from quadrant 1 by strong Uncertainty Avoidance, which means *security motivation* (performance plus security). The countries on the feminine side of Figure 7 distinguish themselves by a focusing on quality of life rather than on performance and on relationships between people rather than on money and things (see Figure 4). This means *social motivation*: quality of life plus security in quadrant 3, and quality of life plus risk in quadrant 4. Now, Maslow's hierarchy puts self-actualization (achievement) plus esteem above social needs above security needs. This, however, is not the description of a universal human motivation process — it is the description of a value system, the value system of the U.S. middle class to which the author belonged. I suggest that if we want to continue thinking in terms of a hierarchy for countries in the lower righthand corner of Figure 7 (quadrant 2), security needs should rank at the top; for countries in the upper lefthand corner (quadrant 4), social needs should rank at the top, and for countries in the lower lefthand corner (quadrant 3) *both* security and social needs should rank at the top.

One practical outcome of presenting motivation theories is the movement toward humanization of work — an attempt to make work more intrinsically interesting to the workers. There are two main currents in humanization of work — one, developed in the United States and called *job enrichment*, aims at restructuring individual jobs. A chief proponent of job enrichment is Frederick Herzberg. The other current, developed in Europe and applied mainly in Sweden and Norway, aims at restructuring work into group work — forming, for example, such semiautonomous teams as those seen in the experiments at Volvo. Why the difference in approaches? What is seen as a "human" job depends on a society's prevailing model of humankind. In a more masculine society like the United States, humanization takes the form of masculinization, allowing individual performance. In the more feminine societies of Sweden and Norway, humanization takes the form of femininization — it is a means toward more wholesome interpersonal relationships in its deemphasis of interindividual competition.

LEADERSHIP

One of the oldest theorists of leadership in world literature is Machiavelli (1468–1527). He described certain effective techniques for manipulation and remaining in power (including deceit, bribery, and murder) that gave him a bad reputation in later centuries. Machiavelli wrote in the context of the Italy of his day, and what he described is clearly a large Power Distance situation. We still find Italy on the larger Power Distance side of Figure 5 (with all other Latin and Mediterranean countries), and we can assume from historical evidence that Power Distances in Italy during the sixteenth century were considerably larger than they are now. When we compare

Machiavelli's work with that of his contemporary, Sir Thomas More (1478–1535), we find cultural differences between ways of thinking in different countries even in the sixteenth century. The British More described in *Utopia* a state based on consensus as a "model" to criticize the political situation of his day. But practice did not always follow theory, of course: More, deemed too critical, was beheaded by order of King Henry VIII, while Machiavelli the realist managed to die peacefully in his bed. The difference in theories is nonetheless remarkable.

In the United States a current of leadership theories has developed. Some of the best known were put forth by the late Douglas McGregor (Theory X versus Theory Y), Rensis Likert (System 4 management), and Robert R. Blake with Jane S. Mouton (the Managerial Grid®). What these theories have in common is that they all advocate participation in the manager's decisions by his/her subordinates (participative management); however, the initiative toward participation is supposed to be taken by the manager. In a worldwide perspective (Figure 5), we can understand these theories from the middle position of the United States on the Power Distance side (rank 15 out of 40 countries). Had the culture been one of larger Power Distance, we could have expected more "Machiavellian" theories of leadership. In fact in the management literature of another country with a larger Power Distance index score, France, there is little concern with participative management American style, but great concern with who has the power. However, in countries with smaller Power Distances than the United States (Sweden, Norway, Germany, Israel), there is considerable sympathy for models of management in which even the initiatives are taken by the subordinates (forms of industrial democracy) and with which there's little sympathy in the United States. In the approaches toward "industrial democracy" taken in these countries, we notice their differences on the second dimension, Uncertainty Avoidance. In weak Uncertainty avoidance countries like Sweden, industrial democracy was started in the form of local experiments and only later was given a legislative framework. In strong Uncertainty Avoidance countries like Germany, industrial democracy was brought about by legislation first and then had to be brought alive in the organizations ("Mitbestimmung").

The crucial fact about leadership in any culture is that it is a complement to subordinateship. The Power Distance Index scores in Figure 5 are, in fact, based on the values of people as *subordinates*, not on the values of superiors. Whatever a naive literature on leadership may give us to understand, leaders cannot choose their styles at will; what is feasible depends to a large extent on the cultural conditioning of a leader's subordinates. Along these lines, Figure 8 describes the type of subordinateship that, other things being equal, a leader can expect to meet in societies at three different levels of Power Distance — subordinateship to which a leader must respond. The middle level represents what is most likely found in the United States.

Neither McGregor, nor Likert, nor Blake and Mouton allow for this type of cultural proviso — all three tend to be prescriptive with regard to a leadership style that, at best, will work with U.S. subordinates and with those in cultures — such as Canada or Australia — that have not too different Power Distance levels (Figure 5).

_____

FIGURE 8   Subordinateship for Three Levels of Power Distance

Small Power Distance	Medium Power Distance (United States)	Large Power Distance
Subordinates have weak dependence needs.	Subordinates have medium dependence needs.	Subordinates have strong dependence needs.
Superiors have weak dependence needs toward their superiors.	Superiors have medium dependence needs toward their superiors.	Superiors have strong dependence needs toward their superiors.
Subordinates expect superiors to consult them and may rebel or strike if superiors are not seen as staying within their legitimate role.	Subordinates expect superiors to consult them but will accept autocratic behavior as well.	Subordinates expect superiors to act autocratically.
Ideal superior to most is a loyal democrat.	Ideal superior to most is a resourceful democrat.	Ideal superior to most is a benevolent autocrat or paternalist.
Laws and rules apply to all and privileges for superiors are not considered acceptable.	Laws and rules apply to all, but a certain level of privileges for superiors is considered normal.	Everybody expects superiors to enjoy privileges; laws and rules differ for superiors and subordinates.
Status symbols are frowned upon and will easily come under attack from subordinates.	Status symbols for superiors contribute moderately to their authority and will be accepted by subordinates.	Status symbols are very important and contribute strongly to the superior's authority with the subordinates.

In fact, my research shows that subordinates in larger Power Distance countries tend to agree more frequently with Theory X.

A U.S. theory of leadership that allows for a certain amount of cultural relativity, although indirectly, is Fred Fiedler's contingency theory of leadership. Fiedler states that different leader personalities are needed for "difficult" and "easy" situations, and that a cultural gap between superior and subordinates is one of the factors that makes a situation "difficult." However, this theory does not address the kind of cultural gap in question.

In practice, the adaptation of managers to higher Power Distance environments does not seem to present too many problems. Although this is an unpopular message — one seldom professed in management development courses — managers moving to a larger Power Distance culture soon learn that they have to behave more autocratically in order to be effective, and tend to do so; this is borne out by the colonial history of most Western countries. But it is interesting that the Western ex-colonial power with the highest Power Distance norm — France — seems to be most appreciated by its former colonies and seems to maintain the best postcolonial relationships with most of them. This suggests that subordinates in a large Power Distance culture feel even more comfortable with superiors who are real autocrats than with those whose assumed autocratic stance is out of national character.

The operation of a manager in an environment with a Power Distance norm lower than his or her own is more problematic. U.S. managers tend to find it difficult to collaborate wholeheartedly in the "industrial democracy" processes of such countries as Sweden, Germany, and even the Netherlands. U.S. citizens tend to consider their country as the example of democracy, and find it difficult to accept that other countries might wish to develop forms of democracy for which they feel no need and that make major inroads upon managers' (or leaders') prerogatives. However, the very idea of management prerogatives is not accepted in very low Power Distance countries. This is, perhaps, best illustrated by a remark a Scandinavian social scientist is supposed to have made to Herzberg in a seminar: "You are against participation for the very reason we are in favor if it — one doesn't know where it will stop. We think that is good."

One way in which the U.S. approach to leadership has been packaged and formalized is management by objectives (MBO), first advocated by Peter Drucker in 1955 in *The Practice of Management*. In the United States, MBO has been used to spread a pragmatic results orientation throughout the organization. It has been considerably more successful where results are objectively measurable than where they can only be interpreted subjectively, and, even in the United States, it has been criticized heavily. Still, it has been perhaps the single most popular management technique "made in U.S.A." Therefore, it can be accepted as fitting U.S. culture. MBO presupposes:

- That subordinates are sufficiently independent to negotiate meaningfully with the boss (not-too-large Power Distance).
- That both are willing to take risks (weak Uncertainty Avoidance).
- That performance is seen as important by both (high Masculinity).

Let us now take the case of Germany, a below-average Power Distance country. Here, the dialogue element in MBO should present no problem. However, since Germany scores considerably higher on Uncertainty Avoidance, the tendency toward accepting risk and ambiguity will not exist to the same extent. The idea of replacing the arbitrary authority of the boss with the impersonal authority of mutually agreed-upon objectivities, however, fits the small Power Distance/strong Uncertainty Avoidance cultural cluster very well. The objectives become the subordinates' "superego." In a book of case studies about MBO in Germany, Ian R. G. Ferguson states that "MBO has acquired a different flavor in the German-speaking area, not least because in these countries the societal and political pressure towards increasing the value of man in the organization on the right to co-determination has become quite clear. Thence, MBO has been transliterated into Management by Joint Goal Setting (Führung durch Zielvereinbarung)." Ferguson's view of MBO fits the ideological needs of the German-speaking countries of the moment. The case studies in his book show elaborate formal systems with extensive ideological justification; the stress on *team* objectives is quite strong, which is in line with the lower individualism in these countries.

The other area in which specific information on MBO is available is France. MBO was first introduced in France in the early 1960s, but it became extremely popular for a time after the 1968 student revolt. People expected that this new technique would lead to the long-overdue democratization of organizations. Instead of DPO (Direction par Objectifs), the French name for MBO became DPPO (Direction *Participative* par Objectifs). So in France, too, societal developments affected the MBO system. However, DPPO remained, in general, as much a vain slogan as did Liberté, Egalité, Fraternité (Freedom, Equality, Brotherhood) after the 1789 revolt. G. Franck wrote in 1973 ". . . I think that the career of DPPO is terminated, or rather that it has never started, and it won't ever start as long as we continue in France our tendency to confound ideology and reality. . . ." In a postscript to Franck's article, the editors of *Le Management* write: "French blue- and white-collar workers, lower-level and higher-level managers, and 'patrons' all belong to the same cultural system which maintains dependency relations from level to level. Only the deviants really dislike this system. The hierarchical structure protects against anxiety; DPO, however, generates anxiety. . . ." The reason for the anxiety in the French cultural context is that MBO presupposes a depersonalized authority in the form of internalized objectives; but French people; from their early childhood onward, are accustomed to large Power Distances, to an authority that is highly personalized. And in spite of all attempts to introduce Anglo-Saxon management methods, French superiors do not easily decentralize and do not stop short-circuiting intermediate hierarchical levels, nor do French subordinates expect them to. The developments of the 1970s have severely discredited DPPO, which probably does injustice to the cases in which individual French organizations or units, starting from less exaggerated expectations, have benefited from it.

In the examples used thus far in this section, the cultural context of leadership may look rather obvious to the reader. But it also works in more subtle, less obvious ways. Here's an example from the area of management decision making: A prestigious U.S. consulting firm was asked to analyze the decision-making processes in a large Scandinavian "XYZ" corporation. Their report criticized the corporation's decision-making style, which they characterized as being, among other things, "intuitive" and "consensus based." They compared "observations of traditional XYZ practices" with "selected examples of practices in other companies." These "selected examples," offered as a model, were evidently taken from their U.S. clients and reflect the U.S. textbook norm — "fact based" rather than intuitive management, and "fast decisions based on clear responsibilities" rather than the use of informal, personal contacts and the concern for consensus.

Is this consulting firm doing its Scandinavian clients a service? It follows from Figure 7 that where the United States and the Scandinavian culture are wide apart is on the Masculinity dimension. The use of intuition and the concern for consensus in Scandinavia are "feminine" characteristics of the culture, well embedded in the total texture of these societies. Stressing "facts" and "clear responsibilities" fits the "masculine" U.S. culture. From a neutral viewpoint, the reasons for criticizing the U.S. decision-making style are as good as those for criticizing the Scandinavian style. In complex decision-making situations, "facts" no longer exist independently from the people who define them, so "fact-based management" becomes a misleading slogan. Intuition may not be a bad method of deciding in such cases at all. And if the implementation of decisions requires the commitment of many people, even a consensus process that takes more time is an asset rather than a liability. But the essential element overlooked by the consultant is that decisions have to be made in a way that corresponds to the values of the environment in which they have to be effective. People in this consulting firm lacked insight into their own cultural biases. This does not mean that the Scandinavian corporation's management need not improve its decision making and could not learn from the consultant's experience. But this can be done only through a mutual recognition of cultural differences, not by ignoring them.

ORGANIZATION

The Power Distance × Uncertainty Avoidance map (Figure 5) is of vital importance for structuring organizations that will work best in different countries. For example, one U.S.-based multinational corporation has a worldwide policy that salary-increase proposals should be initiated by the employee's direct superior. However, the French management of its French subsidiary interpreted this policy in such a way that the superior's superior's superior — three levels above — was the one to initiate salary proposals. This way of working was regarded as quite natural by both superiors and subordinates in France. Other factors being equal, people in large Power Distance cultures prefer that decisions be centralized because even superiors have strong dependency needs in relation to their superiors; this tends to move decisions up as far as they can go (see Figure 8). People in small Power Distance cultures want decisions to be decentralized.

While Power Distance relates to centralization, Uncertainty Avoidance relates to formalization — the need for formal rules and specialization, the assignment of tasks to experts. My former colleague O. J. Stevens at INSEAD has done an interesting research project (as yet unpublished) with M.B.A. students from Germany, Great Britain, and France. He asked them to write their own diagnosis and solution for a small case study of an organizational problem — a conflict in one company between the sales and product development departments. The majority of the French referred the problem to the next higher authority (the president of the company); the Germans attributed it to the lack of a written policy, and proposed establishing one; the British attributed it to a lack of interpersonal communication, to be cured by some kind of group training.

Stevens concludes that the "implicit model" of the organization for most French was a pyramid (both centralized and formal); for most Germans, a well-oiled machine (formalized but not centralized); and for most British, a village market (neither formalized nor centralized). This covers three quadrants (2, 3, and 4) in Figure 5. What is missing is an "implicit model" for quadrant 1, which contains four Asian countries, including India. A discussion with an Indian colleague leads me to place the family (centralized, but not formalized) in this quadrant as the "implicit model" of the organization. In fact, Indian organizations tend to be formalized as far as relationships between people go (this is related to Power Distance), but not as far as workflow goes (this is Uncertainty Avoidance).

The "well-oiled machine" model for Germany reminds us of the fact that Max Weber, author of the first theory of bureaucracy, was a German. Weber pictures bureaucracy as a highly formalized system (strong Uncertainty Avoidance), in which, however, the rules protect the lower-ranking members against abuse of power by their superiors. The superiors have no power by themselves, only the power that their bureaucratic roles have given them as incumbents of the roles — the power is in the role, not in the person (small Power Distance).

The United States is found fairly close to the center of the map in Figure 5, taking an intermediate position between the "pyramid," "machine," and "market" implicit models — a position that may help explain the success of U.S. business operations in very different cultures. However, according to the common U.S. conception of organization, we might say that *hierarchy is not a goal by itself* (as it is in France) and that *rules are not a goal by themselves*. Both are means toward obtaining results, to be changed if needed. A breaking away from hierarchic and bureaucratic traditions is found in the development toward matrix organizations and similar temporary or flexible organization systems.

Another INSEAD colleague, André Laurent, has shown that French managers strongly disbelieve in the feasibility of matrix organizations, because they see them as violating the "holy" principle of unit of command. However, in the French subsidiary of a multinational corporation that has a long history of successful matrix management, the French managers were quite positive toward it; obviously, then, cultural barriers to organizational innovation can be overcome. German managers are not too favorably disposed toward matrix organizations either, feeling that they tend to frustrate their need for organizational clarity. This means that matrix organizations will be accepted *if* the roles of individuals within the organization can be defined without ambiguity.

The extreme position of the United States on the Individualism scale leads to other potential conflicts between the U.S. way of thinking about organizations and the values dominant in other parts of the world. In the U.S. Individualist conception, the relationship between the individual and the organization is essentially calculative, being based on enlightened self-interest. In fact, there is a strong historical and cultural link between individualism and capitalism. The capitalist system — based on self-interest and the market mechanism — was "invented" in Great Britain, which is still among the top three most Individualist countries in the world. In more Collectivist societies, however, the link between individuals and their traditional organizations is not calculative, but moral: It is based not on self-interest, but on the individual's loyalty toward the clan, organization, or society — which is supposedly the best guarantee of that individual's ultimate interest. "Collectivism" is a bad word in the United States, but "individualism" is as much a bad word in the writings of Mao Tse-tung, who writes from a strongly Collectivist cultural tradition (see Figure 6 for the Collectivist scores of the Chinese majority countries Taiwan, Hong Kong, and Singapore). This means that U.S. organizations may get themselves into considerable trouble in more Collectivist environments if they do not recognize their local employees' needs for ties of mutual loyalty between company and employee. "Hire and fire" is very ill perceived in these countries, if firing isn't prohibited by law altogether. Given the value position of people in more Collectivist cultures, it should not be seen as surprising if they prefer other types of economic order to capitalism — if capitalism cannot get rid of its Individualist image.

CONSEQUENCES FOR POLICY

So far we have seriously questioned the universal validity of management theories developed in one country — in most instances here, the United States.

On a practical level, this has the least consequence for organizations operating entirely within the country in which the theories were born. As long as the theories apply within the United States, U.S. organizations can base their policies for motivating employees, leadership, and organization development on these policies. Still, some caution is due. If differences in environmental culture can be shown to exist between countries, and if these constrain the validity of management theories, what about the subcultures and countercultures within the country? To what extent do the familiar theories apply when the organization employs people for whom the theories were not, in the first instance, conceived — such as members of minority groups with a different educational level, or belonging to a different generation? If culture matters, an organization's policies can lose their effectiveness when its cultural environment changes.

No doubt, however, the consequences of the cultural relativity of management theories are more serious for the multinational organization. The cultural maps in Figures 5, 6, and 7 can help predict the kind of culture difference between subsidiaries and mother company that will need to be met. An important implication is that identical personnel policies may have very different effects in different countries — and within countries for different subgroups of employees. This is not only a matter of different employee values; there are also, of course, differences in government policies and legislation (which usually reflect quite clearly the country's different cultural position.) And there are differences in labor market situations and labor union power positions. These differences — tangible as well as intangible — may have consequences for performance, attention to quality, cost, labor turnover, and absenteeism. Typical universal policies that may work out quite differently in different countries are those dealing with financial incentives, promotion paths, and grievance channels.

The dilemma for the organization operating abroad is whether to adapt to the local culture or try to change it. There are examples of companies that have successfully changed local habits, such as in the earlier mention of the introduction of matrix organization in France. Many Third World countries want to transfer new technologies from more economically advanced countries. If they are to work at all, these technologies must presuppose values that may run counter to local traditions, such as a certain discretion of subordinates toward superiors (lower Power Distance) or of individuals toward in-groups (more Individualism). In such a case, the local culture has to be changed; this is a difficult task that should not be taken lightly. Since it calls for a conscious strategy based on insight into the local culture, it's logical to involve acculturated locals in strategy formulations. Often, the original policy will have to be adapted to fit local culture and lead to the desired effect. We saw earlier how, in the case of MBO, this has succeeded in Germany, but generally failed in France.

A final area in which the cultural boundaries of home-country management theories are important is the training of managers for assignments abroad. For managers who have to operate in an unfamiliar culture, training based on home-country theories is of very limited use and may even do more harm than good. Of more importance is a thorough familiarization with the other culture, for which the organization can use the services of specialized crosscultural training institutes — or it can develop its own program by using host-country personnel as teachers.

Selected Bibliography

The first U.S. book about the cultural relativity of U.S. management theories is still to be written, I believe — which lack in itself indicates how difficult it is to recognize one's own cultural biases. One of the few U.S. books describing the process of cultural conditioning for a management readership is Edward T. Hall's *The Silent Language* (Fawcett, 1959, but reprinted since). Good reading also is Hall's article "The Silent Language in Overseas Business" (*Harvard Business Review*, May–June 1960). Hall is an anthropologist and therefore a specialist in the study of culture. Very readable on the same subject are two books by the British anthropologist Mary Douglas, *Natural Symbols: Exploration in Cosmology* (Vintage, 1973) and the reader *Rules and Meanings: The Anthropology of Everyday Knowledge* (Penguin, 1973). Another excellent reader is Theodore D. Weinshall's *Culture and Management* (Penguin, 1977).

On the concept of national character, some well-written professional literature is Margaret Mead's "National Character," in the reader by Sol Tax, *Anthropology Today* (University of Chicago Press, 1962), and Alex Inkeles and D. J. Levinson's, "National Character," in Lindzey and Aronson's *Handbook of Social Psychology*, second edition, volume 4 (Addison-Wesley, 1969). Critique on the implicit claims of universal validity of management theories comes from some foreign authors: An important article is Michel Brossard and Marc Maurice's "Is There a Universal

Model of Organization Structure?" (*International Studies of Management and Organization*, Fall 1976). This journal is a journal of translations from non-American literature, based in New York, that often contains important articles on management issues by non-United States authors that take issue with the dominant theories. Another article is Gunnar Hjelholt's "Europe Is Different," in Geert Hofstede and M. Sami Kassem's reader, *European Contributions to Organization Theory* (Assen, Netherlands: Von Gorcum, 1976).

Some other references of interest: Ian R. G. Ferguson's *Management by Objectives in Deutschland*, (Herder and Herder, 1973) (in German); G. Franck's "Epitaphe pour la DPO," in *Le Management*, November 1973 (in French); and D. Jenkin's *Blue- and White-Collar Democracy* (Doubleday, 1973).

Note: Details of Geert Hofstede's study of national cultures has been published in his book *Culture's Consequences: International Differences in Work-Related Values* (Beverly Hills: Sage Publications, 1980).

READING 4

Zen and the Art of Management

Richard Tanner Pascale*

For many in the West, the term Zen connotes puzzling aspects of Eastern culture. This article attempts to unlock these puzzles as they apply to management of organizations. In the most exhaustive study to date of Japanese-managed companies in the United States and Japan, the author finds that when technology and government factors are equal, the Japanese companies' U.S. subsidiaries do not outperform their American counterparts (despite what has been reported in the U.S. press). Furthermore, and contrary to the conventional wisdom, American managers use a participative decision-making style as often as Japanese managers do. The author explores nuances of the administrative process that appear to account for more effective organizational functioning. He concludes that the arts employed by successful Japanese and American managers include subtle ways of dealing with others in the organization, such as permitting a certain situation to remain ambiguous instead of striving for a premature conclusion. While American managers are often as skillful in these areas as the Japanese, an Eastern perspective makes many of these tools more tangible and their potential more evident.

$\mathbf{F}$or 20 years or more students of management have labored to minimize its mystique, reduce our dependence on "gut feel," and establish a more scientific basis for managerial behavior. All the while, practitioners have been cautious in embracing these pursuits; casting a wary eye on "textbook" solutions, they assert that management is an art as much as a science.

Yet even the most skeptical admit that some benefit has accrued from these efforts. All realms of management, from finance to human relations, have felt the impact of analytical inquiry.

Reprinted by permission of *Harvard Business Review*. "Zen and the Art of Management," by Richard Tanner Pascale, March–April 1978. Copyright © 1978 by the President and Fellows of Harvard College; all rights reserved.

*Author's note: I wish to thank the National Commission on Productivity and the Weyerhaeuser Foundation for support of the research that formed the basis for this article, and Anthony G. Athos for his helpful comments on the manuscript.

One common theme in this evolution of a "management science" has been the desire to make explicit the tools and processes that managers have historically employed intuitively. With just such a goal in mind, I embarked in 1974 on a study of Japanese-managed companies in the United States and Japan. The purpose was to ascertain what elements of the communications and decision-making processes contributed to the reported high performance of Japanese companies.

A number of respected observers of Japanese ways had attributed their success in part to such practices as "bottom-up" communication, extensive lateral communication across functional areas, and a pronounced use of participative- (or consensus-) style decision making that supposedly leads to higher quality decisions and implementation. The research consisted of interviews of and questionnaires administered to more than 215 managers and 1,400 workers in 26 companies and 10 industries.

I made communication audits of the number of telephone calls and face-to-face contacts initiated and received by managers of Japanese companies in Japan, of their subsidiaries in the United States, and of near-identical American companies matched on an industry-by-industry basis. I took pains to document the size and length of meetings and the volume of formal correspondence and informal notes, to observe the frequency of interaction in managerial office areas, and to obtain managers' perceptions of the nature and quality of the decision making and implementation process.

What did I find? First, Japanese-managed businesses in both countries are not much different from American-owned companies: they use the telephone to about the same degree and write about the same number of letters. In their decision-making processes, both in their U.S. subsidiaries and in Japan, the Japanese do not use a participative style any more than Americans do. Actually, I discovered only two significant differences between Japanese and American companies:[1]

1. Three times as much communication was initiated at lower levels of management in the Japanese companies, then percolated upward.
2. While managers of Japanese companies rated the quality of their decision making the same as did their American counterparts, they perceived the quality of *implementation* of those decisions to be better.

These findings puzzled me. How could the style of decision making (in particular, the degree of participation) and quality of decisions be the same in the two groups, yet the quality of implementation be different? Evidently, the greater reliance by the Japanese on bottom-up communication played a role, but the causal relationship remained unclear.

A senior executive at Sony provided a clue. "To be truthful," the Japanese manager said, "probably 60 percent of the decisions I make are my decisions. But I keep my intentions secret. In discussions with subordinates, I ask questions, pursue facts, and try to nudge them in my direction without disclosing my position. Sometimes I end up changing my position as the result of the dialogue. But whatever the outcome, they feel a part of the decision. Their involvement in the decision also increases their experiences as managers."

Many others, American as well as Japanese, alluded in interviews to the same technique. "It does not make so much difference," reflected an American who ran a ball-bearing plant in New Hampshire, "if decisions are top down as it does how the top-down decision maker goes about touching bases. If he begins with an open question, he can often guide his subordinates to a good solution."

In these statements, and in others like them, is the genesis of this paper. The important discovery of this research was not, as expected, that Japanese do some things differently and better. While that is true to a limited extent, the more significant finding is that successful managers, *regardless of nationality*, share certain common characteristics that are related to subtleties of the communications process.

The term Zen in the title of this article is used figuratively to denote these important nuances in interpersonal communication often enshrouded in a veil of mystique. The phenomenon does not correspond to the analytical dimension of consecutive deductive responses. Nor is it directly akin to the human relations dimension that highlights the virtues of problem confrontation, participation, and openness. I refer to this Zenlike quality as the *implicit* dimension. It is as distinct from the other, better-known dimensions of management as time is from the other three dimensions of physical space.

In trying to explain the implicit dimension, I find that the traditional language of management gets in the way. To work around the difficulty, it is helpful to explore this dimension through the lens of the Eastern metaphor. After many interviews with American and Japanese managers, I have come to believe that the perspective imbedded in Eastern philosophy, culture, and values helps make the implicit dimension more visible. Whereas Japanese managers find certain insights within easy reach of the Eastern way of thinking, American managers, while often just as skillful, must swim upstream culturally, so to speak.

AMBIGUITY AS A MANAGERIAL TOOL

Much of the lore of management in the West regards ambiguity as a symptom of a variety of organizational ills whose cure is larger doses of rationality, specificity, and decisiveness. But is ambiguity sometimes desirable?

Ambiguity may be thought of as a shroud of the unknown surrounding certain events. The Japanese have a word for it, *ma*, for which there is no English translation. The word is valuable because it gives an explicit place to the unknowable aspect of things. In English we may refer to an empty space between the chair and the table; the Japanese don't say the space is empty but "full of nothing." However amusing the illustration, it goes to the core of the issue. Westerners speak of what is unknown primarily in reference to what is known (like the space between the chair and the table), while most Eastern languages give honor to the unknown in its own right. Consider this Tao verse:

> Thirty spokes are made one by holes in a hub
> Together with the vacancies between them, they comprise a wheel.
> The use of clay in moulding pitchers
> Comes from the hollow of its absence;

Doors, windows, in a house
Are used for their emptiness:
Thus we are helped by what is not
To use what is.[2]

Of course, there are many situations that a manager finds himself in where being explicit and decisive is not only helpful but necessary. There is considerable advantage, however, in having a dual frame of reference — recognizing the value of both the clear and the ambiguous. The point to bear in mind is that in certain situations ambiguity may serve better than absolute clarity.

When an executive has access to too much data for human processing, he needs to simplify. If he has examined, say, different pricing schemes for 12 months and has identified all the choices available to him, the time has probably come to decide on one of them. "Deciding" in these circumstances has the benefit of curtailing the wheel spinning, simplifying things, and resolving anxiety for oneself and others.

But there is another kind of problem — for example, merging the production and engineering departments — where experience may suggest that the issue is more complicated than the bare facts indicate. Frequently the issue crops up around changes that arouse human feelings. Under these circumstances the notion of ambiguity is useful. Rather than grasping for a solution, the administrator may take the interim step of "deciding" how to proceed. The process of "proceeding" in turn generates further information; you move toward your goal through a sequence of tentative steps rather than bold-stroke actions. The distinction is between having enough data to *decide* and having enough data to *proceed*.

If an executive's perception of the problem and the means of implementation involve groups of persons at different levels of the organization with different mandates (like unions and professional groups) and the distribution of power is such that he lacks full control, successful implementation usually requires tentativeness. The notion of ambiguity helps make tentativeness legitimate.

Ambiguity has two important connotations for management. First, it is a useful concept in thinking about how we deal with others, orally and in writing. Second, it provides a way of legitimizing the loose rein that a manager permits in certain organizational situations where agreement needs time to evolve or where further insight is needed before conclusive action can be taken.

Cards off the Table

To watch a skilled manager use ambiguity is to see an art form in action. Carefully selecting his words, constructing a precise tension between the oblique and the specific, he picks his way across difficult terrain. In critiquing a subordinate's work, for example, the executive occasionally finds it desirable to come close enough to the point to ensure that the subordinate gets the message but not so close as to "crowd" him and cause defensiveness.

A Japanese manager conducts the dialogue in circles, widening and narrowing them to correspond to the subordinate's sensitivity to the feedback. He may say, "I'd like you to reflect a bit further on your proposal." Translated into Western thought patterns, this sentence would read, "You're dead wrong and you'd better come up with a better idea."[3] The first approach allows the subordinate to exist with his pride intact.

Part of our drive for the explicit stems from the Western notion that it's a matter of honor to "get the cards on the table." This attitude rests on the assumption that, no matter how much it hurts, it's good for you; and the sign of a good manager is his ability to give and take negative feedback.

No doubt there is a good deal of merit in this conventional wisdom. But between the mythology of our management lore and our foibles as human beings often lies the true state of things. It is desirable to get the facts and know where one stands. But it is also human to feel threatened, particularly when personal vulnerability is an issue.

There is no reason to believe that Westerners have less pride than the Japanese have or feel humiliation less poignantly than the Japanese do. An American Management Association survey indicates that issues involving self-respect mattered greatly to more than two-thirds of the persons sampled.[4] Eastern cultures are sensitive to the concept of "face"; Westerners, however, regard it as a sign of weakness. Yet look back on instances in organizations where an individual, publicly embarrassed by another, hurt himself and the organization just to even the score. The evidence suggests that explicitly crowding a person into a corner may in many instances be not only unwarranted but also counterproductive.

Delivering oneself of the need to "speak the truth" often masks a self-serving sense of brute integrity. "Clearing the air" can be more helpful to the "clearer" than to others who are starkly revealed. The issue of brute integrity is not just an outcome of a certain cultural tendency to speak plainly and bluntly, nor is it wholly explainable in terms of our assumptions about authority and hierarchy and the relationships between bosses and subordinates. At a deeper level, it has a sexist component. In our culture, simple, straightforward, simplistic confrontation — a kind of high noon shoot-em-out — is mixed with notions of what masculinity is. Unfortunately, shoot-em-outs work best when the other guy dies. If you have to work with that person on a continuing basis, macho confrontations complicate life immensely.

In contrast, ambiguity, in reference to sensitivity and feelings, is alleged in the Western world to be female. But if we set aside the stereotypes and contemplate the consequences of these two modes of behavior on organizational life, we may discover that primitive notions of masculinity work no better in the office over the long-term than they do in bed.

Are brute integrity and explicit communication worth the price of the listener's goodwill, open-mindedness, and receptivity to change? Explicit communication is a cultural assumption, not a linguistic imperative. Many executives develop the skills necessary to vary their position along the spectrum from explicitness to ambiguity.

More 'Ura' than 'Omote'

Earlier I noted the value of ambiguity in permitting time and space for certain situations to take clearer shape or reach an accommodation of their own. A certain looseness in the definition of the relationship between things can permit a workable arrangement to evolve, whereas premature action may freeze things into rigidity. For example, one of the most persistent afflictions in American organizations is the penchant to make formal announcements. Most things one does announce themselves.

The Japanese manager comes culturally equipped with a pair of concepts, *omote* (in front) and *ura* (behind the scenes). These ideas correspond to the Latin notions of de jure and de facto, with one important distinction: the Japanese think of *ura* as constituting *real life; omote* is the ceremonial function for the benefit of others. The Japanese relegate the making of announcements to a secondary place that follows after all the action has taken place behind the scenes.

"You Americans are fond of announcing things," said one Japanese manager in the study. "It sets everything astir. The other day we decided to try out having our personnel department handle certain requests that traditionally had been handled by the production people. Our American vice president insisted on announcing it. Well, the production department had always handled its own personnel affairs and got its back up. Rumors commenced about whether the personnel people were in ascendance, building an empire, and so forth. Given the tentativeness of the system we were trying out, why not just begin by quietly asking that certain matters be referred to personnel? Before long, the informal organization will accustom itself to the new flow. Clearly you can't do this all the time, but some of the time it certainly works."

To announce what you want to happen, you have to make statements concerning a lot of things that you don't know about yet. If certain processes and relationships are allowed to take their own shape first, however, your announcement will probably have to be made just once because you will only be confirming what has already happened. Consider how differently attempts at organizational change might proceed if they embraced the Eastern orientation. Instead of turning the spotlight on the intended move, parading the revised organization charts and job descriptions, management would reassign tasks incrementally, gradually shift boundaries between functions, and issue the announcement only when the desired change had become a de facto reality. In some situations this is the better way.

"Impossible!" some will argue. "People resist change. Only by announcing your intentions can you bring the organization into line." But is it really "into line?" Unquestionably, decrees have their part to play in some organizational actions. But more often than not, the sudden lurch to a new order belies an informal process of resistance that works with enduring effectiveness. One has only to look at the Department of Health, Education, and Welfare for an illustration of this phenomenon. A congressional mandate and 20 years' worth of frustrated presidents have not greatly altered the character of the three distinct bureaus comprising that agency.

The notion of achieving gradual change, rather than launching a head-on assault, runs deep in Eastern culture. It provides a manager with a context for thinking about outflanking organizational obstacles and in time letting them wither away. "It is well to persist like water," counsels the Tao saying. "For back it comes, again and again, wearing down the rigid strength which cannot yield to withstand it."[5]

With such an orientation one can accept the inevitability of obstacles rather than view them with righteous indignation — as some Western managers are inclined to do. And as the Tao saying suggests, acceptance does not convey fatalistic resignation. Rather, it points toward the value of patiently flowing with a solution while in due time it overcomes the obstacles in its path.

TO GET RECOGNITION GIVE IT AWAY

One way of thinking about the rewards employees receive is in terms of a triad: promotion, remuneration, and recognition. Of the three forms of reward, the first two are relatively unresponsive in the day-to-day operation of an organization. Promotions and wage hikes seldom come oftener than six months apart. On a daily basis, recognition is the reward most noticed and sought after. In the American Management Association survey to which I alluded earlier, 49 percent of the respondents indicated that recognition for what they did was their most important reward.

Recognition may become an increasingly important "fringe benefit" since a central problem facing American society is how to reward people in a period of slowed growth when employees win promotions and raises less often. Enriching our understanding of recognition and the role it plays may provide some helpful guidance.

Recognition is a powerful operating incentive. People who live in organizations develop uncanny sensitivity to where it is flowing. If you ask a person to change, one of the most relevant rewards you can provide in return is recognition. If, on the contrary, you try to induce change but you are seen as unwilling to share the recognition, you are not apt to get very far. It is an ironic axiom of organization that if you are willing to give up recognition, in return you gain increased power to bring about effective change.

The Eastern frame of thinking embodies the dual nature of recognition, as this Tao proverb shows:

A wise man has a simple wisdom
Which other men seek.
Without taking credit
Is accredited.
Laying no claim
Is acclaimed.[6]

We are all acquainted with "expressed" recognition, the big prize that modern organizational knights vie for. "B.L.T." is the recognition sandwich . . . "bright lights and trumpets," that is. When you receive a B.L.T., everybody knows about it. But Eastern thinking reminds us of a second variety, which might be called implied recognition. It is subtle but no less tangible, and it is acquired over time.

In its positive form it is the reputation of being trustworthy, skilled in making things happen in the organization, and accomplished in getting things done through people. In its negative manifestation a person is regarded as using people, prone to cutting corners, and out for one's self. Implied recognition can be given in a variety of ways that may seem insignificant, except to the recipient. An effort to seek another's opinion, for example, communicates respect for his insight. So does an invitation to participate in a significant meeting from which the person might otherwise have been excluded.

The phenomenon of implied recognition generally plays an important role in organizations that run smoothly. Problems arise when organizations overemphasize incentives that rivet attention on expressed recognition and undermine regard for implied recognition. As a result, all the members of the "team" try to grab the ball and nobody blocks. They seldom win consistently. But why grab from others what they will give you voluntarily? When you make sure you get the credit you deserve, in the long run you get less of it than you would otherwise.

Eastern perspective provides a further insight. It reminds us that the real organization you are working for is the organization called yourself. The problems and challenges of the organization that you are working for "out there" and the one "in here" are not two separate things. They grow toward excellence together. The sense of the "implied" for accommodation and timing and the sense of the "expressed" for the jugular must be woven together like strands in a braided rope, alternatively appearing and disappearing from sight but part of the whole. Good executives master the art *and* the science of management — not just one or the other.

LEADERS GO STRAIGHT — AROUND THE CIRCLE

Western concepts of leadership embrace a number of images — strength, firmness, determination, and clarity of vision. In American management lore, leaders are seen as lonely figures capable of decisive action in the face of adversity.[7] Eastern thinking views leadership in significantly different ways. Whereas Western leaders are supposedly selected from among those who are outstanding, Eastern culture values leaders who stand "in" rather than stand "out."

In Judeo-Christian cultures, words very nearly possess sacredness. Men are willing to sacrifice for, live by, and die for words. We cling to them and make them swell with meaning; they are shafts of light that give form to our experimental darkness. Anthony G. Athos of the Harvard Business School notes the distinction between two everyday words, choice and decision. Managers, we are taught, "make decisions"; lovers "choose." The former term implies mastery; the latter conveys a difficult selection among choices, in which we can gain some things only by giving up others.[8]

Athos' insight is particularly important for managers because the word "decision" and the phrase "decision making" conjure up an extensive mythology of meaning. Good decision makers, our mythology tells us, have command of the facts, are aware of the options, and select from among them the best one.

The Japanese, however, do not even have a term for decision making in the Western sense. This linguistic curiosity reflects something deeper, a tendency of the culture to acknowledge the ambivalence experienced when our mastery of situations is imperfect. Faced with difficult trade-offs, Japanese "choose" one over the other; Westerners like to think they "decide."

The lore of Eastern management more fully acknowledges the inevitable sense of incompleteness that stems from having to choose. It sensitizes its managers to the illusions of mastery and trains them to suspect the accompanying belief that anything is ever truly decided. Whereas the mythology of Western management tends to cast solutions as fixed and final, Eastern philosophical tradition emphasizes individual accommodation to a continuously unfolding set of events.

Think of the consequences of these outlooks as managers of these two cultures go about living up to their cultural imperatives. Eastern managers accept ambivalence. When faced with the necessity to "juggle," they do so with reassurance that the experience is congruent with what management is all about. Faced with the same set of events, some American managers may feel uneasy. This problem is exacerbated by the absence of cultural underpinnings for thinking about certain activities in which mastery of the situation is either impossible or downright undesirable. (Also, their language is not attuned to expression of this mode of thinking.)

The Western notion of mastery is closely linked with deep-seated assumptions about the self. The professional life of some Westerners, and certainly many who move into management positions, is dedicated to strengthening the ego in an effort to assert and maintain control over their environment and their destiny. In contrast, the Eastern frame of reference views pragmatically appropriate limitations of the ego as a virtue.

To the Easterner, overt strength is not unequivocally a desired attribute. This notion of strength may be likened to the endurance of coral reefs that survive the massive forces of sea and wind during typhoons. Reefs do not attempt to resist the sea like defiant walls of man-made steel and concrete. Instead, the reef extends wedges out in a seaward direction. The waves deflect off these wedges, one against the other. Consequently their power, rather than directed at the reef, is turned against itself. The reef does not insist on standing higher than the sea. In times of typhoon, the waves wash over the reef. And it survives.

Let things flow. "Success is going straight — around the circle," says the Chinese adage. How often in organizations does the forcing of events precipitate needless resistance and even crisis? Yet the Western notion of leadership, fueled by the high value placed on logical, purposive, goal-blinded action, impels many to leap before they look.[9]

Dam up a river. In time the water rises until a trickle finds its way around the obstruction, gradually increasing in flow and force until its original course is resumed. Managers, of course, do not have to watch torrents of frustration and energy needlessly build up behind an organizational obstruction. But perhaps the solution is not always to dynamite away the obstruction; sometimes it is to trace a way around it with a light touch, enough to get a trickle flowing. Let the flow of events do the rest of the work. By embracing an alternative concept of leadership, managers can choose, where appropriate, to seek a contributing place in the flow of things rather than impose a false sense of mastery over events.

FOR EMPLOYEES, IDIOSYNCRASIES VS. SYSTEMS

The typical Western organization prides itself on having made a science of the secular virtues of efficiency and impartiality. In trying to cope with the slowed growth and economic uncertainty of recent years, organizations have intensified the emphasis on efficiency. A different set of forces has put emphasis on impartiality — among them the regulations aimed at eliminating discrimination of all kinds. The dilemma is how to treat people as equal without treating them as the same. Many organizations appear to be insensitive to this distinction. As a result they, like white bread or pure sugar, become bland and somewhat unhealthful; all the vital human elements seem to get refined away.

I should acknowledge that many Western executives show deep concern for the people working for them. In a survey of American managers, psychologist Jay Hall found that those most highly rated in interpersonal skills were generally regarded as the most competent by their bosses. "Good managers," Hall wrote, "use an integrative style of management in which production goals and people's needs are equally important."[10]

Obviously, organizations need efficient systems to accomplish their tasks. But enough is enough, and more may be too much. The human touch is often lacking, and its absence breeds isolation and detachment. Lonely people perform instrumental functions as if they truly were interchangeable parts in a great machine. The explanation, I suppose, is that the increasing physical density of workers in our landscaped offices and automated factories has nothing to do with the psychic distances. Hard-edged procedures enhance this sense of aloneness.

Japanese companies, despite their evident prowess at adopting Western technology, have not followed the Western pattern where trade-offs between human relationships and secular efficiencies are concerned. Of more than 600 American employees of Japanese corporations interviewed in my study (including 100 managers and 500 workers) almost all expressed an awareness of the more personalized approach of their employers. The Japanese have a word describing a special quality of master potters who make the "perfect" bowl. The bowl is endowed with an ever-so-slight imperfection — a constant reminder of the object's relation to the humanity of the maker. The master knows that the perfection of mass-produced bowls is less satisfying than ones that lean a little. In this context, it might be said that Japanese companies lean a little.

The Japanese distinguish between our notion of "organization" and their notion of "the company." In their minds, the term organization refers only to the system; their concept of the company includes its underlying character as well. A company's character describes a shared sense of values long held by members and enforced by group norms. The result is an institutional way of doing things that is different from what efficiency alone would require. The "company" may accomplish the same tasks as an "organization" does, but it occupies more space, moves with more weight, and reflects a commitment to larger ends than just the accomplishment of a mission.

In Japan, companies are thought of as taking all of an employee. (In the United States the prevailing notion is that they take a piece of an employee.) The relationship is akin to the binding force of the family. Lacking such a philosophy, Western organizations tend to rely on what bureaucracies do best — championing "systems solutions" — rather than deal with the idiosyncratic requirements of human nature. The result can isolate people into the lonely illusion of objectivity.

Is the Bottom Line the Measure?

From the Japanese vantage point, the sense of incompleteness in our working lives stems from a divergence between what many people seek and what most Western organizations provide. Most people bring three kinds of needs to their organizational existence: a need to be rewarded for what they achieve, a need to be accepted as a unique person, and a need to be appreciated not only for the function performed but also as a human being. The term "reward," as used here, refers to the tangible payments one receives from an organization (such as salary and promotions) in exchange for services provided.

I use this narrow, rather instrumental definition of rewards to distinguish it from "acceptance" and "appreciation," which represent other kinds of benefits sought. In this context, acceptance refers to the quality of being known in a human sense rather than simply valued for the function one performs. The worker feels acceptance when people and organizations know him for who he is and make allowance for that uniqueness in their relationship with him. Appreciation goes a step further, conveying not only an acknowledgement by others of a person's distinctness but also a valuation of it in a positive and supportive way.

In an effort to express their commitment to people, the Japanese companies in the United States that I studied spent on average more than three times as much per employee on social and recreational facilities and activities than their American counterparts ($48.85 per employee per year versus $14.85). Some of these programs were probably largely symbolic, but many also fostered increased off-the-job contact among employees. The benefit was to "personalize" the particular company.

Perhaps a more direct vehicle for providing acceptance and appreciation is the Japanese policy of supporting spans of control at the supervisory level. This practice resulted in twice as much contact between workers and their foremen as in American companies, measured by employees per first-line supervisor (30.1 versus 13.5). The supervisors in Japanese-managed companies more often worked alongside the subordinates, engaged in personal counselling more extensively, and permitted more interaction among workers than the American companies did.[11]

What was the outcome? The evidence is sufficiently mixed to gratify both skeptics and advocates. There was no difference in production; the average output per unit of labor was about the same. Moreover, the Japanese companies experienced somewhat higher levels of tardiness and absenteeism. In respect to job satisfaction, the results were more favorable for Japanese-managed business in the United States. Their managers and workers expressed much more satisfaction with their jobs than did their counterparts in American companies.

Why bother, it might be asked, if the result has no impact on the bottom line? By Eastern standards the bottom line misses the point. It was Socrates (not an Eastern philosopher) who observed that "man is the measure of all things." Eastern perspective brings his meaning into fuller view. To the Eastern mind, it is "man," not the "bottom line," that is the ultimate measure of all things. He is not the source of all things, as some who view man in total command of his destiny might proclaim. Nor is he the objectified contributor to all things, as some organizations appear to presume in weighing his contributions against their costs.

A Japanese, while concerned with the bottom line, is not single-minded about it as many Westerners are. Rather, he proceeds with a dual awareness — that there is a second ledger in which "success" is debited or credited in terms of his contribution to the quality of relationships that ensue. So the professional manager defines his role not only as one who accomplishes certain organizational tasks but also as an essential intermediary in the social fabric.

ARE FEATHERS MORE EFFECTIVE
THAN SLEDGEHAMMERS?

This discussion has utilized Eastern ideas as a metaphor for exploring the process of management. One central theme is that it is not just particular notions — such as ambiguity or implied recognition — that can be helpful but the cultural context underlying these notions as well. I have tried to suggest that a combination of culture, words, philosophy, and values provides each of us with a particular outlook. The Eastern outlook is adopted not because it is "best" but because it sheds a different light on certain aspects of management. The Eastern perspective provides not so much a new set of tools (for, as I have noted repeatedly, many skilled American managers use these tools) but rather legitimacy for using these tools in some situations where they are appropriate.

From the Eastern vantage point, process is where managers live. This vantage point dwells on the chemistry of human relationships, as well as on the mechanics of human accomplishment, and it provides a way of thinking that assigns a particular value to human needs as well as to systems and economic requirements. Appreciation of the underpinnings of this outlook is fundamental to the thrust of this article. For if they are bounded by our traditional set of Western assumptions, many of the ideas here become empty techniques.

Management assumptions act as fences — keeping some things in and other things out of our awareness. As we have seen, there are many fences, not of wood but shaped by our words, values, and management ideology. I submit that a nontrivial set of management problems might be better understood if viewed from the other side of our Western fence. Undoubtedly, a very high degree of personal development is necessary to embrace both of these outlooks, to know when each is appropriate and to acquire the skills which each requires.

This suggests a cautionary note for the Western manager: in addition to approaching things purposively, defining problems crisply, and identifying his objectives explicitly (which are desirable but not necessarily sufficient traits to manage all problems skillfully), he may also wish to bear in mind that our Western world view diminishes our sensitivity and skill in managing certain kinds of problems. Such insight may enable us to avoid using sledgehammers when feathers will do. Eastern ideas provide a metaphor for the acquisition of such skill. "Truth lurks in metaphors."[12]

Notes

1. For a detailed report of these findings see my article, "Communications and Decision Making Across Cultures: Japanese and American Comparisons," *Administrative Science Quarterly*, in press.

2. Witter Bynner, *The Ways of Life According to Lao Tzu* (New York: Capricorn Books, 1944), p. 30.

3. Frank Gibney, "The Japanese and Their Language," *Encounter*, March 1975, p. 33.

4. G. McLean Preston and Katherine Jillson, "The Manager and Self-Respect," *AMA Survey Report* (New York: AMACOM, 1975).

5. Bynner, *The Way of Life According to Lao Tzu*, p. 74.

6. Bynner, *The Way of Life According to Lao Tzu*, pp. 28 and 38.

7. For a discussion of the myths versus the realities of management behavior and leadership, see Leonard Sayles, *Managerial Behavior* (New York: McGraw-Hill, 1964), especially pp. 41–45; also see Henry Mintzberg, "The Manager's Job: Folklore and Fact," HBR July-August 1975, p. 49.

8. Anthony G. Athos, "Choice and Decision," unpublished working paper, 1973.

9. For a discussion of this "flowing" phenomenon in a Western context, see James D. Thompson, *Organizations in Action* (New York: McGraw-Hill, 1967), p. 149.

10. Jay Hall, "What Makes a Manager Good, Bad, or Average? *Psychology Today*, August 1976, p. 52.

11. Richard Tanner Pascale and Mary Ann Maguire, "The Company and the Worker: Japanese and American Comparisons," Graduate School of Business, Stanford University, 1977.

12. Anthony G. Athos, "Satan is Left-Handed," *Association of Humanistic Psychology Newsletter*, December 1975.

CASE 1

Bhiwar Enterprises[1]

Gordon Brannan and Joseph J. DiStefano

Pratap Bhiwar had been working as a consultant to the family business between the two years of his M.B.A. program. Near the end of his summer's efforts he had prepared a report for his cousin who was Managing Director of the Rori Company, one of several businesses owned and operated by the Bhiwar family. His recommendations were intended to rationalize company operations to increase effectiveness and efficiency. Instead, they seemed to have stimulated a rash of arguments among his cousins and uncles that threatened to destroy forty years of solidarity and business success. As the time drew near to return to North America, Pratap wondered what he could do to resolve the problems his report had generated.

HISTORY OF THE BHIWAR
FAMILY IN AFRICA

Mohan Bhiwar emigrated from India with his wife and family to avoid starvation and to start a new life in the British colony of Kenya. However, in Kenya Mohan could not farm as his family had done in India. Agriculture, especially the cultivation of cash crops, was a white man's monopoly. Africans and Asians[2] were prohibited from farming by the colonial government. Mohan, therefore, became a retail peddler in the area around the village in which he had settled.

For twenty years Mohan rose daily at 4:00 A.M. and rode his bicycle into the countryside, where he purchased surplus fruit and vegetables from Africans. Mohan brought the produce back to his village and sold it. Then he purchased hardware and cloth, which he sold in the more rural villages.

After a few years Mohan was able to afford to bring over from India his three younger brothers — Anil, Vijay, and Sanjay — and their families. Together the brothers expanded the retail operation and assured themselves of economic survival in their adopted country. The family relationships are shown in Figure 1.

All four brothers and their families lived together under one roof. In addition to the economic benefits, this arrangement was also a form of social security. For

FIGURE 1   Bhiwar Family Structure*

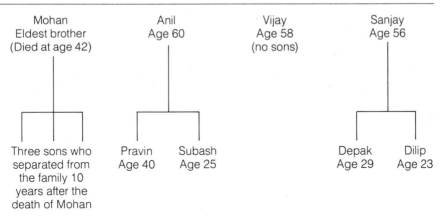

*None of the four senior brothers had a formal education. All started working at about the ages of 12 or 13. Each of the older surviving brothers became a millionaire. Pravin, the elder son of Anil, completed high school in Kenya. His brother Subash went to Europe to study business administration before joining the Rori Company. Depak, Sanjay's older son, completed high school in Europe, and his younger brother Dilip finished high school in Kenya.

example, in the case of accident or sickness other members of the family were available to help. This role of the extended family was particularly important in Kenya where no state welfare structure existed. Living together was also culturally acceptable in the Asian community.[3]

For years the brothers continued their retail peddling and saved a little money from the business every year. Eventually the family bought its first car, and three years later they purchased their first truck. When Mohan died of a heart attack, the family leadership passed to Anil, the oldest surviving brother.

The year Mohan died was also the year the fortunes of the family business picked up. In October a group of African freedom fighters (or terrorists according to the colonists) began a campaign to end colonial rule and white domination in Kenya. The colonial government, which represented white interests in the colony, responded to the terrorism by declaring a state of martial law. As part of its response, the government constructed large prison camps in which to confine captured rebels. These camps had to be supplied with food, clothing, and other provisions. Competitive bids were invited from various firms for the monopoly of supplying the camps. Through an elaborate system of bribery, a common practice in the colony, the Bhiwar brothers successfully obtained the contract.

Their business dealings, however, were not confined to the government. The rebels needed materials for the manufacture of weapons which the brothers were able to supply. The Bhiwars did not consider these activities treasonable. As Asians, they identified neither with the Europeans nor Africans. They saw the relationship as merely buyer-seller. In their dealings with both the rebels and the government, the brothers were able to name their own prices since their services were in such high demand.

Because of their success during the rebellion and the fact that the brothers had established valuable contacts, they were in a favorable position to buy up surplus agricultural produce to sell to European wholesalers in Kenya. The surpluses resulted from improved agricultural techniques introduced after the rebellion had ended. The techniques were part of an economic revitalization program to reduce inequalities which had been central in bringing about the conflict originally. However, although many farmers were able to produce a surplus, few had the transportation facilities necessary to move their goods to market. The Bhiwar brothers, on the other hand, had both equipment and capital. They were, therefore, able to take advantage of this unusual opportunity.

FAMILY BREAKUP
AND A NEW COMPANY

Five years after the rebellion had ended, the older generation of brothers — Anil, Vijay, and Sanjay — decided to retire from active participation in the business. According to tradition, the leadership of the family should have passed to Mohan's oldest son. However, since Anil had been the head of the family unit, his influence and guidance were powerful forces in the transition of leadership. Furthermore, only two of the three sons of Mohan were involved in the business, and both of these were located some distance from the head office where Anil's sons operated.

As the health of the older generation declined, Pravin showed increasing initiative. In addition he received recognition and credit for the steady success of the business by virtue of his physical location, position in the firm, and family status as Anil's older son. As the gradual transition in leadership occurred, it became clear that Pravin would succeed his father. Mohan's sons, resentful of being deprived of a right they saw as belonging to their oldest brother, refused to work in the family business any longer. Their feelings of bitterness were heightened by their judgment that the surviving uncles had not done a conscientious job of looking after them (one was expected to protect the sons of a deceased brother). The result was the breaking away of Mohan's widow and sons from the main body of the Bhiwar family. To some extent this was encouraged by the mother who, according to the Bhiwars, never had liked her brothers-in-law.

The breakup of the family was psychologically traumatic for all parties concerned. Such an event was unusual and discouraged in the Asian community. Socially, it was considered a sign of deterioration in the stability of the family. Personally, it diminished the reputations of all the individuals involved. Within the family it left a great deal of bad feeling between the parties.

After the breakup Pravin, on the advice of his father and uncles, bought a food processing business (Rori Company) from another Asian family. There were two reasons for this acquisition. First, the Bhiwar brothers felt that they could process food cheaply and add to their revenues. Secondly, the purchase of Rori would provide the sons of Anil and Sanjay with an opportunity to develop a business of their own.

FIGURE 2   Organization of Rori Company

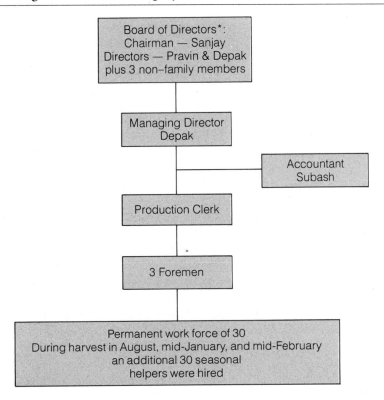

* Note: The Board of Directors never met.

Two years after the acquisition Depak, Sanjay's older son, was made Managing Director of the Rori Company when he returned from finishing his education in Europe. Over the next decade, he expanded the business primarily through his successful marketing efforts in the United States and Canada. But, in spite of this success, Depak was not entirely satisfied because his cousin Pravin would not permit him to have full control over operations. All changes proposed by Depak had to be reviewed and ratified by Pravin before being implemented. An organization chart for the company is shown in Figure 2.

The situation worsened when Pravin's younger brother, Subash, returned to Kenya following completion of his education and was made accountant of the Rori Company. Subash used his position to spy on Depak for his brother Pravin, whose interference in the business and ultimate control of all financial allocations in the family business kept Depak from operating autonomously and efficiently in his own sphere of responsibility. The situation was exacerbated by the fact that personal relations between Depak and the two brothers were strained. Further, it appeared that Pravin was to some extent envious of Depak's ability to work hard and make a success of his operation.

A NEPHEW AS CONSULTANT

Pratap Bhiwar, a nephew through marriage to the older generation (Anil, Vijay, and Sanjay), was home in Kenya for a vacation. He was currently an M.B.A. student in a North American university. While he was visiting with his uncle Sanjay, his cousin Depak arrived and asked him how his studies were going. As the two men began to talk about business in general and the operations of the Rori Company in particular, it occurred to Pratap that he might be able to help Depak with some of the problems he was having in the business. He suggested to Depak that he be hired to do consulting work while he was home for the vacation. Depak was delighted and consulted with his father, Sanjay. The older man also thought the idea had merit, but said that it would be necessary to check with Pravin, who after all was the head of the family interests now that the older generation of men had retired. Pravin made some remarks about outside interference in the affairs of the family, but did not attempt to stop Pratap from helping.

As Pratap started the consulting job, he approached his work using the tough-minded framework of analysis that he was being taught in North America. He viewed the consulting assignment as an opportunity to implement rigorous North American management practices. He decided that any inefficiencies in the operation would be uprooted. He would recommend the firing of poor performers.

After making some preliminary investigations of the operation, Pratap concluded that although the marketing system that Depak had set up was good, the company's costing system was sloppy. In addition, the production setup of the plant was not well integrated with the rest of the operation because of poor planning and haphazard expansion. However, Pratap told Depak, in order to proceed further, it would now be necessary to analyze in some detail the past financial statements of the company. Depak told him that would be difficult since he did not have the data. In fact, he continued, he had never seen any of the financial statements of the Rori Company. He told Pratap that Pravin kept all the statements to himself. Pratap then asked Depak how, as Managing Director of Rori Company, he made his financial decisions. Depak replied that it was simple. Whenever it was necessary to make an expenditure, he relayed his request for money through Subash who then made the representation to his older brother on Depak's behalf. Pravin would then make a decision and tell Subash what it was. Subash would, in turn, inform Depak.

A little amazed by this system, but quite prepared to work within its constraints for the time being, Pratap approached Subash and asked him to obtain the financial statements. Subash, however, misrepresented Pratap to Pravin, who refused to issue the statements. Pratap then approached his uncle Sanjay to help him. Sanjay went to Pravin and persuaded him to hand over the statements. Pravin, however, was not happy about the whole affair. While reluctantly parting with the financial data, he insinuated that Pratap was simply out to make trouble.

After Pratap had analyzed the financial statements, he discovered that a substantial amount of money had disappeared. When asked, Depak said he didn't know anything about it, since he had no control over expenditures. Pratap told Depak that as Managing Director of Rori it was his responsibility to know how and where money was spent. Depak agreed and went to see Pravin. But when he asked Pravin about the money, Pravin exploded in anger and told Depak that he was inefficient as a Managing Director, knew nothing of the business, and had wasted his last six years in the firm. Depak retorted that Pravin had never helped him with the business, so how could he expect him to learn. He added heatedly that whenever he asked Pravin a few questions, he never received any answers. As usual, the meeting ended without Pravin answering any of Depak's questions, and bad feelings continued to exist between the two men.

In these circumstances Pratap felt that the quarrel over the missing money was not worth further straining the family relationships. He told Depak that he would be able to complete his report with the information he had available.

PRATAP'S REPORT

Several days later Pratap finished the report. He had come to two major conclusions. First, the capital acquisition policy of the Rori Company was poor and bore no relation to the overall profit objectives of the firm. He felt the reason was Pravin's absolute financial control. Depak was unable to make necessary capital acquisitions because he could not obtain the money or approval from Pravin. Secondly, Pratap found that Subash was incompetent as an accountant. In failing to gather and to analyze properly the cost data essential to the business, Subash had proven useless to Depak. In short, Pratap concluded that the Rori Company could function neither efficiently nor effectively. The power to make critical financial decisions was in the hands of a man who for all practical purposes was an absentee landlord who refused to listen to his manager.

It was clear to Pratap that he should make two recommendations.

1. Pravin should give Depak control of the financial statements and decisions related to Rori and
2. The incompetent Subash should be removed.

When Pratap showed his report to Depak, Depak said it should be hidden. He felt that the recommendations to rationalize the operations were unacceptable and would result in family conflict. Pratap admitted that he knew it to be true, but was interested in approaching the business problems rigorously and pushing through to logical conclusions. Agreeing that there were some parts of the report that could be implemented without disturbing the family, both men were willing to let the full report "die" in Depak's office.

However, the matter was not resolved so easily. Sanjay kept inquiring about the progress of the report and told Pratap that he would like to see it when it was completed. Eventually, under continual pressure from Sanjay, Pratap brought the report to his uncle. But since Sanjay could not read English, Pratap read the report aloud to him. When Pratap finished, Sanjay agreed with his nephew's conclusions and asked for his recommendations.

Pratap answered that in his opinion the Rori Company should be separated from the Bhiwar Enterprises and placed under the complete control of Depak. He said Depak should be totally responsible for profits and free from outside interference. He also stated that Subash should be fired, since he was incapable of doing his job.

Sanjay listened to the recommendations quietly, but told Pratap that they were unacceptable. If Subash were fired, Sanjay continued, Anil would ask why his son had been discharged. If told that his son was incompetent, he would most certainly become angry, and conflict among the elder brothers would inevitably result. Besides, in the eyes of the Asian community in Kenya, Subash was a big executive. What would they think of the solidarity of the Bhiwar family if he were fired from the family business? Sanjay asked if it would be worth breaking up a close partnership between the brothers that had lasted for forty years just for the sake of more efficiency. Was it really worth all this trouble, Sanjay concluded, for a few thousand dollars of inefficiency?

Although Pratap said that he understood his uncle's point of view, he asked the older man if it was worth sacrificing Depak's future in a business where he was going to be constantly constrained. Pratap argued that Depak would eventually become fed up with the whole situation. In fact, he was fed up now. But as the elder son with the burden of responsibility for the Sanjay household in the Bhiwar family, he was unlikely to rebel against a situation that helped preserve the stability of the extended family as a strongly integrated social unit. Pratap concluded that Depak would likely leave Rori in frustration. Sanjay replied that he understood all this, but could not really accept the solution proposed by Pratap.

Another factor in the situation was Dilip, the younger brother of Depak. Unlike Depak, he had gone into business on his own, although he worked out of the premises of the Rori Company. Dilip was disgusted with watching his older brother being dominated by Pravin and Subash. He felt so strongly that he stated if his father did not resolve the problem soon, he was going to tell Sanjay that he would not speak to him again until he broke away from Anil.

Pratap felt partially responsible for the state of near-crisis in the Bhiwar family and business, since his report had surfaced these problems that had previously remained suppressed. Furthermore, he knew that any additional action by him would have to be taken soon, since he had to return to North America shortly. As the time to make flight reservations drew near, Pratap wondered what he should do.

Appendix A: A Note on Asians Among Africans and Europeans in Kenya

When the English colonists originally came to Kenya, they came to farm fertile land. Although the native Africans were displaced from their land by the whites in the early days before World War I, the small numbers involved had minimal effects especially since there was plenty of land. As time passed, however, the whites took more and more land — mainly through the legislative mechanism of the colonial government, which favored the powerful, agricultural white minority. The African majority in the colony helplessly watched this encroachment and stealing of the land for which they received no remuneration. The Africans were generally regarded as savages by the whites, and, in the colony, had no significant political or economic rights. For the most part Africans were forced either to farm noncash crops on poor land (cash crops were a white monopoly) or to find work in the towns that sprung up in Kenya as the century progressed.

In this social system of inequality, the Asian community formed a third group. Many Asians had first come to the colony as contracted labor before World War I primarily to build the railway. After their contracts had expired, many chose to remain in the colony rather than return to India and be faced with poor land and widespread starvation. In the colony, however, Asians like Africans, were prohibited from farming cash crops. Consequently, many Asians met the growing demand for civil servants, merchants, and professionals. The Asians proved to be brilliant commercial entrepreneurs and, by the 1930s, virtually monopolized the commercial life of Kenya — principally as retail merchants in the towns.

However, although they were a successful commercial community, they were politically less powerful than the whites. During the first half of the twentieth century they constantly fought for equal rights in Kenya. At the same time, as a community, they remained socially aloof from both the whites and the Africans, identifying strongly with their traditional Indian background. Many hoped one day to return to India after they had become financially successful. Because of this orientation to their homeland, their involvement and identity with the colony was limited to what they regarded as being in their interest for political and economic survival.

Their aloofness, economic success, and constant battle for political recognition endeared them neither to the Europeans nor to the Africans. The whites saw them as a threat to their political and economic dominance, while the Africans coveted the Asian commercial success and advancement in the professions and civil service, which many Africans regarded as rightfully belonging to them.

During the colonial period, therefore, the Asians were discriminated against by white legislation which denied them equal access to the political arena. After independence, which followed the rebellion, the new black majority government sought to weaken Asian privileges in the colony by taking over Asian enterprises and giving them to African entrepreneurs. Although there currently are many Africans involved in business, the Asian community has remained an important part of commerce and industry in Kenya. Out of economic necessity, the government of Kenya tolerates Asian businesses and merchants. The number of Africans capable of running commercial operations has been growing constantly so the position of the Asians remains insecure. Intense nationalism among some African governments also has weakened the status of Asians, as the unilateral expulsion of Asians from Uganda in 1972 illustrated. Taking all these factors together, Asians in Kenya today face a dramatically different situation from the colonial period when, at least in the retail sector, their economic survival was certain.

Appendix B: The Extended Family System

Traditionally, the Asian communities in Kenya were organized according to the extended family system. This consisted of all the brothers of a generation and their sons living together either under one roof or in close proximity. By staying together in this way the males of one family were able to maintain a powerful social unit. In the case of marriage, the wives lived with their husbands' family.

This tightly knit kinship structure was closely bound up with the commercial enterprises of the families. For example, the structure of the business organization was based less on the ability of the various personnel in the firm than on the family relationships of the personnel to each other. Given this type of organization, it was possible for a family containing a great deal of business talent to be a very unified and powerful force in commercial affairs.

Within the extended family, the leadership traditionally lay with the eldest brother of the oldest generation still in power. In the case of the Bhiwar brothers this power originally was in Mohan's hands. When he died, the power stayed in his generation and was passed to Anil. When the older brothers retired, tradition dictated that the family leadership be passed to the oldest son of the oldest brother. Note that this does not read "oldest son of the oldest *surviving* brother," which was the rule of succession used by the Bhiwars and resulted in the first family breakup. As head of the household, the oldest man of any generation holding power was the ultimate authority on all matters relating to the family. This power was exercised in many areas including marriage decisions.

Recently the extended family structure has been challenged. Although not yet widespread, there is a growing tendency for some Asians to break from the traditional extended family and adopt the North American nuclear form consisting of a father and mother and their children. Sometimes this breaking away can be done in a way that leaves the parties on amicable terms. More often, however, it is accompanied by considerable trauma, since it is not a practice widely accepted by the Asian community at present.

Notes

1. Names of people, places, and companies have been disguised.
2. In this country blacks are referred to as Africans. Asian is a term that refers to people of East Indian origin, and European is the term used for Caucasians. See Appendix A for a brief discussion of the Asian experience in this multiracial milieu.
3. Appendix B contains a description of some elements of the extended family system.

CASE 2

Footwear International

R. William Blake

John Carlson frowned as he studied the translation of the front-page story from the afternoon's edition of the *Meillat*, a fundamentalist newspaper with close ties to an opposition political party. The story, titled "Footwear's Unpardonable Audacity," suggested that the company was knowingly insulting Islam by including the name of Allah in a design used on the insoles of sandals it was manufacturing. To compound the problem, the paper had run a photograph of one of the offending sandals on the front page. As a result, student groups were calling for public demonstrations against Footwear the next day. As Managing Director of Footwear Bangladesh, Carlson knew he would have to act quickly to defuse a potentially explosive situation.

FOOTWEAR INTERNATIONAL

Footwear International is a multinational manufacturer and marketer of footwear. Operations span the globe and include more than eighty-three companies in seventy countries. These include shoe factories, tanneries, engineering plants producing shoe machinery and moulds, product development studios, hosiery factories, quality control laboratories, and approximately 6300 retail stores and 50,000 independent retailers.

Footwear employs more than 67,000 people and produces and sells in excess of 270,000,000 pairs of shoes every year. Head office acts as a service center and is staffed with specialists drawn from all over the world. These specialists, in areas such as marketing, retailing, product development, communications, store design, electronic data processing and business administration, travel for much of the year to share their expertise with the various companies. Training and technical educa-

Reproduced by permission of the author. © R. William Blake, Faculty of Business Administration, Memorial University of Newfoundland, St. Johns, Canada A1B 3X5

tion, offered through company-run colleges and the training facility at headquarters, provide the latest skills to employees from around the world.

Although Footwear requires standardization in technology and the design of facilities, it also encourages a high degree of decentralization and autonomy in its operations. The companies are virtually self-governing, which means their allegiance belongs to the countries in which they operate. Each is answerable to a board of directors which includes representatives from the local business community. The concept of "partnership" at the local level has made the company welcome internationally and has allowed it to operate successfully in countries where other multinationals have been unable to survive.

BANGLADESH

With a population approaching 110,000,000 in an area of 143,998 square kilometers (see Figure 1), Bangladesh is the most densely populated country in the world. It is also among the most impoverished, with a 1987 per capita gross national product of $160 U.S. and a high reliance on foreign aid. More than 40 percent of the gross domestic product is generated by agriculture and more than 60 percent of its economically active population works in the agriculture sector. Although the land in Bangladesh is fertile, the country has a tropical monsoon climate and suffers from the ravages of periodic cyclones. In 1988 the country experienced the worst floods in recorded history.

The population of Bangladesh is 85 percent Moslem, and Islam was made the official state religion in 1988. Approximately 95 percent of the population speaks Bengali with most of the remainder speaking tribal dialects.

Bangladesh has had a turbulent history in the twentieth century. Most of the country was part of the British-ruled East Bengal until 1947. In that year it joined with Assam to become East Pakistan, a province of the newly created country of Pakistan. East Pakistan was separated from the four provinces of West Pakistan by 1,600 kilometers of Indian territory and, although the East was more populous, the national capital was established in West Pakistan. Over the following years widespread discontent built in the East whose people felt that they received a disproportionately small amount of development funding and were underrepresented in government.

Following a period of unrest starting in 1969, the Awami League, the leading political party in East Pakistan, won an overwhelming victory in local elections held in 1970. The victory promised to give the league, which was pro-independence, control in the National Assembly. To prevent that happening the national government suspended the convening of the Assembly indefinitely. On March 26, 1971, the Awami League proclaimed the independence of the People's Republic of Bangladesh and civil war quickly followed. In the ensuing conflict hundreds of thousands of refugees fled to safety across the border in India. In December India, which supported the independence of Bangladesh, declared war and twelve days later Pakistan surrendered. Bangladesh had won its independence, and the capital of the new country was established at Dhaka. In the years immediately following indepen-

FIGURE 1   Bangladesh

dence industrial output declined in major industries as the result of the departure of many of the largely non-Bengali financier and managerial class.

Throughout the subsequent years, political stability proved elusive for Bangladesh. Although elections were held, stability was threatened by the terrorist tactics resorted to by opposition groups from both political extremes. Coups and counter coups, assassinations, and suspension of civil liberties became regular occurrences.

Since 1983 Bangladesh had been ruled by the self-proclaimed President General H. M. Ershad. Despite demonstrations in 1987, that led to a state of emergency being declared, Ershad managed to retain power in elections held the following year. The country remains politically volatile, however. Dozens of political parties continually maneuver for position and alliances and coalitions are the order of the day. The principal opposition party is the Awami League, an alliance of eight political parties. Many of the parties are closely linked with so-called opposition newspapers, which promote their political positions. Strikes and demonstrations are frequent and often result from cooperation among opposition political parties, student groups, and unions.

FOOTWEAR BANGLADESH

Footwear became active in what was then East Bengal in the 1930s. In 1962 the first major investment took place with the construction of a footwear manufacturing facility at Tongi, an industrial town located 30 kilometers north of Dhaka. During the following years the company expanded its presence in both conventional and unconventional ways. In 1971 the then Managing Director became a freedom fighter, while continuing to oversee operations. He subsequently became the only foreigner to be decorated by the government with the "Bir Protik" in recognition of both his and the company's contribution to the independence of Bangladesh.

In 1985 Footwear Bangladesh went public and two years later spearheaded the largest private-sector foreign investment in the country, a tannery and footwear factory at Dhamrai. The new tannery produced leather for local Footwear needs and the export market, and the factory produced a variety of footwear for the local market.

By 1988 Footwear Bangladesh employed 1,800 employees and sold through 81 stores and 54 agencies. The company introduced approximately 300 new products a year to the market using their in-house design and development capability. Footwear managers were particularly proud of the capability of the personnel in these departments, all of whom were Bangladeshi.

Annual sales in excess of 10,000,000 pairs of footwear gave the company 15 percent of the national market in 1988. Revenues exceeded $30 million U.S. and after tax profit was approximately $1 million. Financially, the company was considered a medium contributor within the Footwear organization. With a population approaching 110,000,000, and per capita consumption of one pair of shoes every two years, Bangladesh was perceived as offering Footwear enormous potential for growth both through consumer education and competitive pressure.

The Managing Director of Footwear Bangladesh was John Carlson, one of only four foreigners working for the company. The others were the managers of production, marketing, and sales. All had extensive and varied experience within the Footwear organization.

THE INCIDENT

On Thursday, June 22, 1989, John Carlson was shown a copy of that day's *Meillat*, a well-known opposition newspaper with pro-Libyan leanings. Under the headline "Footwear's Unpardonable Audacity," the writer suggested that the design on the insole of one model of sandal produced by the company included the Arabic spelling of the word "Allah" (see Figure 2). The story went on to suggest that Footwear was under Jewish ownership and to link the alleged offense with the gunning down of

---

FIGURE 2   Translation of the *Meillat* Story[1]

Unpardonable Audacity of Footwear

In Bangladesh a Sandal with Allah as Footwear trade mark in Arabic designed in calligraphy has been marketed although last year Islam was made the State Religion in Bangladesh. The Sandal in black and white contains Allah in black. Prima facie it appears it has been designed and the Alif "the first letter in Arabic" has been jointly written. Excluding Alif it reads LILLAH. In Bangladesh after the Satan Rushdies[2] Satanic Verses which has brought unprecedented demonstration and innumerable strikes (Hartels). This International shoe manufacturing organization under Jewish ownership with the design of Allah has made religious offence. Where for sanctity of Islam one million people of Afganistan have sacrificed their lives and wherein occupied Palestine many people have been gunned down by Jews for sanctity of Islam in this country the word Allah under this guise has been put under feet.

Last night a group of students from Dhaka university came to Meillat office with a couple of pairs of Sandal. The management staff of Footwear was not available over telephone. This sandal has got two straps made of foam.

[1]The translation is identical to that with which Carlson was given to work.
[2]Salman Rushdie was the author of the controversial book *The Satanic Verses*. The author had been sentenced to death, in absentia, by Ayatollah Khomenei, the leader of Iran, for crimes against Islam.

---

many people in Palestine by Jews. The story highlighted the fact that the design was on the insole of the sandal and therefore, next to the bottom of the foot, a sign of great disrespect to Moslems.

Carlson immediately contacted the supervisor of the design department and asked for any information he could provide on the design on the sandals. He already knew that they were from a medium-priced line of women's footwear that had the design on the insole changed often as a marketing feature. Following his investigation the supervisor reported that the design had been based on a set of Chinese temple bells that the designer had purchased in the local market. Pleased by the appearance of the bells, she had used them as the basis for a stylized design, which she submitted to her supervisor for consideration and approval (see Figure 3).

All the employees in the development and marketing department were Moslems. The supervisor reported that the woman who had produced the offending design was a devout Bengali Moslem who spoke and read no Arabic. The same was true of almost all the employees in the department. The supervisor confirmed to Carlson that numerous people in the department had seen the new design prior to its approval and no one had seen any problem or raised any objection to it. Following the conversation Carlson compared the design to the word Allah, which he had arranged to have written in Arabic (see Figure 4).

Carlson was perplexed by the article and its timing. The sandals in question were not new to the market and had not been subject to prior complaints. As he

FIGURE 3   The Temple Bells and the Design Used on the Sandal

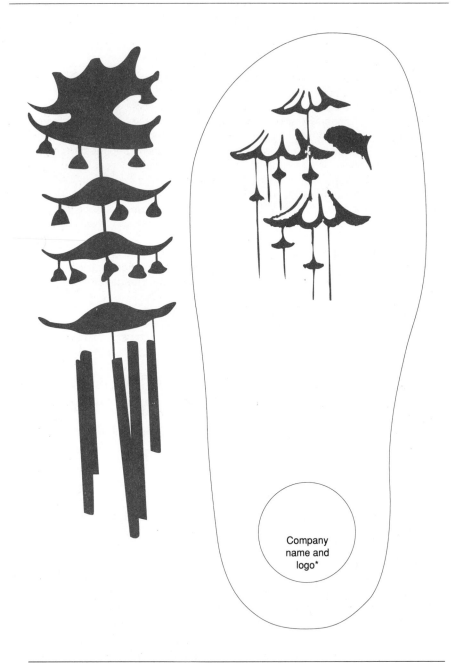

*The company's name and logo appeared prominently on the insole of the sandal. Both of the images in the exhibit were redrawn from copies of facsimiles sent to headquarters by John Carlson.

FIGURE 4   The Arabic Spelling of *Allah*

1. This exhibit was redrawn from a facsimile sent to headquarters by John Carlson.

reread the translation of the *Meillat* article, he wondered why the Jewish reference had been made when the family that owned Footwear International was Christian. He also wondered if the fact that students from the university had taken the sandals to the paper was significant.

As the day progressed the situation got worse. Carlson was shown a translation of a proclamation that had been circulated by two youth groups calling for demonstrations against Footwear to be held the next day (see Figure 5). The proclamation linked Footwear, Salman Rushdie, and the Jewish community and ominously stated that "even at the cost of our lives we have to protest against this conspiracy."

More bad news followed. Calls had been made for charges to be laid against Carlson and four others under a section of the criminal code that forbade "deliberate and malicious acts intended to outrage feelings of any class by insulting its religion or religious believers" (see Figure 6). A short time later Carlson received a copy of a statement that had been filed by a local lawyer, although no warrants were immediately forthcoming (see Figure 7).

While he was reviewing the situation Carlson was interrupted by his secretary. In an excited voice she informed him that the Prime Minister was being quoted as calling the sandal incident an "unforgivable crime." The seriousness of the incident seemed to be escalating rapidly and Carlson wondered what he should do to try to minimize the damage.

FIGURE 5   Translation of the Student Group's Proclamation[1]

The audacity through the use of the name "Allah" in a sandal.

Let Rushdies Jewish Footwear Company be prohibited in Bangladesh.

Dear people who believe in one God It is announced in the holy Quran Allahs name is above everything but shoe manufacturing Jewish Footwear Shoe Company has used the name Allah and shown disrespect of unprecedented nature and also unpardonable audacity. After the failure of Rushdies efforts to destroy the beliefs of Moslems in the Quran, Islam and the prophet (SM) who is the writer of Satanic verses the Jewish People have started offending the Moslems. This time it is a fight against Allah. In fact Daud Haider, Salman Rushdie Viking Penguin and Footwear Shoe Company all are supported and financed by Jewish community. Therefore no compromise with them. Even at the cost of our lives we have to protest against this conspiracy.

For this procession and demonstration will be held on 23rd. June Friday after Jumma prayer from Baitul Mukarram Mosque south gate. Please join this procession and announce we will not pardon Footwear Shoe Companys audacity. Footwear Shoe Company has to be prohibited, don't buy Jewish products and Footwear shoes. Be aware Rushdies partner.

Issued by Bangladesh Islamic Jubashibir (Youth Student Forum) and Bangladesh Islamic Satrashbir (Student Forum)

[1] The translation is identical to that with which Carlson was given to work.

FIGURE 6   Section 295 of the Criminal Code

[295-A. *Deliberate and malicious acts intended to outrage religious feelings of any class by insulting its religion or religious believers*. Whoever, with deliberate and malicious intention of outraging the religious feelings of any class of [the citizens of Bangladesh], by words, either spoken or written, or by visible representations insults or attempts to insult the religion or religious beliefs of that class, shall be punished with imprisonment . . .

. . . In order to bring a matter under S. 295-A it is not the mere matter of discourse or the written expression but also the manner of it which has to be looked to. In other words the expressions should be such as are bound to be regarded by any reasonable man as grossly offensive and provocative and maliciously and deliberately intended to outrage the feelings of any class of citizens. . . . If the injurious act was done voluntarily without a lawful excuse, malice may be presumed.

FIGURE 7   The Statement of the Plaintiff

The plaintiff most respectfully states that:

1) The plaintiff is a lawyer, and a Bangladeshi Citizen and his religion is Islam. He is basically a devout Moslem. According to Islamic tradition he regularly performs his daily work.

2) The first accused of this . . . is the Managing Director of Footwear Shoe Company, the second accused is the Production Manager of the said company, the third accused is the Marketing Manager, the fourth accused is the Calligrapher of the said company and last accused is the Sales Manager of the said company. The said company is an international organization having shoe business in different countries.

3) The accused persons deliberately wanted to outrage the religion of Muslims by engraving the calligraphy of "Allah" in Arabic on a sandal thereby to offend the Religion of majority this Muslim Country. By marketing this sandal with the calligraphy of "Allah" they have offended the religious feelings of millions of Muslims. It is the solemn religious duty and responsibility of every devout Muslim to protect the sanctity of "Allah." The plaintiff first saw the sandal with this calligraphy on 22nd June 1989 at Elephant road shop.

The accused persons collectively and deliberately wanted this calligraphy under the feet thereby to offend the religion of mine and many other Muslims and have committed a crime under provisions of section 295A of the Penal Code. At the time of hearing the evidence will be provided.

Therefore under the provisions of section 295A of the Penal Code the accused persons be issued with warrant of arrest and be brought to court for justice.

The names of the Witnesses

1)
2)
3)

CASE 3

The Canada–China
Computer Crisis (A)[1]

Joseph J. DiStefano

John Stevens, Director of the International Division of Software Services, Ltd., was attempting to clear up his desk before leaving for a week's selling trip. As he left his office to clarify a question with a programmer, he was nearly bowled over by Dr. Paul Horn, who was striding down the hallway in the opposite direction. "You're just the man I want to see," the project leader blurted out with uncharacteristic intensity. "We've got a very serious problem with Yulan Sun. She's deliberately erased the whole program for the interactive graphics package for the multishift scheduling problem we've been working on, and I'm madder than hell! It will take us several months to reconstruct the work. Worse than that, I'll miss the deadline for the project's completion and for the upcoming annual trade fair, which would give our work the perfect publicity we need to launch it successfully."

John was stunned, since he knew that Yulan Sun, a visiting expert from China, had spent several months working on the project. He felt his own blood pressure rise as he replied, "I guess I had better see her right away, Paul. What's behind this and what do you want me to do?"

After a brief explanation of what had transpired over the past week, Paul Horn suggested that John sit tight. "Before you talk to her, I want to get to the bottom of the story myself and try to resolve the problem. I'll talk to her and put something on paper for you before you get back."

By the middle of the next week, John was on the telephone listening to his secretary read the letter Paul Horn had written to Yulan (see Figure 1). He shuddered at the probable consequences not only for Paul's project, but also for the overall agreement with the People's Republic of China (PRC), which John had been working on for the past fifteen months. In his letter, Paul presented his view of the events leading to the present crisis and challenged Yulan to reply by the end of the week AND to turn over the floppy disk on which he knew she had saved a copy of the program. John's secretary had learned from Lindsay Tan, a Software systems analyst, that Yulan had refused to reply to Paul's letter until she met with John, preferably the day he was to return from his selling trip. John knew that on his first morning back at Software he faced a major presentation to the executive committee

FIGURE 1   Paul's Memo to Yulan, Software — Internal Memorandum

DATE: May 8
TO: Yulan Sun
FROM: Paul Horn
SUBJECT: Your VI Model for Nurse Scheduling

Following our conversation on May 6, I think it advisable to lay out my expectations in writing.

First, let me congratulate you on the OPTIK Visual Interactive (VI) Nurse Scheduling model that you have written during your stay at Software. This model represents a useful initial step towards a VI decision support system to address this important and difficult problem. I'm sure, however, that you recognize that the work is still incomplete. In particular, the system does not meet the needs of the manager and further development and testing must take place to prove both the approach and the model.

To continue development of this model, we require the source code (program) that you have developed. While there is no question that the program itself is your work, let me remind you that the project idea was mine, I provided the team of people already experienced with the SAGE equipment and OPTIK software and Software's goodwill secured the cooperation of Ms. McLeod at the Hospital. Further, we worked together during your writing of the program and you used Software's computers and the OPTIK software licensed to the company through me. In short, there is a substantial investment of Software's resources and my time in your program. I, THEREFORE, EXPECT YOU TO PROVIDE US WITH A COMPLETE VERSION OF THE SOURCE CODE FOR THIS MODEL.

I further expect that, when we have completed this work, (hopefully later this summer) a decent presentation for the trade show will result. Your contribution to this work will be recognized in this presentation. Of course, it is not possible TODAY to guarantee that this presentation will be ready or will be accepted by the trade show — technical or managerial problems could still occur since considerable work remains to be done.

Finally, I restate our agreement concerning the OPTIK software. This is a valuable, privately-owned commercial product which we use under license. You must not take away from Software any OPTIK manuals, copies of any manuals, any machine readable OPTIK programs, subroutines or floppy disks or ANY LISTINGS OF OPTIK PROGRAMS OR SUBROUTINES.

We are now upgrading the operating system on the SAGE IV to the new version. The object program that you left on the SAGE will not run after this upgrade. Further, any floppies written under the old OS are not readable under the new OS.

It is, therefore, imperative that we have THE SOURCE CODE FOR YOUR MODEL BY FRIDAY, MAY 10. We can then down load it to our mainframe using the existing OS and reload it to the SAGE under the new OS.

I look forward to your cooperation in providing this program.

(signature)

PH:lm
c.c. John Stevens

of one of his important customers, so he asked his secretary to defer the meeting with Yulan until the next day. He wanted time to confer with Lindsay and Paul before meeting with Yulan. Furthermore, he worried about meeting alone with Yulan. Prior experience taught him that misunderstandings were likely to increase, rather than be resolved, if all parties weren't present. But as tempers seemed to be rising in this situation, he wasn't sure if a joint meeting would be productive either. He knew that whatever he decided to do, the stakes were high and that he had better think through his approach carefully.

SOFTWARE SERVICES AND THE PRC COOPERATION PROGRAM

Software Services, Ltd., was a successful computer software company. The company had grown rapidly from its founding in the early 1970s and had carved a special niche developing custom programs for particular clients that could be generalized to other related problems and sold more widely. An example was Paul Horn's current project in multishift scheduling, which had been started for a hospital client interested in improved scheduling of its nursing staff. Software's competitive edge derived in part from their decision to invest in the latest hardware and to develop software for this equipment that they thought would likely be adopted by their current customers. Suppliers of the new technology understood that they could take advantage of Software's programming skills and market network, so relations between Software and its suppliers were excellent.

The company had about sixty full-time technical specialists with advanced training and skills and about twenty other professional staff, most with B.Sc. degrees who were contracted on a part-time basis. Another fifteen professionals served the marketing and commercial functions in the company. About half of these had moved from the technical areas as the company had grown. The balance of the sales and marketing ranks consisted of M.B.A.s with technical undergraduate degrees or experience. Support functions (accounting, technicians, clerical staff, etc.) consisted of about forty full-time employees, and the senior executive team made up the balance of the personnel in the company.

To operate efficiently and to keep the highly skilled employees challenged and occupied, the company had adopted a matrix structure. The marketing side was organized by industry specialization. The industry managers drew project leaders from the technical groups, which were oriented toward specialized products and applications such as modeling, decision support systems, and operations research. As part of the market differentiation, the company also had an international division, which, in recent years, had added to the firm's ability to attract and retain bright, young professionals in an increasingly competitive market.

The international division was the home for the PRC Cooperation project and where it was now causing considerable frustration. About fifteen months earlier Software had been approached by a nongovernment organization (NGO) in Ottawa which provided placement services for the Canadian International Development Agency (CIDA). CIDA had sponsored a project at the request of the Ministry of Foreign Economic Relations and Trade of the PRC, and the NGO was seeking to place in Canadian industry advanced computer experts, some less experienced programmers, and recent graduates of Chinese technical universities. It was to be a four-year program, the objective of which was to update the experienced people who had fallen significantly behind during the Cultural Revolution between the mid-1960s and mid-1970s. The less experienced graduates were to get exposure to modern equipment and techniques and to gain experience in dealing with real-world problems. The program would simultaneously provide the participants with an understanding of the capitalist system and forge potential commercial links with Canada. Both of these results were consistent with CIDA's policies, which had increasingly shifted toward trade-related aid in recent years.

In this particular project CIDA provided a contribution to overhead to the companies and travel money, salaries, living allowances, language training, and medical insurance to the Chinese visitors. The company was expected to provide facilities and management time in return for the work and output of the Chinese during each visitor's one-year stay. As one of the companies cooperating with CIDA, Software had agreed to accept ten advanced specialists and twelve inexperienced programmers over the four-year contract. In addition to CIDA's paying for this additional manpower and providing overhead allowances to the company, Software executives also hoped, perhaps naively they acknowledged, that establishing direct relationships with the people and government of the PRC would provide them with business advantages in the future. The dramatic opening of China to the West and increasing trade activity might offer new market opportunities for Software's international division.

While reading the newspaper, John Stevens had learned of a similar strategy by one of Canada's leading law firms. The firm had hired and paid the expenses of two Chinese law students for each of the past four years in the hope that the law firm would learn about Chinese regulations and evolving legal system, make important connections with the trainees who would be among the few Chinese to know Western laws, and through them be well-placed to serve the emerging markets for corporations doing business with the PRC. The firm had initiated the idea because of Canada's long relationship with the PRC. Canada had been one of the earliest western nations to recognize the PRC, and China had reciprocated by establishing an embassy in 1972. John believed that establishing relationships with Chinese experts of high standing made excellent marketing sense for the long run. He therefore had urged his own firm to accept CIDA's request for cooperation and had been happy to assume the responsibility for the agreement as an additional activity.

THE PEOPLE

Paul Horn

Dr. Paul Horn, one of Software's most competent technical specialists, was an extremely valuable member of the Software team. Paul had been with the firm for several years. He joined the operations research department and soon established himself as a high producer, who met deadlines. He often worked simultaneously on a number of different projects, and frequently saw new applications for the techniques he developed. In addition, Paul was highly visible in his profession outside the company. He was a regular contributor to professional meetings and published in the most prestigious academic and managerial journals in the world. This was seen as highly desirable by the Software executives, who were anxious to expand the firm's reputation internationally. Because of Paul's record of accomplishments, he had recently been promoted to a project leader. Further, the R&D committee, consisting of the Vice President for R&D and two industry managers and department heads, had responded positively to Paul's frequent requests for equipment, assistants, and financial support for new ideas. The company encouraged such proposals, but the R&D committee scrutinized the requests carefully and demanded clear evidence of performance before extending or renewing its support. More recently, Paul had extended his sources of support by obtaining special grants from various levels of government to help businesses acquire new technology. He had also hired assistants for his work through government-supported training programs.

Paul had obtained a B.A. (Honours) and M.A. from Oxford University and had come to North America to pursue his M.B.A. and Ph.D. at the University of Chicago where he specialized in Operations Research. As many other doctoral candidates had discovered, the process was painfully long. In spite of the financial support from the university, he found it necessary to obtain employment before his dissertation was completed. For a year he worked part-time as an instructor in a nearby institution and then full-time as a lecturer in a university in the Southwest. Paul finished his doctorate and quickly came to enjoy his comfortable life. Both his children were born while he was a faculty member at this university. However, it was primarily the deplorable state of the local schools that prompted his decision to join Software and move to Canada. Paul Horn, determined to see his children in a good educational environment, reluctantly left his idyllic situation at the time his older child approached school age.

In switching to the private sector from a university and to Canada from the United States, Paul expected to make some adjustments. But holding impressive degrees from prestigious universities, Paul also expected more rapid advancement than he initially received at Software. He attributed the delay to misrepresentations by Software, whom he felt had not always lived up to its initial agreement with him. Because of this, he had had sharp exchanges with some of his supervisors and had aired his disagreements openly. However, the strong R&D support, his recent promotion to project leader, and visible successes during the past two or three years had seemed to overcome his earlier frustration. Only rarely did flashes of his earlier feelings break through. His testiness when impatient was no secret in the company, but there was no question that his colleagues enjoyed Paul's company and respected his knowledge, skill, and commitment to his work.

Throughout the company Paul had a reputation as a very hard worker who was frequently seen in his office or the lab facilities early in the morning and on weekends, as were all of Software's most successful project leaders. Within his department he was known as particularly helpful to the young technical specialists brought in by the company on a contract basis. Paul also regularly joined his fellow workers at the staff lounge for lunchtime and coffee break conversations. Paul could always be counted on for incisive remarks and some cutting comments when the repartee and humor became good-naturedly competitive, as it often did when friendly rivalries surfaced.

Paul and his wife, Joan, seemed to enjoy life in the suburbs. Paul played golf and as President of the local chapter of the Optimists, he had led the efforts to raise money to buy microcomputers for elementary schools in his area. He was equally active in his professional societies and served as an officer in one of the national organizations of computer specialists. When the PRC project had been discussed in the company, Paul had been one of a dozen or so technical professionals who had expressed to John an interest in becoming involved.

Yulan Sun

Sun Yulan had been quick to suggest that her Canadian hosts reverse the traditional Chinese ordering of surname first and call her by her given name, Yulan. She had arrived in Canada late the previous July. CIDA had provided a six-week orientation to Canada at the University of British Columbia for a large group of Chinese ranging in age from early twenties to late forties. These people were all participating in development programs of varying duration across the country. Yulan's first few weeks were spent adjusting to an incredibly different world from that which she had known in China. The abundance of consumer goods, the richness of the homes and apartments, the conspicuous wealth, the many yachts in Vancouver harbor, even the expanse of the boulevards, highways, bridges, and neon signs, all overwhelmed her senses. Initially she struggled with her comprehension of English; the speed, accents, and colloquialisms used by the woman in whose home she was staying and by her teachers and acquaintances at the university confused her. They were so different from the part-time, textbook training in English she had had in Beijing. In addition to the disorienting language and cultural differences, Yulan struggled with her dislike for Western food and learned to cope in a city that experienced a public transportation strike that lasted nearly the whole time she was there.

Gradually she became accustomed to her new surroundings, but she felt contradictions in most of her observations and experiences. The bungalow where she lived was modest by Canadian standards, yet seemed wasteful with so many rooms, color TV, telephone, appliances, and furnishings all for the one owner who lived there. Yulan wondered about a society that could generate such wealth, but still leave her host so financially insecure that she had to rent a room to Yulan in order to survive her divorce and unemployment. The media surprised and shocked her, too. How could a country allow insulting commentaries about government officials to appear in print and on TV? How was it possible for radio stations to broadcast music with lewd lyrics and for TV videos to display even more suggestive dancing and revealing costumes?

Yulan experienced this mix of thoughts and feelings from the perspective of living forty-eight years in China. Born just before World War II of reasonably well-to-do parents in Shanghai, Yulan showed a keen aptitude for science and engineering during her middle school years (1948–1954) and was among the few to attend university in the tumultuous years following the revolution. Even more special was her selection to a prestigious Chinese university known throughout North America as "China's MIT," which drew its student body from among the best students in the country. Yulan majored in engineering in the automatic controls department and graduated in 1959. She was immediately taken onto the faculty and was active in research and teaching until 1965 when she was transferred to the computer engineering department. There she quickly established her special talents by teaching and doing research in a variety of areas dealing with both hardware and software. Yulan was the author of two books and several articles on computers.

During her years on the faculty, Yulan met her husband, also an engineering professor. They had their only child, a daughter, in 1968. Their happiness as a family was short-lived, however, because the Cultural Revolution dramatically disrupted their lives. The university was closed for almost a decade, and Yulan was "sent down." This euphemism meant that she had been forcibly removed from her family and sent to a rural area where she had done manual labor in agriculture and had undergone "reeducation" and "self-criticism." She had not seen her husband or daughter for three years. No sooner had she been pronounced "rehabilitated" and permitted to return than her husband had been subjected to two years of the same treatment, during which he had fallen victim to a parasitic disease while planting rice. The debilitating effects of his illness were still visible in his physical frailty, but his spirit remained undiminished.

Perhaps as a consequence of such difficult experiences, Yulan often appeared rigid to John. Particularly when her wishes were thwarted, she became impatient and did not hesitate to raise her voice in anger or to use the traditional Chinese technique of "shaming" the source of her aggravation into acquiescing to her will. This aggressiveness seemed especially marked in her dealings with individuals she perceived as lower in status than herself. Occasionally she seemed slightly paranoid, but John dismissed most incidents as misunderstandings caused by language or cultural difficulties. Notwithstanding these annoyances, John also saw Yulan as an adoring and devoted mother to her daughter and a dedicated, hardworking professional, much admired by her colleagues.

As she emerged from the difficult period of the Cultural Revolution, Yulan's fortunes improved. She and her husband returned to the academic life, which they enjoyed. They were provided an apartment in a five-story walkup, typical of the many such blocks that housed faculty and staff on the university campus. The campus itself represented a "work unit" or "danwei," the basic structure around which all society was organized in the PRC. Everyone who worked or studied at the university lived on campus under the authority of the work unit.

In 1978 as China opened to the West under the leadership of Deng Xiaoping, the university began to develop a capability in the field of management. From a fledgling department of economic management engineering (in North American terms, a bit like a combination of industrial engineering and economics) a rapidly expanding faculty was being built and a need for computer expertise was identified by the senior university administrators. In 1981 Yulan was transferred to the Economic Management Engineering Department as its first director of the Management Information Laboratory. It was in this capacity that she was also selected as the first visitor to Canada on the CIDA-sponsored program with Software.

John Stevens

John Stevens had been with Software almost from its inception. He had joined the firm after graduating with an M.B.A. His interests and studies had emphasized international business and marketing. Prior to beginning his M.B.A., John had completed a mathematics degree and had worked overseas as a volunteer in a developing country. He followed this internship with an extensive period of world travel. Upon returning home, he developed an interest in electronics and computers which led him to a challenging job in computer sales. Ambitious and hardworking, John was a natural achiever in business but soon recognized his need for more formalized training in order to make it into the upper echelons of the corporate world. On the advice of his many contracts and friends, he applied to, and was accepted by the M.B.A. Program at the University of Western Ontario.

Upon graduation John started in a general marketing job at Software before the company had grown so large. The industry specializations had not been as distinct then and the relations between the marketers and technical specialists were not as formalized. Few people in the company had heard of a matrix organization. John's gregarious style and broad education made it easy for him to relate to the variety of people working at Software. His success at marketing the firm's products and securing cooperation from project leaders and their team members gave him significant informal influence in the organization. As the company grew, John's career advanced steadily and he became a manager of one of the industry groups soon after the matrix structure was adopted.

A few years later, the size and complexity of the company required a full-time manager of the human resource function and John was asked to take the job. Seeing the opportunity to do something new and challenging, John agreed, but indicated that he would eventually want to move back into a marketing job.

Seen as a basically easygoing person, some of his tough decisions and recommendations about the careers of some of Software's less outstanding performers surprised some managers. Others were disconcerted at John's volatility in expressing his anger when things didn't go well. During the first two years in the job, John took pride in the policy initiatives he had taken, in the talent that he had helped recruit, and in establishing a relatively smooth-running organization. But he also chafed under the mounting paperwork and regulations imposed by various governmental agencies concerned with human resource issues. What had seemed like a challenging job, tapping some of his natural abilities and core values, had turned into an exasperating routine.

Fortunately for him, the senior executives of Software were just about to create the International Division as a separate entity when John's frustrations crested and he informed the President of his desire to be reassigned to a line job within the next year. The timing and match with John's interests and background were perfect and he jumped at the opportunity to head the new division.

John undertook his international responsibilities with renewed vigor. At the end of the first year, he had been successful in building a solid team and doubling Software's international billings. He credited much of the growth to the excellent performance of the technical professionals in the company, the Paul Horns and Lindsay Tans who turned out exceptional work. They, in turn, commented on the reappearance of the more relaxed John Stevens, whom they had known earlier.

Just at this point, the PRC Cooperation project surfaced and the President asked John to join him on an exploratory trip to China just before Christmas. John had long ago developed an interest in China. As a teenager, John had read about China with fascination. When the PRC Embassy was first established in Ottawa and a few Canadians had reported on their travels, John had written several inquiries trying to arrange a visit. Although none of his letters had been answered, his interest had remained undiminished. Over the previous two years, he had read four books dealing with Chinese political history from the time of World War II through to the excitement of the "Democracy Wall" posters of the early 1980s. No one was surprised at the President's selection of him, nor at his quick reply of "When do we leave?"

The exploratory talks were so successful that he and the President returned with a signed agreement that they had negotiated during their five-day stay. They knew that such a quick agreement was unusual. But they also knew that the Chinese had everything to gain and very little to lose. So they understood that their closing a deal quickly ought not to be seen as a special achievement. Nonetheless, John returned from the trip personally exhilarated and enthusiastically took on the PRC project in addition to his regular duties. Since then John had handled a number of difficult problems and many routine issues. His low tolerance for bureaucracies led to renewed frustrations in dealing with the Canadian government's and Chinese demands for paperwork and reports. As the first year of the project wore on, some of John's enthusiasm abated. But the appearance of the first visitor, Yulan, the following August regenerated his interest. Now that her visit was culminating with a difficult problem, John had a sense of *déjà vu*.

Lindsay Tan

Lindsay Tan was a systems analyst with Software who had been close to Yulan since her arrival. Lindsay was born and raised in Hong Kong and educated in Australia and Canada. She had taken her undergraduate degree in computer science and had been involved in some project work for Software through her senior thesis. Her work had been helpful to the company and her enthusiasm had caught the attention of several people. She was offered a permanent job upon graduation and after a few months' vacation in Hong Kong with her family, she had joined the company full time. Although she did not speak Mandarin, the fact that she was Chinese provided a natural rapport with Yulan. During the first few months, they were often seen together during breaks, and after work. Lindsay spent a number of hours introducing Yulan to the area, helping her get settled in her apartment, and generally being friendly. During this time, she often relayed information about Yulan's progress to

John and her role as an objective and helpful intermediary came to be accepted and relied on by both John and Yulan. Her voluntary call to John's secretary about Yulan's reaction to Paul's letter was typical of the informal role she had played.

YULAN'S ARRIVAL AND EARLY MONTHS OF PRC COOPERATION

Yulan Sun had arrived in Vancouver in late July and was due to fly East to start work with Software in mid-August following the orientation. John was scheduled to go to the Far East in early August and would not be in Toronto for her arrival, so he arranged to see her in Vancouver. John arrived late in the evening and had clients to see from 10:00 A.M. until his flight to Tokyo later that afternoon. Yulan had orientation meetings also, so they met at the hotel to get acquainted over breakfast. Although Yulan was a bit nervous and hesitant, John had no trouble understanding her English and they exchanged pleasantries about her experience during the orientation and joked about enduring the "Canadian disease" of strikes. John noted her discomfort with the food, but was encouraged at her curiosity about his pancakes and blueberries and her apparent willingness to try them when he offered a taste. After talking about plans for her first few weeks at Software, John gave her the airplane tickets that she needed; received a package of pictures, audio tapes, and letters to take to China for Yulan; and arranged for a taxi to return her to the University.

John had decided to stop in China during his trip to meet the first two programmers and an experienced systems analyst whom the Chinese had proposed as visitors starting the following January. He also expected to interview a number of recent computer graduates who would be potential candidates for a subsequent period at Software. Yulan said that the authorities would either arrange for him to meet her husband and sixteen-year-old daughter, or they would deliver the photos and other personal items on his behalf.

The visit went well. John was impressed with the two young computer graduates. They were bright and outgoing and acted as translators during his stay. He quickly approved their projected arrival in Toronto the following January. He was also very favorably impressed at the extensive experience of the second expert, a colleague of Yulan's who had managed a very large factory. But he was worried about her English abilities and urged that she be given more time in the intervening months to strengthen her communication skills. He emphasized that this was important so that both they and Software could obtain the full benefits of the cooperation. He underlined this point about language preparation by rejecting the other graduates because of inadequate English. The Chinese had surprised him by proposing that some additional programmers join the other two who were to go to Canada in January. But he was sure that it would be impossible for them to function in English, so John was firm in his refusal.

In addition to these interviews and the sightseeing that his Chinese hosts graciously provided, John discussed the desires of two senior officials to visit the Software offices the following November. As part of the original agreement, they were to spend a week with Software and a second week visiting other companies in related industries throughout Canada.

At the end of John's stay, Yulan's husband and daughter met him and extended an invitation for lunch in their home, which he accepted with pleasure. When he arrived in the spartan apartment, his thoughts raced back to Toronto and the accommodations he had arranged for Yulan. Even though he had deliberately picked the smallest, least expensive three-room (plus bath and balcony) apartment near the office, he knew it would be luxurious compared to her home. He had thought it would be larger than her home, but had rationalized that since two visiting experts would be in it for most of the time, it wouldn't be embarrassing. Now his stomach tightened in the realization that he had probably erred. But knowing there was little he could do, he turned his attention to his hosts. They provided him with a seemingly unending flow of delicious dishes. He was stunned at the end of the meal by homemade ice cream. He discovered that making ice cream was one of Yulan's hobbies and promised to treat her to the surfeit of flavors at Baskin and Robbins when he returned. At the end of the meal, Yulan's daughter played the violin for him and then proudly played a rock tape on her radio cassette player. She had just returned from a youth camp with American teenagers and had received several tapes as gifts.

The two multiuse rooms were small, grey concrete cubicles and it had shocked John to realize that Yulan would undoubtedly have the best of what was available. Glad for the privilege of being invited, he walked down the four flights savoring the experience and still sensing the genuine warmth that overcame the drabness of the blocks of apartments through which he wound his way back to the University for his final afternoon of meetings. He had had doubts about the worth of taking time from his business calls to stop at the University. But given the special hospitality he had just enjoyed and the importance of face-to-face meetings with the proposed visitors, he was convinced that the detour had been invaluable.

On the same evening he returned to Toronto, he picked up his children and drove to Yulan's temporary room to deliver photos. Two nights later John and his wife took Yulan out for ice cream, starting a close relationship, which built over the early months of her stay. Initially, John saw Yulan briefly two or three times a week at the Software offices, often running into her in the halls or seeking her out for an informal brown-bag lunch. Yulan was quickly immersed in the activities of two different project groups to which she was assigned to learn the computer languages and hardware. She learned quickly and worked long hours on her own. She also attended English classes for recent immigrants in a nearby branch library once a week.

Yulan quickly became accustomed to the fast pace in the company and was invited to several homes for dinner during the first few weeks of her stay. By mid-September she had moved into the apartment John had sublet for her. She obtained the few essential items of furniture with Lindsay's help and seemed to be adjusting to her new environment. John and his family had her to their home several times, and his wife and Yulan seemed to get along especially well. Both were extremely direct people and often laughed about their tendency to ask questions that others found either intimidating or impolite.

In October Yulan attended a course, "Computer Technology, Management and Change." The course was part of a program funded by CIDA to expose the Chinese to Canadian managers and industries across the country. The company visits took place in November.

Fall was also a busy time for John. But he received positive reactions from Yulan, from the two project leaders with whom she worked, and from Lindsay and other Software employees who had made her acquaintance. So he was satisfied that things were going according to the plans and objectives that had been described in detail in the CIDA agreement.

VISIT OF SENIOR CHINESE TO SOFTWARE

John received the shock of his life when the two senior Chinese, with whom he and Software's president had signed the agreement, tried to renegotiate substantial parts of the contract during the very first meeting. They wanted to use the Software contract as the vehicle to send eight of their experts and new graduates to other companies and industries in Canada. They claimed that shifting priorities in China made it critical that different technical specialties be developed. But they wanted all the arrangements to be conducted through Software!

John had been through a few negotiations in his years, but was unprepared for this. He had read and reread Lucian Pye's *Chinese Commercial Negotiating Style*, a study of United States and Japanese executives' experience in China. Although it warned that attempts to renegotiate were normal, John thought he had settled the issue in August when it had also arisen. Then the Chinese had opened it as a possibility, but had not specified the numbers of people or the fields of specialty. John had said "No," but wondered in retrospect if he had been direct or firm enough.

He explained carefully to his counterparts that Software's primary objective in the cooperation project was the direct and extended contact with the Chinese visiting experts. The Chinese visitors pushed their demands and then backed off; then they repeated the cycle of pushing and backing off several times. After a stalemate, the conversation turned to Software's assistance in purchasing a minicomputer for the Faculty of Economic Management. CIDA limited its contribution to $150,000, but the equipment the Chinese wanted was estimated to cost about $200,000. The Chinese tried to reduce the number of trainees to make up the difference. After four hours of discussions, other equipment funds in the contract were used and John agreed to give up a less-experienced visitor to fund the balance needed for the computer purchase.

Then the Chinese returned to their original request to divert several of the trainees to other companies and fields. Again John explained and argued about preserving Software's interests in the agreement. The Chinese finally relented and the meeting ended. The next morning when meetings resumed, John listened incredulously to their raising the issue again. During the previous evening he had thought a lot about his responses to their pressure and had developed a contingency plan which he now acted on. Standing up, he slapped the table, raised his voice and said in a steely tone, barely controlling his anger, "Look, if that is what you want, you should have negotiated contracts with those companies. I am NOT going to do all the work for the benefit of our competitors. If you want to do that, fine. But I will tear up the contract and you can start again with them. I am prepared to rip it up right now. Tell me 'yes' or 'no,' but let's settle it now." Evidently he had gotten through to them, because after some agitated discussion among themselves, they quickly retreated and pronounced the issue closed.

THE MULTISHIFT SCHEDULING PROJECT

As the year progressed, Yulan's adaptation to the technical aspects of Software's activities was excellent. Although she showed some signs of impatience during management and planning meetings of the project groups, she clearly was a very capable professional with the ability to make a significant contribution to Software's business. So at the beginning of the new year, about half way through her stay, John asked Paul Horn if he would be interested in Yulan's joining his team as a full partner in their activities. Paul knew of Yulan's work and he agreed to have her help devise a visual interactive system for scheduling several shifts of workers. It was a problem that Yulan was keenly interested in, since China had many enterprises with three-shift operations. She knew that enormous amounts of time were spent in doing work-force scheduling and that the results were often suboptimal.

After an introductory meeting with Paul, she met with the full-time project member who had been working with the latest SAGE equipment and received a series of briefings on the project, the state-of-the-art hardware, and the software requirements. Then Paul took Yulan to the research site where he introduced her to the supervisor who did the scheduling of the nurses. As he explored the problem with the scheduler, Paul tried very hard to include Yulan in the conversation so she would be able to start her part of the work. He found the exchanges went very slowly with much head-nodding from Yulan and lots of pauses. When Paul thought they were finished, he asked Yulan if she had any remaining comments. Paul was shocked when she responded by asking the scheduler what the problem was. This required going back over the previous 45-minute conversation, which embarrassed Paul. Paul concluded from this experience that Yulan understood very little of a casual conversation, but he also felt that she was unlikely to admit it.

Yulan retreated to her cubicle and began to learn about the sophisticated system. With help from the project team members and a major effort from her (she still continued working on two other projects), she pushed ahead. By late March, she had done an enormous amount of work in developing the basic equations for solving a specific problem of scheduling shifts of nurses over several weeks, and in programming the solution to be displayed in color in a visual interactive model.

This provided the scheduler with the ability to make adjustments easily to several variables and to see the results in graphic form instantly. To translate the accomplishment into terms that John Stevens could easily grasp, Yulan explained that the program was 1,000 lines of FORTRAN and the results converted work currently taking one scheduler a full month to complete into an hour's task. At the same time, it provided much greater flexibility for subsequent manipulation of various decision components.

Even though the work was only partially complete, Yulan's demonstration for John and Lindsay proved to be most impressive. John was doubly pleased because Yulan had been able to describe the context of the work and set up the demonstration of the model in clear, succinct terms. It was also very important to the success of future Chinese visitors that the first collaboration yielded positive results. John was so happy at what he had seen that his first stop after leaving Yulan's presentation was to the president's office to report the results and his second stop was to Paul's office to laud the progress. He also dictated a brief note of praise to Yulan's superior in China. Then he left for home feeling that it had been a most encouraging day.

The results were even more important in light of a meeting Yulan had initiated with John two or three weeks earlier. She had come into his office obviously tense. She felt overwhelmed with the tasks needing to be completed in the short time remaining before her departure. She was negotiating with vendors regarding the purchase of the minicomputer, which took enormous amounts of time detailing the specifications; coordinating with the purchasing department; and reviewing the proposals. She had project work through early April with the other two teams and had another three-week project management course she wished to attend in May. In June she planned to spend time at Waterloo University's computing center, and she was fitting in industry visits near Toronto whenever she could. She also wished to see Montreal and Ottawa and to return to China via Boston, New York, and Washington.

John tried to help her think through priorities and to make trade-off decisions, but everything seemed to be top priority to her. Yulan knew she had much more work to do on the project for Paul if it were to be fully completed, but she also realized that she was running out of time. This pressure was reflected in her eyes, which filled with tears as John talked through the activities with her. Although her reserve and her pride kept her from crying, it was the most emotion Yulan showed at any time other than when she spoke of her daughter. John finally ended the meeting by suggesting that she work on the scheduling project until she and Paul thought that his team could take over her portion and complete it. John agreed to set up a three-way meeting as soon as Yulan thought she had progressed sufficiently to pass on her work to Paul and his assistants.

Two weeks later they had such a meeting in Paul Horn's office. Prior to the meeting John had described to Paul the pressures Yulan was under and the approach he had suggested. In the meeting he summarized the issues and asked Yulan to describe the status of her work up to that point. She did so and indicated that she was not happy to stop then. She realized more testing and debugging were needed, but just didn't have enough time. Paul indicated that if Yulan were to provide briefings to his assistant and to the project member with whom Yulan had worked most closely, they would probably be able to complete the work. He pointed out that she would still be available if questions or problems emerged during the final stages. Although all three recognized that it was not the ideal solution, they also seemed to agree that it was practical.

The discussion included Paul's plan to include the work in the company's presentation for the upcoming trade show on decision support systems. It seemed clear to John that this had been the plan from the beginning, but he also noted that Yulan and Paul had difficulty in understanding each other throughout the meeting. Their accents seemed impenetrable to each other and John had found himself "translating" several times during the meeting. He had been surprised in the meeting that neither Yulan nor Paul had acknowledged their difficulty. Several times he noticed Yulan's blankness at Paul's comments, but Paul only tended to repeat his comments when this happened. Similarly, he spotted Paul's puzzlement at Yulan's pronunciation, but she seemed oblivious to his inability to understand her. So John intervened by testing their understanding and rephrasing and repeating their comments until they each indicated comprehension. The incident dissolved in his memory when soon after this meeting with Paul, Yulan had put on such an impressive display of her work. He had also heard from both Paul and Lindsay that Yulan had conducted a similarly successful demonstration for the scheduling manager of the client hospital. The health administrator had spotted one or two problems in the algorithms and had requested some color changes in the graphic displays, but had been overwhelmingly positive in her reaction to the work and to its potential for scheduling nurses. Although Paul and Lindsay independently had reported the enthusiasm of the hospital administrator to John, they also both had noted that Yulan had not seemed satisfied with her presentation. Each told John of Yulan's denials when they had commented on the success of the presentation. Each had been puzzled by her apparent dismissal of their genuine compliments. Paul had reported with a combination of annoyance and puzzlement that Yulan had abruptly cut him off with an "I don't think so!" when he had observed that her presentation had gone very well. Again, John recalled these comments, which only now seemed significant, even though he wasn't at all sure how to interpret them.

OTHER CONCURRENT EVENTS

Between January and April two other events occurred which John thought influenced what was going on between Paul and Yulan. First, an additional expert and the first two computer graduates had arrived at Software in early January. Although their presence provided instant relief for Yulan's loneliness, complications about financing arrangements and housing had arisen. John held a series of meetings to explain the budgets in greater detail and to work out equitable financial arrangements to cover furniture purchases and rental fees now that Yulan had been joined by another woman who was sharing the apartment. Although he tried hard to be fair, there was no question that Yulan had borne a disproportionate amount of financial burden by being the first visitor and by living alone for the first few months. Another possible inequity might have been that the new graduates were provided the same monthly stipends as the older, more experienced visitors. John wasn't sure how this was perceived, but thought that it might have irritated Yulan.

However, a series of abrasive exchanges between Yulan and John left no ambiguities as to her feelings. In a meeting with John many months earlier, Yulan had expressed an interest in visiting the University of Waterloo which she knew to be a world leader in computers. By March, she held a firm opinion that John had *guaranteed* a two-month visit at the University of Waterloo. But John distinctly recalled only promising to *try* to arrange such a visit and recalled the duration as being much more open-ended, more like "one or two months." He was sure about saying only that he would attempt to arrange a visit, because he had no close friends there and was uncertain of the faculty's willingness to spend time with Yulan. But when these differences in perceptions surfaced, Yulan was adamant about her view being accurate and was very angry with John, even when he repeated that he would do his best to help. At one point in their discussions, the exchange got quite heated. John understood how such a misunderstanding could occur, but was baffled at Yulan's anger and at her apparent lack of appreciation at John's point of view or his willingness to attempt to set up the visit.

After this incident, they had had an even more explosive disagreement over the funding of Yulan's intended Montreal and Ottawa trips. Several significant budget overruns had occurred and John felt as if he had given in on many items. So when Yulan pressed him to cover all expenses for these visits, he balked and then added some conditions to which she reacted with extreme displeasure. At one point they were shouting at each other and both took some time to recover their composure. The amount at stake was not large, but John saw the principles and precedents as critical. Similarly, from Yulan's point of view she felt strongly that her understanding of the agreement was being violated, so she too felt it to be a matter of principle. Neither had had much ability to see the other's perspective and it remained the single point of unresolved rancor during the nine months. So John wondered if this had any bearing on Yulan's erasing the disk. "Perhaps," he thought, "Paul is paying for my sins!" But as he puzzled about the possible connection, he doubted its relevance. His experience with Yulan suggested that she was inclined to be direct on such matters, at least with him. Still, he had prevailed regarding the funding and reporting arrangements for the visits, so the possibility remained that she was displacing her anger onto Paul. Even if this were the case, John wasn't sure how it would help him to deal with the current problem.

THE IMPASSE

Paul had discovered that Yulan had erased all traces of her program from the system disks when he had sent his young assistant to Yulan's cubicle to pick up the program and to be briefed on the project. This was part of the previous agreement that Paul would manage the necessary follow-up and completion of the work Yulan had done. Yulan had refused to give the program to Paul's assistant. When Paul subsequently met with Yulan he learned she had taken a copy of it and erased the original. She said she wanted a guarantee that Paul would credit her work and have the presentation made at the trade fair. When Paul demurred and said that he wanted to have a successful display at the trade fair as much as she, but that he couldn't promise it would be accepted, Yulan became even more insistent. She defended her actions by stating several times that the programming was her work, and as such she had the right to do anything she wanted with it. Paul reminded her with some force that *his* earlier efforts had secured the equipment, *his* project team had supplied the briefings, and that *he* and *his* team members had worked with her during the writing of the program. He added that it had been *his* negotiating skill and *his* reputation that had secured the license for the software. Their exchange had deteriorated to an impasse shortly before Paul had run into John in the hallway. Shortly afterwards, Paul sent the memo in Figure 1 to Yulan.

After his secretary read the memo to him by telephone, John called Lindsay. Lindsay confirmed Yulan's refusal to respond to Paul or to his memo until she met with John. But Lindsay also added that in her view Yulan was also annoyed at Paul's claim that the research was a joint, cooperative effort and was offended at the implication in his memo that she would violate the copyright or licensing arrangements. In conversations with Lindsay, Yulan had repeatedly referred to the long hours of extra work on nights and weekends. She noted that she had done so even without the possibility of bonuses the others would likely receive if the project was successful. She seemed adamant about her position.

From his conversations with Paul he knew, too, that Yulan's work was important to the project. Although it would be possible to reconstruct the programming for the model, it would take three or four months and critical deadlines would be missed. Of importance, too, was the fact Paul had planned on showing the evolution of the ideas and programming as part of the trade show in July. It was there that the package would receive the critical exposure it needed for commercial success.

John knew he had to act before too long, since Yulan would soon be leaving for her three-week management course. Paul's project and trade fair deadlines loomed as additional pressures to act soon. John also knew that the future of the PRC Cooperation Project would also be seriously threatened if the problem were not solved. He even wondered if he should threaten to "pull the plug" on Software's China activity as a way to indicate the gravity of the situation to Yulan. John felt intense loyalty to Paul and appreciated his willingness to have Yulan join his team. At the same time he felt personally committed to the PRC activity and to Yulan's success as the first visitor. He wanted very much to see the collaborative effort between Yulan and Paul yield the rich results that up until a few days ago had looked so promising. From his perspective, neither party could have done what had been done without the other, and the best results could only be obtained by getting this impasse resolved in a cooperative way.

"How to do it?" was the question that confronted him now. "That's what I'm paid for," John thought, as he turned his attention to framing the approaches he should consider in order to make a decision and plan its implementation.

Note

1. The names of the company, its employees, and the Chinese visitors and some of the locations in Canada and China have been changed.

CASE 4

Javitt Industries[1]

Joseph J. DiStefano and Peter Green

George Glett, Director of Personnel of Javitt Industries Incorporated, flew to Japan to study concerns about compensation and benefits in Javitt's Japanese partner, especially in the Plastics Division. Upon arrival, he also was requested to investigate and submit recommendations to Mr. J. J. Rand, President—Western Hemisphere, about a senior management dispute in Javitt Japan, which, if not quickly resolved, could result in the resignations of many key personnel.

Mr. Glett had visited Japan previously and in his reports of these visits had noted several areas of potential conflict among the staff of the Plastics Division. However, though the dispute was not entirely unexpected, the intensity of the feelings and the clandestine meetings did surprise him.

BACKGROUND

Javitt Japan was a joint venture with Javitt personnel responsible for manufacturing and the Japanese partner responsible for the marketing.

The marketing organization was divided into four divisions: the three major product areas and Research and Development. Each of the four divisions — Plastics, Synthetic fibers, Polyester, and Research and Development — was headed by a General Manager. However, only two General Manager positions were currently filled. The General Managers reported to an Area Manager, John Miya, based in the Philippines, but also maintained direct relationships with the President of the Western Hemisphere in Delaware. This practice of reporting to the President had developed during the early stages of establishing Javitt in Japan (see Figure 1).

Recruitment of staff was the responsibility of Javitt Japan's management. Eighty percent of the management personnel had been hired through friendships with other Javitt employees, and the remainder had been drawn from the Japanese labor pool. Javitt did not recruit in the traditional Japanese manner of hiring graduates from educational institutions. The General Manager was consulted on all management recruitment.

FIGURE 1 Javitt Industries Organizational Chart

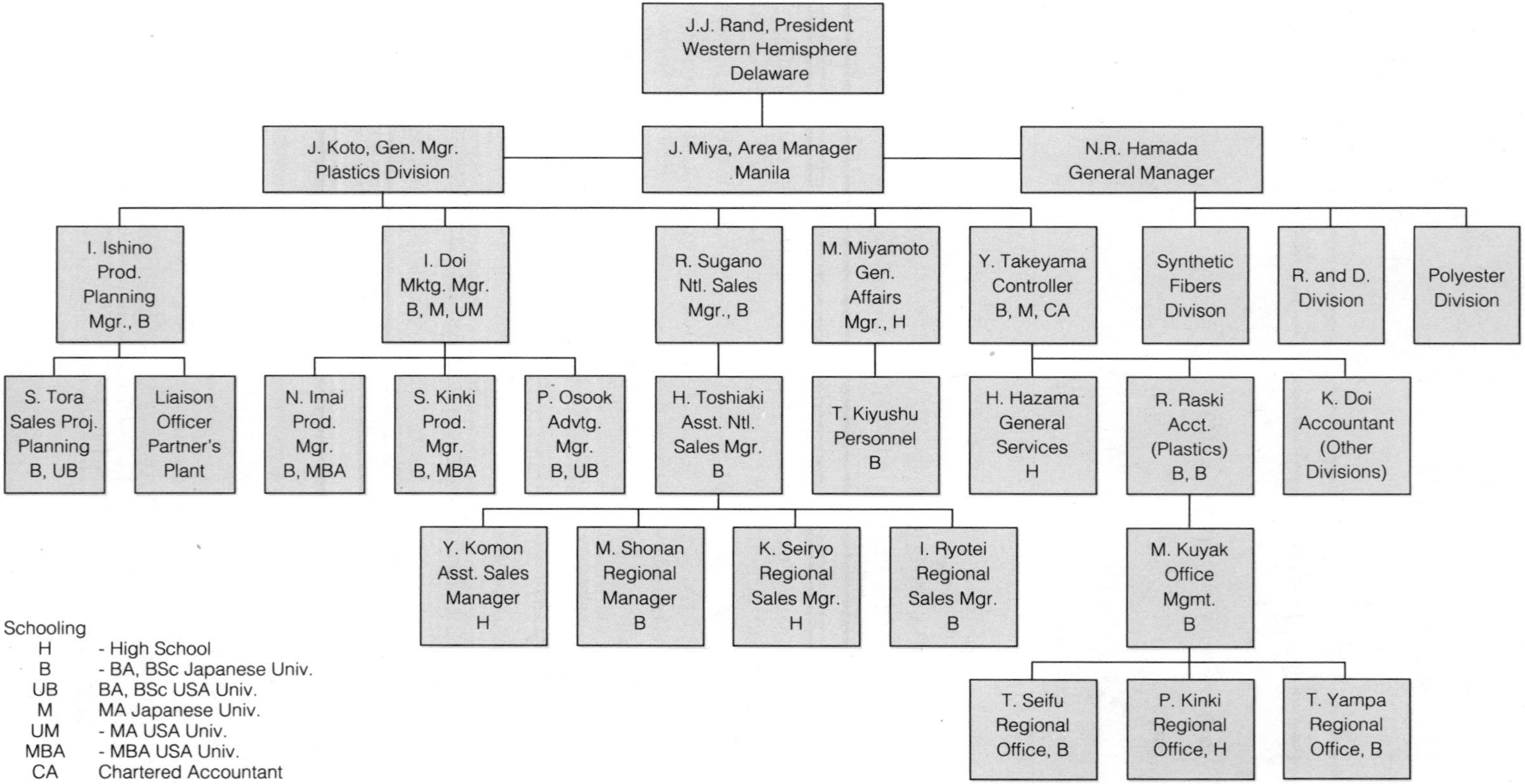

J.J. Rand, President Western Hemisphere Delaware

J. Miya, Area Manager Manila

N.R. Hamada General Manager

Polyester Division

R. and D. Division

Synthetic Fibers Division

Y. Takeyama Controller B, M, CA

M. Miyamoto Gen. Affairs Mgr., H

R. Sugano Ntl. Sales Mgr., B

J. Koto, Gen. Mgr. Plastics Division

I. Doi Mktg. Mgr. B, M, UM

K. Doi Accountant (Other Divisions)

R. Raski Acct. (Plastics) B, B

H. Hazama General Services H

T. Kiyushu Personnel B

H. Toshiaki Asst. Ntl. Sales Mgr. B

M. Kuyak Office Mgmt. B

I. Ishino Prod. Planning Mgr., B

Liaison Officer Partner's Plant

N. Imai Prod. Mgr. B, MBA

S. Kinki Prod. Mgr. B, MBA

P. Osook Advtg. Mgr. B, UB

I. Ryotei Regional Sales Mgr. B

K. Seiryo Regional Sales Mgr. H

M. Shonan Regional Manager B

T. Yampa Regional Office, B

P. Kinki Regional Office, H

T. Seifu Regional Office, B

S. Tora Sales Proj. Planning B, UB

Y. Komon Asst. Sales Manager H

Schooling
H   - High School
B   - BA, BSc Japanese Univ.
UB - BA, BSc USA Univ.
M   - MA Japanese Univ.
UM - MA USA Univ.
MBA - MBA USA Univ.
CA - Chartered Accountant

Job descriptions were formalized but no attempt had been made to introduce an employee appraisal system. The compensation and benefit system was designed to conform with the traditional Japanese system: salary increases were automatic and based on education and seniority, not on performance.

Each division operated independently with little need for any cooperation. Two supporting departments existed: one headed by the Controller and the other by the General Affairs Manager (responsible for Personnel and certain legal matters). These employees were responsible to the General Manager of the Plastics Division but had duties that required them to conduct staff work for the other divisions.

Eighteen months earlier, the Plastics Division, which was the largest division in Javitt Japan, moved from an old building on the outskirts of Tokyo to the lower two floors of a prestigious downtown building already occupied by the other three divisions.

THE MANAGERS

John Koto: General Manager Plastics Division

John Koto was forty-one years old, married, and lived in a luxurious home owned and occupied by his in-laws. As the first General Manager of the Plastics Division, John established operating procedures in a "North American management style." Unlike traditional Japanese managers, John did not avoid making decisions; however, he was so concerned about his prestige that he was unwilling to introduce any program that might increase expenses and reduce profits. For example, John delayed raising salaries, was willing to accept a smaller, less luxurious office than Mr. Hamada's (the General Manager of the Synthetics Division) and had his chauffeur double as a credit collector.

After his first trip to Japan, two years ago, Mr. Glett had reported to Mr. Rand that Mr. Koto:

> . . . unquestionably enjoys a challenge, responsibility, and authority. He perceives himself as a hardworking, effective manager, and when the results of his division's performance are reviewed, he must be credited with a great deal of effort.

> His greatest frustration is his lack of independence from his in-laws. His Japanese pride and need for independence does not permit him to enjoy the luxury of a home and extra finances belonging to his wife. Another reflection of his extreme pride is his concern about the marketing course he is to attend, and whether or not he will be required to write exams.

> John appears to have extreme loyalty to the company. The Japanese concept of total allegiance to a company is now being criticized in Japan, especially where it exists at the expense of the employees. I sense John has more loyalty to the company than to his Japanese staff.

> It would be critical to the Plastics Division if we should lose Mr. Koto over the next two years. Replacements are scarce but, more important, his leaving would have a negative effect on other senior employees.

Mr. Robert Hamada:
General Manager Synthetics Division

Mr. Robert Hamada was forty-one years old. He had been in Japan for five years prior to the time of his appointment, by Mr. Rand, to the position of General Manager of the Synthetics Division. Hamada was a Hawaiian Japanese. He had been educated in Hawaii and had attended university on the United States mainland where his daughter was now going to school.

As a second-generation Japanese (Nisei—Japanese face, but not Japanese mind), Mr. Hamada was immediately subject to open social discrimination. Expressions of the position of Nisei in Japan, and in particular of Hamada's status, had been conveyed to Mr. Glett by Koto and his staff and had ranged from dislike to open hatred. Mr. Hamada had been appointed to a division staffed entirely by Japanese nationals and his assistant had informed several people that the position ought to have been his as he had been with the division since its creation.

Mr. Martin Miyamoto:
General Affairs Manager

Martin Miyamoto was forty-one years old, a high school graduate, totally fluent in English and, in Mr. Glett's opinion, an extremely diligent, affable, and competent man. Hired by Mr. Koto as General Affairs Manager, Miyamoto had responsibility for all Personnel matters, certain legal affairs and general office functions. A helpful man, he offered to assist Mr. Hamada on many personal matters (e.g., income taxes) and had conducted a number of detailed studies for Mr. Hamada. These studies, which affected the entire company, had not been circulated through the other divisions.

A SECRET MEETING

On Thursday, the day after arriving, Mr. Glett learned, from discussions with Mr. Koto, that he suspected Mr. Hamada, his counterpart in the Synthetic Fibers Division, of being in league with Mr. Miyamoto, the General Affairs Manager, to take over his job. Mr. Koto accused Hamada and Miyamoto of hiring an agency to conduct an investigation into his background to identify issues that would justify his dismissal. Later, Mr. Glett confronted Hamada and Miyamoto and received negative responses to his question about their knowledge of an investigation.

On that same day, Mr. Glett received a letter from Y. Takeyama, Controller; I. Doi, Marketing Manager; R. Sugano, National Sales Manager; and I. Ishino, Product Planning Manager, requesting that he attend a meeting at an unspecified location where, "We members of the divisional management personnel would like to be given the opportunity to discuss privately and secretly problems critical to the company . . ."

On Saturday, after having been delivered by taxi to an unknown destination, it was with some surprise that Mr. Glett found not only the four cosigners of the invitation but, as well, twenty-eight members of the Plastics Division Marketing and Sales Management staff in attendance at the meeting. Although ostensibly called to Tokyo for the "First National Sales and Office Managers meeting," the chairperson, Mr. N. Imai, immediately announced that the meeting had been convened to discuss the rumors of Mr. Koto's resignation. In reply to several questions, Mr. Glett assured everyone that he knew of no resignation and that Mr. Rand had recently conveyed to Mr. Koto total confidence in both his management ability and leadership capacity.

Several members of the sales staff then asked why Mr. Hamada and Mr. Miyamoto had hired private investigators to "snoop" on Mr. Koto. The Sales Manager from Osaka added the information that he had been shown the agency receipt by Mr. Koto and told that Mr. Koto had spoken with an investigator, who did not specifically designate Mr. Miyamoto as the person requesting the study, but who did not deny it.

Mr. Takeyama, the Controller, then accused Hamada and Miyamoto of conspiring to oust Mr. Koto, whereafter Takeyama and eleven other managers presented testimonials attesting to Mr. Koto's diligence and leadership. Throughout the testimonials and previous discussion, Mr. Glett received the impression that if Mr. Koto resigned, others would resign with him and that his resignation would damage relationships with the trade.

In replying, Mr. Glett attempted to show that a resignation would be Mr. Koto's own decision. He emphasized that the company would not flounder without Mr. Koto as it had a large pool of expertise on which to draw. Mr. Glett added that Mr. Hamada and Mr. Miyamoto would not be qualified to take over Mr. Koto's position and that the sales and marketing managers should think of their responsibilities not only to the company as a whole but to their families as well. Mr. Glett left the meeting believing he had convinced the managers that Mr. Koto's resignation would not have the serious implications they predicted and that they realized no proof of their accusations yet existed. On the Monday following the meeting, his suspicion that Mr. Koto had been involved in organizing the gathering was confirmed when Mr. Koto greeted him with, "How was the meeting?"

Because of the conviction of the various managers at the meeting, Mr. Glett again approached Miyamoto and Hamada asking whether they had initiated the investigation. Mr. Miyamoto denied complicity, but that evening Mr. Hamada came to Mr. Glett's hotel and embarrassedly admitted hiring an investigator. In a subsequent letter of apology to Mr. Koto (see Figure 2) written at Mr. Glett's suggestion, Mr. Hamada explained that he had hired the investigator to gather information on Mr. Koto's management style. Mr. Miyamoto, he said, had had nothing to do with the investigation which Hamada claimed was for the purpose of giving himself insight and a means to improve his working relationship with Mr. Koto.

In conversation with Mr. Hamada, Mr. Glett learned that Mr. Hamada had been unable to open any communication, formal or informal, with Mr. Koto, even though Hamada's office was only one floor above Koto's.

A copy of the apology was given to the four managers who had openly supported Mr. Koto. In commenting upon the contents of the letter, the managers said,

FIGURE 2   Javitt Industries — Letter of Clarification

TO: Mr. Koto
FROM: Mr. Hamada

Dear John:

This memo is written in hopes that it will clarify some points that have come to my attention concerning yourself, Mr. Miyamoto, and myself.

As you are well aware, unfortunately, there have been signs which tend to indicate that the relationship between the two of us is far from being ideal. Hoping that time will improve our relationship as we get to know each other, I attempted to keep an open mind and ignored matters even when they were of a rather unpleasant nature. Unfortunately, however, the situation progressed from bad to worse. Being new with the company, I am sure you can appreciate my concern and desire to overcome the misunderstandings which existed between us as soon as possible.

A thought occurred to me that if I could get to know you better, we might be able to understand each other and overcome our problems. Unfortunately I know of no out-of-company person who knows you and I felt that your past employer and fellow workers are most qualified in informing me of your ''style'' while at work. Hence the request was made to the credit agency. I wish to strongly emphasize that the agency was told precisely that I had no interest in matters of a personal nature and to avoid them. The parties contacted were personnel from the two companies you were associated with in the past and no one else. This I am sure can be very easily verified by the agency.

I understand Mr. Miyamoto was questioned in connection with my request to the agency. It was most unfortunate that he was implicated in this matter. I would like to make it clear once and for all that Mr. Miyamoto had absolutely nothing to do with it. I myself alone made the decision and took action.

Also there have been speculations that I was anxious to ''take over'' the Plastics Division. Nothing can be further away from the truth than this. My interest lies in the Synthetic Fibers Division and my efforts will continue to be concentrated in this area exactly as my job description states. The rumor of my interest in the Plastics Division is groundless and false.

One other point that I think should be clarified pertains to the R and D operation. I have in no way approached the management to have myself appointed to look after the R and D operation. It came to me as a surprise just as much as it did to many people. This arrangement is only a temporary one and we are presently looking for someone to run it. The sooner we find this person the happier I will be.

I hope this memo clarifies some of the questions you may have had in your mind. Should there be any other questions or should there be any need for further explanation, please feel free to inform me. I will be most happy to reply.

Sincerely

N. Robert Hamada

NRH/sk
c.c. Messrs. J.J. Rand
          G. Glett
          M. Miyamoto

"Nobody but a psychopath could be capable of working out justifications for Mr. Hamada's ridiculous reasoning." Besides suggesting that Mr. Hamada might be covering up for Miyamoto, the managers said that they had been given the impression that Mr. Hamada might have been prompted to initiate the investigation by International Headquarters. This latter thought was rationalized because Mr. Hamada, "could not have taken such an imprudent attitude as to admit his responsibility in writing."

These managers, and some area sales managers, joined together to reconfirm their loyalty to Mr. Koto, and submitted a further memo that recommended dismissing Mr. Miyamoto, and that set out the conditions of acceptance of a new General Manager should Mr. Koto actually resign. (See Figure 3.)

In order to gain a clearer perspective, Mr. Glett called upon Mr. Koto and asked him to discuss his reasons for wishing to resign. The reasons given were:

A. Problems existed with Hamada and Miyamoto.
   1. Hamada hired an investigator.
   2. Hamada criticized Koto's management style and policy proposals.
   3. Miyamoto had created personal problems between Koto, Hamada, and other staff and had aligned himself with Hamada against Koto.
   4. Miyamoto's dual reporting responsibilities made disciplinary action impossible.
B. Management had lost confidence in Koto.
   1. Business had not performed to expectations.
   2. Polyester was promised to Koto but was given to Hamada.
   3. Responsibility for R&D had been temporarily delegated to Hamada.
C. Koto had three employment offers — one American, one Japanese, and one with his father-in-law; if accepted, any one of the offers would double his present salary.
D. Koto resented Hamada, a Nisei, and was suspicious of his intentions, actions, and relations with the International Headquarters.
E. Koto had lost touch with International Headquarters as a result of Mr. Graham's appointment to Mexico (Graham was Rand's predecessor).

After the interview, Mr. Glett returned to his hotel to draft a report with his recommendations based on one or more of the following assumptions:

   1. Koto's responsibility was in excess of his capability and he was reacting emotionally rather than logically in his response to a bad business year.
   2. His traditional, autocratic management style was becoming less effective in dealing with new, young, capable Japanese and he was frustrated.
   3. He was tired and saw an opportunity for higher salary, stock options, job security, and less stress in another company.
   4. In order to resign from the company and still retain his honor in the business community, he was clouding his weaknesses by promoting and spreading negative information relative to Mr. Hamada and Mr. Miyamoto.

FIGURE 3   **Javitt Industries — Memo from Managers**

TO: Mr. Glett
FROM: R. Sugano, Y. Takeyama, I. Doi, I. Ishino, H. Toshiaki, Y. Komon, T. Seifu,
         M. Shonan, H. Hazama, I. Ryotei.
RE: Our Personal Opinion

A. *Mr. J. Koto's Resignation*
   Without Mr. J. Koto, it will be very difficult to make this subsidiary into a
   profitable operation for the following reasons:

   1. *Leadership*
      The operation of an industrial products organization is more difficult than
      others making the leadership ability of the General and Sales Managers
      very critical. No one has more leadership qualities than those possessed by
      Mr. Koto.
   2. *Profit*
      We know that Mr. Koto is a business–minded person who has strived to
      make our operations profitable both in the short and long range points of
      view. No other manager is as profit–oriented as Mr. Koto and no other
      manager will be able to view our business in the same way he has.
   3. *Weakness of Our Division*
      Mr. Koto knows every aspect of our division and has tried to improve all the
      areas of weakness. He could have successfully completed this but has
      been constantly frustrated by "heartless, non–business–minded, jealous
      managers such as Hamada and Miyamoto."
   4. *Personal Relations*
      Most of our managers decided to join our company because they were
      impressed with Mr. Koto's management philosophy. Upon his resignation
      most of the really capable, business–minded managers may leave the
      company unless his replacement is as good as Mr. Koto.

B. *Mr. Koto's Replacement*
   Without a General Manager who knows the traditional distribution sytstem of
   industrial products in Japan it would be very difficult to run our business
   effectively. None of the present personnel in the Plastics Division will accept a
   General Manager who will be directly or indirectly influenced or directed by the
   General Manager of the Synthetic Fibers Division. Because everyone has been
   influenced by Mr. Koto's good management, they will only accept a new
   General Manager who is supported and recommended by Mr. Koto.*

C. *Mr. Miyamoto's Dismissal*
   We all strongly recommend that Mr. Miyamoto be dismissed. If he is not
   dismissed several employees as well as members of management will be
   forced to resign their positions.

*In conversation with several of the writers Mr. Glett learned that they would accept anyone as
long as he was not a Nisei, but that if a Japanese national could not be recruited they would prefer
a North American who was physically very big.

FIGURE 3 **Continued**

Our recommendation is based on the following:

1. Miyamoto has created personal distrust in his involvement with Mr. Hamada in his efforts to oust Mr. Koto.
2. His connection with this division is unnecessary.
   (a) Legal problems can be handled by the General Manager of Marketing Department with Legal Counsel's advice.
   (b) Recruitment of personnel can be handled by a junior personnel officer.
3. During Mr. Koto's absence he took the opportunity to impose bitter criticism on Mr. Koto in front of salesmen and clerks. This behavior disheartened Mr. Koto who is unable to discipline Mr. Miyamoto because he also reports to Hamada.
4. Mr. Koto insists he will resign if either Mr. Hamada or Mr. Miyamoto are permitted to remain in the organization.
5. Miyamoto is suspected of involvement in the investigation of Mr. Koto. This technique of obtaining information is alien to Japanese business custom.
6. Miyamoto submitted a report on personnel administration without consulting with the managers in the division.
7. Miyamoto abused his authority by raiding other managers' areas of responsibility.

Using this ploy, he created sympathy for himself and justification for his resignation.

Mr. Glett was puzzled. What recommendations should he make to Head Office? His experiences when visiting Japan two years ago had been very different from the ones he had had on this visit. How was he going to deal with all of the conflicting evidence which presented itself this time?

Note

1. All names and other data that would identify the company have been disguised.

CASE 5

Karen Leary (A)

Jaan Elias and Linda A. Hill

It did not surprise Karen Leary that her lunch with Ted Chung had turned into a somewhat uncomfortable experience. Although a year had passed since she hired Chung to be a financial consultant (FC), Leary sensed that there was a wide gulf between them. She had tried to get to know him better, but Chung had always distanced himself from her and the other FCs in the office. Leary had hired the Taiwan-born Chung to attract customers from the thriving community of Taiwanese entrepreneurs that had sprung up around Elmville, a Chicago suburb. In his first year at Merrill Lynch, Chung opened the $6 million account of a Taiwanese industrialist and had traded the account actively, generating substantial commissions.

Over lunch, Leary and Chung reviewed Chung's performance during the past year. Leary told him that she was pleased that he had opened such a big account. She reminded him of her concern about the appropriateness of some of his trades. The client was new to the American market, and she questioned Chung's investments in risky stocks and his use of margin. She also cautioned Chung not to spend all his time with this one account; she expected him to develop other Taiwanese customers.

Chung explained that he had been actively developing relationships with wealthy Taiwanese businesspeople and expected to bring in more accounts soon. He also reassured Leary that the Taiwanese industrialist was fully aware of how his account was being handled. Chung then said, in reviewing his own performance, that he was certainly gong to be one of the most important producers in Leary's branch, and therefore, he deserved and needed a private office.

Leary was taken aback by Chung's request. Of the 45 FCs at the Elmville branch, only eight had private offices and they were the best and most experienced brokers. Even FCs doing substantial business in their twentieth year sometimes did not have private offices. Although Chung appeared headed toward a successful career at Merrill Lynch, several elements in Chung's performance over the past year worried Leary. Given her expectations of the Taiwanese market's potential and her aggressive goals for the office, Leary wondered how she should respond to his request.

MERRILL LYNCH BACKGROUND

In 1985, Merrill Lynch, one of the nation's largest wirehouses, found itself in the midst of a fiercely competitive battle in the retail financial services industry. Government deregulation of major financial institutions and increased innovation in financial instruments had unleashed a head-on clash among a diverse group of players. Merrill Lynch, Citicorp, Prudential, American Express, and Sears had built up impressive arrays of consumer financial services through expansion and acquisition.

From the 1940s when Charles Merrill had pioneered the concept of bringing "Wall Street to Main Street," Merrill Lynch had been in the forefront of bringing one-stop financial shopping to all Americans. The core of Merrill's approach to providing financial services had always been the tight bond that brokers formed with their clients. The company had set up a large network of branch offices and supported its brokers with extensive training and topnotch research. Through its efforts, Merrill created the mold for the modern professional broker.[1] FCs responded by showing fierce pride in the company. Most of senior management, including many of the past CEOs, had started out as brokers.

The increased competition, however, had Merrill's top management leading its brokers in new directions. The decision to retitle account executives *financial consultants* was more than cosmetic; it reflected a transition in the way Merrill marketed its services. (Brokers at Merrill Lynch were first called *account executives* by Charlie Merrill in the 1940s. In 1983, they were retitled *financial consultants*.) According to the Merrill Lynch 1985 Annual Report, the company had been moving toward a customer-oriented rather than a product-centered structure. Services were to be "wrapped around the customer." Accordingly, the company introduced a menu of new products, ranging from real estate investments and insurance to centralized cash management accounts. Salaried product specialists had been dispatched to branch offices to aid FCs in pinpointing the proper mix of financial instruments to respond to a client's needs. The new lineup of products necessitated additional training in financial planning practices and profiling the customers' long-term financial goals.

Increased competition and consumer sophistication had also meant smaller margins, and concern about the high fixed cost of operating a large brokerage system. (Merrill Lynch estimates that it takes $100,000 a year to support one broker.) Upper management had targeted goals of cost control and increased productivity per broker while continuing to offer the most professional financial advice possible to the client. The compensation system was restructured to reward asset gathering and top brokers. To be profitable, Merrill's management believed the company must enhance an FC's ability to add value by recognizing and properly satisfying a customer's long-term financial objectives.

Some industry analysts, however, provided a sharp counterpoint to the new strategies being employed by financial service firms. One commented, "People still do business with brokers because they like them. You need the entrepreneurial type of guy. What happens if some of a firm's big ideas don't work?" Another observed, "For most brokers, trading remains the most glamorous part of the business; it provides the high-stakes financial rewards and excitement that motivated them to become brokers." Many thought trading would always be a broker's bread and butter. One broker commented, "The industry is always restructuring. It'll probably happen again in a few years, but the bottom line will still be how much you can bring in with commissions."[2]

TAKING OVER THE BRANCH OFFICE

Leary's Background

Leary joined Merrill Lynch as a financial consultant in 1975, after having managed a family business for several years. Besides quickly building her own client list, Leary took on various leadership roles, such as product coordinator, in the San Francisco branch where she worked.

> I truly enjoyed working with my clients and helping them fulfill their dreams, such as getting the money for a new home or funding the investments that would make it possible for a child to go to college. But I always knew that I wanted to go further in the industry.

After six years as an FC, Leary went to the Merrill Lynch assessment center and passed the grueling set of exercises designed to evaluate management skills. She was assigned to a downtown Chicago branch as sales manager. In 1983, she became resident vice president and general manager at the Elmville branch, a substantial office for a first-time branch manager.

> When I took over the office, there was a large group of people here who had been in production for maybe ten years or more. Many were average producers who did a lot of options and small trades. A few were oriented toward just getting a commission dollar and were having difficulty implementing a financial planning approach. I felt I would have to change this, that the culture was one that would not allow growth. I knew that even if I brought in new, good people their growth would be inhibited by the prevailing culture. . . . Some managers have the philosophy: "If a person is moderately profitable for the firm and no trouble, then fine." I'm not saying that is a bad approach. The firm makes money, the FCs make money, and the manager makes money. It is just that I am more aggressive and my goals are higher. I wanted to build a winning team that would

be recognized for the quality and professionalism of its people, that would excel in matching clients with the products, and that would utilize the full range of Merrill Lynch services. I don't want to be a little country office out in Elmville.

Leary terminated eight of the FCs that she inherited, some of whom had been with Merrill Lynch for over six years. She believed that these were people who could not follow the firm's strategy. In many instances it was a difficult decision, and Leary helped some FCs find positions with other brokerage houses.

Leary initially focused on hiring experienced brokers to fill the vacancies.

I interviewed some younger people who had been brokers with other firms. They were already fully registered and for one reason or another had not fit into their firms. To train a person with no experience, it costs Merrill Lynch $30,000, and it is at least six to eight months before an inexperienced person is at all productive. So it is a long-term, expensive proposition. The people I interviewed were fully registered and knew a little about the business. So I took a risk. It was a business decision; it cost Merrill Lynch little. I hired four or five of them and two made it. . . . But I learned you really can't do it that way and build what I want. It exposes the rest of the office to unsuccessful people and the office needs to view themselves as a collection of successful professionals. So, while it did not cost the firm financially, I think it cost the firm in other areas.

Leary's Management Style

Leary made a point of getting out of her office and on to the floor of the boardroom as often as she could. For at least two hours every day, she navigated among the cubicles, where the FCs were talking with clients on the phone and monitoring market indicators and current events on Quotron screens.

I do a lot of coaching and counseling informally. I find it's effective and less threatening than to be called into the manager's office and asked to explain yourself. So, I'll frequently sit down at a person's desk and just say "Hi. How's it going. Let me see what you're working on. That looks interesting. Have you seen the new tax-free bonds up on page eight of the Quotron?" or I will ask them about a problem they had or a stock that they are watching.

"Karen is by far the most sales-oriented manager I've ever seen," a veteran Merrill Lynch FC commented. "Literally every day, she finds just the right investment for a client. Now a good broker can get on the phone and use that immediately. . . . Some managers are content to just check the mail and do the administration. Not Karen. She really is very aggressive in trying to motivate the FCs."

Leary's superiors praised her development of innovative sales and training programs. She created a voluntary program of partnerships/internships for FCs both to motivate top, older producers and to help young FCs get started.

Some of these older people are doing five or six hundred thousand a year in production and have their business set. They get kind of complacent. At that point in their career, it is very difficult to get these people to prospect or develop new business. On the other hand, younger people need strong role models who are willing to teach them more about the business. I think this program provided a unique opportunity for less experienced FCs to learn firsthand about superior customer service and prudent money management.

Leary persuaded a few of her more experienced FCs to take on younger brokers or trainees as junior partners. The young brokers agreed to make the cold calls and draw up the client profiles needed to gather more assets, while the older FCs helped with the clients and with servicing the accounts. Leary hoped that the program would help reinvigorate the careers of some of her older producers while giving younger ones much-needed experience and supervision.

Leary stressed training her corps of younger brokers. She often came in before the market opened or on Saturdays to lead seminars designed to familiarize young FCs with financial planning techniques. Through case-by-case review, Leary led spirited discussions of Merrill Lynch products and techniques for profiling customer needs. She also leaned on her young FCs, keeping tabs on their cold calling (they were expected to make 200 calls a day) and overseeing the development of their own customer strategies.

Overseeing brokers' trades was an important part of a Merrill Lynch manager's responsibilities, and many of the FCs in Leary's office gave her high marks for staying on top of compliance issues.[3] The branch manager was considered the key to a brokerage house's compliance effort, since he or she was in the best position to monitor brokers. Branch managers were charged with guarding against a wide range of broker malfeasance, including churning (doing more trading in an account than warranted), misrepresentation (failing to properly convey the risks of an investment), unauthorized trading, and unsuitability (recommending investments not in keeping with an investor's financial position).

One of Leary's first moves on taking over the Elmville office was to bring in a new chief compliance officer, one she felt would get to know brokers better and evaluate their trades. Daily, Leary reviewed all of her FCs' account activity and often questioned FCs about their trades. Leary observed, "There is a great deal of concern about protecting our customers. So it is very important to me that we do quality business for them and make sure their investments are right and proper. We deal with money and are very tightly regulated."

Leary's aggressive approach to sales and compliance appeared to have paid off. During her first year, business increased by 30%. However, her style had some FCs grumbling. "She rides all the FCs hard," one commented, "She is always pushing you and looking over your shoulder." Leary hoped her innovative approach to management would be beneficial to and recognized by Merrill Lynch. From the Elmville office, her specific goals in 1985 included completing an office renovation, opening another satellite office, and developing the small business trade. Generally, she wanted to build "a high-producing, successful group of professionals who help one another and work together to provide clients with complete service in meeting their long-term financial goals. All recognizing, of course, that we're dealing with egos and that it takes a very strong ego to be successful."

DEVELOPING THE TAIWANESE MARKET

Hiring and Training Ted Chung

Leary hired Chung to develop the Taiwanese market for Merrill Lynch. "The Taiwanese are not really assimilated into the American system, so we needed a person with a Taiwanese background who spoke Chinese to begin to develop this market. I put some general ads in the papers, and Ted Chung was one of many who answered the ad and one of several Taiwanese." Numerous Taiwanese-owned and -operated businesses had sprung up throughout the Chicago area during the 1970s. Unlike other waves of immigrants to the United States, these Taiwanese had a strong network of contacts and sufficient capital to set up businesses. Through hard work and determination, family-run, first-generation Taiwanese businesses had built up substantial positions in a relatively short time. Many active Taiwanese community organizations had formed, and businesses tailored to the Taiwanese had opened their doors.

The other Taiwanese applicants were young, and Leary felt she needed a more experienced broker to work with Taiwanese businesspeople.

> Chung was in his early forties and he appeared mature, stable, and responsible. He was married with four children, and his wife was a computer programmer. In his seven years in the United States, he had been a very successful salesman for a real estate company and had owned his own moving business. He was independently wealthy. He had been born in Taiwan, yet he was westernized in many ways.

Leary described hiring new FCs as one of the most important functions of a branch manager. She frequently interviewed people three or four times before making a final decision. She met with Chung eight times in various settings before hiring him.

> I felt I didn't really know the whole person, but I wrote that off to the fact that he was Asian and I was not, or maybe there was some concern over my being a woman (though he never expressed any concerns). So after a period of time where I could not put my finger on anything that was wrong, I made the decision to hire him because I felt there were so many areas where he fit. I knew his wife, met his children, knew where he lived, and investigated his background, and there was nothing there that appeared negative.

Newly hired FCs went through an intensive four-month training program. During the first two months, they prepared for the rigorous General Securities exam, and in their third month they learned additional subjects such as portfolio management and selling techniques. The first three months of the program were spent in the branch office, and Leary saw this as a time when trainees could learn how the office operated. Trainees were often asked to fill in for sales assistants or to help in operations.

Chung studied hard and did well on his tests; however, Leary noticed that he bristled and found other things to do when staff members asked for his help.

I called him in and said, "You were asked to sit at the sales assistant's desk this morning, and it appeared that you were uncomfortable with this request, and you found some way not to fulfill it. Let's talk about that." He then described how his feelings were hurt. It came out that he didn't like to do those things; that he frankly considered it to be beneath him, particularly if an underling asked him. He told me that if I asked him he would do it for me. I said, "Well, Ted, this is an office and a business. As a trainee, you are here to learn and to develop, and I would like you to do that."

In their fourth month of training, FCs were sent to the Merrill Lynch training center at One Liberty Plaza in New York City. (Merrill Lynch opened a training center in late 1985 in Princeton, New Jersey.)

When Ted went there, he was very well prepared. He had received excellent scores on all of his tests. Before he went, he and I discussed strategies. I told him there were very fine research people there and gave him names of those people and told him he should develop relationships. And he did.

Leary noted that Chung was very good at establishing contacts with the Merrill people in New York:

Whenever he would go in to meet with a research person, he would bring them something to eat: coffees for both of them, and a doughnut or a bagel. He always made sure to call the person's secretary to find out how they took their coffee and any other preferences. After the meeting, he would send a note along with a little gift, such as a Merrill Lynch pen or cup. He had gone out and bought a whole slew of Merrill Lynch paraphernalia, and he used it effectively.

Bringing in the Big Account

After four months as trainees, FCs began the often arduous process of gaining clients. Most FCs spend their first months back from training making up to 200 cold calls a day. They also gave and attended seminars on personal investing, identifying clients who could benefit from their expertise. Chung, however, felt that the Taiwanese market had to be developed differently.

Ted felt that he could develop the Taiwanese market, but that it was a different market and had to be approached according to Taiwanese tradition. He assured me that in time he would develop very substantial accounts, but that he wouldn't do a lot of business in the beginning, opening what he called "chicken-feed" accounts. I said fine. This is a responsible person who wants to be successful. This is the game plan he wants to use, and it makes sense to me.

Unlike his peers, Chung did not make cold calls and spent much of his time outside of the office, attending events in the Taiwanese community. He felt that the way to develop the Taiwanese market was to increase his own visibility and prestige. In the first three months after he had completed his training, Chung had yet to open his first account. Leary became increasingly concerned about his lack of prospective clients and business. She met with him occasionally, and he reassured her that he was developing relationships that would lead to substantial accounts.

Over time, Leary was becoming more aware of Chung's stiff formality and need for privacy. Leary noted:

> Everything about his desk was spotless. He brought in all kinds of items from past lives, framed pictures of himself from magazines and other displays of his importance. No one was allowed to use his desk. People here can be a little touchy [about their desks], but he was really excessive. He didn't want people using his phone, he didn't want people working at his desk. Normally, an FC will have his desk the way he wants it, and if we are going to have someone else sit there, we usually do the person a courtesy and ask them. But sometimes you just can't. Nobody usually minds. . . . Once you sat at Ted's desk, nothing was an informal meeting. If I sat down there to chat with him, he'd get up and clear all of his papers away and arrange his coat and get everything all set before he would start to talk.

In his fourth month after training, Chung set the office buzzing by bringing in a $6 million account.

> I congratulated him, and we made sure that the account was set up properly. I then made calls to New York to three very good Merrill Lynch analysts and set up some private meetings to support him. I talked to him about the possibility of having the account managed by Merrill Lynch Asset Management, a Merrill Lynch subsidiary that manages substantial amounts of money. I was very uncomfortable with the idea of a brand-new FC handling that kind of money. He insisted the client only spoke Chinese, that there was no way he would allow anyone else to work with him. Chung said he had come to Merrill Lynch only because of him and the fact that they were from the same village in Taiwan. Chung insisted that he could do it.

Leary and her administrative manager, Fred Lewin, began watching the account closely. (The administrative manager is also the chief compliance officer at the branch.) At Leary's request, Chung wrote a letter, in Chinese, to the investor detailing a financial plan that Leary had approved. Chung proposed a conservative stock purchase plan and option-writing program with money (which was coming out of CDs [certificates of deposit] held at a local bank) equally distributed between equities and conservative fixed-income strategy. Leary commented:

> Initially, the investments were pretty good. His first five or six investments were appropriate; they were fixed income and good quality stocks. Then he began to get into takeover stocks. It was an explosive time in the market when takeover rumors about many stocks were booming. While most of the stocks he was purchasing had takeover rumors circulating about them, he initially made sure that the stock was still a Merrill Lynch–recommended security. The stocks Merrill recommends are fundamentally fine, well-managed companies, and have nothing to do with the rumor mill. But the direction he was going in was becoming clear. I'd see his purchases show up on the computer screen and call him in. He would swear, "No, no, no, he's buying it because it's good quality stock, love the earnings," et cetera.

More and more of the account was being invested in equities, and Chung actively used margin borrowing. He also began purchasing stocks not recommended by the Merrill Lynch research department. FCs were not allowed to recommend these stocks to their clients and could not buy them unless the purchases were unsolicited. After making non–Merrill-Lynch–recommended purchases, Chung presented typed, signed, certified letters to Leary from the client attesting that Chung had not suggested the stock and that the purchase order had come at the customer's insistence.

> When Chung's handling of the account departed from the initial strategy, I told Ted I would need to meet the customer. The customer, a Taiwanese industrialist, spoke little English. Chung brought the customer in, but it was a fairly uncomfortable meeting because our communication was limited. The customer smiled and indicated that he was pleased with Chung's work. Ted interceded after about five minutes and said the industrialist had to catch a plane. Translating for him, Chung told me the client had enjoyed meeting me and thanked me for my hospitality.

Leary was now checking Chung's trades every morning. The account was trading actively, and Chung had generated a substantial amount of commissions. Chung was careful to document all of his trading activity formally and to fulfill standard compliance procedures. As time went on, however, Chung became more annoyed with Leary and Lewin's monitoring. He resisted questioning and occasionally became angry at Lewin's inquiries.

The other FCs were very impressed with Chung's achievement. In handling the account, Chung had made some good trades and had followed compliance procedures. Although he had not brought in any other accounts, Chung hinted that additional substantial accounts were on the way. Leary commented:

> When the trades were good, I would call him in and tell him he was doing a good job. I also kept urging him to try to develop other areas. I was always available to him if he needed consultation, and I got him through to people in New York who could help him with the account. These were people most first-year FCs don't ever get to sit down with.

Back at Lunch

Following Chung's request for an office, Leary mentally reviewed the situation. She felt uncomfortable with several aspects of his performance, and the lunch was doing little to ease her worries. She did not know how involved Chung's client was with the account, and because of the language barrier and Chung's close relationship with the client, she could not check with the client more directly. Chung's growing displays of "ego and temper" also worried her. His request for a private office was totally inappropriate. Leary observed:

> It usually takes a person a substantial amount of time to get a private office here. They go to very special people who have really earned their spurs through a lot of good quality business and longevity with the firm. So while the FCs in the office were amazed

by the business Ted was doing, they also needed to think of the office as their family, where things were basically fair.

FCs frequently stated that they considered a private office an important success symbol and worked hard to achieve it. One private office was available, and Chung clearly had his eye on it.

Leary talked with Chung on numerous occasions about her expectations and about her views on how FCs should build their business. Chung never openly disagreed with her, but it was difficult to gauge exactly what he was thinking. Although she once had some qualms about Chung's slow start, he was now a strong producer (with this one account), and Leary knew that the Taiwanese market could be further developed. Leary wondered how she should respond to Chung's request, and what impact her answer would have on the rest of the office.

Notes

1. *Business Week*, January 16, 1984.
2. At large wirehouses, brokers received between 30% and 45% of the business they generated. Branch managers were compensated as a percentage of what the brokers they managed produced. Brokers prized relationships with large customers since over 80% of the commission dollars were produced by 20% of the customers.
3. *Compliance* is the name given to surveillance against broker fraud and to the maintenance of integrity in the brokerage industry.

CASE 6

Karen Leary (B)

Jaan Elias and Linda A. Hill

After Ted Chung asked for the vacant office, Leary could hardly conceal her surprise. However, she took a deep breath and explained that she considered a private office a reward not only for current production credits but also for consistent, long-term service to Merrill. She added that he had made an excellent start but that he needed to develop his business before she could consider his request. Chung nodded that he understood and little else was said during lunch.

The next morning, Leary, as usual, was in her office fielding questions and comments from the many FCs who dropped by. Chung also stopped by her office and requested a private meeting. Leary agreed and shut her office door. Chung then tendered his resignation saying that although he valued his tenure in Leary's branch of Merrill Lynch, he could not continue working there without a private office. He added that he expected to transfer to another Merrill Lynch office in the Chicago area.

Leary knew that it was not accepted practice to permit interbranch transfers at Merrill Lynch. As she talked with Chung, however, she decided not to mention this. "I wanted to see what was in his head," Leary explained, "because I was thinking about what I was building for the long term. I didn't want to be put in a position where I would have to fight fires with an uncontrollable person at every turn."

Leary responded, "Ted, let's be reasonable. I think you are making a mistake by threatening to leave because of this office." She then restated her position as expressed at the previous day's lunch: it was too soon for Chung to be given a private office. Leary explained that if he continued to develop his business, eventually he would be in line to receive his own office.

Chung insisted on immediate guarantees for the unoccupied office. He told Leary that he recognized his importance to the branch and to Merrill Lynch and that she would have to accept his demands. He added how much he desired to stay and expressed his admiration of Leary's management of the office. However, if she did not grant his request, he would be forced to transfer to a branch where his abilities were properly recognized.

Leary ended the 20-minute meeting by saying, "I'll think about it overnight." It was unclear whether Chung was directly challenging her authority or simply did not understand her reasoning.[1]

> I was looking for some kind of apology or recognition by Chung that he was overplaying his hand. But there wasn't even the hint of an apology. I gave him openings, thinking that this was the way he is accustomed to dealing with people and if we discussed it a bit, he would learn that he couldn't deal with the situation that way.

Note

1. Brokers at some financial service firms were known to test managers, to see if they could get additional resources, such as secretarial help.

II

Putting Policy
into Practice:
Selected
Operating Issues

GOING INTERNATIONAL

In keeping with the theme of putting policy into practice, this book's primary focus is on the process of implementing strategic or policy decisions and operating in foreign environments to achieve the intended results of those decisions. Putting strategy or policy into practice is not a simple or automatic process but, rather, one filled with details and, often, problems. Proper implementation requires time, effort, planning, and thought.

There are many ways of organizing to conduct business internationally. Firms can import or export products or they can license foreign companies to produce their products. As a company seeks to develop its own operations in other countries, it has a range of options — from sales offices to manufacturing plants. If it wants to retain control it may choose to use wholly owned subsidiaries or it can opt to give up some ownership control and enter into joint ventures with local firms or even alliances with other foreign firms.

Costs and benefits are associated with each of these operating modes and ownership structures.[1] The costs to be considered usually include capital, management time and commitment, impact on strategy, and the cost of enforcing agreements. Some benefits include repatriation of profits, political security, contribution to parent company knowledge, and local distribution capability.

The existence of these potential costs and benefits suggests that the rational manager will weigh them in coming to his or her decision and choose the "right" one. However, what appears to be a rational, straightforward process may not work in practice. In some circumstances, managers may not have a choice, as suggested by theory, and the decision may, in effect, be made for them. For example, many developing countries want investment and employment, just as we do in North America, and simply exporting products to them may not be a long-term option. Some countries may require joint ventures with local partners so that there will also be local ownership to the industrial capacity of the country and a transfer of technology. In developing countries, such as China, the joint venture process is controlled and the firm may have a government partner. However, the majority of developing countries are market economies and, although they may require some amount of local ownership, firms can choose a local partner for a joint venture or find other ways of providing for local ownership.

Once the decision has been made for a firm to initiate international operations, to expand its international activities, or to change its mode of operations, the issues become ones of implementation and action. Someone has to travel to another country to negotiate a contract, arrange a distributorship, or to work with people from another culture to make a project or joint venture a reality. Once a person leaves the office to negotiate the contract in Europe or to start up the plant in Southeast Asia, what really takes place? Assuming that a joint venture has been decided upon, for example, there are a lot of questions to ask and issues to be faced before it becomes a reality. How does one choose a partner? Where does one look? What characteristics should a partner have? What are one's expectations? What are the potential partner's expectations? The reading, "Partner Selection Criteria for Developed Country Joint Ventures," provides some excellent insights into these issues.

Very often costs are underestimated at the start of the project and do not become apparent until later, when they outweigh the expected benefits. The authors believe that North Americans, in particular, have a tendency to overestimate the benefits and to underestimate the costs of doing business internationally. When the true costs become apparent, a firm begins to learn whether or not it has the commitment and staying power to carry on.

For example, in establishing joint ventures, particularly in developing countries, managers often make some common mistakes. One is that the emphasis is likely to be placed on the "visible" inputs to the decision and the "tangible" aspects of the business. These visible inputs include the legal structure of the venture, the financial considerations of ownership and pro forma operating statements, and the market analyses — all the things managers, and specialists like lawyers and accountants, learned in school and deal with daily. These are important considerations and need to be given careful thought, but they are not the only considerations.

There are many operational issues to be considered in establishing a joint venture that go beyond the legal and economic ones. The "invisible," "intangible," or "nonquantifiable" components of the venture are often ignored or overlooked. Issues like trust, commitment, and partners' expectations are overlooked, possibly because these are not usually part of the manager's prior training. The operating and relationship issues involved may not be given careful thought in advance and may be left to be solved as problems arise. Relationships, in particular, are worthy of special note. Often in North America, relationships are viewed as instrumental, as a means to ends, if they are thought of at all in a business context. In contrast, throughout much of the world outside the United States and Canada, relationships are valued in themselves. They form a basis of trust and linkage upon which a business activity might be built. Given such striking differences in outlook on relationships, it is not surprising that partnership problems are one of the most frequently cited reasons for failure.[2] The situation is analogous to an iceberg in that approximately one-ninth of it is visible above the water's surface, and eight-ninths is below the surface. The results of not knowing what is hidden can be disastrous for ships, and for companies.

Behrman and Grosse suggest that what really distinguishes international business from domestic business is *cross-cultural differences* and the different policies and operations of local *governments* that exercise their soveignty differently than the home country government, or governments of other countries in which the multinational is operating.[3]

Perspectives about operating in foreign environments need to be expanded from primarily conceptual, economic, and cost-benefit orientations to include an understanding of an organization's relationship to and involvement with the local culture — including the social, political, and governmental institutions and processes. Understanding this "social interaction" dimension of international business is important because it has a direct impact on implementation and operating effectiveness. As such, it needs to be considered in any analysis.

This social interaction dimension is not a new dimension of international business or of operating abroad, but rather another perspective that increases one's comprehension of what it really takes to do business internationally. It offers an essential view of constraints and realities that become encapsulated in operating costs including management time, organizational commitment, and the costs associated with enforcing agreements.

STRUCTURES AND SYSTEMS

Once firms have internationalized and have subsidiaries abroad, executives face decisions about how to structure their organization. Typical structures include the international division, product or project, geographical (regional), and transnational or matrix, which combines regional and product foci. Each of these structures has its strengths and weaknesses, and would be appropriate for different situations. The two main factors to be considered are the pressures to be responsive to the local country and culture (localization), and the forces pushing toward global integration (globalization).

Crookell has identified three of the globalization pressures: declining tariffs and easier world trade; international communications, which have led to similar tastes in some products and international standards for these products; and easier international coordination due, again, to modern communication systems.[4] On the other side of the scale are the pressures for localization: nontariff barriers, foreign exchange shortages, cultural differences that influence consumer tastes and preferences even as some products become global, and flexible production technology that reduces the cost advantage of large-scale production while permitting greater local customization. This book does not attempt to pursue an exposition of the advantages and disadvantages of each structure in detail. There are many books on international organization and organization design that cover these issues comprehensively.[5]

Beyond considering the strategic advantages or disadvantages of the various structural forms a company can use, one needs to recognize the cultural values and assumptions upon which these structures may be based. Organizational structures are not free from the influence of culture. Each structure carries with it identifiable assumptions about the legitimacy of certain practices and relationships and defines the locus of authority, responsibility, and basis of power differently. Each legitimizes a different pattern of communications and interaction. In addition to fitting certain competitive situations or product characteristics, some structures may be more acceptable than others in a given culture, as some may require behavior and interactions that are inappropriate in that culture. In Part I, the article "Motivation, Leadership, and Organization: Do American Theories Apply Abroad?" provides some insights into the impact of cultural differences on organizational structures.

Laurent also has investigated the relationship between culture and organizational structure.[6] He believes that attempts to communicate alternative management processes and structures to managers will fail unless the "implicit management gospels" that they carry in their heads are addressed. He became convinced of this when he was trying to explain matrix organizations to French managers to whom the idea of reporting to two bosses was "so alien that mere consideration of such organizing principles was an impossible, useless exercise."

The proposition that guided Laurent's research was that the national origin of managers significantly affected their views of what they considered proper management. His research uncovered differences in the basic conception of organization and found that these differences clustered by nationality. He demonstrated differences on four dimensions of organization: organizations as political systems, authority systems, role-formalization systems, and hierarchical-relationship systems. In another study comparing French and American managers, the results indicated that the two groups held very different views regarding structure.[7] Americans held an instrumental conception of structure while the French held a social conception. A comparison of these two views is presented in Table 1.

In addition to structure, there are a large number of systems that companies employ to manage their people and operations. These include evaluation and reward systems, selection and development systems, and reporting systems. Negotiating styles, decision making, and management styles are also important components of the management process. As with structure, each system or preferred behavioral

---

TABLE 1   **Two Views of Organization[8]**

Instrumental	*Social*
1. Positions are defined in terms of tasks.	Positions are defined in terms of social status and authority.
2. Relationships between positions are defined as being ordered in any way instrumental to achieving organizational objectives.	Relationships defined as being ordered by a hierarchy.
3. Authority is impersonal, rational, and comes from role or function. It can be challenged for rational reasons.	Authority comes from status. It can extend beyond the function and cannot be challenged on rational grounds.
4. Superior-subordinate relationships are defined as impersonal and implying equality of persons involved. Subordination is the acceptance of the impersonal, rational, and legal order of the organization.	Superior-subordinate relationships are personal implying superiority of one person over the other. Subordination is loyalty and deference to the superior.
5. Goal attainment has primacy over power acquisition.	Achievement of objectives is secondary to the acquisition of power.

style has its own set of cultural assumptions on which it is based. The Kluckhohn and Strodtbeck framework and the Hofstede framework (presented in Part I) both highlight some of the cultural underpinnings of management systems and styles.

An important decision facing management in international operations is whether existing systems, structures, and styles can be transferred from one culture to another, or whether they must be changed and adapted in some way when they appear to be in conflict with the norms of another culture.

The answer is not always to change a system or structure, however. Sometimes people in another culture simply need to be trained to use a system. Neither is the answer always to assume that training is all that is needed. Each response has a proper time and place. The decision should be the result of careful, informed judgment based on understanding the cultural biases of the systems and the cultural norms of the country in which the operations are located. Are there rules? Not really, but careful analysis can help sort out the issues and help managers solve the problem. Questions such as "How important is it that we do it identically to the way it's done at home?" can guide one's decisions. It may not be important that the procedures be exactly the same; rather, results may be more important. Just because it's the way headquarters does it, or wants it done, does not mean that it is right for a different cultural environment. What is important is the outcome.[9]

Systems and structures are *tools* to help managers do their job. They are not, nor should they be, ends in themselves. They are culturally determined tools in their assumptions about human motivation and behavior. When they become ends in themselves, they often become barriers to effective performance. This is true in one's own culture and even more so when they are in conflict with the values and beliefs of other cultures.

PEOPLE

The authors believe that firms fail abroad not because their strategy or structures necessarily were wrong, but because the operating plan may have been ill conceived, or executives may not have been prepared thoroughly, resulting in poor implementation. Failure may come when executives are sent overseas and are not able to understand the new culture or to function in their new environment. In Part I, frameworks for thinking about the interactions of people from two or more cultures were presented. The readings, text, and cases showed how different assumptions could lead to different conclusions, and possibly, to conflict.

In a period of globalization, even more businesspeople are going to be interacting in more complex ways with people from other cultures. Expatriates employed in a foreign subsidiary will be working with host country nationals at many levels in the organization and, most likely, from government. Headquarters personnel will interact with local country managers and staff members from other cultures as headquarters and regional offices become more "international." Preparation for these cross-cultural encounters is important, since the costs of failure can be high, either in terms of lost contracts and sales, or in out-of-pocket costs like premature returns from long-term assignments.

The reading "Expatriate Selection, Training and Career Pathing: A Review and Critique" points out two dimensions of "cultural exposure," degree of integration and duration of stay. The integration dimension represents the intensity of the exposure. A person could be sent to a foreign country on a short-term, technical, troubleshooting matter and experience little significant contact with the local culture. On the other hand, a person could be in Japan for only a brief visit to negotiate a contract, but the cultural interaction could be very intense and require a great deal of cultural fluency to be successful. Similarly, an expatriate assigned abroad for a period of years is likely to experience a high degree of interaction with the local culture from living there.

Estimates of expatriate failure rate run between 20 and 50 percent, and the average cost per failure to the parent company ranges from $55,000 to $150,000[10]. Careful selection and preparation of expatriates for their foreign assignments should be high priority issues for multinationals. Unfortunately, this is not always the case.

North American companies went through a period of reducing the number of expatriates they sent overseas because of the expense associated with relocating them and their families. Their salaries are usually higher than those of local managers, and they usually receive benefits to make a move abroad attractive. Benefits often include items like housing or housing allowance, moving expenses, tax equalization, and schooling for children. Many of these benefits are not usually provided to local employees.

Now corporations must reconsider their human resource management policies, including expatriation, in light of globalization. Cross-cultural understanding and experience are essential in today's business environment, and foreign assignments can be a critical part of a manager's development. The reading "International Strategy from the Perspective of People and Culture: The North American Context" addresses the issues to be faced in international human resource management in the coming years. Sending expatriates abroad is not as simple as it once was. Most countries are concerned about the employment of their own people and work permits are usually required for expatriates.

An increasingly important decision to be considered by North American companies is the international assignments of female managers. This has become an issue as more women have graduated from business schools and decided that they want international careers. The reading "Pacific Basin Managers: A Gaijin, Not a Woman" focuses on this subject and calls into serious question some of the myths about barriers to women working internationally.

When a firm operates in a foreign environment, it is not just expatriate policies that comprise the human resource management issues. There are local laws governing the hiring and firing of employees that may be unfamiliar to the firm. There could be substantial financial ramifications for firing a person. Consistent with the culture-general orientation adopted in this book, the specifics of various laws will not be covered here. Whether it will cost two years' salary if a person is fired, or six months' salary, is not the issue. The specifics of laws of all countries are subject to continual change. What is important is that the firm recognizes that such laws exist and that these laws are significant constraints on management discretion. A manager in a foreign country has to know the laws governing personnel practices.

In some countries, hiring quotas — laws requiring the hiring of people of specified ethnic or racial backgrounds — may be in force. These laws are similar in concept to the affirmative action laws in North America. Usually, these quotas have high political sensitivity and significant impact on foreign corporations that are guests in the host country. What does the manager do when the best person for the job is from a particular group, but he or she cannot hire any more people from that group? How does one manage in this situation? Does the manager try to avoid the issue, ignore it, procrastinate, actively recruit — and at what cost? How does the manager maintain cooperation and discipline in an organization when employees come from distinct subgroups that historically have been adversaries?

Where quotas exist, corporations usually are under pressure to employ local people not just at low levels, but in the higher managerial ranks as well. In a number of countries, serious localization pressures are experienced. What is the firm's plan for building local management capacity? How is the firm going to carry out this plan? What price is the firm prepared to pay? The firm's answers to these questions, and its localization policy can significantly contribute to success or failure in a foreign environment.

The use of local managers has increased. In many developing countries, larger pools of better-educated management talent are appearing. In developed countries, where sufficient management talent exists, there are employment and immigration laws with which a firm must comply. In all cases, to attract competent local management, a firm has to offer competitive wages, benefits, working conditions, development, and advancement opportunities.

Finally, interpersonal differences and the potential for conflict exist, not just between expatriates and locals, but also between local groups based on ethnic, tribal, language, or religious differences. The citizenry of many countries is not homogeneous in terms of culture, language, and religion. However, an outsider naively may believe that the inhabitants of a country think and behave similarly. Such conflict between local people is apparent in countries of South and Southeast Asia, Africa, the Middle East, and parts of the Americas.

The cases in this part of the book will put the reader in management positions where he or she must deal with many of the issues discussed above and will have to make decisions about how to respond to these problems. The reader will experience managing intercultural relations in the workplace between expatriates and locals, and also between locals themselves; trying to maintain discipline and managing interpersonal conflict among members of local subgroups; and facing government pressure to increase the number of local managers in an organization. The cases will provide insight into initiating and managing international ventures.

The cases in Part I of the book, and in this part, present seemingly difficult problems. However, they essentially are normal business issues compounded by cultural differences and government policies: geographical expansion, accounting systems, reward systems, interdepartmental and interpersonal conflict, an overseas assignment, conducting a consulting assignment, and establishing joint ventures. As a manager or potential manager, whether in the field or at headquarters, one may face problems of implementing one's business practices in situations of cultural and political diversity. Prior thought and carefully considered policies will make operations run more smoothly.

▬ MANAGING IN SITUATIONS
▬ OF ADVERSITY

In addition to dealing with "normal" operating problems under relatively "normal" conditions, executives also find themselves managing under conditions of considerable tension that usually reflect historical events and cultural factors of a given country or region. Many countries experience some form of social turmoil that could translate into threats against corporate assets, or into physical dangers to employees and, possibly, their families.

Security problems related to criminal activity are a reality in many large cities in both developed and developing countries. Countries in the developing world, particularly, are often thought of as being less safe than North America. Some people may ascribe this condition to poverty and to large income differentials between the "have's" and "have not's" in those countries. Similar conditions prevail in North America, but North Americans tend not to notice them. It would be difficult to convince two couples, friends from Kenya, who were robbed and assaulted in New York City, that the United States is safer than Kenya.

However, problems with security may be more pronounced in developing countries. Expatriates usually are more visible and are well off financially. As such, they are more obvious targets, or come to perceive that they are singled out as targets. There is a social dynamic that contributes to this perception. News spreads through the expatriate grapevine quickly when problems occur. Also, newspapers are more likely to report crimes against the high-status, highly visible expatriates. And embassy officials may complain about security problems publicly, which makes news.

One consequence often is an exaggerated sense of separation on the part of expatriates. By developing a dichotomous viewpoint of "we" (the expatriates) versus "them" (the local people), expatriates may create a barrier to adaptation in addition to the ones that already exist. There may be a tendency to become more insular and isolated. Expatriates may develop increasingly negative attitudes toward the local population that hinder their adaptation to the country and culture. If corporate executives must interact with local people as part of their jobs, such attitudes may impair their effectiveness in establishing good relationships. If a negative, insular attitude develops in an executive's family, then this attitude will continually press on the executive and may impact his or her effectiveness.

Terrorism can be a concern. Politically motivated terrorists have committed murders and bombed airports, airplanes, and buildings in developed and developing countries. Executives of major companies like Renault and Deutsche Bank have been assassinated in Europe. These executives were perceived as being representatives of their corporations, and these corporations were identified as specific targets. Reports of incidents like these a few years ago by North American media contributed to the perception that Europe was not safe and led to mass cancellations of prearranged holidays in Europe. As unfortunate and despicable as these acts are, those who have lived in France or Germany are not likely to let these acts cloud their perceptions of these countries as civilized and safe countries in which to live and do business.

North Americans, generally, are not accustomed to political violence or terrorism, nor are people in many other countries, and they are shocked and scared by it. Violence in North America tends to be criminal in nature rather than political. People may lack experience in or knowledge about other countries and, coupled with unbalanced media reports, develop distorted perceptions. The media tends to report acts of violence and terrorism and these situations grab attention. They are news. If all one ever hears about a particular country is reports about bombings, killings, starvation, and political scandals, one most likely will develop a distorted view of that country.

These things happen in North America, too. However, when they do occur, people put them in perspective. They see these acts as localized and isolated incidents that are exceptions of the rule. This is known from day-to-day experience living in Canada or the United States, for example. However, this perspective is often missing when people read a newspaper or watch television in North America and learn of events in other countries. North Americans may lack the contextual information that enables them to weigh an occurrence relative to normal events in another country.

Companies also operate in countries experiencing social unrest, coup d'états, and even full-scale wars. The physical threat to employees is obvious. It is clearly more dangerous to work in countries where civil wars are in progress than it is to work in Toronto or Boston.

There are many reasons for unrest. In some countries there are separatist movements; in other countries there may be language, religious, or tribal differences. The unrest may stem from economic conditions — some people have a lot and others have nothing. Beyond economic disparity, there are other reasons for strife, such as differing political philosophies like extreme right- and left-wing ideologies vying for control of a country. Whatever the reason, there are numerous countries experiencing social turmoil.

Recently there was hope that the world was becoming a better and easier place in which to live and to do business. China had opened up to the rest of the world, Mikhail Gorbachev was espousing perestroika and glasnost, the Cold War had ended and countries in Eastern Europe were permitted to decide their own destiny, Germany was reunited, Nelson Mandela had been released from prison in South Africa, and Iran and Iraq had ended a long, bloody war. Then suddenly, the situation changed. There was the massacre at Tiananmen Square. Now, as this section is being written, the Soviet Union is facing massive internal disruptions and the possibility of civil war has been raised by some observers. Yugoslavia appears to be disintegrating and a number of other Eastern countries face similar problems of ethnic-based tensions. The Persian Gulf War has ended, but tension and uncertainty remain in the Middle East. India has significant religious differences that have flared up again and are tearing at the country. As one looks at a list of troubled countries, one could say, "Well, obviously North Americans should do business only in North America, Europe, and Japan."

It is interesting to note that countries such as China and the Soviet Union became "darlings" for investment by foreign companies. Then, when the political climate changed in China, for example, companies started to leave. Will it happen in the Soviet Union also? And what about Eastern Europe where Western companies have been scrambling to get a piece of the action?

The authors believe that international business is a long-term proposition and activity. Companies cannot succeed internationally by jumping in and out of countries when the going gets a little tough. Not only is it expensive, but customers and government officials remember when they were deserted.

Many countries could be considered impossible places in which to do business — bad risks. However, not all of them may be as bad as they appear from a distance and some of them may present good business opportunities. The more one learns about other countries, the better one understands the risks involved in those countries. This enables better decisions to be made about entering a certain country and the steps necessary to manage the risks in that country.

The following story illustrates this well. One of the authors was having dinner with the president of a British bank's Canadian subsidiary and was describing some of his activities in East Africa to the bank president. The bank president commented about how risky it was to operate in Africa. This comment surprised the author, who understood the difficulties involved but had thought it possible to manage them. The bank president then described all the countries in South America in which the bank was operating and making money. To the author, South America had to be one of the riskiest places to operate and he said so. The bank president replied, "Not really; the bank has been there for a long time and we understand the situation." Therein lies the moral: Familiarity and understanding of a country provide the necessary perspective for accurately assessing risks, determining acceptable levels of risk, and managing those risks.

It seems that companies can make two major mistakes when dealing with difficult environments. The first is entering a country for the wrong reason ("It's going to be easy"), and the second is leaving it for the wrong reason ("It's a lot more difficult to work there than we first figured"). One must have a realistic attitude toward difficult situations and learn to live and work in a world of uncertainty and risk. Companies need to have strategic and tactical plans for managing those risks. Also, as corporations face decisions about whether or not to operate in some of these difficult countries and regions, a strategic philosophy is needed. A global viewpoint, an understanding of the culture, political situations and risks, and a long-term commitment to international operations are essential.

It is advocated that large companies develop specialists in assessing such risks to contribute to informed decision making, and that others access specialist firms or consultants for information relevant to specific decisions. Companies also are advised to listen to expatriates and locals working in the field to provide systematic assessments of their environments as part of the normal business plan required periodically by head office. Individual managers can add to the quality of their own decision making by reading broadly, understanding the history of regions in which they operate, and by seeking and paying attention to information from international field personnel. As globalization increases, more international representation in the senior ranks of corporate headquarters personnel may increase the ability to assess country risks.

Not all management problems are associated with war and violence. There may be situations in which a new regime has come into power, not necessarily by coup d'état, and that regime has a very different orientation towards foreign enterprises and their responsibilities to the host country than the corporations operating there have. In these situations, nationalization of assets and corporations can take place. What is the right response to this situation? The authors have heard of one company that had its operations in South America nationalized and then got them back. It then went through a second full cycle of nationalization and return. Although the company contested and fought the actions as best it could, their attitude was one of patience, knowing that these things happen and that, eventually, the regime would change and the assets would be returned. This company has had a real commitment to international business and a long-term perspective, both of which have contributed to their unusual success.

There is a range of possible perspectives on, and orientations to, these difficult situations. At one extreme there is the cavalier attitude. Ignore them—"There won't be any problems for me; it's no big deal!" Another extreme is the "Fortress North America attitude." Stay at home—"We have a good market; we're making money and growing. Who needs all those problems?" Neither extreme is realistic. The proactive, positive leadership and a long-term approach are probably the most appropriate orientations for the future.

We live in a small world—a "global village." Even if North Americans choose not to do business in another country, it is quite clear that corporations from countries with strong global orientations are penetrating North American domestic markets. How does one combat that reality? Drawing the wagons into a tight circle will not work any more. A company has to get into the world and compete in the global marketplace with all the associated risks, be they financial or physical.

International business is different from domestic business and those differences must be understood. It's not something a corporation, or manager, should jump into casually. The costs of entering the game can be high. But the experience can be rewarding financially for the corporation, and personally and professionally for the manager.

Notes

1. Raymond Vernon and Louis T. Wells, Jr., *Manager in the International Economy* (Englewood Cliffs, N.J.: Prentice Hall, 5th Edition, 1986, 21.
2. Paul W. Beamish, *Multinational Joint Ventures in Developing Countries* (London: Routledge, 1988); Henry W. Lane and Paul W. Beamish, "Cross-cultural Cooperative Behav-

ior in Joint Ventures in LDC's," *Management International Review* (Special Issue 1990): 87–102.

3. "Toward a Theory of International (vs. Domestic) Business," Jack N. Behrman and Robert Grosse; paper presented before the Academy of International Business, San Diego, October 1988.

4. Harold Crookell, "Organization Structure for Global Operations," Chapter 6 in *International Management: Text and Cases*; Paul W. Beamish, J. Peter Killing, Donald J. Lecraw, and Harold Crookell (Homewood, Ill.: Richard D. Irwin, 1991).

5. See for example, *Managing Across Borders: The Transnational Solution*, C. A. Bartlett and S. Ghosal (Boston: Harvard Business School Press, 1989); and C. K. Prahalad and Y. L. Doz, *The Multinational Mission: Balancing Local Demands and Global Vision* (New York: The Free Press, 1987).

6. Andre Laurent, "The Cultural Diversity of Western Conceptions of Management," *International Studies of Management & Organization* 13, No. 1–2 (1983): 75–96.

7. Giorgio Inzerilli and Andre Laurent, "Managerial Views of Organization Structure in France and the USA," *International Studies of Management & Organization* 13, No. 1–2 (1983): 97–118.

8. Ibid.

9. This statement is a good example of the North American instrumental orientation.

10. Mark E. Mendenhall, Edward Dunbar, and Gary R. Oddou, "Expatriate Selection, Training and Career Pathing: A Review and Critique," *Human Resource Management* 26, No. 3 (Fall 1987).

READING 5

Partner Selection Criteria for Developed Country Joint Ventures

J. Michael Geringer

Selecting partners with compatible skills is not necessarily synonymous with selecting compatible partners. This article identifies and discusses several criteria executives may employ when evaluating suitability of partners for joint ventures with a long-term, non-transitional orientation.

A small technology company, although it is real we will call it Alpha Inc. to conceal its real identity, developed an advanced design for a piece of computer equipment. Lacking the manufacturing and marketing acumen as well as the financial muscle necessary to commercialize this breakthrough rapidly, Alpha's managers decided to seek assistance via a joint venture (JV). They approached several firms and, after painstakingly analyzing the technical compatibility between their own and prospective partners' companies, agreed to venture with one of the industry's dominant firms. Their decision was announced amidst great fanfare — press releases, a companywide celebration, champagne. Analysts lauded the decision and predicted spectacular results. Alpha's stock nearly doubled in value.

Another success story from the Silicon Valley, right? Wrong! Within a year the JV was dissolved, Alpha's stock price tumbled and the executives who help set up the venture had departed for greener pastures. What happened? According to survivors of this debacle, the JV confronted problems from the start. Because of differences in the partners' sizes and management styles, members of the JV teams constantly complained of an inability to work together. Managers from Alpha, accustomed to making quick decisions and then acting upon them, were frustrated by the slow moving bureaucracy of their larger partner. Alpha's designs were repeatedly, and their employees thought unnecessarily, subjected to modifications by the partner's researchers. Product introduction was delayed by several months when the partner unexpectedly transferred several critical personnel to another project.

Reprinted by permission of the *Business Quarterly*, published by The Western Business School, The University of Western Ontario, London, Canada, Vol. 53, No. 1 (Summer 1988).

Complaints to the partner's headquarters frequently appeared to be ignored. To make matters worse, the delays enabled a competitor to beat them to the market with a similar product.

Alpha's managers had not adequately considered the differences between selecting a partner with compatible skills and selecting a compatible partner. They had wanted to establish a JV which would achieve corporate objectives, but this meant different things to the two firms.

The Alpha example is especially insightful because a surprising number of managers do not sufficiently probe the issue of compatibility between their own and prospective partners' companies. They think they are building a strong relationship — but they are not. Establishing a lasting JV relationship is a complex endeavor, and compatibility between partners is only one variable influencing that process. Yet, although selecting a compatible partner may not always result in a successful JV, selection of an incompatible partner virtually guarantees that venture performance will be unsatisfactory.

Previous studies have devoted most of their attention to motivations for forming a JV and managing the venture once it is established. In contrast, this article identifies and discusses several criteria executives should employ when evaluating a company's suitability as a long term JV partner. The discussion is based primarily on a series of interviews with over 100 senior corporate executives regarding the JV experiences of their firms.[1] Overall, these executives had been intimately involved in identifying and selecting partners for more than 300 JVs.

Defining a set of criteria for selecting the "right" partner is roughly analogous to telling a person how to pick the "right" spouse — certainly a difficult, if not an impossible, proposition. Selection of a partner who will be compatible in the long term, rather than for a short-term, transitional "fling" is a complex and individualistic endeavor. Yet, there seem to be common elements to many JVs and experiences of other managers provide guidelines for selecting partners with long-term potential. Several considerations regarding selection criteria — including complementarity of technical skills and resources; mutual need; financial capability; relative size; complementarity of strategies and operating policies; communication barriers; compatible management teams; and trust and commitment between partners — are discussed below.

SEEK COMPLEMENTARY TECHNICAL SKILLS AND RESOURCES

The primary selection criterion should be a potential partner's ability to provide the technical skills and resources which complement those of the firm seeking the partner. If prospective partners cannot provide these capabilities, then formation of a JV is a questionable proposition. Therefore, technical complementarity should be viewed as a *minimum* qualification for selecting a partner.

Technical complementarity is determined by analyzing the key success factors — those few areas strongly influencing competitive position and performance — confronting the proposed JV. Evaluation of your firm's current and anticipated future competitive position relative to these factors should then be performed. Areas where deficiencies exist can serve as the basis for assessing technical complementarity of a partner. However, the analysis should identify more than merely a financial deficiency; such resources may often be accessed via other options which will not entail the extensive managerial involvement of a partner. Although initially appealing, a JV based solely on a partner's financial contributions is unlikely to foster long-term compatibility.

Technical complementarity can assume many forms. A common alliance consists of one parent's supplying technology and another's furnishing marketing capabilities. For example, a U.S. medical equipment firm wanted to expand sales of its product line to Europe. Due to its small size and limited name recognition, however, the company was apprehensive about trying to penetrate the European market on its own. Instead, it sought assistance from a JV partner. Strategic analysis of the proposed investment suggested the partner must be a recognized player in the medical supplies industry, have substantial financial and marketing resources, and embody the technological sophistication necessary to demonstrate the technical advantages of the American firm's products. Companies not satisfying these criteria were rejected as possible co-venturers.

MUTUAL DEPENDENCY: A NECESSARY EVIL

Seeking a partner with complementary technical skills and resources can permit each partner to concentrate resources in those areas where it possesses the greatest relative competence while diversifying into attractive but unfamiliar business arenas. Rather than intensifying weaknesses, JVs can thus be a means of creating strengths. Many managers view dependency on other organizations as undesirable, however, and have avoided such situations when possible. Yet, with proper matching, both partners should perceive a vested interest in keeping the JV working rather than resorting to some non-JV form of investment. There should be some identifiable mutual need, with each partner supplying unique capabilities or resources critical to JV success. When one partner is strong in areas where the other is weak, and vice versa, mutual respect is fostered and second-guessing and conflict can be mitigated. (See Figure 1.)

There should be a "middle level" of dependency between partners. If the level of dependency is too small, the JV is unlikely to survive difficult times. Yet, too much dependency, such as when small firms enter JVs with much larger partners, may prove unstable because of potential consequences of loss of a partner. A small firm might feel insecure, since it may be unable to fully exploit a market opportunity by itself, or only at a much slower rate and greater risk. In addition, as with the Alpha example, association with a prominent partner may influence the smaller firm's stock price. This is particularly worrisome if later termination of the JV is attributed to unsuccessful commercialization of the smaller firm's technology. While the larger firm may emerge relatively unscathed, JV termination might severely disable the small firm by causing customers, employees, and the stock market to question the firm's viability. The resulting damage to its reputation could cause

FIGURE 1 **Prospects for Long-Term Joint Venture Survival**

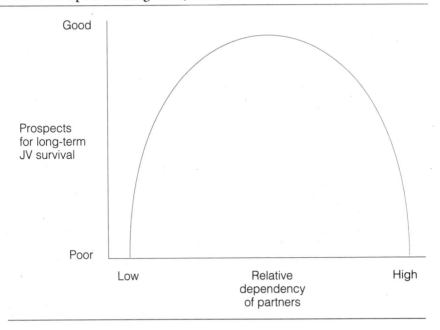

a precipitous decline in its stock value, harm morale, and limit the available strategic options.

Painful lessons about relative dependency of partners were learned by several firms which, in the late 1970s and early 1980s, formed JVs with Asian firms as a means of rapidly accessing cheap labor or new markets. Frequently Canadian and United States corporations contributed initial technology and capital and trained their partners in the intricacies of running the business. Several ventures were subsequently dissolved and the partners used the newly acquired capabilities against their former allies.

Numerous options are available to help ensure that partners will continue to perceive themselves as mutually dependent. One method is to establish some means of "exchanging hostages." For instance, the JV agreement might stipulate that a unilateral decision to break up the corporate marriage prematurely will result in a substantial charge of some sort, "alimony" payments if you will, as well as covenants against engaging in competing activities within a specified time period. The agreement might also guarantee cross purchases of specified volumes of products or services by the partners. This option can reduce the impact of a break-up upon a more-dependent firm by guaranteeing access to critical raw materials or sales revenues during the painful readjustment period. By employing techniques such as these, threats posed by dependency on a partner can be reduced substantially.

AVOID "ANCHORS"

When contemplating a JV, be sure the prospective partner can generate sufficient financial resources to maintain the venture's efforts. Managers frequently note their avoidance of potential "anchors" — partners likely to slow venture growth and development due to inability or unwillingness to provide their share of the funding. As the executive vice president of a major manufacturing concern remarked, "Partners will almost always have differences of opinion regarding expansion. A small company may have fewer financial resources available for shouldering its portion of an expansion or have to pay a higher financing rate than does the larger partner. This can not only cause operating problems, but might also result in some bruised egos, which can further intensify the difficulties."

A firm's inability to fulfill its financial commitments, due to small size, financial difficulties in its other operations, or existence of different discount rates and time horizons, can create turmoil for its partner. Particularly in the JV's early stages when large negative cash flows are most common, the presence of an "anchor" can jeopardize an entire project. Commenting on his company's experiences, a division vice president noted, "The JV was functioning quite smoothly and was meeting or surpassing both companies' projections until the financial demands exceeded (the other firm's) capabilities . . . Resulting animosities ultimately caused the venture to be dissolved."

Although not always possible to identify, several symptoms might indicate potential "anchors." The vice president–international of a large multinational suggested, "You have to look at the partner's balance sheet and ask: 'Is it a financially solid company?' You have to look at their plans for growth and their profit orientation. Is there a difference in the strategic importance placed on the JV's activities? Is the partner likely to encounter financial problems in one or more divisions? If so, what will be the effect upon other activities of the partner, especially the JV?"

A partner's resource constraints can constitute a significant hurdle to establishment of a successful JV. If precautions are observed, however, a partner with meager financial resources need not prevent JV formation or yield premature buyout or termination, especially when insufficient financial contributions are not due to financial insolvency. For example, the agreement may include penalties if either partner attempts to sidestep its financial obligations. To reduce perceived inequities resulting from disparities in financial contributions, the agreement might dictate that shareholdings or payouts be contingent upon each partner's contributions. The agreement might also stipulate that a firm can not engage in similar activities for a specified time period. These types of mechanisms can reduce undesirable effects of an "anchor" upon JV activities.

RELATIVE COMPANY SIZE: THE ELEPHANT AND THE ANT COMPLEX

Although exceptions are numerous, JVs often have the best chance of long-term success if both parties are comparable in sophistication and size, preferably large. If a small firm decides to enter a JV with a similarly-sized partner, the firms may magnify each other's weaknesses. This is less often the case between two large firms, which are likely to have similar values and control systems, similar tolerances for losses, and similar appetites for risk. Crises are less common in large firms, particularly in regard to short-term cash flow. Thus, larger companies typically offer greater "staying power," being able to commit a greater volume of resources over a longer time horizon.

Yet, sometimes JVs between firms of different sizes seem warranted. A smaller firm with innovative technology may venture with a large corporation which offers the financial and marketing clout necessary to commercialize that technology, as with the Alpha example. Similarly, Nike, an innovative designer of athletic shoes, teamed up with Nissho Iwai, Japan's sixth-largest trading company. And in 1978, Advanced Micro Devices, with $62 million in sales, formed a JV with Siemens, West Germany's largest electrical company, to produce a line of microcomputer systems and related products.

When size differences are significant, dubbed "the elephant and the ant complex" by an executive, managers must be aware of problems which could result. One frequently voiced concern is the possible domination of one firm over the other, as addressed earlier during discussion of mutual need. A related problem is that partners' different operational environments and corporate cultures might appear incompatible. For instance, the bureaucratic environment of many large firms, with a relatively slow decision-making apparatus and a voracious appetite for information gathering and analysis, contrasts sharply with the more entrepreneurial and quick-response orientation characteristic of small firms. A small firm, accustomed to reacting within short time frames, can feel paralyzed by the seemingly glacial pace at which the larger company operates. Yet, the small firm's prodding and sense of urgency may make the large partner nervous. The large company might interpret its smaller partner's Spartan environment and informality as indicative of a fly-by-night operation. In addition, the larger firm could perceive that it bears most or all of the risk—educating a sales force and customers about a new product's features; assuming responsibility for warehousing, distribution, or production; lending credibility to the product; and enhancing the prestige and financial status of the smaller firm. In response to its partner's impatience, the larger firm may exercise even greater caution, further exacerbating the problem.

Differences in management style, decision-making orientation, and perspective on time might effectively result in corporate culture shock, frustrating management from each partner and hindering development and maintenance of good rapport. Therefore, a JV between companies of widely different sizes often necessitates creation of a special environment in order to foster successful venture development. For instance, effects of partner size differences might be reduced by giving the JV virtually a free hand in product development or other activities, minimizing administrative red tape and permitting quicker response time. This emphasis on autonomy is particularly appropriate for ventures which confront rapidly changing environments, where slow response would be akin to a kiss of death. Willingness of a partner to allow this autonomy might be a critical consideration in the partner selection decision.

Even if managers strongly desire partners with similar "systems" orientations, that need not dictate JVs between same-size firms. On the contrary, the relevant measure often is not absolute corporate size, but relative size of the respective business units. Therefore, managers may seek partners of similar size at the business or division level. Another option for minimizing effects of size differences is for a small firm to identify a large firm which is both hungry and has the marketing, financial, or technical muscle necessary for a successful JV. This might require greater diligence in identifying and contacting partners, however, since these are attributes which tend to be found in certain individuals or business units rather than in an organization as a whole. Yet, their presence helps ensure the larger partner will be sufficiently aggressive to maintain respect from customers and competitors. As well there is greater likelihood that both partners will have similar perceptions of time as a vital component in the JV's success.

STRATEGIC COMPLEMENTARITY: A PREREQUISITE FOR LONG-TERM SUCCESS

Although a major concern, relative size tends not be as important as achieving a fit between partners' strategic goals for the JV. From the onset of discussions, each partner must try to understand what other participants desire from the union. As one seasoned veteran commented, "It is remarkable how many JVs are consummated where one or both partners do not clearly state their objectives. Under these circumstances, venture failure is almost inevitable."

Having different objectives in forming the JV, including the timing and level of returns on their investments, frequently produces conflicts of interest among partners. For instance, reflecting upon a previous JV involving his company and a Japanese firm, an executive noted the lack of strategic fit between the partners' goals: His company sought rapid market access and a high rate of dividend repatriation so its stock price would be maximized, enhancing an expansion strategy based on exchanges of stock. In contrast, the partner sought transfer of technology and long-term market development, rather than rapid financial returns. As a result of these differences, the JV performed poorly and was abandoned within two years. The partner later used the acquired technological expertise to expand its own market position in Asia.

As partners' objectives diverge, there is increasing risk of dissatisfaction and associated problems. This risk may be heightened when the JV's environment is characterized by a high level of uncertainty, since, under the circumstances, changes in a JV's operations are more likely. Unexpected events can cause problems because of a difficulty in formulating a mutually acceptable response to change. A power game can result and the JV can collapse if the partners cannot reach agreement on an appropriate course of action.

Divergence of corporate goals, however, can lead to a venture's downfall even if performance is satisfactory. For example, Dow-Badische was formed in 1958 as a 50/50 JV between Dow Chemical and BASF and was profitable over much of its life. Nevertheless, despite $300 million in annual sales, the JV was ultimately dissolved. BASF wanted to expand the venture, but, since the JV's activities did not fit the firm's strategic focus, Dow was reluctant to contribute additional funds. This gap between corporate goals prompted BASF to buy out Dow in 1978 and transform the JV into a wholly-owned subsidiary.

Although determining a prospective partner's objectives is often difficult, it is an essential task. Failure to do so increases prospects for later problems. The analysis needs to address not only the firm's current situation and goals, but also scenarios of its likely future position. JVs frequently encounter changes in their operating environments and it is essential to anticipate how a partner is likely to be affected by, and respond to, these changes. JVs tend to work only as long as each partner believes it is receiving benefits or is likely to benefit in the relatively near future. Because of differences in goals what is good for one firm may be a disaster for another. A compatible partner ideally, therefore, is one with similar values and goals, in both a short- and a long-term sense. Such a relationship enhances the ability of managers to interpret one another's sales forecasts, development schedules, cost estimates and so on. This is particularly critical as the strategic stakes — size of investment, potential effect on corporate image, or relationship to the firm's core technologies — increase in scale.

EVALUATE COMPATIBILITY BETWEEN PARTNERS' OPERATING POLICIES

Another consideration during partner selection is similarity of partners' operating policies. During the interviews on which this article is based executives related several instances where differences between partners' policies caused significant problems for JVs. For instance, one JV was nearly dissolved because inconsistencies between partners' accounting systems repeatedly produced disagreement regarding timing of purchases, allocation of costs, and so forth. Since the JV was only marginally profitable, the method of reconciling disagreements could determine whether or not it would appear on the parent's books as a profitable operation, an important consideration for division-level management. Similarly, another executive reported that differences in vacation policies between his firm and a European partner created serious difficulties for their JV because the latter company shut down virtually all operations for a month each summer whereas his firm allowed employees to schedule their own vacation time. As a result the JV repeatedly encountered difficulties.

Partners should be clear regarding the types of policies with which they will be comfortable working. For example, firms from Canada, the U.S. and Europe are typically accustomed to operating with lower debt-to-equity ratios than is the case in Japan. Such policies should be addressed thoroughly before the JV is formed. Differences in operating approaches often result from cultural biases, and managers, not conscious of the existence of these biases, may take for granted that there is a "right" way to do things. As one Japanese manager stated, "Many American executives attempt to force their Japanese partners to adopt American methods of operation in disregard of the distribution structure and other financial and management methods which have prevailed in Japan for a long time. For this reason, many JVs in Japan ultimately fail." As these examples illustrate, compatibility of partners' operating policies should be considered before forming a venture.

POTENTIAL COMMUNICATION BARRIERS

Communication is another potential problem area. By nature, JVs tend to be fragile agreements and communication problems make their operation even more difficult. Such problems can occur as a result of differences between national or ethnic cultures, including language, as well as differing corporate cultures. Cultural differences can impede development of rapport and understanding between partners. The importance of a partner with adequate English (or French) language capability, or the Canadian firm's facility with the language of the partner should not be overlooked. The simple ability to communicate with one's counterpart in a partner firm often makes a significant difference in a JV's prospects for success; the absence of this ability has caused more than a few disasters.

Because of cultural or language differences, subtle nuances might be more difficult to communicate, leading to greater expenditures of time in negotiations, possibly delaying negotiations or major post-formation decisions. The use of buzzwords common to many industries tends to compound language problems and can lead to misunderstandings of each company's role. Especially in technology-oriented fields, commonly used terms might not have the same connotations for each partner. For example, specifications for the Boeing 767 jetliner called for fuselage panels to have a "mirror finish." Boeing's Japanese partners interpreted that specification too literally and engaged in excessive polishing efforts. As a result, labor costs for the initial panels were too high, necessitating further discussions to resolve the misunderstanding. To avoid misinterpretation, managers should consider substituting simple, "Dick-and-Jane" terminology for technical jargon during negotiations and follow-up discussion.

Existence of different cultural perspectives implies value systems which are not necessarily compatible; it is hazardous to assume that promoting interests from one perspective will necessarily promote interests from another. Managers should avoid the alternative assumption that different value systems will necessarily be incompatible, however. Values associated with different perspectives may be similar, even if only slightly, or they might be irrelevant to each other; it is not common for them to be in complete opposition. Language and culture tend not to be insurmountable barriers, particularly for partners from developed nations, though they can be an important handicap. Cultural barriers are often considered when evaluating prospective partners, especially when choosing between two otherwise equivalent partner prospects, but they seldom function as the dominant selection criterion.

COMPATIBLE MANAGEMENT TEAMS HELP REDUCE PROBLEMS

There is much to be said for selecting a partner whose management team is compatible with your own. Personal rapport between the principal decision makers is often important in the selection decision and inability of management to "take to each other" is frequently cited as the basis for rejecting a prospective partner or for terminating a JV. Close personal relationships, particularly among senior operating level managers, help nurture the level of understanding necessary for a successful JV relationship. Managerial compatibility can enhance the partners' ability to achieve consensus on critical policy decisions and to overcome roadblocks encountered during JV formation and operation. Though building relationships between partners' managers takes time, it is an invaluable element of most long-term ventures. This particularly characterizes JVs with Japanese firms, for whom establishment of close personal rapport is customarily a prerequisite to concluding business negotiations.

In many respects, it seems unfortunate that JVs are so heavily dependent on personal rapport between a few individuals. Because of the informal nature of these relationships, including extensive utilization of unwritten "gentlemen's agreements," reliance on executive rapport can lead to unnecessary disputes and conflicts of interests at a later date. To reduce prospects for such difficulties, an additional consideration when selecting a partner is the prospect for continuity among the critical personnel within a partner's management team. Turnover among key management personnel can hinder establishment and maintenance of close relations among partners' managers.

TRUST AND COMMITMENT: ESSENTIAL ELEMENTS OF LONG-TERM RELATIONSHIPS

Forming and operating a JV over the long term requires more than cordial relations between partners' management teams. The partner's perceived trustworthiness and commitment are also pivotal considerations,[2] especially if the proposed JV involves one firm's core technologies or other proprietary capabilities which are the essence of the firm's competitive advantage. Given the inherent fragility of JVs, today's partners could become tomorrow's competitors and a manager might understandably react with some initial distrust regarding potential partners' motives. As one CEO noted, "You've got to be sure you're working with earnest and ethical people who aren't trying to undermine your company. Usually, a partner will have access to your trade secrets. He might attempt to complete a few projects, learn what you do, then exclude you from future deals."

Exposing its technological core to a partner who is unable to protect this knowledge adequately from technological theft or bleed-through can threaten a firm's competitiveness. As a result, one approach is to seek majority control, if not full ownership, of any venture,[3] and to hover over every decision the "child" might make. Given the likelihood of some misunderstanding between the partners, another common response is to have lawyers structure the JV agreement to address every conceivable contingency. Yet, these responses are unlikely to promote compatibility. Often, particularly for JVs involving the Japanese, demands to develop extensive formal contracts dealing with every conceivable dispute might be viewed as evidence of mistrust, threatening the venture from the start.

As an alternative, managers experienced in JVs emphasize the building of mutual understanding and trust, which make the formal written agreement more a symbol of a commitment to cooperate than an actual working document. As one CEO commented, "(partners generally) don't start looking at the specifics of the venture agreement until the relationship starts breaking down and you're contemplating getting out." Regardless of protections written into the JV agreement no legal document is fail-safe. "You can write all sorts of legal contracts and other formal agreements but the partners must trust each other and be committed to the venture in order for it to work. A partner may be able to muster a virtual battalion of lawyers, making it very expensive for you to take a grievance to court, much less to win it," he said. Therefore, each partner needs to be comfortable that the other will honor the spirit, not just the letter, of the agreement. A JV relationship is delicate at best and complicated at worst. Without fundamental trust and commitment by each party, there is little hope for a successful working relationship.

CONCLUDING REMARKS

Although the preceding discussion presents a rather long list of criteria, managers with JV experience probably can add others. Admittedly, these suggestions constitute an ideal set of conditions and there may be few situations where each of these will be fully achieved. Nevertheless, the above provides a foundation for identifying and evaluating the potential long-term compatibility of prospective JV partners.

References

1. The ongoing JV study from which this article is adapted is discussed more thoroughly in J. Michael Geringer, *Joint Venture Partner Selection: Strategies for Developed Countries* (Westport, Conn.: Quorum Books, a division of Greenwood Press, September 1988).
2. The importance of commitment to venture performance is addressed in Chapter Four of Paul W. Beamish, *Multinational Joint Ventures in Developing Countries* (London: Routledge, 1988).
3. The merits of dominant versus shared control JVs are discussed in J. Peter Killing, *Strategies for Joint Venture Success* (New York: Praeger, 1983).

READING 6

International Strategy from the Perspective of People and Culture: the North American Context

Nancy J. Adler and Fariborz Ghadar

I. INTRODUCTION

North American firms frequently conduct the worldwide management of people as if neither the external economic and technological environment nor the internal structure and organization of the firm had changed during the last two decades. While new approaches to managing research and development (R&D), production, marketing, and finance incorporating today's global realities are occurring rapidly, an equivalent evolution in conceptualizing and managing international human resource systems appears absent. According to Evans (1987):

> A review of research since the late 1960s shows that our understanding of the human resources strategies of multinational firms has advanced little since the pioneering studies of Perlmutter into the meaning of multinationalism that led to his Ethnocentric-Polycentric-Regiocentric-Geocentric typology [see Heenan and Perlmutter, 1979].

What is compelling about such apparently unchanging human resource practices is that the 1980s have made it mandatory for corporations to use global strategies if they are to succeed.[1] As Rugman (1988) states:

> The competiveness of the world's dozen leading nations is today largely determined by the effectiveness of their multinational enterprises. Although there are over 16,000 multinationals in the world, the largest 200 account for some 80% of all the world's foreign direct investment, see Stopford and Dunning (1983). There is intensive global competitive rivalry between these 200 multinationals, of which about 70 come from the United States, 60 from Europe, 40 from Japan, 10 from Canada, and the remainder from third world nations (page 47).

To understand economic conditions and the role of human resource management within the Canadian context, it is necessary to understand the role and dynam-

Research in Global Business Management, Volume 1, pages 179–205. Copyright © 1990 by JAI Press Inc., Greenwich, Conn. ISBN: 1-55938-131-0.

ics of American multinationals and extent of trade between Canada and the United States. According to Rugman and Verbeke (1988):

> Canada is tremendously dependent on the U.S. economy and . . . the U.S. stake in Canada is also of major global importance (page 5). . . . In 1986, three-quarters of Canada's exports went to the United States, an overwhelming level of reliance (page 4). . . . Similarly, in the last decade, two-thirds of Canada's imports have come from the United States (page 5).

The same is true for foreign direct investment (FDI). By 1985, three-quarters of the FDI in Canada was American owned (Rugman and Verbeke, 1988, p. 8). Similarly, about 72% of Canadian owned FDI is in the U.S. (Rugman and Verbeke, 1988, p. 8). Even prior to the advent of free trade talks between the two countries, it had become incumbent upon Canadians to understand the continuing evolution of American multinationals if they were to understand the dynamics of their own economy, multinationals, and human resource systems.

In this chapter, we ask three fundamental questions. First, *as a context for addressing human resource management issues, what is the evolution of the multinational enterprise and, most predictably, where will it go from here?* While today's top executives and management scholars can impeccably detail the post-World War II evolution of multinationals, albeit focusing on areas other than human resource management (HRM) and culture, they are less articulate about the future. Have managers allowed themselves to predict the future as merely repeating the most advanced stages of the present? Have management scholars implicitly assumed that today's most advanced global firms represent a final stage of development beyond which neither the firm as a whole, nor any one subsystem, will evolve? If so, we explicitly question this assumption. The widely accepted three-phase model explaining the evolution of multinational enterprises (MNEs) appears, in fact, to go beyond Phase Three.

Second, *how does national culture affect the firm and, thereby, its management of people?* One of the central questions facing international human resource professionals is the influence, or lack thereof, of culture on the management of people worldwide. In Canada, with an explicit policy of domestic multiculturalism, understanding cross-cultural dynamics is a function of all managers, not just those working for MNEs (see Adler and Graham, 1987; and Kanungo, 1980, among others). Still, discussions concerning the influence of culture on strategic efficacy remain time-lagged, disconnected from other corporate realities. We continue to ask *if* culture impacts organizational functioning rather than the more relevant *when*, or under what conditions, it does so. Perhaps we would give more attention to the second question if we placed our inquiry within the context of the evolving strategies and structures of global firms, rather than confining it to the more static assumptions that have governed international personnel decisions for years. The second question thus investigates the consequences of culture at each phase in the evolution of the multinational firm.

Third, *what does each phase of the firm's evolution imply for effectively managing people?* What are the implications for traditional human resource management decisions as well as for those decisions that will only make sense when taken from within a future perspective? Issues needing to be addressed include the cultural homogeneity of top executive teams, the purpose and process of expatriation, the firm's recognition and use of cultural diversity, and the overall management of geographic dispersion. Based on this third question, we suggest some more appropriate approaches to managing people within today's and tomorrow's multinational enterprises (MNEs).

This chapter focuses on global strategy from the perspective of people and culture. It uses the development of American multinationals as a base, starting with the product life cycle in international trade and investment, and proceeding to a commonly accepted three-phase model[2] describing the evolution of multinational enterprises (MNEs) from World War II to the present. Then, going beyond the third phase, it outlines some of the possible characteristics of future Phase Four MNEs. Within this framework of the evolving multinational firm, the chapter suggests some new and more powerful approaches to manage human resource systems and the cultural diversity engendered in global operations. It suggests that we can compete successfully in the global economy, but we can no longer do so without fundamental change.

II. THE MODEL

During the two decades following World War II, United States' multinational corporations dominated international trade. Canada and the United States emerged from the war as the only economically developed nations with their industrial sector unscathed. Ouchi (1984) described U.S. corporations during this post-war period as earning monopoly profits, and their workers as earning monopoly wages; not due to the superiority of American management techniques, but, rather, primarily due to the U.S. being the "only game in town." Recognizing the presence today of vigorous foreign competition, Ouchi predicts that Americans will never again earn the monopoly profits and wages that characterized the decades immediately following World War II. Based on this economic background, we review the three-phase model documenting the evolution of the multinational firm, and then investigate the role of culture and people within that model.

A. The Product Life Cycle
in International Trade and Investment

One way that has been used to understand the evolution of international firms is through the products they produce. The changes a product undergoes in the course of its life cycle have several important implications for the firm's relationship with the external environment as well as its international functioning. At each stage, a product's characteristics dictate the environment in which it can be produced, and, to a certain extent, the environment dictates the possible products. In the United States and Canada, post World War II economic conditions played a determining role in the way business approached the development, manufacturing, and marketing of products. Vernon first described these forces in 1966, just as international markets were beginning to change. He astutely observed that one could divide the international product life cycle for trade and investment into three principal phases: high tech, growth and internationalization, and maturity. As shown in the expanded framework in Table 1, these form the basis of a three-phase development model for multinational enterprises.

Phase One: A Product Orientation

The salient characteristics of Phase One's high tech products are that they are new and unique. Hence, they depend on research and development (R&D); that is, on the application of advances in science and engineering to product development. By definition, Phase One products have never been produced successfully before. Moreover, at most, only a handful of companies are capable of developing and manufacturing any specific product. High tech products are purchased by a highly specialized and limited market. Not surprisingly, given their uniqueness and the few companies capable of producing them, Phase One products generally command a high price relative to direct costs.

Phase Two: A Market Orientation

The entrance of competition marks the beginning of Phase Two, growth and internationalization. All firms embarking on this phase must now focus on expanding their markets and production. Frequently, they expand internationally. Initially, the firm supplies new foreign markets through exports from the home country. Gradually, production shifts to those countries with the largest domestic markets, with firms erecting foreign plants and assembly lines to supply local demand. As these foreign markets grow, more is produced locally and exports from the original home country begin to diminish.

Thus, as products reach Phase Two, market penetration and control replace research and development as the most important functions. Because the product technology has been perfected in Phase One, R&D as a percentage of sales decreases. The firm's activity no longer centers on developing the product, but rather on refining the means of production. Consequently, the focus moves from product engineering to process engineering, although the firm still may address specialized engineering problems associated with design modifications to suit the product for international markets. With other firms continuing to enter the market as producers, competition increases and drives down both price and the proportion of price to cost.

Phase Three: A Price Orientation

Products enter Phase Three, maturity, when standardization of the production process makes further reductions in production costs impossible. The product has become completely standardized. The technology inherent in both the product

TABLE 1 International Product Life Cycle

	Phase I (high tech)	Phase II (growth and internationalization)	Phase III (multinationalization)	Phase IV (globalization)
Competitive strategy	Domestic	Multidomestic	Multinational	Global
Importance of international	Marginal	Important	Dominant	Continual
Primary orientation	Product	Market	Price	Strategy
Product	New, unique, and nonstandard	More standardized	Completely standardized (almost a commodity)	Mass customized
	Engineering content high	Process engineering emphasized	Engineering not emphasized	Product and process engineering
Technology	Proprietary	Shared	Widely shared	Instantly, extensively shared
R&D/sales	High: 10–14%	R&D decreasing	Little R&D	High
Price/cost	High	Decreasing	Approaching 1.0	Initially High
Manufacturers				
• Number	One	Two or more	Many	Few
	Little to no competition	Competition increases	Highly competitive	Extremely competitive
• Location	Domestic production	Driven by market size and potential	Determined by production costs	Determined by production costs
• Decision rule	Manufacturing at home (U.S.) for home market	International manufacturing in prime markets	Multinational manufacturing where factor costs are least	Based on strategy, given production costs, markets, competitors, external political and economic environment

(Continued)

TABLE 1 Continued

	Phase I (high tech)	Phase II (growth and internationalization)	Phase III (multinationalization)	Phase IV (globalization)
Market	Small	Large	Larger	Largest
	Domestic	International	Multinational	Global
Export market	None to small	Growing with high potential	Multinational, large and saturated	Globally large and saturated
Home (U.S.) source	High, with few exports	High, with many exports	Low, with many imports	Low, with imports and exports
Typical ownership	Wholly owned	Joint ventures	Foreign-owned	Alliances

itself and the production process has become widely available; hence, R&D drops off completely. Moreover, the market, while large, is completely saturated with competitors. The potential for growth in either market or market share therefore becomes severely limited. Due to the competition, price often falls to a bare minimum above cost.

Given these conditions, Phase Three firms can gain a competitive advantage only by managing factor costs; that is, by shifting production to those countries in which the elements of production are least expensive. Market considerations no longer determine location, but rather production costs. Because product development occurs in countries with a high standard of living and relatively high labor costs, by Phase Three home country production usually ceases to be competitive and therefore declines markedly. As a result, the home country market now is supplied primarily by production imported from offshore plants.

B. The Accelerated Product Life Cycle

In the years immediately following the Second World War, products developed by North American companies took between fifteen and twenty years to move through the international product life cycle described above. During these years, products progressed gradually through the three phases from high tech development to maturity. Their evolution seemed inevitable. With technological developments originating primarily in the United States and the potential of the American market second to none, U.S. firms naturally supplied their home market first. They gradually moved abroad as the markets of America's allies opened, first establishing links with English-speaking countries — Canada and Great Britain — and then with Western Europe. Typically, these foreign operations were initially 100% or majority owned and limited to assembly plants, with most parts still manufactured in the United States.[3]

Gradually, however, European markets grew sufficiently to support local competition. Simultaneously, the manufacturing technology involved matured and became widely disseminated. As a result, many multinationals found themselves in Phase Two. At this point, while firms could choose strategies that would allow them to remain in Phase One or would help them to succeed in Phase Two, they could not choose to continue Phase One strategies and succeed in a Phase Two economic environment. To prolong their Phase One monopoly position, firms had to invest in products requiring new technology. If not, they had little choice but to accept Phase Two competitive pressures and a weakened market position. Given the increased power of local markets, firms operating in a Phase Two economic environment often had to accept joint ventures with local business partners.

Throughout the twenty-year period following World War II, the international product life cycle provided a reliable guide to business strategy. By the 1970s, however, its acceleration made the need for new strategies and models, and thus for new kinds of multinational enterprises, imminent. By the 1980s, instead of taking fifteen to twenty years for a product to move through the cycle from development to maturity, it generally took three to five years. For some products, it now takes less than six months. While the changes in strategy, structure, production, and marketing are evident, what has been less clear is how these changes effect human resource management systems.

C. The Future: A Possible Phase Four

Many scholars are attempting to describe the future of society, and of corporations within that society (e.g., Naisbitt, 1982). One particularly insightful management scholar, Stan Davis, in his most recent book *Future Perfect* (1987), tells us that we are headed for an era of mass customization, with products being designed to meet individual needs but assembled from components sourced worldwide. Firms will need to understand and respond to individual clients' needs by delivering top-quality products and services at the least cost. Successful firms will be responsive; that is, they will listen to clients, accurately identify trends, and respond quickly. In many ways, firms will compete in Phases One, Two, and Three simultaneously.

To succeed in such a Phase Four environment, firms must become simultaneously more highly differentiated and more integrated. Structurally, successful firms will have passed far beyond the international divisions and foreign subsidiaries of Phase Two, as well as the global lines of business offering mature, standardized products of Phase Three to global heterarchies[4] (Hedlund, 1986) that weave together complex networks of joint ventures, wholly-owned subsidiaries, and organizational and project defined alliances (Galbraith and Kazajian, 1986). Managers in this type of environment will use multifocal approaches combining Phase Two's demands for increased local responsiveness with Phase Three's opportunities for global integration (Doz and Prahalad, 1986). To maintain responsiveness, successful firms will develop global corporate cultures that recognize cultural diversity and its impact on the organization (Adler and Jelinek, 1986), thus allowing them to integrate culture specific strategic choices within a global vision of the firm (Laurent, 1986). Appropriate approaches to human resource management in these types of cooperative ventures will have to be redefined (Lorange, 1986).

III. THE CONSEQUENCES OF CULTURE

How important are cultural differences to organizational effectiveness? To what extent must firms differentiate their products and operations by country and region, versus maintaining global products and integrated, undifferentiated worldwide operations? Integration versus differentiation: the dilemma is certainly not new. Some observers of corporate behavior say cultural differences are not at all important, while others claim them to be extremely important. Those adherents of the cultural convergence perspective argue that organizational characteristics across nations are free, or becoming free, from the particularities of specific cultures. This position suggests that as an outcome of "common industrial logic" — most notably of technological origin — institutional frameworks, patterns, and structures of organizations, and management practices across countries, are converging (Adler, Doktor, and Redding, 1986, pp. 300–301.)[5] By contrast, others argue that organizations are culture-bound, rather than culture-free, and remaining so. They conclude that there is no one-best-way to manage across all cultures, but rather many equally effective ways exist, with the most effective depending, among other contingencies, on the cultures involved (Adler, Doktor, and Redding, 1986, p. 301).[6]

Perhaps this dilemma has not been resolved because we have been asking the wrong question. Using the four phase model described above as a guide, we can ask *when* culture has an impact on organizational functioning, rather than *if* it does or does not. As shown in Table 2, the importance of cultural differences depends on the phase of the life cycle in which the firm operates. Phase One firms can operate appropriately from an ethnocentric perspective, and ignore most cultural differences they encounter. These firms have a unique product that they offer primarily to their own domestic market. The Phase One product's uniqueness and the absence of competitors negate the firm's need to demonstrate sensitivity to cultural differences. If the firm exports the product, it does so without altering it for foreign consumption. Cultural differences are absorbed by the foreign buyers, rather than by the home country's product design, manufacturing, or marketing teams. In some ways, the implicit message Phase One firms send to foreigners is "We will *allow* you to buy our product," and, of course, the more explicit assumption is that the foreigners will want to buy.

By Phase Two, competition brings the need to market and to produce overseas. Consequently, sensitivity to cultural differences becomes critical to implementing an effective corporate strategy. As Phase One's product orientation shifts to Phase Two's marketing orientation, the firm must address each foreign market separately. Whereas the unique technology of Phase One products fits well with adopting an integrated, ethnocentric, one-best-way approach, the competitive pressures of Phase Two fit better with an equifinality approach: that is, with assuming that many-good-ways to manage exist, with the best being contingent on the particular cultures involved. Successful Phase Two firms can no longer expect foreigners to absorb cross-cultural mismatches between buyers and sellers, but rather must modify their own style to fit with that of their foreign clients and colleagues. While managing cultural differences becomes important in designing and marketing culturally appropriate products, it becomes critical in producing them in foreign factories.

As firms enter Phase Three, the environment again changes, and with it the demands for cultural sensitivity. By Phase Three, many firms produce the same, almost undifferentiated product. Firms compete almost exclusively on price. This price competition reduces the importance of most cross-cultural differences, along with almost any advantage the firm could have gained by sensitivity to them. The appropriate Phase Three assumption for product design, production, and marketing can not remain one-best-way or even many-best-ways, but rather must become one-least-cost-way. With primary markets having become global, there is little market segmentation based on culture or other national considerations. Firms gain competitive advantage almost exclusively through process engineering, sourcing

TABLE 2 A Cultural Perspective on the International Product Life Cycle

	Phase I (high tech)	Phase II (growth and internationalization)	Phase III (multinationalization)	Phase IV (globalization)
Perspective	Ethnocentric	Polycentric or regiocentric	Multinational	Global-multicentric
Cultural sensitivity	Unimportant	Critically important	Marginally important	Very important
Who absorbs differences	Foreigners, customers	Home country employees and managers	Differences ignored	Foreign and home country executives and managers
Culturally differentiated marketing	No, unique technology negates its importance	Yes, it creates competitive advantages	No, price negates its importance	Yes, it enhances competitive advantage and is critical to mass customization
Primary orientation	Product	Market	Price	Strategy
Primary product design and market assumption	"One-way" or "one-best-way"	Equifinality or "many-best-ways"	"One-least-cost-way"	Many simultaneous best-ways based on one-best-way

National market segmentation	No	Yes	No	Yes, including subcultures within nations
Primary market	Domestic	Multidomestic	Multinational	Global
Typical organizational structure	Centralized-functional divisions	Country sales offices; then international division	Global lines of business	Global heterarchy
	Home country	Home and host countries	Home country	Global
	Functional divisions	International divisions and individual operations; matrices	Global lines of business	Multicentric
Control	Integrated/centralized	Differentiated/decentralized	Integrated/centralized	Coordinated and differentiated

critical factors on a worldwide basis, and benefiting from the resultant economies of scale. During Phase Three, price competition reduces culture's influence to negligible.

By Phase Four, top-quality, least-possible-cost products and services become the minimally acceptable standard. Competitive advantage comes from sophisticated global strategies based on mass customization. Firms draw product ideas, as well as the factors and locations of production, from worldwide sources. Firms tailor final products and their relationship to clients to very discrete market niches. One of the critical components on which Phase Four firms segment the market again becomes culture. Successful firms understand their potential clients' needs, quickly translate them into products and services, produce those products and services on a least-possible-cost basis, and deliver them back to the client in a culturally appropriate and timely fashion. By Phase Four, the product, market, and price orientations of prior phases almost completely disappear, having been replaced by a strategic orientation combining responsive design and delivery with quick, least-possible-cost production. Firms continually scan the globe, often including geographically dispersed and culturally diverse alliance partners. Since a strategic orientation requires firms to develop global R&D, production, and marketing networks, it forces them to manage cultural diversity within the organization as well as between the organization and its supplier, client, and alliance networks. Attention to cultural differences becomes critical for managing both the firm's organizational culture and its relationships outside of the firm (see Figure 1).

Does culture impact the organization? The question has no single answer. The impact of culture varies with the type of environment and the firm's overall strategy. In Phase One, culture has a minimal impact; in Phase Two, a maximal impact; in Phase Three, again a low impact; and in Phase Four, again a pronounced impact.

FIGURE 1   **Location of Cross-Cultural Interactions**

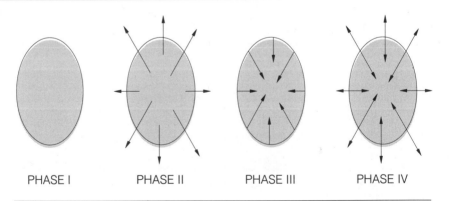

PHASE I   PHASE II   PHASE III   PHASE IV

Similarly, the location of the impact varies with the firm's environment and strategy. In Phase One, cultural diversity effects neither the organizational culture nor the relationships with clients. By Phase Two, cultural differences strongly affect relationships with the external environment, especially with potential buyers and foreign workers. By Phase Three, there is less recognition of cultural differences outside of the firm, but a growing awareness of culture diversity within the firm. And by Phase Four, the firm must manage cultural diversity both within the firm and between the firm and its external environment. This progression from culture's lack of importance, to its critical importance with respect to the firm's external environment, and then with respect to its organizational culture underlies the efficacy of various international human resource management strategies (see Table 2).

IV. INTERNATIONAL HUMAN RESOURCE MANAGEMENT

International human resource management (HRM) involves the worldwide management of people (see Tung, 1984, and Miller et al., 1986, among others). Traditionally, it has focused on the selection, training and development, performance appraisal, and rewarding of international personnel. The effectiveness of particular HRM approaches and practices depends directly on the firm's environment and strategy. As summarized in Table 3, who the firm considers an international employee, who it selects for international assignments, how it trains them, what criteria it uses to assess their international performance, and what impact international experience has on employee careers, should all fit the external environment in which the firm operates and its strategic intent. The central issue for MNEs is not to identify the best international HRM policy per se, but rather to find the *best fit* between the firm's external environment, its overall strategy, and its HRM policy and implementation. Unfortunately, many firms continue to use Phase One and Two approaches to managing human resources, while operating in Phase Three and Four environments. The following section describes which approaches to managing people best fit each phase in the firm's development.

A. Phase One

In Phase One, the firm produces a unique product and sells it primarily to its own domestic market. Given this domestic focus and the absence of competition, the firm's needs for internationally sophisticated people are minimal. The firm generally sends few employees on international business trips, and none on expatriate assignments. Those few are almost always home country nationals sent abroad on marketing assignments. For them, neither cross-cultural management nor language training is essential, because potential buyers have few options other than the particular firm for purchasing Phase One products. This monopoly situation forces

TABLE 3 International Human Resource Management

	Phase I (high tech)	Phase II (growth and internationalization)	Phase III (multinationalization)	Phase IV (globalization)
Primary orientation	Product	Market	Price	Competitive strategy
International mission	Allow foreigners to buy products	Increase market internationally Transfer technology to produce abroad	Source, produce, and sell multinationally	Operate globally based on strategic competitive advantages derived worldwide
Staffing selection				
• Expatriates	Few or none	Many	Some	Many
• Why sent	To sell	To sell, control, and transfer technology	To control	To develop global managers who will integrate global firm
• Who sent	Salespeople	Salespeople, country director, financial officer and technical experts	Country director, financial officer	High-potential managers, top executives
	Home country nationals	Home country nationals	Third and home country nationals	Top performers from all nations
• Level	Marginal performers	Good, not great	Very good performers	Top performers

• Purpose	To get job done	To get job done	To get job done and career development	To get job done, career development, and organizational integration and coordination
Training and development				
• Training	None	One week (maybe)	Longer	Continuous throughout career
• Foreign language competence	None	Language fluency required	English relied on as international business language	Multilingualism a prerequisite
• Career impact	Bad for career	Bad for domestic career	Important for global career	Essential to reach executive suite
• Reentry	Somewhat difficult	Extremely difficult	Less difficult	Professionally easy
Performance appraisal	Corporate bottom line	Subsidiary bottom line	Corporate bottom line	Corporate bottom line and strategic positioning
Rewarding	Extra money to compensate for hardships	Extra money to compensate for hardships	Less generous compensation and benefit packages	Global packages
• Motivation assumptions	Money motivates	Money motivates	Challenge and opportunity motivate	Challenge and opportunity motivate
Career "fast track"	Domestic	Domestic	Some international	Global
Executive "passports"	Home country	Home country	Home country with token foreigners	Multinational

potential buyers (rather than the seller) to absorb the cross-cultural mismatches. Foreign buyers must speak English (or in Quebec's case, French) and accept business practices appropriate to the home environment, while altering products and services, once purchased, to fit their needs. Not surprisingly, the majority of firms operating under Phase One assumptions provide no cross-cultural or predeparture training for those few assigned to work internationally. As one manager aptly describes this Phase One perspective:

> Managing a company is a scientific art. The executive accomplishing the task in New York can surely perform as adequately in Hong Kong [Baker and Ivancevich (1971, p. 40), as reported in Mendenhall, Dunbar, and Oddou (1987)].

Based on Phase One assumptions, firms select candidates for international work almost exclusively on product- or project-specific technical competence (see Mendenhall, Dunbar, and Oddou, 1987).

In the past, understandably ethnocentric assumptions underlying Phase One strategies have led to numerous linguistic and human resource blunders (see Ricks, 1983). While foreign buyers rarely appreciate being forced to accommodate to the seller's language and culture, Phase One firms get away with such ethnocentric behavior because they are "the only game in town"!

Since domestic sales have traditionally dominated Phase One profits, firms generally do not assign their best people to the few international positions. In selecting people for international travel, the firm's primary consideration is "getting the job done." Neither international career development for the employee, nor international organizational development for the firm, is considered important because international is not important. Consequently, in evaluating employees, most Phase One firms ignore international experience or, worse yet, treat it as hindering potential career advancement. As one manager of a Phase One firm said, "It is best to get your international experience standing next to the globe in the president's office."

B. Phase Two

Unlike Phase One, Phase Two firms face competition and respond by expanding from domestic to international operations, including actively marketing internationally, and beginning to assemble and to produce overseas. Phase Two firms are polycentric. They are differentiated into distinct national markets and operations, and only minimally integrated beyond the regional level. To maintain home country dominance, Phase Two firms often have overseas personnel reporting to an international division. Since executive decisions are generally made at a level above the international division, international is rarely considered either central or of primary importance.

Phase Two firms frequently select and send home country sales representatives to market products overseas, technical experts to transfer technology to overseas production sites, and managing directors and financial officers to control overseas operations. Since most R&D, and thus most innovation, still takes place at home, firms view foreign operations primarily as sites for replicating that which has already been done at home. Therefore, while not selecting marginal performers, Phase Two firms rarely send their very best people abroad.

Selection criteria for Phase Two should emphasize cross-cultural adaptability and sensitivity. In reality, companies often continue to use Phase One's primary criterion — technical competence — supplemented by a willingness to go. As Torbiorn (1982, p. 51) bemoans:

> The mass of possible selection criteria proposed in the literature is rarely likely to be matched by a wide range of available candidates and the man chosen is often simply the man who happens to be there.

This approach would be inconceivable if international activities were truly considered central. Consistent with this view of international is the lower stature and influence generally granted Phase Two's international personnel managers.[7]

Unlike the prior phase, cross-cultural sensitivity and language skills become extremely important for Phase Two manager effectiveness. Given the competition, firms create a comparative advantage by producing culturally appropriate products, using culturally appropriate management techniques, and marketing in culturally appropriate ways. To effectively implement these culturally appropriate strategies, international managers themselves need to develop cross-cultural skills. To this end, a number of techniques have been developed to reduce cultural shock and enhance both cross-cultural adaptation and effectiveness.[8]

Unfortunately, however, while numerous techniques exist, American firms generally have not recognized the importance of cross-cultural training to international effectiveness. Schwind (1985) claims that "a majority of companies involved in international trade do not provide any preparatory training for managers and employees destined to work abroad." Consistent with Schwind's observation, Mendenhall and Oddou (1986, p. 77) note that "there is a marked deficiency on the part of U.S. firms in offering comprehensive cross-cultural training to their employees who are assigned overseas." Tung (1981) corroborates others' observations with empirical evidence,[9] reporting in 1982 that only 32% of U.S. companies conducted formal international training programs, as compared with 57% of Japanese companies, and 69% of European companies. Ronen (1986) has noted that the 32% reported in Tung's 1982 study is the same figure as reported in earlier research by Baker and Ivancevich (1971): "This figure has remained virtually unchanged over the last two decades even though large numbers of overseas managers have indicated that proper predeparture preparation is absolutely necessary to improve overseas performance" (Ronen, 1986, p. 548). This low and unchanging level of expatriate training in U.S. companies again exposes Phase One assumptions ill-fitted to the Phase Two (Three and Four) environment. Unfortunately, Canadian companies are not consistently better than American firms.

Moreover, this low and unchanging level of training also probably explains the high expatriate failure rates of American firms — 25 to 40% (Mendenhall and Oddou, 1985) — when compared with those of the Europeans and the Japanese (see Tung, 1982). What it does not explain is the acceptance of such high rates, especially when Tung (1982) has found a correlation of -0.63 between expatriate failure rates and the rigor of the selection and training procedure used. Once again, the problem appears to be that firms operating in a Phase Two environment continue to make Phase One assumptions as an unquestioned convenience in their human resource planning. Needless to say, the consequences of this mismatch between environmental realities and HRM assumptions are quite serious.

While the firm sends expatriates from the home country to fill positions designed for integration and control (those of managing director, financial officer, and, sometimes, technical expert), it often includes host nationals in marketing and personnel positions. The selection of host nationals for positions in their own countries gives some recognition to the importance of cultural understanding and language fluency, even if this recognition is not extended to most home country employees. Kobrin (1988, p. 43) found that over half the U.S. firms surveyed had significantly decreased their expatriates over the past decade. Similarly, Berenbeim (1983, p. v) found that 80% of U.S. firms had local nationals heading the majority of country operations.

Phase Two firms generally evaluate expatriates' performance based on that of the foreign operation, but even the best evaluations rarely lead to significant career advancement. Most returnees from oversees assignments find reentry extremely difficult. While abroad, the firm frequently views them as out-of-sight and out-of-mind. As returnees, it sees them as out-of-date and unimportant. To returnees' disappointment, their colleagues often evaluate them as somewhat inconsequential to the domestic mainstream [see Schein's (1971) discussion linking centrality in the organization to career advancement]. The home organization generally neither values nor uses their understanding of overseas operations or the external international environment (see Edstrom and Galbraith, 1977). For ambitious managers who want to make it to the top of Phase Two firms, going abroad is generally a bad career strategy (for a discussion of reentry, see, among others, Howard, 1973; Adler, 1981; Harvey, 1982).

Similarly, host nationals rarely, if ever, make it to the top of Phase Two firms. In most cases, an invisible ceiling stops them at the level of the country managing director. To get beyond the invisible ceiling, one must hold a passport of the home country. The almost complete absence of non-Americans on the boards of directors of American firms (and the similar absence of non-Japanese on Japanese boards) underscores the strength of the invisible ceiling. Hewlett Packard is currently one of the few major American corporations with a Japanese national on its Board of Directors (Peters, 1986).

C. Phase Three

By Phase Three, the competitive environment again changes. Price, rather than either product or market, allows Phase Three firms to survive in the now global markets. Geographical dispersion often increases, and with it the firm's need to integrate. This geographical dispersion not only includes divisions within the firm, but also worldwide supplier, manufacturer, and distributor networks external to the corporation. Phase Three firms accomplish integration primarily through centralizing and standardizing as many aspects of their products, processes, and structure as possible.

Given the critical role that multinational production and operations play in corporate survival, Phase Three firms attempt to select their best, rather than their marginal, employees for international positions. Specifically, rather than limiting selection to home country employees, they choose managers for international positions from throughout their worldwide organization. Integrating this diversity of employees, however, is not easy. One of the explicit purposes of international assignments, beyond getting-the-job-done, therefore, now becomes firmwide integration. The firm uses international positions to develop an integrated, global organization through the international career development of high potential managers, and thus the creation of a global cadre of executives. Similar to the role global lines of business play in integrating Phase Three products and markets worldwide, the international cadre of executives takes on the central role of integrating the firm through its top managers.[10]

Whereas Phase Three makes international experience essential to firmwide management and career advancement, the importance of cross-cultural sensitivity and language skills diminishes somewhat. Rather than using cultural diversity, Phase Three firms often either assume or create similarity when attempting to integrate the global firm. For example, they frequently assume that consumer tastes are essentially similar worldwide, thus allowing the firm to create generic products and services, and to benefit from substantial economies of scope and scale (see Leavitt, 1983, for an excellent exposition of this position). Similarly, Phase Three firms recognize that price substantially determines both market and market share, hence negating their need to differentiate products and services for individual or culture-specific tastes. Likewise, internal to the organization, Phase Three firms generally adopt English as a common language. Interestingly, for North American firms, this linguistic assumption of similarity forces all nonnative English speakers to become bilingual, but fails to impose similar linguistic requirements on native English speakers.

Moreover, organization culture is assumed to dominate national culture. Under the rubric of organization culture, firms generally require foreign nationals to accommodate to parent company — and, implicitly, parent culture — styles of interacting. The underlying assumption is that cultural differences either can be ignored because the organizational culture has molded nationals of all countries into similar employees — professionals who are "beyond passport" — or must be minimized because they cause problems (see Adler, 1983). The first assumption becomes apparent in the lack of recognition for varying cultural styles of conducting business; that is, in the firm's cultural-blindness. The second assumption becomes apparent in such behaviors as the decision to use English exclusively, or the selection of host nationals who exhibit attitudes and behaviors typical of the parent company's culture. Many North American companies traditionally have recruited host nationals from U.S. and Canadian college campuses to insure that new hires would have an excellent command of English and an adequate socialization into American ways of doing business. In this way, North American firms have been able to hire Americanized foreigners and those familiar with Canada, rather than those more typical of their home country and culture.

As shown in Figure 1, Phase Three differs fundamentally from prior phases in that the primary location of cross-cultural interaction moves inside the organization. Phase One firms encountered little cross-cultural interaction because both their employees and their clients are from the same domestic environment. Phase Two firms encounter cultural differences when interacting with their external environment, primarily as home company nationals attempt to market abroad and to manage foreign workers. By contrast, Phase Three firms, having hired people from around the world and integrated them into the overall organization, encounter cultural differences within the firm's internal organizational culture. The human resource management systems should reflect the location of the cultural diversity. Unfortunately, however, as has been described, Phase Three firms often attempt to assume away the culture differences by choosing to believe that organizational culture overrides differences in national perspective and behavior. Research, however, has shown this assumption of similarity to be incorrect. Organizational culture neither dominates nor erases national culture, but rather, in the case of multinational corporations, appears to accentuate it.[11]

Reentry in this environment poses less of a problem than in prior phases. Because firms value international experience, they often select top people to send overseas, recognize their international accomplishments, and bring them back to significant positions. Rather than hurting the expatriate's career, international assignments often become essential to career success.

D. Phase Four

In Phase Four, which combines aspects of Phases One, Two, and Three, firms face severe competition on a global scale. Successful strategies involve producing least-cost, top-quality products that, while differentiated for individual tastes, are produced globally and marketed globally. The increased severity of global competition forces multinationals to reexamine their traditional (Phase One, Two, and Three) approaches to human resource management (see Pucik, 1984).

The Phase Four environment requires firms to assign their best people to international positions, because, by this time, the overwhelming dominance of the domestic market has become a relic of the past. Key employees must be multilingual and culturally sensitive to identify the needs of culturally differentiated market segments, and to respond quickly and appropriately to each. Moreover, top-quality, least-cost production necessitates worldwide operations, with location dictated by strategic, political, and economic constraints, along with the supply of inputs and market access. Hence, people from all over the world constantly must communicate and work with each other; in the vernacular, they must "think globally" to become global managers (see Murray and Murray, 1986). Boundaries between expatriate and local personnel become obsolete (Doz and Prahalad, 1986). Neither cultural forms of control emphasizing more homogeneous selection, socialization, and training, nor more bureaucratic forms of control can independently address the needs for integration and differentiation (see Jaeger, 1983, and Baliga and Jaeger, 1984). The first emphasizes integration through eliminating differences, while the second emphasizes integration by controlling differences. The former is more appropriate to Phase Three's highly centralized organization, while the latter fits best with Phase Two's emphasis on decentralization. Because neither simultaneously emphasize integration and differentiation, neither fits particularly well in Phase Four.

Effectively managing such a culturally diverse organizational culture becomes an essential Phase Four skill. As Doz and Prahalad (1986) note, multinational corporations must find new ways to manage the dichotomy of cultural diversity and global integration, of national responsiveness and centralized coordination and control. One of the firm's major competitive weapons is its ability to use global human resources along both dimensions, to enhance national responsiveness and global integration.

By Phase Four, as shown in Figure 1, cross-cultural interaction takes place both within the firm and between the firm and its external environment. Consequently, understanding and managing cultural differences has become essential both internally and externally. The firm's home country culture can no longer dominate its organization culture. Ignoring or minimizing cultural diversity has become a luxury of the past, as the firm must now continually recognize and manage it. Beyond recognition, successful Phase Four firms develop skill at identifying those situations in which cultural diversity can be used as an asset, and those in which it must be regarded as a liability. Managers can then choose to accentuate and use differences, or attempts to minimize them, according to the particular situation. In no case does the firm ignore the differences (see Adler, 1983).

Cultural diversity, by increasing differentiation, makes integration more difficult. If managed appropriately, however, cultural differences become a key Phase Four resource. For example, when they need differentiation, firms that recognize cultural diversity can use the differences to gain multiple perspectives, develop wider ranges of options and approaches, heighten creativity and problem solving skills, and thereby increase flexibility in addressing culturally distinct client and colleague systems. Simultaneously, however, these same firms must be able to create similarity from the diversity when they need integration. This consciously created universality, Phase Four's form of organization culture, goes beyond cultural differences to heighten coordination and control.[12] Unlike firms in the prior phases, global Phase Four firms never assume similarity nor rely on naturally occurring universality to heighten integration; they create similarity — "universals."

For Phase Four managers, the salient question is not *if* there is cultural diversity, but rather *how* to manage it. They constantly use cultural diversity to balance three organizational tensions. First, they minimize the impacts of cultural diversity when integration is needed. Second, they use cultural diversity to differentiate products and services when culturally distinct markets or workforces must be addressed. And third, they use cultural diversity as a primary source of new ideas when innovation is needed. Thus, cultural diversity clearly takes on a role of primary importance in Phase Four. To achieve the appropriate balance, managers must become acutely sensitive to cultural nuances and highly skilled at managing culturally diverse environments.

Balancing cultural integration and differentiation affects all aspects of the human resource management system. For example, when firms promote managers from the local culture to positions of significant power in their own country, they are using cultural diversity to increase differentiation. By contrast, when they design multinational career paths for high potential managers and bring them together to create new approaches to managing innovation, production, finance, and marketing, they are using the diversity to create cultural synergy, Phase Four's powerful form of integration.

Phase Four firms no longer have an international division; rather, similar to Phase Three, they are international. They select their best people for global assignments and responsibility. They continually train them in the skills necessary for national responsiveness and culturally synergistic integration. Promotions go to those managers who skillfully assess and balance the needs for differentiation and integration; those who are continually learning, and therefore capable of continually making new choices. Reentry problems diminish significantly given the centrality of global operations and the need for highly trained, experienced, and sophisticated international managers. Given this global perspective, international human resource management is no longer marginal, but becomes central to firmwide success. Without a human resource system well integrated into the firm's global strategy, the Phase Four firm will not succeed. With anything other than a global perspective, the human resource system will cause the Phase Four firm to fail.

IV. IMPLICATIONS: FUTURE TRENDS

As has happened over the past two decades, the world has again changed. Many of today's firms now face a global economy. "Fully 70% of . . . [U.S.A.] industries, up from 25% only a dozen years ago, are under full-scale attack by foreign competitors" (Peters, 1986, p. 11). The United States proportion of world GNP has fallen from a post-war high of 75% to today's 22%. Some firms have changed, while most will have to change significantly to compete successfully in the 1990s and the twenty-first century. Unfortunately, whereas most other functional areas have already begun to respond, many firms' human resource systems have failed to adapt sufficiently to this changing environment. In all too many firms, human resource systems are managed as if they were in Phase One, Two, or Three — the domestic, international, or multinational worlds that were — not in the global world that is, nor in the multiphase world that will be. In one particularly astute indictment, Kobrin (1988) challenged the fundamental premise on which American firms base their overall human resource management policies and their specific expatriate decisions:

> Both managers and academics note a number of good business reasons for the replacement of expatriates by local nationals including environmental competence and cost reduction. . . . I dissent . . . Although all of the reasons given for the phasing out of

expatriates are valid, I suggest one that is not discussed actually dominates: the difficulty many Americans have had adapting to overseas assignments and the abysmally high failure rates they have experienced. Put simply, Americans have not been able to handle working and living in other cultures and U.S. MNCs have found it easier to replace them with foreign nationals than to make an effort to solve the underlying problem (p. 1).

Already today, and certainly in the future, firms must understand cultural differences to successfully implement global R&D, global marketing, global production, and global financial strategies. Cultural awareness has become essential not only within global firms, but also for coordinating and integrating activities among alliance partners of often differing national origins. If executives do not recognize and manage cultural diversity appropriately, their firms will not survive.

To compete globally, people involved in all aspects of the firm must not only think globally, they must realize that competition — and, perhaps more importantly, collaboration — is now on an equal footing. For most North American firms, significant comparative advantage based on technology, production, or market share is rapidly becoming a vestige of the past.

V. CONCLUSION

The research agenda is clear. Management scholars need to study human resource management in context. They must study international HRM within the context of changing economic and business conditions. Similarly, they must study international HRM within the context of the industry and the firm's other functional areas and operations. Studying HRM out-of-context is not only no longer helpful, it has become misleading. Similarly, management scholars need to use multiple levels of analysis when studying international HRM: the external social, political, cultural, and economic environments; the industry; the firm; the subunit; the group; and the individual. Research in isolation is misleading: It fails to advance understanding.

Notes

1. See, among others, Doz (1985); Doz, Bartlett, and Prahalad (1981); Doz and Prahalad (1987); Dunning (1985); Gluck, Kaufman, and Walleck (1980); Grub, Ghadar, and Khambata (1986); Hammel and Prahalad (1985); Hood, Schendel, and Vahlne (198x); Hout, Porter, and Rudden (1982); Leavitt (1983); Porter (1980, 1985, 1986); Porter and Millar (1985); Prahalad and Doz (1981); and Watson (1982).
2. While originally espoused by Vernon in 1966, this argument has been picked up by many commentators; see also Vernon (1971, 1981) and Ghadar (1977, 1985, 1986), among others.
3. See Stopford and Wells (1972).
4. Heterarchies, as used by Hedlund (1986), describe nonhierarchically organized systems: e.g., holographic coding where entire systems are represented or "known" within each component of the system.
5. Among the most notable proponents of this position are Kerr et al. (1952); Hickson et al. (1974, 1979); Form (1979); Negandhi (1979, 1985); Child (1981); Child and Tayeb (1983); and Levitt (1983), among many others.

6. Proponents of the culture specific perspective include Laurent (1983); Lincoln, Hanada, and Olson (1981); Hofstede (1980); Bass et al. (1979); England (1975); Heller and Wilpert (1979); and Haire, Giselli, and Porter (1966), among many others.

7. For a discussion of Phase Two selection practices see, among others, Baker and Ivancevich (1971); Miller (1973); Hawkes and Kealey (1981); Tung (1981); Church (1982); Torbiorn (1982); Abe and Wiseman (1983); Oddou and Mendenhall (1984), Mendenhall and Oddou (1985); and Zeira and Banai (1985).

8. For a discussion of cross-cultural training approaches and techniques, see, among others, Hall (1959); Oberg (1960); Smalley (1963); Byrnes (1966); Guthrie (1967); Higbee (1969); Torbiorn (1982); Ratiu (1983); Oddou and Mendenhall (1984); Mendenhall and Oddou (1985).

9. For similar observations, see Korn/Ferry International (1981); Runzheimer (1984); Dunbar and Ehrlich (1986); and Mendenhall, Dunbar, and Oddou (1986).

10. See Edstrom and Galbraith (1977) for a discussion of the use of international transfers as an organizational development strategy.

11. See Hofstede (1980) for a study of the cultural diversity within IBM's corporate culture, and Laurent (1983) for a study of cultural differences within a number of major American corporations.

12. For a discussion of cultural synergy, see Adler (1986, Chapter 4).

References

Abe, H., and R. L. Wiseman (1983) A cross-cultural confirmation of the dimension of intercultural effectiveness, *International Journal of Intercultural Relations*, 7(1):53–68.

Adler, N. J. (1980) *Re-entry* UCLA dissertation, unpublished, Los Angeles.

Adler, N. J. (1981) Re-entry: Managing cross-cultural transitions, *Group and Organization Studies*, 6(3):341–356.

Adler, N. J. (1983) Organizational development in a multicultural environment, *Journal of Applied Behavioral Science*, 11(3):349–365.

Adler, N. J. (1986) *International Dimensions of Organizational Behavior* (Boston: PWS-KENT Publishing).

Adler, N. J., and J. L. Graham (1987) Business negotiations: Canadians are not just like Americans, *Canadian Journal of Administrative Sciences*, 4(3):211–238.

Adler, N. J., and M. Jelinek (1986) Is "organization culture" culture bound? *Human Resource Management*, 25(1):73–90.

Adler, N. J., R. Doktor, and S. G. Redding (1986) From the Atlantic to Pacific century: cross-cultural management reviewed, *Journal of Management*, 12(2):295–318.

Baker, J. C., and J. M. Ivancevich (1971) The assignment of American executives abroad: systematic, haphazard, or chaotic? *California Management Review*, 13(3): 33–44.

Baliga, B. R., and A. M. Jaeger (1984) Multinational corporations: control systems and delegation issues, *Journal of International Business Studies*, 15(2):25–40.

Bartlett, C. (1983) How multinational organizations evolve, *Journal of Business Strategy*, 4(1):10–32.

Bass, B. M., C. Burger, R. Doktor, and B. V. Barrett (1979) *Assessment of Managers* (NY: Free Press).

Berenbeim, R. E. (1983) *Managing the International Company: Building a Global Perspective* (NY: The Conference Board).

Byrnes, F. C. (1966) Role shock: An occupational hazard of American technical assistants abroad, *The Annals*, 368:95–108.

Child, J. (1981) Culture, contingency and capitalism in the cross-national study of organizations, in *Research in Organizational Behavior,* Vol. 3, L. L. Cummings and B. M. Staw, eds. (Greenwich, CT.: JAI Press), pp. 303–356.

Child, J. and M. Tayeb (1983) Theoretical perspectives in cross-national organizational research, *International Studies of Management and Organization,* (12)4:23–70.

Church, A. T. (1982) Sojourn adjustment, *Psychological Bulletin,* 91(3):540–571.

Davidson, W. H., and P. Haspeslagh (1982) Shaping a global product organization, *Harvard Business Review,* 60(4):125–132.

Davis, S. (1987) *Future Perfect* (Reading, MA: Addison-Wesley).

Doz, Y. L. (1985) *Strategic Management in Multinational Companies* (Oxford: Pergamon Press).

Doz, Y. L., C. A. Bartlett, and C. K. Prahalad (1981) Global competitive pressure vs. host country demands: Managing the tensions in MNCs, *California Management Review,* 23(3):63–74.

Doz, Y. L., and C. K. Prahalad (1986) Controlled variety: A challenge for human resource management in the MNC, *Human Resource Management,* 25(1):55–72.

Doz, Y. L., and C. K. Prahalad (1987) *Multinational Companies' Missions: Balancing National Responsiveness and Global Integration* (NY: The Free Press).

Dunbar, E., and M. Ehrlich (1986) *International Human Resource Practices, Selecting, Training, and Managing the International Staff: A Survey Report.* The Project on International Human Resources (NY: Columbia University-Teachers College).

Dunning, J. (1985) *Multinational Enterprises, Economic Structures and International Competitiveness* (NY: John Wiley & Sons).

Edstrom, A., and J. R. Galbraith (1977) Transfer of managers as a coordination and control strategy in multinational organizations, *Administrative Science Quarterly,* 22(2): 248–268.

England, G. W. (1975) *The Manager and His Values: An International Perspective from the USA, Japan, Korea, India and Australia* (Cambridge: Ballinger).

Evans, P. A. L. (1986) The strategic outcomes of human resource management, *Human Resource Management,* 25(1):149–168.

Evans, P. A. L. (1987) Strategies for human resource management in complex MNCs: A European perspective. In V. Pucik's Academy of Management Proposal "Emerging Human Resource Management Strategies in Multinational Firms: A Tricontinental Perspective," pp. 9–11.

Form, W. (1979) Comparative industrial sociology and the convergence hypothesis, *Annual Review of Sociology,* 5:1–25.

Galbraith, J. R., and R. K. Kazajian (1986) Organizing to implement strategies of diversity and globalization: The role of matrix designs, *Human Resource Management,* 25(1): 37–54.

Ghadar, F. (1977) *The Evolution of OPEC Strategy* (Lexington, MA: Lexington Books).

Ghadar, F. (1985) Political risk and the erosion of control: The case of the oil industry, in *Political Risks in International Business: New Directions for Research, Management, and Public Policy,* T. Brewer, ed. (NY: Praeger).

Ghadar, F. (1986) Strategic considerations in the financing of international investment, in *The Multinational Enterprise in Transition,* revised edition, P. Grub, F. Ghadar, and D. Khambata, eds. (Princeton, NJ: The Darwin Press).

Grub, P., F. Ghadar, and D. Khambata, eds. (1986) *The Multinational Enterprise in Transition,* third edition (Princeton, NJ: The Darwin Press).

Gluck, F. W., S. P. Kaufman, and A. S. Walleck (1980) Strategic management for competitive advantage, *Harvard Business Review,* 58(4):154–161.

Guthrie, G. M. (1967) Cultural preparation for the Philippines, in *Cultural Frontiers of the Peace Corps,* R. B. Textor, ed. (Cambridge, MA: MIT Press).

Haire, M., E. G. Ghiselli, and L. W. Porter (1966) *Managerial Thinking: An International Study.* (NY: Wiley).

Hall, E. T. (1959) *The Silent Language.* (NY: Doubleday).

Hammel, G., and C. K. Prahalad (1985) Do you really have a global strategy? *Harvard Business Review,* **63(4):** 139–148.

Harvey, M. G. (1982) The other side of foreign assignments: dealing with the repatriation dilemma, *Columbia Journal of World Business,* **17(1):**53–59.

Hawes, F., and D. J. Kealey (1981) An empirical study of Canadian technical assistance, *International Journal of Intercultural Relations,* **5(3):**239–258.

Hedlund, G. (1986) The hypermodern MNC — a heterarchy? *Human Resource Management,* **25(1):**9–36.

Heenan, D. A., and H. V. Perlmutter (1979) *Multinational Organizational Development: A Social Architectural Approach* (Reading, MA: Addison-Wesley).

Heller, R. A., and B. Wilpert (1979) Managerial decision making: An international comparison, in *Functioning Organizations in Cross Cultural Perspective,* G. W. England, A. R. Negandhi, and B. Wilpert, eds. (Kent, OH: Kent State University Press).

Hickson, D. J., C. R. Hinnings, C. J. M. McMillan, and J. P. Schwitter (1974) The culture-free context of organization structure: a tri-national comparison, *Sociology,* **8(1):**59–80.

Hickson, D. J., C. J. McMillan, K. Azumi, and D. Horvath (1979) Grounds for comparative organization theory: quicksands or hard core? In *Organizations Alike and Unlike,* C. J. Lammers and D. J. Hickson, eds. (London: Routledge & Kegan, Paul), pp. 25–41.

Higbee, H. (1969) Role shock — a new concept, *International Educational and Cultural Exchange,* **4(4):**71–81.

Hofstede, G. (1980) *Culture's Consequences: International Differences in Work-Related Values* (Beverly Hills, CA: Sage).

Hood, N., D. Schendel, and J.-E. Vahlne, eds. *Strategies in Global Competition.*

Hout T., M. E. Porter, and E. Rudden (1982) How global companies win out, *Harvard Business Review,* **60(5):**98–108.

Howard, C. G. (1973) The expatriate manager and the role of the MNC, *Personnel Journal,* **48(1):**25–29.

Jaeger, A. M. (1983) The transfer of organizational culture overseas: An approach to control in the multinational corporation, *Journal of International Business Studies,* **14(2):** 91–114.

Jaeger, A. M., and B. R. Baliga (1985) Control systems and strategic adaptation: Lessons from the Japanese experience, *Strategic Management Journal,* **6(2):**115–134.

Kanungo, R. N. (1980) *Biculturalism and Management* (Toronto, Butterworth).

Kerr, C. J., T. Dunlop, R. Harbison, and C. A. Myers (1952) *Industrialism and Industrial Man* (Cambridge, MA: Harvard University Press).

Kobrin, S. J. (1988) Expatriate reduction and strategic control in American multinational corporations, *Human Resource Management,* Vol. 27(No. 1), Spring 1988, pp. 63–75.

Korn/Ferry International (1981) A study of the repatriation of the American international executive (New York).

Laurent, A. (1983) The cultural diversity of Western management conceptions, *International Studies of Management and Organization,* **8(1–2):** 75–96.

Laurent, A. (1986) The cross-cultural puzzle of international human resource management, *Human Resource Management,* **25(1):**91–102.

Leavitt, T. (1983) The globalization of markets, *Harvard Business Review,* **61(3):**92–102.

Lincoln, J. R., M. Hanada, and J. Olson (1981) Cultural orientations and individual reactions to organizations: A study of employees of Japanese-owned firms, *Administrative Science Quarterly,* **26(1)**:93–115.

Lorange, P. (1986) Human resource management in multinational cooperative ventures, *Human Resource Management,* **25(1)**:133–148.

Mendenhall, M. E., and G. R. Oddou (1985) The dimensions of expatriate acculturation: a review, *Academy of Management Review,* **10(1)**:39–47.

Mendenhall, M. E., E. Dunbar, and G. R. Oddou (1986) The state of the art of overseas relocation programs in U.S. multinationals. Academy of International Business Meetings (London, England).

Mendenhall, M. E., E. Dunbar, and G. R. Oddou (1987) Expatriate selection, training and career-pathing: A review and critique, *Human Resource Management,* **26(3)**:331–345.

Mendenhall, M. E., and G. R. Oddou (1986) Acculturation profiles of expatriate managers: Implications for cross-cultural training programs, *Columbia Journal of World Business,* **21(4)**:73–79.

Miller, E. L. (1973) The international selection decision: a study of some dimensions of managerial behavior in the selection decision process, *Academy of Management Journal,* **16(2)**:239–252.

Miller, E. L., S. Beechler, B. Bhatt, and R. Nath (1986) The relationship between the global strategic planning process and the human resource management function, *Human Resource Planning,* **9(1)**:9–23.

Murray, F. T., and A. H. Murray (1986) Global managers for global businesses, *Sloan Management Review,* **27(2)**:7–80.

Naisbitt, J. (1982) *Megatrends* (NY: Warner Books).

Negandhi, A. R. (1979) Convergence in organizational practices: An empirical study of industrial enterprise in developing countries, in *Organizations Alike and Unlike,* C. J. Lammers and D. J. Hickson, eds. (London: Routledge & Kegan Paul), pp. 323–345.

Negandhi, A. R. (1985) Management in the third world, in *Managing in Different Cultures,* P. Joynt and M. Warner, eds. (Oslo, Norway: Universitetsforlaget), pp. 69–97.

Oberg, K. (1960) Culture shock: adjustment to new cultural environments, *Practical Anthropology,* **7**:177–182.

Oddou, G., and M. Mendenhall (1984) Person perception in cross-cultural settings: a review of cross-cultural and related literature, *International Journal of Intercultural Relations,* **8(1)**:77–96.

Ouchi, W. (1984) *The M-Form Society* (Reading, MA: Addison-Wesley).

Peters, T. (1986) Competition and compassion, *California Management Review,* **28(4)**: 11–26.

Porter, M. E. (1980) *Competitive Strategy: Techniques for Analyzing Industries and Competitors* (NY: Free Press).

Porter, M. E. (1985) *Competitive Advantage* (NY: Free Press).

Porter M. E., ed. (1986) *Competition in Global Industries* (Boston: Harvard University Press).

Porter, M. E., and V. E. Millar (1985) How information gives you competitive advantage, *Harvard Business Review,* **63(4)**:149–160.

Prahalad, C. K., and Y. L. Doz (1981) An approach to strategic control in MNCs, *Sloan Management Review,* **22(4)**:5–13.

Pucik, V. (1984) The international management of human resources, in *Strategic Human Resource Management,* C. Fombrun, N. Tichy, and M. A. Devanna, eds. (NY: John Wiley).

Pucik, V. (1985) Strategic human resource management in a multinational firm, in *Strategic Management of Multinational Corporations: The Essentials,* H. V. Wortzel & L. H. Wortzel, eds. (NY: John Wiley & Sons), pp. 424–435.

Pucik, V., and J. H. Katz (1986) Information, control and human resource management in multinational firms, *Human Resource Management,* 25(1):103–132.

Ratiu, I. (1983) Thinking internationally: a comparison of how international executives learn, *International Studies of Management and Organization,* 13(1–2):139–150.

Ricks, D. A. (1983) *Big Business Blunders: Mistakes in Multinational Marketing* (Homewood, IL: Dow Jones-Irwin).

Ronen, S. (1986) *Comparative and Multinational Management.* New York: John Wiley.

Rugman, A. M. (1988) Multinational enterprises and strategies for international competitiveness. In *Advances in International Comparative Management,* Volume 3 (Greenwich, CT: JAI Press), pp. 47–58.

Rugman, A. M., and Alain Verbeke (1988) Canadian business in a global trading environment. Paper presented at the "International Business Research for the Twenty-First Century: Canada's New Research Agenda", Ontario Centre for International Business, University of Toronto, Canada.

Runzheimer Executive Report (1984) 1984 Expatriation/Repatriation Survey. Number 31. (Rochester, Wisconsin).

Schein, E. H. (1971) The individual, the organization, and the career: A conceptual scheme. *Journal of Applied Behavioral Science,* 7(4), 401–426.

Schwind, H. F. (1985) "The state of the art in cross-cultural management training". In R. Doktor (ed.) *International Human Resource Development Annual,* 1:7–15. Alexandria, Virginia: American Society for Training and Development.

Smalley, W. A. (1963) Culture shock, language shock, and the shock of self-discovery, *Practical Anthropology,* 10:49–56.

Stopford, J. M., and J. H. Dunning (1982) *U.S. Competitiveness in the World Economy* (Boston: Harvard Business School Press).

Stopford, J. M., and L. T. Wells (1972) *Managing the Multinational Enterprises: Organization of the Firm and Ownership of the Subsidiaries.* New York: Basic Books.

Torbiorn, I. (1982) *Living Abroad: Personal Adjustment and Personnel Policy in Overseas Settings.* New York: John Wiley.

Tung, R. (1981) Selection and training of personnel for overseas assignments. *Columbia Journal of World Business,* 16(1), 68–78.

Tung, R. (1982) Selection and training procedures of U.S., European and Japanese multinationals. *California Management Review,* 25(1), 57–71.

Tung, R. (1984) Strategic management of resources in the multinational enterprise. *Human Resource Management,* 23(2), 129–144.

Vernon, R. (1966) International investment and international trade in the product cycle. *Quarterly Journal of Economics,* 80(2), 190–207.

Vernon, R. (1971) *Sovereignty at Bay: The Multinational Spread of U.S. Enterprises* (NY: Basic Books).

Vernon, R. (1981) Sovereignty at bay ten years after, *International Organization,* 35(5): 517–529.

Watson, C. M. (1982) Counter-competition abroad to protect home markets, *Harvard Business Review,* 60(1):40–42.

Yackley, A. and W. E. Lambert (1971) Inter-ethnic Group Competition and Levels of Aspiration. *Canadian Journal of Behavioral Science,* 3(2):135–147.

Zeira, Y., and M. Banai (1985) Selection of expatriate managers in MNCs: the host-environment point of view, *International Studies of Management and Organization,* 15(1): 33–51.

READING 7

Expatriate Selection, Training, and Career-Pathing: A Review and Critique

Mark E. Mendenhall, Edward Dunbar,
and Gary R. Oddou

In order to delineate the current state of the art of overseas relocation programs in U.S. multinational corporations, the extant literature was reviewed in the areas of expatriate personnel selection, training and career-pathing. The implications of the study's findings for U.S. MNCs are discussed and recommendations for policy change are offered.

Expatriates confront numerous obstacles, both in the overseas workplace and in the foreign society in which they reside: culture shock, differences in work-related norms, isolation, homesickness, differences in health care, housing, schooling, cuisine, language, customs, sex roles, and cost of living, to name but a few. Given the barrage of cross-cultural obstacles that every expatriate must confront, it is not surprising that many expatriates fail to complete the full term of their overseas assignment.

Estimates of the number of aborted overseas assignments vary, since it is difficult to get such data from MNCs. It has been estimated (Copeland and Griggs, 1985; Desatnick and Bennett, 1978; Lanier, 1979; Mendenhall and Oddou, 1985; Misa and Fabricatore, 1979; Torbiorn, 1982; Tung, 1981; Zeira and Banai, 1985) that between 20 to 50 percent of personnel sent abroad return prematurely from their overseas assignment. The financial costs of such premature returns are significant. The average cost per failure to the parent company has been observed to range between $55,000 to $150,000 (Copeland and Griggs, 1985; Edwards, 1978; Harris and Moran, 1979; Holmes and Piker, 1980; Misa and Fabricatore, 1979; Zeira and Banai, 1985). Edwards (1978) notes that "senior management in some organizations estimate that when unrealized business is added, losses total close to a quarter of a million dollars per expatriate failure" (p. 36). Copeland and Griggs (1985) state that

Human Resource Management, 26, No. 3, (Fall 1987): 331–345. © 1987 by John Wiley & Sons, Inc. Reprinted by permission of John Wiley & Sons, Inc.

245

... American companies are losing $2 billion a year in direct costs [on expatriate failures]. There is no figure for costs of lost business and damaged company reputation caused by these expatriates . . . We can assume the figures to be frightening (pp. xix).

In order to avoid the financial and emotional costs associated with the premature return of an expatriate manager, many U.S. MNCs have instituted overseas relocation programs in their human resource divisions. The purpose of these programs is to: 1) select for overseas assignments employees who, because they possess certain skills that are critical to cross-cultural success, reflect a high probability of being effective expatriate employees; 2) provide training for these candidates in cross-cultural skills that will enable them to anticipate (and thus deal effectively with) problems that are unique to the overseas employee; and 3) provide them with a clear idea of how they will fit into the company upon repatriation, and how their overseas experience will fit into their future career path.

Despite the existence of such programs, the problem of expatriate failure and premature return continues to plague MNCs. This state of affairs suggests that for some reason, either because they exist infrequently in MNCs or because their content is of poor quality, these programs are not effectively fulfilling their organizational mission.

The purpose of this paper is to delineate the "terrain of failure" of these programs in United States MNCs, and based on the findings of the review, offer recommendations that would improve current human resource practices in this area. To this end, a review of the international human resource literature was conducted in the areas of expatriate selection, training and career-pathing.

EXPATRIATE PERSONNEL SELECTION IN U.S. MNCs

Every company that sends employees on overseas assignments conducts a selection process; however, some companies are more effective than others in designing valid overseas personnel selection programs. Criteria that are predictive of acculturation and productivity in the overseas assignment have been delineated by a number of authors (Abe and Wiseman, 1983; Church, 1982; Hawes and Kealey, 1981; Mendenhall and Oddou, 1985; Oddou and Mendenhall, 1984; Ratiu, 1983; Stening, 1979; Torbiorn, 1982; Tung, 1981; Zeira and Banai, 1985), and are summarized in Table 1.

Despite the importance of all of the criteria to overseas success, United States firms seem to focus their selection efforts on one single criterion, that of "technical competence." The assumption behind this unidimensional approach to expatriate selection is aptly summarized by a statement of a respondent in Baker and Ivancevich's 1971 study: "Managing [a] company is a scientific art. The executive accomplishing the task in New York can surely perform as adequately in Hong Kong" (p. 40). This rigid tendency in U.S. overseas personnel policy has been noted by many studies (Baker and Ivancevich, 1971; Hayes, 1974; Mendenhall and Oddou, 1985; Miller, 1971, 1972; Tung, 1981), all of which call for more comprehensive selection procedures when staffing overseas assignments. Tung (1981) found

TABLE 1   **A Three-Dimensional Approach to Understanding Expatriate Acculturation**

Factor 1 *SELF- ORIENTATION*	Factor 2 *OTHERS- ORIENTATION*	Factor 3 *PERCEPTUAL- ORIENTATION*
Stress Reduction	Relationship Skills	Flexible Attributions
Reinforcement	Willingness to	Broad Category Width
Substitution	Communicate	High Tolerance for
Physical Mobility	Non-Verbal	Ambiguity
Technical Competence	Communication	Being Non-
Dealing with Alienation	Respect for Others	Judgemental
Dealing with Isolation	Empathy for Others	Being Open-Minded
Realistic Expectations		Field-Independence
Prior to Departure		

Note: For a more in-depth discussion of these variables, see Mendenhall and Oddou, 1985; Oddou and Mendenhall, 1984.

that only 5 percent of the firms in her study administered tests to determine the relational/cross-cultural/interpersonal skills of their candidates. She concluded that

> It is surprising that an overwhelming majority of the firms included in the study failed to assess the candidate's relational abilities when they clearly recognize that relational abilities are important for overseas work and when research has shown that "relational abilities" to be crucial to success in overseas assignments. Given the increasing demand for personnel who could function effectively abroad and the relatively high incidence of "failure," there certainly appears to be room for improvement in this area (Tung, 1981, p. 75).

Another overlooked feature in the selection process for overseas personnel is the adaptability potential of the spouse and other family members. A spouse or family member who is undergoing severe culture shock and/or selecting inappropriate behaviors to deal with the stress of relocation, affects the morale and performance of the expatriate manager (Grain and Cooper, 1981; Gaylord, 1979; Harvey, 1982, 1985; Tung, 1982).

The implication of these studies suggest that screening potential expatriate managers on the criteria in Table 1 is not sufficient, but that their spouses and children should be screened on the criteria as well. Studies that looked at the family as an important variable in the selection process reported that 40% to 52% of the firms studied interviewed the candidate's spouse (Gaylord, 1979; Hays, 1971; Tung, 1981, 1982); however, it should be noted that this interview — as in the case of the expatriate manager — did not exhaustively screen the spouse on the several criteria found to be critical to overseas success. Rather, the interview was peripheral to these criteria, focusing mainly on general issues of willingness to relocate, to support the spouse in his/her new assignment, etc.

A trend seems to have developed in the 1970s and has continued into the present decade, namely, that human resource divisions in U.S. MNCs consistently overlook key criteria that are predictive of overseas success in their recruiting and screening of potential overseas workers. Related to this trend is the corollary tendency to give peripheral screening to the candidates' spouses and family in terms of the same criteria. Researchers have consistently called for changes in this system based on their findings, yet the trend continues.

THE CROSS-CULTURAL TRAINING OF EXPATRIATES

A number of studies (Dunbar and Ehrlich, 1986; Korn/Ferry International, 1981; Mendenhall and Oddou, 1985; Runzheimer, 1984; Schwind, 1985; Tung, 1981) report a marked deficiency on the part of U.S. firms in offering comprehensive cross-cultural skills training to employees and their families prior to their overseas assignments. Tung (1981) found that of the MNCs in her study, only 32% of the firms offered formal training programs to prepare people to live and work overseas; 68% of the companies offered no training at all. Dunbar and Ehrlich (1986) reported that 56% of the companies in their study did not offer cross-cultural training as part of their relocation programs. As Schwind (1985) notes, "the fact that a majority of companies involved in international trade do not provide any preparatory training for managers and employees destined to work abroad is surprising" (p. 7). A variety of reasons have been given by MNC personnel for not focusing efforts and resources to the cross-cultural training of expatriates; they are:

1. The belief that cross-cultural training programs are not effective (Baker and Ivancevich, 1971; Mendenhall and Oddou, 1985; Schnapper, 1973; Schwind, 1985; Tung, 1981; Zeira, 1975).
2. Trainee dissatisfaction with the training programs (Brislin, 1979; Mendenhall and Oddou, 1985; Schnapper, 1973; Zeira, 1975).
3. The lack of time between selection and relocation prohibits in-depth cross-cultural training because there is not enough time to expose the expatriate to "quality" training (Baker and Ivancevich, 1971; Mendenhall and Oddou, 1985; Schwind, 1985; Tung, 1981).
4. The perception that because the overseas assignment is relatively short (1–3 years) it does not warrant budget expenditures on training (Schwind, 1985; Tung, 1981).
5. The trend toward employing local nationals in management (Schwind, 1985; Tung, 1981).
6. No perceived need for such programs on the part of top management (Runzheimer, 1984).

Companies that do offer cross-cultural training programs generally provided training that was not comprehensive in nature; that is, the training emphasized environmental briefing, basic culture orientation, and some language training

(Dunbar and Ehrlich, 1986; Runzheimer, 1984; Tung, 1981). Also, spouses of expatriates tend to be left out of whatever type of training is offered by the company. The 1984 Runzheimer survey reported that 80% of the firms in their study included only the employee in their cross-cultural training program; none of the companies surveyed included the children.

The duration of cross-cultural training programs tend to be relatively short considering the amount of knowledge and skills that need to be taught to the expatriates — the majority are given in one week or less (57%), 29% are given in a 2–3 week time period, and 14% take a month to complete (Runzheimer, 1984). Once overseas, companies tend to not provide much follow-up training in cross-cultural skills (Kohls, 1985; Runzheimer, 1984). The Runzheimer study (1984) reported that of the firms they studied, 49% offered no follow up training at all, 36% offer follow-up training in language skills only, 12% offer no training once overseas but assign the family a "counselor," and only 3% have a comprehensive training program for their overseas employees (Runzheimer, 1984).

CAREER-PATHING AND EXPATRIATION

There is much variation in expatriates' experience with the effects of expatriation on their career. Because very few empirical studies have been conducted on expatriation and career development, their relationship is not clear. No models of career stages have included expatriation as a key variable. Nevertheless, research on careers in general may provide a framework for studying this complex relationship.

For example, Schein's career model (1978) views career movement within an organization as falling into one of three dimensions: 1) *vertical movement*: movement "up" or "down" in the organization; classically, a promotion or a demotion; 2) *radical movement*: the degree of centrality to the organization, which mediates the organizational power of the employee; and 3) *circumferential movement*: the horizontal move across functional areas (e.g., transfer from sales to product development).

Schein (1971) links centrality in the organization to career advancement. The overseas assignment poses an interesting dilemma to this. While one is moving geographically away from the corporate headquarters when assigned overseas, one might or might not be moving away from the center of the organization in terms of the overseas position's influence upon the core business of the company.

The impact on one's career of a geographical move away from corporate headquarters is not clear. In most cases, expatriates tend to perceive an overseas assignment as an opportunity to advance vertically in the organization. Edstrom and Galbraith (1977), for example, found that expatriates viewed the purpose of their overseas assignment as development for future executive responsibility. Some research supports this notion. Brett and Werbel (1980) found that domestic relocation often does result in career advancement, Korn/Ferry (1981) found that 46% of the expatriates they studied were promoted upon return to the U.S.

Gonzalez and Negandhi (1966), however, found mixed results. In looking at managers who had returned for 5, 10, and 15 years from their assignment, there were significant differences in career advancement after repatriation. A third of the former expatriates were found to be in senior executive positions, while roughly one-half of the 100 were in low-level executive positions 15 years later. The majority of subjects in their study were "company men," one-half of them having progressed through their careers in one organization, with an additional 25% having reached managerial and executive positions with only one change of organizations.

Howard (1973) studied the career problems of 81 repatriated U.S. managers. He found the following to be problems for the expatriates:

1. No job existed for the manager upon return.
2. There was a loss of authority and professional freedom in decision making.
3. There was a loss of career and promotional opportunities.
4. There was resentment from colleagues upon return.
5. Uncertainty had existed about the length of the overseas stay.

Further, one-third of the expatriates in Edstrom and Galbraith's 1977 study felt the home office did not utilize their understanding of the overseas operation upon return; they also indicated that they did not feel corporate headquarters placed much emphasis or value on understanding the external and internal environment of overseas operations. This finding was also noted in a study of the Conference Board (La Palombara and Blank, 1977), particularly in Third World markets. The devaluation of this knowledge and expertise was documented as a source of dissatisfaction for the expatriate manager. Finally, Korn/Ferry's 1981 study found that 69% of the managers surveyed reported they felt isolated from domestic operations while abroad.

In general, then, repatriated managers report that the overseas assignment is a haphazard, ill-planned affair that is usually accompanied with vertical advancement. Yet upon return, many have difficulty in readjusting to domestic operations, experience lowered self-efficacy in their domestic position, and on occasion find themselves without a job. Human resource professionals may be unaware of the challenges facing the repatriated employee, thus career obstacles persist for the expatriate.

In summary, the relationship between expatriation and career development/advancement is not clear. With varying results in terms of advancement, it appears as though there is no standard interpretation of the importance of an overseas assignment. The impetus for overseas staffing seems to be more to meet immediate manpower needs than to create an integrated career development strategy for future corporate executives.

Improving Overseas Relocation Programs

While there are no easy, quick and cheap solutions to the problems discussed above, solutions do exist. Some MNCs already have in place the programs that will be discussed hereafter—most do not. While the human resource situation in any organization is unique, the following recommendations are general enough in nature to be adaptable to meet specific needs within a wide range of organizations.

RECOMMENDATIONS FOR
IMPROVING EXPATRIATE SELECTION

1. The criterion of "technical competence" should be retained and added to it should be the criteria listed in Table 1. The fact that overseas acculturation and productivity are multidimensional phenomena should be reflected in the strategy of the selection process and procedures (Hawes and Kealey, 1981; Mendenhall and Oddou, 1985; Oddou and Mendenhall, 1984; Tung, 1981; Zeira and Banai, 1985).

2. The selection process should focus on the measurement and evaluation of the candidate's current levels of expertise in all the aforementioned criteria. Psychological tests, stress tests, evaluations by the candidate's superiors, subordinates, peers, acquaintances, and professional evaluations from licensed psychologists can all aid in ascertaining the candidate's current level of ability in interpersonal and cross-cultural skills. The use of specifically designed assessment centers for international management simulations would be helpful in evaluating existing skill levels on the criteria as well (Heller, 1980; Howard, 1974; Mendenhall and Oddou, 1985; Rahim, 1983; Tung, 1981).

3. The candidate's spouse and children should undergo modified versions of recommendations 1 & 2. Modifications would be necessary in the instrumentation design as spouses and children confront slightly different challenges overseas than do managers. Important factors that need to be covered in "family adaptability screening" are: level of marital stability, responsibilities for aged parents, chemical dependencies on the part of anyone in the household, existence of learning disabilities in a child, behavioral problems in teenagers, emotional stability of family members, strength of family's ties to the community, other family members, friends, local church and children's attachment to extra-curricular activities, and family cohesiveness (Grain and Cooper, 1981; Gaylord, 1979; Harvey, 1982, 1985; Mendenhall and Oddou, 1985; Tung, 1982).

4. International manpower planning should occur in concert with strategic planning. Often, expatriates are selected in a "knee-jerk" fashion to quickly staff an unanticipated vacancy in an overseas subsidiary. Global succession planning requires the accurate forecasting of human resource needs worldwide and the maintenance of a pre-selected pool of candidates to draw from so as to negate lengthy screening processes each time a vacancy arises. In order to create such a pool of expatriate candidates, "internationally-oriented" MBA graduates should be a high priority item for corporate recruiters; once hired, these individuals can be groomed for overseas assignments over time and can be assisted in designing career-paths within the organization that include service abroad (Mendenhall and Oddou, 1985; Tung, 1984).

RECOMMENDATIONS FOR IMPROVING CROSS-CULTURAL TRAINING PROGRAMS

In order for cross-cultural training programs to be successful, top management must support them—both financially and politically. Every study cited concluded that more emphasis on valid and rigorous training programs is needed. In order to encourage top management in this direction, a variety of strategies should be employed.

1. Human resource staffs need to do a better job of quantifying in dollars and cents the full impact on the firm of aborted overseas assignments and the early return of overseas employees. Deficient aspects of current training programs (if they exist) should be documented and communicated to management. Also, a prospectus of a comprehensive training program should be presented to management; however, elements of the program should be prioritized along with attendant costs for each element. Thus, if management is unwilling to fund the entire program, elements can be added incrementally, over time, until the full program can be realized. This gives management flexibility in terms of manpower and financial commitment. Finally, human resource directors should actively market the firm's training program to both line and staff management. Often, line management has some control over funding some training for their people, so maintaining contact with different departments/divisions that have overseas personnel needs is a must. Staff management needs to be reassured that the company's resources are being well spent (Runzheimer, 1984).

2. Cross-cultural training programs ideally should cover the key dimensions of overseas productivity and acculturation (see Table 1). The skills needed are numerous, and the methods by which they are best learned are varied. Brislin (1979) categorized cross-cultural learning methodologies into three types: 1) the "cognitive" or "information-giving" approach (the learning of information or skills from a lecture-type orientation); 2) the "affective" approach (the learning of information/skills via techniques that raise affective responses on the part of the trainee which results in cultural insights); and 3) the "behavioral/experiential" or "immersion" approach (a variant of the affective approach—techniques that provide realistic simulations or scenarios to the trainee, such as assessment centers, field simulations, etc.). An in-depth, comprehensive training program would utilize all these approaches to cross-cultural skill learning.

3. A mediating factor to the above recommendation would be the length of time the expatriate will be stationed overseas and the degree of integration within the host culture that is necessary for the successful completion of the overseas assignment (see Figure 1). Degree of integration refers to the level of cultural fluency the expatriate will need to be successful. Some short-term business negotiations may require high levels of cultural fluency in some regions of the world (e.g., Japan, Saudi Arabia) compared to others (e.g., England, Canada, Australia). Despite the fact that some cultures are easier to adjust to than others (Mendenhall and Oddou, 1985) a long-term overseas stay, even in

a country that is similar to the U.S. (e.g., England, Australia), requires training at the affective level.

As Figure 1 indicates, with an increased need for degree of integration with the host-culture, the type of training should increase in depth from being strictly information-giving in nature to being increasingly affective and immersion-oriented. Also, as degree of integration increases, length of time needed for training increases as well (Mendenhall and Oddou, 1986).

FIGURE 1   1. Relationship Between Degree of Integration into the Host Culture and Rigor of Cross-Cultural Training. 2. Relationship Between Length of Overseas Stay and Length of Training and Training Approach.

LENGTH OF TRAINING		CROSS-CULTURAL TRAINING APPROACH
1–2 months+	High	**Immersion Approach** Assessment center Field experiences Simulations Sensitivity training Extensive language training
1–4 weeks	LEVEL OF RIGOR	**Affective Approach** Culture assimilator training Language training Role-playing Critical incidents Cases Stress reduction training Moderate language training
Less than a week	Low	**Information-giving Approach** Area briefings Cultural briefings Films/books Use of interpreters "Survival-level" language training

	Low	Moderate	High

DEGREE OF INTEGRATION

Length of stay	1 month or less	2–12 months	1–3 years

4. When the family is accompanying the expatriate overseas, they should be given training as well — even the children (Gaylord, 1979; Harvey, 1982, 1985; Mendenhall and Oddou, 1985; Runzheimer, 1984; Walker, 1976). Training programs to some degree will have to be adapted to meet the needs of these individuals, but the evidence that the acculturation level of spouses and children significantly impacts the early return of the expatriate worker suggests that these people cannot be overlooked in the training process.

RECOMMENDATIONS FOR IMPROVING CAREER-PATHING IN MNCs

There is a need to assist the expatriate manager in managing his/her career. By putting in place policies and procedures toward that end, an organization can both more efficiently manage human resources globally and encourage more employees to accept foreign transfers. The fundamental nature of such a system must be comprehensive; that is, the emphasis should not solely be upon pre-departure activities. The ideal international career management program should assess (and give feedback and preparation on) career and skill issues prior to departure, during the assignment, and subsequent to repatriation. The following recommendations illustrate aspects of such a program:

1. In concert with the expatriate, a succession plan should be developed that would identify probable length of stay, projected responsibilities while abroad, and subsequent job position upon repatriation.

2. The firm should establish and coordinate a support system between repatriated staff and expatriates. This "network" should function to provide information on both cultural-specific topics (preferably pre-assignment) and organizational information on the politics and day-to-day activities of the domestic operation while the expatriate is overseas. Other techniques to reduce the "out-of-sight-out-of-mind" dilemma would include distribution of company newsletters to staff abroad as well as other announcements that provide information to domestic employees. Such activities/programs would enable the expatriate to stay in the flow of the day-to-day activities of the home office.

3. MNCs should monitor the training and development needs of expatriates; all too frequently foreign operations lack the resources to provide expatriate employees (and their families) with classroom or informal learning opportunities. Providing management training at a regional headquarters can reduce the logistical problems of training and still guarantee that expatriate staff are current in their technical knowledge or capacity to manage others in cross-cultural work settings.

4. MNCs also could require staff, during their home leave, to update their existing succession plans and examine their future (domestic) career plans. Six months prior to the termination of the expatriate assignment, an internal position search could be initiated on behalf of the expatriate. This essentially would

be a personal job-posting program for the employee. The primary goal would be to involve the employee in determining what position will be most suited to his/her needs after the overseas assignment.

The purpose of such succession planning would be to acquaint the employee with the realities of the current in-house job market, as well as providing job market projections for the next 2–3 years. Far too often expatriates find themselves in unfortunate career dilemmas through lack of planning, career information, and/or outdated promises from superiors as to what their position would be in the company upon return.

The aforementioned interventions are relatively inexpensive to implement — with the exception of overseas staff training programs — requiring more than anything else attention and vigilance of domestic human resources staff to expatriate needs. It is recommended, however, that prior to the initiation of these or any other career pathing activities, the firm define the realities of expatriate career development. This can best be accomplished by surveying former expatriates and staff currently assigned abroad. Furthermore, actual data should be integrated into such a study to assist in determining the level of retention of repatriated staff, the average length of the overseas assignment, and the subsequent career movement of repatriated personnel.

CONCLUSION

The management of an overseas employee relocation program requires the concerted efforts of a variety of functional areas in the human resources group. Not only must personnel selection and training, manpower planning, and employee relations activities be coordinated, but the personnel activities of company headquarters, divisions, and foreign-based subsidiaries need to be coordinated as well if an organization wishes to significantly improve the success of expatriates. Presently, the complex coordination between business units, and within human resource departments, is not occurring. There is much to be done in this area — both by researchers and practitioners — to bring order to the present chaotic state of international human resource staffing.

A final issue worth consideration by both international management scholars and human resources practitioners concerns the potential long-term benefits to be derived from the international assignment. The enhancement of senior management's knowledge of foreign market constraints, cultural values and norms, and the administration of product lines across regional boundaries is of increasing value to the firm today. The proper selection, relocation, repatriation, and prudent reintegration of the international employee provides a valuable means to "internationalize" senior management and executive decision-making, particularly in cases where organizations are committed to retaining an exclusively "domestic" executive staff.

While there are no "model" programs yet in industry today, there is an increasing clarity of what the primary components are which facilitate effective international relocations. Human resource staffs should begin to design overseas relocation programs based on these components rather than relying on past practices that are ineffective, yet comfortable.

References

Abe, H., and Wiseman, R. L. A cross-cultural confirmation of the dimensions of intercultural effectiveness. *International Journal of Intercultural Relations* 7(1983): 53–68.

Baker, J. C., and Ivancevich, J. M. The assignment of American executives abroad: Systematic, haphazard, or chaotic? *California Management Review* 13, No. 3(1971): 39–41.

Brett, J. M., and Werbel, J. D. *The effect of job transfer on employees and their families*. Employee Relocation Council, 1980.

Brislin, R. W. Orientation programs for cross-cultural preparation. In A. J. Marsella, G. Tharp, and T. J. Ciborowski (Eds.), *Perspectives on cross-cultural psychology* (Orlando, Fl.: Academic Press, 1979), 287–304.

Church, A. T. Sojourn adjustment, *Psychological Bulletin* 91, No. 3 (1982): 540–571.

Copeland, L., and Griggs, L. *Going International* (New York: Random House, 1985).

Desatnick, R. L., and Bennett, M. L. *Human resource management in the multinational company* (New York: Nichols Publication Company, 1978), 173.

Dunbar, E., and Ehrlich, M. *International human resource practices, selecting, training, and managing the international staff: A survey report*. The Project on International Human Resources (New York: Columbia University—Teachers College, 1986).

Edstrom, A., and Galbraith, J. R. Transfer of managers as a coordination and control strategy in multinational organizations, *Administrative Science Quarterly* 22, No. 2(1977): 248–263.

Edwards, L. Present shock, and how to avoid it abroad, *Across the Board* 15, No. 2(1978): 36–43.

Gaylord, M. Relocation and the corporate family, *Social Work* (May 1979): 186–191.

Gonzalez, R. F., and Negandhi, A. R. *The United States overseas executive: His orientations and career patterns* (Michigan State University Institute for International Business and Economic Development Studies, Division of Research, 1966).

Grain, R. H., and Cooper, J. F. The morale-productivity relationship: How close? *Personnel* (January–February 1981): 57–62.

Harris, P. R., and Moran, R. T. *Managing cultural differences* (Houston, TX: Gulf, 1979).

Harvey, M. G. The executive family: An overlooked variable in international assignments, *Columbia Journal of World Business* (Spring 1985): 84–93.

Harvey, M. G. Executive stress associated with expatriation and repatriation, *Academy of International Business Proceedings* (December 1982): 540–543.

Hawes, F., and Kealey, D. J. An empirical study of Canadian technical assistance, *International Journal of Intercultural Relations* 5(1981): 239–258.

Hays, R. D. Expatriate selection: Insuring success and avoiding failure, *Journal of International Business Studies* 5(1974): 25–37.

Hays, R. D. Ascribed behavioral determinants of success-failure among U.S. expatriate managers, *Journal of International Business Studies* 2(1971): 40–46.

Heller, J. E. Criteria for selecting an international manager, *Personnel* (May/June 1980): 47–55.

Holmes, W. F., and Piker, F. K. Expatriate failure-prevention rather than cure, *Personnel Management* 12, No. 12(1980): 30–32.

Howard, C. G. Model for design of a selection program for multinational executives, *Public Personal Management* (March/April 1974): 138–145.

Howard, C. G. The expatriate manager and the role of the MNC. *Personnel Journal* 48, No. 1(1973): 25–29.

Kohls, R. Intercultural training. In William R. Tracey (Ed.), *Human resources management and development handbook* (New York: American Management Association, 1985).

Kohls, R. *Intercultural training: Don't leave home without it* (Washington, D.C.: SIETAR, 1984).

Korn-Ferry International, A study of the repatriation of the American international executive, New York, 1981.

Lanier, A. R. Selecting and preparing personnel for overseas transfers, *Personnel Journal* 58, No. 3(1979): 160–163.

La Palombara, J., and Blank, S. Multinational corporations in comparative perspective, *The Conference Board*, No. 725(1977).

Mendenhall, M., and Oddou, G. Acculturation profiles of expatriate managers: Implications for cross-cultural training programs, *Columbia Journal of World Business* 21, No. 4(1986): 73–79.

Mendenhall, M., and Oddou, G. The dimensions of expatriate acculturation: A review. *Academy of Management Review* 10(1985): 39–47.

Miller, E. L. The overseas assignment: How managers determine who is to be selected, *Michigan Business Review* 24, No. 3(1972): 12–19.

Miller, E. L. The international selection decision: A study of some dimensions of managerial behavior in the selection decision process, *Academy of Management Journal* 16(1971): 239–252.

Misa, K. F., and Fabricatore, J. M. Return on investment of overseas personnel, *Financial Executive* 47, No. 4(1979): 42–46.

Oddou, G., and Mendenhall, M. Person perception in cross-cultural settings: A review of cross-cultural and related literature, *International Journal of Intercultural Relations* 8(1984): 77–96.

Rahim, A. A model for developing key expatriate executives, *Personnel Journal* (April 1983): 312–317.

Ratiu, I. Thinking internationally: A comparison of how international executives learn, *International Studies of Management and Organization* 13(1983): 139–150.

Runzheimer Executive Report, 1984 Expatriation/Repatriation Survey, No. 31, Rochester, Wisconsin, 1984.

Schein, E. H. The individual, the organization, and the career: A conceptual scheme, *Journal of Applied Behavioral Science* 7(1971): 401–426.

Schein, E. H. *Career Dynamics: Matching individual and organizational needs* (Reading, Mass.: Addison Wesley, 1978).

Schnapper, M. Resistances to intercultural training. Paper presented at the 13th Annual Conference of the Society for International Development. San Jose, Costa Rica, 1973.

Schwind, H. F. The state of the art in cross-cultural management training. In *International HRD Annual (Volume 1)*, Robert Doktor (Ed.), 7–15 (Alexandria, Va.: ASTD, 1985).

Stening, B. W. Problems in cross-cultural contact: A literature review, *International Journal of Intercultural Relations* 3(1979): 269–313.

Torbiorn, I. *Living abroad: Personal adjustment and personnel policy in the overseas setting* (New York: John Wiley, 1982).

Tung, R. L. Strategic management of human resources in the multinational enterprise, *Human Resource Management* (Summer 1984): 129–143.

Tung, R. L. Selection and training procedures of U.S., European, and Japanese multinationals, *California Management Review* 25, No. 1(1982): 57–71.

Tung, R. L. Selection and training of personnel for overseas assignments, *Columbia Journal of World Business* 16, No. 1(1981): 68–78.

Walker, E. J. 'Til business us do part?' *Harvard Business Review* (1976): 94–101.

Zeira, Y. Overlooked personnel problems of multinational corporations, *Columbia Journal of World Business* 10, No. 2(1975): 96–103.

Zeria, Y., and Banai, M. Selection of expatriate managers in MNCs: The host-environment point of view, *International Studies of Management and Organization* 15, No. 1(1985): 33–51.

READING 8

Pacific Basin Managers:
A *Gaijin*,* Not a Woman

Nancy J. Adler

Pacific Rim business is the fastest growing in the world. To remain competitive, no major North American firm dare ignore Asia. Traditionally, very few women have held managerial and executive positions in Asia. Can North American female managers be successful in Asia, or must firms limit their international management positions to men?

To answer this question, 52 women who had held at least one management position in Asia were interviewed. They were overwhelmingly successful. This study describes who the women are, how they were chosen, and their professional experience as female expatriate managers in Asia.

> It doesn't make any difference if you are blue, green, purple, or a frog. If you have the best product at the best price, they'll buy.
>
> — American female manager based in Hong Kong.

About the single most uncontroversial, incontrovertible statement to make about women in international management is that there are very few of them. The evidence is both subjective and objective [1. p. 58]. As the international personnel vice-president for a North American company, would you choose to send an American or Canadian woman to Asia as an expatriate manager? Would she succeed? Would it be fair to the company and to the woman to send her to Asia? Would it be wiser not to send·her?

International commerce has become vital to North American prosperity. Robert Frederick, chairman of the U.S. National Foreign Trade Council, has stated that

---

*Gaijin means foreigner (i.e., non-Japanese), either male or female.

Human Resource Management, 1987 Vol. 26(2): 169–191. © 1987 by John Wiley & Sons Inc. Reproduced by permission of John Wiley & Sons Inc. This paper is an adaptation that was published in *Women in Management Worldwide*, Nancy J. Adler and Dafna N. Izraeli, editors (M. E. Sharpe Inc., 1988), 226–249.

80 percent of United States industry now faces international competition. Already by the beginning of this decade, approximately 70 percent of all U.S. firms were conducting a portion of their business abroad [2]. Canada provides an even more dramatic example of the importance of international business. By 1980, more than five hundred Canada-based companies had foreign subsidiaries, an increase of more than forty-three percent in just six years [3]. Canadians import nearly one-quarter of all the goods they consume and export a slightly larger proportion of their gross national product. Moreover, foreigners own more than half of Canada's manufacturing capacity [4].

Internationally, Pacific Rim business is the fastest growing in the world. Asian economies, most notably those of the "Four Tigers" — Hong Kong, Korea, Singapore, and Taiwan — have been among the most rapidly developing in recent economic history. At the same time, the People's Republic of China now commands the attention of Western economies, if for no other reason than the size of its potential market; and Japan continues to dominate global economic activity across a widening range of industries. To remain competitive, no major North American firm dare ignore Pacific Rim business.

Along with the globalization of business, stories about women's changing role in society have gained prominence during the last decade. The United Nations Decade for Women emphasized both what needs to be done for women to reach equality and the many changes already under way. Within this pattern of changes, what role do, and will, female managers play in Asia?

One wonders if North American companies should respect Asian countries' apparent cultural norms and send only male managers to those countries. Yet, with the increasing importance of international business, can North American firms afford to limit their personnel selection decisions to one gender? Women's role in international management has become one of the most important questions facing human resources managers of multinational firms. Owing to the economic significance of Pacific Rim business and the apparent dearth of female managers, both local and expatriate, the question assumes particular importance. This chapter examines the role of North American women working in Asia for North American firms. It reports the findings of a series of studies investigating Canadian and U.S. women's role as expatriate managers in Asia.

DO ASIANS DISCRIMINATE AGAINST WOMEN IN MANAGEMENT?

All cultures differentiate male and female roles, expecting women to behave in certain ways, and men, in others; for women to fill certain roles, and men, others. In many cultures the traditional female role supports attitudes and behaviors contradictory to those of a manager. Therefore, women in many parts of the world have failed to aspire to become managers, and men have blocked their pursuit of such careers. Asia is no exception. Few Asian women are managers; even fewer have achieved prominence as managers. Using Canada and the United States as a point of comparison, let us look at the role women play as managers in a selection of Asian countries.

Already two decades ago in the United States, more than fifteen percent (15.8 percent) of working women held managerial and administrative positions, while in Canada almost ten percent (9.5 percent) held such positions.[1] By 1982, American women occupied over a quarter (27.9 percent) of all managerial and administrative positions [6]. Yet, top management positions still elude women: even in the 1980s, American women represent only 5 percent of top executives [7].

By comparison, the number of female managers in Asia, especially those visible to the international business community, remains infinitesimally small. Female managers are almost nonexistent within the corporate structure and, more broadly, within the leadership ranks of the business sector. Women constitute less than one percent of the senior managers in Southeast Asian corporations.[2] But our North American statistics, focusing primarily on major corporations, have missed some of the involvement of female entrepreneurs and women managing smaller and family-owned Asian companies. For example, Japan has more than twenty-five thousand female company presidents, all of whom manage small to medium-size firms; none are CEOs of multinationals.[3] Similarly, a number of women control major family-owned firms in Thailand and Indonesia, although none hold top positions within corporate structures. Notwithstanding this overlooked involvement, neither the numbers nor the status of Asian women in management equals those of their male counterparts. Why? The reasons are cultural, legal, and economic, with the emphasis varying from each specific Asian nation to another.

Indonesia

In Indonesia, only one in five women (20.8 percent) participates in the paid labor force, compared with 60 percent in Sweden, 53 percent in the United States, 51 percent in Canada, 46.7 percent in Japan, and 45.5 percent in Australia [8]. This compares with a male labor-force participation rate of over seventy percent in the United States (77 percent), Canada (78.3 percent), Sweden (74 percent), Japan (80 percent), and Australia (79 percent). Although a few Indonesian women hold highly prestigious leadership positions, the vast majority remain outside the corporate and managerial hierarchy.

As in most areas of the world, Indonesian managers come from the ranks of the educated. In Indonesia only 5 percent of the total population has graduated from high school, and fewer than one percent from an academy or university [9]. Although the proportion of those educated is rising rapidly—and considerably faster for women than for men—women remain half as likely as men to be highly educated.[4] Not surprisingly, the highly educated women have the highest labor-force participation rate, government administration being the second most common occupation after teaching in rural areas and sales in urban areas. Yet almost twice as many educated men as women hold such positions. In the private sector, four times as many men as women hold managerial positions.

Japan

Despite Japan's highly acclaimed advanced industrialization, private industry excludes women from most responsible managerial positions [10]. In 1955, the proportion of professionals and managers in the entire female labor force was 3.5 percent, rising to only 8.5 percent by 1977 [11]. By the 1980s, primarily because of women's reentering the work force after rearing their families, the proportion of women working had risen to one of the world's highest, now constituting almost 40 percent (39.7 percent) of the work force [12], approximately on a par with Sweden [13,14]. Yet, women continue to hold few managerial positions, especially in major corporations.[5] For example, the 1983 *Who's Who in Japanese Business*, covering the 1,754 major companies listed in Japan's 8 Stock Exchanges, included only 68 women among the 160,764 Japanese managers.[6] Moreover, 50 percent of all Japanese firms have no female managers, and that proportion has remained constant since 1955 [11]. Of the Japanese women who have attained managerial status, almost all work for small or medium-size businesses, not for multinational corporations. Despite recent legal changes, no major increase in the number of women in the latter category is predicted.

While cultural and legal constraints partly explain the role of women in Japanese management, the lifetime employment system accounts for their absence from major corporations. Culturally, a well-known Confucian saying states: "A women is to obey her father as daughter, her husband as wife, and her son as aged mother" [11]. Not surprisingly, given this tradition, the Japanese have viewed women neither as authority figures nor as decision makers. Strong cultural norms have made it difficult for Japanese companies to send a woman on domestic or international business trips with a male colleague if not accompanied by a second man. Laws, including the Labor Standards Act, restrict certain positions to men and preclude women from working overtime or at night in many professions.

In general, Japanese society expects women to work until marriage, quit to rear children, and return, only as needed, to low-level and part-time positions after age 40. Thus, by 1985 women constituted a little over 70 percent (70.7 percent) of all part-time workers [12]. Clearly, in Japan, while the home continues to be women's domain, the workplace remains the domain of men. Given this pattern, combined with major Japanese corporations' lifetime employment and promotions systems, most firms have not considered it worthwhile to develop women for significant management positions. Major corporations generally place women on separate career paths from men, frequently treating them differently in terms of wages, promotion, and retirement. Today, Japanese women seeking managerial careers often must take positions in foreign, rather than Japanese, firms [15].

The People's Republic of China

Although one Chinese saying is that "Women hold up half of the world," numerous other traditional folk sayings and proverbs belittle women and disparage their leadership abilities. For example, when a woman becomes a leader, some Chinese say that it is like "a donkey taking the place of a horse, which can only lead to trouble" [16]. Since the 1970s, the anti-Confucian and Lin Piao campaigns have tried to create more favorable conditions for women by identifying obstacles to redefining women's role and improving their status [17]. The media have reported men's and women's groups "as coming to a new awareness of an old problem through the recognition of their ideological constraints originating in the Confucian principle of male supremacy" [16]. Nevertheless, women are still underrepresented in political and leadership positions, receive unequal pay in rural areas, and are bound by traditional courtship and marriage customs that maintain work-related gender differentiation and disproportionate shares of household work [16,18].

Given the rapidly changing political and economic environment in China and its increasing openness to international markets, it is difficult to assess the exact proportion of women currently holding managerial and executive positions. My own interviews with female Chinese managers in 1986 confirmed the continued pattern of placing women's primary responsibility in the home, equality at work being most accessible to those in lower positions and those whose children were grown up and thus beyond the need for daily maternal care.[7] Whereas physical labor knows few gender boundaries in the People's Republic of China, access to top managerial positions in industry and government remains largely the domain of men.

India

Although women have been guaranteed constitutional equality and have occupied prominent positions in government since India's independence, in 1947, only recently have they begun to assume managerial positions in business organizations. A limited survey of 33 female executives across a wide range of industries led to the conclusion that Indian women have fewer opportunities for promotion than men; but once promoted, they perform as well as men in executive positions. However, despite the fact that these Indian women believed they could successfully combine the roles of wife and executive, some questioned the appropriateness of continuing to work if they had small children [19].

Singapore

Singapore has been one of the most rapidly developing "newly industrialized countries" in the Pacific Basin. To overcome critical human-resource shortages, the government launched a major campaign, in the early 1980s, to encourage Singaporean women to rejoin the work force. This effort included supporting quality child-care services, flexible work scheduling and incentives, training and retraining programs, and improved societal attitudes toward career women [20]. By 1983, Singaporean women constituted more than a third (35.5 percent) of the labor force and more than a sixth (17.8 percent) of the administrators and managers (up from 7 percent in 1980). Chan[8] attributes the increases to prosperous economic conditions, the government's development policies encouraging women's participation in the work force, and women's own career aspirations. She views Singapore's rapid growth as an enabling condition, but also notes the 1984 economic downturn's disproportionately adverse effect on women.

The Philippines

Although women from prominent families clearly hold influential positions in Filipino political and economic life, the overall situation for women differs little from that in other Pacific Rim countries. The Philippine Labor Code prohibits discrimination against women with respect to rates of pay and conditions of employment [21]. Yet, while women accounted for approximately a third of the labor force by 1976, less than three percent (2.7 percent) of the working women held administrative or managerial positions in government or business — a figure representing less than one percent of the total managerial positions [22]. Their numbers have not increased.

Philippine society still holds deeply rooted beliefs regarding the role of women at home and at work [23]. Social pressures in Philippine society, in which both men and women frequently support strongly differentiated sex-role stereotypes, make it difficult for a Filipina to choose a career instead of a family or to combine marriage, career, and motherhood successfully [24–26].

WOMEN IN INTERNATIONAL MANAGEMENT

Given the culturally mandated scarcity of local female managers in most Asian countries, can female expatriate managers from North American companies function successfully in Asia? More specifically, should Canadian and American companies send women to Japan, Korea, Hong Kong, the Philippines, the People's Republic of China, Singapore, Thailand, India, Pakistan, Malaysia, or Indonesia? Is the experience of local women — i.e., their relative absence from the managerial ranks — the best predictor of success, or lack thereof, for expatriate women?

The research summarized here presents the story of a noun, *women*, that appears to have gotten mixed up with an adjective, *female*, when describing managers. The study is the unfolding of a set of assumptions about how Asians would treat North American female managers, based on North Americans' beliefs concerning Asians' treatment of their own women. The problem with the story is that the assumptions have proven to be false, that they fail to reflect reality.

THE STUDY

This research on female managers is part of a four-part study on the role of North American women as expatriate managers. In the first part, 686 Canadian and American firms were surveyed concerning the number of women they had sent overseas as expatriate managers. The survey identified over thirteen thousand (13,338) expatriate managers, of whom 402, or 3 percent, were women — that is, 3.3 percent of American and 1.3 percent of Canadian expatriate managers were female. Overall, North American firms send 32 times as many male as female managers overseas [27,28].

Not surprisingly, larger companies send proportionately more women than do smaller companies, with financial institutions leading other industries. However, the 3 percent, although representing significantly fewer than the proportion of North American women in domestic management, should not be viewed as a poor showing, but rather as the beginning of a trend. The vast majority of North American female managers who have ever been sent abroad in expatriate status are currently overseas.

The second, third, and fourth parts of the study attempted to explain why so few North American women work as international managers. Each part was structured around one of the three most common "myths" about women in international management:

Myth 1: Women do not want to be international managers.
Myth 2: Companies refuse to send women overseas.
Myth 3: Foreigners' prejudice against women renders them ineffective, even when they are interested in overseas assignments and succeed in being sent.

These beliefs were labeled "myths" because, although widely held by both men and women, they had never been tested.

Women's Interest in International Careers

Are women less interested than men in pursuing international careers? The second part of the study tested this myth by surveying 1,129 graduating M.B.A.s from 7 management schools in the United States, Canada, and Europe. The overwhelming result was an impressive case of no significant difference: male and female M.B.A.s displayed equal interest or disinterest, in pursuing international careers. Eighty-four percent of the M.B.A.s said they would like an international assignment at some time during their careers. Both males and females, however, agreed that the opportunities were fewer for women than for men, and fewer for women pursuing international compared with domestic managerial careers. Although there may have been a difference in the past, today's male and female M.B.A.s appear equally interested in international work and expatriate positions [29,30].

Corporate Resistance to Assigning Women Overseas

To test the corporate resistance myth, personnel vice-presidents and managers from 60 major North American multinationals were surveyed [31]. According to their responses, over half of the companies (54 percent) hesitate to send women overseas. This is almost four times as many as those hesitating to select women for domestic assignments (54 percent compared with 14 percent). Almost three-fourths (73 percent) believe foreigners are prejudiced against female managers. Similarly, 70 percent believe that women, especially married women in dual-career marriages, would be reluctant to accept, if not totally uninterested in, a foreign assignment. With respect to certain locations, the personnel executives expressed concern about the women's physical safety, the hazards involved in traveling in underdeveloped countries, and, especially in the case of single women, the isolation and potential loneliness. These findings concur with those from a survey of 100 top managers in *Fortune* 500 firms operating overseas in which the majority believed that women faced overwhelming resistance when seeking management positions in international divisions of U.S. firms [2].

Foreigners' Reactions to Female Expatriate Managers

Why do three-quarters of the North American firms believe foreigners are prejudiced against expatriate women managers? Perhaps, owing to their lack of experience, companies anticipate female expatriates' success, or lack thereof, on the basis of the role and treatment of local women within the particular foreign culture. Perhaps the scarcity of Asian women working as managers has led North American companies to conclude that North American women would not receive the respect necessary to succeed in managerial or professional positions. When interviewed, many international personnel executives declared that it would be fair to neither the woman nor her company to send a female manager to Asia when the treatment of local women suggested that she would have difficulty succeeding. The fundamental question was, and remains, Is this a valid basis for predicting female expatriate managers' effectiveness?

Foreign Female Managers in Asia

To investigate the third myth, that foreigners' prejudice against women render the latter ineffective as international managers, 52 female expatriate managers were interviewed in 1983 while in Asia or after returning from Asia to North America. Owing to multiple foreign postings, the 52 women represented 61 Asian assignments. The greatest number was based in Hong Kong (34 percent), followed by Japan (25 percent), Singapore (16 percent), the Philippines and Australia (5 percent each), Indonesia and Thailand (4 percent each), and at least one each in Korea, India, Taiwan, and the People's Republic of China. Since most of the women held regional responsibility, they worked throughout Asia rather than just in their country of foreign residence.

Of those working in Asia, financial institutions sent the vast majority (71 percent). Other industries sending more than two women to Asia included publishing (7 percent) and petroleum (6 percent). Those sending one or two women were engaged in advertising, film distribution, service industries (including accounting, law, executive search, and computers), retail food, electronic appliances, pharmaceuticals, office equipment, sporting goods, or soaps and cosmetics.

On average, the female expatriates' assignments lasted 2.5 years (19.7 months), though they ranged from 6 months to 6 years. Salaries in 1983, not counting benefits, varied from U.S. $27,000 to $54,000, averaging $34,500. The female expatriate managers supervised from 0 to 25 subordinates, the average falling between four and five (4.6). Their titles and levels in the organization varied considerably: some held very junior positions, e.g., "trainee" or assistant account manager, while other held quite senior positions, including one regional vice-president. In no case did a female expatriate hold the company's number-one position in the region or in any country.

Female Expatriates: Who Are They?

As the above description indicates, the female expatriates were fairly junior within their organizations and careers. Their ages ranged from 23 to 41 years, the average being under thirty (28.8). Nearly two-thirds (62 percent) were single; only 3 had children. Five of the women married while overseas — all to other expatriates.

Although the women were considerably younger then the typical male expatriate manager, their age probably does not reflect any systematic discrimination for or against them. Rather, it is an artifact of the relatively high proportion of women sent by financial institutions — an industry that selects fairly junior managers for overseas assignments — and the relatively low proportion in manufacturing, in which international employees are generally quite senior (e.g., country or regional directors).

The women were very well educated and quite internationally experienced. Almost all held graduate degrees, the M.B.A. being the most common. Over three-fourths had had extensive international interests and experience before their present company had sent them overseas. For example, 77 percent had traveled internationally, and almost two-thirds (61 percent) had had an international focus in their studies before joining the company.

On average, the women spoke between two and three languages (average, 2.5), some speaking fluently as many as six. In subjective observations during the interviews, the women, as a group, had excellent social skills and, by Western standards, were very good-looking.

The Decision to Go Overseas

How did the companies and the female managers decide on the overseas transfers? In the majority of cases, the female expatriates were "firsts": only 5 women (10 percent) followed another woman into the international position. Of the 90 percent who were "firsts," almost a fourth (22 percent) represented the first female manager the firm had ever sent abroad. Fourteen percent were the first women sent to Asia, 25 percent were the first sent to the particular country, and 20 percent were the first to fill the specific position. Clearly, neither the women nor the companies had the luxury of role models; few could follow previously established patterns. Except in the case of a few major New York–based financial institutions, both the women and the companies found themselves experimenting, in hope of uncertain success.

The decision process leading a company to send a female manager to Asia could be described as one of mutual education. In more than four of five cases (83 percent), the women had initially introduced the idea of an international assignment to her boss and company. In only 6 instances (11 percent) had the company initially suggested the assignment; in another 3 cases (6 percent), the suggestion had been "mutual."

The women had used a number of strategies to "educate" their companies. Many had explored the possibility of an overseas assignment during their original job interview and had eliminated from consideration companies that were totally against the idea. In other cases, women had informally introduced the idea to their bosses and continued to mention it informally "at appropriate moments" until the company ultimately decided to offer them an overseas position. A few women had formally applied for a number of overseas positions before actually being selected.

Some of the female managers admitted to having employed various strategies to make their careers international, primarily attempting to be in the right place at the right time. For example, one woman who foresaw that Hong Kong would be her firm's next major business center arranged to assume responsibility for the Hong Kong desk in New York, leaving the rest of Asia to a male colleague. The strategy paid off: within a year, the company sent her, not her male colleague, to Hong Kong. Overall, the women described themselves as needing to encourage their companies to consider the possibility of giving overseas posts to women in general and themselves in particular. In most cases they claimed that their companies simply had failed to recognize the possibility of giving women overseas assignments, not as having thoroughly considered the idea and then rejected it. Generally speaking, the obstacle was naiveté, not conscious rejection.

Many women confronted some corporate resistance before being sent abroad. For example:

> *Malaysia*. According to one woman being considered for an assignment in Malaysia, "Management assumed that women didn't have the physical stamina to survive in the tropics. They claimed I couldn't hack it."
>
> *Thailand*. "My company didn't want to send a woman to that 'horrible part of the world.' They think Bangkok is an excellent place to send single men, but not a woman. They said they would have trouble getting a work permit, which wasn't true."
>
> *Japan and Hong Kong*. "Everyone was more or less curious if it would work. My American boss tried to advise me, 'Don't be upset if it's difficult in Japan and Korea.' The American male manager in Tokyo was also hesitant. Finally, the Chinese boss in Hong Kong said, 'We have to try!'"
>
> *Japan*. "Although I was the best qualified, I was not offered the position in Japan until the senior Japanese manager in Tokyo said, 'We are very flexible in Japan.' Then they sent me."

A few women described severe company resistance to sending female managers abroad. To these women it seemed that their firms offered them positions overseas only after all potential male candidates for the positions had turned them down. For instance:

> *Thailand.* "Every advance in responsibility is because the Americans had no choice. I've never been chosen over someone else."
>
> *Japan.* "They never would have considered me. But then the financial manager in Tokyo had a heart attack, and they had to send someone. So they sent me, on a month's notice, as a temporary until they could find a man to fill the permanent position. It worked out, and I stayed."

Although most of the women had been sent in the same capacity as male expatriates, some companies demonstrated their hesitation by offering temporary or travel assignments rather than true expatriate positions. For instance:

> *Hong Kong.* "After offering me the job, they hesitated: 'Could a woman work with the Chinese?' So my job was defined as temporary, a one-year position to train a Chinese man to replace me. I succeeded and became permanent."

This may appear to be a logically cautious strategy, but in reality it tends to create an unfortunate self-fulfilling prophecy. As a number of women reported, if the company was not convinced a women could succeed (and therefore offered her a temporary rather than a permanent position), this decision itself communicated the company's lack of confidence to foreign colleagues and clients as a lack of commitment. The foreigners then mirrored the home company's behavior by also failing to take the women managers seriously. Assignments became very difficult, or could even fail altogether when companies' initial confidence and commitment were lacking. As one women in Indonesia said, "It is very important to clients that I am permanent. It increases trust, and that's critical."

Many women claimed that the most difficult hurdle in their international career involved getting sent overseas in the first place, not — as most had anticipated — gaining the respect of foreigners and succeeding once there.

Did It Work? The Impact of Being Female

When describing their actual working experience in Asia, almost all (97 percent) of the North American women said it had been a success; their descriptions were, admittedly, strictly subjective; but a number of more objective indicators suggest that most assignments were, in fact, successful. For example, most firms — after experimenting with their first female expatriate manager — decided to send other women overseas. Moreover, many companies promoted the women on the basis of their overseas performance and/or offered them other international assignments following completion of the first one.

In only two cases did women report experiences of failure: one in Australia, and the other in Singapore. For the first woman, it was her second international posting, after a successful experience in Latin America, and was followed by an equally successful assignment in Singapore. For the second woman, the Singapore assignment was her only overseas posting.

Prior to conducting the interviews, I had expected the women to describe a series of difficulties caused by their being female and a corresponding set of creative solutions to each difficulty. This was not the case. Almost half of the women (42 percent) reported that being female served more as an advantage than a disadvantage; 16 percent found it to have both positive and negative effects; 22 percent saw it as "irrelevant" or neutral; and only 20 percent found it to be primarily negative.

Advantages

The women reported numerous professional advantages to being female. Most frequently they described the advantage of being highly visible. Foreign clients were curious about them, wanted to meet them, and remembered them after the first encounter. It therefore appeared easier for the women than for their male colleagues to gain access to foreign clients' time and attention. The women described this high visibility, accessibility, and memorability with comments such as the following:

> *Japan.* "It's the visibility as an expat, and even more as a woman. I stick in their minds. I know I've gotten more business than my two male colleagues. [My clients] are extra interested in me."

> *Thailand.* "Being a woman is never a detriment. They remembered me better. Fantastic for a marketing position. It's better working with Asians than with the Dutch, British, or Americans."

> *India and Pakistan.* "In India and Pakistan, being a woman helps in marketing and client contact. I got in to see customers because they had never seen a female banker before. . . . Having a female banker adds value to the client."

The female managers also described the advantages of good interpersonal skills and mentioned their belief that men could talk more easily about a wider range of topics with women than with other men. For example:

> *Indonesia.* "I often take advantage of being a women. I'm more supportive than my male colleagues. . . . [Clients] relax and talk more. And 50 percent of my effectiveness is based on volunteered information."

> *Korea.* "Women are better at treating men sensitively, and they just like you. One of my Korean clients told me, 'I really enjoyed the lunch and working with you.'"

In addition, many of the women described the higher status accorded women in Asia and said that that status was not denied them as foreign female managers. They often felt that they received special treatment that their male colleagues did not receive. Clearly, it was always salient that they were women, but being a woman did not appear to be antithetical to succeeding as a manager.

> *Hong Kong.* "Single female expats travel easier and are treated better. Never hassled. No safety issues. Local offices take better care of you. They meet you, take you through customs, . . . It's the combination of treating you like a lady and a professional."

Japan. "It's an advantage that attracts attention. They are interested in meeting a *gaijin*, a foreign woman. Women attract more clients. On calls to clients, they elevate me, give me more rank. If anything, the problem, for men and women, is youth, not gender."

Moreover, most of the women claimed benefits from a "halo effect." Most of their foreign colleagues and counterparts had never met or previously worked with a female expatriate manager. At the same time, most of the foreign community was highly aware of how unusual it was for American and Canadian firms to send female managers to Asia. Hence, the Asians tended to assume that the women would not have been sent unless they were "the best," and therefore expected them to be "very, very good."

Japan. "Women are better at putting people at ease. It's easier for a woman to convince a man. . . . The traditional woman's role . . . inspires confidence and trust, less suspicion, not threatening. They assumed I must be good if I was sent. They become friends."

Indonesia. "It's easier being a woman here than in any place in the world, including New York City. . . . I never get the comments I got in New York, like 'What is a nice woman like you doing in this job?'"

No Impact

Other women found being female to have no impact whatever on their professional life. For the most part, these were women working primarily with the Chinese:

Hong Kong. "There's no difference. They respect professionalism . . . including in Japan. There is no problem in Asia."

Hong Kong. "There are many expat and foreign women in top positions here. If you are good at what you do, they accept you. One Chinese woman told me, 'Americans are always watching you. One mistake and you are done. Chinese take a while to accept you and then stop testing you.'"

Disadvantages

The women also cited a number of disadvantages in being a female expatriate manager. Interestingly enough, the majority of the disadvantages involved the women's relationship with their home companies, not with their Asian clients. As noted earlier, a major problem involved difficulty in obtaining the foreign assignment in the first place. A subsequent problem involved the limited opportunities and job scope the home company allowed once the woman was overseas. More than half of the female expatriates described difficulty in persuading their home companies to give them latitude equivalent to that given their male colleagues, especially initially. Some companies, out of concern for the women's safety, limited their travel (and thus their region of operation), excluding very remote, rural, and underdeveloped areas. Other companies, as mentioned previously, limited the duration of the women's assignments to six months or a year, rather than the more standard two to three years. For example:

Japan. "My problem is overwhelmingly with Americans. They identify it as a male market . . . geisha girls. . . ."

Thailand (petroleum company). "The Americans wouldn't let me on the drilling rigs, because they said there were no accommodations for a woman. Everyone blames it on something else. They gave me different work. They had me working on the sidelines, not planning and communicating with drilling people. It's the expat Americans, not the Thais, who'll go to someone else before they come to me."

Another disadvantage that some companies placed on the women was limiting them to work only internally with company employees, rather than externally with clients. The companies' often implicit assumption was that their own employees were somehow less prejudiced than were outsiders. Interestingly, the women often found the opposite to be true; they faced more problems within their own organization than externally with clients. One American woman described her situation thus:

Hong Kong. "It was somewhat difficult internally. They feel threatened, hesitant to do what I say, resentful. They assume I don't have the credibility that a man would have. Perhaps it's harder internally than externally because client relationships are one on one, and internally it's more of a group, or perhaps it's harder because they have to live with it longer internally, or perhaps it's because they fear that I'm setting a precedent or because they fear criticism from their peers."

Managing foreign clients' and colleagues' initial expectations proved difficult for many of the women. Some described initial meetings with Asians as "tricky." Since most Asians had previously never met a North American expatriate woman holding a managerial position, there was considerable ambiguity as to who she was, her status, her level of expertise, authority, and responsibility, and therefore the appropriate form of address and demeanor with respect to her.

Hong Kong (Asia Region). "It took extra time to establish credibility with the Japanese and Chinese. One Japanese manager said to me, 'When I first met you, I thought you would not be any good because you were a woman.' . . . The rest of Asia is O.K."

People's Republic of China. "I speak Chinese, which is a plus. But they'd talk to the men, not to me. They'd assume that I, as a woman, had no authority. The Chinese want to deal only with top-, top-, top-level people, and there is always a man at a higher level."

Since most of the North American women whom Asians had met previously had been male expatriate managers' wives or secretaries, the Asians naturally assumed that the new woman on the scene was not a manager. Hence, the women said, initial conversations often were directed to male colleagues, not to the newly arrived female managers. Senior male colleagues, particularly those from the head office, became very important in redirecting the focus of early discussions back toward the women. If this was well done, old patterns were quickly broken, and smooth ongoing work relationships were established; if this problem was ignored or poorly managed, the challenges to credibility, authority, and responsibility became chronic and undermined the women's potential effectiveness.

The North American women clearly had more difficulty gaining respect from North American and European men working in Asia than from the Asians themselves. Some even suggested that the expatriate community in Asia had attracted many "very traditional" men who were not particularly open to the idea of women in management — whether at home or abroad. For example:

Singapore. "Colonial British don't accept women; very male. There are no women in their management levels. I got less reaction from the Chinese. The Chinese are interested only in whether you can do the job."

Hong Kong. "British men . . . you must continually prove yourself. You can't go to lunch with U.K. expat company men. The senior U.K. guys become uncomfortable, and the younger U.K. guys get confused as to whether the lunch is a social or a business occasion. So I hesitate inviting them. Interaction is just tenuous from both sides."

Hong Kong. "The older men had trouble imagining me with the bank in ten years."

As mentioned earlier, many women described the most difficult aspect of the foreign assignment as getting sent overseas in the first place. Overcoming resistance from North American head offices frequently proved more challenging than gaining foreign clients' and colleagues' respect and acceptance. In most cases, assumptions about Asians' prejudice against female expatriate managers appear to have been exaggerated: the anticipated prejudice and the reality did not match. Why? Perhaps foreigners are not as prejudiced as we think.

THE *GAIJIN* SYNDROME

Throughout the interviews, one pattern became particularly clear. First and foremost, foreigners are seen as foreigners. Like their male colleagues, female expatriates are seen as foreigners, not as local people. A woman who is a foreigner (a *gaijin*) is not expected to act like the local people. Therefore, the rules governing the behavior of local women that limit their access to management and managerial responsibility do not apply to foreign women. Although women are considered the "culture bearers" in all societies, foreign women in no way assume, or are expected to assume, that role. As one woman in Japan said, "The Japanese are very smart: they can tell that I am not Japanese, and they do not expect me to act as a Japanese woman. They will allow and condone behavior in foreign women that would be absolutely unacceptable in their own women." Similarly, Ranae Hyer, a Tokyo-based personnel vice-president of the Bank of America's Asia Division, said, "Being a foreigner is so weird to the Japanese that the marginal impact of being a woman is nothing. If I were a Japanese woman, I couldn't be doing what I'm doing here. But they know perfectly well that I'm not" [32].

Many interviewees related similar examples of female expatriates' unique status as "foreign women" rather than as women per se. For example:

Japan and Korea. "Japan and Korea are the hardest, but they know that I'm an American woman, and they don't expect me to be like a Japanese or Korean woman. It's possible to be effective even in Japan and Korea if you send a senior woman, with at least three to four years of experience, especially if she's fluent in Japanese."

Japan. "It's the novelty, especially in Japan, Korea, and Pakistan. All of the general managers met with me. . . . It was much easier for me, especially in Osaka. They were charming. They didn't want me to feel bad. They thought I would come back if they gave me business. You see, they could separate me from the local women."

Pakistan. "Will I have problems? No! There is a double standard between expats and local women. The Pakistanis test you, but you enter as a respected person."

Japan. "I don't think the Japanese could work for a Japanese woman, . . . but they just block it out for foreigners."

Hong Kong. "Hong Kong is very cosmopolitan. I'm seen as an expat, not as an Asian, even though I am an Asian American."

It seems that we may have confused the adjective and the noun in predicting Asians' reactions to North American women. We expected the primary descriptor of female expatriate managers to be "woman" and predicted their success on the basis of the success of the Asian women in each country. In fact, the primary descriptor is "foreign," and the best predictor of success is the success of other North Americans in the particular country. *Asians see female expatriates as foreigners who happen to be women, not as women who happen to be foreigners.* The difference is crucial. Given the uncertainty involved in sending women into new areas of the world, our assumptions about the greater salience of gender (male/female) over nationality (foreign/local) have caused us to have false expectations concerning women's potential to succeed as managers in foreign countries.

RECOMMENDATIONS

It is clear from the experience of the women described and quoted in this paper that North American female expatriates can succeed as managers in Asia. In considering them for overseas assignments, both the companies and the women themselves should bear in mind a number of aspects of such an assignment.

First, do not assume that it will not work. Do not assume that foreigners will treat expatriate female managers the same way they treat their own women. Our assumptions about the salience of gender over nationality have led to totally inaccurate predictions. Therefore, do not confuse adjectives and nouns; do not use the success or failure of local women to predict that of foreign women.

Similarly, do not confuse the role of a spouse with that of a manager. Although the single most common reason for male expatriates' failure and early return from overseas assignments has been the dissatisfaction of their wives, this does not mean that women cannot cope in a foreign environment. The role of the spouse (whether male or female) is much more ambiguous and, consequently, the cross-cultural adjustment is much more demanding than that for the person in the role of employee. Wives (female spouses) have had trouble adjusting, but their situation is not analogous to that of female managers, and therefore is not predictive.

Second, do not assume that a woman will not want to go overseas. Ask her. Although both single and married women need to balance private- and professional-life considerations, many are greatly interested in taking overseas assignments. According to the expressed attitudes of today's graduating M.B.A.s, the number of women interested in working overseas will increase, not decrease, in the next decade.

Given that most expatriate packages have been designed to meet the needs of traditional families (working husband, nonworking wife, and children), companies should be prepared to modify benefits packages to meet the demands of single women and dual-career couples. Such modifications might include increased lead time in announcing assignments, executive search services for the partner in dual-career couples, and payment for "staying connected"—including telephone and airfare expenses—for couples that choose some form of commuting rather than relocating overseas.

Third, give a woman every opportunity to succeed. Accord her full status from the outset—not that of a temporary or experimental expatriate—with the appropriate title to communicate the home office's commitment to her. Do not be surprised if foreign colleagues and clients direct their comments to male managers rather than to the new female expatriate in initial meetings, but do not accept such behavior: redirect discussion, where appropriate, to the woman. The foreign colleagues' behavior should not be interpreted as prejudice, but rather as a reaction to an ambiguous, nontraditional situation.

The female expatriates had a number of suggestions for other women following in their footsteps. First, presume naiveté, not malice. Realize that sending women to Asia is new, perceived as risky, and still fairly poorly understood. In most cases companies and foreigners are operating on the basis of untested assumptions, many of which are faulty, not on the basis of prejudice. The most successful approach is to be gently persistent in "educating" the company to the possibility of sending a woman overseas and granting her the status and support usually accorded male peers in similar situations once sent.

Second, given that expatriating women is perceived as risky, no woman will be sent abroad if she is not seen as technically and professionally excellent. According to the interviewees, beyond being extremely well qualified, it never hurts to arrange to be in the right place at the right time.

Third, for single women, the issue of loneliness, and for married women, the issue of managing a dual-career relationship, must be addressed. Contact with other expatriate women has proven helpful in both cases. For dual-career couples, most women considered it critical that they (1) had discussed the possibility of an international assignment with their husbands long before it became a reality, and (2) had created options that would work for them as a couple, which, for most couples, meant creating options that had never, or rarely, been tried in their particular company.

Global competition is, and will continue to be, intense in the 1980s and '90s, and companies need every advantage to succeed. The option of limiting international management to one gender is an archaic luxury of the past. There is no doubt that the most successful North American companies will call on both men and women to manage their international operations. The only question is how quickly and how effectively companies will manage the introduction of women into their worldwide managerial work force.

Acknowledgments

I should like to thank the Social Sciences and Humanities Research Council of Canada for its generous support of this research. I owe special thanks to Ellen Bessner and Blossom Shafer for their assistance in all phases of the research and to Dr. Homa Mahmoudhi for her help, creativity, and professional insight in conducting the Asian interviews.

Notes

1. International Labour Office (1970) "Statistical Information on Women's Participation in Economic Activity" (mimeographed). Geneva: International Labour Office. Table VIII. Cited by Galenson [5].
2. E. R. Singson (1985) "Women in Executive Positions." Paper presented at the 1985 Congress on Women in Decision Making, the Singapore Business and Professional Women's Association, 22–23 September.
3. See Steinhoff and Tanaka in Nancy Adler and Dafna N. Izraeli, editors, *Women in Management Worldwide*, M.E. Sharpe, 1988.
4. See Crockett in Adler and Dafna.
5. See Steinhoff and Tanaka in Adler and Dafna.
6. N. Suzuki and V. Narapareddy (1985) "Problems and Prospects for Female Corporate Executives: A Cross-cultural Perspective." Working paper, University of Illinois at Urbana-Champaign.
7. Interviews were conducted in Tianjin with female managers from all parts of the People's Republic of China in a management seminar sponsored jointly by the PRC's State Economic Commission and the U.S. Department of Commerce.
8. See Chan in Adler and Dafna.

References

1. Caulkin, S. (1981) "Women in Management." *Management Today*, February, pp. 80–83.
2. Thal, N. L., and Cateora, P. R. (1979) "Opportunities for Women in International Business." *Business Horizons*, 22(6), 21–27.
3. Dun & Bradstreet Canada (1980) *Canadian Key Business Directory 1980*. Toronto: Dun & Bradstreet Canada Ltd.
4. Dhawan, K. C., Etemad, H., & Wright, R. W. (1981) *International Business: A Canadian Perspective*. Reading, MA: Addison-Wesley.
5. Galenson, M. (1973) *Women and Work: An International Comparison* (ILR Paperback No. 13). Ithaca, NY: New York State School of Industrial and Labor Relations, Cornell University. P. 23, Table 4.
6. U.S. Department of Labor, Bureau of Labor Statistics (1982) "Current Population Survey." In *Employment and Training Report of the President*. Washington, DC: U.S. Government Printing Office.
7. Trafford, A., Avery, R., Thorton, J., Carey, J., Galloway, J., and Sanoff, A. (1984) "She's Come a Long Way—Or Has She?" *U.S. News & World Report*, 6 August, pp. 44–51.
8. Sorrentino, C. (1983) "International Comparisons of Labor Force Participation, 1960–81." *Monthly Labor Review*, February, pp. 23–26.
9. Indonesia Biro Pusat Statistic [Central Bureau of Statistics] (1982) *Population of Indonesia*, Series S, no. 2: *Results of 1980 Population Census*. Cited by Crockett in this volume.

10. Dahlby, T. (1977) "In Japan, Women Don't Climb the Corporate Ladder." *The New York Times*, 18 September, Section 3, p. 11.

11. Osako, M. M. (1978) "Dilemmas of Japanese Professional Women." *Social Problems*, 26, 15–25.

12. [Japanese] Women's Bureau (1986) *Fuin Rodo no Jitsujo* [The Actual Condition of Women Workers]. Tokyo: Ministry of Finance Printing Office.

13. Hiroshi, T. (1982) "Working Women in Business Corporations: The Management Viewpoint (Japan). *Japan Quarterly*, 29(July/September), 319–23.

14. Cook, A. H. (1980) *Working Women in Japan: Discrimination, Resistance and Reform.* Ithaca, NY: New York State School of Labor and Industrial Relations, Cornell University.

15. Kaminski, M., and Paiz, J. (1984) "Japanese Women in Management: Where Are They?" *Human Resource Management*, 23(3), 277–92.

16. Croll, E. A. (1977) "A Recent Movement to Redefine the Role and Status of Women. *China Quarterly*, 69, 591–97.

17. "Let All Women Rise Up" (Editorial) (1974) *Jen-min jih-pao*, 8 March.

18. Davin, D. (1976) *Women Work: Women and the Party in Revolutionary China.* London: Oxford University Press. Pp. 53–69, 210–13.

19. Singh, D. (1980) "Women Executives in India. *Management International Review*, 20, August, pp. 53–60.

20. Singapore National Productivity Council, Committee on Productivity in the Manufacturing Sector (1985) *Report of the Task Force on Female Participation in the Labor Force.* Singapore: National Productivity Council.

21. Foz, V. B. (1979) *The Labor Code of the Philippines and Its Implementing Rules and Regulations.* Quezon City: Philippine Law Gazette.

22. Ople, B. F. (1981) *Working Managers, Elites: The Human Spectrum of Development.* Manila: Institute of Labor and Management.

23. Miralao, V. (1980) *Women and Men in Development: Findings from a Pilot Study.* Quezon City: Institute of Philippine Culture.

24. University of the Philippines, Department of Sociology (1977) *Stereotype, Status, and Satisfaction: The Filipina among Filipinos.* Quezon City: University of the Philippines.

25. Castillo, G. T. (1977) *The Filipino Woman as Manpower: The Image and Empirical Reality.* Laguna: University of the Philippines.

26. Gosselin, M. (1984) "Situation des Femmes aux Philippines." *Communiqu'elles*, January, pp. 11–12.

27. Adler, N. J. (1979) "Women as Androgynous Managers: A Conceptualization of the Potential for American Women in International Management." *International Journal of Intercultural Relations*, 3(4), 407–435.

28. Adler, N. J. (1984) "Women in Management: Where Are They?" *California Management Review*, XXV(4), 78–89.

29. Adler, N. J. (1984) "Women Do Not Want International Careers: And Other Myths about International Management." *Organizational Dynamics*, XIII(2), 66–79.

30. Adler, N. J. (1986) "Do MBAs Want International Careers?" *International Journal of Intercultural Relations*, 10(3), 277–300.

31. Adler, N. J. (1984) "Expecting International Success: Female Managers Overseas." *Columbia Journal of World Business*, XIX(3), 79–85.

32. Morgenthaler, E. (1978) "Women of the World: More U.S. Firms Put Females in Key Posts in Foreign Countries." *Wall Street Journal*, 16 March, pp. 1, 17.

CASE 7

Manners Europe[1]

Joseph J. DiStefano

John Wilman, Managing Director of Manners Europe, was reviewing the progress he had made since his arrival in the Netherlands two and a half years earlier. The building supplies and home improvement retail outlets for which he was responsible had expanded rapidly in the four years the company had operated in Europe. Now as he thought about the problems and opportunities that he faced during the balance of his assignment in Europe, he set high priority on solving current operational problems and planning future expansion. He knew that both of these objectives would involve increasing the efficiency and effectiveness of the finance and control aspects of the business, an area to which he and Tom Steiger, Director of Finance, had been devoting a fair amount of attention. In addition, there were business problems in several countries with which he had to deal. He looked forward to the challenge of the next several months.

BACKGROUND OF THE COMPANY

Manners Europe is part of a large United States corporation. Although the parent company operates worldwide in several different industries, a large percentage of its several hundred million dollar annual sales comes from manufacturing, wholesale, and retail activities in the United States involving lumber and forest-related products. In this main area of its business the company is one of the largest of its kind in the world.

As the company's main business matured in the United States top executives became interested in the possibilities of entering the European market. Because of previous activity in the Netherlands involving the Manners agricultural division, they sent a person experienced in retailing to assess the potential. Taking advantage of a capability in four languages, this person made a two-month study culminating in a recommendation that European operations be started with the Netherlands as the base. The decision was made and this same person was soon named to direct

278

the start-up. He spent the first year and a half establishing the legal requirements, choosing a site for the head office and generally dealing with time-consuming business-government relations. With these preliminaries completed the first store was opened. A second outlet was added nearby just before John Wilman took over. John explained the relatively slow pace of development by noting, "United States management was cautious because they understood that European patterns of business were different. They knew that Sears had experienced unexpected difficulties in Spain and that J.C. Penney had problems in Belgium. Wanting to avoid the errors of overestimating the transferability of United States business practices made by these experienced retailers, Manners' home office management was initially conservative about the rate of growth in Europe."

CURRENT EUROPEAN OPERATIONS

Since John arrived, sales volume had risen from $1.5 million (United States) to $10 million from four stores in the Netherlands, three in Belgium, and three in the United Kingdom (operated on a joint venture basis with a British firm). In keeping with the company policy of hiring employees and managers from the country where the stores were located, only two of the 225 employees were American. Happy with the autonomy granted from home office, John noted that he had complete freedom over site selection and personnel matters and much greater authority in capital expenditures than his United States counterparts. With the rapid growth of the parent corporation, John's reporting relationship to the United States had varied. Most recently his superior had been changed from the Vice President for Financial Services to Mr. Ralph Jennings, Executive Vice President of the Manners Corporation.

The retail outlets for which John was responsible were self-service stores featuring some 10,000 lumber, building supplies, and home improvement products usually organized in eight groups over 20,000 square feet of interior space. Cashiers and an information counter were located in the front of the stores with an outside storage area for masonry supplies and heavier building materials. In describing their operations John said, "The idea of a one-stop outlet for all do-it-yourself home improvement products is key. The large variety of items combined with lower prices give us the competitive edge. Our size allows us to buy directly from manufacturers or importing agents," he went on, "thereby cutting out the middleman in cases where he is not providing a valuable service. In addition, our competitors here are more specialized and look for higher margins. By the way," John added, "tradesmen and small contractors are an important market segment besides the regular do-it-yourself customers."

Except for the first store all the outlets on the continent were modern, newly built structures with paved parking lots. They each averaged 20 to 25 employees.

It was at these individual stores where the annual planning cycle started each August. Describing this process John said, "Preparation of our objectives and budget is on an M.B.O.-like basis starting with individual salesmen on the floor and working up. For each outlet general objectives such as market share, store climate, and development of management are included as well as quantitative financial targets. These are all correlated here at headquarters."

The fifteen staff members for the European operations were located in a house that had been converted to offices, which was located next to the first outlet. In addition to the two Americans, this group included the Directors of Operations and Administration (personnel, insurance, credit, etc.) and their staffs together with two Merchandise Managers who served the individual stores and coordinated marketing activities. Figure 1 is an organization chart for Manners Europe.

GROWTH OF THE EUROPEAN OPERATIONS

Sales volume in the two Dutch stores was about $700,000 when John arrived in March. A third store was added and the fourth was scheduled to be opened in June. John decided that his early emphasis would be on getting these stores operating efficiently as a base from which to expand (the tentative target was to have twenty stores in Europe by the end of three years). At the time he arrived, sales volume was good, but there were no profits. Start-up expenses were high and there were operating difficulties.

As he started to address the problems, he soon realized their gravity. The Controller could not balance the books and there had never been an audit or physical inventory taken. John had the first inventory taken the moment he arrived and it indicated a shrinkage of 5 percent. In May he asked the division he reported to for help, and in September internal systems consultants spent two weeks going over the problems. Tom Steiger, who subsequently became Director of Finance, was among those who did the study summarized in Figure 2. Figures 3 and 4 provide background data about John Wilman and Tom Steiger, respectively.

Based on this study the company decided that it was important to have internal accounting and control systems similar to those in the United States. They felt that the Dutch personnel in the company at that time were inadequate for implementing the systems without long-run assistance. The Executive Vice President and Senior Vice President also visited the Netherlands in November and recommended organizational changes which resulted in separate Directors for Finance, Operations, and Administration. After weighing the costs, United States management with John Wilman's concurrence asked Tom Steiger to take on the finance job.[2]

Tom arrived on January 1 and soon found that the situation was worse than he had thought the previous fall (see Figure 5). In particular, the controller about whom Tom had been skeptical during his September study now appeared completely inadequate. "Rather than work on an important problem like reconciling our accounts receivable with customer invoices, I'd find him sorting pop bottles!" said Tom. "And he was a compulsive talker; he'd spend hours chatting in the halls and offices. After several reviews and attempts to alter his behavior, I had to fire him when he wouldn't change." However, he brought his dismissal before the Labor

FIGURE 1 Partial Organization Chart

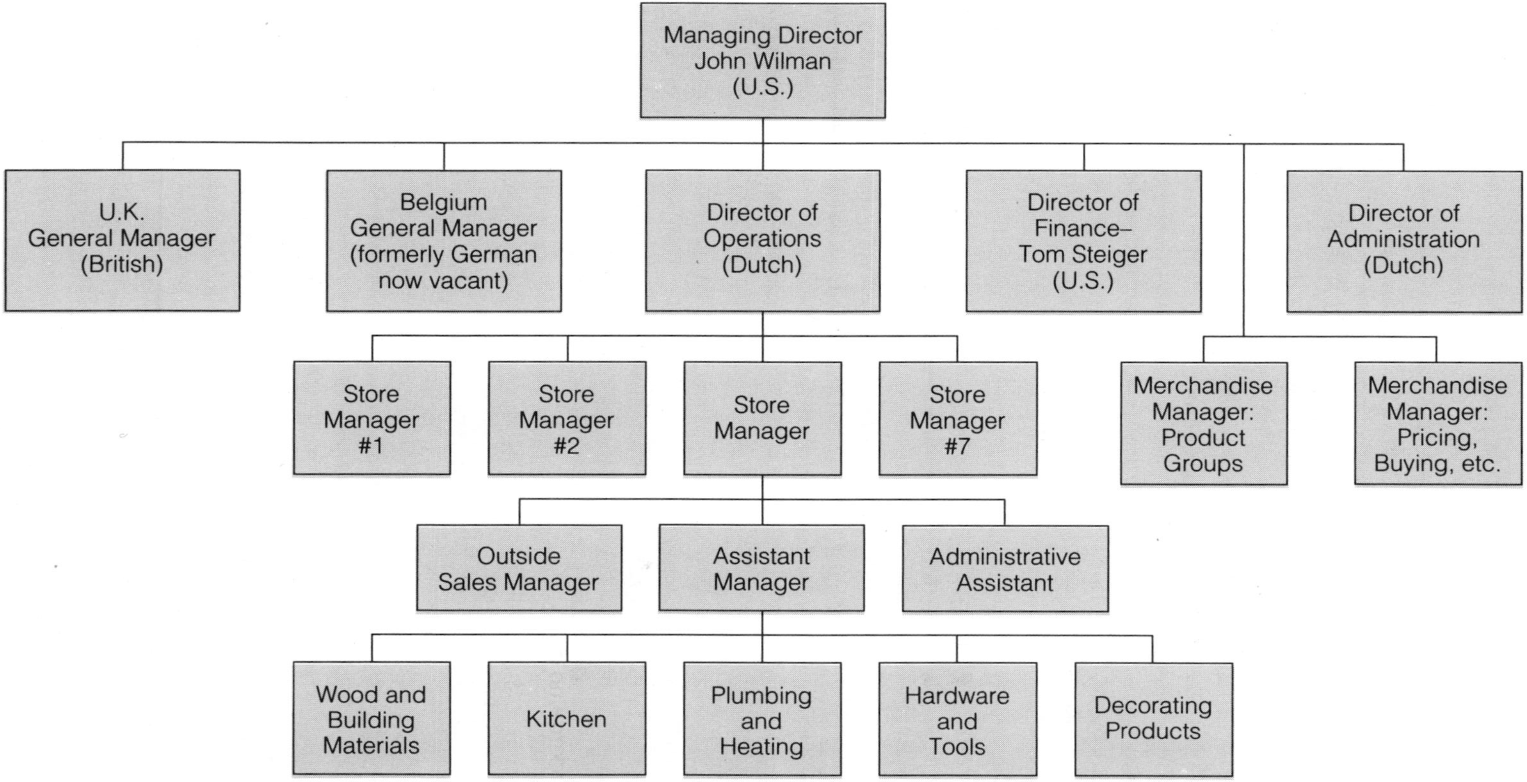

Managing Director
John Wilman
(U.S.)

U.K.
General Manager
(British)

Belgium
General Manager
(formerly German
now vacant)

Director of
Finance—
Tom Steiger
(U.S.)

Director of
Administration
(Dutch)

Director of
Operations
(Dutch)

Merchandise
Manager:
Product
Groups

Merchandise
Manager:
Pricing,
Buying, etc.

Store
Manager
#1

Store
Manager
#2

Store
Manager

Store
Manager
#7

Outside
Sales Manager

Assistant
Manager

Administrative
Assistant

Wood and
Building
Materials

Kitchen

Plumbing
and
Heating

Hardware
and
Tools

Decorating
Products

FIGURE 2 **Systems and Procedures Review Summary**

(Prepared by three corporate systems consultants including
Tom Steiger, dated September 21.)

SECTION I

I. *Evaluation — Existing System*

   A. *Accounts Payable*
      - Lack of control over receivers, vendor's invoices and open accounts payable balance.
      - Delayed match-up of payables documents and disbursements to vendors.

   B. *Margin Determination*
      - Lack of procedure for recording the effect of markdowns.
      - Lack of controls over physical inventory cut-off and processing.
      Physical Inventories
      - No control over cut-off (receivers, sales, vendor's invoices, etc.).
      - Delay in updating book inventories and lack of control over accounts payable function.
      Reporting of Sales (Sales Ticket and Cash Register Operation)
      - Group codes not entered on sales tickets. Cashier must decide correct codes for entry into register.
      - No group distribution made for some sales tickets.
      - Sales discounts not always shown on sales tickets.

   E. *Daily Sales Audit*
      - No home office audit function in connection with Daily Business Report.

   F. *Accounts Receivable*
      - No daily or monthly control.
      - No bad debt reserve.
      - No formal procedure for credit limits or approvals.

   G. *Purchase Order System*
      - Many uncoded items distorts margin determination.

   H. *Procedures*
      - No written branch operating procedures, i.e., operation of cash registers, preparation sales tickets, etc.

   I. *General*
      - Disorganization of office function due to:
      - Lack of experienced personnel
      - Absence of priorities and work schedule
      - Varied demands on Chief Accountant's time

SECTIONS II–IV

Section II contained recommendations and modifications to the existing system in outline form matching items A through H in Section I. It also listed recommendations regarding personnel and gave a list of priorities. Section III contained recommendations regarding mechanized systems. Section IV made longer-range recommendations assuming a total of twenty stores in two and one-half years.

FIGURE 3 **Background Data: John Wilman**

Career with Manners
- Eight years with Manners.
- Training program for management development in lumber and building supplies division as follows.
  - Six months in field operations (lumber yard).
  - Six months in head office.
  - Seven months as assistant manager at a supply center.
  - Seven months as buyer in lumber merchandising.
- One of two-person corporate planning (a new function in company).
- Controller in new corporate activity: land development (recommended by corporate planning).
- Then named as head of European operations (after five years with company).
- John described his jobs in Manners as emphasizing operations management (lumber and store experiences), marketing (store experiences), finance (planning job), and control (land development responsibility).

Personal Background
- International experience: Visited parents during summers of college years (father was President of United States firm in Antwerp). Three months working construction in Switzerland. Speaks some Spanish, and Dutch, the latter through course work since arrival in the Netherlands.
- Family: Married, two children, one in Dutch school and one in international school. Wife very favorably inclined to taking European position. Wife has good language capacity in Dutch and French.
- Education: Undergraduate liberal arts in midwestern college. M.B.A. earned part-time while working for Manners . . . marketing and finance emphasis.

Bureau. After seven months of bureaucratic procedures and negotiations between employer, employee, and the Labor Bureau, a satisfactory termination time was agreed to.[3] "But in spite of these difficulties, we have made progress," Tom added.

SYSTEMS AND PROCEDURES

Of the several internal and external problems faced by John and Tom, actual compliance with systems and procedures once they had been set up seemed to be difficult to accomplish. "Operating a business by numbers and controls just doesn't seem to be part of the orientation of the managers or employees," Tom noted. "Following a procedural manual for pricing, or reporting timeliness or accuracy is second place. Getting things done on time is a big headache . . . and it shows outside the business too. It takes 10 minutes to get a hamburger at McDonald's; they prepare them to individual orders instead of on a fast-food basis! And the 'starter' at the golf course sometimes simply doesn't show up on a Saturday morning."

FIGURE 4   Background Data: Tom Steiger

Career with Company
- Twenty-two years with Manners, successive positions as:
  - Internal auditor,
  - General books supervisor,
  - Controller, agriculture and lumber division,
  - Management Systems and Programs,
  - Internal Systems Consultant — Manners Europe,
  - Director of Finance — Manners Europe,
- Tom's comments about his career: "The company has always treated me right. As long as they do, I'll always work hard to the best of my ability."

Personal Background
- Tom and wife born, raised, and lived in same city in northwestern United States their whole lives. Had not moved in 16 years. Built own home in a big field with woods in the back.
- Wife always willing to move with the job. Children (boy and girl both 12) cried and had problems initially . . . now O.K. Extremely happy at prospect of vacation back in United States, but not unhappy in the Netherlands.
- Family weighed the disadvantages (second-class citizens, fewer material conveniences, no summer cottage, loss of friends) vs. the opportunity to see Europe and favored latter.
- Views of the Dutch people are quite different. Personally they are extremely polite (much more so than Americans), but outside the office in public settings (crowds, supermarkets, highway, golf course) if they do not know you, watch out!
- Language: Biggest problem is language barrier. Company should insist on three months of Dutch courses. Cannot read paper for local news where we live, wait anxiously for English-speaking TV shows, difficult to make friends. If you do not have language before arriving, low incentive to learn since you can get by. But for business and personal life, should do it before.

Tom gave several examples of problems that concerned his department. "Receivers are an important tool for controlling payment to suppliers. It was taking from several days to weeks for us to get receiver notices from the stores, so we set up inventory receipt procedures and put a 48-hour limit on reporting receipt of goods to headquarters. It's taken a whole year to get the stores to comply and even now it isn't unusual to experience one or two week delays. We watch their accuracy and push for updating when stores fall behind. But they seem to *talk* more than to *do*; it sometimes takes five or six requests before we get action."

Another example had to do with the Chief Accountant for Belgium. Tom worked out a plan to shift the individual store bank balances (which were positive and drawing a low interest rate) to the main corporate account in Belgium (which often had a negative balance that was costing the company 11½ percent interest). The stores' banks were not cooperating on the overdraft arrangements, and Tom requested the accountant to contact them to correct it. "I talked to him in the

---

FIGURE 5   **Summary of Administrative Report**

Prepared by Tom Steiger for U.S. Senior Vice President, dated March 6.

Problems: The problems listed on the September 21st report (Figure 2, Section I) were described in detail. The summary paragraph read as follows:

"To sum up the problems, there has been no control of activities, either at the stores or at the head office, no real account system, and therefore no accurate financial reporting except by accident. Some of the manipulations in the books and on the financial statements lead us to suspect fraud, but as yet we find no real evidence of that. We will watch for it as we continue to check everything out."

REASONS FOR PROBLEMS (Verbatim from report)
The basic problem seems to be that, from the beginning of operations, the personnel and equipment necessary for even a minimum of controls and for an adequate accounting system were considered an expense that this company could not afford. Working in this atmosphere, it has become a way of life for everyone that the preparation of documents, their accuracy and timeliness, and finally their recording on the books is something to be done only when and how it is convenient. This is by no means an overstatement, as the facts prove. Consider the keeping of a general ledger system having six profit centers and a total of between four and five hundred accounts. With the manual system being used, one single error in posting, adding, bringing balances forward, etc. results in an out–of–balance condition which is next to impossible to find. The installation of a simple bookkeeping machine a year or two ago would have made that job and its accuracy many times easier. Consider also, the problem of an accountant in establishing a cutoff for physical inventory when the stores prepare and send in receivers when it is convenient and with little regard for accuracy. And he had inadequate manpower, so that he is months behind in his regular work and therefore has not time to really dig into the problems. He soon throws up his hands and only goes through the motions.

Changing this way of life will undoubtedly be our biggest problem. It will be a long and hard educational process to make everyone, especially store personnel, realize the importance of doing things accurately and promptly.

The other major problem is the Controller. As stated above, probably no one could have done the job expected of him with the manpower and equipment provided. And yet there seems to be an inability on his part to regulate his own and his peoples' activities so as to get the most out of what he has. Scheduling has been nonexistent. Many things that he has done, such as some of the statement adjustments, have taken much more of his time in the long run than if he had booked the proper entries in the first place. His people are doing things which, with only a few minutes thought, could be improved upon so as to save 50 percent or more of the time spent on a particular job. Offsetting these deficiencies, though, is the acknowledgment by all that he is a very intelligent man. (But intelligence in speaking seven languages and in accounting principles might not mean intelligence in managing an accounting department.) For the time being we

(Continued)

FIGURE 5**Continued**

---

are giving him the benefit of the doubt because of the extenuating circumstances, and also because so much information is not recorded but is only in his head, so his leaving now would be a setback in straightening things out. We are watching this situation closely.

Plans for Solving Problems: This section of the report is summarized as follows.

The former manager of our first outlet was appointed Director of Administration — Europe. The appointment was described as "the real key in quickly bringing order out of the present chaos." His assignment in addition to personnel, insurance, and expansion was to work with me in designing and implementing controls and better procedures both in head office and in the stores. Other staffing changes were noted.

Plans for preparing for automation and running the automated system in parallel with the existing one were described. Details such as speeding up the processing of vendor invoices in order to take discounts were included. This was estimated to add ½ to ¾ of a percent to the margin.

Detailed accounting adjustments to correct old errors in order to present accurate financial statements and reports were described.

The controller was given target dates for completion of specified activities and was warned that failure to meet deadlines would jeopardize his continued employment. Some pessimism was expressed regarding the probability for his success.

The report concluded with the following list of long range plans.

"a. Continued evaluations of procedures in head office and stores to provide better controls and more efficiency.
 b. Procedures for taking physical inventory and cutoff of accounting records.
 c. Investigation of different handling of collections of customers accounts receivable.
 d. Installation of full retail system of accounting.
 e. Preparation of procedure manuals for other countries and implementation of procedures there.
 f. Functional audit procedures for all stores and other countries' head offices.

I hope that all of this has given you some idea of what the problems are here and how we are attacking them. When you are here in person we can discuss them in detail and will, of course, welcome any suggestions you might have."

---

morning," Tom said. "He called our Director of Administration at headquarters but still hadn't taken any action to call the bank. After a few rather heated comments from me, he replied, 'I need to understand everything clearly before I do something.' I guess language difficulties are part of it," Tom said, "but sometimes I have to act the part of the 'bad buy from the States' to get any action. They're great in theory and talk, but there seems to be a gap when it comes to action."

He also had similar difficulties in the Netherlands. One of the store managers whom Tom described as "a fairly good manager, but an extremely strong-willed man" was deliberately not following procedures. "On three different occasions in the past few months, he deviated from important policies. We have a policy of no credit except to contractors, but we found that he was selling to his employees and using C.O.D. arrangements to carry them. This is used normally to handle accounts for a day or two where a customer might not be home, but he was stretching it to one or two months for some employees, effectively making it a charge account. I called him on the phone and John called him in. He was told to clear all these from the C.O.D. account, collect from the employees, and stop the practice. Two months later he had made additional sales to employees the same way.

"One of the men he sold to was our Director of Operations who happens to live near the store. I was shocked to find this out when I was reviewing the records, and since his office is right next to mine I told him so. He just laughed saying, 'Those rules don't apply to everybody, only regular employees.' I tried to explain what a difficult position that put the store manager in. It meant that he had to disobey me and the policy or offend his boss (the Director of Operations). He just mumbled without any admission that he shouldn't have done it nor with any promise to stop. His attitude seemed to be that it was nice to have procedures, but they really weren't important and didn't apply to him!

"But getting back to the store manager . . . he also ignored our instructions that any equipment purchase of over a specified amount must be cleared at head-quarters. Last week he bought a pricing machine costing well over his limit without checking with us and in a month it will be useless because we're switching over to new procedures.

"His third offense was to ignore our inventory procedures. We recommend that all stores start to prelist their merchandise one month prior to the actual inventory. By listing all the items by name on the inventory sheets in advance, this saves a lot of time on inventory day. He started the prelisting the morning of the inventory and when I asked him why, he gave an excuse about having too much sickness among his employees. We checked his records and he had had only four employee-days of absence during the previous month.

"With these three incidents happening one right after another, I decided to raise the issue at the next administrative clinic we had (a periodic meeting called by Tom to review procedures). I recalled the events and said that I got the impression he followed only procedures that he agreed with or liked. He replied, 'Maybe so.' I spent a fair amount of time explaining the reasons for the procedures and showing the serious implications of their not being followed as we add more stores. He then promised to do better, but I still have problems getting the cooperation of the Dutch managers."

MOTIVATION TO WORK

In talking about other problems John Wilman noted that the achievement and production orientation in the United States was just not the same in the Nether-lands. After the first two years of operating an M.B.O. kind of system, he had tried to tie it to compensation and felt that it had failed. "The incremental tax rate kills incentive," he explained. "A person may only take home 20 percent of an increase. Besides, many Dutch have a different view of compensation. They argue from an assumption that everyone gives 100 percent of their effort all the time, so they should be paid 100 percent as a normal exchange, not given a bonus."

Tom was concerned about obtaining the commitment of employees to work overtime on the few occasions when it was necessary. He cited an example from the previous week when they were trying to meet the time schedule for accounting reports to the United States office. The computer services company delivered the data at 9:00 PM on Friday (Tom said they were often late in spite of his complaints), and Tom and two of the employees worked into the evening and agreed to return at nine the next morning. After working for two hours on Saturday, the more junior of the two, who had only been with the company a few months, said that he had to leave for a tennis lesson since he had missed the previous week's lesson. He returned some time after two o'clock that afternoon. Later Tom asked the Dutch Chief Accountant about the incident, noting that it was the first overtime requested of the man in two months. He answered that it had puzzled him too and cited a similar experience with the employee. So on the following Monday Tom decided to ask about it. The following exchange took place.

> *Tom:* "You know, you shocked me greatly when you left for tennis on Saturday. We needed you to get that report out and relied on you. I want you to develop."
>
> *Employee:* "Yes, I realize that. But my wife is also taking lessons and she won't go without me. I want her to get over her shyness and am trying to encourage her to get out."
>
> *Tom:* "It's understandable that you want to help her, but the chips were down. That report had to be finished. Social life has to take a second place in emergencies. I like to enjoy life, too . . . golf and bridge are my favorites, yet I missed my golf game on Saturday without any questions."
>
> *Employee:* "Yes, yes, but my wife was involved."
>
> *Tom:* "Well, if you had a family emergency, the company would understand and take second place. So when the company has an emergency, we expect you to help us. We need to rely on you."
>
> *Employee:* "O.K."

John cited another example saying, "It's not just internal operations that get affected by this attitude. We have problems with the contractor in building our new stores, too. And this is true even though we've used the same contractor on all the jobs and might be able to expect a little extra consideration. Although we've put all the buildings out for bids, he's the only one who will agree to meet our time specifications of three months from start to completion. The nearest another bidder has come has been five months. We were concerned about his last job and were especially anxious to get the parking lot paved. It had been delayed by eight straight days of rain. We got one day of good weather for laying the asphalt and what happens? He and his workers went to the beach!!"

Tom gave another example. "We're releasing the Accounts Payable Manager (who was at the end of a six-month trial period). He's forty-five years old and can't find a job, but still has priced himself out of the market. He's unreliable; I have to check everything. I can't even trust him to balance out the check totals with the invoice totals each day."

Three or four months ago it was necessary to work on a Saturday morning, so I warned the people involved on the previous Thursday. He simply said, 'No, I won't be in the city Saturday.' He didn't tell me what I already knew — that he goes horseback riding every Saturday. He's one that has always taken the employees' part on this issue claiming that it is against Dutch customs to work overtime."

We had a run-in over a religious holiday too. For many businesses it was a holiday, but our stores were to be open for half the day. So John sent a memo to the headquarters staff saying that as long as the store employees had to work, it would be good for all of us to come in the half day, too. After all, they could see if we weren't here and how would that look? Anyway, this Accounts Payable Manager and two of his people didn't show up. The next day I asked about it. He said, 'They took it as part of their holiday allowance, and as for me, I marched in the parade with the band.' When I asked if he had seen John's memo, he gave me a cold stare, said 'Yes,' and walked away. To him personal life came first."

COMPENSATION

John also discussed the relation between motivation and compensation. "As I mentioned, we've had difficulty linking pay with achievement of objectives. At the store manager level I first had difficulty when I introduced the idea. But I found that if I talked about it as an increase, as an add-on basis, it was more attractive. We link it to the sales and income of the particular product groups in their stores. But there is still the feeling that a bonus is demeaning, since it suggests to them that we think they weren't working up to 100 percent at their regular pay level. This is so strong that I've had some of our best Dutch sales personnel refuse commission arrangements and work for less on a nonincentive basis."

For the sales personnel in charge of product groups, we relate their monthly bonus half to the overall sales of the store and half to their meeting the product group objectives. We added the cashiers, outside sales representatives, and warehouse staff to the bonus scheme and initially got a good response. The hourly employees have a fixed potential bonus. The outside reps' bonus is a percentage of sales, but their base salary is larger than it would be in the United States. But so far, I'm not satisfied with the way we're using it, nor do I think it's producing tangible results. Of course, much depends on how the individual manager uses it . . . on the quality and frequency of feedback to these people."

Belgium was more oriented to financial incentives according to John. The bonus scheme had been installed there and the response had been encouraging.

Salary increases were a problem, too. John told of a recent incident involving two accountants. Accountant A was married and in his late twenties and was considered a low producer. Accountant B was single, aged seventeen, and produced at least five times the work of A. His salary was 25 percent less than A's. Yet when salary review came up, the Chief Accountant and the Director of Administration recommended a greater increase for A than for B. Tom refused their advice, gave A only the mandatory cost-of-living increase and added the remainder of the increase recommended for A to B's raise. Both the Director of Administration and Chief Accountant were visibly upset and voiced their disapproval. When A came in and angrily asked why he hadn't gotten an increase, Tom flatly told him he wasn't worth it. He had done poor work and refused to work overtime. Then A questioned B's raise saying that since he was single, he didn't need it. John indicated that A seemed to think that if he were paid more, then he would work harder. "It contradicts the assumption that we hold," John concluded, "that you get rewarded after you demonstrate your accomplishments. Education, age, marital status, and financial need have more influence on salary here than in the United States."

RECRUITING

With the expansion of operations and employee turnover, recruiting was an issue that concerned both managers. Part of the problem came from the very low rate of unemployment in the Netherlands, which averaged 2 percent across the country but was virtually zero in several of the regions where stores were located or planned. Newspaper ads for clerks or cashiers went unanswered. Job titles were inflated to add status and prestige. For example, the accounts payable supervisor was listed as "manager" and people with little or no office experience would apply for the position. Tom commented that the Controllers for both the Netherlands and Belgium probably had had no supervisory experience at all.

Another reason for recruiting problems had to do with Manners being a United States company. Tom estimated that only about 10 percent of the Dutch aggressively sought employment with United States firms. Some wanted to learn United States business methods, while others liked the less dictatorial climate. But he thought that the vast majority viewed United States companies as too heartless, too demanding, and requiring too much hard work. The new Accounts Payable Manager told Tom openly that his family had criticized him for joining a United States company.

John agreed that it was difficult to find people willing to work for multinational companies. He thought they were viewed as being different from local companies in vague ways and were generally stereotyped as expecting more from people than did European firms.

But John noted that this varied within Europe, too. He said that the Belgian operations had been started with a German as General Manager. But soon letters directed to him from Belgian employees arrived with complaints about the autocratic practices of the German General Manager. They were resentful of German supervisors. Some Belgian customers even complained about a "German firm" being in Belgium. Differences in national attitudes contributed to the complications of recruiting.

It was also difficult to obtain people with the level of education desired by the company. There wasn't the supply of generally educated B.A.s as in North America. Some people had higher status degrees in which case they usually refused supervisor's positions as "beneath" them. Others had attended night classes and received "business school" diplomas which were hard to judge and generally meant minimum training in a narrow area such as bookkeeping.

Hiring experienced people from other firms was also subject to uncertainties, partially influenced by Dutch laws. An admittedly extreme example was described by John who told of receiving a request from a Dutch bank for a reference about a former Manners employee who had been fired for stealing. But according to the law, John was forbidden to say anything negative or to refer to the discharge. "I simply replied that the person worked for us from date x to date y," John said. "But it gives you some idea of the problem we face in screening people for jobs."

Besides the problem of finding skilled people in a situation of a limited and underqualified supply, other government regulations added to the risks. They prohibited the company from firing anyone with more than two months' seniority except with clear proof of fault for a limited number of offenses (such as theft). Because of this John had directed that all new employees at the supervisory level or above be required to sign a six-month contract which, in effect, lengthened this trial period by four months.

OTHER PROBLEMS EXTERNAL TO THE COMPANY

But not all the operating or planning problems dealt with internal activities. One critical dimension involved supplier relations. John remarked about the "organized" nature of the supply situation with cartels, informal agreements, etc. "Ironically," he noted, "what was a strength at the sales end of our business—that is, our low price—turned out to be a distinct handicap at the supply end. Suppliers balked at shipping to a low-price retail organization that would force a cut in margins among their established customers. The fact is that we threatened two sets of the large suppliers' clients: both the traditionally smaller, more specialized, Dutch retail merchants and the middlemen vendors who we bypassed because of our large quantity buying. In addition to 'breaking the rules,' as newcomers we were hardly 'members of the club.' This is still a problem that I have to stay on top of.

"The supply issue in Belgium is a bit different," John added. "Initially we had trouble even getting vendors to talk with us, much less supply our stores. Slowly we realized that the way of doing business there was quite different. It meant being less direct, more informal, and entertaining more. We changed our manner of dealing with them and saw a dramatic improvement in both price and delivery. It was amazing.

"Business and government relations and the political environment represent another area where we have to adapt. This is particularly important to our plans for expansion. With the scarcity of land in the Netherlands building permits are *very* tightly controlled. Permission to build a store requires elaborate zoning regulations and a series of approvals. There's no under-the-table action either. And although we don't suffer any more than Dutch firms, the procedures are heavy and the red tape often causes delays that hurt us. On top of that, the city council of most local governments is controlled by small business people, shopkeepers, and other retail merchants from the center-city. Our kind of store directly challenges all that these people value and prize. That hardly helps us," John understated wryly.

"In Belgium it's very different from here . . . more like the United States. You can be driving along and see property that looks good and in a reasonable time get favorable zoning and buy it. It's less bound by fixed rules and regulations; much more political. The flexibility is reflected by a more rapid growth there. Of course, our competitors grow more quickly, too."

Shifting from this subject, John turned to some of the characteristics of the Manners Europe sales that concerned him. One item was that of product mix. He noted that plumbing and carpeting had shown strength in the Netherlands and Belgium but had been the slowest portions of their product line in England.

He was also concerned about the relative proportions of sales between consumer sales versus contractors and professionals. While the do-it-yourself acceptance of the Manners concept was encouraging, the contractors and professionals represented a definite problem. Traditionally in the Netherlands these people bought from special wholesalers called builders' merchants. Manners had broken this distribution channel and the professionals were resisting the change. They resented the fact that Manners wanted to sell both to them and direct to the consumer on a do-it-yourself appeal. In fact, this new pattern not only disrupted their long-standing relations with the builders' merchants, but also created new competition for the contractors and tradesmen — namely, the do-it-yourself consumer who would now use professionals less frequently.

John knew from direct experience that it was hard to sell the contractors on the merits of the Manners outlets and it was even tougher to sell the store managers on developing this market segment. Examining the comparative sales data he had assembled (see below), he felt that further action was necessary.

Percentage of Sales by Market Segment and Country

Market Segment	*Country*			
	U.S.	Netherlands	Belgium	United Kingdom
Professional	50%	20%	5%	40%
Do-It-Yourself	50%	80%	95%	60%

In citing the discrepancies across countries John noted that the General Manager's position in Belgium was still vacant, though he was leaving for Belgium the very next day to continue work on finding the right person. The relative success of the English operation with small builders was partially explained by the fact that Manners' partner in the joint venture there was one of England's largest builders' merchants.

In comparing the countries on other dimensions, he stated that the Dutch stores were characterized by a smaller average sale per customer, but a larger number of customers relative to Belgium where fewer people bought more goods per stop.

In England both figures were smaller than either the Netherlands or Belgium data, but their success in tapping the smaller builder market more than made up for this. John said that one survey at a store in the Netherlands indicated that 20 percent of their customers did not own a car. Eight percent shopped at the store by bicycle. Closing the review with a grin, John chuckled, "You ought to see the stuff they tow away on a bike . . . the most amazing scene I've witnessed is a man who bought a bathtub and managed to cycle away!"

SOME PRESSURES TO ACT

One of the facts that added to the pressures for John to establish some priorities among these problems and start to deal with them was top management's policy of limiting United States executives to three years overseas. This meant that Tom Steiger's experience and expertise was available to the European operation only for an additional twelve to eighteen months. Yet future expansion depended on sound accounting and control systems. In addition, it meant another decision for John to make — whether to recommend an American or European as Tom's successor. At this time he couldn't see an inside candidate of the necessary caliber, and the market conditions made the price of obtaining the right outsider in Europe so high as to offset the cost disadvantages of bringing over a younger American. He also wondered if an American might be more willing and able to fight the battle of implementing change and obtaining cooperation than would a European.

On the other hand, he knew that a European would be more acceptable on several grounds. First, there was the publicly stated policy of being a fully European operation. This was generally known to the Manners' employees. John also knew that his boss, Ralph Jennings, was committed to the notion of European management. Then there were the cultural problems of adapting home office practices to the foreign operations. This, he knew, could be used to argue either side of the choice. He wanted to have a recommendation ready on this question prior to his next scheduled return to the United States in early August. He would be meeting with Mr. Jennings then to review the European operations and wanted to be prepared if asked about this issue.

Perhaps of even greater urgency was the question of his own status. The three years limit on being overseas was a well-established policy about which the United States executives felt rather strongly. The Dutch employees were sensitive to this, too, and John neither wished to be a "lame duck" director, nor did he want to alienate them by leaving the issue unresolved. While he obviously wished to avoid antagonizing top management, he wasn't beyond lobbying tactfully for an extension for a year or two to consolidate into a firm base the expansion he had spearheaded since his arrival.

As he thought about his own career with Manners and about the lengthy list of issues turned up by his and Tom's review of their work in Europe, he knew he faced a busy period of analysis, decisions, and action in the next two months before his trip back home.

Notes

1. Names of the company and people have been disguised.
2. Tom estimated that it cost the company from two and a half to three times as much to have an American in the position than a local person. The difference was due to the basic salary difference plus foreign location bonus, travel, moving expenses, and education, cost of living, and housing allowances.
3. Approval of the Labor Bureau must be obtained and termination times and payment can be quite large (two years' salary). Also when a person is fired, he or she may receive 80 percent of his or her salary for up to three years as unemployment compensation paid by the government.

CASE 8

Urban Architecture (A)

Neil Abramson, Mark Chow
and Henry W. Lane

Keith Johnson, President of Urban Architecture, had settled into his transatlantic flight and was reviewing in his mind the incredible two weeks he had just spent in Milan negotiating to become the sole American distributor for the Italian furniture company Memphis Milano.

He was extremely pleased, yet worried. He had the outline of a contract with Memphis and he was excited to have the opportunity to be the sole United States distributor. He was worried because he still had to convince his partner that the deal could work and get his approval. Keith had learned a lot in Milan, but not all of what he learned was encouraging. He now had questions about the viability of Memphis and its line that he never had before. And the irrevocable letter of credit could still prove to be the undoing of the deal. He had avoided having to give in on this point, but it was still an open issue to Memphis.

The deal could still fall apart and he did not want that. He believed in the furniture, and he knew he could sell it. How he presented the situation to his partner would be critical. He was beginning to think that he should just gloss over or even ignore the problems that he uncovered that were now nagging him. But then, he wondered, maybe his passion for the furniture was getting in the way of his judgment. Maybe being the sole United States distributor for Memphis was not going to be worth the time, effort, and money that he was going to have to invest. Maybe he should forget it and concentrate his efforts on finding other companies to represent. He had to decide before he got to the office the next day.

THE ART FURNITURE INDUSTRY

Art furniture was highly stylized furniture, lighting systems, and artifacts that were notable for their unique design and high fashion. The product range included fabrics, chairs, lighting fixtures, tables, sofas, beds, mirrors, cabinets, dishes, and ceramics. Products could be positioned as artifacts, as limited editions, or as commissioned one-of-a-kind pieces.

Most art furniture was designed and manufactured in Italy, Sweden, Denmark, Great Britain, and France. There were some designers in Japan but very little Japanese art furniture was exported. The list of high-design furniture companies included Memphis Milano, Driade, Zanotta, Cassina, B & B Italia, Wendell Castle, Massimo Iosa Ghini, Pallucco, and Alchimia. The most important annual display of all types of art furniture was at Italy's Salon Internazionale del Mobile. This was the world's premier art furniture fair held each September in Milan. Keith Johnson described that fair as 'Christmas in the furniture world.'

Art furniture was a unique hybrid of the 1980s. There was a dramatic increase in the value of the pieces, the designers, and the companies associated with art furniture. In some respects, the more exclusive designers had positioned themselves as selling 'instant antiques.' Prices generally began in the $200 to $2,000 range and could escalate to more than $50,000.

THE MARKET FOR ART FURNITURE

For many years art furniture mainly was available in big urban centers such as New York, Los Angeles, and Chicago and only through architects or designers who used these products in their designs. Consumers were not allowed to purchase directly from distributors and had to go through an architect or designer at a considerable mark-up.

In the United States, art furniture was often displayed in museums as an exclusive form of collectible. In some respects, the curators of places like the Brooklyn Museum, the Denver Museum, the Detroit Institute of Arts, and the Virginia Museum of Fine Arts had become trendsetters.

Art furniture was not for everyone. The majority of furniture sold in the United States was very traditional and it was unlikely that art furniture would appeal to most people. The clients sought were already educated about art furniture. However, Johnson felt that some people outside this segment just needed a little encouragement.

The major markets of New York, Los Angeles, and Chicago were served by a wide range of art furniture dealers. Many of these dealers also were entering the newly developing markets of Dallas, Boston, Seattle, San Francisco, and Miami. They were finding that consumers of art furniture could be found across the United States and that pieces so avant-garde they were a hard sell in New York could be sold in places like Baton Rouge. As Keith put it, "They were discovering that there were people of character and good taste all over." Also, art furniture was now becoming available in up-scale retail establishments.

ART FURNITURE INDUSTRY
SEGMENTS

Art furniture could be positioned as a residential product or an office system. As a residential product it was sold as an exclusive collectible, a high-style houseware, or a fashionable home furnishing. As an office system, art furniture was intended to replace traditionally designed office furniture. This later segment was particularly important, since sales of office systems surpassed $20 billion in 1986. Steelcase and Herman Miller were examples of traditional office system manufacturers. Steelcase's sales, at the time, were approximately $2 billion. Westinghouse, which had just purchased design harbinger Knoll International, was providing Steelcase and Herman Miller with some competition also.

Art furniture was sold mainly in the United States market for residential purposes. Even with this avant-garde market there were more conservative and more radical products available. For example, Crate and Barrel furniture was intended to help consumers build their self-confidence while experimenting with art furniture. It emphasized a mix of safe American classics and eclectic collections from around the world. Crate and Barrel helped customers pull together disparate pieces with panache.

The home furnishings segment remained traditional in the sense that it catered to those who were interested in having everything match. Ralph Lauren Home Collection stores and Laura Ashley Home Stores were large and expanding chains. Gear, with The Guild Hall, added to their position, offered a totally coordinated look for the home. Other established competitors included Conran's, Domain, Roche-Bobois, and Palazzetti.

Another approach to the residential market was the mass merchandising of IKEA. This company began to enter the United States market after having secured much of Europe's midmarket segment. IKEA provided inexpensive, well-designed furniture ready for immediate delivery and use. Imitators included STOR, Expressions, and Stylus.

The most radical approach to art furniture was to furnish the entire home with stand-alone products that did not match except in the sense of being avant-garde, artistic, and of dramatic design. Any object that could stand alone, with a functional, philosophic, and artistic purpose that contributed to the furnishing of a house, could be considered a piece of art furniture.

KEITH JOHNSON'S ENTRY INTO ART FURNITURE

Keith Johnson's education included art and art history, and he was drawn to purchasing and renovating old properties in Detroit. His brother Craig, an interior design architect, assisted him. Craig interested Keith in using art furniture, especially lighting and furniture, in his renovations. Keith, who felt that the spaces should be filled with period pieces, was eventually won over by Craig's argument that good design tenets don't change over the centuries.

Keith used more and more Italian art furniture in his projects. Eventually, he was noticed by Atelier International of New York when he placed a $90,000 order for the most radically designed pieces sold by the firm. The pieces chosen were those that were hard to sell even in New York. Atelier International quickly had its Chicago representative visit Keith. Keith, after impressing the representative with his knowledge of art history, was recommended to be an Atelier dealer. Keith's entry into the art furniture market was made almost on a lark, but he quickly became a very effective salesman and spokesman for art furniture. His building, according to one source, became "an Italian palazzo filled with zany, eye-popping, didactic things!"

Keith also acquired a minority partner, Ladislav Jerga, who had a business background. Keith was the intuitive optimist ready to rush into deals based on his feelings. Ladislav analyzed each deal and identified all the pitfalls and dangers. If Keith could persuade Ladislav that the deal was sound, then the chances were they had covered the important risks.

Keith Johnson was the Midwest distributor for Atelier International for four years, from 1984 to 1988. He was responsible for increasing Atelier's sales from $90,000 to $900,000. However, Keith was not entirely happy with the situation. He made a 10 to 15 percent commission, which had to support his sales staff and showroom. He felt he was taking more risk than Atelier, but they were getting the majority of the profits. In addition, although Keith was supposed to have the Midwest as an exclusive territory, he found that Atelier was selling into his area — possibly as much as $800,000 over the four years. He was competing with the "house."

Urban Architecture proved very successful in selling all kinds of European art furniture in the Midwest. Within six months of becoming Atelier's representative, the company represented a number of other lines on behalf of domestic importers based in New York and Chicago. These lines included Memphis Milano, which was imported by Artemide Lighting Inc. of New York.

THE MEMPHIS MILANO LINE

The Memphis line began in 1981, primarily as a result of the dissatisfaction of one industrial designer — Ettore Sottsass. Sottsass had been the creative genius behind Olivetti's trademark chrome and steel and the leather and glass look. However, Sottsass came to lament the limitations of this pattern and declared that shiny perfectionism was not a reflection of the real world.

Persuading investors in key design firms to finance operations, he began a new, independent enterprise. His success in Milanese design shows soon captured the attention of the design industry and also the public imagination. In Keith Johnson's opinion, Memphis furnishings were "the most radical rupture with modernism in furniture in this half century." Memphis products were primarily aimed at the residential furnishings market and were mainly stand-alone objects of the most revolutionary artistic and functional design.

In April 1988 as Keith was departing on a holiday, Guido Burrato, Executive Vice President of Artemide, phoned to ask him if he would like to take over complete distribution of Memphis Milano for the United States. Keith felt the offer was made because Artemide salespeople were having trouble selling Memphis, and Artemide held a large inventory of Memphis objects. Keith, however, had been very successful selling Memphis.

Keith took his Martinique holiday and ten days later returned with the decision that he would negotiate to become Memphis Milano's United States distributor. He gave notice to the other American distributors whose European art furniture he was selling that Urban Architecture now would self-import only. Then he made plans to go to New York to arrange the terms of the deal with Guido Burrato.

Although Ladislav thought that Artemide was offering only Urban Architecture the chance to be their American agent for Memphis Milano and would remain a middleman in charge of importing, advertising, and market positioning, Keith was confident that Artemide wanted nothing more to do with Memphis Milano. Keith felt that Artemide had hurt the United States market for Memphis Milano. Artemide salespeople preferred to sell European lighting systems because it was so much easier and required no art or architectural historical base. They seemed to sell Memphis almost begrudgingly or with indifference. It was even hard for dealers to get Memphis Milano catalogues from Artemide (Keith could get only 10–15 a year, which went to his very best clients). Artemide preferred the agents to focus on lighting systems, as there was more money in contract lighting.

When Keith and Ladislav met with Guido Burrato to negotiate terms, Keith was proved right. Burrato said he wanted Keith to take Milano over completely. Keith was offered all the several thousand Milano catalogues Artemide was holding. Keith also asked to take Artemide's Milano inventory on consignment. Burrato wanted better terms than these, but Keith's offer was very close to the final deal Burrato accepted.

However, for Urban Architecture to become the sole United States distributor of Memphis, the deal also had to be approved by the Italian owners of Memphis Milano. The owners were Ernesto Gismondi and his architect wife, Carlotta de Bevilacqua. In practice, the deal also had to be approved by Alberto Albrici as well. Alberto was the Italian export manager who ran Memphis worldwide on a day-to-day basis.

After Keith, Ladislav, and Burrato had come to an understanding, they arranged a conference call with Alberto in Milan. Alberto gave Keith tentative approval to proceed but made it clear that the deal was conditional on further negotiations between Keith, Alberto, Ernesto, and Carlotta. Alberto wanted these negotiations to take place during the Internazionale del Mobile fair in September. Keith knew that the Italians had no information about him except that he was an American furniture dealer. Keith felt he had three months, from June to September, to make a good impression by showing he could sell Memphis in the United States.

Keith decided he would try to sell the Memphis inventory he had obtained from Artemide to his most important clients in the Michigan area at a price that was just above the FOB Milan cost to Artemide. He told the dealers they had a one-time-only opportunity to build a nice Memphis collection at a discount of almost 50 percent. The price would represent no discount to Memphis Milano, who would receive their normal profit margin, but Urban Architecture would cover only costs and make no profit. Keith had no idea how his clients would respond, but his goal was to go to Italy with a large number of sales, which would make him look good to the Italians.

Keith's clients bought all the Memphis being offered. In September 1988, Keith went to Milan with a binder containing 100 orders worth over $80,000 to Memphis to negotiate the final deal with Alberto. Alberto would then decide whether to recommend Keith to Ernesto and Carlotta. Keith expected that there would be long sessions of numbers and analysis — offers and counteroffers — because Alberto had trained in business at the Milan Polytechnic and worked as a manager at Colgate Palmolive Milan. Keith dreaded this sort of strict management-type process, since he was more of a "people person," but he intended to do his best.

Also, Keith had discovered that Urban Architecture was not the sole company interested in distributing Memphis in the United States. North American distributors of other art furniture lines, with considerably more capital than Keith, were apparently willing to pay for the distribution rights because they thought art furniture was becoming a hot new fad in the United States and Memphis would become a popular commodity. Keith was going to have to persuade the Memphis people that he was the best person for the job even if he could not afford to offer an up-front payment.

NEGOTIATING WITH MEMPHIS MILANO

Keith was surprised at the way the negotiations were conducted. No business was discussed for three days. Keith visited the homes of Alberto, Ernesto, and Carlotta and enjoyed many fine meals. They went to shows, nightclubs, and the beach. Much time was spent getting to know each others' attitudes and personal philosophies. Initially Keith was pleased at this country-club approach. Then he began to worry that they would never get any work done. They were not developing any guidelines for the contract. He also worried that time was wasting and Ladislav would worry or get upset at the delay.

Then he realized that they were at work. The Italians had no intention of talking business until they knew what kind of a person Keith was. In three or four days of intense living together, they were going to find out. If Keith was pretending to be other than he was, eventually he would slip up. Keith commented:

> It's very much like the Saudis and the Japanese. They do not jump in there and start doing business right away. They want to know your character first: your goals in life; what you have done with your life. The question is, Why should they do business with you?

Keith knew he was being tested. He thought he might have a small edge over others who wanted the distributorship because Guido Burrato liked him and had recommended him. But Burrato had told him that these people would make up their own minds.

Finally, the business discussions started between Keith and Alberto; they went on for four or five days. The two would sit talking and drink cappuccino coffee from 8 A.M. until late each night. At lunch they were off for three hours — half an hour for lunch and two and one-half hours talking about life. Keith was sure Alberto wanted to know Keith's philosophy of life as a clue to how Keith would represent Memphis' image when Keith was in the United States.

The first issue of concern in the business discussions was the question of inventory. Alberto wanted Urban Architecture to carry inventory in the United States and wanted to write up a large order for Keith to sign before the discussions were over. Alberto said he felt Keith would be more committed to Memphis if he had inventory. Keith, who did not have a lot of capital, wanted to put his money in advertising and order only what he sold.

Keith used his binder of sales as a bargaining chip to fend off Alberto's pressure to buy inventory. Keith said the binder proved he could sell Memphis and Alberto would have to trust Keith's proven selling ability based on the large order the binder represented. Alberto asked to see the binder and Keith said he would not show it until the negotiations were concluded, but he told Alberto the value of the sales. Keith said he would not give him the orders from the binder until he had a contract as the Memphis distributor for the United States.

The binder became the focus of discussions. Alberto got upset, feeling that Keith was playing with him. Finally, Ernesto got involved, asking about the binder at dinner. Keith traded the binder for the agreement that he would not have to carry inventory. Keith commented:

> The timing was perfect. Alberto had been pressing me for an agreement on inventorying Memphis, which I didn't want to do at all. At the time, I just didn't have a feel for what would happen — you know, what would sell well and in what quantities. I knew what sold well in Michigan, but I couldn't anticipate what would sell across the country.

A second point of disagreement was the method of payment. Memphis wanted Keith to set up an irrevocable letter of credit for $100,000. Memphis would ship merchandise and the value would be deducted from the letter of credit. This was a normal custom in Europe and the arrangement Memphis had with its distributors in Germany, Switzerland, France, and elsewhere. This arrangement would protect Memphis if Urban Architecture went bankrupt because Memphis would not have to pay the freight to have the goods returned to Italy. Also, Memphis' payment on the furniture would be secure and immediate. Urban Architecture could not delay paying. Keith had different thoughts:

> They love the idea of an irrevocable letter of credit. Although large firms in the United States use it, the practice is not standard for small firms because it's very expensive. Your accountants have to prepare statements every month for the bank to review. It's an added expense. Also, in the Midwest, you are not going to get a bank that you can characterize as being liberal, like Chase Manhattan or Chemical, that may not understand the trends of a rather new industry but will still take a chance. I'm dealing with banks that barely want to lend money to Chrysler. To say you want an irrevocable letter of credit means you almost wind up putting the money in escrow and then they lend to you against that. So what do you gain? Most importers like me buy "cash against documents." When the goods arrive in the United States, the customs broker calls and you courier a certified check to the broker to get the goods out of customs. As far as I was concerned, Memphis was going to have to take the risk. I was too small to put $100,000 into escrow.

The pressure to buy inventory and the insistence for quick cash gave Keith the feeling that Memphis was not as prosperous as he had believed. He knew that Memphis had distributorships in Switzerland, Germany, France, and Japan and he tried to find out how well these distributors were doing.

> We talked about the other dealers in the world. I asked Alberto what they were selling in terms of volume, but he wouldn't discuss it with me in any detail.

However, as Keith was introduced to other Memphis dealers from around the world, who were also attending the Salon Internazionale del Mobile, he began to understand why his file of new sales was of such interest to Alberto. In simple terms, the other dealers described to him how few key clients Memphis truly had around the world. The company on which he wanted to base his business was not nearly as profitable as he had originally thought.

The dealers told Keith that in each of their markets Memphis could not be sold unless the distributor got the best possible price from Memphis Milano and sold at a big discount to their best clients. This made Keith worry that the market for Memphis might be glutted. It was his opinion that a good art furniture line could remain avant-garde for about ten years until the rest of art furniture design caught up and made them look ordinary. Perhaps Memphis was "old hat" after eight years. Keith remembered:

> I spoke with the Memphis dealers at parties and at dinners and they were pretty candid. None of them were able to sell much of it, except to a handful of key clients who were canny collectors. At this point I became nervous. I was prepared to put all my eggs in this one basket, and now I could see that maybe it would be a bust.

Keith also started to get the feeling that Ernesto Gismondi, the owner, might be feeling a bit disillusioned with Memphis and that Alberto needed large American orders to rekindle Ernesto's enthusiasm. Keith still felt that Memphis would be a good investment for him. His personal belief was that the United States market had been badly handled through a late introduction, poor specifications, no flexibility, and poor service to clients and that the problems with broken and late shipments could be corrected. He believed he could sell enough to be important to Memphis and to develop enough economic clout so that they would listen to him.

However, as he went back to negotiations he was unsure about the long-term viability of Memphis. He wondered whether Urban Architecture could afford so much risk when a large company like Artemide had seemingly given up. Yet he continued the negotiation because of his conviction that Memphis represented quality and that he had seen himself that he could sell it to his major clients.

While the negotiations were going on, Keith decided to learn more about the rest of the operations of Memphis Milano. He understood you could learn a lot about a company by meeting with its employees and asking them what it is like to work there. So he talked to people working at all levels of Memphis. He learned what control systems were used. He learned what sold best from what was most often shipped. He learned what pieces were most likely to break in transit. The secretaries even told him about Alberto's emotional states — "Don't call him in the morning when he is moody and cranky; call after lunch when he is 'dancing on air.'" Keith felt he was not only finding out useful information, but he was also building working relations and dispelling the idea that he was an ugly, bottom-line American. Several box lunches eaten on the loading dock helped dispel that image.

After four days of discussions it seemed that the Memphis people were satisfied with Keith. Alberto began to set aside much of his work and spent a week with Keith teaching him the details of importing Memphis from Italy, which Keith had not expected. To understand the distribution systems and how to deal with brokers, Keith was walked through the system by Alberto. Alberto came across as a disciplined patrician and was extremely thorough and erudite in his questioning of Keith. His English was impeccable. All possible problems related to product line, distribution, and materials handling were discussed. Alberto instructed Keith how to handle quotas, inventories, dealers, advertising, marketing, placement of prototypes in cultural institutions, and exhibitions. Alberto insisted on going over each area repeatedly and in such detail that Keith began to regard him as somewhat of a pest who was overly concerned about mistakes.

KEITH'S STRATEGY

Keith's intuition about Memphis Milano was that the line could be very successful if it could be sold at a more reasonable price directly to the consumer rather than only through architects and designers. Memphis would have to be made as accessible in the United States as it was to consumers in Europe. This would be in contrast to, say, Atelier International of New York, for example, whose margin on United States sales to their distributors was about 300 percent at wholesale over their FOB Milan cost. This was the reason art furniture was so expensive. By the time a Le Corbusier sofa that cost $900 reached the public, it might cost $9,600. People were learning about this because the shelter magazines, such as *Metropolitan Home*, were telling them.

The most radical art furniture usually was available for sale only to architects and designers, who would purchase pieces of furniture they wanted placed in their plans for buildings. The general public was excluded from these art furniture showrooms and could not buy art furniture except through an architect or designer who could charge a large markup. This would have been Atelier's strategy for selling Memphis, if they had the line.

Urban Architecture would allow the public into their showrooms. The public then would have a choice of buying at retail prices or going to architects or designers in order to have them buy a piece for them. Architects and designers could purchase from Urban Architecture at a lower price, and in turn sell to the public with a design fee margin if they chose to. In this manner, accessibility for the public would be increased without undercutting reasonable margins for the architects and designers.

Keith also had ideas for his own retail store. He would set it up, refine the ideas, and then franchise it. He had a modest, three-tier pricing system worked out. He would mark up the products 100 percent to his dealers, 150 percent to architects and designers (the trade), and 200 percent to the public. He saw the need for a lot of third-party credibility. He would have to get the shelter magazines excited and writing about him, Memphis Milano, and his reasonable prices. He would advertise his prices, even brag about them.

Keith knew it would work, but would Ladislav believe him? Could Keith convince him, or should he even try to convince him?

CASE 9

Solartron (B)[1]

R. William Blake and
Henry W. Lane

Bob Allan was relieved to hear Andre Marcil, President of Solartron, answer the phone. Since receiving an early morning phone call from Nairobi, Kenya, Allan had spent the day tracking Marcil down, finally tracing him to Paris, France.

> "Andre, I had a call from Rick Douglas this morning; he's in Nairobi and he feels the situation at the Lubango Development site is critical and that the contract is in jeopardy. The contractor is hassling the work crews and the architect is saying that some of the components in the Solartron Kenya system are unacceptable. Rick says it's essential that you go to Nairobi for a day or two to sort things out."

> "Bob, it just doesn't sound that serious. I'm sure it's nothing that George Beida (Marcil's Kenyan partner) can't handle. Besides, I have to go to Geneva tomorrow, I really don't think I can get to Nairobi."

> "Look, Andre, I don't think you realize how serious this could be. You know Rick; he doesn't usually panic but he was sure concerned this morning. I really think you should go."

SOLARTRON

Solartron was one of the largest manufacturers of solar systems in Canada. From its conception four years earlier, the company had grown rapidly, and sales now exceeded $2,000,000.

The driving force behind Solartron was Andre Marcil, a young dynamic entrepreneur with a master's degree in solar engineering, who had overseen the expansion of the company in Canada and had personally negotiated the first entry into the international market.

The turning point in the development of Solartron occurred when the Canadian government, in an effort to develop alternative sources of energy, implemented a multimillion dollar program to promote the introduction of solar systems. Solartron was one of ten companies selected to receive federal grants.

Solartron became a public company through the takeover of a semidormant company with minor oil and gas interests. The resulting company was structured into two divisions — oil and gas, and solar. Marcil left the running of the oil and gas interests to the existing management and continued to focus his attention on the solar division, which now offered a full line of solar systems.

Despite the rapid growth of Solartron to a position of dominance in the Canadian solar industry, Marcil recognized that the country's geographic location limited the potential use of solar. If Solartron was to expand it would have to do so internationally. Ignoring the highly competitive United States market, Marcil signed a licensing agreement for the manufacture and sale of Solartron's low-temperature pool collectors in France. He then turned his attention to the "Sunbelt" countries of the developing world.

Solartron bid successfully against fifty-two companies from thirty-five countries for a contract to install domestic hot water systems in a housing project in Algeria and was awarded 400 of the 1,000 units. This contract established its credibility in the international marketplace.

Solartron's success in Algeria impressed Dave Matthews, Director of the Africa Division of the Industrial Cooperation Division of the Canadian International Development Agency (CIDA). Solartron was one of the smallest companies to win a tender in Algeria and Matthews approached Solartron to participate in a number of international technology shows with CIDA sponsorship.

SOLARTRON KENYA

At the urging of Matthews, and funded by a CIDA grant, Solartron exhibited at the Technology for the People show held in Geneva. Later that year while traveling in Kenya with Rick Douglas of the World Three Consultants[2] and discussing the potential for renewable energy in Kenya, Matthews described Solartron's Geneva exhibit and suggested that Douglas and Marcil meet. In Nairobi, Douglas introduced Matthews to George Beida. Beida was a very successful businessman and a personal friend of Douglas. The two men had met when Beida was studying at university in the early 1960s, and they had maintained a close relationship over the years. Following his university training, Beida had returned to the newly independent Kenya and accepted a position with Universal Enterprises, the largest nongovernment employer in the country, with more than 2,000 employees. Working as an assistant to the general manager, Beida planned and implemented the transfer of the retail and distribution operations of the company to local Africans.

After seven years with Universal, Beida struck out on his own. Over the following years he built up a group of thirteen companies in such diverse fields as finance, trucking, refrigeration, and cattle ranching. At the time of Matthews's visit, Beida's flagship company, Kenya Construction, was one of the largest real estate development companies in Kenya with over 1000 homes under construction. Matthews' description of Solartron's products intrigued Beida and he expressed an interest in learning more about solar systems.

On his return home, Matthews met with Solartron and described the potential solar market in Kenya. World Bank studies indicated the need for the development of 10,000 new homes in Kenya over the following ten years. He told Marcil about Kenya Construction and offered Solartron a grant to go to Kenya to install some systems on site. Subsequently Douglas met with Solartron, offered an introduction to Beida, and agreed to meet Marcil in Nairobi on a future trip. Shortly thereafter the technology transfer grant was approved and Solartron shipped the components for several systems to Nairobi.

After his next visit to Algeria, Marcil flew to Kenya to meet with businesspeople and government officials and to get a feel for the country. He found Kenya beautiful and the people friendly and relaxed. He was well received and generated considerable interest in solar by installing demonstration systems at the University, the Ministry of Energy, and on two of Beida's model homes.

The Canadian High Commission[3] was particularly impressed by Solartron's product line. After a number of meetings it agreed to support a proposal to the Department of External Affairs in Ottawa for the installation of solar hot water systems on nine staff quarter houses (SQ) owned by Canada. It was hoped to have the systems installed in time for display during the World Energy Show to be held in Nairobi eight months later in August. To ensure that the required components arrived in time to be installed, the Canadian government had them brought into the country as a diplomatic shipment like everything destined for the show. This meant bypassing the usual customs delays and allowing the components to enter the country duty free.

Marcil was very pleased with the prospect of installing systems on the SQ houses. He had already developed strong links with the government for domestic contracts and he hoped that the successful installation of systems on the SQ houses would lead to further orders from External Affairs to install systems on their buildings around the world. Such an opportunity would give Solartron invaluable publicity and the chance to expand its international operations.

During the visit Solartron also negotiated an agreement with the International School of Kenya (ISK) for the installation of pool collectors and hot water collectors for the showers. Because the Canadian government provided substantial funding for ISK, it was permissible for these systems to be included in the shipment for the Canadian High Commission, also.

Beida was very impressed by Marcil. The two men had a series of meetings during which they discussed the potential for solar in Kenya, concluding that the country offered an ideal market. There was no oil or coal in Kenya and the country was being financially strained by the cost of imported oil, which was taking 40 percent of its limited foreign exchange. Furthermore, the abundant sunshine resulting from the country's geographical location made solar energy feasible year round. These factors, combined with a good industrial base and the prediction of tremendous growth in housing development,[4] seemed to promise a ready market for domestic solar hot water systems.

When the discussion turned to the consideration of different ways in which the men could work together, Beida was adamant. He felt strongly that Solartron should establish a joint venture in Kenya. He was not interested in a straight licensing agreement and felt that the potential for success would be maximized if Solartron were to take a Kenyan partner. He believed a local company would have a competitive edge bidding on government contracts if there was significant Kenyan participation. The joint venture was important for him as he knew the company's success in Kenya would depend on continued involvement by his partner in technical and management matters. Beida also wanted Solartron to invest in the venture. Marcil and Beida agreed that $150,000 capitalization, or $75,000 each, would be sufficient. If the deal proceeded, Solartron's input would be in technology rather than cash. Beida would provide cash, plant space, local knowledge, and contacts that would facilitate the penetration of the Kenyan market.

In Ottawa, Marcil discussed the situation with Rick Douglas, who vouched for Beida's integrity and ability as a businessman. Marcil was excited by the potential Kenya appeared to offer and was eager to move ahead. As a first step he approached External Affairs and negotiated a contract to install solar hot water systems on the SQ houses in Nairobi. Oral commitment was also given for the ISK components to be included in the diplomatic shipment, and that the government would pay the freight charges involved.

Marcil next approached CIDA for funding to conduct a viability study on the proposed joint venture. Despite the attraction of the Kenyan market, he had some reservations about the local economic climate. Although Kenya welcomed foreign investment, economic problems brought on by the energy crunch and falling commodity prices, which were the country's principal foreign exchange earners, were causing concern for foreign investors. The shortage of foreign exchange had led to delays in the release of funds for dividend repatriation[5] and to the refusal of numerous requests for allocations for import licenses. These actions had reduced inventories to critical levels for many companies and Marcil was concerned about putting money into such an environment.

Marcil also had reservations about entering a joint venture. His partners would be inexperienced in solar; this, combined with the necessity to provide supervision and to work to maintain a good relationship, would put a strain on his limited time. He also believed that a joint venture would be a higher risk financially than licensing, as he would have to invest in Kenya, but that success would result in a much higher long-term profit. People would be the key to success. Marcil felt that Beida had the qualities he was looking for: honesty, reliability, flexibility, credibility, good contacts, and a willingness to work hard. In entering negotiations, Marcil was adamant on only two points, the value of his technology and the requirement for a fifty-fifty split. If no one had control, he thought, the partners would be forced to sit down and talk together to resolve any differences.

In late June, Marcil returned to Kenya. In a series of meetings, George Beida, Rick Douglas, and Marcil mapped out a joint venture proposal and Beida and Marcil signed a letter of intent that would establish a fifty-fifty partnership in Solartron Kenya (STK) between Solartron and Freezeking, a refrigeration systems company controlled by Beida. They also discussed the formation of a holding company, Solartron Africa (STA), to license Solartron Kenya and other companies in English-speaking Africa.

A problem arose during this period. Beida's lawyer warned that the government was unlikely to accept Solartron's technology as its total capital input and that

Solartron would probably have to put up some cash. On the positive side, the Canadian High Commission appeared to have cleared the way to import a container of Solartron collector components, thus allowing for the installation on the SQ houses and their demonstration at the World Energy Show.

Although the June meetings were productive, they were also extremely hectic. Marcil was in Nairobi for only four days and Rick Douglas, who had, by common assent, assumed the role of coordinator, was hard-pressed to get him together with Beida often enough to iron out the details of the proposed venture.

On the last day of the visit many details remained to be settled. Marcil and Beida finally managed to get together at 9 P.M., and the intense discussion that followed lasted through the evening and continued during the high-speed drive to the airport. Arriving at the airport fifteen minutes before his scheduled departure, Marcil managed to complete exit formalities in record time and made the flight with minutes to spare.

Although the two men had managed to touch on most of the major points of the proposed venture during the meeting, neither had kept notes. A detailed feasibility study was to be prepared as the next step and to ensure that all parties were aware of what they had undertaken, Rick Douglas put together a memorandum outlining the division of tasks. It had been agreed that the identification of an expatriate to work for Solartron Kenya was a high priority and the memorandum included a description of the type of person Marcil was to look for.

> Someone from Canada will be hired to work full-time for the company for part of a year in Kenya. This person should be an engineer, preferably mechanical, with at least two to three years experience in industry. He or she must also have good management skills. The engineering background, although necessary, will be secondary. Management and organization abilities are crucial.

> This person will undertake two months of training in Ottawa. The person will be encouraged to be available for the August World Energy Show. It may be that he or she will use vacation time to attend the show, go back and finish up at the present job, and then join on a full-time basis sometime later. Bob Allan and Andre Marcil should begin recruiting such a person immediately. This person will play a role in getting the company physically in operation and will assist with the feasibility study. When the person finishes in Kenya he or she would be available to work in Algeria or in another African country for STA. George Beida will have to explore the possibility of a work permit for such a person and Bob Allan will explore the personal taxation difficulties.

On his return to Ottawa, Marcil completed the feasibility study for his board of directors. It was his hope that Solartron Kenya would be functioning with an on-site manager by October and that the first Kenyans would be arriving for training at that time.

To assess the progress of the venture, Marcil reviewed the steps that had been taken and his expectations for the future. Solartron Kenya would be involved primarily in supplying domestic hot water systems for new housing developments. Initially, systems would be shipped already assembled, but the plan was to shift rapidly to a knocked-down version and, as soon as practicable, to start sourcing some components locally. Key components, such as the tube and fin, would continue to be supplied from Ottawa, due to the extremely high cost of the machinery used in their manufacture. Solartron hoped to bring technicians from Kenya for a two-week training course at the Ottawa plant as soon as possible. These men would work closely with the technical manager, to be appointed from Canada. Based on the World Bank housing projection, Marcil hoped that the new company would have sales in the next two years of $1,200,000 and $2,100,000, respectively, of which 20 percent would be export sales in neighboring countries.

Marcil had been pleased with his dealings and choice of partner. He thought George Beida was an entrepreneur who made things happen and he was "counting on Beida to make Solartron Kenya the African base." He realized that Beida had no knowledge of the solar industry and, with his numerous business interests, little time to spend on day-to-day management. This would be done by Dr. Harold Kamina, a Ph.D. in engineering and managing director of Freezeking. Andre felt that Kamina was technically strong but would need help marketing the systems. Marcil's main expectation of Beida was that he would use his considerable influence in the business and government community to get business for Solartron Kenya. He was not concerned about Beida's willingness to perform this function as he knew Beida would lose credibility if his first major international industrial deal fell through. In short, Marcil felt that he would have Beida's cooperation, but that he would have to fight for his time.

Marcil expected his own job would be primarily marketing, negotiating licenses in other African countries as well as setting guidelines and providing on-going research and development. He expected to make two trips to Kenya each year.

In addition to the Kenyan venture, Solartron was preparing another major expansion. Although the international expansion was providing solar markets, Andre knew the company was made vulnerable by its reliance on solar. If the field attracted major corporations such as the oil companies, Solartron would have trouble competing. To minimize this risk and to further the growth of the company, Marcil planned to make Solartron a total renewable energy company. Areas of proposed expansion included biomass and wood energy. As a first step in this direction Solartron negotiated a license with an Austrian company to produce a "thermo bio" boiler designed to burn wet and/or dry wood or other agricultural waste materials, thereby turning waste products into useful energy. With the introduction of the product Marcil planned to create a bioenergy division. Marcil's plans for the company were ambitious and included a solar subdivision, expansion into the United States, and a number of technical innovations.

A JOINT VENTURE AGREEMENT

In August, Marcil was in Nairobi for the World Energy Show. Ten Canadian companies, including Solartron, were exhibiting at the show.

Marcil had hoped to ship a container of systems to Nairobi prior to the show to allow Solartron to install the SQ and ISK units for display during the show.

Bureaucratic delays in Canada had blocked the shipment of the container and, for a time, it appeared the agreement would be canceled. When it became known that the Prime Minister would attend the show, the contract was rushed through and the container shipped. Because of the late action, however, it was necessary for the government to air-freight four systems to Nairobi and Marcil received a frantic call to get them installed for the Prime Minister's inspection. As a result Marcil and his installer worked through the night, finishing the installation one hour before the Prime Minister's visit to the site.

During August Marcil and Beida had further talks about the joint venture. Rick Douglas made it clear that the Kenyan authorities would not accept technology and training as Solartron's only contribution; it would have to put up cash. During the meetings the two men also discussed the structuring of the proposed venture. They decided that Solartron Kenya would be a licensee of Solartron Africa and that the holding company would grant licenses and provide technical support and services in other African countries. This structure was suggested in response to emerging political and cultural problems associated with conducting business between Kenya and some other African nations. It was their hope that the holding company, Solartron Africa, would be viewed as a nonaligned company.

Marcil had some reservations about the financing of the venture. He still did not like the idea of investing cash in Kenya, but he accepted the government's rejection of a technology-only package. He believed that Freezeking had an excellent chance of obtaining an order for 1,000 solar domestic hot water systems for a new housing project (Lubango) and hoped that this would lead to further orders for the company.

After further discussions with George Beida and Rick Douglas during a visit by Beida to Ottawa in September, a proposal for further restructuring of the venture was developed. Solartron Kenya would be a licensee of Solartron Africa but would buy the collectors and/or components directly from Ottawa. Marcil and Beida would share the profits of Solartron Africa and Solartron Kenya equally. Marcil also would realize a profit on the components or collectors sold by Solartron to the various licensees, including Solartron Kenya, which would technically be a joint venture licensing from Solartron Africa.

The only other significant change was that Beida would now hold 51 percent of Solartron Kenya and Marcil would hold 49 percent. Although this went against Marcil's stated policy of not holding less than 50 percent, he trusted George Beida and acknowledged that this structure would greatly ease the company's ability to function in the Kenyan environment and, because it would be a Kenyan company, would make it easier to borrow money locally.

LUBANGO

In mid-October, Marcil received good news. Freezeking had been awarded a contract to provide and install 500 of the 1,000 solar domestic hot water systems to be installed at Lubango, located outside Nairobi. Lubango was the largest housing project ever proposed for Kenya. Plans called for 6,000 houses to be constructed in six phases with 1,000 houses being built during each phase. The overall development was funded by the Scandinavian Development Fund[6] and was to be administered by Kenyan Development Agency (KDA). If Freezeking performed well, it would have established itself solidly in the local market and Solartron Kenya would become a prime contender for future contracts. With this in mind, Beida and Kamina resolved to ensure the project was an unqualified success.

Freezeking had been fortunate to receive the contract as it had entered the running late in the process and before Solartron Kenya had been structured or incorporated. The fact that Freezeking was not known as a solar company had made the successful result all the more remarkable. According to Kamina:

> We really came in very late on this particular project. The architects had their nominated suppliers for the solar equipment and letters had already been written long ago, even, I think, before Andre Marcil ever showed up on the scene. The first thing we did when we knew we were going to go into solar was to initiate action so we could at least be cited in correspondence as suppliers of solar equipment. Since we are a local company we were requested to quote also.

During his June visit, Marcil had met with people from the Kenyan Development Agency. Specifications for the solar systems had not been written and KDA was waiting for the Ministry of Energy to develop them. KDA felt specifications were necessary to ensure fair and objective comparisons. Marcil had offered the specifications for his equipment as a model. When the Ministry of Energy eventually issued its solar specifications, most of Solartron's had been accepted and used as the standard.

The initial meeting with KDA was set up by Beida:

> We introduced Marcil to KDA at a luncheon. I knew he was good and the people at the Ministry of Energy had been very impressed. KDA thought they would require this information and they were happy to have it. Of course the Solartron equipment had a technical advantage but the specifications were technically rigorous and would ensure good equipment for the project.

Kamina did the tender costing for the Freezeking bid. He initially added a minimal profit margin because the project was seen as an opportunity to establish the company rather than as a significant money-maker.

The Freezeking bid had not yet been submitted when Marcil arrived for the World Energy Show. During the show, Freezeking's strongest competitor approached the Solartron booth and enquired of Marcil if there was the possibility of licensing Solartron technology. Unaware of Solartron's link with Freezeking, the man went on to boast that his company was assured of receiving a contract to supply 1,000 collectors for a "local project," even going so far as to reveal the price he had submitted in his tender. Kamina expanded on this chance encounter:

> Andre's questions were a bit loaded. He was quite inquisitive because the tender had not been closed and our competitor seemed so sure of winning the tender. Up to that time

our operations were not known to most people and our competitor did not know of our plans to go into business with Solartron. So he revealed his bid and we learned that our tender would not get the job. His equipment was not as good as ours, but we couldn't take a chance. We had to be sure that we were not out of the price range, so we calculated his price per unit and went just a little bit lower on ours. What we eventually bid was not absolutely realistic. There was no profit, but this was deliberate."

Having submitted what he believed was the low tender, Kamina commenced work on a technical comparison of Solartron's equipment and that of their nearest competitor.

What helped us tremendously was our comparative analysis. Solar is a new thing in Kenya and the evaluation of the tender took some effort so we prepared a technical comparison of the competing systems. We had our competitor's brochure and were able to point out weaknesses. We made this available to the consultants who were evaluating the tenders and we came out clear winners. We should have received the entire job, but I think the client eventually decided that they would award it to two companies, so we got 500 units and our competitor got the other 500 units.

The receipt of the Lubango contract signaled the beginning of a series of problems for Freezeking. Because the bid had been submitted before the new company, Solartron Kenya, was fully operational, there were numerous opportunities for difficulties to develop. These were compounded by the actions of their competitors, who were incensed at losing "their project" and who now tried to discredit Freezeking and have the whole contract awarded to them. Kamina complained:

The politicking to get the business was the major problem at Lubango. Because even after we got the tender many attempts were made to discredit us; little issues became mountains.

Beida commented:

In the first place, we got the tender before we were ready. And when we got it, we won it on merit, because the standard was set and the specifications were set. But having won, everybody wanted to say you never installed solar heaters before, you never did this, you never did that. A contractor will blame you, everybody will blame you — for a simple reason. This was only the beginning — there were a thousand houses in the first phase. They have another five thousand to go. And whoever makes a good deal of this will get them. Plus, the project is owned 50 percent by SDF. They aren't going to support Canada. The other competitors were Scandinavian and British.

Kamina expanded:

We went into the project as an unknown entity. Also, we suspected all along that there may have been some meeting of minds between some people close to the project and a certain company to supply solar equipment. It's interesting, because the people whom I think they had in mind eventually didn't get a piece of the job.

Now, when we got in, the atmosphere was not really conducive to us because there was an element of resentment. The given specifications against which we tendered were quite clear. So when we went in, they tried to make things almost impossible. We are not really highly experienced in tendering procedures and working in that field. My own background is in consulting engineering work, not really in contracting work. I think — in hindsight — if we had more experience we would have called their bluff in the beginning. But initially they were more or less playing with us. You know, "Do this!" and we'd run until we were breathless to try to fulfill their demands. "When will you finish this? When will you do that?" It was very, very, very harassing.

But the major area of difficulty was with the water tank. The systems are installed in basically three components: the collectors and connectors, supplied from Canada, and the storage tank, which we were to make locally. Solartron had proposed a tank for us that really would not work here. This caused a confidence gap, because the drawing brought from Canada was for a nonpressurized tank. When we actually saw the thing, we realized it wouldn't work. So we had to change it to a pressurized tank. That involved a lot of additional equipment and created an element of doubt in the minds of the architects as to whether we were competent and knew what we were doing. Of course, we were sure ourselves, but they're entitled to feel that, especially given the fact that we were the last to appear on the scene.

Then these project architects insisted that we had to carry out a pressure test on the tanks. They wrote up a specification that would have been good for a steam boiler, with six-gauge steel plate construction and pressure specifications that were really out of this world. They did not conform to the normal specifications. So if we followed these specifications — and that was their idea — we would have gone bust because the cost of producing these tanks would be prohibitive. So that was one problem, but they tried to put all sorts of hurdles in our way.

It soon became clear that some of the project's backers were hoping that Freezeking would withdraw their bid before the final contract was signed. This backstage pressure continued on several fronts, with queries from the project architects on every small aspect of the design and installation and demands for a concrete example of the system proposed. Letters were written containing innuendos on Freezeking's ability to perform, in an attempt to undermine the company's credibility. It took Beida's contacts and Kamina's connections in the local engineering community to ensure that Freezeking would weather the storm.

During the month following the awarding of the contract and prior to the actual signing, more problems, including the tank design, developed. Despite requests to Solartron (Canada) for technical information, communications seemed to have broken down, and little help was forthcoming. Pressure continued to mount for Freezeking to demonstrate an operating system, but none of the required special fittings supplied from Canada were available despite the fact that large numbers of fittings were physically in the country. These fittings were in the container that had been brought into the country as a diplomatic shipment by the Canadian High Commission. Although the container had more components than were required for the SQ houses and ISK, concerns about the use of these duty-free items on other projects prevented Freezeking from gaining access to the surplus components.

When Rick Douglas arrived in Nairobi in early November, he found progress stalled and Freezeking under intense pressure from their competitors, the project consultants and the architects. Although Beida had managed to ensure that the contract was signed, this had not stoped the attacks. Kamina explained:

> It was a struggle to sign the contract; some people had not given up the fight to try to get the job all for themselves. Letters were being written to the client about us that were not accurate. We saw copies and by pointing out what the facts of the matter were, we were able to neutralize them and the contract was signed.

A renewed round of attacks, made primarily on technical grounds, convinced Douglas that it was essential for Marcil to fly to Nairobi. Neither Beida nor Douglas had a technical background, and Kamina was not sufficiently well acquainted with the Solartron products to counter the attacks. KDA was becoming confused and desperately wanted to sort out the mess. They had gone for help to advisors in the Ministry of Energy, who were seconded from a Scandinavian agency. The advice was to go with the Scandinavian systems. People at KDA wondered if they were being manipulated, but they did not have the technical knowledge to know for sure; they were getting ready to acquiesce. Although a Canadian solar engineer had recently been hired to work for Solartron Kenya, he was not due to arrive in Nairobi until the end of December, so that would not help.

In mid-November, Douglas called his colleague, Bob Allan, at their office in Toronto.

> Bob, the situation here is critical. The crews at the work site are being hassled and the architect is saying some of the system components are unacceptable, no one here is capable of refuting the attacks and we're in danger of losing the contract. Try to contact Andre and tell him that he's got to get down here.

Notes

1. The names of all people and companies have been changed as have the names of organizations and some locations in Kenya.
2. World Three Consultants was formed to promote the development of joint ventures and other business relationships between Canadian and African businesspeople. The group's initial strategy had been to focus on one country, Kenya, which was well known to Rick Douglas and his partner, Bob Allan.
3. In Commonwealth countries, the embassies of other Commonwealth countries are called High Commissions.
4. Kenya had one of the highest rates of population growth in the world; the country's population was expected to more than double to 44,000,000 by the year 2000.
5. The government also had imposed a temporary limit on dividend repatriation that was eventually lifted.
6. The SDF is a government sponsored organization whose mandate is to fund projects in countries of the developing world.

Solartron (C)[1]

R. William Blake and Henry W. Lane

DECEMBER 24

Rick Douglas sat at his desk reading the note from Andre Marcil, President of Solartron:

> Pierre and Lise left at 9:45 P.M. and we accomplished quite a bit in the three hours prior to his flight; as usual, when the pressure's on the work gets done. He looked very happy and excited, and I feel that he is going to be a very good addition to the group and that he will definitely help Solartron Kenya really get off the ground.

APRIL 22

As the plane carrying Pierre and Lise lifted off from Kenyatta International Airport, Pierre was both relieved and depressed. What had seemed like such a wonderful opportunity when he joined Solartron Kenya had ended. Now he was leaving Kenya, after less than four months.

The reasons for the early departure were complex and, depending on who was asked, could be attributed in part or in whole to a number of people. It seemed to Pierre that things had gotten off to a bad start from which he had never recovered.

PIERRE BLONDEAU

Pierre Blondeau was a lanky, easygoing solar engineer. His work experience included the preparation of feasibility studies; conducting energy conservation surveys, computer simulations, and field work; and supervision. Pierre's grin and his shaggy hair gave him a boyish appearance that belied his technical competence. At the age of thirty, he had already completed a master's degree in solar and mechanical engineering and, although he enjoyed his job with a consulting engineering firm, he was ready for a new challenge.

In recent years, his personal life had been turbulent. His divorce was finalized nine months ago, and since that time, he had been living with Lise Rivard, a writer, in a house they had purchased together. Lise was an ardent feminist whose fiery personality and volatility had attracted Pierre the first time they met.

Blondeau had attended a contractors' meeting in Ottawa. During lunch, he got into a discussion with Alain Marcil, Sales and Marketing Manager for Solartron, one of the largest manufacturers of solar systems in Canada. Blondeau had dealt often with Solartron, and was impressed by its products and professionalism. Marcil told him that Solartron was expanding its operations overseas and mentioned that he was looking for an engineer to work for Solartron Kenya, a joint venture that had just been established.

Blondeau was excited by the description of the opportunity. The following week he telephoned Alain's brother, Andre Marcil, Solartron's founder and President, and arranged for an interview.

SOLARTRON KENYA

Rick Douglas, Director of the World Three Consultants[2] (WTC) had been introduced to Andre Marcil through the offices of the Canadian International Development Agency. The two men discussed the potential for solar energy in Kenya, and Douglas offered an introduction to George Beida, a Kenyan businessman who was very active in housing development. Marcil subsequently made three visits to Kenya, the result of which was a joint venture agreement with Beida. The agreement called for the creation of two new companies, Solartron Africa (STA), a holding company, and Solartron Kenya (STK), an operating company that would service the Kenyan market. Following the development of STK, the men hoped to expand into other African countries through STA.

During a series of meetings the details of the agreement were finalized. The partners hoped to introduce Solartron's products into Kenya through a three-phase program. Initially, the systems would be exported to Kenya. In the second phase, products would be shipped completely knocked down for local assembly, and in phase three, all assembly and the bulk of component manufacture would be done locally.

During discussions, Beida made it clear that he considered the provision of an engineer for STK from Solartron to be a very high priority:

> If we have an engineer from the parent company working for us, our clients will have confidence in us. The type of engineer we really need is a person who can sell—you know, a marketer. Because if it's a question of just producing drawings, we can get the staff locally and send them to Canada. What we require is a human being with a good personality, you know, good public relations. Because all business as far as I'm concerned, relates to or revolves around charm.

Marcil initially did not understand or share Beida's concern about the credibility of the new company in the eyes of other Kenyan executives.

> Hiring a Canadian for STK would be overkill, and I can't afford to lose a person right now anyway. Harold Kamina (who was to be Managing Director of STK) is a Ph.D engineer. Send us a Kenyan and we'll train the person to work with Harold.

But as the discussion progressed, it became clear to Marcil that the presence of a Canadian offered significant advantages to STK in terms of credibility and the availability of technical competence. He agreed to look for a suitable candidate and Douglas subsequently prepared a memorandum which outlined the type of person Marcil was to look for:

> Someone will be hired to work full time for the company for a part of a year in Kenya. This person should be an engineer, preferably in mechanical, with at least two to three year's experience in industry. He or she must also have good management skills.
>
> The engineering background, although necessary, should be secondary. Management and organization abilities are crucial as this person will play a role in getting the company physically in operation and will assist with the feasibility study.

Marcil started looking for a suitable candidate, and over the next three months, interviewed six people. Included among the candidates was Pierre Blondeau.

THE HIRING OF PIERRE BLONDEAU

Andre Marcil was impressed by Blondeau's background and the initiative he had shown in requesting an interview. The two men were immediately comfortable with each other and, as the discussion progressed, Andre became convinced that Blondeau was the most impressive candidate he had met and would be a great asset to STK. At the conclusion of the meeting, he told Blondeau that he was offering him the job and suggested that he talk it over with Lise before making a decision.

Lise was Blondeau's major concern. She had been reserved when he first mentioned the idea of moving to Africa but was unwilling to be separated from him for the six to twelve months he would be away. If he decided to accept, she would go with him.

English was the business language of Kenya and most people spoke it. Although Blondeau spoke fluent English, Lise spoke little, and her native French was a language seldom heard in Kenya. This, combined with the anticipated cultural and social changes, dampened her enthusiasm for the adventure.

Blondeau wanted very much to accept the offer. After discussing the options with Lise, he informed Marcil that he would accept if Solartron agreed to provide return airfare for both him and Lise, and if English lessons could be arranged for Lise in Nairobi. He discussed Lise's hesitancy with Marcil, and it was agreed that if she did not enjoy Nairobi, she would return home alone.

Marcil was extremely pleased to have hired someone as qualified as Blondeau. In a final meeting, the two men agreed on the terms of employment and signed a contract (Figure 1).

In a subsequent letter to Rick Douglas, Marcil said of Blondeau:

> We have come to the conclusion that he offers the most potential for the position as Manager of Solartron Kenya. His background and experience in solar engineering are quite strong, and to me, this was a nonnegotiable. On the management side, even though he has been responsible for some important projects, he will have to be supervised and directed quite closely, at least to get the organization going.

FIGURE 1

(This is a translation from the French original)
CONTRACT BETWEEN: SOLARTRON INC.
AND
PIERRE BLONDEAU

The present contract is for the hiring of Pierre Blondeau as a consultant on the following conditions:

1. He will be paid a salary totaling $36,000 or $3,000 per month.

2. The salary after taxes must total $25,000.

3. This contract may have a duration of one year, from January 1 to December 31. The minimum duration is six months.

4. A car and a place to live will be furnished by STK.

5. Pierre Blondeau will also be added to our benefits program in the same proportion as the employees of Solartron Inc.

6. Return airfare for Pierre Blondeau and his companion will be paid by Solartron Inc.

7. The stipulated salary (See Item 1) will be paid every two weeks.

WRITTEN AND SIGNED THIS TWENTY-THIRD DAY OF OCTOBER.

The terms of the agreement called for Blondeau to work in Solartron's Ottawa facility two or three days a week until mid-December. This would allow him to familiarize himself with the company's products and processes and the details of the African operation. He was to start work in Nairobi on January 1.

THE BRIEFING

Rick Douglas and Andre Marcil had agreed that the person chosen to work for STK would spend two or three days talking with members of the World Three Consultants. The purpose of the visit would be to brief the person on the geography, history, and culture of Kenya. Shortly after accepting the job, Blondeau agreed that he and Lise spend two days with the consultants. Last-minute scheduling problems resulted in the couple arriving late and it became necessary to compress the briefings into a day and a half.

The focus of the briefings was primarily on the country. There was little said about the job. Since it was a start-up situation, everything would need to be done and anything could be expected to happen. Rick Douglas met first with the pair, giving them an overview of the work of WTC and its involvement with Solartron, and then talking at length of his experiences in Africa and of the differences to be expected and opportunities to be enjoyed. His love for the country was evident in his animated discussion of life in Kenya.

Rick's colleague, Bob Allan, took a somewhat harder line in his briefings. He dwelled at length on the problems of living in a developing country, of coping with being a minority, language hassles, security problems, how to deal with a houseboy, and the myriad of other little things that can frustrate Westerners. During the afternoon, Lise was visibly tired and her limited ability with English made it difficult for her to follow the discussion. After two hours, she retired for a nap, rejoining the others for supper and the evening talks.

The briefings were generally positive and painted a picture of Kenya as a beautiful and stable country offering the expatriate a good standard of living, and the opportunity to visit some of the finest game parks and resorts in Africa. Balancing this, however, was a warning to Lise and Pierre that there would inevitably be hassles, and that flexibility and adaptability would be necessary if they were to make the most of the experience.

Bob Allan had mixed feelings about their visit:

> Pierre was a pleasant person and obviously strong technically, but he was short on management skills. Lise seemed largely disinterested in the briefings and was unsure whether she should go with him.

Allan mentioned his misgivings about Lise to Douglas, who agreed with his concerns but hesitated to mention them to Marcil. Solartron Kenya had won a contract to install 500 domestic hot water systems the previous week and intense pressure was coming from STK to get someone out there. He felt that the pair could cope, and that the language lessons he arranged for Lise would allow her to interact in the local society and enjoy her time in Africa.

DECEMBER 29

As the KLM flight commenced its final approach to Kenyatta International Airport, Pierre Blondeau wondered what the coming weeks would bring. He and Lise had spent the previous week vacationing in Amsterdam and, although tired after the overnight flight, he was excited at the prospect of actually arriving in Africa and the challenge his new position would offer.

Blondeau had high expectations of Kenya. Marcil had said they would spend the month of January at River Court, the spacious three-bedroom apartment used by the World Three Consultants. During that time, they would choose their apartment residence to be furnished complete to the cutlery and which would have a houseboy. Although local transportation would not be immediately available, Blondeau was to purchase a station wagon or pickup truck for STK and use it as his personal vehicle outside working hours. Even used cars were expensive in Kenya and it would be impractical for him to buy one for a one-year appointment. Having the use of the STK vehicle would give Blondeau and Lise the freedom to explore Kenya in their free time.

Blondeau was looking forward to his new job. Marcil had given him a job description and he was eager to see STK make the transition into a successful operating company. After a few days off to get settled and celebrate New Year's, he expected to be at his desk bright and early Monday morning.

ERICA BECK

Erica Beck was looking forward to meeting Pierre and Lise. As WTC's resident consultant in Nairobi, she had been actively involved in the process that had led to the establishment of STK. Since the awarding of the contract for 500 domestic hot water systems in October, her involvement had been almost full-time as she assisted STK's managing director, Harold Kamina, with a wide range of activities. Erica was not an engineer, and although she had found the activities of the previous months highly stimulating, she had other projects underway that needed her attention. With Pierre's arrival, she would be able to bow out of day-to-day involvement with STK.

At age thirty-three, Erica was a veteran of Africa. She previously had lived four years in Swaziland where she established a cooperative garment manufacturing plant. During this time, she had traveled widely and had developed a deep affection for the continent and its people.

On her return to North America from Africa, Erica enrolled in an M.B.A. program. On graduation, she joined WTC and was sent to represent the company in Nairobi.

Erica had discussed Pierre and Lise at length with Rick Douglas during his recent visit to Nairobi. To ensure a smooth transition for the couple, he asked her to arrange for a suitable apartment and to help them through the first weeks in the country.

In late November, Erica started looking for an apartment. Her intention was to locate the pair in a middle-class area with a mixed population and easy access to public transportation. Such an apartment would be reasonably priced and offer a diverse and interesting cultural experience.

Although Erica had located two apartments to fit her criteria, both had been ruled as unsuitable by George Beida. After persistent questioning by Erica, he made it clear that he felt Blondeau should be free to choose his own apartment. He also had Erica telex Solartron to suggest the couple bring their own linens as those available in Kenya were more expensive and of lower quality.

December had flown by and now Erica was at the airport waiting for Blondeau and Lise to complete entry formalities. Although she knew how tiring the overnight flight from Europe could be, Erica was expecting the couple to be excited, positive, and enthusiastic about their arrival in Kenya.

Blondeau and Lise appeared tired as they struggled out of customs under the weight of their baggage. Erica's initial impression was that he was easygoing, but Lise seemed a little distant. After introducing herself, she led the way to her Volkswagen, where it became obvious that it would be impossible to get all the luggage in. As she and Blondeau discussed alternatives, she was surprised to see Harold Kamina pull up in his Mercedes.

HAROLD KAMINA

Although he knew that Erica Beck would be meeting Pierre and Lise, Harold Kamina had decided to drive to the airport to welcome them to Kenya.

Kamina was excited at the prospect of meeting Pierre Blondeau. As Managing Director of STK, he had been under tremendous pressure to get the new company operational, and since the awarding of the contract, he had been struggling to get the installation of the 500 domestic hot water systems running smoothly. Solartron Kenya had added tremendously to his workload, and his other obligations did not leave him the time he needed to devote to the start-up. In addition to a refrigeration contracting company, he owned a bakery and a heavy equipment distributorship, both of which required a lot of attention.

As he drove to the airport, Kamina was preoccupied with his latest dilemma; Solartron Kenya had no solar collectors available for installation at Lubango. Although a container destined for the project had arrived the previous week, Kamina had been horrified to discover that no Société Générale du Surveillance (SGS) inspection certificate had been obtained prior to shipment from Canada. Now Kenya customs were refusing to clear it, and it was possible the container would have to be returned. Although his crews were at work installing water storage tanks on the Lubango houses, it would be necessary to start adding the collectors to complete the systems very soon. As an interim measure, Kamina had hoped to borrow some collectors from the Canadian High Commission. The High Commission had arranged to bring a container full of systems into Kenya as a diplomatic shipment prior to the World Energy Show in August. The systems were destined for installation on Canadian staff quarter housing and at the International School of Kenya. The container contained more systems than these projects required and the school's system had yet to be installed. Kamina was expecting another container to arrive in three weeks; however, he was under mounting pressure from the project engineers to meet his installation commitments. To date, he had been unable to convince the High Commission to release the excess systems to him, and he was hoping Blondeau might be able to resolve the problem. Kamina also wanted Blondeau to prepare an inventory of the contents of the container, because much of the copper piping had "disappeared" since arriving in Kenya.

Bringing in an engineer from Canada had been important to Kamina:

> I felt very strongly that we had to have a representative from the manufacturing company. Somebody had to be there to represent the interests of the parent company and see to things on their behalf because it is a joint venture. That's one point. The other point, which was crucial to me, was that we needed a technical person just for sheer credibility. When we go to sell ourselves, to present ourselves, we also wanted to say, this fellow is the manufacturer of the equipment. If I'm the client, I don't want to talk to a middleman. Also, a technical person would support somebody in charge of administration. So you need a technical arm to lean on, apart from somebody local. This is why we needed two engineers, one expatriate and one local. This is just a market feeling from the business point of view. From the technical point, I can assure you there is nothing I could not do, if I could only have a week or two training. Technically, it's quite ordinary; it's more or less following the rules of the game and adapting from one

environment to another. We have a young man eminently suited for that. So technically, even for installation, we don't require help from Canada. We require support in design, not for domestic equipment, but for industrial projects. But as I say, the idea of a Canadian was for the transitional period.

There are so many tremendous problems setting up a new company. . . for example, trying to translate North American business and manufacturing procedures into local terms. This is the first stage of a three-stage project. So this person's role was really to set up all this and also do business for us — look for clients and things like that and oversee our installations.

Kamina arrived at the airport as Erica and Pierre were discussing what to do with the baggage. Enthusiastically pumping Blondeau's hand, he welcomed the pair to Kenya and immediately started discussing the problems facing STK. Quickly taking charge of the situation, he bundled the remainder of the bags into his car and, taking Blondeau with him, headed for River Court, leaving Erica and Lise to follow in the Volkswagen.

On the drive to River Court, Erica began to feel apprehensive about Lise, who was incensed at having been separated from Pierre and whose general conversation seemed to indicate a very inflexible attitude. Erica was concerned that this could cause problems in the very traditional Kenyan culture. It was still pretty much a man's world. Women's lib had not yet arrived in Kenya, and no one knew better than Erica the amount of effort, thought, and flexibility it took to adapt. The couple visibly brightened on seeing the River Court apartment, but their smiles disappeared when Erica told them they would have to vacate in two days. Blondeau expected to have a month at River Court, during which time he could search for an apartment, and the prospect of finding an apartment so quickly did not appeal to him.

Less than an hour later the phone rang. Kamina, now back at the office, was pressing Pierre to come to work. Pierre hung up totally perplexed. He expected to have some time off to settle in and had been surprised when Kamina talked business in the car. Now it appeared he was not to have any time off at all.

Erica felt strongly that Pierre and Lise should go to the office, if only for half an hour, just to be polite. Despite her efforts, Lise refused and although Pierre went, he did so reluctantly.

SETTLING-IN PROBLEMS

Pierre and Lise's introduction to their new lifestyle was far from tranquil. Although there were numerous minor problems and irritants, these were overshadowed by major problems which developed in four areas: housing, transportation, work routine, and personal life.

Housing

From the moment Erica Beck explained the necessity to vacate River Court within two days, housing was foremost in Blondeau's mind:

I expected to spend a month in River Court, which would leave us enough time to find a place with no rush. The company was supposed to take charge of providing all the furniture and everything because I didn't carry that stuff—you see I was expecting to have everything when I arrived here. He said Erica would be staying the month at River Court also. This is also a delicate point. I didn't know Erica at all, you see. I like her; she's okay. But when you have to live together, there may be some friction. It really is a gamble to get two different people together, and if you force them to live together, it may be too much.

Harold Kamina commented:

When they arrived, they were put up in a flat whose lease was running out in two days. So within those two days, we moved them to another flat. They said it was not suitable, so we said, "Okay, we will now move you to another place." Which is where they are now. So, there was just a question of three or four days in this transition. But I think they didn't take very well to it.

Pierre Blondeau was not impressed by the apartment search:

Erica arranged with Beida. We went to three different places and they were all too far away from the city center, so we decided to go for the apartment that was downtown and ready, but there were no household goods, just the furniture, and nothing to cook with.

George Beida commented:

I said, "What would you wish? Where would you like to live?" He said, "You know my wife's not working. I would like to live downtown." Downtown. I said, "In what type of accommodation?" He said he would like two bedrooms. I said, "Why two bedrooms?" He replied, "Because when Andre comes, we would like him to stay there." I didn't believe that, but it's not the issue. But then, I said, "In Nairobi, we don't have anything like that downtown. There are very few places that are downtown. However, we do have a two-bedroom flat, which will be ready in February. It's on top of Nairobi House near the theatre, near to the restaurants, next to everything. It's not ready yet, but there's a one-bedroom flat in the same building. Go and look at it! If you like it, and you want to stay there, being inconvenienced for one month, then you can move upstairs into the two-bedroom flat. Then you'll be downtown and your wife will have no problem with transportation." He went to look at it. He didn't even come back to the office. He just went and moved his things there. So I figured the guy is happy.

But Pierre and Lise were soon back in the housing market.

We couldn't stand it for more than one week. It was very noisy. The buses around there made a lot of noise. It was small and dark, and I saw big cockroaches running around. Dirty, dirty—cockroaches and everything.

We then found a place that was two kilometers outside of the city, but at least there was bus service and it was a serviced apartment. During the first week, I had to buy some household goods, and we had to argue because the company didn't want to reimburse me.

George Beida was perplexed by Blondeau's behaviour:

Now he decided he didn't want downtown anymore. I said, "Okay, go look at furniture you want for the flat." But halfway through, I knew this would never work. He said Andre promised him cutlery. Andre promised him, you know. He was promised linen and so on and so forth. I knew that was not correct. Because when I talked with Erica, I said, "Erica, can you ask these fellows to bring their own linen because it's cheaper in Canada." Anyway, I did not bother to argue about it, and I knew the problem would never be solved. I could not let my partner down. So, I said, "Okay, if you were promised that, what else were you promised? A fellow to clean your flat. What else?" I said, "Well, okay, we will provide that too. The only thing — downtown is not possible." It's a fact, there are few flats in downtown Nairobi. So I took him in my car. We went to look for serviced apartments, which had cutlery and staff. I said, "Look at this. If you like it, you move in as soon as you want to move in." He said he would take Lise to see it. He said they liked it, so they moved in. And even then, he was not satisfied. Things are not right. You know, the color is not right. He should have said so when they first went there. He can't expect me to go to decide on the color. He went to the flats. He said he's happy, he's comfortable.

Transportation

While the accommodation was being settled, Blondeau had started work. Progress on the Lubango installations was at a standstill while STK and Blondeau tried to borrow collectors from the container imported by the Canadian High Commission. He was also involved in conducting an inventory of the contents of the container, a significant portion of which had disappeared. Blondeau's work required him to be mobile and the lack of a vehicle for his use quickly replaced the housing issue as a point of contention.

Andre told me I was supposed to purchase a vehicle for the company. He told me I could use that vehicle for my personal use and when I was working, the vehicle would be used for company purposes. The first weekend I was able to borrow Kenya Construction's Volkswagen and Mr. Beida told me, no problem, you can take the Volkswagen every night to travel back and forth. But the next week the car broke down and there was no alternative solution. He kept telling me, you will get your own vehicle in two weeks anyway and then it was at the end of the month, and after that it was another two weeks and so on. The Volkswagen was used by the people in Kenya Construction and if one of them had a meeting, he might come back at 7:00 P.M., so I would spend all my time here waiting for the vehicle. I couldn't plan. I'd make an appointment with someone and then realize I had no transportation.

Harold Kamina was not sympathetic to Blondeau:

Each time there was a problem, it really swung around the vehicle, so much that all his memos are related to that.

These are pool vehicles you know — you can't have them to yourself. So whether he wanted something for himself exclusively, we don't know. Maybe he was promised a vehicle and he interpreted it too literally.

George Beida commented:

When he said he needed a car, we provided him with a car. Then the car broke down. He came to the office immediately and asked for another car. I said, "How can we provide another car? We don't have cars all over." And we started seeing the problem coming. The company was not yet finalized, so we could not borrow money. In fact, we could not start operating the company without the Foreign Investment License which we were still waiting for. So I told him, "Listen! Anything we do before the formalities are finalized will cause problems." Because our problem is that we started operating, we started doing business, before we were finalized. So it became a big issue. For example, he said he needed a car to go shopping at night. How can he say that? It's all crazy! There is no shopping at night in Kenya. Anyway, he has a car. If it breaks down it has to be repaired. And as it went on, quite frankly, I started losing interest because I started seeing this man is not going to fit in here. So what's the point in me buying a car when that money could be used to clear the solar heaters at the port. He should be able to understand. He was very negative.

Harold Kamina:

The vehicle was available. During working hours, he might not have it to himself, but to come in to work and to go to his house, he had it. He had it everyday, everyday. When it broke down, he took it so badly. But even a new vehicle has to go to the garage sometime.

Working Conditions

Although the technical aspects of his new job were much as he had anticipated, Blondeau was surprised by the administration he was expected to handle:

Andre gave me a priority list and a job instruction list that included, of course, technical stuff, but also managing, marketing, administration, keeping the inventory and everything. I don't think I realized all the implications of that because it is really a big task to ask someone who has a technical background to be a good administrator at the same time.

He told me there would be staff to do most of the work. I was just to be able to understand what they were doing. When I arrived here, I realized that there was not much staff. I thought that the partners here were going to be more involved in the administration.

I didn't suspect that I would spend so much energy just to get things going, to get the proper tools to do my job and try to convince the directors that I was here to work and that I needed some tools to do that.

To add to Blondeau's frustration, he had been sent home to his apartment to work for three weeks, shortly after his arrival, because he did not have a work permit. Harold Kamina explained:

Before we got approval for the permit, he could not come here to work. So he stayed away for about three weeks until we got approval.

By the time approval was received, Blondeau had decided to leave STK, and Kamina then decided he did not want to put up the security bond and pay for the permit for such a short period of time:

> For his dependent and himself, we would have to put up a bond of $3,000. We can't put that much up for three months; it doesn't make sense. But he took offense to things like that.

With a shortage of collectors and STK short on working capital as it waited for official approval from the Foreign Investment Review Committee, Blondeau felt very constrained in what he could accomplish. He also found that he could not get away as easily as he wished. He discovered that his expectations were unacceptable to Kamina, who said:

> And then he wanted to be excused from working on Saturdays, because he wanted to see the country. We said "No, we work on Saturdays here. Even if you don't work Saturdays in Canada, we cannot afford not to. We can't help it!" But all the same, he still had to go up country almost every weekend.

Pierre Blondeau commented:

> When I arrived here and I realized that I couldn't get these things, at least for the first few months, I wondered how I could go on safari and enjoy myself. When you decide to come to Africa, I think there is the challenge of the job, but there is also your personal life to consider; you want to be able to travel and enjoy the country. It is a new country to discover.

Personal Life

Blondeau's frustration at his situation did not greatly move George Beida, who had been unimpressed from their first meeting.

> He was shaggy, disorganized. . . . The way he was dressed, he looked like a hippie traveling around. When he arrived, we had a problem with the solar collectors being held by the Canadian High Commission, and we were waiting for him to sort it out. The day he arrived he said, "You know, I'm very tired. I'd like to relax for a few days before I do anything." And you know, sure like hell, he had to take four or five days off before he'd look at it. His attitude was not right.

Pierre Blondeau had a different view of the situation.

> Rick Douglas told me I would have at least a week off to get familiar with the country and the people. But almost the moment I was off the plane, they required me in the office because they had some problems on a deadline. I could have refused because my contract didn't start until January 1st, but I was in a bad position, and I also had to come to the office to solve my lodging problems.

Beida was also concerned about Lise.

> I called the man and said, "Listen, we are going to have a lot of problems. You have a young wife. She cannot be expected to be sitting at home doing nothing. Even my wife cannot sit at home doing nothing. So either she gets involved in some voluntary organizations or something else. She's French — she could go to the French Embassy or the French cultural center and find out what can be done there; or be involved in the university. Something — so that she's busy. Otherwise, she will be looking at the watch for you. Is there anything I can help with?" I even tried introducing them to people around, but it just couldn't work. It just couldn't work.

Despite the attempts of Beida and Beck to draw Lise out and make her feel more comfortable, she remained aloof and made little attempt to develop friends or socialize in the local community. She seemed to spend most of her time in the flat writing, and Beida felt certain that she was behind much of Blondeau's discontent.

> One weekend I invited him and Lise to my house for lunch. I had some visitors, including some Cabinet Ministers. During lunch Lise asked if she could see me. I said, "Sure why not? Come to my office." So she's the one who came in, in fact, to tell me — to give me a lecture about the apartment. This is why I knew it would not work. The bloody fellow should have told me himself. Unfortunately for me, I managed it badly. I should have kicked her out of my office. Because after that, he started writing me letters also.

Blondeau's frustration with the housing and transportation problems was increased by his contact with other expatriates.

> I met people from France, from Brazil, from all sorts of places, and most of them told me that they enjoyed Kenya. So I tried to discover why they did, and most of them said that they could not afford the same standard of living anywhere else. I feel that I live much better when I am in Canada. I have my own transport. I don't have to beg to get it. I don't have to account to anybody. I have a house that I like.

By mid-February, Blondeau and Lise had decided to leave Africa. Pierre Blondeau explained his decision.

> I would say an accumulation of frustrations made me decide to go back, I didn't see any way that things would really improve. I just felt I had had enough and also there were some other adaptation problems, because we came as a couple and for the man it is usually easier because you have work — you have a job — at least you know how to spend your time for at least eight hours a day. Lise didn't speak much English, which added to the difficulty.
>
> Also, we didn't know many people and you have to live a certain time in a place before getting to know people. At night, we didn't have much to do. There weren't many movies there, and if you don't like going to nightclubs, then it restricts activities. As you live in a place, you find more and more to do, but I think for Lise, it was a lot harder than it was for me. But I had difficulties as well. I'm not so sure that even if I had gone there alone . . . I maybe would have left early anyway.

George Beida commented:

He saw himself coming here, quite frankly, much more to see the country than to do the work. I think his problem is culture shock more than anything else, and I think the major problem is that he's highly dominated by his lady.

Harold Kamina was more concerned with the Lubango project:

I would like really to see Solartron coming up with a replacement for Blondeau as soon as possible because we are in a critical stage where the next twelve months will mean a pruning away of certain companies involved in the energy field.

The experience with Blondeau had frustrated Andre Marcil. He was uncertain as to what to attribute the early return, but he was sure on one thing: the brief stay had cost him at least $20,000 with little to show for it. Now he sat at his desk rereading a telex from George Beida. The tone of the telex was urgent and the message was clear. Beida and Kamina both felt it was crucial to the survival of STK that a replacement for Blondeau be sent immediately. Marcil's instinctive reaction was that such a step would be unnecessary and costly. Despite his reluctance, however, he respected his partners' views and wanted the venture to succeed. If he decided to replace Blondeau, he wondered, what should he do differently?

Notes

1. The names of companies, their employees, and some places have been changed.
2. The World Three Consultants had been formed to promote the development of business opportunities with African businessmen. The primary focus of the company was Kenya, although development work was underway in other African countries.

CASE 11

Ellen Moore (A): Living and Working in Bahrain

Gail Ellement, Martha Maznevski,
and Henry W. Lane

The General Manager had offered me a choice of two positions in the Operations area. I had considered the matter carefully, and was about to meet with him to tell him I would accept the Accounts Control position. The job was much more challenging than the Customer Services post, but I knew I could learn the systems and procedures quickly and I would have a great opportunity to contribute to the success of the Operations area.

It was November 1989, and Ellen Moore was just completing her second year as an expatriate manager at the offices of a large American financial institution in Manama, Bahrain. After graduating with an M.B.A. from a leading business school, Ellen had joined her husband, who was working as an expatriate manager at an offshore bank in Bahrain. Being highly qualified and capable, she had easily found a demanding position and had worked on increasingly complex projects since she had begun at the company. She was looking forward to the challenges of the Accounts Control position.

ELLEN MOORE

Ellen graduated as the top female student from her high school when she was sixteen, and immediately began working full-time for the main branch of one of the largest banks in the country. By the end of four years, she had become a corporate accounts officer and managed more than twenty large accounts.

I remember I was always making everything into a game, a challenge. One of my first jobs was filing checks. I started having a competition with the woman at the adjacent desk who had been filing for years, except she didn't know I was competing with her. When she realized it, we both started competing in earnest. Before long, people used to come over just to watch us fly through these stacks of checks. When I moved to the next job, I used to see how fast I could add up columns of numbers while handling phone conversations. I always had to do something to keep myself challenged.

While working full-time at the bank, Ellen achieved a Fellowship in the Institute of Bankers after completing demanding courses and exams. She went on to work in banking and insurance with one of her former corporate clients from the bank. When she was subsequently promoted to manage their financial reporting department, she was both the first female and the youngest person the company had ever had in that position.

Since she had begun working full-time, Ellen had been taking courses towards a bachelor's degree at night in one of the city's universities. In 1983 she decided to stop working for two years to complete her degree. After she graduated with a major in accounting and minors in marketing and management, she entered the M.B.A. program.

> I decided to go straight into the M.B.A. program for several reasons. First, I wanted to update myself. I had taken my undergraduate courses over ten years and wanted to obtain knowledge on contemporary views. Second, I wanted to tie some pieces together — my night-school degree left my ideas somewhat fragmented. Third, I wasn't impressed with the interviews I had after I finished the bachelor's degree, and fourth, I was out of work anyway. Finally, my father had already told everyone that I had my M.B.A., and I decided I really couldn't disappoint him.

Just after Ellen had begun the two year M.B.A. program, her husband was offered a position with an affiliate of his bank, posted in Bahrain beginning the next spring. They sat down and examined potential opportunities that would be available for Ellen once she completed her M.B.A. They discovered that women could work and assume positions of responsibility in Bahrain and decided they could both benefit from the move. Her husband moved to Bahrain in March, while Ellen remained to complete her M.B.A. Ellen followed, with M.B.A. in hand, eighteen months later.

BAHRAIN

Bahrain is an archipelago of thirty-three islands located in the Persian Gulf (see Figure 1). The main island, Bahrain, comprises 85 percent of the almost 700 square kilometers of the country and is the location of the capital city, Manama. Several of the islands are joined by causeways, and in 1987 the 25-kilometer King Fahd Causeway linked the principal island to the mainland of Saudi Arabia, marking the end of island isolation for the country. In 1971, Bahrain gained full independence from Britain, ending a relationship that had lasted for almost a century. Of the population of more than 400,000 people, about one-third were foreigners.

Bahrain has had a prosperous history. Historically, it has been sought after by many countries for its lush vegetation, fresh water, and pearls. Many traditional crafts and industries were still practiced, including pottery, basket making, fabric weaving, pearl diving, dhow (fishing boat) building, and fishing. Bahrain was the pearl capital of the world for many centuries. Fortunately, just as the pearl industry collapsed with the advent of cultured pearls from Japan, Bahrain struck its first oil.

FIGURE 1 Maps of the Middle East

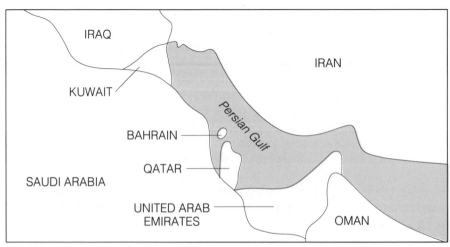

Since the 1930s, the oil industry had been the largest contributor to Bahrain's gross national product. The country was the first in the Persian Gulf to have an oil industry, established with a discovery in 1932. Production at that time was 9,600 barrels a day. Eventually, crude output reached over 40,000 barrels a day. Bahrain's oil products included crude oil, natural gas, methanol and ammonia, and refined products like gasoline, jet fuels, kerosene, and asphalts.

The Bahraini government had been aware for several years that the oil reserves were being seriously depleted. It was determined to diversify the country's economy away from a dependence on one resource. Industries established since 1971 included aluminum processing, shipbuilding, iron and steel processing, and furniture and door manufacturing. Offshore banking began in 1975. Since Bahraini nationals did not have the expertise to develop these industries alone, expatriates from around the world, particularly from Western Europe and North America, were invited to conduct business in Bahrain. By the late 1980s, the country was a major business and financial center, housing many Middle East branch offices of international firms.

Expatriates in Bahrain

Since Bahrain was an attractive base from which to conduct business, it was a temporary home to many expatriates. Housing compounds, schools, services, shopping and leisure activities all catered to many international cultures. Expatriates lived under residence permits, gained only on the basis of recruitment for a specialist position that could not be filled by a qualified and available Bahraini citizen.

To Ellen, one of the most interesting roles of expatriate managers was that of teacher. The Arab nations had been industrialized for little more than two decades and had suddenly found themselves needing to compete in a global market. Ellen believed that one of her main reasons for working in Bahrain was to train its nationals eventually to take over her job.

> Usually the teaching part was very interesting. When I first arrived in the office, I was amazed to see many staff members with microcomputers on their desks, yet they did not know the first thing about operating the equipment. When I inquired about the availability of computer courses, I was informed by a British expatriate manager that "as these were personal computers, any person should be able to use them, and as such, courses aren't necessary." It was clear to me that courses were very necessary when the computer knowledge of most employees consisted of little more than knowing where the on/off switch was located on a microcomputer.

> Although it was outside of office policy, I held "Ellen's Introduction to Computers" after office hours, just to get people comfortable with the machines and to teach them a few basics.

> Sometimes the amount of energy you had to put into the teaching was frustrating in that results were not immediately evident. I often worked jointly with one of the Bahraini managers, who really didn't know how to develop projects and prepare reports. Although I wasn't responsible for him, I spent a great deal of time with him, helping him improve his work. Initially there was resistance on his part, because he was not prepared to subordinate himself to an expatriate, let alone a woman. But eventually he came around and we achieved some great results working together.

The range of cultures represented in Bahrain was vast. Expatriate managers interacted not only with Arab nationals, but also with managers from other parts of the world, and with workers from developing countries who provided a large part of the unskilled labour force.

> The inequality among nationalities was one issue I found very difficult to deal with during my stay in Bahrain. The Third World immigrants were considered to be the lowest level possible in the pecking order, just slightly lower than nationals from countries outside the Gulf. Gulf Arabs, being of Bedouin origin, maintained a suspicious attitude towards "citified" Arabs. Europeans and North Americans were regarded much more highly. These inequalities had a major impact on daily life, including the availability of jobs and what relations would develop or not develop between supervisors and subordinates. Although I was well acquainted with the racial problems in North America, I haven't seen anything compared to the situation in Bahrain. It wasn't unusual for someone to be exploited and discarded, as any expendable and easily replaceable resource would be, because of their nationality.

Although many expatriates and their families spent their time in Bahrain immersed in their own cultural compounds, social groups, and activities, Ellen believed that her interaction with the various cultures was one of the most valuable elements of her international experience.

MANAGING IN BAHRAIN

Several aspects of the Middle Eastern culture had tremendous impact on the way business was managed, even in Western firms located in Bahrain. It seemed to Ellen, for example, that "truth" to a Bahraini employee was subject to an Arab interpretation, which was formed over hundreds of years of cultural evolution. What Western managers considered to be "proof" of an argument or "factual" evidence could be flatly denied by a Bahraini; if something was not believed it did not exist. Also, it seemed that the concept of "time" differed between Middle Eastern and Western cultures. Schedules and deadlines, although sacred to Western managers, commanded little respect from Bahraini employees. The two areas that had the most impact on Ellen's managing in a company in Bahrain were the Islamic religion and the traditional attitude towards women.

Islam[1]

Most Bahrainis are practicing Muslims. According to the Muslim faith, the universe was created by Allah, who prescribed a code of life called Islam, and the Qur'an is the literal, unchanged Word of Allah preserved exactly as transcribed by Muhammad. Muhammad's own acts as a prophet form the basis for Islamic law and are second in authority only to the Qur'an. The five Pillars of Islam are belief, prayer, fasting, alms giving, and pilgrimage. Muslims pray five times a day. During Ramadan, the ninth month of the Islamic calendar, Muslims must abstain from food, drink, smoking, and sexual activity from dawn until dusk in order to master the urges that sustain and procreate life. All Muslims are obliged to give a certain proportion of their wealth in alms for charitable purposes; the Qur'an stresses that the poor have a just claim on the wealth of the prosperous. Finally, if possible, all Muslims should make a pilgrimage to Mecca during their lives, in a spirit of total sacrifice of personal comforts, acquisition of wealth, and other matters of worldly significance.

> Certainly the Muslim religion had a tremendous impact on my daily working life. The first time I walked into the women's washroom at work I noticed a tap about three inches off the floor over a drain. I found this rather puzzling; I wondered if it was for the cleaning crew. When a woman came in, I asked her about the tap, and she explained that before going to the prayer room, everyone had to wash all uncovered parts of their bodies. The tap was for washing their feet and legs.
>
> One time I was looking for one of my employees, Mohammed, who had a report due to me that afternoon. I searched for him at his desk and other likely spots throughout the office, but to no avail; he just wasn't around. I had had difficulties with Mohammed's work before, when he would submit documents long after deadlines, and I was certain he was attempting to slack off once again. I bumped into one of Mohammed's friends and asked if he knew Mohammed's whereabouts. When he informed me that Mohammed was in the prayer room, I wasn't sure how to respond. I didn't know if this prayer room activity was very personal and if I could ask questions, such as the length of time one generally spends in prayer. But I needed to know how long Mohammed would be away from his desk. Throwing caution to the wind, I asked the employee how long Mohammed was likely to be in prayers and he told me it usually takes about ten minutes. It wasn't that I felt I didn't have the right to know where my employee was or how long he would be away; I just wasn't certain my authority as a manager allowed me the right to ask questions about such a personal activity as praying.
>
> During Ramadan, the hours of business are shortened by law. It is absolutely illegal for any Muslim to work past two o'clock in the afternoon, unless special permits are obtained from the Ministry of Labor. Unfortunately, business coming in to an American firm does not stop at two, and a majority of the non-Muslim workers are required to take up the slack.

Unlike religion in Western civilization, Islam permeates every function of human endeavor. There does not exist a separation of church, state and judiciary. Indeed, in purist circles, the question does not arise. The hybrid systems existing in certain Arab countries are considered aberrations created by Western colonial influences. Accordingly, to function successfully, the expatriate must understand and learn to accept a very different structuring of a society.

Women in Bahrain

Bahrain tended to be more progressive than many Middle Eastern countries in its attitude towards women. Although traditions were strong, Bahraini women had some freedom. For example, all women could work outside the home, although the hours they could work were restricted both by convention and by the labor laws. They could only work if their husbands, fathers, or brothers permitted them, and could not take potential employment away from men. Work outside the home was to be conducted in addition to, not instead of, duties performed inside the home, such as child rearing and cooking. Most women who worked held secretarial or clerical positions; very few worked in management.

Bahraini women were permitted to wear a variety of outfits, from the conservative full-length black robe with head scarf, which covers the head and hair, to below-the-knee skirts and dresses without head covering.

> Arab women who sincerely want change and more decision-making power over their own lives face an almost impossible task, because the male influence is perpetuated not only by men but also by women who are afraid to alter views they understand and with which they have been brought up all their lives. I once asked a female coworker the reason why one of the women in the office, who had previously been "uncovered," was now sporting a scarf over her head. The response was that this woman had just been married, and although her husband did not request that she become "covered," she personally did not feel as though she was a married woman without the head scarf. So she simply asked her husband to demand that she wear a scarf on her head. It was a really interesting situation; some of the more liberal Bahraini women were very upset that she had asked her husband to make this demand. They saw it as negating many of the progressive steps the women's movement had made in recent years.

Although Bahrainis had been exposed to Western cultures for the two decades of industrial expansion, they were still uncomfortable with Western notions of gender equality and less traditional roles for women.

> One day a taxi driver leaned back against his seat and, while keeping one eye on the road ahead, turned to ask me, "How many sons do you have?" I replied that I didn't have any children. His heartfelt response of "I'm so sorry" and the way he shook his head in sympathy were something my North American upbringing didn't prepare me for. My taxi driver's response typifies the attitude projected toward women, whether they are expatriates from Europe or North America or Bahrainis. Women are meant to have children, preferably sons. Although Bahrain is progressive in many ways, attitudes on the role of women in society run long and deep, and it is quite unlikely these sentiments will alter in the near, or even distant, future.

> Another time I was greeted with gales of laughter when I revealed to the women in the office that my husband performed most of the culinary chores in our household. They assumed I was telling a joke, and when I insisted that he really did most of the cooking, they sat in silent disbelief. Finally, one woman spoke up and informed the group that she didn't think her husband even knew where the kitchen was in their house, let alone would ever be caught touching a cooking utensil. The group nodded in agreement. Although these women have successful business careers — as clerks, but in the work force nonetheless — they believe women should perform all household tasks without the assistance of their husbands. The discovery that this belief holds true in Bahrain is not remarkable, as I know many North American and European businesswomen who believe the same to be true. What is pertinent is these women allow themselves to be completely dominated by the men in their lives.

> The one concept I faced daily but never accepted was that my husband was regarded as the sole decision maker in our household. He and I view our marriage as a partnership in which we participate equally in all decisions. But when the maintenance manager for

our housing compound came by, repairs were completed efficiently only if I preceded my request with "my husband wants the following to be completed." It's a phrase I hated to use because it went against every rational thought I possess, but I frequently had to resort to it.

These attitudes also affected how Ellen was treated as a manager by Bahraini managers:

> One manager, I'll call him Fahad, believed that women were capable only of fulfilling secretarial and coffee-serving functions. One day I was sitting at my desk, concentrating on some documents. I didn't notice Fahad having a discussion with another male manager nearby. When I looked up from my papers, Fahad noticed me and immediately began talking in French to the other manager. Although my French was a bit rusty, my comprehension was still quite serviceable. I waited for a few moments and then broke into their discussion in French. Fahad was completely dismayed. Over the next few years, Fahad and I worked together on several projects. At first, he was pompous and wouldn't listen to anything I presented. It was a difficult situation, but I was determined to remain above his negative comments. I ignored his obvious prejudice towards me, remained outwardly calm when he disregarded my ideas, and proceeded to prove myself with my work. It took a lot of effort and patience but, in time, Fahad and I not only worked out our differences, but worked as a successful team on a number of major projects. Although this situation had a happy ending, I really would have preferred to have directed all that energy and effort toward more productive issues.

Bahraini nationals were not the only ones who perpetuated the traditional roles of women in society. Many of the expatriates, particularly those from Commonwealth countries, tended to view their role as "the colonial charged with the responsibility to look after the developing country." This was reflected in an official publication for new expatriates that stated: "Wives of overseas employees are normally sponsored by their husbands' employers, and their Residence Permits are processed at the same time. . . ."[2] However, wives were not permitted to work unless they could obtain a work permit for themselves.

> The first question I was often asked at business receptions was "What company is your husband with?" When I replied that I worked as well, I received the glazed-over look, because they assumed I occupied myself with coffee mornings, beach, tennis, and other leisure activities as did the majority of expatriate wives.

> Social gatherings were always risky. At typical business and social receptions the men served themselves first, after which the women selected their food. Then women and men positioned themselves on opposite sides of the room. The women discussed "feminine" topics, such as babies and recipes, whereas the men discussed the fall (or rise) of the dollar and the big deal of the day. At one Bahraini business gathering, I hesitated in choosing sides: Should I conform and remain with the women? But most of these women did not work outside their homes, and, consequently, they spoke and understood very little English. I joined the men. Contrary to what I expected, I was given a gracious welcome.

> However, on another occasion I was bored with the female conversation, so I ventured over to the forbidden male side to join a group of bankers discussing correspondent banking courses. When I entered the discussion, a British bank general manager turned

his nose up at me. He motioned towards the other side of the room and told me I should join the women. He implied that his discussion was obviously over my head. I quickly informed him that although I personally had found the banking courses difficult to complete while holding a full-time banking position, I not only managed to complete the program and obtain my Fellowship but at the time was the youngest employee of my bank ever to be awarded the diploma. The man did a quick turnabout, was thoroughly embarrassed, and apologized profusely. Although it was nice to turn the tables on the man, I was more than a little frustrated with the feeling that I almost had to wear my résumé on my sleeve to get any form of respect from the men, whether European, North American, or Arab.

A small percentage of Bahraini women had completed university degrees in North America and Europe. While residing in these Western cultures, they were permitted to function as did their Western counterparts. For example, they could visit or phone friends when they wished without first obtaining permission. After completing their education, many of these women were qualified for management positions; however, upon returning to Bahrain they were required to resume their traditional female roles.

The notion of pink M.B.A. diplomas for women and blue for men is very real. Although any M.B.A. graduate in North America, male or female, is generally considered to have attained a certain level of business sense, I had to constantly "prove" myself to some individuals who appeared to believe that women attended a special segregated section of the university with appropriately tailored courses.

Ellen discovered that, despite being a woman, she was accepted by Bahrainis as a manager as a result of her Western nationality, her education, and her management position in the company.

Many of my male Arab peers accepted me as they would any expatriate manager. For example, when a male employee returned from a vacation, he would typically visit each department, calling upon the other male employees with a greeting and a handshake. Although he might greet a female coworker, he would never shake her hand. However, because of my management position in the company and my status as a Western expatriate, male staff members gave me the same enthusiastic greeting and handshake normally reserved for their male counterparts.

Ellen also found herself facilitating Bahraini women's positions in the workplace.

Because I was the only female in a senior management position in our office, I was often asked by the female employees to speak to their male superiors about problems and issues they experienced in their departments. I also had to provide a role model for the women because there were no female Bahraini managers. Some of them came to me not just to discuss career issues but to discuss life issues. There was just no one else in a similar position for them to talk to. On the other hand, male managers would ask me to discuss sensitive issues, such as hygiene, with their female staff members.

The government of Bahrain introduced legislation that restricted the amount of overtime hours women could work. Although the move was being praised by the (female) Director of Social Development as recognition of the contribution women were making to Bahraini industry, Ellen saw it as further discriminatory treatment restricting the choices of women in Bahrain. Her published letter to the editor of the *Gulf Daily News* read:

> . . . How the discriminatory treatment of women in this regulation can be seen as recognition of the immense contribution women make to the Bahrain work force is beyond comprehension. Discrimination of any portion of the population in the labor legislation does not recognize anything but the obvious prejudice. If the working women in Bahrain want to receive acknowledgment of their indispensable impact on the Bahrain economy, it should be through an increase in the number of management positions available to qualified women, not through regulations limiting the hours they work. All this regulation means is that women are still regarded as second-class citizens who need the strong-arm tactics of the government to help them settle disputes over working hours. Government officials could really show appreciation to the working women in Bahrain by making sure that companies hire and promote based on skill rather than gender. But there is little likelihood of that occurring.

The letter was signed with a pseudonym, but the day it was published one of Ellen's female employees showed her the letter and claimed, "If I didn't know better, Ellen, I'd think you wrote this letter."

Career Decisions

When Ellen first arrived in Bahrain, she had great expectations that she would work somewhere she could make a difference. She received several offers for positions and turned down, among others, a university and a high-profile brokerage house. She decided to take a position as a Special Projects Coordinator at a large American financial institution.

> In fact, the records will show I was actually hired as a "Financial Analyst," but this title was given solely because at that time, the government had decided that expatriate women shouldn't be allowed to take potential positions away from Bahraini nationals. The expertise required as a Financial Analyst enabled the company to obtain a work permit for me as I had the required experience and academic credentials, although I performed few duties as an analyst.

In her special projects role, Ellen learned a great deal about international finance. She conducted efficiency studies on various operating departments. She used her systems expertise to investigate and improve the company's microcomputer usage and developed a payroll program that was subsequently integrated into the company's international systems. She was a member of the Strategic Review Committee, and produced a report outlining the long-term goals for the Middle East market, which she then presented to the Senior Vice President of Europe, Middle East, and Africa.

After one year, Ellen was rewarded for her achievements by a promotion to Manager of Business Planning and Development, a position that reported directly to the Vice President and General Manager. She designed the role herself and was able to be creative and quite influential in the company. During her year in this role, she was involved in a diverse range of activities. She managed the Quality Assurance department, coordinated a product launch, developed and managed a senior management information system, was an active participant in all senior management meetings, and launched an employee newsletter.

At the end of her second year in Bahrain, Ellen was informed that two positions in operations would soon be available, and the General Manager, a European expatriate, asked if she would be interested in joining the area. She had previously worked only in staff positions and quickly decided to accept the challenge and learning experience of a line post. Both positions were in senior management, and both had responsibility for approximately thirty employees.

The first position was for Manager of Accounts Control, which covered the Credit, Collection, and Authorization departments. The Manager's role was to ensure that appropriate information was used to authorize spending by clients, to compile results of client payment, and to inform management of nonpayment issues. The Manager also supervised in-house staff and representatives in other Gulf countries for the collection of withheld payments.

The second post was Manager of Customer Services, New Accounts, and Establishment Services. The Manager's role was to ensure that new clients were worthy and that international quality standards were met in all Customer Service activity. The Manager also worked with two other departments — Marketing, to ensure that budgets were met, and Sales, to manage relationships with the many affiliate outlets of the service.

After speaking with the two current Managers and considering the options carefully, Ellen decided that she would prefer working in the Accounts Control area. The job was more oriented to financial information, the Manager had more influence on operations at the company, and she would have the opportunity to travel to other countries to supervise staff. Although she was not familiar with the systems and procedures, she knew she could learn them quickly. Ellen went into her meeting with the General Manager excited about the new challenges.

Ellen Meets with the General Manager

Ellen told the General Manager she had decided to take the Accounts Control position and outlined her reasons. Then she waited for his affirmation and for the details of when she would begin.

"I'm afraid I've reconsidered the offer," the General Manager announced. "Although I know you would probably do a terrific job in the Accounts Control position, I can't offer it to you. It involves periodic travel into Saudi Arabia, and women are not allowed to travel there alone." He went on to tell Ellen how she would be subject to discriminatory practices, would not be able to gain the respect of the company's Saudi Arabian clients, and would experience difficulty traveling there.

Ellen was astonished. She quickly pointed out to him that many businesswomen were representatives of American firms in Saudi Arabia. She described one woman she knew of who was the sole representative of a large American bank in the Eastern Province of Saudi Arabia who frequently traveled there alone. She explained that other women's experiences in Saudi Arabia showed professional men there treated professional women as neither male nor female, but as businesspeople. Besides, she continued, there were no other candidates in the company for either position. She reminded the General Manager of the pride the company took in its quality standards and how senior management salaries were in part determined by assuring quality in their departments. Although the company was an equal opportunity employer in its home country, the United States, she believed the spirit of the policy should extend to all international offices.

The General Manager informed her that his decision reflected his desire to address the interests of both herself and the company. He was worried, he said, that Ellen would have trouble obtaining entry visas to allow her to conduct business in Saudi Arabia and that the customers would not accept her. Also, if there were ever any hostile outbreaks, he believed she would be in danger, and he could not have lived with that possibility.

Ellen stated that as a woman, she believed she was at lower risk of danger than her Western male counterparts since in the event of hostility, the Saudi Arabians would most likely secure her safety. There was much greater probability that a male representative of the firm would be held as a hostage.

The General Manager was adamant. Regardless of her wishes, the company needed Ellen in the Customer Service position. New Accounts had only recently been added to the department, and the bottom-line responsibility was thus doubled from what it had been in the past. The General Manager said he wanted someone he could trust and depend upon to handle the pressure of New Accounts, which had a high international profile.

Ellen was offered the Customer Service position and then dismissed from the meeting. In frustration, she began to consider her options.

Take the Customer Service Position

The General Manager obviously expected her to take the position. It would mean increased responsibility and challenge. Except for a position in high school where she managed a force of sixty student police, Ellen had not yet supervised more than four employees at any time in her professional career. On the other hand, it went against her values to accept the post, since it had been offered as a result of gender roles when all consideration should have been placed on competence. She knew she had the abilities and qualifications for the position. She viewed the entire situation as yet another example of how the business community in Bahrain had difficulty accepting and acknowledging the contributions of women to international management, and she didn't want to abandon her values by accepting the position.

Fight Back

There were two approaches that would permit Ellen to take the matter further. She could go to the General Manager's superior, the Senior Vice President of Europe, Middle East, and Africa. She had had several dealings with him and had once presented a report to him with which he was very impressed. But she wasn't sure she could count on his sympathy regarding her traveling to Saudi Arabia, as his knowledge of the region was limited, and he generally relied on local management's decisions on such issues. She could consider filing a grievance against the company. There were provisions in Bahraini Labor Law that would have permitted this option in her case. However, she understood that the Labor Tribunals, unlike those held in Western countries, did not try cases based on precedents or rules of evidence. In other words, the judge would apply a hodgepodge of his own subjective criteria to reach a decision.

Stay in the Business Planning and Development Job

Although the General Manager had not mentioned it as an option, Ellen could request that she remain in her current position. It would mean not giving in to the General Manager's prejudices. Since she had been considering the two Operations positions, though, she had been looking forward to moving on to something new.

Leave the Company

Ellen knew she was qualified for many positions in the financial center of Bahrain and could likely obtain work with another company. She was not sure, though, whether leaving her present company under these circumstances would jeopardize her chances of finding work elsewhere. Furthermore, to obtain a post at a new company would require a letter of permission from her current employer, who, as her sponsor in Bahrain, had to sanction her move to a new employer who would become her new sponsor. She was not sure that she would be able to make those arrangements, considering the situation.

> I always tell my employees: "If you wake up one morning and discover you don't like your job, come to see me immediately. If the problem is with the tasks of the job, I'll see if I can modify your tasks. If the problem is with the department or you want a change, I'll assist you in getting another position in the company. If the problem is with the company, then I'll help you write your résumé." I have stated this credo to all my employees in every post I've held. Generally, they don't believe that their manager would actually assist with résumé writing, but when the opportunity arises, and it has, and I do come through as promised, the impact on the remaining employees is priceless. Employees will provide much more effort towards a cause that is supported by someone looking out for their personal welfare.

Ellen's superior did not have the same attitude towards his employees. As she considered her options, Ellen realized that no move could be made without a compromise either in her career or her values. Which choice was she most willing to make?

Notes

1. "Resident in Bahrain," Vol. 1, 1987, *Gulf Daily News*, pp. 61–63.
2. "Resident in Bahrain," Vol. 1, 1987, *Gulf Daily News*, p. 57.

CASE 12

Canada Royal (International) (A)[1]

R. William Blake and Henry W. Lane

OVERVIEW

For eighteen months, Doug Strong, Area General Manager for Latin America, had been searching for a joint venture partner for Canada Royal's (CanRoy) Malindranian subsidiary. During the last year, he had been heavily involved in negotiations with the Miranda family. After endless discussions, revisions to agreements, and countless telexes back and forth to headquarters, Doug finally had reached agreement with Carlos Miranda. When they finished signing the documents, Doug was surprised to discover that Carlos did not have the downpayment as required. It was an even greater shock when Carlos exploded in anger when Doug asked him to provide a guaranty of payment before giving the shares to Miranda.

Doug faced a difficult choice between jeopardizing the deal (and his own business objectives for the year) and acquiescing to another unreasonable move by Carlos Miranda. (A summary of the people in the case and a partial organization chart can be found at the end of the case.)

BACKGROUND

The Early Days

The army tanks were still in the streets of San Raphael as the Red Cross plane, carrying Bill Anthony, touched down at the international airport. Revolutionary forces were in the process of ousting the dictator who had ruled Malindrania for eight years. The only way that Bill, the newly appointed President of CanRom (Canada Royal de Malindrania), could get to San Raphael was to fly from a neighboring country on a Red Cross flight. On the ride to the company's office, Bill observed the broken windows and rubble that street mobs had left behind.

CanRom was basically a sales office that generated profit from the 3 to 5 percent commission charged to customers on products sourced from CanRoy plants worldwide and sold to Malindranian customers on irrevocable letters of credit with payment in United States dollars. No warehousing or distribution facilities existed.

343

During a size-up of the company and market opportunities, Bill saw potential on a number of fronts. He opened a warehouse and stocked it with CanRoy products. This move required CanRom to assume the administrative problems of clearing shipments through customs and paying duty but, by selling this "nationalized" stock and cutting out the middleman, profit margins increased to 25 percent. Next, Bill began accepting payment in pesos, rather than hard-to-obtain United States dollars, and sales increased rapidly.

José Dalmau

Bill hired José Dalmau to replace the existing sales manager and possibly to be Bill's own successor. Under Dalmau's guidance, CanRom's sales increased dramatically. Bill was impressed by Dalmau:

> José was very bright — maybe even brilliant — and he could sell refrigerators to Eskimos. He was also ambitious and wanted to make money. He had outside business activities, but we had an understanding about no conflict of interests.

> José was high-strung. Latins are very different from North Americans. They are more emotional. You have to understand this when you work with them.

Bill eventually was replaced by a financial specialist sent from Canada. Soon afterwards José Dalmau also left Malindrania, and for the next few years, he worked for CanRoy companies in Argentina, Mexico, and Venezuela. José became unhappy in Venezuela and announced his intention to resign. He was offered the job of running CanRom, to which he returned.

Dalmau's aggressiveness and entrepreneurial flair meshed well with the local business environment and sales boomed. However, another side of the man was starting to appear. One executive who knew Dalmau well described his perception of the man:

> José was a real tiger, a fantastic businessperson. He really built up the business, but by some pretty unscrupulous means. He was also a one-person show. He had to lick all the stamps himself.

Although Dalmau was a prime reason for CanRom's profitability, he ran the company as his personal fiefdom, a style that eventually brought him into conflict with the Area office. A CanRoy executive reported:

> He was a superb businessperson, an entrepreneur. He did everything himself — his own way. He didn't relate all that well to the big corporation. He kept CanRoy at arm's length, but he ran a tight ship. He thought it was his company and people had to be 100 percent loyal to José. The company was CanRoy in name only.

> You wouldn't get a reply to your letters and he never did an annual plan. He knew we (Area office) had to do it and eventually would send someone to do it for him.

CanRoy itself was undergoing change at this time. An internal study recommended geographical decentralization, and a new organizational structure was implemented. Ian Ferguson was named Area General Manager for Latin American

(CanRoy S.A.). José Dalmau was given the title of General Manager of CanRom, reporting to Ferguson. During Dalmau's tenure, CanRom developed new products (molded plastic fittings) and sales were strong and profits rose. A new extrusion line was set up. CanRoy borrowed 90 percent of the cost of the installation locally and paid off the loan in two years.

Doug Strong Arrives

Doug Strong replaced Ferguson as Area General Manager for Latin America. During his three years with CanRoy, Strong had been Chief Planning Officer in the United States. Prior to joining CanRoy, Strong had been a Certified Public Accountant, a management consultant, and Managing Director of a large automotive supplies firm, and had worked for extended periods of time on a number of overseas assignments.

The Area office, a home in suburban Montevideo, was staffed by four officers responsible for planning, finance, personnel, and technical services. The planning officer had been in Latin America less than a year. The personnel officer had three weeks left before moving to his next assignment.

Within two weeks of arrival, Strong decided to move the office. He reasoned that the current location was too far from operations in Mexico and that travel was easier from Sao Paulo. Also since CanRoy, at that time, did not manage any businesses in Uruguay, the Area office had to rely on headquarters for financing and could not take advantage of the blocked profits in countries where CanRoy did have operations. The office also was sprayed with machine gun bullets during the attempted assassination of the next-door neighbor. Strong commented on this event:

> The office was peppered with bullet holes. I can't say this was the reason we moved, but it certainly helped us concentrate on the idea.

On a trip to Brazil, Strong contacted Pedro Vargas, the recently retired CEO of CanRoy Brazil, to arrange for an estate agent to meet him in Sao Paulo to find a new Area office. After a day in Sao Paulo, Doug had signed contracts for the new Area office headquarters and for his own apartment.

Later that month, Strong established the Sao Paulo office with considerable help from Vargas in recruiting staff and solving the numerous administrative difficulties that arose with the government. Strong subsequently convinced Vargas to join the Canroy S.A. staff as liaison with the Brazilian government.

Doug Strong Encounters José Dalmau

One of the briefings Strong received after becoming Area General Manager concerned CanRom. By then, it was a profitable company[2] operating the newest equipment. Although the company showed an excellent ROI, Dalmau was not operating the CanRoy way and was running the business with almost total disregard of CanRoy's desires. He was suspected of paying illegal commissions, and also had a new extrusion line in operation for which the capital expenditure request had not been prepared.

At his first meeting with Dalmau, Strong presented a list of administrative problems for José to correct. José became angry. Doug gave him a month to straighten the problems out and asked for a phone call every two weeks:

> I never heard a word from him. I sent him a telex to come to the Area office, which he ignored. Finally, I got on the phone and told him to get down here. I gave him a real up and down. That never happened to him before. He was white with rage. He didn't like being told what to do. He was awfully proud.
>
> I know he worked hard — all the hours God gave. He built the company, but it wasn't a CanRoy company.

While on a trip to Colombia, Strong learned that José had quit and announced his intention to start a company competing with CanRom. The sales manager, administration manager, and the sales force all quit at the same time. According to Doug, José even took the sales records:

> When I asked for them back, he said he wanted a termination bonus. I told him that I hadn't fired him. He agreed, but told me that I had made his life miserable.

A New CEO for CanRom — Rodrigues Floriano

Strong needed a seasoned General Manager to replace Dalmau and to rebuild the sales force. He offered the job to Rodrigues Floriano, the CEO in Paraguay during the previous six years. Regardless of whether or not he accepted the job permanently, Strong directed Floriano to be in San Raphael within forty-eight hours.

Rodrigues Floriano was forty-eight years old, had degrees in business and mechanical engineering from U.C.L.A., and had done an excellent job in Paraguay despite serious weight and related medical problems. During his time in Paraguay, he carried two guns at all times, because he had been a constant target for a revolutionary group. Later he discovered his secretary had been a member of the group.

Floriano was described by many people as an intelligent, honest man who was very knowledgeable and who had solid operating experience. One executive who was close to him commented:

> Rodrigues is very intelligent — there's a touch of the genius in him. But despite his United States education, a strong North American veneer, and a Canadian wife, he is very Spanish, very macho, and very strong willed.

Floriano accepted the job. During the following months, total sales declined 35 percent and CanRom lost 50 percent of its molded products business as Dalmau took some of CanRom's customers and Floriano instituted a no-kickback policy. By the end of his first year, however, Floriano had rebuilt the sales force, and sales were back to projected levels. Strong explained:

> We had the business because of illegal payments; Rodrigues eventually got it all back on a straight basis.

A CHANGE IN OWNERSHIP STATUS

The Decision to Latinize

In May 1981, a few months prior to Dalmau's abrupt departure, Doug Strong had decided the time had come to comply with the Latin American Common Market legislation. Article 15, effective January 1, 1978 required "foreign" firms to become "mixed' or "national" companies within 12 years.[3] Article 15 restricted dividend repatriation for foreign companies to 14 percent of their registered capital base and limited the growth of the capital base to 5 percent per year. Profits in excess of the 14 percent were "limbo profits," which could neither be repatriated nor reinvested in Malindrania. Shifting CanRom to "mixed" company status would eliminate these restrictions and permit repatriation of the retained earnings accumulating in Malindrania.

In addition to limbo profits, CanRoy was experiencing pressure from the government. The National Investment Institute (INI), which administered Article 15, would not allow CanRom to register its investment in a second extrusion line until it had seen the company's transition plan to "mixed" status. About the same time, CanRoven in Venezuela was also being asked for its Latinization plan in support of one of its proposed investments.

CanRoy S.A.'s Planning Officer completed a strategic study for CanRom and the companies in countries bordering Malindrania and concluded:

> We could take a lot of time to make the transition if we wanted to continue as we were, but if we wanted to grow, we had to Latinize.

The Search for a Joint Venture Partner

José Dalmau, at his last meeting with Strong before quitting, stated he was prepared to be a shareholder along with a local bank. Strong never considered Dalmau's proposal seriously:

> In my mind I rejected his offer. He wasn't straight with me. He wasn't transparent; he was opaque. I place great importance on knowing what people are thinking and their knowing what I am thinking. That's what I mean by "transparent."

The bank, however, was not interested in CanRom, which it thought was overpriced. Strong and Ian Ferguson, who was now a CanRoy Executive Vice President and Doug's boss, agreed on a value for CanRom of seven times the current year's earnings, which would prevent CanRoy from taking a write-off. At that time, Malindranians were investing at a multiple of two to four times earnings, and a large bottling company had just gone public at a multiple of two and a half.

Contacts for two potential partners came from an international bank in Malindrania and CanRom's law firm. Strong and Vargas visited both in San Raphael.

The Carrasco family owned 7-Up bottling plants, a newspaper, and finance and real estate companies among its many investments. As with the previous exploration, neither side was enthusiastic about the possible deal. After two meetings and a letter formally stating CanRoy's position, the Carrascos lost interest. They wanted management control over companies in which they invested. Strong, for his part, was not satisfied with the family because he felt they were not primarily industrialists with experience in manufacturing.

Discussions were held with a company that assembled automobiles and distributed spare parts and farm machinery. Managed by a German, the company appeared very efficient and impressed Strong and Vargas. However, discovery that American Industries (CanRoy's major competitor) was a significant, although not controlling, shareholder ended discussions. Pedro Vargas commented that the General Manager was a man who believed he knew everything and who also wanted to run CanRom.

Because Vargas had no connections in Malindrania, he turned to business contracts in Sao Paulo for help. The most promising recommendation came through the Brazilian Foreign Office — a Malindranian who had been Ambassador to Canada, Antonio Souza. Souza, in turn, recommended the Miranda family — Henrique and Carlos, two brothers who held prominent positions in the Malindranian business scene.

Strong enquired about the Mirandas and received excellent reports. The family was held in high esteem in Malindrania. The bank had glorious words of praise for Henrique who was President of a large insurance company. At a cocktail party, the International Director of a large multinational corporation described an excellent joint venture with Henrique.

Doug was heartened by the reports. It was not easy finding a partner in Malindrania even though most of the industrial and commercial base was controlled by a handful of families. It seemed that everyone wanted management control even though they knew nothing about plastics. Strong's experience with the Trade Commissioner at the Embassy in finding a partner had been disappointing, and he ruled out a partnership with the Malindranian government unless forced into it. Government posts were political plums and everyone would change when the regime changed. The Mirandas looked like the best bet.

Carlos Miranda, the older of the brothers, although not as financially successful as his younger brother, had an estimated personal worth of $20 million. His wife was equally wealthy. Carlos's main business was real estate development — an industry where it was not uncommon to see extremely rapid paybacks due to a combination of inflation and petrodollar financed expansion. In keeping with the tradition of numerous Latin American countries, Carlos, as the oldest male, was the head of the family. Pedro Vargas recommended that he and Doug meet with Carlos.

Negotiations with Carlos Miranda

The meeting in San Raphael in October 1981 was amicable and addressed the process by which "mixed" company status would be reached. CanRoy's original idea was to progress in stages with an initial sale of 20 percent of the equity. Carlos, however, was eager to move to 51 percent participation in one step. It was financially attractive to Strong, who agreed in principle. Following the meeting, Strong cabled headquarters proposing a reduction of CanRoy's holding in CanRom to 49 percent as a way of circumventing a possible confrontation with INI which insisted on being a party to any negotiations involving the transfer of shares in foreign-owned companies in Malindrania.

CanRoy S.A. proposed to headquarters a joint primary/secondary share offering. A value of U.S. $10.2 million was placed on CanRom's shares. The proceeds from a secondary placement of 32 percent of the shares would be repatriated, and the new shares would be subscribed to by the Miranda group. Proceeds of the primary issue would finance new projects, all of which had been discussed with Miranda during negotiations. The estimated cost of these projects was $2.8 million.

Strong wrote headquarters urging quick action on the proposal. In addition to a problem of limbo profits, CanRom could not register a recent investment in new equipment as part of its capital base and was forecasting peaking profit growth. The prospect of peaking earnings could hurt in negotiating the final price since a company was worth only what it could earn.

Besides making a financially attractive deal, Strong thought Carlos Miranda seemed to be the right partner:

> I was looking for Malindranian partners to help in the domestic environment, who could take an interest in the direction of the business, but would recognize that CanRoy was running it on a day-to-day basis and at Board meetings would recognize the complexity of our business.

Carlos agreed openly that he did not want to run the company, reassuring Strong with statements like, "I don't want to be involved in something I don't understand" and "You don't expect me to drive three hours to the plant site and bother the CEO, do you?" Pedro Vargas recalled that an important factor in Carlo's favor was his agreement not to be actively involved in daily management.

Some Legal Considerations

Xavier Domtila, a Brazilian who was CanRoy S.A.'s legal officer, now became heavily involved in the negotiations. Xavier's first problem was to find a local lawyer since CanRoy S.A. was not satisfied with its existing law firm. CanRoy had been offered a deal by which it could become a mixed company and ensure control, according to Domtila:

> When you have a proposal to reduce your holdings to 49 percent and you still want to guarantee keeping management control, the solution in Latin America — where most, if not all, countries prohibit management contracts — is to have your lawyer own 2 percent of the stock. Every lawyer has a little company around the corner which is a holding company for such shares. It is a common practice in Latin America. Many MNC's work this way. Our lawyer said he had many companies doing it.

The resulting ownership from such a deal would be: CanRoy — 49 percent, CanRoy's lawyer — 2 percent, the local partner — 49 percent. Domtila commented on the legality of this approach:

In some countries, it's more than illegal. It's an infringement of their sovereignty, a usurping of their nationality. It's a very serious offense in Malindrania, perhaps more so than in any other country.

Carlos suggested that he and CanRoy jointly hire a lawyer and he introduced Xavier to a man who was reputed to be an expert on INI. Benjamin Almaro was hired to help the parties put the partnership together.

Negotiating the Price

As in previous negotiations, price proved a problem. Another large MNC had just made the transition to "mixed" company status at three times earnings. Miranda balked at a multiple of seven. Throughout the negotiations, Strong remained steadfast — everything was negotiable except price. Carlos eventually agreed to the price.

In November, Strong sent a request to headquarters for approval of the sale. Reactions to the request were generally favorable. But questions were raised about the rationale for a secondary issue, about dealing with only one partner and whether or not a better price and more effective control over CanRoy's investment might not be possible via a public offering of the stock.

Plans for a secondary issue were revised since headquarters viewed it as a partial withdrawal from Malindrania, and Miranda's resistance to the idea raised the likelihood of an unfavorable reaction to it. Doug included in his letter three scenarios involving primary stock issues and their resultant dividend flows (see Figure 1). Strong also indicated that Miranda only was interested in acquiring 51 percent and that a public sale of stock was complicated. The offering was too large for the poorly organized stock exchange to handle and that, in any event, "it will never be as profitable as the proposed sale to Miranda." Besides, as Pedro Vargas pointed out, slow development of Malindrania's technical and managerial class made it difficult to find anyone other than the government or powerful family groups with the money and interest in owning businesses. By December 24, Doug had rewritten and resubmitted the request, proposing an all primary stock issue. The covering letter again urged quick action.

By February, Doug Strong believed he had reached agreement with Carlos. CanRoy would issue new shares and sell its subscription rights to the Miranda group for approximately U.S. $2.6 million. The Miranda group would purchase the new issue and, in the process, become the majority shareholder.

Despite concurrence by Doug and Carlos on the main features of the joint venture agreement, negotiations continued during the following months as the two sides tried to agree on the details of the final contract.

Control of the Joint Venture

In May 1982 headquarters raised the issue of control of the proposed venture. Because local regulations prohibited management contracts, CanRoy proposed to control the operations of CanRom through measures incorporated in a technical cooperation agreement. The use of the CanRoy trademark and name would be

FIGURE 1 **Dividend Analysis**
Canada Royal de Malindrania (CanRom)

Hypothesis I — Status quo maintained (CanRoy 100%)

REGISTERED CAPITAL BASE

Position at 31st Dec. 1980	P 11,512,669
ADD: Automatic Increase of 5%	575,633
Position at 31st Dec. 1981	12,088,302
ADD: Automatic Increase of 5%	604,415
Position at 31st Dec. 1982	12,692,717
ADD: Automatic Increase of 5%	634,635
Position at 31st Dec. 1983	13,327,352
ADD: Automatic Increase of 5%	666,367
Position at 31st Dec. 1984	P 13,993,719

SUMMARY OF DIVIDENDS

1981	14% ON	P 11,512,669 =	P 1,611,774
1982	14% ON	12,088,302 =	1,692,362
1983	14% ON	12,692,717 =	1,776,980
1984	14% ON	13,327,352 =	1,865,829
1985	14% ON	13,993,719 =	1,959,121
			8,906,066
			US $ 2,473,907

Hypothesis II — Primary Issue (CanRoy 49%)

ASSUMPTIONS

1) Registration of past limbo profits permitted by INI.
2) Profits constant at US$ 1,325,000 p.a. plus 20% before tax on injection of primary issue for next four years.

REGISTERED CAPITAL BASE at 31.12.80 equal:

To Total Equity	P 20,535,747
ADD: New Investment	3,146,493
Position at 31st Dec. 1981	23,682,240
ADD: 49% of Profit	2,337,300
Position at 31st Dec. 1982	26,019,540
ADD: 49% of Profit	4,514,000
Position at 31st Dec. 1983	30,533,540
ADD: 49% of Profit	4,514,000
Position at 31st Dec. 1984	P 35,047,540

SUMMARY OF DIVIDENDS

1981	14% ON	20,535,747	2,875,005
1982	14% ON	23,682,240	3,315,513
1983	14% ON	26,019,540	3,642,736
1984	14% ON	30,533,540	4,274,696
1985	14% ON	35,047,540	4,906,655
			P 19,014,605
			US $ 5,281,839

(Continued)

FIGURE 1   **Continued**

Hypothesis III — Primary Issue (CanRoy 49%)

ASSUMPTIONS
1) Registration of new equipment only permitted.
2) Profits constant at US $ 1,325,000 p.a. plus 20% before tax on injection of
   primary issue for next four years.

REGISTERED CAPITAL BASE

Position at 31st Dec. 1980	P 11,512,669
ADD: New Equipment Investment	3,136,493
Position at 31st Dec. 1981	14,649,162
ADD: 49% of Profit	4,514,000
Position at 31st Dec. 1982	19,163,162
ADD: 49% of Profit	4,514,000
Position at 31st Dec. 1983	23,677,162
ADD: 49% of Profit	4,514,000
Position at 31st Dec. 1984	P 28,191,162

SUMMARY OF DIVIDENDS

1981	14% ON	11,512,669	P 1,611,774
1982	14% ON	14,649,162	2,050,882
1983	14% ON	19,163,162	2,682,842
1984	14% ON	23,677,162	3,314,802
1985	14% ON	28,191,162	3,946,762
			P 13,607,062
			US $3,779,739

restricted to a five-year period and usage would stop if the technical cooperation agreement was violated. It was also suggested that a vote of two-thirds of the shareholders be required before any investment or divestment decision be made. Perhaps the key suggestion made in a letter to Strong was that CanRoy have the unilateral right to cancel the agreement:

> . . . if the non-CanRoy directors and/or shareholders of CanRom force management to act in any manner that would run contrary to CanRoy's interest in guarding its reputation for ethical and sound products, or contrary to any advice CanRoy may give that is not violative of the laws of Malindrania.

The use of the CanRoy name was typical of the difficulties the prospective partners were having in the negotiations. Carlos wanted the unconditional use of the name and trademark for an indefinite period, while CanRoy was only prepared to offer it for a limited time due to its inability, as a minority shareholder, to legally control the company. At Carlos's suggestion, the problem was solved by changing the name of the company to "CaRom" prior to the signing of the agreement.

By August, the parties were still trying to reach final agreement on numerous details. Strong was becoming impatient since documents from the Miranda group continually failed to reflect previously arrived at mutual understandings on important aspects. Strong telexed Miranda about his unhappiness over the delay and suggested a meeting in San Raphael. The meeting focused on the CanRoy name and trademark, the technical cooperation agreement, and CanRoy's position about competing with CaRom in Malindrania.

After the meeting, Strong reiterated his position in a telex. CanRoy was willing to offer a five-year renewable technical assistance agreement with the supply of new technology on a case-by-case basis. The use of the CanRoy name and trademark would be terminated prior to the transfer of shares, and a carefully limited competition clause was included. Miranda's reaction was negative. His understanding was that CaRom would continue to use the CanRoy trademark and anything short of an unlimited noncompetition clause was totally unacceptable. The tone of Carlos's response indicated that negotiations were beginning to frustrate him as well. Miranda's telex ended:

> Remember that from the beginning, our negotiations have been carried out under the principle of equality to both partners and all the documents to be executed in this negotiation should contain this principle.

As the winter dragged on and negotiations continued, Floriano came under increasing pressure from Miranda. In September he informed Strong of concerns raised by Carlos at a recent meeting:

1. Is CanRoy still interested in the Miranda partners or is CanRoy trying to pull out?
2. Is CanRoy looking for a partner or for a front that will run things CanRoy's way only?
3. Miranda is confused that agreements reached here are changed later. He would like to be able to sit with the deciders to shorten the negotiations.

Floriano concluded:

> My personal opinion is that we can force a 50 percent partner into agreeing to conditions he considers unfair if he is interested enough, but we will simply pay for it later in disagreements.

Negotiations continued through 1982. When it looked possible to consummate the deal by year's end and receive payment, Strong pressed Miranda to pay interest on the purchase price. Strong reasoned that since the price had been set almost a year earlier and Miranda would share in a full year's dividends even though he had not put up any money, an interest payment was reasonable. Miranda thought otherwise. He lost his temper and refused outright, threatening to call off further negotiations. Not wanting to lose the deal, Strong acquiesced.

THE PARTNERSHIP AGREEMENT

Domtila first proposed a shareholders' agreement to protect the minority interest and specify that management of the company would always remain with CanRoy. This agreement was not possible since it was against Malindranian law. The response to further suggestions along this line was also negative. Finally, it was decided to write the bylaws of the company in a way that would give CanRoy the maximum possible protection. The basic agreement Xavier Domtila eventually worked out was:

1. (a) 51 percent Class A shares. These can be held by nationals only.
   (b) 49 percent Class B shares. These can only be held by foreigners.
   When sold to nationals, they became Class A shares.
2. The company was to be administered by a board of directors who would elect a chief executive officer (CEO). The board comprises three members elected by Class A shares and two members elected by Class B shares.
3. Four directors comprised a quorum. Decisions could be taken only if at least one Class B director was present and a decision had to be unanimous. This was effectively a veto power.
4. Amendments to bylaws must be approved by 75 percent of the board of four members.
5. Once the CEO was approved, only votes by Class B directors could change him.

According to Malindranian law, CanRoy could not force its choice of CEO, but it was understood that CanRoy would nominate the CEO who would be approved by the national directors. Further, a statement of the general manager's[4] functions and duties were to be approved by the board at its first meeting after Latinization.

Approval of the job description would provide the basis for managing the company without Board interference in day-to-day operations. The Board would set direction, check the implementation of policies, but not intervene in normal management activities.

Finally, a technical assistance agreement was signed. The Miranda family had no skill or experience in plastics. Under this agreement, CanRoy would provide CanRom with trained management through whom CanRoy's technology and skills would be available. A condition of the agreement was that if the Mirandas failed to follow CanRoy's advice, then technical assistance would be cut off. Domtila believed these measures provided CanRoy with the maximum protection and control possible under Malindranian law. Strong also agreed with Carlos's request that CanRoy train one of his sons so that he could be considered for CEO of CanRom someday.

THE JOINT VENTURE IS COMPLETED

The agreement that had been planned for February 1982 was finally signed in December 1982. INI approved the Latinization program on December 16. The final agreement would result in approximately U.S. $1,800,000 (after tax) being repatriated for the stock rights and a significant contribution to CanRom's capital. A dividend would also be declared paying an additional $202,000 to CanRoy and $211,000 to the Miranda group.

The bylaws were written first in English and initialed by the parties to the agreement. This document was then translated into Spanish for signatures. Strong and Domtila were presented with the Spanish version displaying the seal of a public translator on December 18. The two men were in a rush. Unable to buy a return ticket from San Raphael to Sao Paulo on a commercial airline during the Christmas season, they had to settle for a one-way ticket to San Raphael and a private charter plane back to Sao Paulo. The plane had to leave in time to fly over the Amazon during daylight, since it was not permitted to fly over that region at night unless fully equipped with all the gear specified to permit survival and rescue should the plane have to land in the jungle.

There was pressure on December 19 to sign the bylaws, give Carlos the stock, receive payment, and get out of the city. There was also pressure created by the imminent arrival of year's end and the desire to repatriate the cash that year. Finally, one of Strong's primary objectives was to consummate the joint venture. He had agreed with his boss, Ian Ferguson, to do it and he fully intended to succeed (see Figure 2). Commented Doug: "In CanRoy, we bust our guts to reach our objectives."

FIGURE 2   **Performance Assessment Work Sheet**
Canada Royal (International)

Calendar Year 1982

NAME:	D. B. Strong		
POSITION:	President	COMPANY:	CANROY S.A.

MAJOR PERFORMANCE OBJECTIVES

	Target	Achievement
FINANCIAL:		
Consolidated Net Income	41.0	
Levered Return on Equity	20%	
Capital Expenditures	48,000	
Dividend (Gross)	17,700	

NONQUANTITATIVE OBJECTIVES:
1. Execution of Brazil strategy:
   a. Maintain relationship with NPRS.
   b. Keep Beuilaqua on plan.
   c. Develop a Mooca project.
   d. Review fabrication program.
2. Mexico
   a. Achieve Mexicanization if market permits but dependent on growth projects.
   b. Divisionalization.

(Continued)

FIGURE 2   **Continued**

3. Explore joint venture with LATCO Industries in Guatemala.
4. Conclude Malindrania partnership and prepare strategic plan.
5. Colombia: achieve Colombianization.
6. Prepare and update succession plans in all companies.
7. Identify American Industries L.A. objectives.
8. Develop strategy for Argentina.
9. Develop strategy for Central America.

_____   Date: _____
(Signature of Incumbent)
_____   Date: _____
(Signature of Supervisor)

The parties signed the bylaws and Doug gave Carlos a copy of the Argentinian General Manager's job description saying, "We would like something like this for the G.M. of CanRom." Carlos replied, "Okay."

As he was about to hand over the shares, Strong discovered that Miranda did not have the down payment. Carlos said CanRoy would have the money in three or four days. Strong was reluctant to give up the shares and asked for some guaranty or he could not leave the shares. Domtila recalled that Carlos exploded:

My word is enough! You don't need a guaranty — I give up, the partnership is ended!

Strong told Miranda that he wanted to finalize the deal and then asked for Domtila's advice. Miranda left the two to discuss the matter in private.

From a legal point of view, there would be no proof of payment and CanRoy could turn to the courts to force payment. The only risk would be the time involved. It wasn't the legalities that worried Domtila, however. He was becoming increasingly skeptical of Miranda's intentions and he advised Strong to keep the stock and call off the deal. Strong walked across the office and gazed out into the streets of San Raphael contemplating Domtila's advice. He turned as the door opened and Carlos entered saying, "Well, Senor Strong, are we in business or not?"

Notes

1. Names of people, companies, cities, and countries have been disguised. The name of the country, Malindrania, was adopted from *The Adventures of Don Quixote de la Mancha* by M. Cervantes.
2. Sales were U.S. $9.7 million and profits were U.S. $1.3 million

FIGURE 3 Canada Royal (International) (A): Summary of People in the Case and Partial Organization Chart

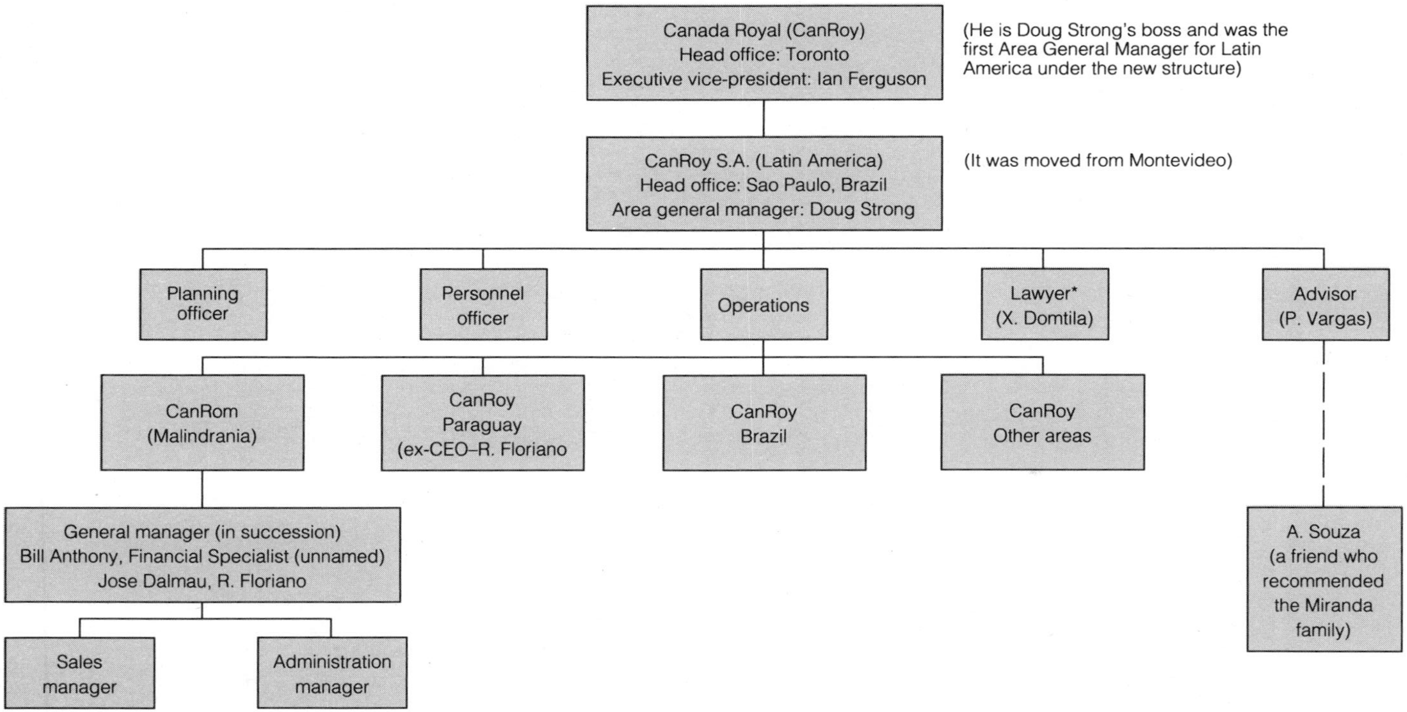

Canada Royal (CanRoy)
Head office: Toronto
Executive vice-president: Ian Ferguson

(He is Doug Strong's boss and was the first Area General Manager for Latin America under the new structure)

CanRoy S.A. (Latin America)
Head office: Sao Paulo, Brazil
Area general manager: Doug Strong

(It was moved from Montevideo)

Advisor
(P. Vargas)

A. Souza
(a friend who recommended the Miranda family)

Lawyer*
(X. Domtila)

CanRoy
Other areas

Operations

CanRoy
Brazil

Personnel
officer

CanRoy
Paraguay
(ex-CEO–R. Floriano

Planning
officer

CanRom
(Malindrania)

General manager (in succession)
Bill Anthony, Financial Specialist (unnamed)
Jose Dalmau, R. Floriano

Sales
manager

Administration
manager

* The other lawyer mentioned in the case, Benjamin Almaro, was an independent lawyer hired jointly by CanRoy and Carlos Miranda.

3. "Foreign" companies were defined as those that were less than 51 percent owned or controlled by national investors; "mixed" companies had 51 to 80 percent local equity and effective local control; "national" companies had 80 percent of the capital held by local investor and proportionate management control.
4. The terms General Manager and CEO are used interchangeably.

CASE 13

International Bank of Malaysia[1]

Joseph J. DiStefano

Near the end of a four-week management development course in Hong Kong, Mr. Ian Dankworth, Branch Manager of the Kuala Lumpur office of the International Bank of Malaysia, was reflecting on a serious personnel problem in his own office. Two of his department heads, Mr. Wong Chin Poh (Credit) and Mr. Zainuddin Bin Abdul Wahab (Administration), were causing serious disruptions to morale and performance through their efforts to discredit each other. Under ordinary circumstances Mr. Dankworth might have dealt with the situation as a "simple personality conflict between two managers." But in this case the problem was complicated by the fact that Wong was of Chinese ancestry while Zainuddin was Malay.[2]

This not only intensified their hostile feelings toward each other but also constrained the options open to Ian for resolving the difficulties. He knew that any action he took would be subject to the scrutiny of the office employees and the Malaysian government, both of whom were sensitive to the delicate relations between these two racial groups that accounted for the bulk of Malaysian citizenry. In fact, the government had moved toward increasing regulation of the racial mix within companies operating in Malaysia. As he considered these issues, Ian knew that he would soon be back in Kuala Lumpur and faced with resolving the problem.

BACKGROUND

International was a worldwide commercial banking organization. Although the headquarters was located in the United States, foreign offices conducted their domestic affairs fairly autonomously within the limits of corporate policies. The Malaysia operation was typical of the bank's organizational approach to international markets. Headquarters was concerned with only those local branch activities that included the administration of truly "international" transactions (e.g., dealings of corporate customers with the foreign offices) and the handling of credit applications that were beyond the approval limit of local management.

359

The Kuala Lumpur Regional Office had been in existence for many years and employed a total of fifty-eight employees. As General Manager, Dankworth was responsible for the overall performance of International's Malaysian affairs. He gave direction to the various Department Heads on corporate matters and when necessary saw to the integration of departmental activities. John White, as Senior Representative, coordinated International's "major business developments," i.e., those areas subject to the immediate interest of head office but ongoing in Malaysia. White also handled certain administrative services rendered to a few important clients. The local bank branches simply administered the details of any large deals prearranged by Dankworth or White.

Cheong Shul Lee, the Regional Manager for the domestic branch network, had responsibility for all local operations and for the integration of International's requirements as dictated by Dankworth and White.

With the exception of Dankworth, White, and Zainuddin, all other managers were Chinese. An organization chart showing the reporting relationships and deployment of personnel is shown in Figure 1. Each manager maintained a staff relationship with the branch managers and provided functional assistance while monitoring branch activities to ensure adherence to precisely defined procedural rules and policies.

The normal work activities varied from department to department. The Credit Department comprised a small group of specialists who performed a critical function. All credit applications from the branches came to them for authorization. If the amount of the application was beyond their own approval limit (as set by their Department Head, Wong, and the Regional Manager), they nonetheless reviewed it and recommended the approval or refusal of the application before passing it on to the next approval level. Also within this department was the Credit Administration group, which was in charge of policing all approved credits through the use of records and security documentation jointly required and coordinated by themselves and Administration. They inspected existing credits issued by the branches, Dankworth, or White to check for discrepancies from approved procedures.

Zainuddin headed the Administration Department, which served two basic functions. It had responsibility for the internal accounting of the regional office itself and exercised central accounting control over all branch offices. This department accumulated and distributed pertinent figures to the other departments (e.g., loan records for credit) and prepared reports for head office. This department also served as the "foreign exchange center," reporting the consolidated branch position to the Southeast Asian foreign exchange control regarding the bank's position (their commitments of local currency for the prearranged future transactions of their clients). They also reviewed and authorized minor deviations from established procedures and/or rates when requested by the branches. Such exceptions were granted when the overall value of the business relationship with the customer warranted compromise on some minor issue.

The Accounting Department was the information center. This function required frequent interaction with and cooperation from the other department heads and personnel. For example, International was a commercial bank but certain clients

FIGURE 1 International Bank of Malaysia — Kuala Lumpur Regional Office Organization Chart

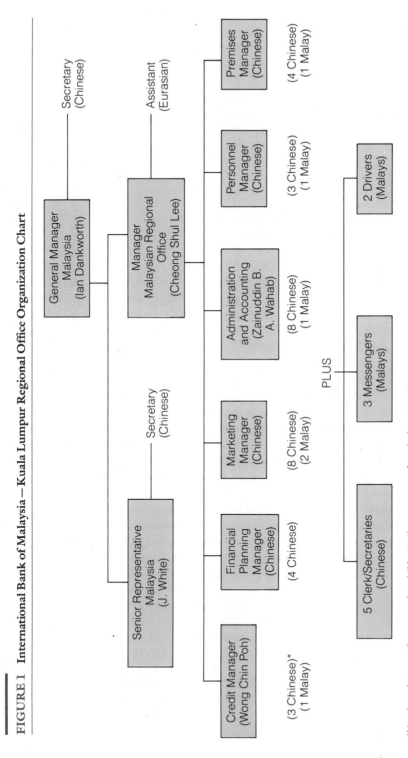

*Numbers in parentheses are in addition to the manager of each department.

pressured for personal loans for their VIPs. Although approval in principle was granted by Dankworth, Zainuddin assessed the marginal cases and provided any non-standard loan documentation such as information on the political or economic ramifications involved with any particular request. Many special applications that originated through White or the domestic branches, via the Credit Department, often required only administrative processing. They did however demand effort, since approval of these applications was usually expected within a brief time after their submission. Zainuddin was quite capable of handling these procedures and had, thus, gradually gained some measure of control over all but the largest domestic cases.

Since these activities together with normal loan and accounting responsibilities required the frequent interaction of the Credit and Administration Department heads, interpersonal difficulties had considerable impact on the effectiveness and efficiency of the operation. Ian reviewed several examples of negative effects resulting from their squabbles.

- The Financial Planning group assessed the profitability of various customer deposit accounts, which was required by the Credit Department as one of their many criteria for setting loan rates. Administration was required to provide several detailed reports concerning loan performance, deposit account balances, and so on. This meant that the Administration group had to deal with the branches in drawing the pertinent records together. Occasionally a competitive situation arose where the Credit Department required precise costing information to assist in pricing an attractive loan opportunity. Administration might then hinder a rapid turnaround citing branch tardiness as the cause.

- Personal loan applications were channeled into the regional office via the Credit Department to be endorsed by them. Since this was an exceptional service for a commercial bank, these applications might be blocked or delayed by Administration. Although the conflicts were based on a genuine difference of opinion regarding the anticipated cost/benefit trade-offs, Administration and Credit were both clearly unwilling to present and negotiate their respective positions in the conciliatory manner. The resulting delays hindered the business development efforts of the Branch Managers.

- "Even our office sports club has been affected," Ian complained. He explained that the club was partially sponsored by the company and that he encouraged participation by office personnel in its activities. Since Wong was on the committee that operated the club, Zainuddin took every opportunity to criticize it. One example occurred when the committee decided to sell two of the carrom boards it owned.[3] They circulated a memo through the office requesting those interested in purchasing a board to submit bids in writing by the following Saturday at noon (the end of the normal five and a half day working week). Zainuddin, who apparently did not see the circular until 9:00 A.M. on the Saturday in question, stopped by the desk of the club secretary and said, "I just heard about the carrom boards and want to make a bid. But I have to leave for an appointment."

When noon arrived and the committee convened to open the bids, she told them of his comment. However, they decided to proceed as planned, opened the bids, and sold the boards. On Monday, Zainuddin gave the secretary his bid (which turned out to be higher than any of those submitted on Saturday) and was furious when he discovered that the boards had already been sold. He exploded in full view of the office staff, yelling that it was obvious that Wong was at the bottom of the decision to deny him a fair chance. Again, Ian was forced to intervene and calm the situation even though he, as patron of the club, normally left the operating details to the employee committee.

ABOUT THE PEOPLE INVOLVED

Ian Dankworth, age forty, had joined International in Australia where he had been born and raised. He first moved to the Far Eastern operations six years later and had been in several locations there. He had received no specific training for his present position, which he had occupied for three years, other than the course he was just finishing. However, he had spent five years in Malaysia before becoming General Manager and had previously served in the Senior Representative post. The terms of service for expatriates were geared to a higher cost of living and therefore allowed them and their families to enjoy a greater degree of luxury and comfort than their United States or European counterparts. Also the Malaysian organization was such that Ian was given greater responsibility than he could have hoped for had he remained in Australia or gone to the United States operation.

Because of the time spent in Malaysia and because of his outgoing personality, Ian had frequent social contact with both Malays and Chinese (more with the latter). He learned to speak Malaysian and found himself a regular visitor to Malay and Chinese homes for festive occasions. In the office he appeared totally in command. He managed the steady stream of people and problems that flowed to his desk with calm and decisive assurance.

As Ian thought about the two men whose behavior was concerning him, he recognized both surface similarities and marked differences in their backgrounds and experience. Zainuddin's history with International dated back thirteen years, since his graduation from school, and included two years in the home office in the United States. He was a native Malay, a "bumiputra" (son of the soil). He was from a very "good" family in Kuala Lumpur where his father was a prominent lawyer. Zainuddin was a Muslim who appeared from his outward behavior (e.g., regular attendance at the Mosque each Friday and observance of all religious duties) to be devout.

Wong came from a well-to-do Chinese business family. He was born in Malaysia, but his ancestors came from China. A university graduate, he had spent a nine-month training period in the United States shortly after joining International.

Wong was Buddhist as were many of the Chinese in Malaysia. He did not appear to be as strict an observer of his faith as Zainuddin was of his.

Both men were married and lived in Petaling Jaya, a very large industrial and residential area approximately five miles outside Kuala Lumpur. They commuted each day by car from P.J., as it was commonly known. Their homes were of similar construction and size — brick with tile roofs — and were provided by the company.

In describing the men Ian characterized Zainuddin as a very nice person with a good sense of humor who often exercised it even at his own expense. "He's likeable, alright," said Ian, "but he's rather idle and he is weak in technical areas." Ian went on, "He's liked by his staff, but is seen as a bit of a 'nit,' a joker, even by them."

Another problem existed that affected the normal office discipline of his staff. Zainuddin would turn up late for work, disappear for hours without an explanation or reason, and take extended lunch hours despite repeated requests, threats, and instructions from management to comply with standard office routine. Naturally, when senior management disciplined other staff on similar matters, they would invariably ask why Zainuddin could get away with it and not them.

Evaluating Zainuddin's effectiveness in the office, Ian said, "Frankly, he's useless, a conclusion shared by every senior representative I've ever had within one month of their arrival. But," he added ruefully, "his presence is a political necessity."

Ian described Wong as "immature, with a childish sense of humor, more given to pranks. He's a hard worker and technically competent," Ian said, "but, his staff senses his immaturity so he doesn't gain the respect that he should have as an executive." Ian concluded, "He makes a contribution and has the potential to develop."

Ian realized that the problem between his Department Heads was not just a personality clash concerning only himself and these two men. More specifically, the government was trying hard to get more Malays into business and industry to improve their standard of living. But the Chinese had the reputation of being the real workers in the country. The commonly held stereotype viewed them as shrewd (sometimes bordering on dishonest) businessmen who would work eighteen hours a day if it was rewarding to them. In contrast, urban Malays were seen as living hand-to-mouth. Malay farmers were viewed as more hardworking, but as being difficult to change and having a short-range perspective. For example, although technical developments made it possible to raise more than one rice crop a year, the paddy planter maintained the one crop pattern, since it was sufficient for his needs.

Conventional wisdom thus explained the steady progression of Chinese to high levels because of their ambition and willingness to work. But because of government action they were kept from the very top positions which political pressure reserved for Malays.

THE GOVERNMENT POSITION

It was only a few months earlier that a Ministry of Labor representative came into the International office and requested to inspect the salary book. From that data he extracted information on the percentage of Malays, Chinese, Indians, and others at each salary level. Later, Ian received a letter saying that the racial composition of the staff did not represent that of the country. It stated that the government's objective was to achieve the following distribution at all levels in the organization:

Malays	30–40%
Chinese	20–30%
Others	Balance

The company was required to give written assurance that they were undertaking to meet these government aims.

Ian knew that when the Labor Ministry representative inspected their records next year he would expect an increase in the proportion of Malays. And, he realized, that the scrutiny would include the executive levels as well as the percentage of total employees. This fact worried him as he thought about how to resolve the problems between Wong and Zainuddin. The situation was further complicated since he knew that Cheong, the Regional Office Manager, would soon be replacing John White, who was being transferred to another post. Ian also knew that, although no serious sanctions had yet been exercised, the government could revoke International's charter in Malaysia if International did not comply with government policy.

Ian had observed the government stand on this issue toughen since the riots in Malaysia. Although these riots were rooted in communal divisions based on racial, economic, social, linguistic, religious, and rural/urban differences their immediate cause was the election results that year. During this election the Alliance Party, a coalition of United Malays National Organization (U.M.N.O.), Malayan Chinese Association (M.C.A.), and Malayan Indian Congress, which had ruled the country since independence from Britain in 1957, suffered unexpectedly heavy losses. Three opposition parties drawing support from Chinese urban electorates and the militant champion of Malay rights (Pan-Malayan Islamic Party) combined to prevent the Alliance Party majority from reaching the two-thirds mark necessary to change the Constitution . . . a change the Alliance Party and Prime Minister Tungku Abdul Rahman had strongly promoted during the campaign.

Immediately after the results were announced, the M.C.A. split from the Alliance, announcing that it could no longer represent Chinese interests within the party. The three Chinese opposition parties responded with great excitement. The following day victory parades were organized and a mood of general celebration spread through the Chinese population. Heckling developed between Chinese and Malay groups. Reportedly, pork was thrown at some Malays, a grave offense to the Muslims, who view it as unclean.

Whatever the immediate cause, serious rioting followed, and the opportunity to vent the racial enmity that had been smoldering for many years was quickly seized by both sides. Conservative government estimates claimed 200 people killed and blamed the rioting on the Communists. Chinese suffered disproportionate casualties, a fact many attributed to the total domination of the police and armed forces by Malays. In the aftermath of the riots the Constitution was suspended and a power struggle continued from May to September. Rahman was accused of being soft on the Chinese, and he counter-attacked by ousting two of his critics from the Alliance. Finally, his resignation was forced (with an appropriate face-saving story) and the legislature was reconvened in February.

The residue of bitterness about these events, which in themselves originated in historical racial friction, could still be seen years later. Ian knew that this bitterness was a force he must consider in deciding what to do about Wong and Zainuddin.

LONG- AND SHORT-RANGE PROBLEMS

Ian realized that he had to deal with the short-run problem of what to do about the two men. But he also knew that how he dealt with them would affect his options on handling the quotas established by the Ministry of Labor. Several alternatives were open to him. He could duplicate positions, pairing a figurehead Malay with a Chinese who would perform most of the tasks. Or, he could simply stall and continue with his present staffing arrangements. Another route would be to attempt to comply with the government requirement as quickly and fully as possible. Additionally, he might plan a judicious mix of these approaches.

As he considered these options, he started to lay out the facts he would need to make a decision. For example there were financial implications. The total bank income had increased the past year from M$12,400,000 to M$15,800,000. Overhead expenses as a percentage of gross income (total revenue less deposit interest) also had increased from 72 percent (M$9,100,000) up to about 76 percent (M$12,008,000). About 50 percent of overhead was taken up by salaries. The executive staff earned between M$1,000 and M$2,000/month (Zainuddin and Wong were both below M$1,500/month). Executive trainees started between M$500 and M$550/month and were increased to M$1,000/month upon completion of the training program, which usually ran from eighteen months to two years.

But financial concerns were not the only factors influencing his decision. Ian worried about the availability of competent Malays, whom he knew constituted a much lower proportion of the high school and university graduates relative to the Chinese. Although primary education was given in Malay, Chinese, and English, it was voluntary and the dropout rate was high. However, the dropout rate was higher among Malays than Chinese.[4]

Because the pressure to attract the few Malay graduates available was felt by all firms, the salary offers were increasing rapidly. Ian knew of two American oil firms who were paying new trainees (some of whom had not graduated from university) as high as M$750/month. And he expected the competitive "bidding" to get worse until the supply of graduates increased significantly. Because of the limited supply of teachers, this was unlikely to occur in the near future despite the increasing enrollments in primary schools and heavy government spending on education.

Enjoying the opportunity to consider these issues away from the day-to-day pressures of the office, he realized that whatever decisions he made had to be put in the context of an increasingly anti-expatriate climate.

A hedge against the future might be to advise head office to sell or to merge with a local banking network through which International's services could be maintained within the local domestic market in an "undisturbed" operating manner. He realized that the number of foreign banks had decreased by about 20 percent and that the Malaysian government might force a continuation of that trend.

CONCLUSION

Considering the problems he faced when he returned home next week, Ian summarized the decisions he needed to make. In the short run he had to resolve the difficulties between Wong and Zainuddin or suffer the consequences of decreasing office morale and efficiency. In the longer run he had to deal with the government pressures to increase the percentage of Malays throughout the Kuala Lumpur office of International . . . and he knew that visible progress had to be made in a reasonable period. As he finished his preparation for the next day's classes and thought about his fellow managers who were already enjoying a cool beer downstairs, he wondered what he should do about these problems that were so closely related to each other.

Notes

1. Names of people and companies have been disguised.
2. Both men are Malaysian citizens. Throughout the case the use of "Chinese" and "Malay" refers to ethnic origin, not citizenship.
3. Carrom is a game roughly comparable to pool. The boards have 4 pockets and "seeds" about the size of checkers are used.
4. At the time of the case the demand for qualified Malays at all but the lowest levels greatly exceeded availability. The requirements for educated manpower at professional, subprofessional, and skilled levels were forecast to increase significantly. Similar situations have been repeated in numerous countries in recent years.

CASE 14

Hazelton International Limited[1]

Lorna L. Wright and Henry W. Lane

John Anderson, Project Manager of the Maralinga-Ladawan Highway Project, was both exasperated and relieved as he drove the jeep up the rutted road to the river where he and Dan Simpson would wait for the ferry. John was taking Dan Simpson, his replacement, on a three-day site check of the project. During this trip John was also going to brief Dan on the history of the project and the problems he would encounter.

John was exasperated because the client had requested two more construction supervisors, and yet, after two years of operation, only 17 kilometers of the 245-kilometer highway were under construction. Hazelton, a consulting engineering company, was only an advisor on the project and so far had had little success in getting the client to heed its advice. John wondered whether the two new people would change anything or if their presence would be justified? A recommendation had to be made to headquarters either to comply with the client's wishes for the supervisors to be on site within a month or to override the request. John was relieved because this problem, and others, would be Dan Simpson's to handle. As they waited for the ferry, John began briefing Dan on the project.

BACKGROUND

Since 1965 Hazelton had successfully completed assignments in forty-six countries across Africa, Asia, Europe, South and Central America, and the Caribbean region. A large proportion of the projects had been in Africa but the company was now turning attention to developing its Asian operations. Since its beginning, Hazelton had done only ten projects in Asia — less than 10% of all its projects.

Hazelton provided consulting services in transportation, housing and urban development, structural engineering, and municipal and environmental engineering, to both government and corporate clients around the world. Specific services included technical and economic feasibility studies, financing, planning, architecture, preliminary and final engineering design, maintenance programming, construction supervision, project management and equipment procurement.

368

Projects ranged from extremely large (building an international airport) to very small, requiring the skills of only a single expert (advising on a housing project in Malaysia). The majority of these projects were funded by international lending agencies (ILAs). The previous year Hazelton's worldwide annual fee volume exceeded U.S. $40 million.

Hazelton staffed its overseas projects with senior members of its permanent staff. In addition, experts with international experience and capabilities in the applicable language were used whenever possible. Both these principles had been adhered to in the Maralinga-Ladawan project.

MARALINGA-LADAWAN HIGHWAY PROJECT

The project required design and construction supervision services for a 245 km highway along the western coast of the island of Tola from Maralinga in the north to Ladawan in the south. (See Figure 1.) Sections of the highway past Ladawan were being reconstructed by other firms funded by aid agencies from Japan and Australia.

FIGURE 1   Map of Soronga (not to scale)

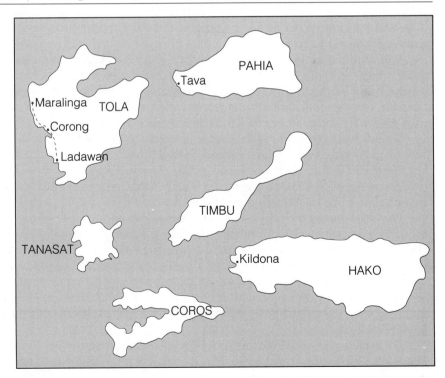

FIGURE 2   Hazelton's Six Largest Projects

	Project	Location	Fee
1.	International airport	Africa	$4 million
2.	Highway supervision	South America	$3.4 million
3.	Highway feasibility	South America	$2.25 million
4.	Highway design	South America	$2.25 million
5.	Highway betterment	Soronga	$1.63 million
6.	Secondary roads: graveling	Africa	$1.32 million

In addition to supervising the actual construction, Hazelton was responsible for a major training program for Sorongan engineers, mechanics, operators, and administrative staff.

This was the fifth largest project ($1.6 million in fees) Hazelton had ever undertaken (see Figure 2). It was a joint venture with two other firms, Beauval Ltd. and McPherson Brothers International (MBI), whom Hazelton involved to strengthen its proposal. Hazelton acted as the lead firm on behalf of the consortium and assumed overall responsibility for the work. Over the life of the project, the three firms would send twenty-two expatriates, including highway designers, engineers, mechanics, and operators.

MBI was involved because it was a contractor and Hazelton felt it might need those types of skills when dealing with a "force account" project. Usually, Hazelton supervised the project and left the actual construction to others. This project was different. Force account meant that the construction workers would be government employees who would not be experienced in construction work.

Beauval had been working in Asia for seventeen years and had established a base of operations in Kildona. It had done several projects on the island of Hako, but this would be the first on the island of Tola. This local experience would help the proposal gain acceptance both in the eyes of the financing agency, and the client, the Sorongan Highway Department (SHD).

The financing agency provided a combination loan and grant for the project and played a significant role in the selection of the winning proposal. The grant portion paid for the salaries of the expatriates working on the project while the loan funds were for necessary equipment.

Under the contract's terms of reference, Hazelton personnel were sent as advisors on the techniques of road construction and equipment maintenance. The training component was to be the major part of the project with the actual construction being the training vehicle.

The project was to last five years with Hazelton phasing out its experts in about four years. The Sorongans would be trained by that point to take over the project themselves. The training program would use formal classroom instruction and a system of counterparts. Each expatriate engineer or manager would have a counterpart Sorongan engineer or manager who worked closely with him in order for the expertise to be passed on. At the mechanic and operator levels, training programs would be set up involving both in-class instruction and on-the-job training.

SHD's responsibilities included providing counterpart staff, ensuring that there was housing built for the expatriates, and providing fuel and spare parts for the equipment that would be coming from Canada.

It was thought that a force account project — with government staff doing the work — would be the best way to marry the financial agency's objective of training with the Sorongan government's aim of building a road. It was one of the first times that SHD had found itself in the role of contractor.

Hazelton was in the position of supervising one arm of the organization on behalf of another arm. It was working for the client as a supervising engineer, but the client also ran the construction. Hazelton was in the middle.

In Soronga's development plans this project was part of the emphasis on developing the transportation and communication sector. It was classed as a *betterment* project, meaning that Soronga did not want undue resources going toward a "perfect" road in engineering terms; merely one that was better than the present one and that would last. An important objective also was to provide employment in Tola and permit easier access to the rest of Soronga, because the province was a politically sensitive area and isolated from the rest of the country.

TOLA

Tola was the most westerly island of the Sorongan archipelago. It was isolated from the rest of the country because of rough terrain and poor roads. It was a socially conservative province and fundamentalist in religion. The majority of Tolanese were very strict Moslems. The ulamas (Moslem religious leaders) played an important role in Tolanese society, perhaps more so than in any other part of Soronga.

Economically, the province lagged behind Hako, the main island. The economy was still dominated by labor-intensive agriculture. Large-scale industry was a very recent development with timbering providing the biggest share of exports. A liquefied natural gas plant and a cement factory were two new industries begun within the past two years.

From its earliest history, Tola enjoyed a high degree of autonomy. In 1821 it signed a treaty with Britain guaranteeing its autonomy in commerce. This was revoked in 1871 when Britain signed another treaty with France, recognizing the latter's sovereignty over the whole of the country.

Tola understood the implications of this treaty and tried to negotiate with the French to retain their autonomous standing. Neither side was willing to compromise, however, and in 1873 France declared war on Tola. This war continued for fifty years, and the fierce resistance of the Tolanese against colonization became a model for Soronga's own fight for independence later. Even after the Tolanese officially surrendered to the French this did not mean peace. Guerrilla warfare continued, led by the ulamas. With the advent of World War II and the arrival of the Japanese, resistance to the French intensified. At the end of the war, the Japanese were expelled and the French returned to Soronga, but not to Tola.

With the independence of Soronga, Tola theoretically formed part of the new nation, but in practice it retained its regional, social, economic, and political control. In 1961, however, the central government in Kildona dissolved the province of Tola and incorporated its territory into the region of West Pahia under a governor in Tava.

Dissatisfaction with this move was so intense that the Tolanese proclaimed an independent Islamic Republic in 1963. This rebellion lasted until 1971, when the central government sought a political solution by giving Tola provincial status again. In 1977 Kildona granted special status to the province in the areas of religion, culture, and education.

Tola's long periods of turmoil had left their mark on the province and on its relations with the rest of the country. It was deeply suspicious of outsiders (particularly those from Hako, since that was the seat of the central government), strongly independent and fiercely proud of its heritage and ethnic identity. Although all Tolanese could speak Sorongan because that was the only language used in the schools, they preferred to use their native language, Tolanese, amongst themselves. The central government in Kildona had recently become concerned about giving the province priority in development projects to strengthen the ties between the province and the rest of the country.

PROGRESS OF THE PROJECT — THE FIRST YEAR

Negotiations on the project took longer than expected, and the project actually began almost a year after it was originally scheduled to begin. Hazelton selected its personnel carefully. The Project Manager, Frank Kennedy, had been successful in a similar position in Central America. He had also successfully cleaned up a problem situation in Lesotho. In September Frank and an administrator arrived in Soronga, followed a month later by the major design team, bringing the total expatriate contingent to ten families. They spent a month learning the Sorongan language but had to stay in Kildona until December because there was no housing in Maralinga. The houses had not been finished; before they could be, an earthquake destroyed the complex. Eventually, housing was rented from Australian expatriates working for another company who were moving to a complex of their own.

Hazelton was anxious to begin work, but no Sorongan project manager had been specified, and the vehicles did not arrive until late December. When the vehicles did arrive, the fuel tanks were empty and there was no fuel available. Neither was there provision in SHD's budget to buy fuel or lubricants that year. The project would have to wait until the new fiscal year began on April 1 to get money allotted to it. Meanwhile, it would be a fight for funds.

YEAR 2

By the beginning of the year the equipment was on site, but the Sorongan counter-part staff still were not. Hazelton wanted to start the design work but there was no Sorongan design staff. The staff that was there would leave on Wednesday for a Friday holiday and return a week later.

Hazelton had no control over SHD staff, since it had no line responsibility. When the SHD Project Manager finally arrived, he was reluctant to confront the staff. Senior SHD people on the project were Hakonese, whereas most of the people at the operator level were local Tolanese. There was not only the Hakonese-Tolanese strain but an unwillingness on the part of the senior staff to do anything that would stir up this politically volatile area.

Frank was having a difficult time. He was a construction man. There were 245 kilometers of road to build and nothing was being done. It galled him to have to report no progress month after month. If the construction could start, the training would quickly follow.

On top of the project problems, Frank's wife was pregnant and had to stay in Singapore, where the medical facilities were better. His frustration increased, and he began confronting the Sorongan Project Manager, demanding action. His behavior became counterproductive and he had to be replaced. The man chosen as his replacement was John Anderson.

John Anderson

John Anderson was a civil engineer who had worked for Hazelton for fifteen years. He had a wealth of overseas experience in countries as diverse as Thailand, Nigeria, Tanzania, and Kenya. He liked the overseas environment for a variety of reasons, not the least of which was the sense of adventure that went with working abroad. "You meet people who stand out from the average. You get interesting points of view."

Professionally, it was also an adventure. "You run across many different types of engineering and different ways of approaching it." This lent an air of excitement and interest to jobs that was lacking in domestic work. The challenge was greater also since one didn't have access to the same skills and tools as at home: As John said, "You have to make do."

Even though he enjoyed overseas work, John had returned to headquarters as Office Manager for Hazelton. His family was a major factor in this decision. As his two children reached high school age, it became increasingly important for them to be settled and to receive schooling that would allow them to enter university. Thus, John had no intention of going overseas in the near future. However, when it became evident that a new Project Manager was needed for Soronga, loyalty prompted him to respond without hesitation when the company called.

He had been the manager of a similar project in Nigeria where he had done a superlative job. He had a placid, easygoing temperament and a preference for operating by subtle suggestions rather than direct demands. Hazelton's top management felt that if anyone could make a success of this project, John could.

PERCEPTIONS OF THE PROJECT

From the description of Maralinga in the original project document, John knew he would face problems from the beginning. However, when he arrived on site, it wasn't as bad as he'd expected. People were friendly, the housing was adequate, and there was access to an international school run by the Australians.

The work situation was different. The equipment that had come from Canada could not be used. Bridges to the construction sites had not been built and the existing ones could not support the weight of the machines. The bridgework was to have been done before the road project started.

Roads had to be widened to take the construction equipment, but no provisions had been made to expropriate the land needed. Instructions were that the road must remain within the existing right-of-way. Technically, SHD could lay claim to fifteen meters, but they had to pay compensation for any crops lost, even though those crops were planted on state land. Because of these problems, the biggest pieces of machinery, such as the crusher plant, had to be taken apart and moved piece by piece. Stripping a machine down for transportation took time, money, and manpower — all in short supply.

The budgeting process presented another problem. It was done on an annual basis rather than for the entire project period. It was also done in meticulous detail. Every liter of fuel and every nut and bolt had to be included. The budget was extremely inflexible, too. Money allocated for fuel could not be used for spare parts if the need arose.

When the project was initially planned, there was plenty of money, but with the collapse of oil prices, the Sorongan economy was hit hard and restrictions on all projects were quickly instituted. Budgets were cut in half. The originally planned money was no longer available for the project.

Further problems arose because the project was a force account. The government bureaucracy could not react quickly and in construction, fast reactions were important. Revisions needed to be approved quickly, but by the time the government approved a change, it was often too late.

The training component of the project had more than its share of problems. Counterpart training was difficult because Sorongan managers would arbitrarily reassign people to other jobs. Other counterparts would leave for more lucrative jobs elsewhere. Among the mechanics, poor supervision compounded the problems. Those who showed initiative were not encouraged and the spark soon died.

ARRIVAL ON SITE

John arrived in Soronga in March. SHD budgets were due soon after. This required a tremendous amount of negotiating. Expenses had to be identified specifically and in minute detail. By September the process was completed, and the project finally, after more than a year, had funds to support it.

Shortly after John's arrival, the project was transferred from the maintenance section of SHD to the construction section. The Sorongan Project Manager changed and the parameters of the job began to change also. SHD would not allow realignment of the road. To change the alignment would have meant getting property rights, which was an expensive, time-consuming process and inconsistent with a project that SHD saw as road improvement rather than road construction.

This meant that half the design team had no work to do. Their roles had to be quickly changed. For example, the Chief Design Engineer became Costing, Programming, and Budgeting Engineer. The new SHD Project Manager was inexperienced in his post and concerned about saving money and staying within budget. Because of this, he was loath to hire more workers to run the machinery because the rainy season was coming and construction would slow down. The workers would have to be paid but little work would be done.

By October, with the rainy season in full swing, it was evident that the money allocated to the project was not going to be spent, and the Project Manager frantically began trying to increase activity. If this year's budget was not spent, it would be very difficult to get adequate funds for the next year. However, it was difficult to spend money in the last months because no preparatory work had been done. It took time to let tenders and hire trained staff.

The new SHD Project Manager was Hakonese, as was his predecessor. Neither understood the local Tolanese situation. Getting access to gravel and sand sites necessitated dealing with the local population, and this was not handled well, with the result that it took a long time to acquire land rights.

The supervisors were also mainly Hakonese and could exercise little control over the work force. Discipline was lax. Operators wouldn't begin doing any constructive work until 9:30. They would quit at 11:30 for a two-hour lunch and then finish for the day at 5:00. Drivers hauled material for private use during working hours. Fuel disappeared at an alarming rate. One morning when a water truck was inspected before being put into service, the Hazelton advisor discovered the water tank was full of fuel. No explanation as to how the fuel got there was forthcoming, and it soon vanished again.

Bridges were a problem. It had been almost two and one-half years since the original plans had been submitted, and SHD was now demanding changes. Substructures were not yet in place and the tenders had just been let. When they were finally received by midyear, SHD decided that Canadian steel was too expensive and they could do better elsewhere. The tendering process would have to be repeated, and SHD had not yet let the new tenders.

Although there was no real construction going on, training had begun. A Training Manager was on site, and the plan was to train the mechanics and equipment operators first. The entire program would consist of four phases. The first phase would involve thirty people for basic operator training. The second would take the best of the first phase and train them further as mechanics. In the third phase, the best mechanics would train others. The fourth phase would upgrade skills previously learned.

However, SHD canceled the second phase of training because they considered it to be too costly and a waste of time. They wanted people to be physically working, not spending time in the classroom. Hazelton felt that both types of training were needed and thus the cancellation raised difficulties with the financing agency, who considered the training needs paramount.

SHD, as a government agency, was not competitive with private companies in wages. It was not only losing its best engineering people to better-paying jobs elsewhere, but it could not attract qualified people at the lower levels. Its people, therefore, were inexperienced and had to be taught the basics of operating mechanical equipment. Ironically, equipment on the project was some of the most sophisticated available.

In June there was a push to get construction underway. There was a need to give the design people something to do and a desire to get the operators and mechanics moving, as well as the equipment, which had been sitting idle for several months. Finally, there was the natural desire to show the client some concrete results.

Hazelton was losing the respect of the people around them. Most people were not aware that Hazelton was acting merely in an advisory capacity. The feeling was that they should be directing the operations. Since Hazelton was not taking charge, the company's competence was being questioned.

SHD was directing the construction, but there didn't seem to be any plan of attack. The SHD Manager was rarely on site and the crews suffered badly from a lack of direction. Time, materials, and people were being wasted because of this. Bits and pieces of work were being started at different points with no consideration given to identifying the critical areas.

The rainy season was due to begin in September and would last until the end of December. This was always a period of slow progress because construction was impossible when it rained. Work had to be stopped every time it rained and frequently work that had been done before the rain had to be redone.

Besides the problem of no progress on construction, some of the expatriate staff were not doing the job they had been sent out to do. Because there was little design work, the design engineer was transformed into a costing and budgeting man. No bridges were being built, so the bridge engineer was idle. No training was being done, so the Training Manager was declared redundant and was sent home.

It was difficult for Hazelton to fulfill even its advisory role because SHD personnel were not telling them what they were doing next. A communication gap was rapidly opening between SHD and Hazelton. Communication between SHD in Tola and SHD in Kildona was poor also. It appeared that the Kildona headquarters was allowing the Tola office to sink or swim on its own. Little direction was forthcoming. It didn't seem as if SHD Kildona was allocating its best people to the project, either.

The one bright spot of the year was that the project was now under the construction section of SHD rather than the maintenance, and thus they could understand things from a construction point of view. The feeling was that things would improve because now the people in headquarters at least understood what the field team was up against and what it was trying to accomplish.

YEAR 3

At the beginning of the year, there was little to be seen for the past year's work.

The Hazelton staff and their Sorongan counterparts worked out of a small two-story building in the SHD office compound in Maralinga. The Sorongans occupied the top floor and Hazelton, the bottom. A field camp and trailer site had been set up in Corong, the halfway point between Maralinga and Ladawan. The plan was to move construction out from this area in both directions.

John, his Mechanic Supervisor, and the Bridge Engineer made the five-hour trip out to the site at the beginning of each week, returning to Maralinga and their families at the end of the week. The Second Mechanic and his wife lived on-site, whereas the erstwhile Design Engineer, now in charge of budgeting and administration, stayed primarily in the Maralinga office.

SHD was beginning to rethink its position on using force account labor. There were signs that in the next fiscal year it might hire a contractor to do the actual work because the force account was obviously not satisfactory. SHD also underwent another change in Project Manager. The third person to fill that position was due on-site in April but arrived at the end of May. The new manager began making plans to move the Sorongan base of operations to Corong. The Hazelton expatriates, for family reasons, would remain based in Maralinga.

The project now also underwent its third status change. It was now being given back to the Maintenance Section again. The budget process had to be started again. Hazelton, in its advisory role, tried to impress on the SHD staff the advantages of planning ahead and working out the details of the next year's work so that there would be funds in the budget to support it.

Construction had at last started, even though in a desultory fashion. However, Ramadan, the month of fasting for Moslems, was looming on the horizon and this would slow progress considerably. This meant no eating, no drinking, and no smoking for Moslems between sun-up and sundown, which had obvious consequences for a worker's energy level. Productivity dropped drastically during this period. This had not been a major problem the previous year because not much work was being done. Following Ramadan, there would be only two months to work at normal speed before construction would have to slow again for the rainy season.

John's briefing of Dan having been completed, they continued the site check. John wanted Dan to inspect the existing bridges as they arrived at them.

Note

1. Names of people, companies, cities, and countries have been disguised.

CASE 15

An International Project Manager's Day[1]

Lorna L. Wright and Henry W. Lane

SITUATION

The Maralinga-Ladawan Highway Project consists of fourteen expatriate families and the Sorongan counterpart personnel. (See Figure 1.) Half of the expatriates are engineers from Hazelton. The other expatriates are mechanics, engineers, and other technical personnel from Beauval and MBI, the other two firms in the consortium. All expatriate personnel are under Hazelton's authority. This is the fifth largest project Hazelton has ever undertaken, with a fee of $1.63 million.

As the new Project Manager, you arrived in Maralinga late on March 28 with your spouse. There was no chance for a briefing before you left. Head office personnel had said John Anderson, the outgoing project manager, would fill you in on all you needed to know.[2] They had also arranged for you to meet people connected with the project in Kildona.

On March 29 you visited the project office briefly and met the accountant/administrative assistant, Tawi, the secretary, Julip, and the office messenger/driver, Satun. You then left immediately on a three-day site check of the 245-kilometer highway with John. Meanwhile, your spouse has started settling in and investigating job prospects in Maralinga.

On your trip you stopped at the field office in Corong. Chris Williams, second mechanic, and his wife, Beth, were living there. Chris was out at the timber company site to get help in recovering a grader that had toppled over the side of a ravine the night before, so you weren't able to see him. However, you met his Sorongan counterpart and he advised you that everything was going well, although they could use more workers.

You noted that Corong did not have any telephone facilities. The only communication link, a single sideband radio, had been unserviceable for the past few weeks. If you needed to contact Chris, it would involve a five-hour jeep ride to Corong to deliver the message. You were able to see the haphazard way the work on the road was proceeding and witnessed the difficulty in finding appropriate gravel sites.

378

FIGURE 1 Organization Chart

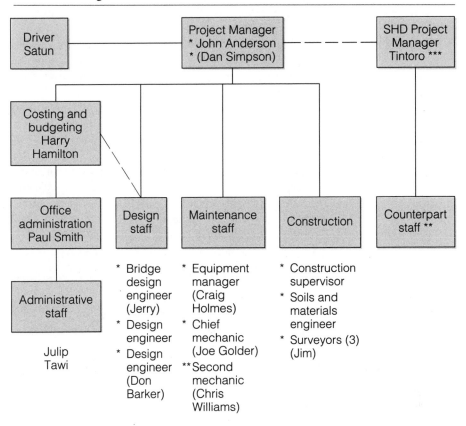

* These people travel to Corong and other locations frequently.

** Stationed in Corong.

*** Located on the floor above Dan Simpson in the same building.

Note: The two expatriates responsible for the training component had been sent home. The remaining six expatriates called for under the contract had not yet arrived in Soronga and the two construction supervisors recently requested by SHD would be in addition to these six people.

Transportation availability: (1) Project-owned: (a) There is one Land Rover for administrative use by HQ staff, (b) one car is shared by all the families, and (c) most trucks are in Corong; however there usually are some around Maralinga; (2) Public: (a) Pedal-cabs are available for short distances (such as getting to work), (b) local "taxis" are mini-van-type vehicles, which are usually very overcrowded and which expatriates usually avoid, and (c) there are a few flights to Kildona each week.

Inspecting some of the bridges you had crossed made you shiver too. Doing something about those would have to be a priority, before there was a fatality.

You returned to Maralinga on April 1 and met some of the staff and their families. Their comments made it clear that living conditions were less than ideal. The banking system made it difficult to get money transferred and converted into local currency (their salaries, paid in dollars, were deposited to their accounts at home), and the only available school was not appropriate for children who would have to return to the North American educational system.

That evening John left for another project on another continent. It is now Tuesday morning, April 2. This morning, while preparing breakfast with your spouse, the propane gas for your stove ran out. You have tried, unsuccessfully, on your way to work to get the gas cylinder filled, and have only now arrived at the office. It is 10:00 A.M. You have planned·to have lunch with your spouse at noon and you are leaving for the airport at 2:00 P.M. for a week in Kildona to visit the Beauval office, the Sorongan Highway Department (SHD) people, and the International Aid Agency (IAA) representative for discussions concerning the history and future of this project (it takes about one-half hour to drive to the airport). This trip has been planned as part of your orientation to the job. Since the IAA representative and the senior manager in the Beauval office were both leaving for other postings at the end of the month, this may be the only opportunity you will have to spend time with them.

On your arrival at the office, Julip tells you that Jim, one of the surveyors, and his wife Joyce, are arriving at 10:30 to discuss Joyce's medical problems with you. This is the first opportunity you have had to get into your office and do some work. You have about thirty minutes to go through the contents of your in-basket and take whatever action you feel is appropriate.

INSTRUCTIONS

For the purpose of this exercise, you are to assume the position of Dan Simpson, the new Project Manager for the Maralinga-Ladawan Highway Project.

Write out the action you choose on a piece of paper. Your action may include writing letters, memos, telexes, or making phone calls. You may want to have meetings with certain individuals or receive reports from the office staff. For example, if you decide to make a phone call, write out the purpose and content of the call. If you decide to have a meeting with one of the office staff or another individual, make a note of the basic agenda of things to be discussed and the date and time of the meeting. You also need to think about establishing priorities for the various issues.

To help you think of the time dimension, a calendar is shown in Figure 2. Also, Maralinga is twelve hours ahead of Eastern Standard Time.

Notes

1. Names of people, companies, cities, and countries have been disguised.
2. See Case 14, "Hazelton International Limited."

FIGURE 2 Calendar

Sunday	Monday	Tuesday	Wednesday	Thursday	Friday	Saturday
March 24	25	26	27	Arrival in Maralinga 28	29 —— Site check with John	30
31	April 1 ↑ Return	TODAY —— 2	3 —— Visit to Kildona	4	5	6
7	8	Return to Maralinga ↑ 9	10	11	12	13
14	15	16	17	18	19	20
21	22	23	24	25	26	27
28	29	30	May 1	2	3	4

*Note: You are in a Muslim area. People do not work Friday afternoons. Saturday morning usually is a workday.

III

Value Conflicts: Selected Ethical and Legal Issues

OVERVIEW

Part II of this book presented selected operating issues that international managers experience. This part presents selected ethical and legal situations that managers as well as managers-to-be are likely to encounter in their careers. The authors have separated the ethical issues from the other operating issues for pedagogical purposes because they felt that the ethical issues do not always receive the attention that they deserve. Emphasizing the ethical problems allows more detailed analytical treatment of the issues and, hopefully, encourages development of a way of thinking about them that managers can use.

The separation of operating and ethical decisions is artificial because problems in the real world do not necessarily come with neat labels attached: here is a finance problem; here is a marketing problem; and now, an ethical problem. Managers may categorize the issues by functional area or break up a complex problem into components such as those mentioned. Usually, however, policy issues and decisions are multifaceted and simultaneously may have financial, marketing, and maybe production components. They also may have ethical dimensions that managers should consider. However, in considering a typical complex problem with more than one dimension, the ethical dimension may be overlooked.

If situations did come with labels on them, a person could apply the techniques and concepts he or she had learned, such as net present value or market segmentation, to arrive at a decision. What would happen when the problem labeled "ethical dilemma" arrived? A manager probably would be in a quandary because he or she most likely would not have a way of analyzing, let alone solving, this type of problem. The decision-making tools for this type of situation probably would be missing. Business schools, traditionally, have not emphasized the teaching of ethics as rigorously as they have the teaching of finance or marketing, for example. Business students and managers generally have not been trained to think about ethical issues as they have been trained in the frameworks and techniques for functional areas of specialization.

One of the first things managers often do when they encounter an ethical problem is avoid it through the process of rationalization. They may focus on some other aspect of the problem. They might transform the ethical problem into some other type of problem — a legal or accounting problem, for instance. The reasoning seems to be that so long as one is behaving legally, or in accordance with accepted accounting practices, for example, nothing else is required. As is discussed later, compliance with laws and professional regulations is probably a minimum requirement for responsible managers.

Another avoidance behavior is to see the problem as only one small piece of a larger puzzle and to assume that someone higher up in the organization must be looking after any unusual aspects, such as ethical considerations. Alternatively, the decision maker might turn it into someone else's problem — perhaps a customer, supplier, or person in higher authority — with the comment that "I am following my boss's orders" or "my customer's instructions." When a customer asks for a falsified invoice on imported goods for his records with the difference deposited in a bank outside his or her country, and you provide this "service," is it only the customer's behavior that is questionable?

Rationalizing one's behavior by transforming an ethical problem into another type, or assuming responsibility for only one specific technical component of the issue, or claiming it is someone else's problem gives one the feeling of being absolved from culpability by putting the burden of responsibility elsewhere.

Who is responsible for ensuring ethical behavior? The authors believe that corporations have a responsibility to make it clear to their employees what behavior is expected from them. This means that executives in headquarters have a responsibility, not just for their own behavior, but for providing guidance to subordinates. However, the person on the spot facing the decision is ultimately responsible for his or her own behavior, even if there is no guidance from headquarters.

Ethical questions can arise in many areas of operations: the type of products produced, marketing and advertising practices, business conduct in countries where physical security is a consideration, hiring and promotion practices in countries where discrimination and racism exist, and requests for payments to secure contracts or sales. As an example, one could look at attempts by the United States government to open up markets in Southeast Asia for North American cigarette manufacturers. Should the government spend money to combat smoking in the United States while also spending it to promote cigarette exports to other countries? One side argues that the United States is exporting death and disease to the developing world.[1] The other side counters that cigarettes are manufactured and sold in countries such as Thailand; therefore American manufacturers would not be introducing these items for the first time. Manufacturing and selling cigarettes is not illegal in Thailand, and American companies should have equal access to the market.[2] But, what about the United States government's attempts to try to change Thai laws that restrict or ban cigarette advertising?[3] Is this acceptable or is it going too far?

At the company level, what obligations should a corporation have regarding advertising in other countries? Should the company follow the local laws even if they are less restrictive than at home, or would there be a responsibility to advertise that cigarette smoking is hazardous to your health and include all warnings required in the United States? All the questions regarding exporting and advertising cigarettes could be treated simply as issues in international trade, or marketing and advertising, if one chose. To do so, however, is to address only part of the question.

Situations in which physical security could be a problem may present ethical issues for managers and employees. Consider a situation in which British expatriate women working in the Middle East training center of a North American–based bank found themselves. They were en route to conduct a training program in Lagos, Nigeria, and were supposed to be met by one of the bank's local staff who would assist them through the hazards presented by the customs authorities at the airport. When the local staff member failed to appear, the women felt forced to pay bribes to bring legitimate training materials and equipment into the country. Soon after paying the money, their taxi was stopped at the darkened perimeter of the airport and machine guns were jabbed at them through the windows by uniformed men. The women were "shaken down" again and felt very vulnerable, particularly with no foreign currency left. After repeatedly showing their documents, denying that they were violating any laws, and playing dumb about the purpose of the delay, the accusing questions, and the threatening gestures, they were finally permitted to pass.

The women were deeply shaken by the experience and vowed never to travel into that country alone again. What responsibility did the local management bear for abandoning them? And what was the ethical responsibility of the experienced managers for whom the women worked who sent them into such a situation so ill prepared? What is a manager's responsibility regarding the implementation of his or her decisions, particularly when the specific action has to be taken by another person?

Discrimination or racism may be deeply rooted in the history and cultures of a country and may be firmly ensconced in a country's laws. In South Africa, the policies of many corporations appear to have lagged behind the views of the broader society where their headquarters operations are located.[4] Since many companies in the United States were only slowly changing their domestic behavior in response to civil rights legislation, it is hardly surprising that their South African operations might not assume leading positions against apartheid. However, as public consciousness on these issues was raised in North America, and pressure for changes in multinational behavior in South Africa increased, some of the larger companies did become more assertive in providing changes in their subsidiaries in South Africa.

Two significant forces that emerged in the United States that accelerated such change in South Africa and caused many companies to adopt similar approaches came from outside the multinationals. The first was the emergence of pressure groups that used proxies at annual meetings to force the issue. These were often led by church groups that invested in the companies in order to apply such pressure. The second was a codification of acceptable behavior, the Sullivan Principles, named for the black minister who led their development. The idea was that if companies agreed to operate in South Africa in accordance with these principles, they would earn the right to be exempt from the pressure group tactics.

In hindsight, even these steps were not sufficient to bring substantial change, leading the Reverend Sullivan to change his position and advocate withdrawal. But unpopular policies of the South African government, political unrest, sanctions of Western countries, and an eroding economic climate finally influenced the multinationals' decisions. Now, many major corporations have divested or are divesting. Some, such as Kodak, even decided not to sell their products in the country. It may well have been the case that *no* corporate policies in and of themselves, no matter when instituted, would have been enough to change the tide of events in South Africa, but executives have an ethical responsibility to diligently address such issues.

There are countries where discrimination against indigenous ethnic and racial groups is not as obvious to the outside world as the situation in South Africa. This removes a significant external pressure for change from a corporation. However, the dilemma still remains and corporations need to develop operating policies for managing in these environments.

Many of the previous examples were drawn from experiences in developing countries. But it would be wrong to think that all ethical dilemmas will be found in the developing world. Ethical problems also arise in the United States and Canada. A case in point involves situations of extraterritoriality, when the United States applies its laws beyond its own boundaries.

Extraterritoriality is the unilateral application of laws by a nation to the conduct of persons or corporations beyond the borders of that nation. This creates conflict with a second nation trying to enforce its laws over people or corporations residing within its territory. More simply stated, two governments claim jurisdiction over the same corporation and issue conflicting and mutually exclusive demands. Management faces a real dilemma! Which law should it break since it cannot obey both? Beyond the legal question may be some ethical ones. Who will be asked or required to actually break the law and, thus, be subject to possible criminal charges and a jail sentence? How can anyone be expected to manage in such a no-win situation?

Although the United States is, perhaps, the country that most visibly applies its laws extraterritorially, it is not the only one. However, the size and importance of the United States consumer and financial markets attract corporations from all over the world and, thus, provide greater opportunity for such action. Case 22 in this book, "The Bank of Nova Scotia (Brady Subpoena)" is one example of the legal and ethical bind in which managers can find themselves. And this situation was almost repeated recently!

In mid-1990, the United States Senate attached a trade-ban amendment (the Mack Amendment) to a bill attempting to control the spread of chemical and biological weapons. The amendment would have made it illegal for any subsidiary of a United States company, including subsidiaries in Canada, to do business with Cuba. Canada did not have the same restriction or concern with trade with Cuba as the United States did, and Canadian companies could do business there. The Canadian government called this amendment an intrusion into Canadian sovereignty that it found "clearly unacceptable" and issued an order forcing these Canadian firms (Canadian because they are incorporated in and resident in Canada) to ignore the United States legislation.[5] Ultimately, President Bush pocket vetoed the bill[6] and the amendment died with it, at least temporarily.

Another dilemma that executives may encounter is a request for a bribe. How should this situation be handled? The issue of bribery has many facets and a more detailed discussion on the topic can be found in Reading 9, "Bribery in International Business: Whose Problem Is It?"

The cases in this part of the book deal with payoffs, such as bribery and pressure to change bid evaluations, and the complications arising from the extraterritorial application of laws. In each case, the reader will have to develop his or her own stance on these difficult issues. The reader is encouraged to think carefully about the problems depicted in the cases and to develop reasoned positions. You may find yourself in a similar situation someday, and you will have to make the decision for real. It is hoped that by working through the decisions in these cases now, you will be better able to deal with similar decisions later.

As the authors encountered ethical dilemmas themselves or heard about others who had experienced them, they wrote cases and developed a managerial framework for thinking about and analyzing the problems. The framework to be presented is not a complete or definitive treatment of the topic of ethics, nor are the cases an exhaustive set of issues that one might face in international business, but together they provide a practical and useful way to address the topic.

ETHICAL VERSUS LEGAL BEHAVIOR

Ethics is the study of morals and systems of morality, or principles of conduct. The study of ethics is concerned with the right or wrong and the should's or should not's of human decisions and actions. This does not mean that all questions of right and wrong are ethical issues, however. There is right and wrong associated with rules of etiquette — for example, in which hand to hold your knife and fork; in the use of language and rules of grammar; and in making a computer work. Holding a fork in the wrong hand or speaking ungrammatically does not constitute unethical behavior.

The ethical, or moral, frame of reference is concerned with human behavior in society and with the *relationships*, *duties*, and *obligations* between people, groups, and organizations. It is concerned with *human consequences* associated with decisions and actions, not solely profits, more sophisticated technology, or larger market share. In this concern for human outcomes it differs from other prespectives such as financial, marketing, accounting, or legal. An ethical perspective requires one to extend *consideration beyond one's own self-interest* (or that of one's company) to consider the interests of a wider community of people including employees, customers, suppliers, the general public, or even foreign governments. It also advocates behaving according to what would be considered better or *higher standards of conduct*, not necessarily the minimum acceptable by law, for example.

The question always arises as to the distinction between legal and ethical behavior. If one acts legally, in accordance with laws, is that not sufficient? Not all of society's norms regarding moral behavior have been codified, or made into law. There can, therefore, be many instances of questionable behavior that are not illegal.[7] It would seem that acting legally is the minimum required behavior for executives. However, society relies on more than laws to function effectively in many spheres of endeavor. In business, trust is essential also. Finally, it should also be recognized that not all laws are moral.

Henderson has provided a useful way to think about the relationship between ethical and legal behavior.[8] He created a matrix based on whether an action was legal or illegal, and ethical or unethical, similar to that shown in Figure 1.

Assuming that executives want to act legally and ethically (Quadrant 4) and want to avoid making decisions, or acting in ways, that are illegal and unethical (Quadrant 2), the decisions that create dilemmas are the ones that fall into Quadrants 1 and 3. For example, consider the decision of a manager of a chemical company who refuses a promotion of a pregnant woman to an area of the company where she would be exposed to toxic chemicals that could damage her child. The manager probably would be acting ethically, but illegally. Maybe he could solve the problem by delaying the promotion, if that was possible. This simple example

FIGURE 1   **Framework for Classifying Behavior**

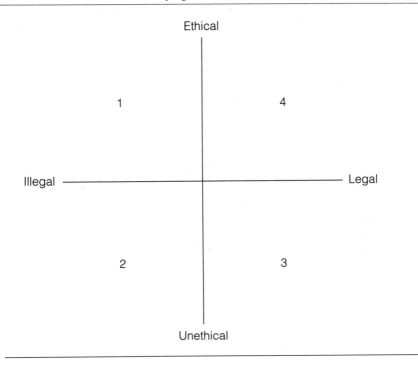

illustrates that a decision can be ethical but not legal, and also that there may be solutions that allow a win-win outcome in which the decision is legal and ethical because of the way it was made.

In Quadrant 3 there would be situations like the marketing of infant formula in developing countries. This activity is not illegal, but a vote of the United Nations [regarding infant formula] declared it unethical.[9] Similarly, apartheid may be legal in South Africa, but it is not ethical. Corporations operating there and following laws that discriminate against black Africans need to consider this distinction carefully.

The last example raises the question about whose laws and values should be followed when there are differences. Although it might seem the authors are avoiding answers, they believe that these are questions each person and company need to answer for themselves. The challenge is to find ways of operating that are consistent with local laws and high standards of conduct. The authors believe that this goal is attainable with thorough analysis and carefully considered action. In those situations where such a win-win outcome is not possible there is always the option of choosing not to operate in that environment. The decision to walk away and lose the business may seem naive, but the authors have met and interviewed a number of executives of very successful companies that have done just that. One described how his company turned down a $50 million consulting contract in Latin America because there was no way to avoid paying a bribe to a government official. Another explained that in his experience if a company developed a reputation for acting ethically it was not usually subjected to unethical demands. Each person has to make his or her own decision and live with the consequences of their actions. The information in the next sections is designed to help in the decision-making process.

 ETHICAL FRAMEWORK[10]

Moral philosophers have developed frameworks for thinking about moral issues and for analyzing ethical problems, but those frameworks generally have not been included in international business curricula. The authors investigated various frameworks for analyzing ethical problems and quickly learned that there are conflicting positions and prescriptions among them. In classes they observed that people advocated actions that represented some of the major frameworks, but without understanding the foundations or strengths and weaknesses of their positions. Consider the following discussion.

> *Person X:* "If we don't pay what he is asking we will lose the contract and people back home will lose jobs. Is that ethical when people can't feed their families?"
> *Person Y:* "I don't care. What you are suggesting is absolutely wrong."
> *Person Z:* "Now hold on, it doesn't seem to be against the rules there. It is different in that culture. Everyone is doing it. They need the extra money to support their families. Besides, we should not impose our system of morality on other cultures."

The reader may have heard or taken part in similar exchanges. These people may not realize it, but they are engaged in a discussion of moral philosophy. It is the type of discussion that tends to excite emotions and generate heat and argument, rather than provide insight and a thoughtful course of action.

The authors hope to make people aware of the ethical frameworks behind the positions they espouse and link everyday reasoning to three different philosophical positions in a way that is instructive and useful. In the brief exchange just portrayed, one sees elements of Kant's categorical imperative, utilitarianism, and cultural relativism. Since the reader may likely take part in similar discussions (or arguments) at some time in his or her career, the authors think that some knowledge of these three frameworks will be useful. The frameworks are very commonly used, which is why they were chosen.

The main categories of ethical theories can be divided into consequential or teleological theories, which focus on the consequences, outcomes, or results of decisions and behavior; rule-based, or deontological, theories, which focus on moral obligations, duties, and rights; and cultural theories, which emphasize cultural differences in standards of behavior. These are discussed briefly here.

Consequential Theories

Consequential theories focus on the goals, end results, and/or consequences of decisions and actions. They are concerned with doing the maximum amount of "good" and the minimum amount of "harm." Utilitarianism is the most widely used example of this type of moral framework. It suggests doing the best for the greatest number of people. Another example is acting in a way so as to provide more net utility than an alternative act. It essentially is an economic, cost-benefit approach to ethical decision making. If the benefits outweigh the costs, then that course of action is indicated. The limitations of this approach are that it is difficult or impossible to identify and account for all the costs and benefits; and since people have different utility curves how does one decide whose curve should be used? In real life, how does one compute this utility curve? Finally, in an effort to weigh the costs and benefits, one relies on quantitative data, usually economic data, and many important variables that should be considered are not quantifiable and, therefore, often ignored.

Rule-Based Theories

Rule-based theories include both absolute, or universal, theories and conditional theories. The emphasis of these theories is on duty, obligations, and rights. For example, if an employee follows orders or performs a certain task, management has an obligation to ensure that the task is not illegal or harmful to that person's health. People in power have a responsibility to protect the rights of the less powerful. These theories are concerned with the universal should's and ought's of human existence — the rules that should guide all people's decision making and behavior wherever they are.

One of the best-known absolute theories is the categorical imperative of Immanuel Kant. Whereas utilitarianism takes a group or societal perspective, the categorical imperative has a more individualistic focus: individuals should be treated with respect and dignity as an end in itself; they should not be used simply as a means to an end. A person should not be done harm, even if the ultimate end is good. The criteria should be applied consistently to everyone. One of the questions to ask is "If I were in the other person's (or group's or organization's) position would I be willing for them to make the same decision for the same reasons that I am going to make?"

A variation of the absolute theories is fundamentalism. In this case, the rules may come from a book like the Bible, Koran, or Torah. In these systems, one is dealing with an authoritative, divine wisdom that has been revealed through prophets. The Golden Rule (Do unto others as you would have them do unto you) would fall into this category. Difficult questions arise when considering which book or prophet to follow and whose interpretation of the chosen book to use. The books are usually interpreted by priests, mullahs, or rabbis who may reflect an elite or possibly isolated group. There can be conflicting interpretations within the same religion as well. Also, the interpretations may be inconsistent with current social and environmental circumstances, as well as large segments of a society. The rules that people choose to follow also can be secular, as well as religious, as in the case of Nazi Germany.

One potential shortcoming of these type of prescriptions is that they permit one to claim that one is not responsible for his or her own behavior: "I was just following orders!" is a common excuse. The end result may be the same — one does not have to think for oneself and make a moral judgment, but can avoid it by claiming to be following a higher authority. As far as secular orders are concerned, the war crimes trials after World War II established that following orders was not an acceptable legal defense for the atrocities committed.

Cultural Theories

With cultural theories, local standards prevail. Cultural relativism is interpreted to mean that there is no one right way; in other words, people should not impose their values and standards on others. The reasoning behind the arguments usually is that we should behave as the locals do. The familiar expression tells us, "When in Rome do as the Romans do." One problem, however, comes from the fact that the local people we are encouraged to emulate may not necessarily be the most exemplary. In one's own culture, it is known that people exhibit different standards of behavior. Does that mean we should advocate that businesspeople coming to the United States act like the people convicted in the Wall Street trading scandals, just because those people are Americans? Adopting this philosophy can encourage denial of accountability and the avoidance of moral choice. Using arguments based on this philosophy, the morality of bribes or actions of repressive regimes, for example, does not have to be examined very closely. These theories are summarized in Figure 2.

How does one choose among these conflicting theories? There is not a simple answer to the question and the authors cannot tell the reader what personal values he or she should hold. Perry studied and described the process of intellectual and ethical development, which provides a partial answer, however. Individuals progress through a series of stages toward higher and more complex levels of ethical development.[11] In Perry's words,[12]

> The scheme begins with those simplistic forms in which a person construes his world in unqualified polar terms of absolute right-wrong, good-bad; it ends with those complex forms through which he undertakes to affirm his own commitments in a world of contingent knowledge and relative values.

The most basic level[13] is *dualism*, in which a dualistic structure of the world is assumed or taken for granted. According to this world view there is right and wrong, good and bad, we and they. These positions are defined from one's own

FIGURE 2 Analytical Frameworks

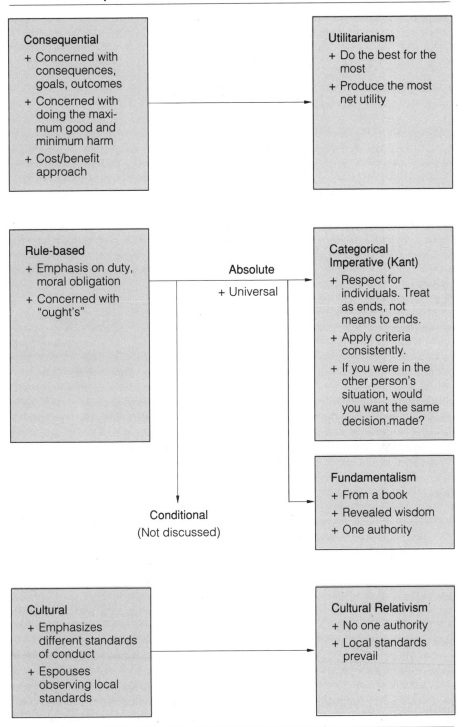

perspective based on membership in a group and belief in and adherence to a common set of traditional beliefs. There is a major transition to the next level, *relativism*, where people begin to see and understand the importance of context, and that knowledge and values are relative. Different people in different parts of the world think and believe differently as we have already seen in earlier parts of this book. Hofstede, in the preface to his book, *Culture's Consequences*,[14] quotes Blaise Pascal to illustrate this point: "There are truths on this side of the Pyrénées which are falsehoods on the other."

The highest level of development is *commitment in relativism* in which a person understands the relativistic nature of the world, but makes a commitment to a set of values, beliefs, and a way of behaving within this expanded world view. The goal is to arrive at the point where one assumes responsibility for one's own actions and decisions based upon careful consideration and the application of the "essential tools of moral reasoning — *deliberation* and *justification*.[15] The dilemma is that progression to this stage is not automatic or guaranteed, and people may become delayed in their development or even stuck in the earlier stages.

SOME GUIDELINES TO CONSIDER

Gandz and Hayes[16] suggested some objectives for teaching business ethics: creating an *awareness* of the ethical components of the decision; *legitimizing* the consideration of ethical issues in the decision process; *analyzing* the ethical components with some framework; and *applying* this technique of ethical analysis to decision situations. To provide a framework for analysis, a series of diagnostic questions and some recommendations are presented. These can be applied to the case situations in the book and, the authors hope, can serve as a guide in the future.

Managers have multiple interests that they must consider because they are embedded in a network of relationships as depicted in Figure 3. The interests, goals and values of the various actors in any situation can potentially conflict. Identifying these relationships helps in structuring one's analysis.

1. Who are the stakeholders that have an interest in, or will be affected by, the decision: shareholders, the home country government, host country governments, customers, suppliers, employees, unions? There are probably others that could be added to that list, but the point is to comprehensively identify the stakeholders and their interests.

2. What are the responsibilities and obligations to these stakeholders? Identify the responsibilities that the organization has, but do not overlook the ones that you, personally, might have to external stakeholders and/or to your own organization.

For example, a decision about whether or not to shut down operations in a country may involve ethical issues. Take the situation of an insurance company selling life insurance in Uganda during a period of civil war.[17] The company had been told years earlier that its operation was nationalized and now was

FIGURE 3   A Manager's Context

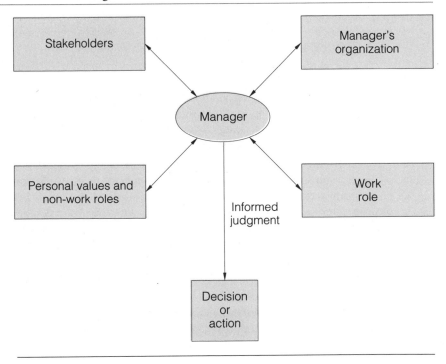

having its ownership restored. The branch in Uganda was not profitable. The decision to shut down, from a profit-and-loss perspective, may have been easy to make, but what were the company's responsibilities to their managers, who ran the company in their interest after it had been nationalized and who were concerned about possible violence to field personnel and to themselves if the company closed its operations? And what were its obligations to its policyholders? The issue may not be whether the company should shut down, but how it should handle its responsibilities, obligations, and commitments to its employees and customers, as well as to its shareholders.

It is important to remember that a company has multiple groups of stakeholders in addition to the investors in the business, and executives need to be clear about their responsibilities and obligations to all these groups. It is easy to ignore some of them, particularly when they are thousands of miles away and probably cannot exert any pressure on the company to behave in their interests. The ethical perspective advocates giving careful consideration to these types of issues and not avoiding them or pretending that they do not exist.

3. In addition to the economic, management, and legal decisions, are there any ethical issues that need to be considered? Be careful not to fall into the trap of transforming ethical decisions into some other type.

4. Do you have the best information possible and the *facts*? Avoid fuzzy thinking. Take the time to get the facts, all of them. Avoid using, or being swayed by, hearsay or unsubstantiated assertions. These are statements that have no specifics to go with them: "Everybody is doing it," "We'll lose business if we don't do it," or "It's a normal practice." When you hear statements like these, push for the analysis and details. Often, you may find that they are unsubstantiated assertions parading as analysis.

5. What assumptions are being made? What ethical framework is being invoked? Whose utility is being maximized? Whose values are being used? Consider multiple (including opposing) viewpoints, but examine them carefully. Weigh the costs and benefits to all stakeholders.

6. Are there options that have not been identified? In trying to identify action possibilities, avoid characterizing decisions to be made using false dichotomies, either/or characterizations that do not have to be win/lose positions. For example, the statement "We need to pay the bribe or lose the business" portrays the situation as win/lose, but it may not be. These positions often develop because the initial analysis was not as complete as it could have been. This mind-set can limit the action possibilities open to the manager. Strive for a win/win situation. Is there a way to solve the problem that satisfies all parties and allows you to fulfill your obligations?

7. How should you, as an individual, act? Is this different from your role as a manager? If there is a conflict, try to resolve it.

8. Do not let people put the monkey on your back. Do not accept responsibility for decisions that are not your responsibility. Some people will try to find a scapegoat to make a particularly difficult, possibly illegal or unethical decision. Do not let them use you. How do you protect yourself? You could ask for it in writing, or suggest an open meeting with other people present to discuss it.

9. Do not avoid making ethical decisions on issues that are your responsibility.

10. Try to avoid dependent relations. If you are too dependent on a particular customer, or if you need the job too badly, you are in a position where you may not have the power to maintain your standards. You may want to be prepared to walk away from these situations.

11. Do not use "culture" as an excuse for not trying to do things the proper way. Just because the local company does not treat its toxic waste properly does not mean that it is acting as a model of behavior for that culture. Also, beware of confusing culture and an individual's personality and character. If a person is asking for something that is illegal, or unethical, that tells you something about that person's character, not necessarily about his or her culture.

12. Some decision criteria to consider include: do the best for all involved stakeholders; fulfill obligations; observe laws and contracts; do not use deception; and avoid knowingly doing harm (physical, psychological, economic, or social).

13. Remember that there can be personal consequences associated with your decision. People have lost their jobs because someone higher in the organization needed a scapegoat, and others have gone to jail for their actions. Look after the interests of your company in your role as manager, but look after your own interests also. You may be the only one that does!

14. Consider the "billboard" or the "light-of-day" tests. When you drive to work in the morning would you be happy to see your decision or action prominently announced on a large billboard for everyone to read and to know about? Or alternatively, would you be willing to discuss your actions in a meeting where you would be subject to questions and scutiny and have to justify them? Would your actions look as reasonable in the light of day as they did when the decision was made behind closed doors?

15. Finally, maintain high standards! When in Rome do as the *better* Romans do.

Notes

1. Philip Smucker, "U.S. Sending Marlboro Man to Rope in Asian Smokers," *The Globe and Mail*, Toronto, Ontario, May 29, 1990. This statement was attributed to Senator Edward Kennedy.
2. Smucker, "U.S. Sending Marlboro Man to Rope in Asian Smokers."
3. Ibid.
4. It should be noted that in February 1991 South African President F. W. de Klerk pledged to eliminate some key components of apartheid by abolishing laws classifying people by race and regulating where they can live and own land. The announcement was not unanimously welcomed in South Africa, however, and right-wing conservatives vowed to fight the move. In June 1991, the Population Registration Act was repealed.
5. Ross Howard, "Branch plants ordered to ignore U.S. bill banning trade with Cuba," *The Globe and Mail*, Toronto, Ontario, November 1, 1990.
6. "Bush's Sanctions Veto snubs Foreign Relations Leaders," *Congressional Quarterly*, (November 24, 1990): 3932.
7. To see examples of this distinction in action in a large Wall Street firm in the 1980s read *Liar's Poker* by Michael Lewis (Penguin Books, 1989).
8. Verne E. Henderson, "The Ethical Side of Enterprise," *Sloan Management Review* (Spring 1982): 37–47.
9. Ibid.
10. This section draws on the following works: Jeffery Gandz and Nadine Hayes, "Teaching Business Ethics," Working Paper No. 86-17R, October, 1986, School of Business Administration, The University of Western Ontario; Tad Tuleja, *Beyond the Bottom Line*, (New York: Penguin Books, 1985); John B. Matthews, Kenneth E. Goodpaster, Laura Nash, *Policies and Persons: A Casebook in Business Ethics* (New York: McGraw-Hill, 1985).
11. William G. Perry, Jr., *Forms of Intellectual and Ethical Development in the College Years: A Scheme*, (New York: Holt, Rinehart & Winston, 1970).
12. Ibid., 3.
13. In Perry's full scheme there are nine stages. The authors have chosen to use only the three major positions in the scheme.

14. Geert Hofstede, *Culture's Consequences*, (Beverly Hills: Sage Publications, 1980).
15. Jeffrey Gandz and Nadine Hayes, "Teaching Business Ethics," *Journal of Business Ethics* 7 (1988): 659.
16. Ibid.
17. "The Europa Insurance Company," David Burgoyne and Henry Lane; Case 9-84-C049, School of Business Administration, The University of Western Ontario.

READING 9

Bribery in International Business: Whose Problem Is It?

Henry W. Lane and Donald G. Simpson

Bribery is a frequently discussed problem in international business. This article looks at the problem from the North American and from the developing country perspective. It describes and analyzes specific cases and highlights recurring patterns of behavior.

The article is based on the experiences of the authors, who have been promoting business in the developing world. In addition to ethical considerations involved with bribery, there are some very practical reasons for not engaging in the practice. There are also real barriers to establishing the relationships necessary to avoid the practice yet continue doing business.

INTRODUCTION

No discussion of problems in international business seems complete without reference to familiar complaints about the questionable business practices North American executives encounter in foreign countries, particularly developing nations. Beliefs about the pervasiveness of dishonesty and the necessity of engaging in such practices as bribery vary widely however, and these differences often lead to vigorous discussions that generate more heat than light. Pragmatists or "realists" may take the attitude that "international business is a rough game and no place for the naive idealist or the fainthearted. Your competitors use bribes and unless you are willing to meet this standard, competitive practice you will lose business and, ultimately, jobs for workers at home. Besides, it is an accepted business practice in those countries, and when you are in Rome you have to do as the Romans do." "Moralists," on the other hand, believe that cultural relativity is no excuse for unethical behavior. "As Canadians or Americans we should uphold our legal and ethical standards anywhere in the world; and any good American or Canadian knows that bribery, by any euphemism, is unethical and wrong. Bribery increases a product's cost and often is used to secure import licenses for products that no longer can be sold in the developed world. Such corrupting practices also contribute to the moral disintegration of individuals and eventually societies."

The foregoing comments represent extreme polar positions but we are not using these stereotypes to create a "straw man" or a false dichotomy about attitudes toward practices such as bribery. These extreme viewpoints, or minor variations of them, will be encountered frequently as one meets executives who have experience in developing countries. Some "realists" and "moralists" undoubtedly are firm believers in their positions, but many other executives probably gravitate toward one of the poles becaue they have not found a realistic alternative approach to thinking about the issue of bribery, never mind finding an answer to the problem.

The impetus for this article came from discussions with executives and government officials in Canada and in some developing nations about whether a North American company could conduct business successfully in developing countries without engaging in what would be considered unethical or illegal practices. It was apparent from these talks that the question was an important one and of concern to business executives, but not much practical, relevant information existed on the issue. There was consensus on two points: first, there are a lot of myths surrounding the issue of payoffs and, second, if anyone had some insights into the problem, executives would appreciate hearing them.

In this article we would like to share what we have learned about the issue during the two years we have been promoting business (licensing agreements, management contracts, joint ventures) between Canadian and African companies. Our intention is not to present a comprehensive treatment of the subject of bribery nor a treatise on ethical behavior. Our intention is to present a practical discussion of some dimensions of the problem based on our experience, discussions and, in some cases investigation of specific incidents.

THE PROBLEM IS MULTIFACETED

It can be misleading to talk abut bribery in global terms without considering some situational specifics such as country, type of business, and company. Our discussions with managers indicate that the payoff problem is more prevalent in some countries than in others. Executives with extensive experience probably could rank countries on a scale reflecting the seriousness of the problem. Also, some industries are probably more susceptible to payoff requests than others. Large construction projects, turnkey capital projects, and large commodity or equipment contracts are likely to be most vulnerable because the scale of the venture may permit the easy disguise of payoffs, and because an individual, or small group of people, may be in a strategic position to approve or disapprove the project. These projects or contracts are undoubtedly obvious targets also because the stakes are high, the competition vigorous, and the possibility that some competitors may engage in payoffs increased. Finally, some companies may be more vulnerable due to a relative lack of bargaining power or because they have no policies to guide them in these situations. If the product or technology is unique, or clearly superior, and it is needed, the company is in a relatively strong position to resist the pressure. Similarly, those firms with effective operational policies against payoffs are in a position of strength. Many senior executives have stated, with pride, that their companies have reputations for not making payoffs and, therefore, are not asked for them. These were executives of large, successful firms that also had chosen not to work in some countries where they could not operate comfortably. These executives often backed up their claims with specific examples in which they walked away from apparently lucrative deals where a payoff was a requirement.

Two other elements of the situational context of a payoff situation that vary are the subtlety of the demand and the amount of money involved. All payoff situations are not straightforward and unambiguous, which may make a clear response more difficult. Consider, for example, the case of a company that was encouraged to change its evaluation of bids for a large construction project. Some host country agencies were embarrassed by the evaluation results since Company X, from the country providing significant financing for the project, was ranked a distant third. The agencies sought a reevaluation on questionable technicalities. The changes were considered but the ranking remained the same. At this point pressure began to build. Phone calls were made berating the firm for delaying the project and hinting that the large follow-on contract, for which it had the inside track, was in jeopardy. No one ever said make Company X the winner or you lose the follow-on.

Although no money was to change hands, this situation was similar to a payoff request in that the company was being asked to alter its standard for acceptable business practices for an implied future benefit. The interpretation of the "request," the response, and the consequences, were left entirely to the company's management. Refusal to change may mean losing a big contract, but giving in does not guarantee the follow-on and you leave the company vulnerable to further demands. In ambiguous situations factors such as corporate policies and the company's financial strength and its need for the contract enter into the decision. In this case the company had firm beliefs about what constituted professional standards and did not desperately need the follow-on contract. Although it refused to change, another company might find itself in a dilemma, give in to the pressure, and rationalize its behavior.

Finally, payoffs range in size from the small payments that may help getting through customs without a hassle up to the multimillion dollar bribes that make headlines and embarrass governments. The payoff situations we discuss in this article are more significant than the former, but much smaller and far less dramatic than the latter. These middle-range payoffs (tens of thousands of dollars) may pose a problem for corporations. They are too big to be ignored but possibly not big enough to be referred to corporate headquarters unless the firm has clear guidelines on the subject. Regional executives or lower level-managers may be deciding whether or not these "facilitating payments" are just another cost of doing business in the developing world.

ON THE OUTSIDE LOOKING IN
(THE NORTH AMERICAN PERSPECTIVE)

"It's a corrupt, payoff society. The problem has spread to all levels. On the face it looks good, but underneath it's rotten." Comments such as these are often made by expatriate businesspeople and government officials alike. The North American executive may arrive in a Third World country with a stereotype of corrupt officials and is presented with the foregoing analysis by people-on-the-spot who, he or she feels, should know the situation best. His or her fears are confirmed.

This scenario may be familiar to some readers. It is very real to us because we have gone through that process. Two cases provide examples of the stories a businessperson may likely be told in support of the dismal analysis.

> *The New Venture:* Company Y, a wholly owned subsidiary of a European multinational, wished to manufacture a new product for export. Government permission was required and Company Y submitted the necessary applications. Sometime later one of Company Y's executives (a local national) informed the Managing Director that the application was approved and the consultant's fee must be paid. The Managing Director knew nothing about a consultant or such a fee. The executive took his boss to a meeting with the consultant—a government official who sat on the application review committee. Both the consultant and the executive claimed to remember the initial meeting at which agreement was reached on the $10,000 fee. A few days later the Managing Director attended a cocktail party at the home of a high-ranking official in the same agency. This official recommended that the fee be paid. The Managing Director decided against paying the fee and the project ran into unexpected delays. At this point the Managing Director asked the parent company's legal department for help. Besides the delay, the situation was creating a problem between the Managing Director and his executives as well as affecting the rest of the company. He initially advised against payment but after watching the company suffer, acquiesced with the approval of the parent company. The fee was renegotiated downward and the consultant paid. What was the result? Nothing! The project was not approved.

> *The Big Sale:* Company Z, which sold expensive equipment, established a relationship with a well-placed government official on the first trip to the country. This official, and some other nationals, assured Company Z representatives that they would have no trouble getting the contract. On leaving the country, Company Z representatives had a letter of intent to purchase the equipment. On the second trip Company Z representatives brought the detailed technical specifications for a certain department head to approve. The department head refused to approve the specifications and further efforts to have the government honor its promise failed. The deal fell through. Company Z's analysis of the situation, which became common knowledge in business and government circles, was that a competitor paid the department head to approve its equipment and that the government reneged on its obligation to purchase Company Z equipment.

While in the country, the visiting executive may even have met Company Z's agent in the "Big Sale," who confirms the story. Corruption is rampant, and in the particular case of the "Big Sale" he claims to know that the department head received the money and from whom. The case is closed! An honest North American company cannot function in this environment—or so it seems.

ON THE INSIDE LOOKING OUT
(THE DEVELOPING COUNTRY'S
PERSPECTIVE)

During his visit the executive may have met only a few nationals selected by his company or government representatives. He probably has not discussed bribery with them because of its sensitive nature. If the businesspeople and the officials he met were dishonest, they would not admit it; if they were honest he probably felt they would resent the discussion. Also, he may not have had enough time to establish the type of relationship in which the subject could be discussed frankly. It is almost certain that he did not speak with the people in the government agencies who allegedly took the payoffs. What would he say if he did meet them? And more than likely he would not be able to get an appointment with them if he did want to pursue the matter further. So the executive is convinced that corruption is widespread having heard only one side of the horror stories.

Had the visitor been able to investigate the viewpoints of the nationals what might he have heard? "I would like to find a person from the developed world that I can trust. You people brought corruption here. We learned the concept from you. You want to win all the time, and you are impatient so you bribe. You offer bribes to the local people and complain that business is impossible without bribing."

Comments like these are made by local businesspeople and government officials alike. If the visiting executive heard these comments he would be confused and would wonder whether or not these people were talking about the same country. Although skeptical, his confidence in the accuracy of his initial assessment would have been called into question. Had he been able to stay longer in the country, he might have met an old friend who knew the department head who allegedly was paid off in the Big Sale. His friend would have made arrangements for the visitor to hear the other side of the story.

The Big Sale Revisited: After the representatives of Company Z received what they described as a letter of intent to purchase the equipment they returned home. On the second visit they had to deal with the department head to receive his approval for the technical specifications.

At the meeting they told the department head that he need not worry about the details and just sign off on the necessary documents. If he had any questions regarding the equipment he could inspect it in two weeks time in their home country. The department head's initial responses were: (1) he would not rubber stamp anything, and (2) how could this complex equipment which was supposedly being custom made for his country's needs be inspected in two weeks when he had not yet approved the specifications.

As he reviewed the specifications he noticed a significant technical error and brought it to the attention of Company Z's representatives. They became upset with his "interference" and inferred that they would use their connections in high places to ensure his compliance. When asked again to sign the documents he refused, and the company reps left saying that they would have him removed from his job.

After this meeting the Premier of the country became involved and asked the company officials to appear before him. They arrived with the Premier's nephew for a meeting with the Premier and his top advisors. The Premier told his nephew that he had no business being there and directed him to leave. The company officials then had to face the Premier and his advisors alone.

The Premier asked if the company had a contract and that if it had, it would be honored. The company had to admit that it had no contract. As far as the Premier was concerned the issue was settled.

However, the case was not closed for the Company Z representatives. They felt they had been promised the deal and that the department had reneged. They felt that someone had paid off the department head and they were quite bitter. In discussions with their local embassy officials and with government officials at home they presented their analysis of the situation. The result was strained relations and the department head got a reputation for being dishonest.

Well, the other side of the story certainly has different implications about whose behavior may be considered questionable. The situation is now very confusing. Is the department head honest or not? The executive's friend has known the department head for a long time and strongly believes he is honest; and some other expatriate government officials have basically corroborated the department head's perception of the matter. But the businesspeople and the government officials who first told the story seemed reputable and honest. Who should be believed? As the visiting executive has learned, you have to decide on the truth for yourself.

PATTERNS OF BEHAVIOR

The preceding vignettes illustrate our position that bribery and corruption is a problem for North American and Third World businesspeople alike. We also have observed two recurring behavioral patterns in these real, but disguised, situations. The first is the predisposition of the North American businessperson to accept the premise that bribery is the way of life in the developing world and a necessity in business transactions. The second behavioral pattern occurs in situations where payments are requested and made.

We believe that many executives visit Third World countries with an expectation to learn that bribery is a problem. This attitude likely stems from a number of sources. First, in many cases it may be true. In some countries it may be impossible to complete a transaction without a bribe and the horror stories about the widespread disappearance of honesty are valid. However, in some instances the expectations are conditioned by the "conventional wisdom" available in international business circles. This conventional wisdom develops from situations like the ones we have described. As these situations are passed from individual to individual, accuracy may diminish and facts be forgotten. This is not done intentionally but happens since it is rare that the story tellers have the complete story or all the facts. Unverified stories of bribery and corruption circulate through the business and government communities and often become accepted as true and factual. The obvious solution, and difficulty, is learning how to distinguish fact from fiction.

Another factor influencing initial expectations are the unfavorable impressions of developing countries and their citizens that are picked up from the media. Often only the sensational, and negative, news items from these countries are reported in North America. We learn of bombings, attacks on journalists and tourists, alleged (and real) coup d'états, and major scandals. These "current events" and the "conventional wisdom" combined with an executive's probable lack of knowledge of the history, culture, legal systems, or economic conditions of a country all contribute to the development of unfavorable stereotypes that predispose the executive toward readily accepting reports that confirm his already drawn conclusions: all Latin American or African countries, for example, are the same and corruption is to be expected.

The stories that constitute "evidence" of corruption may be tales of bribery like the "New Venture" or the "Big Sale," or they may take other forms. The story we have heard most often has the "protect yourself from your local partner" theme. It goes like this: "If you are going to invest in this country, particularly in a joint venture, you have to find a way to protect yourself from your partner. He is likely to strip all the company's assets and leave you nothing but a skeleton. Just look what happened to Company A."

On hearing the "evidence," particularly from expatriates in the foreign country, a visiting businessperson most likely accepts it without further investigation. He has forgotten the old adage about there being two sides to every story. His conclusion and conviction are most likely based on incomplete and biased data.

Is there another viewpoint? Certainly! Many nationals have expressed it to us: "The Europeans and North Americans have been taking advantage of us for decades, even centuries. The multinationals establish a joint venture and then strip the local company bare through transfer pricing, management fees, and royalties based on a percentage of sales rather than profits. They have no interest in the profitability of the company or its long-term development."

The situation is ironic. Some local investors are desperately looking for an honest North American executive whom they can trust at the same time the North American is searching for them. Our experience indicates that this search process is neither straightforward, nor easy. And while the search continues, if it does, it is difficult for the North American to maintain a perspective on the situation and remember that there are locals who may share his values and who are equally concerned about unethical and illegal practices.

In summary, we would characterize the first observed pattern of behavior as a preparedness to accept "evidence" of corruption and the simultaneous failure to examine critically the "evidence" or its source.

The second behavioral pattern appears in the actual payoff process. The request very likely comes from a low- or middle-level bureaucrat who says that his boss must be paid for the project to be approved or for the sale to be finalized. Alternatively, it may be your agent who is providing similar counsel. In either case you are really not certain who is making the demand.

Next, the payoff is made. You give your contact the money, but you never really know where it goes.

Your expectations are obvious. You have approached this transaction from a perspective of economic rationality. You have provided a benefit and expect one in return. The project will be approved or the sale consummated.

The results, however, may be very different than expected. As in the case of the "New Venture," nothing may happen. The only outcome is indignation, anger, and perhaps the loss of a significant amount of money. Now is the time for action, but what recourse do you have? Can you complain? You may be guilty of bribing a government official. And, you certainly are reluctant to admit that you have been duped. Since your direct options are limited, your primary action may be to spread the word: "This is a corrupt, payoff society."

WHY DOES IT HAPPEN?

There are numerous explanations for corruption in developing nations. First, and most obvious is that some people are simply dishonest. A less pejorative explanation is that the cost of living in these countries may be high and salaries low. Very often a wage earner must provide for a large extended family. The businessperson is viewed opportunistically as a potential source of extra income to improve the standard of living. Finally, some nationals may believe strongly that they have a right to share some of the wealth controlled by multinational corporations.

Besides being familiar to many readers, these explanations all share another common characteristic. They all focus on "the other person" — the local national. Accepting that there may be some truth in the previous explanations, let us, however, turn our focus to the visiting North American to see what we find. We could find a greedy, dishonest expatriate hoping to make a killing. But, let us give this person the same benefit of the doubt we have accorded to the local nationals so far.

On closer examination we may find a situation in which the North American executives are vulnerable. They have entered an action vacuum and are at a serious disadvantage. Their lack of knowledge of systems and procedures, laws, institutions, and the people can put them in a dependent position. Unfamiliarity with the system and/or people makes effective, alternative action such as they could take at home difficult. A strong relationship with a reputable national could help significantly in this situation. Quite often the national knows how to fight the system and who to call in order to put pressure on the corrupt individual. This potential resource should not be dismissed lightly. Although the most powerful and experienced MNC's may also be able to apply this pressure, most of us must be realistic and recognize that no matter how important we think we are, we may not be among those handful of foreigners that can shake the local institutions.

Time also can be a factor. Often the lack of time spent in the country either to establish relationships, or to give the executive the opportunity to fight the system contributes to the problem. Because North American businesspeople believe that time is money and that their time, in particular, is very valuable, they operate on a tight schedule with little leeway for unanticipated delays. The payoff appears to be a cost-effective solution. In summary, the executive might not have the time, knowledge, or contacts to fight back and sees no alternative other than pay or lose the deal.

SOME REAL BARRIERS

If, as we think, there are many honest businesspeople in North America and in the developing world looking for mutually profitable arrangements and for reliable, honest partners, why is it difficult for them to find each other? We believe a significant reason is the inability of both sides to overcome two interrelated barriers — time and trust.

Trust is a critical commodity for business success in developing countries. North Americans going to invest in a country far from home need to believe they will not be cheated out of their assets. Nationals have to believe that a joint venture, for example, will be more than a mechanism for the North American to get rich at their expense. But, even before the venture is established trust may be essential if the perspective partners are ever to meet. This may require the recommendation of a third party respected by both sides.

Establishing good relationships with the right people requires an investment of time, money, and energy. An unwillingness of either party to make this investment is often interpreted as a lack of sincerity or interest. The executive trying to do business in four countries in a week (the "five-day wonder") is still all too common a sight. Similarly the successful local businessperson may have an equally hectic international travel schedule. Both complain that if the other was really serious he would find time to meet. Who should give in? In our opinion the onus is on whichever party is visiting to build into the schedule the necessary time to work on building a relationship or to find a trusted intermediary. Also both parties must be realistic about the elapsed time required to establish a good relationship and negotiate a mutually satisfactory deal. This will involve multiple trips by each party to the other's country and could easily take twelve to eighteen months.

THE COST OF BRIBERY

The most quantifiable costs are the financial ones. The cost of the "service" is known. The costs of not bribing are also quantifiable: the time and money that must be invested in long-term business development in the country, or the value of the lost business. However, there are other costs that must be considered.

1. You may set a precedent and establish that you and/or your company are susceptible to payoff demands.
2. You may create an element in your organization that believes payoffs are standard operating procedure and over which you may eventually lose control.
3. You or your agents may begin using bribery and corruption as a personally nonthreatening, convenient excuse to dismiss failure. You may not address some organizational problems of adapting to doing business in the developing world.
4. There are also personal costs. Ultimately you will have to accept responsibility for your decisions and action, and those of your subordinates. At a minimum it may involve embarrassment, psychological suffering, and a loss of reputation. More extreme consequences include the loss of your job and jail sentences.

CONCLUSION

It is clear that bribery can be a problem for the international executive. Assuming you do not want to participate in the practice, how can you cope with the problem?

1. Do not ignore the issue. Do as many North American companies have done. Spend time thinking about tradeoffs and your position prior to the situation arising.
2. After thinking through the issue establish a corporate policy. We could caution, however, that for any policy to be effective, it must reflect values that are important to the company's senior executives. The policy must also be used. Window dressing will not work.
3. Do not be too quick to accept the "conventional wisdom." Examine critically the stories of bribery and the source of the stories. Ask for details. Try to find out the other side of the story and make enquiries of a variety of sources.
4. Protect yourself by learning about the local culture and by establishing trusting relationships with well-respected local businesspeople and government officials.
5. Do not contribute to the enlargement of myths by circulating unsubstantiated stories.

Finally, we would offer the advice that when in Rome do as the *better* Romans do. But, we would add, do not underestimate the time, effort, and expense it may take to find the better Romans and establish a relationship with them.

CASE 16

Valley Farms International (A)[1]

Donald G. Simpson and Henry W. Lane

John Roberts, a university professor of finance, was trying to decide whether to change careers when he took a six-month leave of absence to see if he had an aptitude for international business. He accepted a short-term consulting job to conduct a feasibility study for a milk-processing plant in a country in the Middle East (which will be referred to as the "Republic").

At the time, the country's Regent was still in control, although opposition to his regime was becoming more open. When Roberts made his first trip in August, optimism for the Regent's regime was still high among Westerners and the local middle class. However, by his second trip in November the situation was changing. There were uprisings and demonstrations, but it was considered only "temporary unrest."

Valley Farms, which was to be the supplier of cattle for the milk-processing plant project, was also supplying a small number of cattle for a demonstration farm. It had shipped eighty cattle in November, which arrived during Roberts' visit and during violent demonstrations against the Regent. The airport authorities would not allow the plane to be off-loaded, nor connect the power for the air conditioning. By morning half the cattle had died before Roberts could free them. Crowds, out of control, were frantically attacking the Regent's military and women in Western clothing. Roberts was caught in the demonstration in a taxi. It was a frightening environment, and John commented that it was one of the few times he had been scared.

The feasibility study concluded that the project was economically viable, but not feasible due to the deteriorating political conditions. During the course of the study, Roberts had made the acquaintance of the owner of Valley Farms, a dairy farm and cattle auction operation that was selling a lot of cattle to countries in South America. Since the milk plant project was not going to go forward, Roberts was easily persuaded to complete his leave of absence with Valley Farms and to take on the task of organizing its burgeoning domestic and international operation.

Roberts never returned to his life as a teacher. He remained with Valley Farms as Export Manager and assumed responsibility of arranging financing for the export sales. Eventually a decision was made to split the export and domestic operations, and Valley Farms International (VFI) was incorporated with Roberts being one of the partners. The export operations were driven by three aspects: demand by clients for cattle, which was cyclical; the ability of the client to obtain hard currency; and the ability of Valley Farms International to find successful local agents to represent their interests. Although Roberts was prepared to travel widely to close a deal, the operation depended to a significant degree on the work of local agents. Within a short time of the incorporation, VFI had withdrawn from the South American market as Brazil's holdings of foreign currency declined rapidly. Attention turned to North Africa and the Far East. Small sales were concluded with Morocco and for three years VFI made extensive sales to South Korea. This market was saturated by 1984 and sales ended quickly.

Amazingly, however, Roberts' attention had been drawn back to the Republic. One of his old contacts in that country advised him that the Ministry of Agriculture was in the market looking for cattle. Yogurt, a staple of the diet of people of the Republic, requires substantial milk supplies, and the cattle population had been reduced during the worst days of the revolution. Supply sources were limited mainly to Western Europe or Canada.

In spite of the bad memories of his last involvement in the Republic, Roberts saw a good commercial opportunity. With only a general lead from his contact in the Republic as to where he might find the Ministry of Agriculture delegation, John headed off to Europe. He eventually found them in Holland and learned quickly that he was having to match wits with a group of committed young revolutionaries who behaved like, and no doubt believed that, they were running the show and shaping the rules of the game now. Roberts' intuition, however, was that someone higher up behind the scenes was probably still pulling the strings. Two members of the group had been students in the United States and understood North Americans reasonably well. The others had not been to the United States, and the leader of the group spoke no English and was a hardened revolutionary.

Following their discussions in the Netherlands, Roberts offered to fly the group of six to visit VFI and to pay their expenses while they surveyed the VFI operation. They accepted and came for a week. Roberts was kept busy showing them the dairy operation, the auction barns, and some of the farms from which cattle would be obtained and discussing the technical details of cattle selection, in which these people were not highly experienced. He also found himself in discussion about social responsibilities and the role of morality in one's life.

A deal was reached by the strangest of events. Throughout the week Roberts had spent almost every waking hour touring, dining, and talking with the group in order to build trust. On Sunday, he told them he was going to church, and they were welcome to wait until his return or to go with him. To his surprise they went and sat through the service and the informal coffee time discussion following. Rather than being offended by their exposure to a Christian service, these religious fundamentalists were pleased to know they were dealing with a religious person.

Shortly afterward a $6 million contract was signed with the Ministry of Agriculture. Obtaining the contract had been much easier than Roberts had expected, but no doubt implementing the contract would provide some challenges. A four-person delegation from the Republic arrived to inspect the cattle, which were to be shipped in planeloads of 200 cattle each. Roberts arranged for them to inspect the cattle, which at this point, were being held at different farms in the area. They did not want to see the cattle, only the papers on the cattle. To Roberts this was not a good sign. It suggested they were going to be more concerned with all the paper technicalities rather than viewing the animals to judge the quality.

On the first morning after a cursory examination of the papers, they rejected half the available cattle. Of the half tentatively approved, they visited one small group and rejected almost all of them. One of Roberts' partners, who had been viewing the behavior incredulously, finally lambasted them for their incompetence. The members of the delegation were deeply offended and said that they were leaving for home. It took Roberts three days to calm them down. Although they agreed to stay, the following days with them seriously tested Roberts' patience. Their behavior was wildly erratic. One day they seemed to be happy with the way things were going, and the next day they would be angry. Afterwards Roberts reflected that part of the problem was that they were not confident in the job they were assigned. They took seriously the responsibility that had been given to them, but they were not sure how much to trust the word of this North American stranger.

The first shipment was made in June. A major problem developed when the cattle were tested upon arrival in the Republic. Inspectors claimed that most of the animals in the first shipment had TB and slaughtered them. Almost immediately, Roberts flew to the Republic with a veterinary doctor from the federal Department of Agriculture. Part of the problem was the manner in which the cattle were tested. Also, the cattle were being tested for a TB strain for which North Americans did not test. The testing had to be changed for future shipments. This was done and the shipments were completed to the satisfaction of both the customer and VFI, which made a good profit on the sales.

Two years later, Roberts was back in the Republic to sign a contract to deliver 10,000 cattle. As Roberts described it, negotiating in a revolutionary country was different than anything he had experienced before. The young revolutionaries who had taken over the bureaucracies were working hard to get the best deal for the government. With their bazaar-mentality upbringing, they were prepared to bargain for days at a time. Although these young bureaucrats seemed to believe honestly that they were in charge, Roberts realized that another system was at work. He needed information to understand what was going on. This information came from a contact he had made in prerevolutionary times, a person with earlier Canadian connections who was Westernized, capitalistic, and motivated by money.

To get negotiations started, Roberts needed his help. For a price, this man claimed he would open the gate to the powerful force behind the scenes in the Republic, which Westerners came to call "the Invisible Hand." Although Roberts knew that, according to law of the Republic, agents were forbidden, he understood also that all serious Western companies doing business in the country had a "contact." This man had had previous contacts with Canada and knew something about how North American firms operated. The first information he had offered Roberts was accurate and useful. He had informed VFI that the Ministry of Agriculture was back on the market for cattle, and that the purchasing team was in Europe. From that time on, their conversations had been sprinkled with references to the need for some payment. These discussions were confusing to Roberts, for it was never clear exactly for what he might be paying or even to whom the money would be going.

In convoluted discussions, spread over time, he had been led to believe that "the invisible hand needed to be fed." The inference was that these were powerful people who, of course, could not be identified. However, the clear message was that without their approval Roberts' negotiations would never be treated seriously. Eventually, a figure of $300 a head (approximately 10 percent of the contract price per head) was suggested as an appropriate fee. Payment would be made upon delivery.

Thus Roberts found himself carrying on two sets of negotiations simultaneously . . . one with the buyer and one with his contact. With the latter he kept asking himself "What am I buying?" As he saw it, the payment might be necessary "to get into the game . . . to begin serious negotiations with the buyers." It would be an expensive admission fee and he wondered whether or not it would be worthwhile.

Note

1. Names of people, companies, and some countries have been disguised.

CASE 17

Thurlow Limited[1]

R. William Blake and Henry W. Lane

Bill Carruthers sat back in his chair and reflected on the latest phone call from John Sukiro, Chairman of the Sorongan Economic Development Agency. Obviously, John was under increasing pressure from the Japanese government to purchase Japanese instrumentation for the petrochemical complex under development at Letoro. Bill quickly skimmed the familiar tender comparisons and reached the inevitable conclusion; no matter how the figures were manipulated, Staubing, the German supplier, had the low bid and should be awarded the contract.

Bill was sympathetic with John's predicament. Japan was giving $22,000,000 to the Letoro project, and obviously, expected Japanese manufacturers to be awarded contracts. The final decision on the instrumentation bids could have a profound effect on the future of Japanese aid which Soronga could ill afford to lose. Nevertheless, Bill felt that he was unable to help John. As the manager for the Letoro project, he had personally supervised the preparation of the bid comparisons. Changing the recommendation at this stage could damage Thurlow's credibility and its ability to win future contracts.

Bill's musings were interrupted by the ringing of the phone. The caller was Murray Kerson, Letoro Project Director for the Pacific Rim Development Bank (PRDB). Murray was very concerned about the upcoming lenders meeting. All parties to the project would be there and the instrumentation bids would be discussed. If Yamagata, the Japanese supplier, did not receive the contract for the instrumentation, the financing package for the whole project would be in jeopardy and the complex might never be built. As leader of the lending consortium, the PRDB would be under pressure to produce an acceptable solution. It was clear that Murray blamed the Thurlow bid comparison for creating the problem. "You got us into this bind," he said to Bill, "now how do you help us get out?"

BILL CARRUTHERS

A graduate in chemical engineering from the University of Edinburgh, Bill Carruthers emigrated to North America. Within one month of his arrival, he had joined Thurlow as a design engineer and progressed through increasingly responsible

413

positions. He was Chief Engineer for a major petrochemical development in Brazil. Bill's gift for languages made him a natural choice for overseas assignments, and soon afterwards, he was made Managing Director of Thurlow Far East, a company incorporated in Singapore to handle Thurlow's Australasian operations. In this capacity, Bill had been Thurlow's principal representative on the Letoro project.

THURLOW LTD.

Thurlow Ltd. was founded in the early 1950s by a small group of engineers under the direction of John Thurlow. The firm soon developed a reputation for high-quality consulting engineering within the petrochemical industry. Shortly after its inception, the company won a contract for a major development in Australia. The success of that project led to a policy of actively pursuing international contracts, and in the following years the company became involved in projects all over the world. It developed strong working relationships with the major lending agencies and, working for them, became the first consulting engineering firm to apply its skills on a large scale in the developing world. Because of its leading position in the industry, Thurlow was a favorite with the Pacific Rim Development Bank. Over the years, Thurlow undertook numerous projects on their behalf, and this relationship was reflected in the fact that the PRDB was currently Thurlow's largest single customer, accounting for 25 percent of the company's revenue.

Thurlow and its subsidiary companies offered clients a variety of services. These included all design and engineering services required to construct major plants, the preparation and implementation of construction budgets, purchasing, and the supervision of construction and scheduling. The company also offered management, training, and operating assistance. Thurlow considered itself to be an integrated company capable of taking a project from a feasibility study through start-up operations, including the development of infrastructure and manpower requirements. Subsidiaries included an American operation, the Singapore office, and management consulting company. The group employed over 500 people and had revenues in excess of $60,000,000.

Thurlow's internal organization structure was similar to that of most consulting engineering firms. To ensure that the company had the human resources to respond to opportunities, a permanent nucleus of skilled professionals was maintained, while other personnel were hired on a contract basis. Thurlow had a "stable" of over 300 personnel who worked for them in the past and who could be called on to work on future projects. Because it was in the business of providing professional expertise, Thurlow's ability to vary the size of its staff allowed the firm to remain profitable under all but the bleakest economic conditions. Needless to say, the more people Thurlow had on contract, the greater its revenue, and therefore, its profits would be.

SORONGA

Soronga was a nation located in the Western Pacific. Under its colonial rulers, large-scale agricultural plantations had been developed, and for many years, the country depended on the export of agricultural products as its primary source of foreign exchange. Little attempt had been made to develop an industrial base. When independence was granted, the withdrawal of expatriates left the country with a very limited organizational infrastructure on which to build.

Under its new leader, Francis Madoka, and the new administration, numerous "parastatals" were created. These government corporations were designed to control all significant economic activities in the country. In addition to parastatals, such as SEDA (Sorongan Economic Development Agency), SORA (Sorongan Railway Authority), and SOPA (Sorongan Power Authority) there also were the usual government ministries such as housing, public works, and health and welfare.

A major weakness in the government agencies and in the parastatals was a shortage of educated people to manage them. Although some workers in the forty to fifty age bracket were competent administrators due to their exposure to the colonial administration, many of the younger people lacked education, experience, and motivation. One expatriate characterized the parastatals as "inadequate bureaucracies" in which only one or two people were capable of "vision" and were willing to make decisions. Although there was no enmity among the various parastatals and ministries, there was a strong motivation to build individual power bases. Many bureaucrats were reluctant to make decisions or to allow their counterparts in other departments to initiate actions that might impact on their sphere of influence. The result was a system characterized by a lack of cooperation in which it was difficult to find someone willing to make a decision or to take responsibility for one.

The stability of the new government quickly made it a favorite with the major aid organizations. Notable among these were Japanese and New Zealand agencies which provided numerous large loans and grants to promote development in a variety of industrial sectors. Canadian aid to Soronga focused on power development, transportation, and water supply areas in which Canada had strong domestic capabilities. Although Canada was respected in Soronga, its aid program was small compared to that of many other lenders. As a result, Canada had little influence on government policy or decision making.

LETORO — THE FIRST REPORT

For more than a decade, the Sorongan Agricultural Service (SAS) carried out a development program designed to increase the production of food crops for domestic use. It became evident that significant increases in productivity could be realized through the introduction of chemical fertilizers. Soronga had large reserves of offshore natural gas and this fact, combined with the need for a viable project to contribute to large-scale industrial growth, led the government to hire Thurlow to conduct a preliminary feasibility study and to recommend a location for a nitrogen-based fertilizer plant.

The final report was comprehensive. Thurlow inventoried land resources, estimated future development potential, and assessed the viability of a number of areas based on such factors as resource availability, location, and the complexity of infrastructure requirements.

The report concluded that two areas were suitable for plant development. One was the port city of Kildona on Hako, the largest island in the group, and the other was near Letoro, located 150 miles inland on the same island.

Although Kildona offered a location that was readily accessible and easier to develop, it was a long way from the major agricultural plantations. Because natural gas could be transported for half the price of ammonia, the finished product, it was considered preferable to build the complex near the end user. Letoro was near the center of the development area but would require an infrastructure development program far more expensive and complex than would be needed at Kildona. The major impediments to development at Letoro were the lack of railway service and the absence of a nearby power generating facility. The final report recommended the construction of a plant at Kildona.

Six months after the Thurlow report was submitted, the Sorongan government announced a series of major economic development policies. Prominent among these was a plan to develop a petrochemical fertilizer complex at Letoro. Although no reason was given for choosing the inland site, a subsequent announcement revealed than an aid agency had agreed to construct a new railroad line on Hako. The line would pass very close to the Letoro location. Shortly thereafter, Thurlow was retained to identify the most suitable site for a plant at Letoro.

THURLOW'S SECOND REPORT

After assessing a number of areas, Thurlow recommended a location on the south shore of the Marin River in the heart of the agricultural development zone. The site was three miles from the new railway line and offered ready access to most of the plantations. A road bridge would have to be built across the river to facilitate the supply of fertilizers to the north shore.

At the proposed plant capacity the return on investment would be 10 percent, compared to the industry norm of 17 percent for comparable projects. The Letoro project would be marginally profitable but, since profitability was a secondary concern, there appeared to be a strong possibility that development would take place.

The principal force behind the feasibility studies had been Mr. Rawana, Chairman of the Sorongan Economic Development Agency (SEDA). The fertilizer development was his pet project, and despite government inaction for years, he continued to lobby for its approval. The completion of a major hydroelectric facility and the new rail line the following year, improved the viability of the project. Mr. Rawana increased the pressure to get the concept accepted and funded. He managed to get PRDB funding to expand the plantations at Letoro and from that time, PRDB maintained an agricultural specialist in the area.

Armed with the two Thurlow feasibility studies, Mr. Rawana began to lobby the major aid agencies for funding. He was successful in acquiring a grant to enable SEDA to hire a full-time petrochemical consultant. The consultant, Mr. Janal from India, was to formulate plans for the proposed plant and act as a catalyst to get the project underway. Although he had limited experience in the industry, he knew more than anyone at SEDA, and quickly assumed the role of resident expert.

Government officials saw the Letoro project as a way to supply the need for fertilizers internally while simultaneously providing an addition to Soronga's industrial base that could lead to the development of a lucrative export market.

PROJECT DEFINITIONS

Because of the length of time since the last study (five years), a decision was made to do a third feasibility study. SEDA invited Thurlow to bid and Bill Carruthers got a "clear message" from Mr. Janal who told him, "Get a government grant from your government and you'll get the study." Thurlow approached the government, but since the project fell outside the aid areas Canada was interested in supporting, no funds were forthcoming. The New Zealand government was quick to react. Soronga was one of the key countries in their aid program and they readily agreed to supply the required funds. Although Thurlow submitted a bid on the feasibility study, Bill was not surprised when Napier Engineering, a New Zealand based consulting-engineering firm, was awarded the contract.

Because it was funding the study, the New Zealand government wanted to have a "watchdog" of its own involved. It found one at New Zealand Petro-Planning (NZPP), a Crown corporation with no foreign experience. The man chosen was Mr. Robbins, a research chemist with limited operating experience. He was attached to SEDA, and as had been the case with Mr. Janal, was soon regarded as a "specialist."

At this time, a major personnel change occurred at SEDA. Mr. Rawana was promoted to the Ministry of Finance, a position that allowed him to exert considerable influence on the Letoro project. His replacement at SEDA was Mr. Sukiro, former head of the Sorongan Steamship Line. His knowledge of petrochemical development was negligible and he relied heavily on his advisors. The structure of the increasingly complex "organization" overseeing the third feasibility is shown in Figure 1.

Napier Engineering kept in mind the preferences of agencies that would probably be funding the project. The key design factor in the Letoro plant would

---

FIGURE 1 Feasibility Study: Organizational Relationships

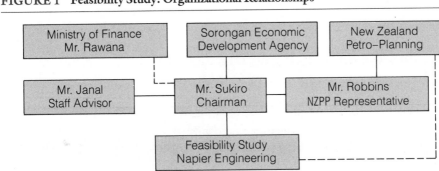

be the use of relatively unsophisticated equipment incorporating the maximum of manual control. The plant would, as far as practical, be labor intensive and designed to use uncomplicated maintenance routines.

The Napier study recommended the construction of a plant to produce a narrow range of fertilizers for domestic Sorongan needs. Although the study indicated that such a plan would be financially viable, representatives of Thurlow felt that it would be marginal at best.

THE LETORO COMPLEX

The proposed plant would be complex to finance. Because of a shortage of development funds in Soronga, the project would depend on foreign funding. The New Zealand International Development Agency (NIDA) was pushing for the project to begin, but was unable, for political reasons, to underwrite the whole project or lead the lending consortium. NIDA had lost a considerable amount of prestige and money in a disastrous project it had funded recently in South America, and the government could not afford to chance a recurrence. Finding an agency to assume the lead role was not difficult. The PRDB was looking for projects to fund and, through the efforts of Mr. Rawana, had been kept well informed of the status of the Letoro project. PRDB offered a low-interest loan of $20,000,000, to be matched by a credit for an equal amount. The credit would be repayable, but the term was open to negotiation, and the only cost would be a service charge of ½ percent. NIDA offered a loan of $26,000,000 at 1½ percent interest and Japan, which had a long history of involvement in Soronga, offered a grant of $22,000,000 through the Japanese Development Fund (JDF). A major condition of the Japanese grant was that the funds be used to purchase the instrumentation for the plant. Other financing came from the Asian Development Bank (ADB), the Australian Investment Bank (AIB), and U.S.A.I.D. Details of the proposed financing package are shown in Figure 2. Total funding of $128,000,000 was pledged, but SEDA was having difficulty getting agreement from all the participants on terms and conditions for the loans and for such key considerations as procurement procedures and methods of payment. It appeared likely that the lenders would agree to a modified version of World Bank guidelines, but until such time as this was settled, the loans would not become cross-effective[2] and the project could not go ahead.

INFRASTRUCTURE REQUIREMENTS

Since the proposed plant site was in an undeveloped area of the country, significant infrastructure development would be necessary to ensure the success of the project. The recent extension of the railway system had pushed the main line close to the proposed site, but a three-mile spur would have to be constructed to the plant. One hundred and eighty miles of electrical transmission line would be required to supply power from the hydroelectric plant, and a bridge would have to be built across the

FIGURE 2   **Thurlow Ltd. Financing Package**

Pacific Rim Development Bank	
— loan @ 7%	$ 20,000,000
— credit @ ½%	20,000,000
Asian Development Bank	
— loan @ 10%	13,000,000
Japanese Development Fund	
— grant*	22,000,000
Australian Investment Bank	
— loan @ 13%	15,000,000
New Zealand International Development Agency	
— loan @ 1½%	26,000,000
U.S.A.I.D.	
— grant	12,000,000
Total — U.S. Dollars	$128,000,000

* To be used in part to purchase instruments.

Marin River. A townsite capable of housing 2,000 people would have to be built to accommodate the families of the workers brought in to run the plant. Because tunnels on the railway line limited the size of equipment that could be transported by rail, 60 miles of road leading to the site would have to be upgraded. A pipeline would also have to be built to move the natural gas from Kildona to Letoro. A final, but crucial, portion of infrastructure development was a plan to provide a trained work force for the new plant. It was estimated that over 600 workers would have to be selected and trained to operate the complex.

From the outset, major problems developed. Although funding sources had been secured for the plant itself, many portions of the infrastructure were still unfunded. Even more troublesome problems were created by the complexity of the project. At least three government agencies and four parastatals were involved in, and had some degree of control over, various aspects of the project. Unfortunately, no single agency or parastatal had overall control of all the elements. The desire by the various officials involved to maintain or build their personal power prevented the desired degree of efficiency or coordination from being achieved.

PROJECT MANAGER

When it appeared that the funding for the complex would be available, SEDA decided to proceed with the selection of a design engineer. Because it had conducted the feasibility study, Napier Engineering was generally acknowledged to be the leading contender for the job. This was in keeping with the goals of NIDA, which hoped to offset its loan through the awarding of equipment contracts to New Zealand suppliers. If Napier won the contract, New Zealand would effectively have a stranglehold on the project, as Napier would be receiving much of its direction from the NZPP advisors to SEDA. This prospect alarmed officials of PRDB who, according to one Thurlow executive, were "concerned that as leader of the lending consortium, they would have no control over the project if it became purely a New Zealand management group." To prevent this from occurring, PRDB insisted that a firm be appointed to act as Project Manager.

Working as a representative for SEDA, the Project Manager would assist in the selection of a design engineer for the battery limits plant,[3] oversee the work of the design engineer, and coordinate all outside infrastructure development. In most development projects, project management is an in-house capacity, but SEDA lacked the ability to carry out the function. According to Bill Carruthers, "the PRDB was quite desperate to get a non–New Zealand company involved at the project management level so that international procurement could effectively take place." At the insistence of PRDB, a request for proposals for the project management contract was issued. The request indicated that the chosen company would act as SEDA's representative in overseeing the project from the choice of the design engineer through the start-up of the plant. At this point, the PRDB asked Thurlow to bid for the contract.

Thurlow felt obligated to respond to this request. As Bill said, "We must have been doing 60 to 70 percent of the PRDB business in this area so we had some obligation, since they appealed to us, to look into it and get involved." By June, Thurlow submitted a detailed proposal to SEDA, describing the company's qualifications and experience, and discussing their perception of the project management function. The most significant recommendation was that plant start-up and operation be placed under the project manager to ensure the efficient coordination and control of the project.

Four companies bid for the contract: Bombay Engineering, an Indian company experienced in the use of appropriate technology; Hoffman, a German firm with no petrochemical experience; Fertech, the New Zealand government agency that had been set up to oversee the ill-fated South American project; and Thurlow.

Thurlow did not receive an immediate response to their proposal, and in December, Bill left for Malaysia for a long overdue vacation. He was tracked down there by his secretary who, on January 5, read him a "frantic" PRDB telex which stated in part, "Why haven't you responded to the invitation to come to talk about your proposal on the 8th of January in Wellington?" Bill immediately returned to Singapore, and then left for Wellington, where he made a presentation that stressed Thurlow's experience and the need for a clearer definition of the role and responsibilities of the project manager. Inquiries into the reason for Thurlow not being informed of the Wellington meeting produced the response that NZPP had "lost" their invitation. Bill believed that in reality the "loss" had been a "last ditch" attempt by the New Zealand interests to exclude someone who they knew would function independently and in the way the PRDB wanted.

The day following the Wellington meeting, Thurlow sent a letter to SEDA repeating its position and urging that to provide more effective coordination and control of the project management and design engineering roles be merged. If this merger were not acceptable, Thurlow would be pleased to function either as project manager or design engineer. In response to this letter, SEDA sent Bill Carruthers an invitation to meetings to be held in Soronga in early February.

At the February meeting, SEDA made it clear that it was interested only in a bid on project management services from Thurlow. Bill Carruthers drafted a letter indicating Thurlow's willingness to participate on that basis and returned to Singapore. During the subsequent days, a major confrontation took place between the PRDB and NIDA. NIDA continued to apply pressure for the contract to be awarded to Fertech, while the PRDB threatened to withdraw from the project if Fertech received it. Without PRDB support, the project could not begin and NIDA wanted the development to proceed. The PRDB prevailed and on February 15, Thurlow was awarded the project management contract.

SELECTION OF THE DESIGN ENGINEER

One of the primary responsibilities of the project manager was to aid SEDA in selecting a design engineer for the petrochemical complex. The design engineer would draw up plans and specifications for the plant, conduct technical evaluations of supplier's bids, and oversee actual construction. Although Napier Engineering was generally considered to be the leading contender for the position, the lenders had agreed to follow World Bank guidelines, which called for open competitive bidding (see Figure 3). A request for proposals sent in June produced three submissions. Thurlow now had to evaluate each and recommend one to SEDA.

The high bid was from Voigt Engineering Ltd. at $8,000,000. Napier Engineering bid $7,500,000, but Huntington (United States) Inc. was the low bidder at $6,000,000. After careful analysis of the bids, experience, and capabilities of the three firms, Bill Carruthers made an oral recommendation favoring Huntington on the basis of both price and experience. NIDA had already lost a significant amount of control over the project and threatened to withdraw its $26,000,000 if Napier was not awarded the contract. In discussing the pressure he was under at the time, Bill talked of Thurlow's corporate policy and said, "When sitting in judgment of fellow consultants, there is only one way to do the job, do it right even if it means getting thrown off." When Thurlow proceeded to put the recommendation in writing, a fresh crisis developed. This time, NIDA was in the stronger position. The PRDB was now committed to the project and needed the NIDA funds. PRDB was not prepared to jeopardize the project for $1,500,000 and decided to bend the guidelines to allow Napier to be awarded the contract. Huntington representatives soon found out what was happening and despite the strong lobbying that followed from United States Congressmen and the American Ambassador to Soronga, Napier Engineering was appointed as design engineer for the project.

FIGURE 3   Thurlow Ltd. — Selected World Bank Procurement Guidelines

General
The bank does not permit a borrower to deny prequalification, if required, to a firm for reasons unrelated to its capacity to supply the goods and works in question; nor does it permit a borrower to disqualify any bidder for such reasons.

Notification
The bank may require that invitations to bid be advertised in well–known technical magazines, newspapers, and trade publications of wide international circulation in sufficient time before bids are to be opened to enable prospective bidders to request bidding documents and prepare bids.

Prequalification of Bidders
A clear statement of the requirements for qualification should be sent to all firms desiring to be considered for prequalification.

Alterations to Bids
. . . no bidder should be permitted to alter his bid after the first bid has been opened. Only clarifications, not changing the substance of the bid, may be accepted.

Evaluation and Comparison of Bids
The bid with the lowest evaluated cost, but not necessarily the lowest submitted price, should be judged the most advantageous offer.

    For comparison of all bids, the currency or currencies of the bid price . . . for each bid should be valued in terms of a single currency selected by the borrower and stated in the bidding documents. The rates of exchange to be used in such valuation should be the selling rates published by an official source, and applicable to similar transactions, on the day bids are opened, unless there should be a change in the value of the currencies before the award is made. In the latter case, the exchange rates prevailing at the time of the decision to notify the award to the successful bidder should normally be used.

Award of Contract
The award of contract should be made, within the period specified, for the validity of bids to the bidder whose responsive bid has been determined to be the lowest evaluated bid, and who meets the appropriate standards of capability and financial resources.

ORGANIZATIONAL STRUCTURE

With the awarding of the design engineering contract to Napier Engineering, the formal organizational structure for the development of the plant was complete. As can be seen from Figure 4, the informal lines of communications were numerous and presented the threat of heavy political involvement in the decision-making process.

FIGURE 4 **Project Structure**

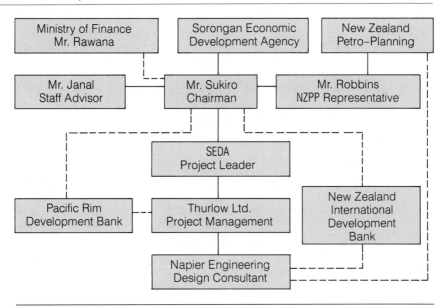

Although it had been agreed that SEDA would provide a project leader to assume responsibility for the project, this position was still vacant. Mr. Sukiro was receiving advice from three primary sources. Mr. Janal provided input as a petro-chemical "expert"; Mr. Robbins of NZPP was giving consulting advice on the overall project; and Thurlow, as project manager, was acting as advisor to SEDA on all aspects of development of the plant and the infrastructure. An overview of the entire project including financing is shown in Figure 5. Thurlow's responsibilities included reviewing and coordinating the work of all consultants, contractors, and suppliers working on the plant and the infrastructure. In addition, it was required to make recommendations on all equipment tenders and to prepare earnings estimates and financial evaluations.

Bill Carruthers in Singapore expected to spend approximately 25 percent of his time acting as Project Director in which capacity he would coordinate policy with SEDA. In addition, six members of his Singapore staff were assigned to the project on a full-time basis. A Sorongan manager was also appointed to coordinate day-to-day progress with SEDA and, when the project entered the construction phase, to coordinate the work of all Thurlow personnel in the country. Having established the basic Thurlow organization, Bill Carruthers pressed to get the project under way. Because of the diversity of financiers, government departments, parastatals, contractors, and suppliers involved in the Letoro project, Bill knew his job would not be an easy one.

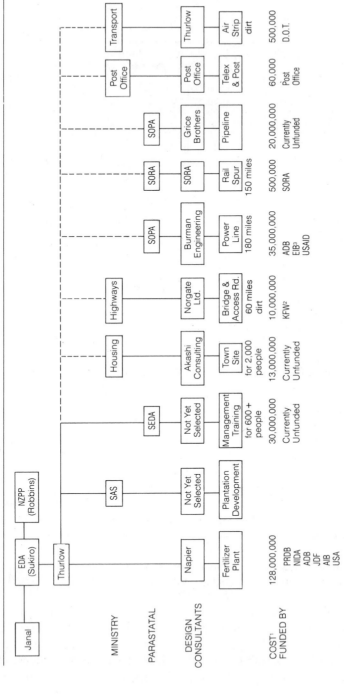

FIGURE 5 Thurlow Ltd. – Letoro Project

Janal — EDA (Sukiro) — NZPP (Robbins)

Thurlow

Transport — Thurlow — Air Strip (dirt)

Post Office — Post Office — Telex & Post

SOPA — Grice Brothers — Pipeline

SORA — SORA — Rail Spur (150 miles)

SOPA — Burman Engineering — Power Line (180 miles)

Highways — Norgate Ltd. — Bridge & Access Rd. (60 miles dirt)

Housing — Akashi Consulting — Town Site (for 2,000 people)

SEDA — Not Yet Selected — Management Training (for 600 + people)

SAS — Not Yet Selected — Plantation Development

Napier — Fertilizer Plant

MINISTRY

PARASTATAL

DESIGN CONSULTANTS

COST[1]

FUNDED BY

- Fertilizer Plant: 128,000,000 — PRDB, NIDA, ADB, JDF, AIB, USA
- Plantation Development: 30,000,000 — Currently Unfunded
- Management Training: 13,000,000 — Currently Unfunded
- Town Site: 10,000,000 — KFW[2]
- Bridge & Access Rd.: 35,000,000 — ADB, EIB[3], USAID
- Power Line: 500,000 — SORA
- Rail Spur: 20,000,000 — Currently Unfunded
- Pipeline: 60,000 — Post Office
- Telex & Post: 500,000 — D.O.T.

[1] The estimated cost of the plant itself was $128,000,000. All other costs shown on this line are in addition to the cost of the plant.
[2] Kuwait Fund.
[3] European Investment Bank.

424

INFRASTRUCTURE DEVELOPMENT

Serious financing problems were becoming evident in the infrastructure planning. The training program, town site, and pipeline were still unfunded and no sources of funding appeared to be immediately available. The most critical of the three was the training and management program. The finished plant and associated operations would require more than 600 Sorongans in positions of varying complexity. Just over 100 of these would be "counterparts" to the skilled expatriates who would be responsible for bringing the plant "on line." It was intended that the chosen counterparts would work with the expatriates one-on-one with the aim of eventually replacing them. Because of the limited number of suitably trained people in the Sorongan work force, selection and training would have to start shortly to ensure the personnel would be available when required.

The value of the training and management package was $30,000,000 over three years. Thurlow was expected to receive the contract and had a clause in its contract as project manager stating that SEDA still had 15 months to declare its intention to negotiate with Thurlow over terms and conditions for providing the required services. The clause further stated that if the parties could not reach agreement four months after declaring its intention, SEDA would be free to negotiate with other parties. Although Thurlow did not anticipate problems in receiving the contract, it was concerned about where the money would come from. PRDB officials had expressed the belief that cash flow from the plant would pay the costs, but Bill Carruthers had calculated that at least $8,000,000 would be required before start-up and that the plant would be hard pressed to allocate any of its cash flow to training during the first few years of operation.

The second major area of concern was the town site. Because the majority of the required personnel would be hired from the populous coastal areas, a town capable of supporting 2,000 inhabitants would be required. To induce the people to move to the cooler climate of the interior, the town would have to be well built and offer excellent facilities. The Ministry of Housing was responsible for planning and construction. Although an architect had completed plans, the $13,000,000 required to build the town was not available. Bill Carruthers estimated that the town would have to be ready one and a half years before the scheduled date for finishing the plant if the start-up were to occur on schedule. He had suggested that the construction camp be upgraded as a temporary measure, but the Ministry of Housing would not accept this plan.

The pipeline was the third major problem area. The $20,000,000 required for construction had not been included in the original estimates and Soronga was having difficulty finding an agency to supply the funds.

THE EQUIPMENT BIDS

Napier Engineering's plant design had been completed and Thurlow was ready to solicit prequalification tenders for the supply of equipment. Industry press advertisements inviting submissions on 20 separate equipment packages stressed the fact that selection would be made on the basis of worldwide competitive tenders. This was in accordance with the World Bank procurement guidelines which all funding agencies agreed to accept. According to the guidelines (see Figure 3), all companies whose prequalification submissions were considered acceptable would be invited to bid on specific packages.

The final choice of contractor would be made in a two-step process. Napier Engineering would conduct a technical evaluation of the tenders and Thurlow would then carry out a commercial evaluation. According to the guidelines, Thurlow's final recommendation to SEDA would be based on "the bid with the lowest evaluated cost, but not necessarily the lowest submitted price." Factors to be considered at arriving at an evaluated cost included "time of completion of construction or delivery, operating costs where applicable, or the efficiency and compatibility of the equipment, the availability of service and spare parts, and the reliability of construction methods proposed."

Of particular interest to the lending agencies were the prequalification submissions received for the instrumentation. The Japanese had made the grant of $22,000,000 expecting that the funds would be used to purchase this equipment. Although the conditions for the grant could have stipulated that the contract go to a Japanese supplier, this had not been done and the JDF had agreed to accept World Bank guidelines. Nonetheless, no one involved with the project doubted that the JDF expected Japanese manufacturers to be the leading contenders to supply the instrumentation.

Twenty companies submitted prequalification statements for the instrumentation, and following a comprehensive review by Napier and Thurlow in June, nine were invited to bid on the instrumentation package. Three months later, the nine tenders were opened publicly and the prices read out. After detailed technical analysis of the bids by Napier, the three lowest bidders, Staubing from Germany; Blois et Fils from France; and Yamagata of Japan, were invited to meet with representatives of Napier and Thurlow for further discussion and clarification. Staubing bid in Deutschmarks, Blois et Fils in United States dollars, and Yamagata in Japanese Yen. For comparative purposes, Thurlow would convert these bids into United States dollars in accordance with World Bank guidelines. In the following weeks, representatives of the three firms met with their counterparts from Napier and Thurlow and attended final meetings at which SEDA and NZPP were also represented.

On October 25, Thurlow distributed its comparison of tenders. The financial comparison, shown in Figure 6, clearly indicated that Blois et Fils, the French company, had the lowest bid. Staubing was within 1 percent of Blois while Yamagata was over by 10 percent. In final discussions, officials of Yamagata made a "cryptic reference" indicating a willingness to drop their price by 8 percent, but had not offered this as an "alternate bid" under the terms of the guidelines. Bill Carruthers did not feel the offer had a significant effect on the final result as its inclusion would still leave Yamagata 2 percent above the Blois bid. In its conclusion, Thurlow recommended that the contract be awarded to Blois et Fils.

FIGURE 6   **Thurlow Ltd. — Tender Comparison**

	Staubing	Blois	Yamagata
October 25			
Equipment	$10,293,725	$10,379,526	$11,581,909
Spares	521,167	520,702	733,645
Erection, Supervision & Start-			
Up Assistance	99,152	149,500	158,345
Freight–In	985,244	895,863	929,500
Building Cost Differential	325,000	357,000	—
Steam Consumption Differential	130,000	—	130,000
	$12,354,288	$12,302,591	$13,533,399
	100.4	100	110
Tender Comparison — January 20			
Equipment	$ 9,952,936	$10,379,200	$12,243,156
Spares	503,198	520,702	760,305
Erection, Supervision & Start-			
Up Assistance	575,913	881,361	955,162
Less: 8% for Yamagata			(1,298,603)
Freight–In	985,244	895,863	929,500
Building Cost Differential	325,000	357,500	—
Steam Consumption Differential	130,000	—	130,000
	$12,472,291	$13,034,626	$13,719,520
	100	105	110
Final Prices After Adjustment for			
Relevant Factors	$13,055,204	$13,502,079	$13,294,703
	100	103	102

Copies of the tender comparison were distributed to the three companies and to SEDA, NZPP, PRDB, NIDA, and JDF. In November, Thurlow received a long telex from SEDA stating that, "Your comparison is incomplete . . . you have not included eight items that would give a truer picture." After listing the factors, the telex concluded by stating, "In considering the eight factors, you will realize that Yamagata has the lowest bid." The technical nature of the factors mentioned indicated to Thurlow that an outside expert was involved and subsequent investigation found that the list had been prepared by a consultant hired by the Japanese government. The telex was the result of strong pressure on SEDA from the Japanese government to have the contract awarded to Yamagata. Japan was one of Soronga's largest aid donors and JDF officials had threatened to curtail future aid programs if Yamagata did not receive the contract. Soronga could not afford to lose Japanese aid, but the low level of Canadian aid to Soronga gave Thurlow little political clout. In response to JDF demands, SEDA began to pressure Thurlow.

After a close examination of the eight factors, Bill sent a telex back to SEDA stating that, "Half had no bearing and were too subjective" while the others "made no appreciable difference to the results." SEDA, however, insisted on a new comparison including the relevant factors and the 8 percent price reduction for Yamagata. In a letter dated January 20, Thurlow provided such a comparison (Figure 6). The comparison did not help Yamagata who remained 2 percent high, but fluctuating exchange rates did make the German bid marginally preferable to that of Blois et Fils. In its conclusion, Thurlow recommended that Staubing be awarded the contract.

Bill Carruthers now found himself under intense pressure to change the comparison. According to Bill, "SEDA didn't want to take the responsibility for making the decision and NZPP wasn't going to take it for them. They wanted Thurlow to tell them to buy the equipment. Then if anything went wrong, it was Thurlow's responsibility." Although SEDA was unwilling to take responsibility for accepting other than the low bid, it was equally unwilling to risk losing further Japanese aid. During the following weeks, Bill received numerous calls from SEDA, JDF, and Yamagata, all of whom wanted Thurlow to change its comparison. For reasons of professionalism and to protect its reputation, Thurlow said, "It's not just ethics, it's pragmatic. You have to protect your professionalism. If you bend, somebody, someday, may be on the other side of the fence and they won't want the rules bent . . . they'll never trust you again!"

THE CURRENT SITUATION

Bill Carruthers was at the center of the growing storm. Although he was confident that his comparison was unbiased and accurately reflected the relative merits of the three bids, he was concerned about the effect it was having on Thurlow's relationship with SEDA. During his latest phone call, Mr. Sukiro had stated that Thurlow was "destroying the spirit of cooperation . . . you are not flexible enough . . . we won't get the project off the ground this way . . . it's costing us dollars." He also implied that he was having second thoughts about awarding the training and management contract to Thurlow. The $30,000,000 contract represented a significant potential source of revenue to the company, and Bill was concerned about jeopardizing Thurlow's position. He was also concerned about the company's ability to function effectively as Project Manager without the total support and cooperation of Mr. Sukiro.

Bill's position was further complicated by the pressure he was receiving from Murray Kerson at the Pacific Rim Development Bank. Standing by his recommendation could harm the good relationship Thurlow maintained with the PRDB, while acquiescence to the SEDA demands could harm Thurlow's credibility and affect the prospect of receiving future contracts. In a recent telephone exchange, Murray had told Bill, "You need to be more flexible." When Bill asked how they should be more flexible, Murray replied, "Well, we can't tell you how to do it. That's your business. You know the area best." Ruminating on his dilemma, Bill said, "You do that to get the monkey off your back and they throw you to the wolves . . . you can't trust anybody." Nonetheless, as he prepared for the forthcoming lenders meeting, Bill wondered if he shouldn't resolve the situation by adjusting the bids. After all, the $250,000 in question was insignificant in the context of the entire project.

Notes

1. The names of people, countries, and agencies have been disguised.
2. When more than one lender is involved in a project, no contracts can be signed or monies disbursed until total financing is in place and all lenders have agreed to each other's terms and conditions. When this occurs, the loans are "cross-effective."
3. The physical plant "inside the fence."

CASE 18

Polysar (A)

R. William Blake and Joseph J. DiStefano

Ian Rush was pensive. As he made a final review of the events leading up to this evening, the President of Polysar contemplated the probable direction the impending audit committee meeting would take. Although he was primarily concerned about possible changes to the footnotes to the consolidated financial statements, Ian was also curious about how the auditors would broach and deal with the rebating practices of Polysar International S.A. (PISA), Polysar's Swiss marketing subsidiary. Although he was aware that Maxwell Henderson, the Auditor General, had some concerns about PISA's handling of these rebates, he also knew that they were standard competitive practice and that, according to his legal advisors, no Swiss laws were being broken by PISA.

Nonetheless, Ian knew that the Auditor General might prove to be difficult. Max Henderson was not easily moved once he had adopted his position on an issue and, in this case, it appeared he disagreed with his coauditors at Peat Marwick who had indicated little concern with the practices. This difference of opinion promised to make the audit committee meeting most interesting and Ian wondered what position he and the Polysar counsel, William Dyke, should take.

HISTORY OF POLYSAR

Polymer Corporation Ltd. was incorporated under the Federal Companies Act on February 13, 1942, to produce synthetic rubber for the Allied war effort. For the duration of the war, the plant in Sarnia, Ontario was operated under contract by other companies with Polymer coordinating operations and paying the operating companies a fixed fee for each pound of material produced.

At the end of the war, the Minister of Trade and Commerce agreed to allow Polymer to remain in business, provided the company could be operated profitably without any special advantages not available to any private sector company. Commencing in 1946, Polymer was operated as an agency of the Crown with the government owning the facilities and appointing the management. Because capacity vastly exceeded Canadian demand, a concentrated effort was launched to develop export markets, and a research facility was built to provide additions to the product line. During the late forties, the name "Polysar" was introduced and the new trademark quickly became identified with Polymer's product.

Between 1945 and 1950 a strong network of independent distributors was built in Europe. With natural rubber now readily available, many companies were inclined to switch back from synthetics, but good work by Polymer's distributors was instrumental in keeping customers for synthetic rubbers.

During the Korean War, the price of natural rubber tripled while that of synthetic remained virtually unchanged. This development caused many users to switch permanently to synthetics and market demand increased steadily.

In 1952, Polymer issued 2,000,000 shares and $8,000,000 in debentures to the Government in exchange for direct control of all assets being operated by the corporation. By the end of 1954, the company had retired the debentures and had paid a further $14,500,000 in dividends and $20,000,000 in income tax.

Strong export demand during the 1950s led to the expansion of capacity and further broadening of the product line. During this period, Polymer appointed distributors in Japan, South Africa, New Zealand, Australia, Central America, and the Middle East. In 1955, the United States government sold its rubber plants to private industry and this provided the first significant export competition for Polymer. Increased competition also appeared in Europe where several new plants were constructed.

By 1960, 125,000 tons of the 157,000 ton capacity of the plant were being exported. New capacity was essential and after a thorough analysis, the company concluded that:

1. Its ex-plant prices, plus freight and delivery charges, exceeded European prices.
2. With the founding of the EEC, discriminatory duties were a strong possibility.
3. Ninety percent of Polymer's special rubbers were sold outside Canada, primarily in Europe.
4. Other firms were starting production in Europe.

To respond to these factors, the company announced that it would build new plants at Antwerp, Belgium and Strasbourg, France. The former would produce butyl rubber and the latter, certain specialty rubbers. Capital investment for the two plants was $25,000,000.

To give European customers better sales and technical service, an International Marketing Group was created. After assessing a number of sites it was decided to locate the new company in Fribourg, Switzerland, to take advantage of favorable tax rates and treaties. The new company, Polysar International S.A., or PISA, would be responsible for marketing the output of the Canada, Antwerp, and Strasbourg plants outside the country in which the producing plant was located. PISA would also contract for the supply of technical assistance and know-how and would maintain a technical service center. For tax reasons and as a final link in the European organizational structure, a holding company, Polysar Nederland B.V. was created to link the European operation to Polymer Corporation Ltd.

By the mid-1960s significant excess capacity had developed in Europe. This was squeezing the margin on SBR's, the basic styrene-butadiene copolymer that accounted for two-thirds of Polymer's production. To ensure future growth, Polymer started to diversify into stereo rubbers and plastics and resins. The 1966 acquisition of Kayson Chemicals, a major Canadian producer of polystyrene and compounder of other plastic materials, was followed by the purchase of a series of small plastic producers in the Eastern United States.

In July 1972, the Canada Development Corporation purchased Polymer and the company's name was changed to Polysar. By 1972 Polysar revenues had grown to $205,376,000. Polysar key management personnel at the end of 1972 are shown in Figure 1.

AUDIT PRACTICES

During the twenty-year period that it was a Crown Corporation, Polymer was subject to the Financial Administration Act of 1951. Under this Act, responsibility for auditing the company fell upon the Auditor General of Canada. Although the Act called for an audit essentially the same as that required in the private sector, there were a number of differences. The most significant difference directed the Auditor General to:

> Call attention to any other matter falling within the scope of this examination that in his opinion should be brought to the attention of Parliament.

The vehicle normally used to carry out this function was the "Annual Report of the Auditor General to the House of Commons." This was submitted in January–February, for the year ended the previous March 31.

The Auditor General was sole auditor for Polymer until 1970, when Peat Marwick became coauditors. This change was implemented at the suggestion of the President of Polymer, and with the concurrence of the Auditor General, Mr. Henderson. Peat Marwick had been coauditors for Polymer's European operations since the incorporation of PISA in 1962 and, because of a shortage of personnel in the Auditor General's office, had been solely responsible for carrying out the physical examinations prior to the joint signing of the financial statements. The 1970 appointment made Peat Marwick coauditors for all the Polymer companies.

PISA

Concurrent with the decision to build plants in Strasbourg and Antwerp it was decided to incorporate companies in Switzerland and the Netherlands. The Swiss company, Polysar International S.A. or PISA, would own Polymer's patents and

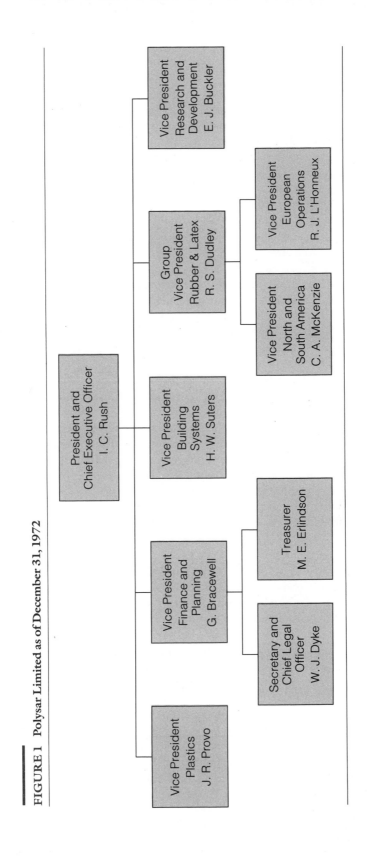

FIGURE 1 Polysar Limited as of December 31, 1972

President and Chief Executive Officer — I. C. Rush

Vice President Plastics — J. R. Provo

Vice President Finance and Planning — G. Bracewell

Secretary and Chief Legal Officer — W. J. Dyke

Treasurer — M. E. Erlindson

Vice President Building Systems — H. W. Suters

Group Vice President Rubber & Latex — R. S. Dudley

Vice President North and South America — C. A. McKenzie

Vice President European Operations — R. J. L'Honneux

Vice President Research and Development — E. J. Buckler

know-how, license or sell these assets to related companies or to third parties, and market the products of plants owned or controlled by Polymer. The Netherlands company was to function as a holding company, owning the capital stock of the Belgian, French, and Swiss companies.

Because Polymer was a Crown Corporation, approval of these plans was required from Privy Council. Approval was given on September 21, 1961, in a statement which read, in part:

> This group of companies will give Polymer direct participation in the two European trading blocs, result in considerable tax savings, place Polymer in an improved competitive position and thereby increase Polymer's earnings.

To guard Polymer's competitive position, a further order was issued in April, authorizing Polymer to "discharge their obligations under the Financial Administration Act with regard to the preparation of annual financial statements and reports on a consolidated basis, as permitted under the Companies Act." This would allow the company to mask detailed financial data and prevent the competition from carrying out regional or product sales analysis.

Under PISA's direction, the distributor network established in the post war years continued to grow. By 1965, distributors in forty countries were selling Polymer products in seventy countries. Distributors were assisted in an advisory capacity by technical service personnel attached to PISA. With new products or applications, a PISA specialist would attempt to satisfy the customer's technical personnel, while the distributor worked with the purchasing agent. Polymer sold the product to the distributors who then had complete control over its ultimate destination. In general, the distributors preferred to sell large-volume items, such as SBRs, rather than the relatively low-volume specialty products, even though the margins on the later were significantly higher. Distributors were paid a marketing commission on sales, and product was shipped directly to the end user who paid PISA.

Polymer's management believed that the key factors in their initial success were product quality, technical service, and price. Because of their early entry into the market, Polymer had built up considerable customer loyalty, but, particularly on commodity rubbers, they found margins shrinking as competitive pressure increased. Although Polymer retained a degree of customer loyalty, the surplus of product on the market increased the importance of price to the customer and Polymer was forced into price competition to maintain its sales.

During the latter half of the 1960s, management's desire to control distribution led to a policy of acquiring some distributors and terminating the agreements with others in major national markets and setting up subsidiary marketing companies. This was facilitated by the existence of clauses which allowed termination of the agreements on 90 days' notice before the year-end.

Sales representatives in the new subsidiaries were on salary with bonuses based on gross yearly sales for the company. Salespeople negotiated prices with customers based on guidelines set down by PISA. Margins were set to maximize profits in

PISA while, at the same time, ensuring that subsidiary profits yielded an adequate return on investment. Large volume customers often negotiated rebates or price cuts. These were paid only when the agreed volume had been taken, and could apply on single orders or be paid on an annual or semiannual basis on orders accrued during that period.

Prices to PISA from the manufacturing plants were set through a process of negotiation and new price lists were provided to PISA sales representatives on a regular basis, normally monthly. PISA had control over the production from all three plants and set production guidelines on a monthly basis.

PISA sales and profits grew steadily through the 1960s. Although budgets continued to be submitted to Canada for approval, operating responsibility was largely delegated to PISA. Corporate management in Canada concentrated on policy planning, strategy, product and process development, and systems implementation, while PISA management set production levels and marketed the companies' products. A degree of corporate involvement was maintained through the election of a member of Polymer senior management to PISA's board of directors.

The organizational structure for PISA in 1972 is shown in Figure 2. Between ten and fifteen sales supervisors, based in Fribourg, were responsible for negotiating end product prices with the representatives in the European subsidiaries and dealt directly with customers in other parts of the world. Sales representatives worked within set price guidelines, but were given latitude in setting the terms of individual contracts.

FIGURE 2   **Polysar International S.A. as of December 31, 1972**

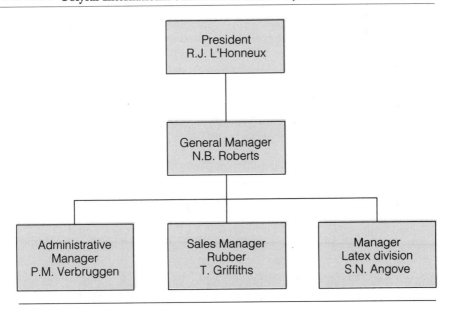

THE 1972 PISA AUDIT

In July 1972, Polymer was sold to the Canada Development Corporation (CDC). Because the sale terminated Polymer's status as a Crown Corporation, it was decided by the Board of Directors that it would be inappropriate to reappoint the Auditor General of Canada after the end of the current fiscal year. CDC, as a Special Act Company, was not a Crown company and was not audited by the Auditor General.

The normal interim examination of the records of PISA began in October 1972. The audit was supervised by Mr. Matthews of Peat Marwick's Zurich office who had just taken over responsibility for PISA. In a meeting held in Fribourg on December 4, he discussed a number of concerns with Mr. Kirkwood of the firm's Toronto office. Foremost among these was the inability of his manager to "confirm"[1] accounts with a number of PISA's customers. Mr. Matthews explained that PISA, as a competitive practice, routinely offered customers rebates for purchases above certain volume levels. Although the vast majority of these rebates were paid directly to the customer, a number of customers were billed at full price and a credit balance for the amount of their rebate was established in PISA's books. Upon payment by the customer, the credit was paid out in compliance with the customer's instructions. In very exceptional cases the credit was either paid out in cash or deposited to the customer's Swiss bank account. Because some of these payments did not appear on the books of the purchasing subsidiary of the customer, Mr. Matthews was unable to confirm the credit balances with these customers and, therefore, had no way of knowing whether they did, in fact, accurately represent the actual PISA liabilities.

The following day, the problem was again discussed at length. In addition to Mr. Matthews and Mr. Kirkwood, this meeting was attended by Mr. Cowperthwaite, Peat Marwick's senior Canadian partner for Polysar, Mr. Bradford, PISA's finance officer, Mr. Verbruggen, European Comptroller, Mr. Erlindson, Polysar's Treasurer, and Mr. Bracewell, Vice President, Planning and Finance, for Polysar. After discussion of the rebate problem it was decided that PISA would submit a letter of representation to Peat Marwick setting forth the following: certification as to the accuracy of a listing of the rebate credit balances on the books; acknowledgment that the company was aware of the degree of involvement of their employees in connection with this kind of transaction; and certification that, to the best of the company's knowledge, the employees had no control over the bank accounts maintained in Switzerland. Mr. Matthews agreed to draft such a letter for review in Canada prior to signature.

Subsequent to this meeting, Mr. Matthews discussed the rebate situation and the letter of representation with Mr. Collins of Peat Marwick's Paris office. Mr. Collins was the senior partner for Europe responsible for professional practices; and as such, advised Mr. Matthews on the format of the letter.

On February 1, 1973, Matthews sent Kirkwood and Collins a letter dealing with the PISA situation (Figure 3). The letter outlined the mechanics of the rebate practice in detail and discussed the advantages involved. Benefits to the customers included, "reduction of local tax liabilities and the provision of a means to maintain, physically, funds outside the control of national exchange regulations." For PISA,

---

FIGURE 3   Peat, Marwick, Mitchell & Co. — Internal Memorandum

---

TO	Mr. Office	J.D. Collins Paris	DATE	February 1, 1973
FROM	Mr. Office c.c.	N.N. Matthews Zurich Mr. W.G. Mecklenburg — Paris Mr. K.H. Kirkwood — Toronto	STENO	MH/MV
SUBJECT		Polysar International SA		

I refer to your memo of January 16 which I deliberately delayed answering until I visited Fribourg and had certain detailed information which I had requested the company to prepare.

It is the practice of Polysar International SA (PISA) to sell and invoice merchandise to certain customers (in accordance with agreements with their customers) at inflated prices. Within the accounts of Fribourg adjustment is automatically made to contra sales accounts and to accrued liabilities to reduce such selling prices to actual terms agreed with the customers. When the customer pays the invoice a transfer is usually made from accrued liabilities to accounts receivable via an internal credit note, a copy of which seldom goes to the customer. A separate subsidiary ledger account is maintained within the accounts receivable ledger for each customer for these liabilities and statements relating to these accounts are virtually never sent outside of Switzerland. Settlement of the liabilities is effected in accordance with the specific instructions of each customer. Such methods vary from bank transfers to numbered Swiss bank accounts to transfers to Swiss affiliates of such customers and from check payments to customers who personally visit Fribourg to international payments to designated beneficiaries.

These transactions, which are effected with customers in a large variety of countries, have certain advantages for both parties. For PISA they help to maintain price levels in certain countries while at the same time they offer incentives to customers which enable them to sell their product. Indeed on the latter point PISA is, we are informed, obliged to do it as it is common practice with all its competitors. The primary advantages for customers are reduction of local tax liabilities and the provision of a means to maintain, physically, funds outside the control of national exchange regulations.

We have discussed the legal aspects of these transactions with company officials, including the in-house legal official, in Fribourg. We have been informed that neither the federal nor tax laws of Switzerland have been violated. The reductions can be justified as price discounts which have to be granted to achieve sales in the normal course of business. No attempt is made in Switzerland to disguise the payments from Swiss authorities. The situation as regards foreign exchange and fiscal regulations, however, appears less clear. From PISA's point of view there could perhaps be the possibility of being subjected to foreign legal action for price fixing. Further, the company might be implicated in an action

(Continued)

FIGURE 3 **Continued**

---

against a customer for evasion of foreign exchange control regulations. The customer is clearly more liable in this area, as he is also in the area of tax evasion. Successful prosecution on these charges could possibly result in penalties and other consequences to certain customers sufficient to prejudice the collectibility of our related accounts receivable.

Further it is to be noted that some 45 percent of the payments in the year are to a _____customer. The group structure in Europe is built round a _____ holding company and even if the _____authorities could not actually take action against PISA they might be able to take action locally against the group and possibly prejudice the European structure.

The extent of these transactions in the year ended December 31, 1972 is as follows:

(1) Rebates granted amounted to approximately SFr.7,000,000 which represents some 1.5 percent of total sales and 2.6 percent of sales to nonaffiliated companies.

(2) Rebates estimated owed at December 31, amounted to SFr.4,000,000 or 3.1 percent of current liabilities.

From an audit point of view we feel that we were confronted with the following aspects:

(1) Were the transactions processed during the year bonafide?
(2) Were payments made in accordance with customer instructions?
(3) Was control over these transactions, and especially the payments adequate?
(4) Is presentation in the statement of earnings proper?
(5) Is the company properly indemnified by the customers in respect of any breach of fiscal, exchange, or other foreign regulations?

We believe that our detailed audit test work, which revealed no exceptions, was satisfactory to positively conclude in respects of points (1), (2), and (3). For point (4) the audited accounts present net sales in the earnings statement. The fifth part is to be covered not only by our discussions, already mentioned above, but also by a specific letter of representation, a draft of which is attached. It has been Mr. Kirkwood's proposal that the Vice President of Finance and Planning, Polysar Corporation, who is also a Director of PISA should sign this letter and we are proposing that Mr. Roberts, the General Manager and Mr. Bradford, Manager of Finance and Accounting should also sign as the two local officials most familiar with the transactions.

Your comments on the foregoing would be much appreciated, particularly as regards the text and signatories of the representation letter.

SIGNED

H. N. Matthews

the practice allowed them to maintain "list" prices while attracting customers with competitive rates. Although the letter indicated that proper records were being kept by PISA, and that no Swiss law was being violated, concern was raised that PISA could be subject to foreign legal action for price fixing or be implicated in an action against a customer for evasion of foreign exchange control regulations. In such an event, the consequences to the customer could be sufficient to prejudice PISA's related accounts receivable. The letter ended with a discussion as to who should be the signator of the letter of representation. Mr. Matthews suggested that Bracewell, Roberts, and Bradford should sign, but requested his colleagues' opinion on the matter.

On receipt of this letter, Mr. Kirkwood sent a copy of the draft letter of representation to Mr. Bracewell (Figure 4). In subsequent discussion, Mr. Bracewell insisted on two deletions. There were sections that acknowledged an awareness by PISA that the rebate payments may be "in breach of fiscal, exchange, and other trading regulations of certain foreign countries or that it may enable a customer to violate such regulations," and that consideration had been given to the possibility that the collection of certain receivables could be prejudiced by the discovery of such transactions.

A copy of Matthews' letter also found its way to the Auditor General on or about February 7. This was the first time that Mr. Henderson had been made aware of the rebate situation and he was very concerned about the possibility of the existence of a "contingent liability." He requested more details from Peat Marwick and, as an interim measure, announced that he would not sign the consolidated financial statements for Polysar on February 15, as originally scheduled.

FIGURE 4   **Polysar International S.A. — Draft Letter from Auditors as Edited by Polysar**

Peat, Marwick, Mitchell & Co.,
8027 Z U R I C H   DRAFT

Gentlemen,

In connection with your examination of our financial statements as of and for the year ended December 31, 1972 you have requested that we make certain representations to you regarding certain marketing allowances and rebates which have been paid or accrued during the year to certain customers. These allowances and rebates, lists of which are annexed as appendices A and B to this letter and initialled by us for purpose of identification, are distinguishable from other similar allowances and rebates as they are paid or credited in accordance with specific customer instructions, to designated bank accounts or beneficiaries who are not persons to whom the related sales invoices are sent. Further such credits are segregated by the company from the accounts receivable ledger.

We inform you to the best of our knowledge and belief that:

(a) Appendix A attached is a complete list of the company's liability for such allowances and rebates accrued at December 31, 1972.

(Continued)

FIGURE 4 **Continued**

(b) The company has carefully considered all the possible legal implications of making payments of the nature referred to and listed in Appendix B attached and it is our opinion that no Swiss regulations, legal, fiscal, or other, have been violated.[1] We are aware that there is the possibility that the making of such payments themselves is in breach of fiscal, exchange, and other trading regulations of certain foreign countries or that it may enable a customer to violate such regulations. We are, in particular, aware of the payments approximating some SFr.3,000,000 in the year to ▓▓▓▓▓▓▓▓▓ —2

▓▓▓▓▓▓▓ 3 ▓▓▓▓▓▓▓

After consideration of all the foregoing possible implications we are also of the opinion that the company does not need to make provision at December 31, 1972 for any contingency arising from such transactions.

2 — Further we confirm that, in considering the adequacy of provision for doubtful receivables, due consideration was given to the possibility that the collection of certain receivables might be prejudiced by action taken and punishment imposed by foreign regulatory authorities in the case of discovery of such transactions.

(c) The company has full knowledge of involvement of its employees in payment of such allowances and rebates. It is aware that Mr._____ and Mr._____ have joint signing authority over the account of ▓▓▓▓▓▓▓▓▓▓ —3 to which payments of this nature are made from time to time. Other than the foregoing case no employees of the company have control over the accounts to which such payments are made.

Yours very truly,
POLYSAR INTERNATIONAL, SA
Not Signed

---

[1] The phrase "by the company" was requested to be added here.
[2] These sections were removed by Polysar.
[3] Shaded areas contained specific names and references to employees or customers that the authors of the case have deleted.

In a telephone discussion of the letter of representation on February 9, Mr. Bracewell asked Mr. Kirkwood to add the words, "by the company" to the phrase, "it is our opinion that no Swiss regulations, legal, fiscal, or other, have been violated." He went on to say that he had discussed the matter with Mr. Rush, President of Polysar, and that they had agreed that Mr. Bracewell's name be deleted from the letter of representation and that Mr. Mahler, legal officer for PISA, be added. To ensure that awareness of the letter was communicated to top management, a copy would be directed to Mr. Dudley, Group Vice President, Rubber and Latex, in Canada.

In a letter dated February 9, Kirkwood transmitted this information to Matthews and Collins (Figure 5). He also discussed PISA's exposure on possible exchange violations by customers, and indicated that the company intended to seek legal advice on this situation. Reference was also made to a statement by Dr. Homberger, PISA's Swiss lawyer, that PISA was not in violation of any Swiss laws. The letter concluded by stating that Polysar's consolidated financial statements were now due to be signed on February 21, and requested that confirmation of the signing of the letter of representation be transmitted by that date.

FIGURE 5   **Peat, Marwick, Mitchell & Co. — Internal Memorandum**

TO: Matthews, Zurich
DATE: February 9, 1973
FROM: Kirkwood
            Toronto

c.c.   Mr. Collins/Paris

SUBJECT: Polysar International S.A.

AIRMAIL — SPECIAL DELIVERY

PRIVATE

Following my telephone conversation with you on Thursday, February 8th I talked with Mr. Collins on Friday, February 9. We are now in agreement with the form of representation letter which should be signed by management. Mr. Bracewell on advice of Mr. Eric E. Homberger (Zurich) has requested that item (b) of the representation letter be further amended to add the words "by the company" after the word violated. Item (b) would then read as follows:

> The company has carefully considered all the possible legal implications of making payments of the nature referred to and listed in Appendix B attached and it is our opinion that no Swiss regulations, legal, fiscal, or other, have been violated by the company. We are also of the opinion that the company does not need to make provision at December 31, 1972 for any contingency arising from such transactions.

You undertook to mail to me on Thursday the two schedules A and B referred to in the representation letter and I trust that such has been done.

Mr. Bracewell has undertaken to furnish us with a copy of the written opinion of Mr. Homberger as to the company's nonviolation of Swiss law and I will forward a copy of the same to you when received or you should arrange to obtain a copy directly from Mr. Homberger (see later).

The purpose of having Mr. Bracewell sign the representation letter was to ensure that management in Sarnia is aware of these transactions in addition to the PISA management. Mr. Bracewell asks that his name be deleted as a signatory and that awareness be communicated by sending a confirmed copy of the letter to Mr. R.S. Dudley in Sarnia, who is the Group Vice President in charge of the Rubber

(Continued)

FIGURE 5 Continued

and Latex Operations. Mr. I.C. Rush, President, with whom all of this has been discussed concurs in this handling. Additionally, we will be advising the Directors at the Audit Committee meeting on February 21, therefore I feel that awareness by all parties is adequately documented.

We are agreed that the financial statements have in no way been affected by the accounting transactions surrounding the handling of marketing allowances and that from an audit standpoint our only concern is to the extent that a possible contingent liability exists. Such contingency would probably be limited to exposure under fiscal or foreign exchange regulations as they could be violated by customers, with Polysar by association considered to be a party thereto.

As Polysar has apparently acted in accordance with written instructions from the customers and we have assurance of nonviolation of Swiss law, their possible exposure only lies with possible association with their customers' practices. They obviously cannot be expected to be their "brothers' keeper" and in the instance of fiscal violation, the customer must take additional action such as expensing the full amount of the invoice in his records which would seem to remove any contingency to Polysar by association.

A foreign exchange violation is somewhat different, as perhaps by doing nothing further beyond entering the original arrangement the customer may be in violation. The company is being asked to assess their possible exposure by seeking advice of outside counsel but I have no assurances that such will be sought at the present time. As a practical matter the corporation transfers large sums between countries, almost on a daily basis, with no contravention of foreign exchange regulations.

Obviously any contingent liability, deemed sufficiently quantitative and reasonably assured, which should be commented on in the PISA statements would also require to be commented on in the consolidated statements. At this point we have only identified a possible contingency, let alone a contingency, and I therefore do not feel that the handling of these transactions should be commented on as a contingency referred to in the accounts of PISA or Polysar consolidated. I trust on reflection that you concur.

As agreed with Mr. Collins, he was to call you on Friday and appraise you of our conversation as well as suggest that more dialogue take place between Dr. Homberger and yourself on these transactions to give you additional assurance. Mr. Bracewell has been advised of his possible meeting and concurs therein.

It is our intention to sign the report to the consolidated financial statements on Wednesday, February 21. I would ask that you telephone me before that date indicating that the representation letter has been signed and that you see no need to comment thereon in the PISA statement or report thereto.

Polysar International S.A.
February 9, 1973

On February 13, Cowperthwaite phoned Henderson to discuss the PISA situation. Although Henderson was still very concerned about the possibility of a contingent liability, Cowperthwaite did not share this concern. He believed that PISA was engaged in a standard business practice and that all transactions were property recorded and had commercial substance. With the legal opinion that PISA was not in violation of Swiss law and given the letter of representation, he felt that it would be possible to give Polysar a "clean certificate." Henderson disagreed and the two men agreed to meet with Mr. Kirkwood for further discussions on the afternoon of February 21, before proceeding to the Polysar audit committee meeting scheduled for that evening.

Prior to the meeting, Cowperthwaite phoned Mr. Rush and Mr. Hampson, Chairman of the CDC, to advise them of Mr. Henderson's concern. At his meeting with Henderson, Cowperthwaite noted, the Auditor General had indicated that he had some problems with the practices and expressed his intention to refrain from signing the consolidated statements unless a footnote was added, admitting to the possibility of a contingent liability or unless Polysar agreed to stop the practice of paying undocumented rebates outside the customer's home country. Cowperthwaite believed however, that he could satisfy the Auditor General's concerns and suggested to Ian that the matter be left to them to sort out.

As Ian Rush reviewed this history and made final preparations for the upcoming meeting of the audit committee, he wondered what position he and the Polysar counsel, William Dyke, should take.

Note

1. The primary function of an audit is to ensure that the financial statements are fairly presented in accordance with generally accepted accounting principles. To accomplish this the auditors establish specific procedures to establish the validity of the transactions processed and recorded during the year. One such procedure is confirmation of accounts which simply asks the customer to confirm that the account receivable or payable on the books of the company agrees with that shown in the customer's records.

CASE 19

Polysar (B)

R. William Blake and Joseph J. DiStefano

On February 21, 1973, the joint auditors of Polysar Ltd. described the rebate practices followed by the Swiss marketing group to a meeting of the Polysar audit committee. Participants in the meeting included Mr. Rush, Mr. Dyke, and two outside Directors from Polysar, and Mr. Cowperthwaite and Mr. Kirkwood from Peat Marwick. Also in attendance were the Auditor General, Mr. Henderson, and the Chairman of the CDC, Mr. Hampson. Although it was made clear to the committee that, in the opinion of the auditors, PISA was not violating laws or regulations and that legal opinion had been obtained that the transactions did not violate Swiss law, Mr. Henderson indicated that he was considering advising the Prime Minister of the matter. The other participants in the meeting did not share Mr. Henderson's concern and it was decided to discuss the matter again at a meeting scheduled for March 7. Discussion of the rebates occupied approximately twenty minutes, the remainder of the two-hour meeting being spent in discussion of proposed revisions to the footnotes to the financial statements.

The following day a meeting of the Board of Directors was held. Included among the topics of discussion were the minutes of the audit committee of the previous day. Mr. Hampson, on behalf of the audit committee, referred to the rebates and advised the meeting of the letter of representation and of the legal opinion that there had been no violation of Swiss laws by PISA. Throughout the discussion at both meetings the concern of the Directors of Polysar was on the possibility of the existence of a contingent liability. Satisfied that no such liability existed and that PISA was following normal competitive practices, the Directors moved on to other matters.

On March 7 Mr. Henderson traveled to Sarnia to sign the consolidated financial statements. He signed them with some reservation, however, and in conversation with Ian Rush indicated that he was still not comfortable and would have to consider the matter further. He again alluded to the possibility of informing the Prime Minister of the rebate practices and of his concern with the situation.

Although he was not pleased with the prospect of a letter to the Prime Minister, Ian Rush was not overly concerned. He was confident that the company was behaving properly and that the substance of the issues was not a problem.

Having signed the statements, on March 22 Mr. Henderson took the unusual step of writing to the Prime Minister to advise him of the existence of "a serious contingent liability of indeterminable proportions arising out of certain transactions of its (Polysar's) Swiss subsidiary" (Figure 1). Copies of the letter were sent, with covering letters, to Mr. Rush and Mr. Hampson.

FIGURE 1   **Letter to Prime Minister from Auditor General**

Auditor General of Canada

Ottawa, Ontario
K1A 0G6
March 22, 1973

The Right Honourable Pierre Elliott Trudeau
Prime Minister of Canada,
Ottawa.

My dear Prime Minister,

I recently signed and transmitted the financial statements of Polymer Corporation Limited and its subsidiaries for the year ended December 31, 1972 to the Honourable Jean–Pierre Goyer, Minister of Supply and Services, and also to Mr. H.A. Hampson, Chairman of the Board of Canada Development Corporation, since this company purchased the outstanding shares of this Crown corporation last July.

The purpose of this letter is to advise you that my examination of Polymer's accounts this year disclosed existence of a serious contingent liability of indeterminable proportions arising out of certain transactions of its Swiss subsidiary, Polysar International S.A. Briefly, this arises from the subsidiary's practice of invoicing certain European customers, by agreement, at inflated prices, with the difference being remitted to the customers or their representatives in cash in Switzerland or placed in numbered Swiss bank accounts as directed. As a result of this practice, the customer is in a position to reduce his tax liabilities in his own country and avoid his country's foreign exchange control regulations, where these exist. Full particulars of the practices surrounding these rebates, payment of which aggregated approximately Sw. Fr. 7,000,000 ($1,900,000) during 1972, can be obtained from Polymer Corporation Limited.

The extent to which Polymer and its subsidiary may be contingently liable for aiding and abetting such transactions largely depends, of course, on whether the customers concerned are apprehended by their respective national authorities. The officials of Polymer and Polysar believe there is little danger of this because the practices followed are not uncommon, in fact they are fairly prevalent today in the operations of multinational corporations in many parts of the world.

(Continued)

FIGURE 1   **Continued**

Nevertheless I consider it my duty to draw your attention to this contingent liability because these corporations are handling public moneys and are owned by the Government of Canada. While it may indeed be possible to defend any claims made against Polymer and Polysar from a corporate standpoint, the fact remains that the publicity attendant on the charges which could be made against a Canadian Crown corporation and/or Canadian Development Corporation could have serious and undesirable consequences.

The reason why, as the auditor of Polymer, I have not insisted on disclosure of the existence of this contingent liability is that to have done so would in my view have been contrary to the best interests of Polymer as a multinational corporation trading in world markets in a highly competitive field. However, I would be remiss in my duty if I did not draw the seriousness of this situation to your attention.

I have sent a copy of this letter to Mr. Ian C. Rush, President of Polymer Corporation Limited, and to Mr. H.A. Hampson, Chairman of the Board of Canada Development Corporation, in accordance with my undertaking to them.

Yours sincerely,

M. Henderson

On March 26, the Prime Minister's Correspondence Secretary wrote simply acknowledging receipt of Mr. Henderson's letter. No further communication was forthcoming from the Prime Minister's office. Later the same day, the Minister of Justice rose in the House to announce that Polysar was no longer a Crown Corporation.

Although he did not reply directly to Mr. Henderson, the Prime Minister wrote to Mr. Drury, President of the Treasury Board, advising him of the letter and suggesting possible courses of action (Figure 2). After telephone discussions with Mr. Hampson, Chairman of the CDC, Mr. Drury apparently took no further action.

At the March 29 meeting of the Board of Polysar, the Auditor General was not nominated as auditor and Peat Marwick became sole auditor for the corporation. Although the Directors believed this was in keeping with Polysar's new status, Mr. Henderson was incensed. In a heated letter to Mr. Rush (Figure 3) he refused to sign the accounts of certain subsidiaries until he was advised whether action had been taken to stop the rebate practice and was provided with an explanation of the "arbitrary way in which the Polysar shareholders fired the Auditor General." According to Mr. Henderson, Polysar was still a Crown Corporation and remained subject to the Financial Administration Act.

FIGURE 2 **Letter from Prime Minister to Treasury Board (with Added Notes)**

Ottawa, K1A 0A2
March 26th, 1973

My dear Colleague:

I am enclosing herewith a copy of a letter dated March 22nd from the former Auditor General which has just come to my attention. It raises a matter about the operations of Polymer Corporation that seems to me to require immediate attention. In the light of your present responsibilities, as well as the experience you have had in this general industrial field, I wonder if the best course might not be for you to organize a discussion of the question with Messrs. Turner, Goyer, and Sharp. These seem to me to be the Ministers whose present jurisdiction and previous experience would suggest that they should be concerned. Perhaps from such a group, there could come a recommendation as to what the government's position ought to be and whether the government has any responsibility to urge a particular course of action on C.D.C. or Polymer.

While there may be no strict breach of law involved in the action that is referred to (I do not know whether that is the case or not), and while the government may not have complete control or direct responsibility because of the status of Polymer and C.D.C., there are obvious possibilities for embarrassment. Perhaps the right course would be for the appropriate Minister on behalf of the government, to draw this to the attention of the management of Polymer and C.D.C. and express the hope that they will give serious consideration to the question whether any modification in the practices of Polymer in its trading arrangements is required. I do not know whether this would be the best course but, in any event, I should appreciate it if you could have this matter given immediate consideration and then let me have your views.
Yours sincerely,

P.E. Trudeau

* * *

The Honourable C.M. Drury,

President of the Treasury Board,
Ottawa.

Called Morrison (CDC Exec VP) 27 March, he has undertaken to get Hampson to justify in writing the future policy of Polysar, Polymer, CDC.
P.S.: I have not made any reply to Mr. Henderson's letter other than the acknowledgment by Mr. Lawless, a copy of which is also herewith. It seems to be that any further reply, if there is to be one, ought to be directed to the Acting Auditor General or the new Auditor General, as the case may be.

FIGURE 3   **Letter from Auditor General to Mr. Rush**

Toronto, Ontario.
M4V 1Y3

October 25, 1973.

Mr. Ian C. Rush,
President,
Polysar Limited,
Sarnia, Ontario.

Dear Ian,

The Office of the Auditor General has sent me sets of accounts of the subsidiaries as at December 31, 1972 with the request I sign and return them. They are dated prior to my retirement from office and prior to the removal of the Auditor General as one of the joint Polysar auditors.

Quite frankly, I do not feel I can sign these without benefit of information on the following two points. I should appreciate it if you would clear them up for me.

The first relates to what action, if any, has been taken to have your European subsidiaries, principally the Swiss one, stop their activities aiding and abetting their customers to avoid their national foreign exchange obligations. I have never had any acknowledgment whatsoever of my letter of March 22, 1973 on this from either the Prime Minister, Hampson, or yourself. I should like to know about this as I understand the practice continues unabated.

The second point relates to the arbitrary way in which the Polysar shareholders fired the Auditor General last May. I do not understand how this action could have been taken not only under the Defence Production Act still extant but also because Polysar still remains a Crown corporation under the Financial Administration Act.

I do not wish to embarrass you and your colleagues over these questions. A great deal of hard work was expended across the years by myself and my staff in helping Polysar and I feel, quite frankly, that I am entitled to an explanation of these actions.

All best wishes,

Yours sincerely,

MAXWELL HENDERSON

In his reply, Mr. Rush sought to placate Mr. Henderson (Figure 4). This was the last discussion of the rebate practice between Mr. Henderson and Polysar and, in management's perspective, the subject was now a dead issue.

FIGURE 4   **Mr. Rush's Reply to Mr. Henderson**

Mr. Maxwell Henderson,   Sarnia, Ontario
Toronto, Ontario. M4V 1Y3   November 8, 1973

Dear Max:

Your letter of October 25, 1973 seeks clarification of two matters arising from your past association with Polysar as one of its joint auditors.

May I first say that I understand your wish to secure further knowledge in the areas of the two points raised. I say with all sincerity, also, that our people at Polysar warmly admired you personally and appreciated your friendly help and professionalism during your years of association with us.

With regard to practices in Europe involving Polysar International's handling of rebates under instructions from customers, we have taken the action to remove our own people from any direct involvement such as assumption and use of signature power. At the same time, we continue to observe instructions given us by certain customers relative to the disposition of funds they own. As long as disposition in this way remains a common competitive practice in Switzerland, we feel we have no alternative but to act according to these particular customers' instructions in order for Polysar to remain competitive.

With respect to the removal of Crown status from Polysar, the government's position was stated by the Minister of Justice to the House on March 26, 1973. The action at Polysar's annual shareholders' meeting on March 29, 1973 not to reappoint the Auditor General as a joint auditor of the firm was a decision which was consistent with this and recognized the change of ownership in mid–1972 whereby Polysar became a wholly–owned subsidiary of the Canada Development Corporation, a company which is not a Crown corporation and which employs only private auditors. Thus, it was an action consistent with Polysar's new ownership status and was intended to bring the practices of the two allied companies into line with one another with respect to auditing arrangements.

I trust that these comments are helpful to you in understanding Polysar's position in both matters.

With very best regards,

Yours very truly,

Ian C. Rush

ICR:IG
b.c.c. Mr. H.A. Hampson
       Mr. E.R. Rowzee
       Mr. G. Bracewell

CASE 20

Polysar (C)

R. William Blake and Joseph J. DiStefano

On November 25, 1976, Maxwell Henderson, former Auditor General of Canada, received a phone call from a reporter in Ottawa. The Capital was still buzzing with allegations of massive bribery and kickbacks on the part of a Crown corporation, Atomic Energy Canada Ltd., in selling a Candu nuclear reactor to South Korea. Newspapers were full of the story and editorials began assaulting the Canadian government's "capacity to ignore morality and propriety."

The reporter was hoping for an equally exciting story about Polysar. He said

> In connection with the bribes and kickbacks that were the subject of the Atomic Energy investigation, we understand you wrote to the prime minister some years ago on the matter of Polysar.

Although Henderson acknowledged writing such a letter, he refused to give a copy to the reporter. That, he said, would be up to the Prime Minister to release.

Determined to pursue this lead the reporter made phone inquiries to the Prime Minister's office. Despite their noncommittal response to the reporter, there was great excitement in the Privy Council Office as the staff set about locating the letter.

The headline in the *Globe and Mail* of November 26 was dramatic: "Foreign firms bribed by Canada and Trudeau told ex-auditor says." Although the story did not mention Polysar by name, it did state that Mr. Henderson had warned the Prime Minister a number of years earlier that Crown corporations were involved in such activities. Later that day, Mr. Trudeau rose in the House of Commons to attack the "misleading and mischievous headlines in the *Globe and Mail.*"

The front-page headline in the next issue of the *Globe and Mail* proclaimed: "Polysar says paybacks normal, still makes them." Another related first page story exclaimed: "No bribery involved, House told. Knew of payments in 1973 Trudeau says." This story gave the viewpoint of an experienced international trader who claimed Polysar should have been "suspicious that it was being made a party to a tax and currency law fiddle." The President of CDC, Mr. Hampson expressed his viewpoint that when a large company is receiving shipments in many countries all of which are aggregated to compute the discount, it can decide where the rebate should be paid. In the story he commented:

> We're not a taxing authority. If the customer wants us to pay the money in Country X that's where we do. It's his money. I don't see anything illegal in that.

An editorial in the *Globe and Mail* entitled, "The Ugly Canadians," observed:

> Canada has been accused of playing games with foreign agents, to cheat and steal and lie and profit. Did we, and if we did, did we put a stop to it? And if we did not put a stop to it, how can this Government stand?

The stories and editorial in the *Globe and Mail* surprised and angered Polysar executives. After the Prime Minister tabled the letters in the House, Ian Rush called the situation "a tempest in a teapot" and stated that "any suggestion of illicit or illegal action is without foundation." Nevertheless, it was clear from the tone of the editorial of November 27 that Polysar would have to respond quickly to minimize potential damage to its reputation. Ian Rush immediately called a meeting of key executives for the following day, Sunday.

At the meeting a consensus was quickly reached that it would be prudent for Polysar to review the practices in question. Accordingly, Mr. Critchley, Vice President Finance, and Mr. Dudley, Group Vice President, Rubber and Latex, were dispatched to Switzerland, with Mr. Buchanen of Peat Marwick, to conduct a preliminary investigation. In the interim a statement was prepared and released to the press (Figure 1).

FIGURE 1 **Polysar Press Release**

Information From
Polysar Limited, Sarnia, Ontario, Canada N7T 7M2
For release: 11:00 P.M., November 28, 1976

"The controversy which has arisen over Polysar International in Europe, following the common commercial practice of allowing rebates, and the unpleasant and inapplicable language used to describe it, are a great disappointment to me as a Canadian," Ian Rush, President of Polysar Limited, said in Sarnia last night.

Mr. Rush stated that all of the transactions were properly recorded in the books of Polysar International S.A., which were under the full scrutiny of independent auditors, thus making any suggestion of secret payments completely ludicrous.

"The customers were fully entitled to the rebates, which were therefore their property, and Polysar International was obligated to act in accordance with the customers' instructions on the handling of those rebates.

"Perhaps a statement given to me yesterday by our auditors, the internationally respected firm of Peat, Marwick, Mitchell & Co., best describes the true situation. They say, and I quote — 'We (PMM) were joint auditors with the Auditor General in

(Continued)

FIGURE 1   **Continued**

1972. We also signed the audit report which gave a clean opinion on the financial statements of the company.

   " 'The transactions in question were rebates to bonafide customers which were fully disclosed to us by the company during the course of the audit.

   " 'No bribes, kickbacks, or illegal payments were involved. The transactions were audited by us in accordance with generally accepted auditing standards and accounted for in accordance with generally accepted accounting principles.

   " 'In our opinion, no contingent liability arose from these rebates.

   " 'Because of the significance of the amounts involved, the matter was raised by the auditors and discussed fully at an Audit Committee meeting of the Board of Directors on February 22, 1973. This was in order to ensure that the Directors understood the practice and, at the request of the auditors, a legal opinion was obtained from the company's international tax and legal counsel confirming the legality of the rebates and the fact that there would be no adverse consequences to the company.

   " 'We are now the sole auditors, know that the practice of rebate continues, and through our normal audit verifications we are satisfied that the rebates are accounted for properly in the company and that no contingent liabilities exist.' "

   "I would therefore reaffirm," Mr. Rush concluded, "that any suggestion of illicit or illegal action on the part of this company is entirely without foundation."

   While the company's internal review progressed in Switzerland, the House of Commons, on November 30, ordered:

> That the subject matter of the letter from the Auditor General of Canada to the Prime Minister of Canada, dated March 22, 1973, tabled November 26, 1976, be referred to the Standing Committee on Public Accounts.

   After two days in Fribourg, Mr. Critchley and Mr. Buchanen reported to a Board of Directors meeting on December 3. Their investigation had shown that all rebates were fully recorded and had been handled according to customers' instructions. Nonetheless some rebates were being paid in other than the customer's home country and sometimes into Swiss bank accounts. This report, coupled with the upcoming Public Accounts meetings led to a long discussion as to just what further action Polysar should take.

CASE 21

Polysar (D)

R. William Blake and Joseph J. DiStefano

The upcoming meeting of the Public Accounts Committee of the House of Commons led Ian Rush, President of Polysar, to order a detailed investigation into the rebate practices and procedures of the Swiss marketing subsidiary for the period 1970 to 1976. In light of the Critchley/Buchanen report he felt this would be the responsible thing to do:

> It was necessary to tear up the floor boards to see if there was anything underneath.

At a Board meeting held on December 15, Ian recommended the appointment of Mr. David Stanley, a Polysar Director, and the Honourable John Aylesworth, a former judge of the Supreme Court of Ontario, as a two-person committee charged with carrying out this task.

After a thorough investigation, including two weeks spent at PISA headquarters in Switzerland, Aylesworth and Stanley presented their report to the Board of Directors on January 31, 1977.

The Committee found that:

1. We discovered that the great bulk of PISA's business, ranging from 80 percent to 95 percent of the annual value of its sales during the period under review, was conducted in a manner which, in our view, could not provide any ground whatever for either legal or moral criticism.

2. We found nothing to indicate any actual or attempted bribery on the part of any employee involved in negotiations with or sales to customers. The marketing activities of PISA are conducted in a highly competitive field, where slight changes in cost of PISA's product to the customer may result in the loss of a customer or in the acquisition of new ones.

3. We did find, however, that objectionable or questionable practices in fact existed in respect of sales to some 13 direct customers and to fourteen of PISA's distributors at one time or another during the period. These practices involved total rebates or similar payments to such customers and distributors equivalent in total to some $4.8

453

million Canadian, (an average of some $700,000 Canadian per year) peaking in the highest single year at slightly in excess of $1.6 million Canadian.

After detailing the transactions of these thirteen customers the report presented the following general findings and recommendations:

1. We are unable to accept the conclusion that PISA has been forced into the above unacceptable invoicing and payment practices because of competitive conditions in the market in which it operates. It is significant to us that the overwhelming proportion of PISA's business is carried on in an unexceptionable way, and we find it difficult to understand why the company should have departed so far from currently acceptable business practice in order to secure the comparatively small volume of marginal business which was available to it by so doing. We recommend discontinuation of such practices.

2. We do not feel that a company with PISA's annual sales volume should attempt to function with the prevailing low level of financial staff in terms of authority and control. It seems clear to us that PISA should be provided with a top-ranking financial officer who should prescribe corporate policy in invoicing and payment practices, more emphatically those related to Latex products, and whose consent should be required in all instances of departure from such prescribed policies. Such an officer should be instructed to refer to the parent company for clearance in exceptional cases.

3. PISA appears to us to be a typical "sales-oriented" company in which success or failure has been measured by gross sales volume rather than by any other yardstick. We must report that we were unable to establish clearly where the ultimate sales authority lies in PISA; that is, in whose hands the ultimate authority lies as to whether any given transaction is acceptable at a given price or on given terms. Clearly the management of Polysar must make a definite determination of this point.

   It was drawn repeatedly to our attention that the sole criterion applied by PISA management to the acceptability of any given manner of doing business was whether or not it was consistent with Swiss law. We cannot report to you that we approve of a criterion that what is acceptable is what one can get away with. In our experience, any business corporation must set certain standards as to what classes of business it is prepared to transact. Again in our experience, we believe that the corporations with the highest standards in this regard are normally those which are most successful. We are not able to commend to you the business standards with which PISA has been content.

4. Since questionable transactions at PISA were first drawn to the attention of the Polysar Audit Committee in February of 1973, it is logical to ask why no action was taken up to the time of our investigation, except for an immaterial change in signing powers of certain PISA officers with respect to the bank account of a small distributor.

In their conclusion Aylesworth and Stanley stated that the legal opinions obtained by Polymer in 1972–73 had been "premised on assumptions of fact which our investigation has demonstrated to have been unwarranted." They also questioned the propriety of Peat Marwick's failure to raise the rebate issue again in subsequent years. "It would seem," the report concluded, "that Polysar's continuing auditors had a somewhat different view of the PISA transactions than that of the former Auditor General."

Ian Rush was surprised at the findings of the Aylesworth/Stanley report — he had never had a marketing responsibility and had accepted the rebate situation as a "normal business practice." Furthermore, the advice he had received both internally and from Peat Marwick had suggested that there was no cause for concern. As he considered the contents of the report, Ian turned his thoughts to the upcoming hearings of the Public Accounts Committee. The Committee was still investigating allegations of massive bribery by Atomic Energy Canada Ltd. and Ian worried that there might be a tendency to tar Polysar with the same brush. The Public Accounts Committee was made up of twenty members drawn proportionately from all parties and chaired by a member from the opposition party. The Committee was empowered to summon and examine witnesses under oath and would make a full report of its findings and recommendations to the House. There was, however, no obligation for the government to implement committee recommendations.

Because the Committee had been dealing with the Atomic Energy of Canada scandal Ian suspected that its members would harbor a considerable amount of skepticism regarding any explanation offered on Polysar's behalf. He was aware that the committee had been frustrated in its attempt to develop a case against AECL and he was concerned that they might be "looking for blood" when they dealt with Polysar. In addition, he had had sufficient dealings with politicians to know that the various committee members would see the situation as a potential opportunity to further their own political ends. Ian wondered how Polysar should present its case to the Public Accounts Committee and what he should do about the issue within Polysar.

CASE 22

Bank of Nova Scotia
(Brady Subpoena) (A)

Henry W. Lane, Errol Mendes,
and Douglas J. Powrie

OVERVIEW

For eight months the Bank of Nova Scotia had been trying to find its way through a legal maze which was beginning to look like it had no way out. A grand jury in the United States had subpoenaed documents located in the Bahamas and Cayman Islands relating to a client of the Bank. The Bank had not been able to get permission from those countries to release the documents, and complying with the subpoena would mean violating their bank secrecy laws. On October 10, 1983, a United States District Court denied an appeal from the Bank and presented it with a choice: comply with the subpoena or face a contempt of court hearing.

THE SUBPOENA

In early 1983, a United States federal prosecutor was attempting to convince a federal grand jury in West Palm Beach, Florida, that there were reasonable grounds to believe that Frank and Paula Brady had been involved in smuggling marijuana into the United States and also had evaded United States taxes on their drug related profits.[1]

On March 1, 1983, this grand jury issued a subpoena to the Bank of Nova Scotia requesting documents maintained by the Bank in the Bahamas, the Cayman Islands, and Antigua. On March 4, 1983, the Bank was served with the subpoena at its agency in Miami, Florida.[2]

The Bank operated in Miami through an agency which can be thought of as a branch with restricted activities. The subpoena served on the Bank's agent in Miami is considered in law to be served on the bank itself. In this situation the agency could have been making loans to United States and foreign companies in Florida and financing trade and, therefore, could have had substantial assets in the United States. However, the Bank is considered to be present in Miami by reason of having an agent there, even if it does not have any substantial assets there.

Before American prosecutors can bring a person to trial for an offense punishable by over one year in prison, they must first convince a grand jury to bring an indictment. A *grand jury* is a group of ordinary citizens (the number varies) who hear and view evidence of an alleged crime compiled by the prosecutors. Their duty is to examine the prosecutors' evidence and to determine whether that evidence shows probable cause for believing that a crime has been committed. If they find probable cause, the grand jury will issue an indictment. An *indictment* is a formal written accusation of the crime that allows the prosecutor to bring the accused before the courts in a criminal trial. The grand jury determines only whether to accuse someone of a crime; it does not determine guilt. The proceedings of a grand jury are completely secret, similar to the deliberations of a jury in the more familiar trial jury.

During its proceedings, the grand jury is empowered by law to compel the appearance of witnesses to give testimony and to compel the presentation of documents. The written command to appear or to present is called a *subpoena*. Failure to comply with a subpoena is considered *contempt* of court (since noncompliance obstructs the administration of justice). United States courts have the power to punish contempt by fine or imprisonment.

The scope of subpoenas can be far reaching. The subpoena served on the Bank required production of virtually all papers, documents, and records for all financial transactions, savings accounts, checking accounts, trust accounts, and other financial accounts, maintained by the Bank of Nova Scotia, at any of its main or branch offices in the specified locations relating to Frank J. Brady, Paula Brady, Frank J. Brady Enterprises, Inc., Brady Farms, Inc., and/or Clay Island Farms, Inc. Moreover, the subpoena required that all documents be originals except where such were not available.[3] The subpoena gave no indication of how the documents would be relevant to the investigation.[4]

THE BANK'S RESPONSE

Upon receiving the subpoena, the Bank's attorneys contacted the United States Attorney General and expressed the Bank's intention to produce the documents in a lawful manner. The United States attorney was also informed of the financial privacy laws in effect in the Bahamas and the Cayman Islands.[5] The Bank also expressed its intention to apply for disclosure in accordance with the laws of the Cayman Islands and provided copies of the applicable Cayman Islands statute and a statement from the Cayman Islands court which explained the type of information necessary to file a successful application. The information necessary to satisfy the Cayman courts was available only from the United States government.[6]

Unfortunately for the Bank, it was a criminal offense under Cayman secrecy law to divulge confidential information originating in the Cayman Islands including bank information and documents about client activities. The penalty for breach of the secrecy law was a fine of up to U.S. $6,100, up to two years imprisonment, and suspension of banking licenses. The penalty could be applied to the Bank itself and to the employee who broke the law on the Bank's behalf.

The United States prosecutor had two alternatives to a subpoena, either of which could have procured the documents. First, he could have applied directly to a Cayman court, requesting that it use its power to waive the secrecy laws and procure the documents to assist the United States investigation. Such an application is called *letters rogatory* and would have required the United States prosecutor to present evidence before the Cayman court showing that the secrecy laws were being used to shield criminal activity.

Second, he could have applied directly to the Cayman government for an executive method of disclosure. The direct application was provided for by a United States–Cayman Islands intergovernmental agreement under which evidence similar to that required by the Cayman courts would have to be supplied before disclosure could be obtained. The United States prosecutor would have to explain the materiality and necessity for the documents. The United States prosecutor did not choose either of these alternatives, claiming that the processes were too time consuming, expensive, and unreliable.

In the Cayman Islands, production of the documentation could also be obtained if the customer agreed to the release of the documents. The Bank did not keep records of customer addresses, and therefore was not able to contact the individuals under investigation to obtain their consent to the production of the documents.[7] Although it probably could have found a way to contact the Bradys through further investigation, such action poses a potential dilemma from the Bank's perspective. On one hand, if it does not contact the customer to obtain consent, it could later be accused of not acting in good faith. On the other hand, if it does contact the customer and he refuses, he can go to court to get an injunction to prevent the Bank from making any disclosures. The Bank could then be accused of "courting the impediment" or creating the situation that reinforces its position that it cannot release the information. It is a potential no-win situation.[8]

The Bank also provided details on how to obtain the documents located in the Bahamas and was willing to cooperate with the United States to have the documents released.[9] Under the Bahamian law, the release of such information was primarily through the traditional system of letters rogatory. However, the Bank of Nova Scotia could not initiate this procedure. Only the United States authorities could initiate the letters rogatory, but they refused. The United States authorities refused to produce affidavits of materiality similar to those required under the Cayman Island's bank secrecy laws.[10]

On March 22, 1983, the Bank's Miami agency sent telexes to the Bank's branches in Antigua, the Cayman Islands, and the Bahamas, requesting that the branches (1) determine whether they had the type of documents sought by the subpoena and (b) transmit any of the documents sought to the Miami agency no later than March 25, 1983.[11] There were ten branches in the Bahamas alone that had to be searched.

Affidavits were received from the Bank's Cayman Islands' branches and the Bahamas' attorneys which stated documents covered by the subpoena had been located at two branches. However, financial privacy laws made it a criminal offense for the Bank or its employees to disclose the documents.[12] The Antigua branch responded that it did not have any of the documents sought by the subpoena. Apparently the United States prosecutors accepted the Antigua branch's statement.[13]

BACK TO COURT

Since the United States was not cooperating in securing the release of the documents, on March 29, 1983, an agent for the Bank appeared before the grand jury and declined to produce the documentation sought.[14] On April 4, the Bank made a motion to quash the subpoena; or, alternatively, for more time to respond, particularly to get the Bahamian and Cayman Island governments' permission to disclose the confidential information; or, alternatively, to have the United States prosecutor provide information which supported the necessity of the documentation for the investigation of the grand jury.[15]

The two critical legal arguments raised by the Bank in the motion to quash the subpoena were as follows: First, the Bank argued that it had acted in good faith, and had done everything in its power to comply with the subpoena, but had not been able to produce the documents because of the lack of cooperation from the United States Attorney's office. A number of United States court decisions seemed to be based on the principle that if you acted in good faith, you could be excused for not complying with a subpoena.[16]

The second argument was that before enforcing the cross-border subpoena, the District Court should balance interests as prescribed by Section 40 of the United States *Restatement (Second) of Foreign Relations*, which had been applied by several federal courts and the Supreme Court in deciding cross-border subpoena cases.[17]

Restatements of the United States law are written by prominent legal scholars in an attempt to clarify the state of the law as passed by the United States legislatures and as interpreted by the United States courts. In the course of producing a restatement, a series of tentative drafts are circulated among interested scholars, allowing their views and comments to be incorporated. A restatement, then, is a consensus of expert opinion and can be influential in arguments before the United States courts. They are not, however, the law. Restatements are updated periodically to reflect developments in the law.

Section 40 of *Restatement (Second) of the Foreign Relations Law of the United States (1965)* states:

> Where two states have jurisdiction to prescribe and enforce rules of law and the rules they may prescribe require inconsistent conduct upon the part of a person, each state is required by international law to consider, in good faith, moderating the exercise of its enforcement jurisdiction, in the light of such factors as:
>
> a) Vital national interests of each of the states.
>
> b) The extent and nature of the hardship that inconsistent enforcement actions would impose upon the person.
>
> c) The extent to which the required conduct is to take place in the territory of the other state.
>
> d) The nationality of the person, and

e) The extent to which enforcement by action of either state can reasonably be expected to achieve compliance with the rule prescribed by the state.

The Bank argued that the most recent draft of the *Restatement* listed specific factors which also should be considered by United States courts:[18]

In issuing an order directing production of documents or other information located abroad, a court in the United States must take into account:

1) The importance to the investigation or litigation of the documents or other information requested.

2) The degree of specificity of the request.

3) In which of the states involved the documents or information originated.

4) The extent to which compliance with the request would undermine important interests of the state where the information is located, and

5) The possibility of alternative means of securing the information.

The Bank also called attention to the notes to this section of the tentative draft of the *Restatement*:[19]

No aspect of the extension of the American legal system beyond the territorial frontiers of the United States has given rise to so much friction as the request for documents associated with investigation and litigation in the United States.

Applying the balancing test in the *Restatement*, the Bank argued that the United States prosecutors had shown no valid reason why the District Court should provoke international friction by forcing a peaceful trader in the United States to violate the criminal laws of a foreign state.[20]

On April 27, the United States District Court of the Southern District of Florida denied the Bank's motion to quash the subpoena on extremely formalistic grounds, citing an earlier case involving the Bank of Nova Scotia in the same judicial district when, under similar circumstances, the Bank produced documents from branches in the Bahamas and the Cayman Islands. However, the District Court made two concessions to the Bank. First, it granted a time extension to May 31, to comply with the subpoena. Second, it required the United States authorities to "provide any reasonable assistance, especially in dealing with foreign governments; however, the government is not required to forward letters rogatory."[21]

Soon after the District Court's decision, the Bank's counsel in Miami requested United States authorities to provide affidavits of materiality so that documentation could be released from the Cayman Island branches. The Bank offered to retain a Nassau solicitor who had acted successfully on behalf of the United States government in the past in obtaining documents in conformity with the Bahamian bank secrecy laws. At one stage, Bank officials even asserted that in a telephone conversation, the Assistant United States Attorney agreed to provide such affidavits.[22]

On learning of this asserted oral agreement, Assistant United States Attorney Blair took a very adversarial stance and denied he had ever agreed to provide such affidavits. He claimed that he could not do this even if he wanted to as this would breach the confidentiality of the grand jury proceedings. He claimed that his only duty under the April 27, Order of the District Court was to let the Caribbean authorities know that the grand jury investigation was proceeding. It seemed that the United States refusal to help came from a belief that any such assistance would be futile in getting the information requested from either Caribbean jurisdiction.[23]

The Bank, seemingly frustrated at the apparent lack of cooperation from the United States prosecutors, asked the Grand Court of the Cayman Islands on May 27 for permission to deliver the documents without the affidavit of materiality in view of the United States District Court Order of April 27, 1983. The Grand Cayman Court responded on May 31, by issuing its own injunction against disclosure, but stated it would rehear the matter, if and when the Bank received more information about the materiality of the documents to the investigation.[24] The Bank did not appeal fearing any such action would be "futile" and "doomed to failure."[25]

On June 1, the Bank again sought an order in the District Court directing the United States authorities to act, or for more time, or to be relieved from further obligations under the subpoena.[26] The Bank presented a status report of events to that date.[27] It argued that: (a) the Bank was making a good faith effort to comply with the subpoena; (b) the Bank needed assistance from someone if it was ever to be in a position to apply to the Grand Court of the Cayman Islands for production of the required documents. It further asserted that this was especially appropriate when the scope of the grand jury's subpoena was so broad; (c) the United States authorities had to be given explicit directions to provide the Bank with assistance in light of the April 27 Order of the District Court, including deadlines to provide such assistance. The Bank asked for a partial waiver of any grand jury confidentiality requirements if such requirements existed; (d) United States authorities should be required to utilize letters rogatory in the Bahamas as the Bahamian Supreme Court had expressly declared that method to be the appropriate procedure and the Bank had been willing to obtain Bahamian counsel to assist in the letters rogatory procedure; (e) in the absence of such assistance from the United States authorities, it should be relieved from further obligations to respond to the subpoena.[28]

The United States Attorney responded in a similar fashion. He asserted that: (a) The Bank had flagrantly refused to comply with the subpoena despite being given extra time to do so between April 27 and May 31, 1983. (b) The Bank had *procured* an order of the Grand Court of the Cayman Islands so that it could reinforce the argument that it could not disclose information under the Cayman bank secrecy laws. (c) The Bank was still asking for the United States authorities to go through the letters rogatory procedure when the District Court in its April 27 order had expressly stated that such authorities need not issue such a request for judicial assistance in the Bahamas.[29]

The United States Attorney requested that the Bank be fined $5,000 per day until the subpoenaed documents were produced, and he specified a particular employee of the Bank in Miami to be jailed for a period not to exceed the term of the grand jury, with the provision that the employee could purge himself of contempt by producing the subpoenaed documents.[30]

At the June hearing, "the government submitted to the District Court for its in-camera review (i.e., the Bank was excluded) on the question of materiality and relevancy, an affidavit by I.R.S. Special Agent McCall as to the known existence of five negotiable instruments which were sought pursuant to the subpoena and further offered the in-camera testimony of Agent McCall with regard to a sixth, which was discovered after the affidavit was drafted."[31]

The United States attorney apparently had no qualms about providing evidence of the materiality and relevancy of the documents requested to the United States District Court, while denying the same to the Grand Court of the Cayman Islands. Any such disclosure by the United States authorities in the Grand Court of the Cayman Islands would also have been on an in-camera basis. The only individual who could leak the in-camera confidential testimony of the United States authorities would be the Judge of the Grand Court of the Cayman Islands.[32]

District Court Judge Paine on October 10, 1983, granted the United States authorities' motion to compel compliance with the subpoena. The Court was of the opinion that the government had done all that it was required to do by law and by the Court's Order of April 27, 1983. Judge Paine again cited the earlier case involving the Bank of Nova Scotia in 1982 as a precedent.[33]

Judge Paine denied the Bank's requests under their initial motion and he directed the Bank to comply with the subpoena no later than October 17, 1983. Furthermore, he stated that a contempt hearing would be held on October 21 unless the Bank complied with the subpoena before that time.[34]

THE BIND

The Bank was caught in a bind. Its choices at this point seemed to be to break the laws of the Bahamas and Cayman Islands, face contempt charges in the United States, or try to appeal the latest ruling.

What about international law? International law anticipates such a conflict and apparently offers a solution. The international standard is that the law which purports to affect conduct beyond the borders of a nation (like the United States subpoena of documents located outside United States borders) should defer to the law of the nation within whose nation the conduct will occur (the Cayman secrecy laws affecting documents in Cayman). Unfortunately for the Bank there is no way to enforce international law. There are no international police or jails, and countries, including the United States, ignore the World Court when they want to.

DÉJÀ VU?

The previous Bank of Nova Scotia case to which Judge Paine referred twice was settled on November 29, 1982. A subpoena had been served on the Bank in Miami on September 23, 1981 requesting documents from its branches in the Cayman Islands, the Bahamas, and Antigua relating to a customer of the Bank. A federal grand jury was conducting a tax and narcotics investigation.

The Bank did not produce the documents claiming that without the customer's assent or an order from the Bahamian courts the Bank would be violating the Bahamian secrecy laws.[35]

A hearing was held on the United States government's request to compel the Bank to comply with the subpoena. Most of the arguments were similar to those in the Brady subpoena discussed earlier. Another issue that emerged in this hearing was the degree of control the Miami agency had over the Nassau branch. The United States argued that all banking transactions for the Nassau branch could be done in Miami and the Bank argued the Miami agency was a one-way conduit for customer communication with Nassau. The District Court required compliance with the subpoena and the Bank appealed.[36]

The judge's conclusion:

> Absent direction from the legislative and executive branches of our federal government, we are not willing to emasculate the grand jury process whenever a foreign nation attempts to block our criminal justice process. It is unfortunate the Bank of Nova Scotia suffers from differing legal commands of separate sovereigns, but as we stated in *Field* (at 410):
>
> "In a world where commercial transactions are international in scope, conflicts are inevitable. Courts and legislatures should take every reasonable precaution to avoid placing individuals in the situation [the Bank] finds (it)self. Yet, this court simply cannot acquiesce in the proposition that United States criminal investigations must be thwarted whenever there is conflict with the interest of other states."

For the reasons stated above, the judgment entered by the District Court was affirmed.

The Bank turned over the documents in apparent violation of Bahamian law after the United States Supreme Court refused to quash the subpoena and the day after the fine was increased from $5,000 per day to $25,000 per day.[37]

INFORMATION ABOUT TAX HAVENS AND THE BANK'S STRUCTURE

Tax Havens — Use and Misuse

A tax haven is defined "loosely to include any country having a low or zero rate of tax on all or certain categories of income and offering a certain level of banking or commercial secrecy."[38] If this definition is applied literally most developed countries fall within its scope — including the United States. However, there are degrees to which a country offers shelter or refuge from taxes and secrecy. There are four general types of tax haven.[39]

1. *No–Tax Havens.* There are virtually no taxes in the Bahamas, Cayman Islands, Turks and Caicos, Nauru, and Vanuatu.
2. *Tax on Local Income Only.* Liberia, Panama, Costa Rica, and Hong Kong do not tax income from foreign sources. They tax only local income.

3. *Low Tax with Treaty Benefits.* Some countries offer a special, low tax rate (such as 3 percent in the Netherlands Antilles) and are party to favorable income tax treaties (such as low withholding tax on dividends) with other countries. Jersey, Guernsey, and the Isle of Man fall into this category.
4. *Special Privileges.* Some countries offer special privileges allowing corporations to be managed, controlled, and earn their income from abroad. Corporations meeting these conditions pay a fixed annual fee in lieu of income tax. This category includes Luxembourg, Netherlands, Switzerland, Liechtenstein, Jersey, Guernsey, Isle of Man, Gibraltar, and Barbados.

In these countries where it is possible to avoid taxes an industry comprised of accountants, tax consultants, lawyers, bankers, and trust officers has developed to help individuals and corporations avoid taxes.[40] There clearly are legal uses of tax havens like tax avoidance and participation in the Eurodollar market free from United States control. However, features of tax havens like secrecy laws also lend themselves to an illegal use such as tax evasion; and for the laundering of money from illegal sources. (Note: At the time of the events in the case, the actual processing of money by a bank from illegal activities of others was not illegal in the United States or Canada.)

Most tax havens encourage foreign banks into offshore banking usually by distinguishing between resident and nonresident banking. Nonresident banking activity usually does not have reserve requirements; is not subject to exchange controls; and is taxed differently, if at all.[41] Foreign banks are important to the economies of tax havens. The Gordon Report stated:[42]

One test of the importance of banking to an economy is the relationship of foreign assets of banks in a country to that country's foreign trade. When compared to foreign trade, foreign assets of deposit banks in tax haven jurisdictions were substantially greater than foreign assets of deposit banks in nontax havens. Special statistics developed to measure the excessive holdings of foreign assets of tax haven banks indicate that these excess assets[43] are very large, and have been growing at a rapid rate. For all tax havens surveyed[44] excess foreign assets grew from $16.7 billion in 1970 to $272.9 billion in 1978. During the same period, excess foreign assets held worldwide grew from 12.5 percent to 29.1 percent. When all jurisdictions were compared, only 13 out of 126 have foreign assets which are excessive relative to the world average in 1979. These 13 are the tax haven jurisdictions studied and the United Kingdom and France. The U.K. is an offshore financial center itself, and its data include the tax havens of the Channel Islands and the Isle of Man which could not be separated from all other U.K. data. France has excess deposits, largely because export financing aid is handled through private banks.

The importance of United States banks to the major Caribbean financial centers is growing. For example, from 1973 to 1979, total assets of U.S. bank branches increased nine times in the Cayman Islands, eight times in the Bahamas, and four times in Panama.[45]

The banking industry has a significant effect on the economy of the tax haven. Financial business yields revenues in the form of fees and modest taxes on financial institutions. The tax haven also benefits from employment of personnel and rental of facilities. The Bahamas Central Bank estimated that expenditures of banks and offshore branches in the Bahamas in 1975 was $32,886,000, including $18,330,000 for salaries. Licenses and other fees amounted to $1.5 million, and the banks employed 1,890 (1,650 Bahamians) people.[46] Informed sources estimate that by early 1978, the banking sector may have employed 2,100 people (1,897 Bahamians), paying them salaries in excess of $26 million per annum. An additional 10,000 jobs may have been indirectly supported.

A comparable survey of the Cayman Islands indicates that, in 1977, total operating expenditures by Cayman branch banks were $10.2 million, of which $5.3 million were for salaries. These branches paid $1.6 million in fees and employed 433 people, of whom 298 were local citizens.[47]

The Gordon Report also provided the following information:

1. Total deposits in banks (United States and foreign) at year-end, 1978 in tax havens in the Western Hemisphere[48] was $160 billion. $100 billion was in branches or subsidiaries of U.S. banks.
2. Total deposits in all banks (United States and foreign) at year end 1978 in all tax havens surveyed[49] was $385 billion of which $131 billion was in United States branches or subsidiaries.
3. Growth in deposits was most rapid in the Bahamas, Cayman Islands, and Panama.

The Gordon study was not able to estimate the level of use of tax havens by drug traffickers and tax evaders. However, it did find 250 criminal cases that were active, or closed within the previous three years involving offshore transactions. It stated that "this number of cases is an indication of a significant level of use." Another indication of the magnitude of the problem is the estimate of the money involved in the narcotics trade — up to $60 billion.[50]

The Bank of Nova Scotia — Structure and Operations[51]

In 1983 the Bank reorganized around its four core business areas:

1. *The Retail Banking and Operations division* is responsible for consumer loans, mortgages, credit cards, savings and checking accounts, cashstop machines, branch operations, and administrative systems and support.
2. *The Canadian Commercial Banking division* provides credit and noncredit (cash management, payroll preparation, etc.) commercial services to small and medium sized Canadian companies.
3. *The North American Corporate Banking division* manages the Bank's relationships with large national and multinational corporations in Canada and the United States. The corporate office is in Toronto and the division maintains offices in three other Canadian cities and nine United States cities (Atlanta, Boston, Chicago, Cleveland, Houston, Miami, New York, Portland, San Francisco). The 1984 annual report stated that the Bank maintains "a leading position among foreign banks in United States corporate relationships. Our activities included lead positions in major acquisition financing, letter of credit supported tax exempt transactions and project financings."

The *Treasury* coordinates the activities of the Treasuries in Europe, the Middle East, the Pacific, and in North America. It also includes a new merchant banking activity.

4. *The International division* of the Bank maintains 174 offices in 51 countries to serve clients around the world. It provides a wide range of financial services to its clients — retail, commercial, corporate, wholesale, and trust. The division is divided into four regions: Caribbean (regional office in Toronto; offices in twenty islands/countries); Central and South America (regional office in Toronto; offices in five countries); Europe, Middle East and Africa (regional office in London; offices in fifteen countries); Pacific (regional office in Manila; offices in eleven countries). The Bank operates through a network of branches, representative offices, agencies, subsidiary and affiliated companies. In 1981 it had a total of 211 offices outside Canada of which 157 were located in the Caribbean region.[52] The Bank's international retail activities are primarily located in the Caribbean where it has been represented since 1889.[53] (Note: It is believed that the bank is the largest financial institution, in terms of offices, in the Caribbean.)

Some selected statistics on the bank's financial performance are shown in Tables 1–4.

TABLE 1 **Net Income ($Millions)**

	1980	1981	1982	1983
Domestic	93	118	92	152
International	142	126	181	196
Total	235	244	273	348

TABLE 2 **Average Total Assets ($Billion)**

	1980	1981	1982	1983
Domestic	19.9	24.2	28.5	28.3
International	18.5	21.1	24.5	25.7
Total	38.4	45.3	53.0	54.0

TABLE 3 **Return on Assets (%)**

	1980	1981	1982	1983
Domestic	.47	.49	.32	.54
International	.77	.60	.74	.76
Total	.61	.54	.51	.64

Source: 1984 Annual Report.

TABLE 4   **Geographic Distribution of Major Earning Assets* ($Millions) 1983**

	$	% OF TOTAL EARNING ASSETS
Middle East, Africa	$ 525	1.0
Japan	1,712	3.4
Other	1,634	3.2
Asia	3,346	6.6
Mexico	988	2.0
Brazil	807	1.6
Venezuela	549	1.1
Other Latin American	1,154	2.2
Total Central & South American	3,498	6.9
Jamaica	792	1.6
Other Caribbean	1,592	3.1
Total Caribbean	2,384	4.7
United Kingdom	2,348	4.7
France	1,925	3.8
West Germany	934	1.9
Belgium	662	1.3
Netherlands	596	1.2
Other Europe	2,467	4.9
Total Europe	8,932	17.8
Total Above	$18,685	37.0
United States	7,065	14.0
Canada	24,700	49.0
Total	$50,450	100.0

*Major earning assets are loans, deposits with banks other than the Bank of Canada, and securities.
Location is based on geographic area or country of borrower or country of residence of guarantor.
Countries exceeding 1% of assets are reported separately.
Source: 1984 Annual Report.

Notes

The legal events presented regarding the Brady subpoena have been taken from a legal record of the case entitled *The Bank of Nova Scotia Case: A Case of U.S. Extraterritorial Information Gathering* (unpublished). It was compiled by Errol P. Mendes, Faculty of Law, The University of Western Ontario from public documents. Footnotes 1–7 and 9–34 were also taken from that record.

1. Jud Harwood, "Bank of Nova Scotia (Brady Subpoena): US Government Lawyers Deceive the Courts." *Taxes International* 65 (March 1985): 3.
2. "Subpoena to Testify Before Grand Jury 83–1 (WPB)". In "The United States District Court for the Southern District of Florida; Selected Court Documents Pertaining to: *The United States of America* vs. *The Bank of Nova Scotia* (Brady)." Prepared by the Economic Law and Treaty Division, Department of External Affairs, Volume 1 (hereafter referred to as "Volume 1").
3. "Attachment to Subpoena: The Bank of Nova Scotia." In Volume 1 (see n. 2).
4. Supra n. 1, p. 4.
5. Jud Harwood and Bruce Zagaris, "Judge Paine Socks-It-To The Bank of Nova Scotia" *Taxes International* 54 (April 1984): 12.
6. Ibid., 12.
7. Ibid., 5–8.
8. R. J. Marshall, Senior International Counsel, Bank of Nova Scotia, Personal Communication.
9. Harwood and Zagaris, "Judge Paine," 12–13.
10. "Memorandum of Law in Support of the Bank of Nova Scotia's Motion Directed to Subpoena 83–1" 1–19, 4. In Volume 1 (see n. 2).
11. "Memorandum of Law in Support of the Bank of Nova Scotia's Motion Directed to Subpoena 83–1," 2. In Volume 1 (see n. 2).
12. Ibid., 2.
13. Ibid., 2.
14. "Government's Motion to Compel Compliance with Grand Jury Subpoena and Answer to Movant's Motion to Quash Grand Jury Subpoena," 2. In Volume 1 (see n. 2).
15. "Memorandum of Law in Support of the Bank of Nova Scotia's Motion Directed to Subpoena 83–1," 1–2. In Volume 1 (see n. 2).
16. Ibid., 7–14.
17. Ibid., 8–13.
18. "Memorandum of Law in Support of the Bank of Nova Scotia's Motion Directed to Subpoena 83–1," 9. In Volume 1 (see n. 2).
19. *Restatement of Foreign Relations Law of the United States* (Revised), S420, reporters' notes at 18 n–1 (Tent. Draft 3, 1980). In Ibid., p. 15.
20. Ibid., 15.
21. "United States District Court, Southern District of Florida, Case No. 83–1 (WPB), April 27, 1983, Order pp. 1–2." In Volume 1 (see n. 2).
22. "Correspondence Between Bank's Attorney and U.S. Department of Justice" (March–June 1983): 1–12. In Volume 1 (see n. 2).
23. Ibid., 9–10.
24. Supra n. 5, p. 13.
25. "Bank's First Appeal Reply Brief" p. 8. In Supra N. 5, p. 13.
26. "Motions of the Bank of Nova Scotia for Order Containing Findings, Directing Government to Act, For Further Enlargement of Time or, Alternatively, to be Relieved from Further Obligations under Order and Subpoena," p. 1. In Volume 1 (see n. 2).
27. "Status Report and Memorandum of Law, In Support of the Bank of Nova Scotia's Motions for Orders Making Findings, Directing Government to Act, for Further Enlargement of Time or Alternatively, to be Relieved from Further Obligations Under Subpoena," pp. 3–8. In Volume 1 (see n. 2).
28. Ibid., 9–10.
29. "Government's Answer to Defendant's Motion for Order Containing Facts, Directing

Government to Act, For Further Enlargement of Time or, Alternatively, to be Relieved from Further Obligations Under Order and Subpoena," 1–3. In Volume 1 (see n. 2).

30. Ibid.

31. "U.S. Attorney's First Appeal Brief, p. 12, footnote 9." In Harwood and Zagaris (n. 5), 13.

32. "The Bank of Nova Scotia's Reply to the Government's Answer to Defendants' Motion for Order Containing Findings, Etc." In Volume 1 (see n. 2). See also Harwood (n. 1), 28–29.

33. "United States District Court, Southern District of Florida, Case No. 83–1 (WPB): Order, October 10, 1983," 1–3. In Volume 1 (see n. 2).

34. Ibid.

35. *Taxes International*, 40 (February 1983): 4.

36. Ibid.

37. Jud Harwood, "Bank of Nova Scotia," 4.

38. *Tax Havens and Their Use by United States Taxpayers—An Overview*. A report to the Commissioner of Internal Revenue, the Assistant Attorney General (Tax Division) and the Assistant Secretary of the Treasury (Tax Policy), by Richard A. Gordon, Special Counsel for International Taxation; January 12, 1981. Chapter 2.

39. Marshall J. Langer, *Practical International Tax Planning*. 3rd ed. (New York: Practicing Law Institute, 1985), 3–4.

40. Ibid., 3–4.

41. *Tax Havens*, A29.

42. Ibid., A29 and A30.

43. Excess assets are those above the worldwide average of foreign assets of deposit banks to worldwide foreign trade. The amount above what this ratio would yield was the excess assets for that jurisdiction. For example, 1978 total foreign assets held by deposit banks in the Bahamas were $95.2 billion. Based on the worldwide average of deposits to world trade, $1.8 billion was needed to finance the foreign trade of the Bahamas. The difference, $93.4 billion, represented excess international assets and is an indication of assets attracted because of the tax haven status of the jurisdiction.

44. Bahamas, Bermuda, Cayman Islands, Hong Kong, Luxembourg-Belgium (the foreign trade data for the two countries could not be separated), Netherlands Antilles, Panama, Singapore, and Switzerland.

45. *See* Hoffman, *Caribbean Basin Economic Survey*. Federal Reserve Bank of Atlanta (May/June/July 1980), at 1.

46. C. Y. Frances, *Central Banking in a Developing Country with an Offshore Banking Centre*, Central Bank of the Bahamas (1978).

47. Cayman Islands, Department of Finance and Development.

48. Bahamas, Bermuda, British West Indies, Barbados, Costa Rica, Cayman Islands, Netherlands, Antilles, and Panama.

49. In addition to those countries listed in (48) add Bahrain, Hong Kong, Luxembourg, Singapore, and Switzerland.

50. *Crime and Secrecy: The Use of Offshore Banks and Companies*. Hearings before the Permanent Subcommittee on Investigations of the Committee on Governmental Affairs, United States Senate, Ninety-Eighth Congress, First Session, March 15, 16 and May 24, 1983; p. 67.

51. Bank of Nova Scotia Annual Reports 1984, 1985.

52. *Offering Circular*, "U.S. $25,000,000, The Bank of Nova Scotia, 15½% Deposit Notes Due June 15, 1986," dated May 27, 1981, p. 7.

53. Ibid.

INDEX

471